Commentaries on the *Laws of England*

William Blackstone

A Facsimile of the First Edition
of 1765–1769

VOLUME II

Of the
Rights of Things
(1766)

With an Introduction by A. W. Brian Simpson

The University of Chicago Press

Chicago & London

The University of Chicago Press, Chicago 60637
The University of Chicago Press, Ltd., London

09 08 07 06 05 04 03 02 01 00   7 8 9 10 11 12

Volume 1: *Of the Rights of Persons,*
    ISBN: 0-226-05538-8 (ppbk)
Volume 2: *Of the Rights of Things,*
    ISBN: 0-226-05541-8 (ppbk)
Volume 3: *Of Private Wrongs,*
    ISBN: 0-226-05543-4 (ppbk)
Volume 4: *Of Public Wrongs,*
    ISBN: 0-226-05545-0 (ppbk)

LCN: 79–11753

INTRODUCTION TO BOOK II

BLACKSTONE, following a scheme devised nearly a century earlier by Sir Matthew Hale,[1] the great seventeenth-century jurist, devotes the second book of the *Commentaries* to what are curiously called the rights of things, *jura rerum*. By this expression are meant "those rights which a man may acquire in and to such external things as are unconnected with his person."[2] The subject matter therefore is property law, so considered as to embrace all rights which do not attach to individuals simply as such, whether naturally or as members of civil society. It would be hard to over-emphasize the contemporary significance, both to professional lawyers and to Blackstone's lay readership, of property law, particularly real property law, as a branch of legal learning. His lectures at Oxford, out of which grew the *Commentaries*, were specifically directed to "gentlemen of independent estates and fortune, the most useful as well as considerable body of men in the nation . . . . It is their landed property, with it's long and voluminous train of descents and conveyances, settlements, entails and incumbrances, that forms the most intricate and most extensive object of legal knowledge."[3] For the propertied classes, land, the permanent endowment of the governors, represented power, status, and security; for the lawyer, whose activities were very largely parasitic on the propertied classes, property law was where the money was to be got. At a theoretical level its importance was again undisputed. In the legal and political thought of the time, an extraordinary significance was attributed to the protection of property; for some indeed this was both the principal function of municipal law and the very reason for the establishment of civil societies. Freedom of property, classed by Blackstone as the third absolute right, inherent in every Englishman, the notion of which was classically expressed in John Locke's *Two Treatises of Government* (1689),[4] was of leading importance in the tradition of liberal thought associated with the French and American revolutions; not until the nineteenth century did freedom of contract come to achieve a similar status. Blackstone's second volume therefore seeks to set out, explain, and justify the way in which the common law of England discharges one of its three principal obligations to its subjects.

The Theory of Property Rights

It is understandable, given the acknowledged primacy of the subject, that Blackstone begins with an incursion into the theory of property, "Of Property in General."[5] Today theories of property appear to excite neither the popular nor the specialist interest they once did. They rarely feature in legal study; much of the writing on the subject belongs to the tradition of natural law, and today few read the writings of authors in this tradition.[6] Such theories are concerned first with historical inquiry of a kind nowadays the preserve of anthropologists rather than historians: how did the institution of property come about? This question Blackstone tackles in a speculative manner, supposing a state of primitive simplicity, as in Genesis, in which all was in common. His views as to how and why private property in moveables, and eventually in immoveables, first emerged are derived from earlier writers, particularly the Swedish jurist Baron Pufendorf, whose *Of the Laws of Nature and Nations*[7] was available in an English edition published by the Oxford University Press in 1710 and widely read.

Theories of property are also concerned with the ethical justification of private property. Here Blackstone, who was primarily interested in property in land, took the orthodox view of the time: the individual's right derived from "occupancy."[8] But this left open the intriguing question of why the act of taking should confer an exclusive right to possession. Why, we might put it, should finding be keeping? Here there was a controversy. One school of thought claimed that the right depended upon some form of implied or tacit social contract, and that property rights therefore derived from the obligation to keep agreements; this was the view, for example, of Sir Robert Filmer,[9] Grotius,[10] and Pufendorf. In opposition was the view, primarily associated with John Locke, that there existed independently of contract, and thus independently of civil society, a *natural* right of property, derived from the individual's expenditure of labor in occupying; a form of this theory is now adopted by Marxists. Blackstone, never at his most lucid in high theory, belittles the controversy but, a theorist in spite of himself, he principally follows Locke, conceiving of property as essentially an institution of natural law, whose extension beyond its natural bounds was due to developments in human, civil law. For example, no form of inheritance seemed to him to be "natural."[11] Blackstone's theoretical views are to be found scattered about Book II, and not simply in the first chapter;[12] they cannot easily be isolated from his general views on the nature of law itself. Opinions may differ as to whether his treatment of the subject is sophisticated in its complexity or merely confused.

Blackstone on Real Property

Blackstone then proceeds, in the following twenty-two chapters, to give an account of the law of real property. Broadly, real property, as opposed to personal property (dealt with in the final nine chapters), was the law of immoveables as opposed to moveables, or land as opposed to chattels. Over the preceding seven centuries the common law judges and sergeants, assisted intermittently by parliamentary legislation (itself the work of common lawyers), had evolved separate bodies of law for real property and personal property. To make matters even more confusing, they had constructed in "chattels real"—typically, leases—a hybrid creature, which Blackstone discusses under the heading of real property. Since the twelfth century, the law of real property, that body of law involved in the resolution of land disputes, had been the predominant concern of the royal courts, where the common law was made, and the common law as an intellectual system evolved from the elaborate procedures through which rights in real property were challenged, tested, and vindicated. The name "real property" itself is taken from the procedures, the real actions, through which landowners' rights were specifically enforced. The dominant status of real property law, early established, long persisted, and in Blackstone's time that body of law, viewed as the mechanism either for the resolution of land disputes, or, as it was used by the expert conveyancers for the cooperative, consensual organization of land ownership, remained the most important and intellectually developed branch of the common law. Extreme intellectual development in law is not necessarily a virtue, and real property law had become the victim of too many able minds refining too many distinctions for too long.

It was of almost incredible complexity; cynics like Oliver Cromwell called it an ungodly jumble. It had become a mystery, unintelligible except to experts.

Its unintelligibility was aggravated by another feature. The basic scheme of concepts in which rights in land had come to be expressed had been settled in the early Middle Ages, when society had been organized feudally; land law was in origin feudal law. In the immense period which had elapsed between the world of Norman feudalism and the world of Blackstone there had of course been many important developments and changes in the law, but at no point had there been any radical break in continuity. Indeed to this very day, both in the country of its origin and in countries to which it was exported in the colonial and imperial periods, the common law remains an essentially medieval body of law that has been unsystematically modified and patched up so as to make the system work, if not always well, as least tolerably. Accidents of history have sometimes produced a situation in which real property law retains more archaic features outside England than at home. The major reforms date from the nineteenth century; in Blackstone's day all these lay in the future, so that the system was in many respects archaic. Its procedures and doctrines were of baffling complexity, and a fear existed that any tinkering with so venerable and ramshackle an edifice could collapse the structure and throw all property into confusion.

Blackstone made what was previously a dark mystery comprehensible to those who did not propose to acquire an understanding of the subject by years of study in conveyancing chambers or attorney's office. To have written, in so brief a compass, a clear, readable account of real property law was an extraordinary achievement. Blackstone's second volume exemplifies his remarkable ability to separate out the essentials, the elements of the subject, from matters of elaboration or refinement. With this ability he combined the equally important gift of succinct, economical expression. It is easy, from reading Blackstone, to be misled into thinking that the law of the time was as simple as he makes it seem; it must be emphasized that this was not the case. A good example of his technique is to be found in chapter 11, where he discusses the doctrines governing contingent remainders, which were soon, in 1772, to be made the subject of a celebrated but esoteric work, Fearne's *Essay on the Learning of Contingent Remainders and Executory*

Devises.[13] Blackstone, after setting out in a few pages the basic principles involved goes on, "It were endless to attempt to enter upon the particular subtilties and refinements, into which this doctrine, by the variety of cases which have occurred in the course of many centuries, has been spun out and subdivided: neither are they consonant to the design of these elementary disquisitions."[14] He knew what had to be cut out to hold his readers' attention.

Blackstone's Predecessors

Blackstone was not the first to compose a treatise on real property law: he had two celebrated predecessors. The first was Sir Thomas Littleton, a fifteenth-century lawyer and later judge, whose *Tenures*, a brief and mainly elementary statement of property law, was one of the earliest lawbooks printed in England, the first of its many editions appearing in about 1481.[15] Though according to tradition the *Tenures* was written for Littleton's son Richard,[16] I suspect that like the *Commentaries* it originated as lectures for students; this would explain its simplicity. Littleton's book was not, however, for laymen; indeed it was written not in English but in the Norman-French then used by lawyers as the private language of their mystery. For over a century it formed the staple diet of young law students.

Then in the early seventeenth century a fate typical of short successful lawbooks overtook the *Tenures,* it was made the subject of an elaborate gloss or commentary. The author was the most learned of all the black letter lawyers, Sir Edward Coke.[17] To Coke the *Tenures* was "the ornament of the common law, and the most perfect and absolute work that was ever written in any human science." In *The First Part of the Institutes of the Laws of England,* always known to lawyers as "Coke on Littleton," he expounded and dissected the words of the master with an incredible display of technical legal learning. Where Littleton's opening paragraph defines the fee simple in a hundred and ninety-four words, Coke's commentary on the same passage extends to over twenty thousand. Later commentators added further material, and in its final form, evolved in the late eighteenth century, Littleton's original text was submerged with notes by Francis Hargrave and Charles Butler superimposed on notes by Lord Nottingham and

Sir Matthew Hale expounding Coke's commentary. As a mine of learning on property law, "Coke on Littleton" was unrivaled, and its dominance continued until late in the nineteenth century. It was, however, a book to consult or study, being far too repulsive to read. If Blackstone's treatment of the subject owes anything to his predecessors, it must be to Littleton, not Coke, but there is no direct sense in which the *Tenures* formed a model.

Blackstone's Scheme

Blackstone himself acknowledged that an expositor of a complex subject, whose aim is simplicity, must hit on and adhere to a simple scheme.[18] After dealing with property in general, he treats of the objects of property (divided, in the case of real property, into corporeal things and incorporeal things), then with the tenures by which these forms of property are held, then with the interests those who hold them can have (the doctrine of estates), then with title to real property, and finally with modes of alienating real property. The scheme was not perfect, the principal difficulty being where to put that most characteristic of all the products of the ingenuity of English property lawyers, the trust. Blackstone's account of this institution is to be found principally in chapter 20, "Of Alienation by Deed,"[19] tucked away in an account of conveyancing forms. The subject is also discussed in chapter 8 ("Of Freeholds Not of Inheritance")[20] and in chapter 18 ("Of Title by Forfeiture").[21] Blackstone's account of the development of the trust from the use is inadequate, and he nowhere gives a clear account of the distinction between property rights established and recognized by the courts of common law as legal, and property rights—typically, the rights of a beneficiary under a trust—recognized in the Court of Chancery as equitable only. Essentially the distinction is that a legal property right is enforceable against the property into whomsoever's hands it has come, whereas an equitable right is liable to be defeated if the property comes into the hands of a purchaser in good faith for value of the legal estate without notice of the existence of the trust. The defective treatment of trusts is the only serious gap in Blackstone's comprehensiveness; it is a fault generated by his scheme of arrangement.

Blackstone and Feudalism

Blackstone's treatment of real property law within his scheme was essentially historical;[22] he believed that "It is impracticable to comprehend many rules of the modern law, in a scholarlike scientifical manner, without having recourse to the antient."[23] He seeks to explain existing law by setting out the manner of its evolution, using history for its explanatory and sometimes for its justificatory force; the majority of treatise writers have followed this technique ever since. Usually the picture is one of steady improvement, but at times Blackstone writes as if there was once a simple golden age of the common law, which thereafter suffered from new-fangled inventions.[24] Monks (Blackstone was hostile to monks) came in for a share of the blame.[25] Blackstone's historicism is particularly in evidence in his treatment of tenure. He emphasized, as he had to do, the feudal origins of English land law, and he begins with a somewhat idealized picture of "the nature and doctrine of feuds," whose principal legal expression is the dogma that all land is held of a feudal lord, and directly or ultimately of the monarch as supreme feudal lord. His historical views are largely derived from Sir Martin Wright's *Introduction to the Law of Tenures* (1730); Blackstone was not himself a historian, but a user of history. But in Blackstone's time the major and economically important consequences of tenure had largely vanished, as had the military tenures which were the typical expressions of Norman feudalism. Blackstone emphasizes feudalism partly because the structure and terminology of the law was still dominated by its origin, and partly because he was at pains to demonstrate that the common law, in spite of its feudal lineage, gave expression and protection to the natural right of individual private property. For feudalism seems, on the face of things, to deny this; subjects "hold" land conditionally from the monarch, they do not "own." Indeed it is part of the modern folklore of real property law that "the king owns all the land," a notion not, however, to be found in Blackstone. He is, however, anxious to demonstrate that feudalism (which he abominated)[26] had been largely deprived of its oppressive character, and that in spite of the survival of feudal elements and the universal doctrine of tenure, the common law does recognize individual private ownership.[27]

Blackstone on the Doctrine of Estates

The second leading characteristic of English land law is the doctrine of estates. The law of tenure having set out those rights, duties, and liabilities of the landholder which sprang from his relationship as tenant with his feudal lord, the doctrine of estates comprises an analysis of the quantum of interest of the landholder in terms of time. The most elegant statement of the doctrine, which Blackstone unfortunately does not quote, is to be found in the sixteenth-century *Walsingham's Case*: "The land itself is one thing and the estate in land is another thing: for an estate in the land is a time in the land, or land for a time: and there are diversities of estates, which are no more than diversities of time; for he who hath a fee simple in the land has a time in the land without end, or land for a time without end; and he who has land in tail has a time in land, or the land for a time, as long as he has issue of his body; and he who has an estate in land for life has no time in it longer than his own life; and so of one who has an estate in land for the life of another, or for years."[28]

The whole corpus of rules defining the estates which could exist, their incidents and manner of creation, and most importantly how they could be put together like an elaborate jigsaw, was enormously complex; Blackstone's simplification is remarkable. It is easy enough to grasp the notion of the fee simple—roughly, "ownership"—and of the estate for years, the familiar lease. What is more baffling is the scheme of estates associated with *family* land-ownership: the life estate, the entail, conditional and determinable fees, and estates in remainder and reversion. All the elaboration here was the product of aristocratic dynastic family landholding. To the wealthy landed classes, real property was the essential endowment not of individuals but of the family, a continuing but constantly changing entity forming and reforming around the basic family events—birth, the attainment of majority, marriage and death—and rendered continuous by the concepts of blood and inheritance. Land was to be exploited in the interests of the family, not the individual, but the mechanism for its exploitation was, paradoxically, a subtle manipulation of individual property rights; the family was never treated as an entity capable of itself owning or possessing rights, nor on the other hand were patriarchal notions carried to the point at which only the father of the family enjoyed rights. In the complex history of the subject was expressed a continuous tension between two strategies. According to one, the family endowment is best secured by permitting individuals, particularly the current head of the family, as little discretion and power of disposition over the family lands as possible. According to the other, the same end was better achieved by a flexible system under which the endowment can be reallocated so as to adapt to changes in the family, catering for personalities and uncovenanted family events. The compromise commonly employed in Blackstone's time, and evolved in the seventeenth century, was the strict settlement under which the land was managed by a succession of life tenants, the settlement being reconstituted each generation to ensure that no single individual ever acquired an unfettered power to appropriate the family capital for his individual purposes. It is remarkable that in spite of Blackstone's exaltation of private *individual* property rights, the landowning class in reality had little use for them.

Of the strict settlement, which all his readers would know in practice, Blackstone gives no general account, though in Appendix II his specimen conveyance by lease and release is a strict settlement of typical form on the occasion of a marriage. For an account of the institution it is necessary to go outside the *Commentaries*.

Blackstone on Title and Modes of Alienation

The remainder of Blackstone's account deals with the principles governing both the establishment of title to real property, and the mechanisms of transfer which themselves constitute steps in the establishment of title. Blackstone presents this intricate body of law, which in reality gave rise to extensive insecurity of title, in the form of a set of exceptions to title by inheritance, which he viewed as "the principal object of the laws of real property in England." A romantic attachment to the hereditary principle, and particularly to the principle of primogeniture, long persisted in England, though the truth of the matter was that the landowning classes, as paradoxically as they shied away from individual property rights, avoided, by settlements either by will or *inter vivos*

(i.e., between the living, taking effect before death), the operation
of the doctrine of inheritance wherever possible. To understand
Blackstone one must appreciate this paradox.

Blackstone on Personal Property

The remainder of the volume deals with personal property, a
branch of the law which was, in Blackstone's time, relatively less
developed than that of real property, but one in which individual
property rights were in reality more respected. The principal and
historical reason for this was partly economic, partly social. The
common law was essentially the law of the aristocratic landed
classes, and in their world, as contrasted with the urban world of
the mercantile classes, moveable, tangible property constituted a
less significant form of wealth than land. In the main their personal property represented expenditure rather than investment.
Blackstone himself makes much of the relative unimportance of
chattels in his explanation for the way in which the law of moveables had evolved on quite different lines than real property law.
In particular, moveables had never been subjected to the doctrines
of tenure or estates, and consequently they could not be subjected
to the elaborate scheme of the family strict settlement; relatively
simple mechanisms were used to ensure that the more permanent
forms of personal property devolved with the land. Blackstone's
whole account of personal property, with its discussion of the problems of the beekeeper and the legal position of partridges in a
mew, smells of the countryside; the law is the law of the country
gentry, not Cheapside. The *Commentaries* reflects the essentially
rural character of the high civilization of the eighteenth century.

Mercantile Custom and Personal Property

Today of course much wealth consists of various forms of intangible personal property: stocks and shares, life insurance policies, negotiable commercial instruments, copyrights, patents, commercial goodwill, and so forth. The legal institutions involved
were essentially emanations of the urban commercial world of
merchants, principally though not exclusively taking the form of

offshoots of commercial contract law. Historically the law merchant had been conceived of as a body of law quite distinct from the common law, as a personal law of those of the merchant class. In Blackstone's time theory had changed; he tells us that the custom of merchants, "however different from the common law, is allowed for the benefit of trade, to be of the utmost validity in all commercial transactions . . . ."[29] Particularly with the chief justiceship of Lord Mansfield (1756–88),[30] there was a major reception of mercantile custom into the common law.

In Blackstone's treatment of personal property this area of law is not emphasized. There is a discussion of copyright and a short account of bills of exchange, promissory notes, and insurance, the first tucked away in the discussion of title by occupancy and the second in the section on title by gift, grant, and contract.[31] In Blackstone's basic analysis of personal property rights, the newer forms of commercial intangible property presented peculiar difficulty. He adopted a traditional distinction between "things in possession" and "things in action," the latter comprising objects of private property rights which are recoverable by legal action, as opposed to being in the actual possession of the owner; an example is a debt. Blackstone supposed that title to all "things in action" had its basis in contract, express or implied.[32] Given this defective scheme it is not easy to see where to place intangibles generally; copyright for example is intangible but not based on contract. Blackstone never thought through the analytical problems, and his scheme is rendered even more difficult by the distinction he draws between "absolute" and "qualified" property.[33] As in the case of the trust, the source of difficulty is the original scheme.

Blackstone on Contract

The received concept of a "thing in action" as a form of property fathered what seems to modern readers to be the most peculiar feature of Book II. Lurking unexpectedly in chapter 30, which is devoted to modes of acquisition of personal property, is Blackstone's account of the law of contract, dealing both with formal contracts by sealed instruments and with the so-called simple or parole contracts by word of mouth, some evidenced by written documents.[34] Contracts are here conceived of as a sort of conveyance; either they pass property in tangible things such as a horse or book (as in the case of chattel sales), or they pass intangible property recoverable in action, such as a debt. Contracts to perform services or other acts, such as marriage, do not fit the analysis, since the right to the services is not technically a "thing in action," and such contracts are consequently hardly mentioned. Blackstone's treatment of contract is unsatisfactory because again he falls victim to the deficiency of his basic scheme which, in its failure to reflect the sophistication of contemporary law, has misled many into supposing that the law of contract was in his time little developed. Blackstone's scheme does, however, reflect the fact that in eighteenth-century legal thought contract had not achieved the status it was to gain in the nineteenth century, when it came to be viewed as the principal civilizing force in social development, and consequently as the branch of the law of the profoundest social significance. Freedom of contract was to overtake freedom of property; Blackstone never of course mentions freedom of contract.

A. W. BRIAN SIMPSON

NOTES

1. (1609–76). Hale's best known works are his *History of the Pleas of the Crown*, and *The History of the Common Law of England*, available in a paperback edition by the University of Chicago Press (ed. C. M. Gray). His *General Analysis of the Civil Part of the Law* was first published posthumously in 1713.
2. Blackstone, *Commentaries* II:1.
3. Id. Introduction I:7.
4. Available in numerous editions, perhaps most usefully in that by P. Laslett (1963).
5. Blackstone ch. 1 of Book II. See also I:138.
6. A useful introduction is A. P. d'Entrèves, *Natural Law* (1951).
7. First published in 1672. Baron Pufendorf (1632–89) was professor of the law of nature and nations at Heidelberg and later professor of jurisprudence at Lund.
8. The term translates *occupatio* of Roman law texts; the equivalent term for moveables is *perceptio*, "taking."

9. The *Patriarcha* and other political writings of Filmer (c. 1588–1653) are available in a modern edition by P. Laslett (1949). His theory of property is set out in § VIII–X. The *Patriarcha* was first published posthumously in 1680.

10. Hugo Grotius (1583–1645), whose *De Iure Belli ac Pacis* appeared in 1625.

11. Blackstone II:10.

12. See on inheritance id. I:134, II:400, IV:9; on occupancy II:258ff, especially the discussion of copyright at 405–7. The long discussion of the legal position of game and the prerogative is at II:410ff. On slavery see I:123 and II:402, discussed in F. O. Shyllon, *Black Slaves in Britain* (1974), in ch. 5. The passage in I:123 was altered in the second edition (1766) to conform more to the doctrine set out for captives at II:402.

13. Fearne went through numerous editions, suffering the fate of the good lawbook; from an original size of under a hundred pages it expanded in the hands of editors to over a thousand.

14. Blackstone II:172.

15. Littleton (c. 1410–81) became a judge in 1466; his effigy may still be seen in Worcester Cathedral.

16. The traditional story to this effect is based on the use of the expression *"mon fils"* in the text, but this was at the time the way one addressed young students generally.

17. (1551–1633).

18. See Blackstone ch. 1 of Book I.

19. Id. II:327–39. Notice also 296–97.

20. Id. II:137.

21. Id. II:271–74.

22. See also id. IV:435, where are set out "some rude outlines of a plan of the history of our laws and liberties."

23. Id. II:44.

24. See, e.g., II:331.

25. See, e.g., id. II:48.

26. See id. II:52.

27. See id. II:104–6.

28. Plowden, *Commentaries* 555 (1578).

29. Blackstone I:75.

30. The only modern life discussing Mansfield's contribution as a lawyer is C. H. S. Fifoot's *Lord Mansfield* (1936).

31. Blackstone II:405 and 458ff.

32. Id. II:397.

33. Id. II:389–91.

34. Blackstone, following Hale's scheme, also discusses contract when dealing with private wrongs.

COMMENTARIES

ON THE

LAWS

OF

ENGLAND.

BOOK THE SECOND.

BY

WILLIAM BLACKSTONE, Esq.

SOLICITOR GENERAL TO HER MAJESTY.

OXFORD,

PRINTED AT THE CLARENDON PRESS.

M. DCC. LXVI.

CONTENTS.

BOOK II.

Of the RIGHTS of THINGS.

CONTENTS.

CHAP.

CONTENTS.

CHAP.

CONTENTS.

CHAP.

CONTENTS.

Chap. XXXII.

Of Title *by* Testament, *and* Administration.   489.

✱✧✱

APPENDIX.

ERRATA.

Page 13, *line* 6 : *before* heir *insert* their immediate
21, *line* 4 : *for* and *read* or
96, *line* 4 : *after* was *insert* virtually
103, *line* 4 : *after* another *insert* and his heirs
121, *line* 3 : *for* specifice state *read* specific estate
149, *line* 17 : *for* at *read* as
199, *line* 9 : *for* alienes to *read* enfeoffs
272, *line* 25 : *for* 32 *read* 23
276, (*note* a *and* b) *for* 152, 153, *read* 252, 253,
309, (*note* w) *for* 90 *read* nº. 24. 1 Vern. 348.
473, *line* 30 : } *for* tradesman *read* trader
474, *line* 12 : }

COMMENTARIES

ON THE

LAWS of ENGLAND.

Book the second.

Of the RIGHTS of THINGS.

Chapter the first.

Of PROPERTY, in general.

THE former book of thefe commentaries having treated at large of the *jura perfonarum*, or fuch rights and duties as are annexed to the perfons of men, the objects of our enquiry in this fecond book will be the *jura rerum*, or, thofe rights which a man may acquire in and to fuch external things as are unconnected with his perfon. Thefe are what the writers on natural law ftile the rights of dominion, or property, concerning the nature and original of which I fhall firft premife a few obfervations, before I proceed to diftribute and confider it's feveral objects.

THERE is nothing which so generally strikes the imagination, and engages the affections of mankind, as the right of property; or that sole and despotic dominion which one man claims and exercises over the external things of the world, in total exclusion of the right of any other individual in the universe. And yet there are very few, that will give themselves the trouble to consider the original and foundation of this right. Pleased as we are with the possession, we seem afraid to look back to the means by which it was acquired, as if fearful of some defect in our title; or at best we rest satisfied with the decision of the laws in our favour, without examining the reason or authority upon which those laws have been built. We think it enough that our title is derived by the grant of the former proprietor, by descent from our ancestors, or by the last will and testament of the dying owner; not caring to reflect that (accurately and strictly speaking) there is no foundation in nature or in natural law, why a set of words upon parchment should convey the dominion of land; why the son should have a right to exclude his fellow creatures from a determinate spot of ground, because his father had done so before him; or why the occupier of a particular field or of a jewel, when lying on his death-bed and no longer able to maintain possession, should be entitled to tell the rest of the world which of them should enjoy it after him. These enquiries, it must be owned, would be useless and even troublesome in common life. It is well if the mass of mankind will obey the laws when made, without scrutinizing too nicely into the reasons of making them. But, when law is to be considered not only as matter of practice, but also as a rational science, it cannot be improper or useless to examine more deeply the rudiments and grounds of these positive constitutions of society.

IN the beginning of the world, we are informed by holy writ, the all-bountiful creator gave to man " dominion over all " the earth; and over the fish of the sea, and over the fowl of " the air, and over every living thing that moveth upon the " earth [a]."

"earth[a]." This is the only true and folid foundation of man's dominion over external things, whatever airy metaphyfical notions may have been ftarted by fanciful writers upon this fubject. The earth therefore, and all things therein, are the general property of all mankind, exclufive of other beings, from the immediate gift of the creator. And, while the earth continued bare of inhabitants, it is reafonable to fuppofe, that all was in common among them, and that every one took from the public ftock to his own ufe fuch things as his immediate neceffities required.

THESE general notions of property were then fufficient to anfwer all the purpofes of human life; and might perhaps ftill have anfwered them, had it been poffible for mankind to have remained in a ftate of primaeval fimplicity: as may be collected from the manners of many American nations when firft difcovered by the Europeans; and from the antient method of living among the firft Europeans themfelves, if we may credit either the memorials of them preferved in the golden age of the poets, or the uniform accounts given by hiftorians of thofe times, wherein " *erant omnia communia et indivifa omnibus, veluti unum cunctis pa-* " *trimonium effet* [b]." Not that this communion of goods feems ever to have been applicable, even in the earlieft ages, to ought but the *fubftance* of the thing; nor could be extended to the *ufe* of it. For, by the law of nature and reafon, he who firft began to ufe it, acquired therein a kind of tranfient property, that lafted fo long as he was ufing it, and no longer [c]: or, to fpeak with greater precifion, the *right* of poffeffion continued for the fame time only that the *act* of poffeffion lafted. Thus the ground was in common, and no part of it was the permanent property of any man in particular: yet whoever was in the occupation of any determinate fpot of it, for reft, for fhade, or the like, acquired for the time a fort of ownerfhip, from which it would have been unjuft, and contrary to the law of nature, to have driven him by force; but the inftant that he quitted the ufe or occupation of it,

---

[a] Gen. 1. 28.
[b] Juftin. *l.* 43. *c.* 1.
[c] Barbeyr. Puff. l. 4. c. 4.

another

another might feife it without injuftice. Thus alfo a vine or other tree might be faid to be in common, as all men were equally entitled to it's produce; and yet any private individual might gain the fole property of the fruit, which he had gathered for his own repaft. A doctrine well illuftrated by Cicero, who compares the world to a great theatre, which is common to the public, and yet the place which any man has taken is for the time his own[d].

But when mankind increafed in number, craft, and ambition, it became neceffary to entertain conceptions of more permanent dominion; and to appropriate to individuals not the immediate *ufe* only, but the very *fubftance* of the thing to be ufed. Otherwife innumerable tumults muft have arifen, and the good order of the world been continually broken and difturbed, while a variety of perfons were ftriving who fhould get the firft occupation of the fame thing, or difputing which of them had actually gained it. As human life alfo grew more and more refined, abundance of conveniences were devifed to render it more eafy, commodious, and agreeable; as, habitations for fhelter and fafety, and raiment for warmth and decency. But no man would be at the trouble to provide either, fo long as he had only an ufufructuary property in them, which was to ceafe the inftant that he quitted poffeffion; --- if, as foon as he walked out of his tent, or pulled off his garment, the next ftranger who came by would have a right to inhabit the one, and to wear the other. In the cafe of habitations in particular, it was natural to obferve, that even the brute creation, to whom every thing elfe was in common, maintained a kind of permanent property in their dwellings, efpecially for the protection of their young; that the birds of the air had nefts, and the beafts of the field had caverns, the invafion of which they efteemed a very flagrant injuftice, and would facrifice their lives to preferve them. Hence a property was foon eftablifhed in every man's houfe and home-ftall; which feem to have been originally mere temporary huts or moveable cabins,

[d] *Quemadmodum theatrum, cum commune fit, recte tamen dici poteft, ejus effe eum locum quem quifque occuparit. De Fin. l. 3. c. 20.*

fuited

suited to the defign of providence for more fpeedily peopling the earth, and fuited to the wandering life of their owners, before any extenfive property in the foil or ground was eftablifhed. And there can be no doubt, but that moveables of every kind became fooner appropriated than the permanent fubftantial foil: partly becaufe they were more fufceptible of a long occupancy, which might be continued for months together without any fenfible interruption, and at length by ufage ripen into an eftablifhed right; but principally becaufe few of them could be fit for ufe, till improved and meliorated by the bodily labour of the occupant; which bodily labour, beftowed upon any fubject which before lay in common to all men, is univerfally allowed to give the faireft and moft reafonable title to an exclufive property therein.

THE article of food was a more immediate call, and therefore a more early confideration. Such, as were not contented with the fpontaneous product of the earth, fought for a more folid refrefhment in the flefh of beafts, which they obtained by hunting. But the frequent difappointments, incident to that method of provifion, induced them to gather together fuch animals as were of a more tame and fequacious nature; and to eftablifh a permanent property in their flocks and herds, in order to fuftain themfelves in a lefs precarious manner, partly by the milk of the dams, and partly by the flefh of the young. The fupport of thefe their cattle made the article of *water* alfo a very important point. And therefore the book of Genefis (the moft venerable monument of antiquity, confidered merely with a view to hiftory) will furnifh us with frequent inftances of violent contentions concerning wells; the exclufive property of which appears to have been eftablifhed in the firft digger or occupant, even in fuch places where the ground and herbage remained yet in common. Thus we find Abraham, who was but a fojourner, afferting his right to a well in the country of Abimelech, and exacting an oath for his fecurity, "becaufe he had digged that well[c]." And Ifaac, about ninety years afterwards, re-claimed this his fa-

[c] Gen. 21. 30.

ther's

ther's property; and, after much contention with the Philiftines, was fuffered to enjoy it in peace [f].

ALL this while the foil and pafture of the earth remained ftill in common as before, and open to every occupant: except perhaps in the neighbourhood of towns, where the neceffity of a fole and exclufive property in lands (for the fake of agriculture) was earlier felt, and therefore more readily complied with. Otherwife, when the multitude of men and cattle had confumed every convenience on one fpot of ground, it was deemed a natural right to feife upon and occupy fuch other lands as would more eafily fupply their neceffities. This practice is ftill retained among the wild and uncultivated nations that have never been formed into civil ftates, like the Tartars and others in the eaft; where the climate itfelf, and the boundlefs extent of their territory, confpire to retain them ftill in the fame favage ftate of vagrant liberty, which was univerfal in the earlieft ages; and which Tacitus informs us continued among the Germans till the decline of the Roman empire [g]. We have alfo a ftriking example of the fame kind in the hiftory of Abraham and his nephew Lot [h]. When their joint fubftance became fo great, that pafture and other conveniences grew fcarce, the natural confequence was that a ftrife arofe between their fervants; fo that it was no longer practicable to dwell together. This contention Abraham thus endeavoured to compofe: " let there be no ftrife, " I pray thee, between thee and me. Is not the whole land be- " fore thee? Separate thyfelf, I pray thee, from me. If thou " wilt take the left hand, then I will go to the right; or if thou " depart to the right hand, then I will go to the left." This plainly implies an acknowleged right, in either, to occupy whatever ground he pleafed, that was not pre-occupied by other tribes. " And Lot lifted up his eyes, and beheld all the plain of Jordan, " that it was well watered every where, even as the garden of the " Lord. Then Lot chofe him all the plain of Jordan, and jour- " neyed eaft; and Abraham dwelt in the land of Canaan."

[f] Gen. 26. 15, 18, &c.

[g] *Colunt difcreti et diverfi; ut fons, ut*   *campus, ut nemus placuit. De mor. Germ.* 16.

[h] Gen. c. 13.

UPON

U p o n the fame principle was founded the right of migration, or fending colonies to find out new habitations, when the mother-country was overcharged with inhabitants; which was practifed as well by the Phaenicians and Greeks, as the Germans, Scythians, and other northern people. And, fo long as it was confined to the ftocking and cultivation of defart uninhabited countries, it kept ftrictly within the limits of the law of nature. But how far the feifing on countries already peopled, and driving out or maffacring the innocent and defencelefs natives, merely becaufe they differed from their invaders in language, in religion, in cuftoms, in government, or in colour; how far fuch a conduct was confonant to nature, to reafon, or to chriftianity, deferved well to be confidered by thofe, who have rendered their names immortal by thus civilizing mankind.

A s the world by degrees grew more populous, it daily became more difficult to find out new fpots to inhabit, without encroaching upon former occupants; and, by conftantly occupying the fame individual fpot, the fruits of the earth were confumed, and it's fpontaneous produce deftroyed, without any provifion for a future fupply or fucceffion. It therefore became neceffary to purfue fome regular method of providing a conftant fubfiftence; and this neceffity produced, or at leaft promoted and encouraged, the art of agriculture. And the art of agriculture, by a regular connexion and confequence, introduced and eftablifhed the idea of a more permanent property in the foil, than had hitherto been received and adopted. It was clear that the earth would not produce her fruits in fufficient quantities, without the affiftance of tillage : but who would be at the pains of tilling it, if another might watch an opportunity to feife upon and enjoy the product of his induftry, art, and labour? Had not therefore a feparate property in lands, as well as moveables, been vefted in fome individuals, the world muft have continued a foreft, and men have been mere animals of prey; which, according to fome philofophers, is the genuine ftate of nature. Whereas now (fo gracioufly

has

has providence interwoven our duty and our happiness together) the result of this very necessity has been the enobling of the human species, by giving it opportunities of improving it's *rational* faculties, as well as of exerting it's *natural*. Necessity begat property; and, in order to insure that property, recourse was had to civil society, which brought along with it a long train of inseparable concomitants; states, government, laws, punishments, and the public exercise of religious duties. Thus connected together, it was found that a part only of society was sufficient to provide, by their manual labour, for the necessary subsistence of all; and leisure was given to others to cultivate the human mind, to invent useful arts, and to lay the foundations of science.

THE only question remaining is, how this property became actually vested; or what it is that gave a man an exclusive right to retain in a permanent manner that specific land, which before belonged generally to every body, but particularly to nobody. And, as we before observed that occupancy gave the right to the temporary *use* of the soil, so it is agreed upon all hands that occupancy gave also the original right to the permanent property in the *substance* of the earth itself; which excludes every one else but the owner from the use of it. There is indeed some difference among the writers on natural law, concerning the reason why occupancy should convey this right, and invest one with this absolute property: Grotius and Puffendorf insisting, that this right of occupancy is founded upon a tacit and implied assent of all mankind, that the first occupant should become the owner; and Barbeyrac, Titius, Mr Locke, and others, holding, that there is no such implied assent, neither is it necessary that there should be; for that the very act of occupancy, alone, being a degree of bodily labour, is from a principle of natural justice, without any consent or compact, sufficient of itself to gain a title. A dispute that favours too much of nice and scholastic refinement! However, both sides agree in this, that occupancy is the thing by which the title was in fact originally gained; every man seising to his own continued use such spots of ground as he found most

agreeable

agreeable to his own convenience, provided he found them un-occupied by any one elfe.

PROPERTY, both in lands and moveables, being thus origi-nally acquired by the firft taker, which taking amounts to a de-claration that he intends to appropriate the thing to his own ufe, it remains in him, by the principles of univerfal law, till fuch time as he does fome other act which fhews an intention to abandon it: for then it becomes, naturally fpeaking, *publici juris* once more, and is liable to be again appropriated by the next oc-cupant. So if one is poffeffed of a jewel, and cafts it into the fea or a public highway, this is fuch an exprefs dereliction, that a property will be vefted in the firft fortunate finder that will feife it to his own ufe. But if he hides it privately in the earth, or other fecret place, and it is difcovered, the finder acquires no property therein; for the owner hath not by this act declared any intention to abandon it, but rather the contrary: and if he lofes or drops it by accident, it cannot be collected from thence, that he defigned to quit the poffeffion; and therefore in fuch cafe the property ftill remains in the lofer, who may claim it again of the finder. And this, we may remember, is the doc-trine of the law of England, with relation to treafure trove[i].

BUT this method, of one man's abandoning his property, and another's feifing the vacant poffeffion, however well founded in theory, could not long fubfift in fact. It was calculated merely for the rudiments of civil fociety, and neceffarily cea-fed among the complicated interefts and artificial refinements of polite and eftablifhed governments. In thefe it was found, that what became inconvenient or ufelefs to one man was highly con-venient and ufeful to another; who was ready to give in ex-change for it fome equivalent, that was equally defirable to the former proprietor. This mutual convenience introduced com-mercial traffic, and the reciprocal transfer of property by fale, grant, or conveyance: which may be confidered either as a con-

[i] See Book I. pag. 285.

tinuance of the original poffeffion which the firft occupant had; or as an abandoning of the thing by the prefent owner, and an immediate fucceffive occupancy of the fame by the new proprietor. The voluntary dereliction of the owner, and delivering the poffeffion to another individual, amount to a transfer of the property; the proprietor declaring his intention no longer to occupy the thing himfelf, but that his own right of occupancy fhall be vefted in the new acquirer. Or, taken in the other light, if I agree to part with an acre of my land to Titius, the deed of conveyance is an evidence of my having abandoned the property, and Titius, being the only or firft man acquainted with fuch my intention, immediately fteps in and feifes the vacant poffeffion: thus the confent expreffed by the conveyance gives Titius a good right againft me; and poffeffion, or occupancy, confirms that right againft all the world befides.

THE moft univerfal and effectual way, of abandoning property, is by the death of the occupant; when, both the actual poffeffion and intention of keeping poffeffion ceafing, the property, which is founded upon fuch poffeffion and intention, ought alfo to ceafe of courfe. For, naturally fpeaking, the inftant a man ceafes to be, he ceafes to have any dominion: elfe, if he had a right to difpofe of his acquifitions one moment beyond his life, he would alfo have a right to direct their difpofal for a million of ages after him; which would be highly abfurd and inconvenient. All property muft therefore ceafe upon death, confidering men as abfolute individuals, and unconnected with civil fociety: for then, by the principles before eftablifhed, the next immediate occupant would acquire a right in all that the deceafed poffeffed. But as, under civilized governments which are calculated for the peace of mankind, fuch a conftitution would be productive of endlefs difturbances, the univerfal law of almoft every nation (which is a kind of fecondary law of nature) has either given the dying perfon a power of continuing his property, by difpofing of his poffeffions by will; or, in cafe he neglects to difpofe of it, or is not permitted to make any difpofition at all,

the

the municipal law of the country then fteps in, and declares who
fhall be the fucceffor, reprefentative, or heir of the deceafed;
that is, who alone fhall have a right to enter upon this vacant
poffeffion, in order to avoid that confufion, which it's becoming
again common would occafion[i]. And farther, in cafe no teftament be permitted by the law, or none be made, and no heir can
be found fo qualified as the law requires, ftill, to prevent the ro-
buft title of occupancy from again taking place, the doctrine of
efcheats is adopted in almoft every country; whereby the fovereign of the ftate, and thofe who claim under his authority, are
the ultimate heirs, and fucceed to thofe inheritances, to which
no other title can be formed.

THE right of inheritance, or defcent to the children and relations of the deceafed, feems to have been allowed much earlier
than the right of devifing by teftament. We are apt to conceive
at firft view that it has nature on it's fide; yet we often miftake
for nature what we find eftablifhed by long and inveterate cuftom.
It is certainly a wife and effectual, but clearly a political, eftablifhment; fince the permanent right of property, vefted in the anceftor himfelf, was no *natural*, but merely a *civil*, right. It is
true, that the tranfmiffion of one's poffeffions to pofterity has an
evident tendency to make a man a good citizen and a ufeful member of fociety: it fets the paffions on the fide of duty, and
prompts a man to deferve well of the public, when he is fure
that the reward of his fervices will not die with himfelf, but be
tranfmitted to thofe with whom he is connected by the deareft
and moft tender affections. Yet, reafonable as this foundation of
the right of inheritance may feem, it is probable that it's immediate original arofe not from fpeculations altogether fo delicate and
refined; and, if not from fortuitous circumftances, at leaft from
a plainer and more fimple principle. A man's children or neareft
relations are ufually about him on his death-bed, and are the

---

[i] It is principally to prevent any vacancy
of poffeffion, that the civil law confiders
father and fon as one perfon; fo that upon
the death of either the inheritance does not
fo properly defcend, as continue in the
hands of the furvivor. *Ff.* 28. 2. 11.

earlieft

earlieft witneffes of his deceafe. They became therefore generally the next immediate occupants, till at length in procefs of
time this frequent ufage ripened into general law. And therefore
alfo in the earlieft ages, on failure of children, a man's fervants
born under his roof were allowed to be his heirs; being immediately on the fpot when he died. For we find the old patriarch
Abraham expreffly declaring, that "fince God had given him no
"feed, his fteward Eliezer, one born in his houfe, was his heir[k]."

WHILE property continued only for life, teftaments were ufelefs and unknown; and, when it became inheritable, the inheritance was long indefeafible, and the children or heirs at law were
incapable of exclufion by will. Till at length it was found, that
fo ftrict a rule of inheritance made heirs difobedient and head-
ftrong, defrauded creditors of their juft debts, and prevented
many provident fathers from dividing or charging their eftates as
the exigence of their families required. This introduced pretty
generally the right of difpofing one's property, or a part of it,
by *teftament*; that is, by written or oral inftructions properly *witneffed* and authenticated, according to the *pleafure* of the deceafed;
which we therefore emphatically ftile his *will*. This was eftablifhed in fome countries much later than in others. With us in
England, till modern times, a man could only difpofe of one
third of his moveables from his wife and children : and, in general, no will was permitted of lands till the reign of Henry the
eighth; and then only of a certain portion : for it was not till
after the reftoration that the power of devifing real property became fo univerfal as at prefent.

WILLS therefore and teftaments, rights of inheritance and
fucceffions, are all of them creatures of the civil or municipal
laws, and accordingly are in all refpects regulated by them; every
diftinct country having different ceremonies and requifites to make
a teftament completely valid : neither does any thing vary more
than the right of inheritance under different national eftablifh-

[k] Gen. 15. 3.

ments.

ments. In England particularly, this diverfity is carried to fuch a length, as if it had been meant to point out the power of the laws in regulating the fucceffion to property, and how futile every claim muft be that has not it's foundation in the pofitive rules of the ftate. In perfonal eftates the father may fucceed to his children; in landed property he never can be heir, by any the remoteft poffibility: in general only the eldeft fon, in fome places only the youngeft, in others all the fons together, have a right to fucceed to the inheritance: in real eftates males are preferred to females, and the eldeft male will ufually exclude the reft; in the divifion of perfonal eftates, the females of equal degree are admitted together with the males, and no right of primogeniture is allowed.

THIS one confideration may help to remove the fcruples of many well-meaning perfons, who fet up a miftaken confcience in oppofition to the rules of law. If a man difinherits his fon, by a will duly executed, and leaves his eftate to a ftranger, there are many who confider this proceeding as contrary to natural juftice: while others fo fcrupuloufly adhere to the fuppofed intention of the dead, that if a will of lands be attefted by only *two* witneffes inftead of *three*, which the law requires, they are apt to imagine that the heir is bound in confcience to relinquifh his title to the devifee. But both of them certainly proceed upon very erroneous principles: as if, on the one hand, the fon had by nature a right to fucceed to his father's lands; or as if, on the other hand, the owner was by nature intitled to direct the fucceffion of his property after his own deceafe. Whereas the law of nature fuggefts, that on the death of the poffeffor the eftate fhould again become common, and be open to the next occupant, unlefs otherwife ordered for the fake of civil peace by the pofitive law of fociety. The pofitive law of fociety, which is with us the municipal law of England, directs it to veft in fuch perfon as the laft proprietor fhall by will, attended with certain requifites, appoint; and, in defect of fuch appointment, to go to fome particular perfon, who, from the refult of certain local

confti-

conftitutions, appears to be the heir at law. Hence it follows, that, where the appointment is regularly made, there cannot be a fhadow of right in any one but the perfon appointed : and, where the neceffary requifites are omitted, the right of the heir is equally ftrong and built upon as folid a foundation, as the right of the devifee would have been, fuppofing fuch requifites were obferved.

B u t, after all, there are fome few things, which notwith-ftanding the general introduction and continuance of property, muft ftill unavoidably remain in common ; being fuch wherein nothing but an ufufructuary property is capable of being had ; and therefore they ftill belong to the firft occupant, during the time he holds poffeffion of them, and no longer. Such (among others) are the elements of light, air, and water ; which a man may occupy by means of his windows, his gardens, his mills, and other conveniences : fuch alfo are the generality of thofe animals which are faid to be *ferae naturae,* or of a wild and un-tameable difpofition ; which any man may feife upon and keep for his own ufe or pleafure. All thefe things, fo long as they re-main in poffeffion, every man has a right to enjoy without dif-turbance ; but if once they efcape from his cuftody, or he vo-luntarily abandons the ufe of them, they return to the common ftock, and any man elfe has an equal right to feife and enjoy them afterwards.

A g a i n ; there are other things, in which a permanent pro-perty *may* fubfift, not only as to the temporary ufe, but alfo the folid fubftance ; and which yet would be frequently found with-out a proprietor, had not the wifdom of the law provided a re-medy to obviate this inconvenience. Such are forefts and other wafte grounds, which were omitted to be appropriated in the general diftribution of lands : fuch alfo are wrecks, eftrays, and that fpecies of wild animals, which the arbitrary conftitutions of pofitive law have diftinguifhed from the reft by the well-known appellation of game. With regard to thefe and fome others, as

diftur-

difturbances and quarrels would frequently arife among individuals, contending about the acquifition of this fpecies of property by firft occupancy, the law has therefore wifely cut up the root of diffenfion, by vefting the things themfelves in the fovereign of the ftate; or elfe in his reprefentatives, appointed and authorized by him, being ufually the lords of manors. And thus the legiflature of England has univerfally promoted the grand ends of civil fociety, the peace and fecurity of individuals, by fteadily purfuing that wife and orderly maxim, of affigning to every thing capable of ownerfhip a legal and determinate owner.

CHAPTER THE SECOND.

OF REAL PROPERTY; AND, FIRST, OF CORPOREAL HEREDITAMENTS.

THE objects of dominion or property are *things,* as contradiftinguifhed from *perfons:* and things are by the law of England diftributed into two kinds; things *real,* and things *perfonal.* Things real are fuch as are permanent, fixed, and immoveable, which cannot be carried out of their place; as lands and tenements: things perfonal are goods, money, and all other moveables; which may attend the owner's perfon wherever he thinks proper to go.

IN treating of things real, let us confider, firft, their feveral forts or kinds; fecondly, the tenures by which they may be holden; thirdly, the eftates which may be had in them; and, fourthly, the title to them, and the manner of acquiring and lofing it.

FIRST, with regard to their feveral forts or kinds, things real are ufually faid to confift in lands, tenements, or hereditaments. *Land* comprehends all things of a permanent, fubftantial nature; being a word of a very extenfive fignification, as will prefently appear more at large. *Tenement* is a word of ftill greater extent; and though in it's vulgar acceptation it is only applied to

houfes

houfes and other buildings, yet in it's original, proper, and legal
fenfe it fignifies every thing that may be *holden*, provided it be
of a permanent nature; whether it be of a fubftantial and fenfible,
or of an unfubftantial ideal kind. Thus *liberum tenementum*,
franktenement, or freehold, is applicable not only to lands and
other folid objects, but alfo to offices, rents, commons, and the
like [a] : and as lands and houfes are tenements, fo is an advowfon
a tenement; and a franchife, an office, a right of common, a
peerage, or other property of the like unfubftantial kind, are, all
of them, legally fpeaking, tenements [b]. But an *hereditament*, fays
fir Edward Coke [c], is by much the largeft and moft comprehenfive expreffion; for it includes not only lands and tenements, but
whatfoever may be *inherited*, be it corporeal, or incorporeal, real,
perfonal, or mixed. Thus an heir loom, or implement of furniture which by cuftom defcends to the heir together with an
houfe, is neither land, nor tenement, but a mere moveable; yet,
being inheritable, is comprized under the general word, hereditament : and fo a condition, the benefit of which may defcend
to a man from his anceftor, is alfo an hereditament [d].

HEREDITAMENTS then, to ufe the largeft expreffion, are
of two kinds, corporeal, and incorporeal. Corporeal confift of
fuch as affect the fenfes; fuch as may be feen and handled by
the body: incorporeal are not the object of fenfation, can neither
be feen nor handled. are creatures of the mind, and exift only in
contemplation.

CORPOREAL hereditaments confift wholly of fubftantial
and permanent objects; all which may be comprehended under
the general denomination of land only. For *land*, fays fir Edward
Coke [e], comprehendeth in it's legal fignification any ground,
foil, or earth whatfoever; as arable, meadows, paftures, woods,
moors, waters, marifhes, furzes, and heath. It legally includeth

---

[a] Co. Litt. 6.   [d] 3 Rep. 2.
[b] Co. Litt. 19, 20.   [e] 1 Inft. 4.
[c] 1 Inft. 6.

alfo all caftles, houfes, and other buildings : for they confift, faith he, of two things ; *land*, which is the foundation ; and *ftructure* thereupon : fo that, if I convey the land or ground, the ftructure or building paffeth therewith. It is obfervable that *water* is here mentioned as a fpecies of land, which may feem a kind of folecifm ; but fuch is the language of the law : and I cannot bring an action to recover poffeffion of a pool or other piece of water, by the name of *water* only ; either by calculating it's capacity, as, for fo many cubical yards ; or, by fuperficial meafure, for twenty acres of water ; or by general defcription, as for a pond, a watercourfe, or a rivulet : but I muft bring my action for the land that lies at the bottom, and muft call it twenty acres of *land covered with water* [f]. For water is a moveable, wandering thing, and muft of neceffity continue common by the law of nature ; fo that I can only have a temporary, tranfient, ufufructuary property therein : wherefore if a body of water runs out of my pond into another man's, I have no right to reclaim it. But the land, which that water covers, is permanent, fixed, and immoveable : and therefore in this I may have a certain, fubftantial property ; of which the law will take notice, and not of the other.

L a n d hath alfo, in it's legal fignification, an indefinite extent, upwards as well as downwards. *Cujus eft folum, ejus eft ufque ad coelum,* is the maxim of the law, upwards ; therefore no man may erect any building, or the like, to overhang another's land : and, downwards, whatever is in a direct line between the furface of any land, and the center of the earth, belongs to the owner of the furface ; as is every day's experience in the mining countries. So that the word " land" includes not only the face of the earth, but every thing under it, or over it. And therefore if a man grants all his lands, he grants thereby all his mines of metal and other foffils, his woods, his waters, and his houfes, as well as his fields and meadows. Not but the particular names of the things are equally fufficient to pafs them, except in the inftance

[f] Brownl. 142.

of

of water; by a grant of which, nothing paſſes but a right of
fiſhing [g] : but the capital diſtinction is this; that by the name of
a caſtle, meſſuage, toft, croft, or the like, nothing elſe will paſs,
except what falls with the utmoſt propriety under the term made
uſe of; but by the name of land, which is *nomen generaliſſimum*,
every thing terreſtrial will paſs [h].

[g] Co. Litt. 4.   [h] *Ibid.* 4, 5, 6.

Chapter the third.

Of INCORPOREAL HEREDITAMENTS.

AN incorporeal hereditament is a right iſſuing out of a thing corporate (whether real or perſonal) or concerning, or annexed to, or exerciſible within, the ſame [a]. It is not the thing corporate itſelf, which may conſiſt in lands, houſes, jewels, or the like; but ſomething collateral thereto, as a rent iſſuing out of thoſe lands or houſes, or an office relating to thoſe jewels. In ſhort, as the logicians ſpeak, corporeal hereditaments are the ſubſtance, which may be always ſeen, always handled : incorporeal hereditaments are but a ſort of accidents, which inhere in and are ſupported by that ſubſtance; and may belong, or not belong to it, without any viſible alteration therein. Their exiſtence is merely in idea and abſtracted contemplation; though their effects and profits may be frequently objects of our bodily ſenſes. And indeed, if we would fix a clear notion of an incorporeal hereditament, we muſt be careful not to confound together the profits produced, and the thing, or hereditament, which produces them. An annuity, for inſtance, is an incorporeal hereditament : for though the money, which is the fruit or product of this annuity, is doubtleſs of a corporeal nature, yet the annuity itſelf, which produces that money, is a thing inviſible, has only a mental exiſtence, and cannot be delivered over from hand to hand. So tithes,

[a] Co. Litt. 19, 20.

if

if we confider the produce of them, as the tenth fheaf or tenth lamb, feem to be completely corporeal; yet they are indeed incorporeal hereditaments: for they, being merely a contingent right, collateral to and iffuing out of lands, can never be the object of fenfe: they are neither capable of being fhewn to the eye, nor of being delivered into bodily poffeffion.

INCORPOREAL hereditaments are principally of ten forts; advowfons, tithes, commons, ways, offices, dignities, franchifes, corodies or penfions, annuities, and rents.

I. ADVOWSON is the right of prefentation to a church, or ecclefiaftical benefice. Advowfon, *advocatio*, fignifies *in clientelam recipere*, the taking into protection; and therefore is fynonymous with patronage, *patronatus*: and he who has the right of advowfon is called the patron of the church. For, when lords of manors firft built churches on their own demefnes, and appointed the tithes of thofe manors to be paid to the officiating minifters, which before were given to the clergy in common (from whence, as was formerly mentioned [b], arofe the divifion of parifhes) the lord, who thus built a church, and endowed it with glebe or land, had of common right a power annexed of nominating fuch minifter as he pleafed (provided he were canonically qualified) to officiate in that church of which he was the founder, endower, maintainer, or, in one word, the patron [c].

THIS inftance of an advowfon will completely illuftrate the nature of an incorporeal hereditament. It is not itfelf the bodily poffeffion of the church and it's appendages; but it is a right to give fome other man a title to fuch bodily poffeffion. The advowfon is the object of neither the fight, nor the touch; and yet it perpetually exifts in the mind's eye, and in contemplation of law. It cannot be delivered from man to man by any vifible bo-

[b] Vol. I. pag. 109.
[c] This original of the *jus patronatus*, by building and endowing the church, appears

alfo to have been allowed in the empire. *Nov.* 56. *t.* 12. *c.* 2. *Nov.* 118. *c.* 23.

dily

dily transfer, nor can corporal poſſeſſion be had of it. If the patron takes corporal poſſeſſion of the church, the church-yard, the
glebe or the like, he intrudes on another man's property; for to
theſe the parſon has an excluſive right. The patronage can therefore be only conveyed by operation of law, by verbal grant, either
oral or written, which is a kind of inviſible, mental transfer:
and being ſo veſted, it lies dormant and unnoticed, till occaſion
calls it forth; when it produces a viſible, corporeal fruit, by in-
titling ſome clerk, whom the patron ſhall pleaſe to nominate, to
enter and receive bodily poſſeſſion of the lands and tenements of
the church.

ADVOWSONS are either advowſons *appendant*, or advowſons
in groſs. Lords of manors being originally the only founders,
and of courſe the only patrons, of churches[d], the right of patronage or preſentation, ſo long as it continues annexed to the
poſſeſſion of the manor, as ſome have done from the foundation
of the church to this day, is called an advowſon appendant[e]: and
it will paſs, or be conveyed, together with the manor, as incident and appendant thereto, by a grant of the manor only, without adding any other words[f]. But where the property of the advowſon has been once ſeparated from the property of the manor,
by legal conveyance, it is called an advowſon in groſs, or at large,
and never can be appendant any more; but is for the future annexed to the perſon of it's owner, and not to his manor or lands[g].

ADVOWSONS are alſo either *preſentative, collative,* or *donative*[h]. An advowſon preſentative is where the patron hath a right
of preſentation to the biſhop or ordinary, and moreover to demand of him to inſtitute his clerk, if he find him canonically
qualified: and this is the moſt uſual advowſon. An advowſon
collative is where the biſhop and patron are one and the ſame
perſon: in which caſe the biſhop cannot preſent to himſelf; but

[d] Co. Litt. 119.
[e] *Ibid.* 121.
[f] *Ibid.* 307.

[g] *Ibid.* 120.
[h] *Ibid.*

he does, by the one act of collation, or conferring the benefice, the whole that is done in common cafes, by both prefentation and inftitution. An advowfon donative is when the king, or any fubject by his licence, doth found a church or chapel, and ordains that it fhall be merely in the gift or difpofal of the patron; fubject to his vifitation only, and not to that of the ordinary; and vefted abfolutely in the clerk by the patron's deed of donation, without prefentation, inftitution, or induction [i]. This is faid to have been antiently the only way of conferring ecclefiaftical benefices in England; the method of inftitution by the bifhop not being eftablifhed more early than the time of arch-bifhop Becket in the reign of Henry II [k]. And therefore though pope Alexander III [l], in a letter to Becket, feverely inveighs againft the *prava confuetudo*, as he calls it, of inveftiture conferred by the patron only, this however fhews what was then the common ufage. Others contend, that the claim of the bifhops to inftitution is as old as the firft planting of chriftianity in this ifland; and in proof of it they allege a letter from the Englifh nobility, to the pope in the reign of Henry the third, recorded by Matthew Paris [m], which fpeaks of prefentation to the bifhop as a thing immemorial. The truth feems to be, that, where the benefice was to be conferred on a mere layman, he was firft prefented to the bifhop, in order to receive ordination, who was at liberty to examine and refufe him: but where the clerk was already in orders, the living was ufually vefted in him by the fole donation of the patron; till about the middle of the twelfth century, when the pope and his bifhops endeavoured to introduce a kind of feodal dominion over ecclefiaftical benefices, and, in confequence of that, began to claim and exercife the right of inftitution univerfally, as a fpecies of fpiritual inveftiture.

H o w e v e r this may be, if, as the law now ftands, the true patron *once* waives this privilege of donation, and prefents to the bifhop, and his clerk is admitted and inftituted, the advow-

---

[i] Co. Litt. 344.
[k] Seld. tith. c. 12. §. 2.
[l] *Decretal. l.* 3. *t.* 7. *c.* 3.
[m] *A. D.* 1239.

fon is now become for ever prefentative, and fhall never be donative any more. For thefe exceptions to general rules, and common right, are ever looked upon by the law in an unfavourable
view, and conftrued as ftrictly as poffible. If therefore the patron, in whom fuch peculiar right refides, does once give up that
right, the law, which loves uniformity, will interpret it to be
done with an intention of giving it up for ever; and will thereupon reduce it to the ftandard of other ecclefiaftical livings.

II. A second fpecies of incorporeal hereditaments is that
of tithes; which are defined to be the tenth part of the increafe,
yearly arifing and renewing from the profits of lands, the ftock
upon lands, and the perfonal induftry of the inhabitants: the
firft fpecies being ufually called *predial,* as of corn, grafs, hops,
and wood[n]; the fecond *mixed,* as of wool, milk, pigs, &c[o], confifting of natural products, but nurtured and preferved in part by
the care of man; and of thefe the tenth muft be paid in grofs:
the third *perfonal,* as of manual occupations, trades, fifheries,
and the like; and of thefe only the tenth part of the clear gains
and profits is due[p].

I T is not to be expected from the nature of thefe general
commentaries, that I fhould particularly fpecify, what things are
tithable, and what not, the time when, or the manner and proportion in which, tithes are ufually due. For this I muft refer to
fuch authors as have treated the matter in detail: and fhall only
obferve, that, in general, tithes are to be paid for every thing
that yields an annual increafe, as corn, hay, fruit, cattle, poultry,
and the like; but not for any thing that is of the fubftance of
the earth, or is not of annual increafe, as ftone, lime, chalk, and
the like; nor for creatures that are of a wild nature, or *ferae naturae,* as deer, hawks, &c, whofe increafe, fo as to profit the
owner, is not annual, but cafual[q]. It will rather be our bufinefs
to confider, 1. The original of the right of tithes. 2. In whom

[n] 1 Roll. Abr. 635. 2 Inft. 649.
[o] *Ibid.*
[p] 1 Roll. Abr. 656.
[q] 2 Inft. 651.

that

that right at prefent fubfifts. 3. Who may be difcharged, either totally or in part, from paying them.

1. As to their original. I will not put the title of the clergy to tithes upon any divine right ; though fuch a right certainly commenced, and I believe as certainly ceafed, with the Jewifh theocracy. Yet an honourable and competent maintenance for the minifters of the gofpel is, undoubtedly, *jure divino* ; whatever the particular mode of that maintenance may be. For, befides the pofitive precepts of the new teftament, natural reafon will tell us, that an order of men, who are feparated from the world, and excluded from other lucrative profeffions, for the fake of the reft of mankind, have a right to be furnifhed with the neceffaries, conveniences, and moderate enjoyments of life, at their expenfe, for whofe benefit they forego the ufual means of providing them. Accordingly all municipal laws have provided a liberal and decent maintenance for their national priefts or clergy : ours in particular have eftablifhed this of tithes, probably in imitation of the Jewifh law : and perhaps, confidering the degenerate ftate of the world in general, it may be more beneficial to the Englifh clergy to found their title on the law of the land, than upon any divine right whatfoever, unacknowleged and unfupported by temporal fanctions.

We cannot precifely afcertain the time when tithes were firft introduced into this country. Poffibly they were cotemporary with the planting of chriftianity among the Saxons, by Auguftin the monk, about the end of the fixth century. But the firft mention of them, which I have met with in any written Englifh law, is in a conftitutional decree, made in a fynod held *A. D.* 786 [r], wherein the payment of tithes in general is ftrongly enjoined. This canon, or decree, which at firft bound not the laity, was effectually confirmed by two kingdoms of the heptarchy, in their parliamentary conventions of eftates, refpective-

---

[r] Selden, c. 8. §. 2.

ly confifting of the kings of Mercia and Northumberland, the bifhops, dukes, fenators, and people. Which was a few years later than the time that Charlemagne eftablifhed the payment of them in France[s], and made that famous divifion of them into four parts; one to maintain the edifice of the church, the fecond to fupport the poor, the third the bifhop, and the fourth the parochial clergy[t].

THE next authentic mention of them is in the *foedus Edwardi et Guthruni*; or the laws agreed upon between king Guthrun the Dane, and Alfred and his fon Edward the elder, fucceffive kings of England, about the year 900. This was a kind of treaty between thofe monarchs, which may be found at large in the Anglo-Saxon laws[u]; wherein it was neceffary, as Guthrun was a pagan, to provide for the fubfiftence of the chriftian clergy under his dominion; and, accordingly, we find[w] the payment of tithes not only *enjoined*, but a *penalty* added upon non-obfervance: which law is feconded by thofe of Athelftan[x], about the year 930. And this is as much as can certainly be traced out, with regard to their legal original.

2. 3. WE are next to confider the perfons to whom they are due. And upon their firft introduction (as hath formerly been obferved[y]) though every man was obliged to pay tithes in general, yet he might give them to what priefts he pleafed[z]; which were called *arbitrary* confecrations of tithes: or he might pay them into the hands of the bifhop, who diftributed among his diocefan clergy the revenues of the church, which were then in common[a]. But, when diocefes were divided into parifhes, the tithes of each parifh were allotted to it's own particular minifter; firft by common confent, or the appointments of lords of manors, and afterwards by the written law of the land[b].

[s] *A. D.* 778.
[t] Book I. ch. 11. Seld. c. 6. §. 7. Sp. of laws, b. 31. c. 12.
[u] Wilkins, pag. 51.
[w] *cap.* 6.
[x] *cap.* 1.
[y] Book I. Introd. §. 4.
[z] 2 Inft. 646. Hob. 296.
[a] Seld. c. 9. §. 4.
[b] *LL. Edgar. c.* 1 & 2. *Canut. c.* 11.

How-

H O W E V E R, arbitrary confecrations of tithes took place again afterwards, and became in general ufe till the time of king John[c]. Which was probably owing to the intrigues of the regular clergy, or monks of the Benedictine and other rules, under arch-bifhop Dunftan and his fucceffors; who endeavoured to wean the people from paying their dues to the fecular or parochial clergy, (a much more valuable fet of men than themfelves) and were then in hopes to have drawn, by fanctimonious pretences to extraordinary purity of life, all ecclefiaftical profits to the coffers of their own focieties. And this will naturally enough account for the number and riches of the monafteries and religious houfes, which were founded in thofe days, and which were frequently endowed with tithes. For a layman, who was obliged to pay his tithes fomewhere, might think it good policy to erect an abbey, and there pay them to his own monks; or grant them to fome abbey already erected; fince for this dotation, which really coft the patron little or nothing, he might, according to the fuperftition of the times, have maffes for ever fung for his foul. But, in procefs of years, the income of the poor laborious parifh priefts being fcandaloufly reduced by thefe arbitrary confecrations of tithes, it was remedied by pope Innocent the third[d] about the year 1200 in a decretal epiftle, fent to the arch-bifhop of Canterbury, and dated from the palace of Lateran : which has occafioned fir Henry Hobart and others to miftake it for a decree of the council of Lateran held *A. D.* 1179, which only prohibited what was called the infeodation of tithes, or their being granted to mere laymen[e]; whereas this letter of pope Innocent to the arch-bifhop enjoined the payment of tithes to the parfons of the refpective parifhes where every man inhabited, agreeable to what was afterwards directed by the fame pope in other countries[f]. This epiftle, fays fir Edward Coke[g], bound not the lay fubjects of this realm; but, being reafonable and juft (and, he might have added,

[c] Selden. c. 11.   [f] *Ibid. c.* 26.
[d] *Opera Innocent. III. tom.* 2. *pag.* 452. [g] 2 Inft. 641.
[e] *Decretal. l.* 3. *t.* 30. *c.* 19.

           being

being correfpondent to the antient law) it was allowed of, and fo became *lex terrae.* This put an effectual stop to all the arbitrary confecrations of tithes; except fome footfteps which ftill continue in thofe portions of tithes, which the parfon of one parifh hath, though rarely, a right to claim in another : for it is now univer- fally held [h], that tithes are due, of common right, to the parfon of the parifh, unlefs there be a fpecial exemption. This parfon of the parifh, we have formerly feen [i], may be either the actual in- cumbent, or elfe the appropriator of the benefice : appropriations being a method of endowing monafteries, which feems to have been devifed by the regular clergy, by way of fubftitution to ar- bitrary confecrations of tithes [k].

3. WE obferved that tithes are due to the parfon of common right, unlefs by fpecial exemption : let us therefore fee, thirdly, who may be exempted from the payment of tithes, and how. Lands, and their occupiers, may be exempted or difcharged from the payment of tithes, either in part or totally, firft, by a real compofition; or, fecondly, by cuftom or prefcription.

FIRST, a real compofition is when an agreement is made be- tween the owner of the lands, and the parfon or vicar, with the confent of the ordinary and the patron, that fuch lands fhall for the future be difcharged from payment of tithes, by reafon of fome land or other real recompence given to the parfon, in lieu and fatisfaction thereof [l]. This was permitted by law, becaufe it was fuppofed that the clergy would be no lofers by fuch compo- fition; fince the confent of the ordinary, whofe duty it is to take care of the church in general, and of the patron, whofe intereft it is to protect that particular church, were both made neceffary to render the compofition effectual: and hence have arifen all fuch compofitions as exift at this day by force of the common law. But, experience fhewing that even this caution was ineffectual, and

---

[h] Regift. 46. Hob. 296.
[i] Book I. pag. 372.
[k] In extraparochial places the king, by his royal prerogative, has a right to all the tithes. See book I. pag. 110.
[l] 2 Inft. 490. Regift. 38. 13 Rep. 40.

the poffeffions of the church being, by this and other means, every day diminifhed, the difabling ftatute 1 3 Eliz. c. 10. was made; which prevents, among other fpiritual perfons, all parfons and vicars from making any conveyances of the eftates of their churches, other than for three lives or twenty one years. So that now, by virtue of this ftatute, no real compofition made fince the 1 3 Eliz. is good for any longer term than three lives or twenty one years, though made by confent of the patron and ordinary : which has indeed effectually demolifhed this kind of traffick; fuch compofitions being now rarely heard of, unlefs by authority of parliament.

SECONDLY, a difcharge by cuftom or prefcription, is where time out of mind fuch perfons or fuch lands have been, either partially or totally, difcharged from the payment of tithes. And this immemorial ufage is binding upon all parties, as it is in it's nature an evidence of univerfal confent and acquiefcence; and with reafon fuppofes a real compofition to have been formerly made. This cuftom or prefcription is either *de modo decimandi*, or *de non decimando*.

A *modus decimandi*, commonly called by the fimple name of a *modus* only, is where there is by cuftom a particular manner of tithing allowed, different from the general law of taking tithes in kind, which are the actual tenth part of the annual increafe. This is fometimes a pecuniary compenfation, as twopence an acre for the tithe of land : fometimes it is a compenfation in work and labour, as that the parfon fhall have only the twelfth cock of hay, and not the tenth, in confideration of the owner's making it for him : fometimes, in lieu of a large quantity of crude or imperfect tithe, the parfon fhall have a lefs quantity, when arrived to greater maturity, as a couple of fowls in lieu of tithe eggs; and the like. Any means, in fhort, whereby the general law of tithing is altered, and a new method of taking them is introduced, is called a *modus decimandi*, or fpecial manner of tithing.

To

To make a good and fufficient *modus*, the following rules muft
be obferved.   1. It muft be *certain* and *invariable* [m], for payment
of different fums will prove it to be no *modus*, that is, no original real compofition; becaufe that muft have been one and the
fame, from it's firft original to the prefent time.   2. The thing
given, in lieu of tithes, muft be beneficial to the *parfon*, and not
for the emolument of *third perfons* only [n]: thus a *modus*, to repair
the *church* in lieu of tithes, is not good, becaufe that is an advantage to the parifh only; but to repair the *chancel* is a good
modus, for that is an advantage to the parfon.   3. It muft be
fomething *different* from the thing compounded for [o]: one load of
hay, in lieu of *all* tithe hay, is no good *modus*: for no parfon
would, *bona fide*, make a compofition to receive lefs than his due
in the fame fpecies of tithe; and therefore the law will not fuppofe it poffible for fuch compofition to have exifted.   4. One
cannot be difcharged from payment of one fpecies of tithe, by
paying a *modus* for another [p].   Thus a *modus* of 1 *d.* for every
milch cow will difcharge the tithe of *milch* kine, but not of *barren* cattle: for tithe is, of common right, due for both; and
therefore a *modus* for one fhall never be a difcharge for the other.
5. The recompence muft be in it's nature as durable as the tithes
difcharged by it; that is, an inheritance certain [q]: and therefore
a *modus* that every *inhabitant* of a houfe fhall pay 4 *d.* a year, in
lieu of the owner's tithes, is no good *modus*; for poffibly the
houfe may not be inhabited, and then the recompence will be
loft.   6. The *modus* muft not be too large, which in law is called
a *rank modus :* as if the real value of the tithes be 60 *l. per annum*, and a *modus* is fuggefted of 40 *l.* this *modus* will not be
good; though one of 40 *s.* might have been valid [r].   For, in thefe
cafes of prefcriptive or cuftomary *modus's*, the law fuppofes an
original real compofition to have been regularly made; which
being loft by length of time, the immemorial ufage is admitted

[m] 1 Keb. 602.
[n] 1 Roll. Abr. 649.
[o] 1 Lev. 179.

[p] Cro. Eliz. 446. Salk. 657.
[q] 2 P. Wms. 462.
[r] 11 Mod. 60.

as

as evidence to fhew that it once did exift, and that from thence fuch ufage was derived. Now time of memory hath been long ago afcertained by the law to commence from the reign of Richard the firft [s]; and any cuftom may be deftroyed by evidence of it's non-exiftence in any part of the long period from his days to the prefent: wherefore, as this real compofition is fuppofed to have been an equitable contract, or the full value of the tithes, at the time of making it, if the *modus* fet up is fo rank and large, as that it beyond difpute exceeds the value of the tithes in the time of Richard the firft, this *modus* is *felo de fe* and deftroys itfelf. For, as it would be deftroyed by any direct evidence to prove it's non-exiftence at any time fince that aera, fo alfo it is deftroyed by carrying in itfelf this internal evidence of a much later original.

A PRESCRIPTION *de non decimando* is a claim to be entirely difcharged of tithes, and to pay no compenfation in lieu of them. Thus the king by his prerogative is difcharged from all tithes [t]. So a vicar fhall pay no tithes to the rector, nor the rector to the vicar, for *ecclefia decimas non folvit ecclefiae* [u]. But thefe privileges are *perfonal* to both the king and the clergy; for their tenant or leffee fhall pay tithes of the fame land, though in their own occupation it is not tithable. And, generally fpeaking, it is an eftablifhed rule, that in *lay* hands, *modus de non decimando non valet* [w]. But fpiritual perfons or corporations, as monafteries, abbots, bifhops, and the like, were always capable of having their lands totally difcharged of tithes, by various ways [x]: as, 1. By real compofition: 2. By the pope's bull of exemption: 3. By unity of poffeffion; as when the rectory of a parifh, and lands in the fame parifh, both belonged to a religious houfe, thofe lands

---

[s] This rule was adopted, when by the ftatute of Weftm. 1. (3 Edw. I. c. 39.) the reign of Richard I. was made the time of limitation in a writ of right. But, fince by the ftatute 32 Hen. VIII. c 2. this period (in a writ of right) hath been very rationally reduced to fixty years, it feems unaccountable, that the date of legal prefcription or memory fhould ftill continue to be reckoned from an aera fo very antiquated. See 2 Roll. Abr. 269. pl. 16.

[t] Cro. Eliz. 511.

[u] *Ibid.* 479.

[w] *Ibid.* 511.

[x] Hob. 309. Cro. Jac. 308.

were

were difcharged of tithes by this unity of poffeffion : 4. By prefcription ; having never been liable to tithes, by being always in
fpiritual hands : 5. By virtue of their order; as the knights templars, ciftercians, and others, whofe lands were privileged by the
pope with a difcharge of tithes[y]. Though, upon the diffolution
of abbeys by Henry VIII, moft of thefe exemptions from tithes
would have fallen with them, and the lands become tithable a-
gain ; had they not been fupported and upheld by the ftatute
31 Hen. VIII. c. 13. which enacts, that all perfons who fhould
come to the poffeffion of the lands of any abbey then diffolved,
fhould hold them free and difcharged of tithes, in as large and
ample a manner as the abbeys themfelves formerly held them.
And from this original have fprung all the lands, which, being
in lay hands, do at prefent claim to be tithe-free : for, if a man
can fhew his lands to have been fuch abbey lands, and alfo immemorially difcharged of tithes by any of the means before-mentioned, this is now a good prefcription *de non decimando*.　But he
muft fhew both thefe requifites : for abbey lands, without a fpecial ground of difcharge, are not difcharged of courfe ; neither
will any prefcription *de non decimando* avail in total difcharge of
tithes, unlefs it relates to fuch abbey lands.

III. C o m m o n, or right of common, appears from it's very
definition to be an incorporeal hereditament : being a profit
which a man hath in the land of another ; as to feed his beafts,
to catch fifh, to dig turf, to cut wood, or the like[z].　And hence
common is chiefly of four forts ; common of pafture, of pifcary,
of turbary, and of eftovers.

1. C o m m o n of pafture is a right of feeding one's beafts on
another's land; for in thofe wafte grounds, which are ufually
called commons, the property of the foil is generally in the lord
of the manor ; as in common fields it is in the particular tenants.
This kind of common is either appendant, appurtenant, becaufe
of vicinage, or in grofs[a].

[y] 2 Rep. 44. Seld. tith. c. 13. §. 2.　　[a] Co. Litt. 122.
[z] Finch, law. 157.

COMMON *appendant* is a right, belonging to the owners or occupiers of arable land, to put commonable beafts upon the lord's wafte, and upon the lands of other perfons within the fame manor. Commonable beafts are either beafts of the plough, or fuch as manure the ground. This is a matter of moft univerfal right; and it was originally permitted [b], not only for the encouragement of agriculture, but for the neceffity of the thing. For, when lords of manors granted out parcels of land to tenants, for fervices either done or to be done, thefe tenants could not plough or manure the land without beafts; thefe beafts could not be fuftained without pafture; and pafture could not be had but in the lord's waftes, and on the uninclofed fallow grounds of themfelves and the other tenants. The law therefore annexed this right of common, as infeparably incident, to the grant of the lands; and this was the original of common appendant: which obtains in Sweden, and the other northern kingdoms, much in the fame manner as in England [c]. Common *appurtenant* is where the owner of land has a right to put in other beafts, befides fuch as are generally commonable; as hogs, goats, and the like, which neither plough nor manure the ground. This, not arifing from the neceffity of the thing, like common appendant, is therefore not of common right; but can only be claimed by immemorial ufage and prefcription [d], which the law efteems fufficient proof of a fpecial grant or agreement for this purpofe. Common *becaufe of vicinage*, or neighbourhood, is where the inhabitants of two townfhips, which lie contiguous to each other, have ufually intercommoned with one another; the beafts of the one ftraying mutually into the other's fields, without any moleftation from either. This is indeed only a permiffive right, intended to excufe what in ftrictnefs is a trefpafs in both, and to prevent a multiplicity of fuits: and therefore either townfhip may enclofe and bar out the other, though they have intercommoned time out of mind. Neither hath any perfon of one town a right to put his

---

[b] 2 Inft. 86.　　　　　　　　　　[d] Co. Litt. 122.
[c] Stiernh. *de jure Sueonum. l.* 2. *c.* 6.

beafts originally into the other's common ; but if they efcape, and
ftray thither of themfelves, the law winks at the trefpafs [e]. Common *in grofs*, or at large, is fuch as is neither appendant nor appurtenant to land, but is annexed to a man's perfon ; being
granted to him and his heirs by deed : or it may be claimed by
prefcriptive right, as by parfon of a church, or the like corporation fole. This is a feparate inheritance, entirely diftinct from
any landed property, and may be vefted in one who has not a foot
of ground in the manor.

ALL thefe fpecies, of pafturable common, may be and ufually
are limited as to number and time ; but there are alfo commons
without ftint, and which laft all the year. By the ftatute of Merton however, and other fubfequent ftatutes[f], the lord of a manor
may enclofe fo much of the wafte as he pleafes, for tillage or
woodground, provided he leaves common fufficient for fuch as are
entitled thereto. This enclofure, when juftifiable, is called in law
" approving ;" an antient expreffion fignifying the fame as " im-
" proving [g]." The lord hath the fole intereft in the foil ; but the
intereft of the lord and commoner, in the common, are looked
upon in law as mutual. They may both bring actions for damage
done, either againft ftrangers, or each other ; the lord for the
public injury, and each commoner for his private damage [h].

2, 3. C O M M O N of pifcary is a liberty of fifhing in another
man's waters ; as common of turbary is a liberty of digging turf
upon another's ground [i]. There is alfo a common of digging for
coals, minerals, ftones, and the like. All thefe bear a refemblance to common of pafture in many refpects ; though in one
point they go much farther : common of pafture being only a
right of feeding on the herbage and vefture of the foil, which
renews annually ; but common of turbary, and the reft, are a
right of carrying away the very foil itfelf.

[e] Co. Litt. 122.
[f] 20 Hen. III. c. 4.   29 Geo. II. c. 36.
and 31 Geo. II. c. 41.

[g] 2 Inft. 474.
[h] 9 Rep. 113.
[i] Co. Litt. 122.

4. C O M-

4. C o m m o n of eftovers (from *eftoffer*, to furnifh) is a liberty of taking neceffary wood, for the ufe or furniture of a houfe or farm, from off another's eftate. The Saxon word, *bote*, is of the fame fignification with the French *eftovers*; and therefore houfe-bote is a fufficient allowance of wood, to repair, or to burn in, the houfe; which latter is fometimes called fire-bote: plough-bote and cart-bote are wood to be employed in making and re-pairing all inftruments of hufbandry: and hay-bote or hedge-bote is wood for repairing of hays, hedges, or fences. Thefe botes or eftovers muft be reafonable ones; and fuch any tenant or leffee may take off the land let or demifed to him, without waiting for any leave, affignment, or appointment of the leffor, unlefs he be reftrained by fpecial covenant to the contrary [k].

T h e s e feveral fpecies of commons do all originally refult from the fame neceffity as common of pafture; viz. for the main-tenance and carrying on of hufbandry: common of pifcary being given for the fuftenance of the tenant's family; common of tur-bary and fire-bote for his fuel; and houfe-bote, plough-bote, cart-bote, and hedge-bote, for repairing his houfe, his inftru-ments of tillage, and the neceffary fences of his grounds.

IV. A f o u r t h fpecies of incorporeal hereditaments is that of *ways*; or the right of going over another man's ground. I fpeak not here of the king's highways, which lead from town to town; nor yet of common ways, leading from a village into the fields; but of private ways, in which a particular man may have an intereft and a right, though another be owner of the foil. This may be grounded on a fpecial permiffion; as when the owner of the land grants to another a liberty of paffing over his grounds, to go to church, to market, or the like: in which cafe the gift or grant is particular, and confined to the grantee alone; it dies with the perfon; and, if the grantee leaves the country, he cannot affign over his right to any other; nor can he juftify

[k] Co. Litt. 41.

taking

taking another perſon in his company[1]. A way may be alſo by preſcription ; as if all the owners and occupiers of ſuch a farm have immemorially uſed to croſs another's ground : for this immemorial uſage ſuppoſes an original grant, whereby a right of way thus appurtenant to land may clearly be created. A right of way may alſo ariſe by act and operation of law : for, if a man grants me a piece of ground in the middle of his field, he at the ſame time tacitly and impliedly gives me a way to come at it ; and I may croſs his land for that purpoſe without treſpaſs[m]. For when the law doth give any thing to one, it giveth impliedly whatſoever is neceſſary for enjoying the ſame[n]. By the law of the twelve tables at Rome, where a man had the right of way over another's land, and the road was out of repair, he who had the right of way might go over any part of the land he pleaſed : which was the eſtabliſhed rule in public as well as private ways. And the law of England, in both caſes, ſeems to correſpond with the Roman[o].

V. Offices, which are a right to exerciſe a public or private employment, and the fees and emoluments thereunto belonging, are alſo incorporeal hereditaments : whether public, as thoſe of magiſtrates ; or private, as of bailiffs, receivers, and the like. For a man may have an eſtate in them, either to him and his heirs, or for life, or for a term of years, or during pleaſure only : ſave only that offices of public truſt cannot be granted for a term of years, eſpecially if they concern the adminiſtration of juſtice, for then they might perhaps veſt in executors or adminiſtrators[p]. Neither can any *judicial* office be granted in reverſion ; becauſe, though the grantee may be able to perform it at the time of the grant, yet before the office falls he may become unable and inſufficient : but *miniſterial* offices may be ſo granted[q] ; for thoſe may be executed by deputy. Alſo, by ſtatute 5 and 6 Edw. VI. c. 16. no public office ſhall be ſold, under pain of diſability to diſpoſe of or hold it. For the law preſumes that he, who buys an

[1] Finch. law. 31.
[m] *Ibid.* 63.
[n] Co. Litt. 56.
[o] Lord Raym. 725. 1 Brownl. 212.

[2] Show. 28. 1 Jon. 297.
[p] 9 Rep. 97.
[q] 11 Rep. 4.

office, will by bribery, extortion, or other unlawful means, make his purchafe good, to the manifeſt detriment of the public.

VI. DIGNITIES bear a near relation to offices. Of the nature of theſe we treated at large in the former book [r] : it will therefore be here fufficient to mention them as a ſpecies of incorporeal hereditaments, wherein a man may have a property or eſtate.

VII. FRANCHISES are a ſeventh ſpecies. Franchiſe and liberty are uſed as ſynonymous terms : and their definition is [s], a royal privilege, or branch of the king's prerogative, ſubſiſting in the hands of a ſubje't. Being therefore derived from the crown, they muſt ariſe from the king's grant; or, in ſome caſes, may be held by preſcription, which, as has been frequently ſaid, preſuppoſes a grant. The kinds of them are various, and almoſt infinite : I will here briefly touch upon ſome of the principal ; premiſing only, that they may be veſted in either natural perſons or bodies politic ; in one man, or in many : but the ſame identical franchiſe, that has before been granted to one, cannot be beſtowed on another ; for that would prejudice the former grant [t].

To be a county palatine is a franchiſe, veſted in a number of perſons. It is likewiſe a franchiſe for a number of perſons to be incorporated, and ſubſiſt as a body politic, with a power to maintain perpetual ſucceſſion and do other corporate aɛts : and each individual member of ſuch corporation is alſo ſaid to have a franchiſe or freedom. Other franchiſes are, to hold a court leet : to have a manor or lordſhip ; or, at leaſt, to have a lordſhip paramount : to have waifs, wrecks, eſtrays, treaſure-trove, royal fiſh, fo feitures, and deodands : to have a court of one's own, or liberty of holding pleas, and trying cauſes : to have the cognizance of pleas ; which is a ſtill greater liberty, being an excluſive right, fo that no other court ſhall try cauſes ariſing within that juriſdiɛtion : to have a bailiwick, or liberty exempt from the ſheriff of the county, wherein the grantee only, and his officers, are to

[r] See Book I. ch. 12.   [t] 2 Roll. Abr. 191. Keilw 196.

[s] Finch. L. 164.   exe-

execute all procefs : to have a fair or market ; with the right of taking toll, either there or at any other public places, as at bridges, wharfs, and the like ; which tolls muft have a reafonable caufe of commencement, (as in confideration of repairs, or the like) elfe the franchife is illegal and void[u] : or, laftly, to have a foreft, chafe, park, warren, or fifhery, endowed with privileges of royalty ; which fpecies of franchife may require a more minute difcuffion.

As to a *foreft :* this, in the hands of a fubject, is properly the fame thing with a chafe ; being fubject to the common law, and not to the foreft laws[v]. But a *chafe* differs from a park, in that it is not enclofed, and alfo in that a man may have a chafe in another man's ground as well as his own ; being indeed the liberty of keeping beafts of chafe or royal game therein, protected even from the owner of the land, with a power of hunting them thereon. A *park* is an enclofed chafe, extending only over a man's own grounds. The word *park* indeed properly fignifies any enclofure ; bnt yet it is not every field or common, which a gentleman pleafes to furround with a wall or paling, and to ftock with a herd of deer, that is thereby conftituted a legal park : for the king's grant, or at leaft immemorial prefcription, is neceffary to make it fo[w]. Though now the difference between a real park, and fuch enclofed grounds, is in many refpects not very material : only that it is unlawful at common law for any perfon to kill any beafts of park or chafe[x], except fuch as poffefs thefe franchifes of foreft, chafe, or park. *Free-warren* is a fimilar franchife, erected for prefervation or cuftody (which the word fignifies) of beafts and fowls of warren[y] ; which, being *ferae naturae,* every one had a natural right to kill as he could :

[u] 2 Inft. 220.
[v] 4 Inft. 314.
[w] Co. Litt. 233. 2 Inft. 199. 11 Rep. 86.
[x] Thefe are properly buck, doe, fox, martin, and roe ; but in a common and legal fenfe extend likewife to all the beafts of the foreft : which, befides the other, are reckoned to be hart, hind, hare, boar, and

wolf, and in a word, all wild beafts of venary or hunting (Co. Litt. 233.)
[y] The beafts are hares, conies, and roes : the fowls are either *campeftres,* as partridges, rails, and quails ; or *fylveftres,* as woodcocks and pheafants ; or *aquatiles,* as mallards and herons. *(Ibid.)*

but

but upon the introduction of the foreſt laws at the Norman conqueſt, as will be ſhewn hereafter, theſe animals being looked
upon as royal game and the ſole property of our ſavage monarchs,
this franchiſe of free-warren was invented to protect them ; by
giving the grantee a ſole and excluſive power of killing ſuch
game, ſo far as his warren extended, on condition of his preventing other perſons.　A man therefore that has the franchiſe
of warren, is in reality no more than a royal game-keeper : but
no man, not even a lord of a manor, could by common law juſtify
ſporting on another's ſoil, or even on his own, unleſs he had the
liberty of free-warren[z].　This franchiſe is almoſt fallen into diſ-
regard, ſince the new ſtatutes for preſerving the game ; the name
being now chiefly preſerved in grounds that are ſet apart for
breeding hares and rabbits.　There are many inſtances of keen
ſportſmen in antient times, who have ſold their eſtates, and reſerved the free-warren, or right of killing game, to themſelves ;
by which means it comes to paſs that a man and his heirs have
ſometimes free-warren over another's ground[a].　A *free fiſhery*,
or excluſive right of fiſhing in a public river, is alſo a royal franchiſe ; and is conſidered as ſuch in all countries where the feodal
polity has prevailed[b] : though the making ſuch grants, and by
that means appropriating what ſeems to be unnatural to reſtrain,
the uſe of running water, was prohibited for the future by king
John's great charter, and the rivers that were fenced in his time
were directed to be laid open, as well as the foreſts to be diſ-
afforeſted[c].　This opening was extended, by the ſecond[d] and
third[d] charters of Henry III, to thoſe alſo that were fenced under
Richard I ; ſo that a franchiſe of free fiſhery ought now to be at
leaſt as old as the reign of Henry II.　This differs from a *ſeveral*
fiſhery ; becauſe he that has a ſeveral fiſhery muſt alſo be the
owner of the ſoil, which in a free fiſhery is not requiſite.　It
differs alſo from a *common* of piſcary before-mentioned, in that

[z] Salk. 637.
[a] Bro. *Abr. tit. Warren.* 3.
[b] Seld. *Mar. clauſ.* I 24. Dufreſne. V.
503. Crag. *de Jur feod.* II. 8. 15.
[c] *cap.* 47. *edit.* Oxon.
[d] *cap.* 20.
[e] 9 Hen. III. c. 16.

the free fifhery is an exclufive right, the common of pifcary is
not fo : and therefore, in a free fifhery, a man has a property in
the fifh before they are caught ; in a common of pifcary, not till
afterwards [f]. Some indeed have confidered a *free* fifhery not as
a royal franchife, but merely as a private grant of a liberty to fifh
in the *feveral* fifhery of the grantor [g]. But the confidering fuch
right as originally a flower of the prerogative, till reftrained by
magna carta, and derived by royal grant (previous to the reign
of Richard I.) to fuch as now claim it by prefcription, may remove fome difficulties in refpect to this matter, with which our
books are embaraffed.

VIII. C o r o d i e s are a right of fuftenance, or to receive
certain allotments of victual and provifion for one's maintenance [h].
In lieu of which (efpecially when due from ecclefiaftical perfons)
a penfion or fum of money is fometimes fubftituted [i]. And thefe
may be reckoned another fpecies of incorporeal hereditaments ;
though not chargeable on, or iffuing from, any corporeal inheritance, but only charged on the perfon of the owner in refpect
of fuch his inheritance. To thefe may be added,

IX. A n n u i t i e s, which are much of the fame nature ;
only that thefe arife from temporal, as the former from fpiritual,
perfons. An annuity is a thing very diftinct from a rent-charge,
with which it is frequently confounded : a rent-charge being a
burthen impofed upon and iffuing out of *lands*, whereas an annuity
is a yearly fum chargeable only upon the *perfon* of the grantor [j].
Therefore, if a man by deed grant to another the fum of 20 *l. per
annum*, without expreffing out of what lands it fhall iffue, no
land at all fhall be charged with it ; but it is a mere perfonal
annuity : which is of fo little account in the law, that, if granted to an eleemofynary corporation, it is not within the ftatutes
of mortmain [k] ; and yet a man may have a real eftate in it,
though his fecurity is merely perfonal.

[f] F. N. B. 88. Salk. 637.
[g] 2 Sid. 8.
[h] Finch. L. 162.
[i] See Book I. ch. 8.
[j] Co. Litt. 144.
[k] *Ibid.* 2.

X. R e n t s

X. RENTS are the laſt ſpecies of incorporeal hereditaments. The word, rent, or render, *reditus*, ſignifies a compenſation, or return; it being in the nature of an acknowlegement given for the poſſeſſion of ſome corporeal inheritance [1]. It is defined to be a certain profit iſſuing yearly out of lands and tenements corporeal. It muſt be a *profit*; yet there is no occaſion for it to be, as it uſually is, a ſum of money: for ſpurs, capons, horſes, corn, and other matters may be rendered, and frequently are rendered, by way of rent [m]. It may alſo conſiſt in ſervices or manual operations; as, to plough ſo many acres of ground, to attend the king or the lord to the wars, and the like; which ſervices in the eye of the law are profits. This profit muſt alſo be *certain*; or that which may be reduced to a certainty by either party. It muſt alſo iſſue *yearly*; though there is no occaſion for it to iſſue every ſucceſſive year; but it may be reſerved every ſecond, third, or fourth year [n]: yet, as it is to be produced out of the profits of lands and tenements, as a recompenſe for being permitted to hold and enjoy them, it ought to be reſerved yearly, becauſe thoſe profits do annually ariſe and are annually renewed. It muſt *iſſue out* of the thing granted, and not be part of the land or thing itſelf; wherein it differs from an exception in the grant, which is always of part of the thing granted [o]. It muſt, laſtly, iſſue out of *lands and tenements corporeal*; that is, from ſome inheritance whereunto the owner or grantee of the rent may have recourſe to diſtrein. Therefore a rent cannot be reſerved out of an advowſon, a common, an office, a franchiſe, or the like [p]. But a grant of ſuch annuity or ſum may operate as a perſonal contract, and oblige the grantor to pay the money reſerved, or ſubject him to an action of debt [q]; though it doth not affect the inheritance, and is no legal rent in contemplation of law.

THERE are at common law [r] three manner of rents; rentſervice, rent-charge, and rent-ſeck. *Rent-ſervice* is ſo called be-

---

[1] Co. Litt. 144.
[m] *Ibid.* 142.
[n] *Ibid.* 47.

[o] Plowd. 13. 8 Rep. 71.
[p] Co. Litt. 144.
[q] *Ibid.* 47. [r] Litt. §. 213.

caufe it hath fome corporal fervice incident to it, as at the leaft fealty, or the feodal oath of fidelity ˢ. For, if a tenant holds his land by fealty, and ten fhillings rent; or by the fervice of plough-ing the lord's land, and five fhillings rent; thefe pecuniary rents, being connected with perfonal fervices, are therefore called rent-fervice. And for thefe, in cafe they be behind, or arrere, at the day appointed, the lord may diftrein of common right, without referving any fpecial power of diftrefs ; provided he hath in him-felf the reverfion, or future eftate of the lands and tenements, after the leafe or particular eftate of the leffee or grantee is expired ᵗ. A *rent-charge*, is where the owner of the rent hath no future intereft, or reverfion expectant in the land ; as where a man by deed maketh over to others his *whole* eftate in fee fimple, with a certain rent payable thereout, and adds to the deed a cove-nant or claufe of diftrefs, that if the rent be arrere, or behind, it fhall be lawful to diftrein for the fame. In this cafe the land is liable to the diftrefs, not of common right, but by virtue of the claufe in the deed : and therefore it is called a rent-*charge*, becaufe in this manner the land is charged with a diftrefs for the payment of it ᵘ. *Rent-feck, reditus ficcus*, or barren rent, is in effect nothing more than a rent referved by deed, but without any claufe of diftrefs.

THERE are alfo other fpecies of rents, which are reducible to thefe three. Rents *of affife* are the certain eftablifhed rents of the freeholders and antient copyholders of a manor ʷ, which can-not be departed from or varied. Thofe of the freeholders are fre-quently called *chief* rents, *reditus capitales* ; and both forts are in-differently denominated *quit* rents, *quieti reditus* ; becaufe thereby the tenant goes quit and free of all other fervices. When thefe payments were referved in filver or white money, they were an-tiently called *white*-rents, or *blanch-farms, reditus albi* ˣ ; in con-tradiftinction to rents referved in work, grain, &c. which were

ˢ Co. Litt. 142.
ᵗ Litt. §. 215.
ᵘ Co. Litt. 143.
ʷ 2 Inft. 19.

ˣ In Scotland this kind of fmall pay-ment is called *blench-holding*, or *reditus albae firmae*.

called

called *reditus nigri*, or *black-maile*[y]. *Rack*-rent is only a rent of the full value of the tenement, or near it. A *feefarm*-rent is a rent-charge issuing out of an estate in fee; of at least one fourth of the value of the lands, at the time of it's reservation[z]: for a grant of lands, reserving so considerable a rent, is indeed only letting lands to farm in fee simple instead of the usual methods for life or years.

THESE are the general divisions of rent; but the difference between them (in respect to the remedy for recovering them) is now totally abolished; and all persons may have the like remedy by distress for rents-seck, rents of assise, and chief-rents, as in case of rents reserved upon lease[a].

RENT is regularly due and payable upon the land from whence it issues, if no particular place is mentioned in the reservation[b]: but, in case of the king, the payment must be either to his officers at the exchequer, or to his receiver in the country[c]. And, strictly, the rent is demandable and payable before the time of sunset of the day whereon it is reserved[d]; though some have thought it not absolutely due till midnight[e].

WITH regard to the original of rents, something will be said in the next chapter: and, as to distresses and other remedies for their recovery, the doctrine relating thereto, and the several proceedings thereon, these belong properly to the third part of our commentaries, which will treat of civil injuries, and the means whereby they are redressed.

[y] 2 Inst. 19.
[z] Co. Litt. 143.
[a] Stat. 4 Geo. II. c. 28.
[b] Co. Litt. 201.
[c] 4 Rep. 73.
[d] Anderf. 253.
[e] 1 Saund. 287. 1 Chan. Prec. 555.

C H A P T E R   T H E   F O U R T H.

O F   T H E   **FEODAL   SYSTEM.**

I T is impoffible to underftand, with any degree of accuracy,
either the civil conftitution of this kingdom, or the laws
which regulate it's landed property, without fome general ac-
quaintance with the nature and doctrine of feuds, or the feodal
law : a fyftem fo univerfally received throughout Europe, upwards
of twelve centuries ago, that fir Henry Spelman [a] does not fcruple
to call it the law of nations in our weftern world. This chapter
will be therefore dedicated to this inquiry. And though, in the
courfe of our obfervations in this and many other parts of the
prefent book, we may have occafion to fearch pretty highly into
the antiquities of our Englifh jurifprudence, yet furely no induf-
trious ftudent will imagine his time mif-employed, when he is
led to confider that the obfolete doctrines of our laws are frequently the foundation, upon which what remains is erected ;
and that it is impracticable to comprehend many rules of the modern law, in a fcholarlike fcientifical manner, without having recourfe to the antient. Nor will thefe refearches be altogether void
of rational entertainment as well as ufe : as in viewing the ma-
jeftic ruins of Rome or Athens, of Balbec or Palmyra, it admi-
nifters both pleafure and inftruction to compare them with the
draughts of the fame edifices, in their priftine proportion and
fplendor.

[a] of parliaments. 57.

T H E

THE conſtitution of feuds [b] had it's original from the military policy of the northern or Celtic nations, the Goths, the Hunns, the Franks, the Vandals, and the Lombards, who all migrating from the ſame *officina gentium*, as Crag very juſtly entitles it [c], poured themſelves in vaſt quantities into all the regions of Europe, at the declenſion of the Roman empire. It was brought by them from their own countries, and continued in their reſpective colonies as the moſt likely means to ſecure their new acquiſitions : and, to that end, large diſtricts or parcels of land were allotted by the conquering general to the ſuperior officers of the army, and by them dealt out again in ſmaller parcels or allotments to the inferior officers and moſt deſerving ſoldiers [d]. Theſe allotments were called *feoda*, feuds, fiefs, or fees ; which laſt appellation in the northern languages [e] ſignifies a conditional ſtipend or reward [f]. Rewards or ſtipends they evidently were ; and the condition annexed to them was, that the poſſeſſor ſhould do ſervice faithfully, both at home and in the wars, to him by whom they were given ; for which purpoſe he took the *juramentum fidelitatis*, or oath of fealty [g] : and in caſe of the breach of this condition and oath, by not performing the ſtipulated ſervice, or by deſerting the lord in battle, the lands were again to revert to him who granted them [h].

ALLOTMENTS thus acquired, naturally engaged ſuch as accepted them to defend them : and, as they all ſprang from the

---

[b] See Spelman of feuds, and Wright of tenures, *per tot.*

[c] *De jure feod.* 19, 20.

[d] Wright. 7.

[e] Spelm. *Gl.* 216.

[f] Pontoppidan in his hiſtory of Norway (page 290) obſerves, that in the northern languages **oþ** ſignifies *proprietas* and **all** *totum.* Hence he derives the **oþal** right in thoſe countries ; and hence too perhaps is derived the *udal* right in Finland, &c. (See Mac Doual. Inſt. part. 2.) Now the tranſ-

poſition of theſe northern ſyllables, **alloþþ**, will give us the true etymology of the *allodium*, or abſolute property of the feudiſts ; as, by a ſimilar combination of the latter ſyllable with the word **fee** (which ſignifies, we have ſeen, a conditional reward or ſtipend) **feeoþþ** or *feodum* will denote ſtipendiary property.

[g] See this Oath explained at large in *Feud. l.* 2. *t.* 7.

[h] *Feud. l.* 2. *t.* 24.

same right of conqueſt, no part could ſubſiſt independent of the whole; wherefore all givers as well as receivers were mutually bound to defend each others poſſeſſions. But, as that could not effectually be done in a tumultuous irregular way, government, and to that purpoſe ſubordination, was neceſſary. Every receiver of lands, or feudatory, was therefore bound, when called upon by his benefactor, or immediate lord of his feud or fee, to do all in his power to defend him. Such benefactor or lord was like-wiſe ſubordinate to and under the command of his immediate benefactor or ſuperior; and ſo upwards to the prince or general himſelf. And the ſeveral lords were alſo reciprocally bound, in their reſpective gradations, to protect the poſſeſſions they had given. Thus the feodal connection was eſtabliſhed, a proper mi-litary ſubjection was naturally introduced, and an army of feuda-tories were always ready enliſted, and mutually prepared to muſ-ter, not only in defence of each man's own ſeveral property, but alſo in defence of the whole, and of every part of this their newly acquired country [i]: the prudence of which conſtitution was ſoon ſufficiently viſible in the ſtrength and ſpirit, with which they maintained their conqueſts.

THE univerſality and early uſe of this feodal plan, among all thoſe nations which in complaiſance to the Romans we ſtill call barbarous, may appear from what is recorded [k] of the Cimbri and Teutones, nations of the ſame northern original as thoſe whom we have been deſcribing, at their firſt irruption into Italy about a century before the chriſtian aera. They demanded of the Ro-mans, " *ut martius populus aliquid ſibi terrae daret, quaſi ſtipen-* " *dium : caeterum, ut vellet, manibus atque armis ſuis uteretur.*" The ſenſe of which may be thus rendered; they deſired ſtipen-diary lands (that is, feuds) to be allowed them, to be held by military and other perſonal ſervices, whenever their lords ſhould call upon them. This was evidently the ſame conſtitution, that diſplayed itſelf more fully about ſeven hundred years afterwards; when the Salii, Burgundians, and Franks broke in upon Gaul,

---

[i] Wright. 8.   [k] *L. Florus. l.* 3. *c.* 3.

the Vifigoths on Spain, and the Lombards upon Italy, and introduced with themfelves this northern plan of polity, ferving at
once to diftribute, and to protect, the territories they had newly
gained. And from hence it is probable that the emperor Alexander Severus [1] took the hint, of dividing lands conquered from
the enemy among his generals and victorious foldiery, on condition of receiving military fervice from them and their heirs for
ever.

Scarce had thefe northern conquerors eftablifhed themfelves
in their new dominions, when the wifdom of their conftitutions,
as well as their perfonal valour, alarmed all the princes of Europe;
that is, of thofe countries which had formerly been Roman provinces, but had revolted, or were deferted by their old mafters,
in the general wreck of the empire. Wherefore moft, if not all,
of them thought it neceffary to enter into the fame or a fimilar
plan of policy. For whereas, before, the poffeffions of their
fubjects were perfectly *allodial*; (that is, wholly independent,
and held of no fuperior at all) now they parcelled out their royal
territories, or perfuaded their fubjects to furrender up and retake
their own landed property, under the like feodal obligation of
military fealty [m]. And thus, in the compafs of a very few years,
the feodal conftitution, or the doctrine of tenure, extended itfelf
over all the weftern world. Which alteration of landed property,
in fo very material a point, neceffarily drew after it an alteration
of laws and cuftoms : fo that the feodal laws foon drove out the
Roman, which had hitherto univerfally obtained, but now became for many centuries loft and forgotten; and Italy itfelf (as
fome of the civilians, with more fpleen than judgment, have expreffed it) *belluinas, atque ferinas, immanefque Longobardorum leges
accepit* [n]

---

[1] " *Sola, quae de hoftibus capta funt, limi-*
" *taneis ducibus et militibus donavit ; ita ut*
" *eorum ita effent, fi haeredes illorum militarent,*
" *nec unquam ad privatos pertinerent : dicens*
" *attentius illos militaturos, fi etiam fua rura*
" *defenderent. Addidit fane his et animalia et*
" *fervos, ut poffent colere quod acceperant ; ne*

" *per inopiam hominum vel per fenectutem defe-*
" *rerentur rura vicina barbariae, quod turpif-*
" *fimum ille ducebat.*" (Æl. Lamprid. *in vita*
Alex. Severi.)

[m] Wright. 10.

[n] Gravin. Orig. *l.* 1. §. 139.

B u t this feodal polity, which was thus by degrees eſtabliſhed over all the continent of Europe, ſeems not to have been received in this part of our iſland, at leaſt not univerſally and as a part of the national conſtitution, till the reign of William the Norman ° Not but that it is reaſonable to believe, from abundant traces in our hiſtory and laws, that even in the times of the Saxons, who were a ſwarm from what ſir William Temple calls the ſame northern hive, ſomething ſimilar to this was in uſe : yet not ſo extenſively, nor attended with all the rigour that was afterwards imported by the Normans. For the Saxons were firmly ſettled in this iſland, at leaſt as early as the year 600 : and it was not till two centuries after, that feuds arrived to their full vigour and maturity, even on the continent of Europe [p].

T h i s introduction however of the feodal tenures into England, by king William, does not ſeem to have been effected immediately after the conqueſt, nor by the mere arbitrary will and power of the conqueror; but to have been conſented to by the great council of the nation long after his title was eſtabliſhed. Indeed from the prodigious ſlaughter of the Engliſh nobility at the battle of Haſtings, and the fruitleſs inſurrections of thoſe who ſurvived, ſuch numerous forfeitures had accrued, that he was able to reward his Norman followers with very large and extenſive poſſeſſions : which gave a handle to the monkiſh hiſtorians, and ſuch as have implicitly followed them, to repreſent him as having by right of the ſword ſeiſed on all the lands of England, and dealt them out again to his own favourites. A ſuppoſition, grounded upon a miſtaken ſenſe of the word *conqueſt*; which, in it's feodal acceptation, ſignifies no more than *acquiſition :* and this has led many haſty writers into a ſtrange hiſtorical miſtake, and one which upon the ſlighteſt examination will be found to be moſt untrue. However, certain it is, that the Normans now began to gain very large poſſeſſions in England : and their regard for the feodal law, under which they had long lived, together

° Spelm. *Gloſſ.* 218. Bract. *l.* 2. *c.* 16. §. 7.   [p] Crag. *l.* 1. *t.* 4.

with

with the king's recommendation of this policy to the Englifh, as the beft way to put themfelves on a military footing, and thereby to prevent any future attempts from the continent, were probably the reafons that prevailed to effect it's eftablifhment here. And perhaps we may be able to afcertain the time of this great revolution in our landed property with a tolerable degree of exactnefs. For we learn from the Saxon Chronicle [q], that in the nineteenth year of king William's reign an invafion was apprehended from Denmark ; and the military conftitution of the Saxons being then laid afide, and no other introduced in it's ftead, the kingdom was wholly defencelefs : which occafioned the king to bring over a large army of Normans and Bretons, who were quartered upon every landholder, and greatly opprefled the people. This apparent weaknefs, together with the grievances occafioned by a foreign force, might co-operate with the king's remonftrances, and the better encline the nobility to liften to his propofals for putting them in a pofture of defence. For, as foon as the danger was over, the king held a great council to inquire into the ftate of the nation [r] ; the immediate confequence of which was the compiling of the great furvey called domefday-book, which was finifhed in the next year : and in the latter end of that very year the king was attended by all his nobility at Sarum ; where all the principal landholders fubmitted their lands to the yoke of military tenure, became the king's vafals, and did homage and fealty to his perfon [s]. This feems to have been the aera of formally introducing the feudal tenures by law ; and probably the very law, thus made at the council of Sarum, is that which is ftill extant [t], and couched in thefe remarkable words : " *ftatuimus, ut omnes liberi* " *homines foedere et facramento affirment, quod intra et extra uni-* " *verfum regnum Angliae Wilhelmo regi domino fuo fideles effe volunt ;* " *terras et honores illius omni fidelitate ubique fervare cum eo, et*

---

[q] *A. D.* 1085.

[r] *Rex tenuit magnum concilium, et graves fermones habuit cum fuis proceribus de hac terra, quo modo incoleretur, et a quibus hominibus. Chron. Sax. ibid.*

[s] *Omnes praedia tenentes, quotquot effent notae*

melioris per totam Angliam, ejus homines facti funt, et omnes fe illi fubdidere, ejufque facti funt vafalli, ac ei fidelitatis juramenta praefti-terunt, fe contra alios quofcunque illi fidos futuros. Chron. Sax. A. D. 1086.

[t] *cap.* 52. Wilk. 228.

" *contra inimicos et alienigenas defendere."* The terms of this law (as fir Martin Wright has obferved [u]) are plainly feodal : for, firft, it requires the oath of fealty, which made in the fenfe of the feudifts every man that took it a tenant or vafal; and, fecondly, the tenants obliged themfelves to defend their lord's territories and titles againft all enemies foreign and domeftic. But what puts the matter out of difpute is another law of the fame collection [w], which exacts the performance of the military feodal fervices, as ordained by the general council. " *Omnes comites, et* " *barones, et milites, et fervientes, et univerfi liberi homines totius* " *regni noftri praedicti, habeant et tenoant fe femper bene in armis et* " *in equis, ut decet et oportet : et fint femper prompti et bene parati* " *ad fervitium fuum integrum nobis explendum et peragendum cum* " *opus fuerit; fecundum quod nobis debent de feodis et tenementis fuis* " *de jure facere; et ficut illis ftatuimus per commune concilium totius* " *regni noftri praedicti."*

THIS new polity therefore feems not to have been *impofed* by the conqueror, but nationally and freely *adopted* by the general affembly of the whole realm, in the fame manner as other nations of Europe had before adopted it, upon the fame principle of felf-fecurity. And, in particular, they had the recent example of the French nation before their eyes; which had gradually furrendered up all it's allodial or free lands into the king's hands, who reftored them to the owners as a *beneficium* or feud, to be held to them and fuch of their heirs as they previoufly nominated to the king : and thus by degrees all the allodial eftates of France were converted into feuds, and the freemen became the vafals of the crown [x]. The only difference between this change of tenures in France, and that in England, was, that the former was effected gradually, by the confent of private perfons; the latter was done at once, all over England, by the common confent of the nation [y].

[u] Tenures. 66.
[w] *cap.* 58. Wilk. 228.
[x] Montefq. Sp. L. b. 31. c. 8.
[y] Pharoah thus acquired the dominion of all the lands in Egypt, and granted them out to the Egyptians, referving an annual render of the fifth part of their value. (Gen. c. 47.)

IN

IN confequence of this change, it became a fundamental maxim and neceffary principle (though in reality a mere fiction) of our Englifh tenures, " that the king is the univerfal lord and original " proprietor of all the lands in his kingdom; and that no man " doth or can poffefs any part of it, but what has mediately or " immediately been derived as a gift from him, to be held upon " feodal fervices." For, this being the real cafe in pure, original, proper feuds, other nations who adopted this fyftem were obliged to act upon the fame fuppofition, as a fubftruction and foundation of their new polity, though the fact was indeed far otherwife. And indeed by thus confenting to the introduction of feodal tenures, our Englifh anceftors probably meant no more than to put the kingdom in a ftate of defence by eftablifhing a military fyftem; and to oblige themfelves (in refpect of their lands) to maintain the king's title and territories, with equal vigour and fealty, *as if* they had received their lands from his bounty upon thefe exprefs conditions, as pure, proper, beneficiary feudatories. But, whatever their meaning was, the Norman interpreters, fkilled in all the niceties of the feodal conftitutions, and well underftanding the import and extent of the feodal terms, gave a very different conftruction to this proceeding; and thereupon took a handle to introduce not only the rigorous doctrines which prevailed in the duchy of Normandy, but alfo fuch fruits and dependencies, fuch hardfhips and fervices, as were never known to other nations [7]; as if the Englifh had in fact, as well as theory, owed every thing they had to the bounty of their fovereign lord.

OUR anceftors therefore, who were by no means beneficiaries, but had barely confented to this fiction of tenure from the crown, as the bafis of a military difcipline, with reafon looked upon thefe deductions as grievous impofitions, and arbitrary conclufions from principles that, as to them, had no foundation in truth [a]. However, this king, and his fon William Rufus, kept up with

[7] Spelm. of feuds, c. 28.   [a] Wright. 81.

a high hand all the rigours of the feodal doctrines : but their succeſſor, Henry I, found it expedient, when he ſet up his pretenſions to the crown, to promiſe a reſtitution of the laws of king Edward the confeſſor, or antient Saxon ſyſtem ; and accordingly, in the firſt year of his reign, granted a charter[b], whereby he gave up the greater grievances, but ſtill reſerved the fiction of feodal tenure, for the ſame military purpoſes which engaged his father to introduce it. But this charter was gradually broke through, and the former grievances were revived and aggravated, by himſelf and ſucceeding princes ; till in the reign of king John they became ſo intolerable, that they occaſioned his barons, or principal feudatories, to riſe up in arms againſt him : which at length produced the famous great charter at Runing-mead, which, with ſome alterations, was confirmed by his ſon Henry III. And, though it's immunities (eſpecially as altered on it's laſt edition by his ſon[c]) are very greatly ſhort of thoſe granted by Henry I, it was juſtly eſteemed at the time a vaſt acquiſition to Engliſh liberty. Indeed, by the farther alteration of tenures that has ſince happened, many of theſe immunities may now appear, to a common obſerver, of much leſs conſequence than they really were when granted : but this, properly conſidered, will ſhew, not that the acquiſitions under John were ſmall, but that thoſe under Charles were greater. And from hence alſo ariſes another inference ; that the liberties of Engliſhmen are not (as ſome arbitrary writers would repreſent them) mere infringements of the king's prerogative, extorted from our princes by taking advantage of their weakneſs ; but a reſtoration of that antient conſtitution, of which our anceſtors had been defrauded by the art and fineſſe of the Norman lawyers, rather than deprived by the force of the Norman arms.

HAVING given this ſhort hiſtory of their riſe and progreſs, we will next conſider the nature, doctrine, and principal laws of feuds ; wherein we ſhall evidently trace the groundwork of many parts of our public polity, and alſo the original of ſuch of our

[b] *LL. Hen. I. c. 1.*   [c] *9 Hen. III.*

OWN

own tenures, as were either abolifhed in the laft century, or ftill remain in force.

THE grand and fundamental maxim of all feodal tenure is this; that all lands were originally granted out by the fovereign, and are therefore holden, either mediately or immediately, of the crown. The grantor was called the proprietor, or *lord*; being he who retained the dominion or ultimate property of the feud or fee: and the grantee, who had only the ufe and poffeffion, according to the terms of the grant, was ftiled the feudatory or *vafal*, which was only another name for the tenant or holder of the lands; though, on account of the prejudices we have juftly conceived againft the doctrines that were afterwards grafted on this fyftem, we now ufe the word *vafal* opprobrioufly, as fynonymous to flave or bondman. The manner of the grant was by words of gratuitous and pure donation, *dedi et conceffi*; which are ftill the operative words in our modern infeodations or deeds of feoffment. This was perfected by the ceremony of corporal inveftiture, or open and notorious delivery of poffeffion in the prefence of the other vafals, which perpetuated among them the aera of the new acquifition, at a time when the art of writing was very little known: and therefore the evidence of property was repofed in the memory of the neighbourhood; who, in cafe of a difputed title, were afterwards called upon to decide the difference, not only according to external proofs, adduced by the parties litigant, but alfo by the internal teftimony of their own private knowlege.

BESIDES an oath of *fealty*, or profeffion of faith to the lord, which was the parent of our oath of allegiance, the vafal or tenant upon inveftiture did ufually *homage* to his lord; openly and humbly kneeling, being ungirt, uncovered, and holding up his hands both together between thofe of the lord, who fate before him; and there profeffing that " he did become his *man*, from " that day forth, of life and limb and earthly honour:" and then he received a kifs from his lord [d]. Which ceremony was deno-

[d] Litt. §. 85.

minated

minated *homagium,* or *manhood,* by the feudifts, from the ftated form of words, *devenio vefter homo* [e].

WHEN the tenant had thus profeffed himfelf to be the man of his fuperior or lord, the next confideration was concerning the *fervice,* which, as fuch, he was bound to render, in recompenfe for the land he held. This, in pure, proper, and original feuds, was only twofold : to follow, or do *fuit* to, the lord in his courts in time of peace; and in his armies or warlike retinue, when neceffity called him to the field. The lord was, in early times, the legiflator and judge over all his feudatories : and therefore the vafals of the inferior lords were bound by their fealty to attend their domeftic courts baron [f], (which were inftituted in every manor or barony, for doing fpeedy and effectual juftice to all the tenants) in order as well to anfwer fuch complaints as might be alleged againft themfelves, as to form a jury or homage for the trial of their fellow-tenants; and upon this account, in all the feodal inftitutions both here and on the continent, they are diftinguifhed by the appellation of the peers of the court ; *pares curtis,* or *pares curiae.* In like manner the barons themfelves, or lords of inferior diftricts, were denominated peers of the king's court, and were bound to attend him upon fummons, to hear caufes of greater confequence in the king's prefence and under the direction of his grand jufticiary ; till in many countries the power of that officer was broken and diftributed into other courts of judicature, the peers of the king's court ftill referving to themfelves (in almoft every feodal government) the right of appeal from thofe fubordinate courts in the laft refort. The military branch of fervice confifted in attending the lord to the wars, if called upon, with fuch a retinue, and for fuch a number of days,

[e] It was an obfervation of Dr Arbuthnot, that tradition was no where preferved fo pure and incorrupt as among children, whofe games and plays are delivered down invariably from one generation to another. (Warburton's notes on Pope. vi. 134. 8°.) Perhaps it may be thought puerile to ob- ferve (in confirmation of this remark) that in one of our antient paftimes (the *bafilinda* of Julius Pollux, *Onomaftic. l.* 9. *c.* 7.) the ceremonies and language of feodal homage are preferved with great exactnefs.

[f] *Feud. l.* 2. *t.* 55.

as

as were ftipulated at the firft donation, in proportion to the quantity of the land.

A T the firft introduction of feuds, as they were gratuitous, fo alfo they were precarious and held at the *will* of the lord [g], who was the fole judge whether his vafal performed his fervices faithfully. Then they became certain, for one or more *years*. Among the antient Germans they continued only from year to year ; an annual diftribution of lands being made by their leaders in their general councils or affemblies [h]. This was profeffedly done, left their thoughts fhould be diverted from war to agriculture ; left the ftrong fhould incroach upon the poffeffions of the weak ; and left luxury and avarice fhould be encouraged by the erection of permanent houfes, and too curious an attention to convenience and the elegant fuperfluities of life. But, when the general migration was pretty well over, and a peaceable poffeffion of their new-acquired fettlements had introduced new cuftoms and manners ; when the fertility of the foil had encouraged the ftudy of hufbandry, and an affection for the fpots they had cultivated began naturally to arife in the tillers ; a more permanent degree of property was introduced, and feuds began now to be granted for the *life* of the feudatory [i]. But ftill feuds were not yet *hereditary*; though frequently granted, by the favour of the lord, to the children of the former poffeffor ; till in procefs of time it became unufual, and was therefore thought hard, to reject the heir, if he were capable to perform the fervices [k] : and therefore infants, women, and profeffed monks, who were incapable of bearing arms, were alfo incapable of fucceeding to a genuine feud. But the heir, when admitted to the feud which his anceftor poffeffed, ufed generally to pay a fine or acknowlegement to the lord, in

---

[g] *Feud. l.* 1. *t.* 1.

[h] Thus Tacitus : *(de mor. Germ. c.* 26.) " *agri ab univerfis per vices occupantur : arva* " *per annos mutant.*" And Caefar yet more fully ; *(de bell. Gall. l.* 6. *c.* 21.) " *Neque* " *quifquam agri modum certum, aut fines pro-* " *prios habet ; fed magiftratus et principes, in*

" *annos fingulos, gentibus et cognationibus ho-* " *minum qui una coierunt, quantum eis et quo* " *loco vifum eft, attribuunt agri, atque anno* " *poft alio tranfire cogunt.*"

[i] *Feud. l.* 1. *t.* 1.

[k] Wright. 14.

horfes,

horfes, arms, money, and the like, for fuch renewal of the feud : which was called a relief, becaufe it re-eftablifhed the inherit-ance, or, in the words of the feodal writers, *" incertam et cadu-* *" cam hereditatem relevabat."* This relief was afterwards, when feuds became abfolutely hereditary, continued on the death of the tenant, though the original foundation of it had ceafed.

FOR in procefs of time feuds came by degrees to be univer-fally extended, beyond the life of the firft vafal, to his *fons*, or perhaps to fuch one of them, as the lord fhould name ; and in this cafe the form of the donation was ftrictly obferved : for if a feud was given to a man and his *fons*, all his fons fucceeded him in equal portions ; and as they died off, their fhares reverted to the lord, and did not defcend to their children, or even to their furviving brothers, as not being fpecified in the donation[1]. But when fuch a feud was given to a man, and his *heirs*, in general terms, then a more extended rule of fucceffion took place ; and when a feudatory died, his male defcendants *in infinitum* were ad-mitted to the fucceffion. When any fuch defcendant, who thus had fucceeded, died, his male defcendants were alfo admitted in the firft place ; and, in defect of them, fuch of his male collateral kindred as were of the blood or lineage of the firft feudatory, but no others. For this was an unalterable maxim in feodal fuc-ceffion, that " none was capable of inheriting a feud, but fuch " as was of the blood of, that is, lineally defcended from, the " firft feudatory[m]." And the defcent, being thus confined to males, originally extended to all the males alike ; all the fons, without any diftinction of primogeniture, fucceeding to equal portions of the father's feud. But this being found upon many accounts inconvenient, (particularly, by dividing the fervices, and thereby weakening the ftrength of the feodal union) and *honorary* feuds (or titles of nobility) being now introduced, which were not of a divifible nature, but could only be inherited by the eldeft fon[n] ; in imitation of thefe, *military* feuds (or thofe we are now defcribing) began alfo in moft countries to defcend ac-

[1] Wright. 17.
[m] *Ibid.* 183.
[n] *Feud.* 2. *t.* 55.

cording

cording to the fame rule of primogeniture, to the eldeft fon, in exclufion of all the reft °.

OTHER qualities of feuds were, that the feudatory could not aliene or difpofe of his feud; neither could he exchange, nor yet mortgage, nor even devife it by will, without the confent of the lord ᴾ. For, the reafon of conferring the feud being the perfonal abilities of the feudatory to ferve in war, it was not fit he fhould be at liberty to transfer this gift, either from himfelf, or his pofterity who were prefumed to inherit his valour, to others who might prove lefs able. And, as the feodal obligation was looked upon as reciprocal, the feudatory being entitled to the lord's protection, in return for his own fealty and fervice; therefore the lord could no more transfer his feignory or protection without confent of his vafal, than the vafal could his feud without confent of his lord �q : it being equally unreafonable, that the lord fhould extend his protection to a perfon to whom he had exceptions, and that the vafal fhould owe fubjection to a fuperior not of his own choofing.

THESE were the principal, and very fimple, qualities of the genuine or original feuds; being then all of a military nature, and in the hands of military perfons : though the feudatories, being under frequent incapacities of cultivating and manuring their own lands, foon found it neceffary to commit part of them to inferior tenants; obliging them to fuch returns in fervice, corn, cattle, or money, as might enable the chief feudatories to attend their military duties without diftraction : which returns, or *reditus*, were the original of rents. And by this means the feodal polity was greatly extended; thefe inferior feudatories (who held what are called in the Scots law " rere-fiefs") being under fimilar obligations of fealty, to do fuit of court, to anfwer the ftipulated renders or rent-fervice, and to promote the welfare of their immediate fuperiors or lords ʳ. But this at the fame time demolifhed

° Wright. 32.   q *Ibid.* 30.
ᴾ *Ibid.* 29.   ʳ Wright. 20.

the

the antient fimplicity of feuds; and an inroad being once made upon their conftitution, it fubjected them, in a courfe of time, to great varieties and innovations. Feuds came to be bought and fold, and deviations were made from the old fundamental rules of tenure and fucceffion; which were held no longer facred, when the feuds themfelves no longer continued to be purely military. Hence thefe tenures began now to be divided into *feoda propria et impropria,* proper and improper feuds; under the former of which divifions were comprehended fuch, and fuch only, of which we have before fpoken; and under that of improper or derivative feuds were comprized all fuch as do not fall within the other defcription: fuch, for inftance, as were originally bartered and fold to the feudatory for a price; fuch as were held upon bafe or lefs honourable fervices, or upon a rent, in lieu of military fervice; fuch as were in themfelves alienable, without mutual licence; and fuch as might defcend indifferently either to males or females. But, where a difference was not expreffed in the creation, fuch new-created feuds did in all other refpects follow the nature of an original, genuine, and proper feud [s].

BUT as foon as the feodal fyftem came to be confidered in the light of a civil eftablifhment, rather than as a military plan, the ingenuity of the fame ages, which perplexed all theology with the fubtilty of fcholaftic difquifitions, and bewildered philofophy in the mazes of metaphyfical jargon, began alfo to exert it's influence on this copious and fruitful fubject: in purfuance of which, the moft refined and oppreffive confequences were drawn from what originally was a plan of fimplicity and liberty, equally beneficial to both lord and tenant, and prudently calculated for their mutual protection and defence. From this one foundation, in different countries of Europe, very different fuperftructures have been raifed: what effect it has produced on the landed property of England will appear in the following chapters.

[s] *Feud.* 2. *t.* 7.

CHAPTER THE FIFTH.

OF THE ANTIENT ENGLISH TENURES.

IN this chapter we fhall take a fhort view of the antient tenures of our Englifh eftates, or the manner in which lands, tenements, and hereditaments might have been holden; as the fame ftood in force, till the middle of the laft century. In which we fhall eafily perceive, that all the particularities, all the feeming and real hardfhips, that attended thofe tenures, were to be accounted for upon feodal principles and no other; being fruits of, and deduced from, the feodal policy.

ALMOST all the real property of this kingdom is by the policy of our laws fuppofed to be granted by, dependent upon, and *holden* of fome fuperior or lord, by and in confideration of certain fervices to be rendered to the lord by the tenant or poffeffor of this property. The thing holden is therefore ftiled a *tenement,* the poffeffors thereof *tenants,* and the manner of their poffeffion a *tenure.* Thus all the land in the kingdom is fuppofed to be holden, mediately or immediately, of the king; who is ftiled the lord *paramount,* or above all. Such tenants as held under the king immediately, when they granted out portions of their lands to inferior perfons, became alfo lords with refpect to thofe inferior perfons, as they were ftill tenants with refpect to the king; and, thus partaking of a middle nature, were called *mefne,* or middle, lords. So that if the king granted a manor to A, and he granted a portion of the land to B, now B was faid to hold of A, and A of the king; or, in other words, B held his lands immediately of A, but mediately of the king. The king therefore was ftiled lord paramount; A was both tenant and lord, or was a mefne lord; and B was called tenant *paravail*, or the loweft tenant; being he who is fuppofed to make avail, or profit, of the land^a. In this manner are all the lands of the kingdom holden, which are in the hands of fubjects: for, according to fir Edward Coke^b, in the law of England we have not properly *allodium*; which, we have feen^c, is the name by which the feudifts abroad diftinguifh fuch eftates of the fubject, as are not holden of any fuperior. So that at the firft glance we may obferve, that our lands are either plainly feuds, or partake very ftrongly of the feodal nature.

A L L tenures being thus derived, or fuppofed to be derived, from the king, thofe that held immediately under him, in right of his crown and dignity, were called his tenants *in capite*, or in chief; which was the moft honourable fpecies of tenure, but at the fame time fubjected the tenants to greater and more burthenfome fervices, than inferior tenures did^d. This diftinction ran through all the different forts of tenure; of which I now proceed to give an account.

I. T H E R E feem to have fubfifted among our anceftors four principal fpecies of lay tenures, to which all others may be reduced: the grand criteria of which were the natures of the feveral fervices or renders, that were due to the lords from their tenants. The fervices, in refpect of their quality, were either *free* or *bafe* fervices; in refpect of their quantity and the time of exacting them, were either *certain* or *uncertain*. *Free* fervices fuch as were not unbecoming the character of a foldier, or a free-

---

^a 2 Inft. 296.
^b 1 Inft. 1.
^c pag. 47.
^d In the Germanic conftitution, the electors, the bifhops, the fecular princes, the imperial cities, &c, which hold directly from the emperor, are called the *immediate* ftates of the empire; all other landholders being denominated *mediate* ones. Mod. Un. Hift. xlii. 61.

man,

man, to perform; as to ferve under his lord in the wars, to pay a fum of money, and the like. *Bafe* fervices were fuch as were fit only for peafants, or perfons of a fervile rank; as to plough the lord's land, to make his hedges, to carry out his dung, or other mean employments. The *certain* fervices, whether free or bafe, were fuch as were ftinted in quantity, and could not be exceeded on any pretence; as, to pay a ftated annual rent, or to plough fuch a field for three days. The *uncertain* depended upon unknown contingencies; as to do military fervice in perfon, or pay an affeffment in lieu of it, when called upon; or to wind a horn whenever the Scots invaded the realm; which are free fervices: or to do whatever the lord fhould command; which is a bafe or villein fervice.

FROM the various combinations of thefe fervices have arifen the four kinds of lay tenure which fubfifted in England, till the middle of the laft century; and three of which fubfift to this day. Of thefe Bracton (who wrote under Henry the third) feems to give the cleareft and moft compendious account, of any author antient or modern [e]; of which the following is the outline or abftract [f]. " Tenements are of two kinds, *frank-tenement*, and " *villenage*. And, of frank-tenements, fome are held freely in " confideration of homage and *knight-fervice*; others in *free-focage* " with the fervice of fealty only." And again [g], " of villenages " fome are pure, and others privileged. He that holds in *pure* " *villenage* fhall do whatfoever is commanded him, and always be " bound to an uncertain fervice. The other kind of villenage is " called *villein-focage*; and thefe villein-focmen do villein fervices, " but fuch as are certain and determined." Of which the fenfe feems to be as follows: firft, where the fervice was *free*, but *uncertain*, as military fervice with homage, that tenure was called

---

[e] *l. 4. tr. 1. c. 28.*

[f] *Tenementorum aliud liberum, aliud villenagium. Item, liberorum aliud tenetur libere pro homagio et fervitio militari; aliud in libero focagio cum fidelitate tantum. §. 1.*

[g] *Villenagiorum aliud purum, alium privile-* *giatum. Qui tenet in puro villenagio faciet quicquid ei praeceptum fuerit, et femper tenebitur ad incerta. Aliud genus vil'enagii di itur villanum focagium; et hujufmodi villani focmanni — villana faciunt fervitia, fed certa et determinata. §. 5.*

the tenure in chivalry, *per fervitium militare,* or by knight-fervice. Secondly, where the fervice was not only *free,* but alfo *certain,* as by fealty only, by rent and fealty, *&c,* that tenure was called *liberum focagium,* or free focage. Thefe were the only *free* holdings or tenements; the others were *villenous* or fervile : as, thirdly, where the fervice was *bafe* in it's nature, and *uncertain* as to time and quantity, the tenure was *purum villenagium,* abfolute or pure villenage. Laftly, where the fervice was *bafe* in it's nature, but reduced to a *certainty,* this was ftill villenage, but diftinguifhed from the other by the name of privileged villenage, *villenagium privilegiatum;* or it might be ftill called focage (from the *certainty* of it's fervices) but degraded by their *bafenefs* into the inferior title of *villanum focagium,* villein-focage.

I. THE firft, moft univerfal, and efteemed the moft honourable fpecies of tenure, was that by knight-fervice, called in Latin *fervitium militare,* and in law French *chivalry,* or *fervice de chivaler,* anfwering to the *fief d' haubert* of the Normans[h], which name is exprefsly given it by the mirrour[i]. This differed in very few points, as we fhall prefently fee, from a pure and proper feud, being entirely military, and the genuine effect of the feodal eftablifhment in England. To make a tenure by knight-fervice, a determinate quantity of land was neceffary, which was called a knight's fee, *feodum militare;* the value of which, not only in the reign of Edward II[k], but alfo of Henry II[l], and therefore probably at it's original in the reign of the conqueror, was ftated at 20 *l. per annum;* and a certain number of thefe knight's fees were requifite to make up a barony. And he who held this proportion of land (or a whole fee) by knight-fervice, was bound to attend his lord to the wars for forty days in every year, if called upon : which attendance was his *reditus* or return, his rent or fervice, for the land he claimed to hold. If he held only half a knight's fee, he was only bound to attend twenty days, and fo in proportion[m]. And there is reafon to apprehend, that this fer-

[h] Spelm. *Glof.* 219.
[i] c. 2. §. 27.
[k] Stat. *de milit.* 1 Edw. II. Co. Litt. 69.
[l] Glanvil. *l.* 9. *c.* 4.
[m] Litt. §. 95.

vice

vice was the whole that our anceftors meant to fubject themfelves to; the other fruits and confequences of this tenure being fraudulently fuperinduced, as the regular (though unforefeen) appendages of the feodal fyftem.

THIS tenure of knight-fervice had all the marks of a ftrict and regular feud: it was granted by words of pure donation, *dedi et conceffi*[n]; was transferred by inveftiture or delivering corporal poffeffion of the land, ufually called livery of feifin; and was perfected by homage and fealty. It alfo drew after it thefe feven fruits and confequences, as infeparably incident to the tenure in chivalry; *viz.* aids, relief, primer feifin, wardfhip, marriage, fines for alienation, and efcheat: all which I fhall endeavour to explain, and fhew to be of feodal original.

1. AIDS were originally mere benevolences granted by the tenant to his lord, in times of difficulty and diftrefs[o]; but in procefs of time they grew to be confidered as a matter of right, and not of difcretion. Thefe aids were principally three: firft, to ranfom the lord's perfon, if taken prifoner; a neceffary confequence of the feodal attachment and fidelity; infomuch that the neglect of doing it, whenever it was in the vafal's power, was, by the ftrict rigour of the feodal law, an abfolute forfeiture of his eftate[p]. Secondly, to make the lord's eldeft fon a knight; a matter that was formerly attended with great ceremony, pomp, and expenfe. This aid could not be demanded till the heir was fifteen years old, or capable of bearing arms[q]: the intention of it being to breed up the eldeft fon, and heir apparent of the feignory, to deeds of arms and chivalry, for the better defence of the nation. Thirdly, to marry the lord's eldeft daughter, by giving her a fuitable portion: for daughters' portions were in thofe days extremely flender; few lords being able to fave much out of their

[n] Co. Litt. 9.

[o] *Auxilia fiunt de gratia et non de jure, — cum dependeant ex gratia tenentium et non ad voluntatem dominorum.* Bracton. *l.* 2. *tr.* 1. *c.* 16. §. 8.

[p] Feud. *l.* 2. *t.* 24.

[q] 2 Inft. 233.

income

income for this purpofe; nor could they acquire money by other means, being wholly converfant in matters of arms; nor, by the nature of their tenure, could they charge their lands with this, or any other incumbrances. From bearing their proportion to thefe aids no rank or profeffion was exempted: and therefore even the monafteries, till the time of their diffolution, contributed to the knighting of their founder's male heir (of whom their lands were holden) and the marriage of his female defcendants [r]. And one cannot but obferve, in this particular, the great refemblance which the lord and vafal of the feodal law bore to the patron and client of the Roman republic; between whom alfo there fubfifted a mutual fealty, or engagement of defence and protection. With regard to the matter of aids, there were three which were ufually raifed by the client; *viz.* to marry the patron's daughter; to pay his debts; and to redeem his perfon from captivity [s].

B u t befides thefe antient feodal aids, the tyranny of lords by degrees exacted more and more; as, aids to pay the lord's debts, (probably in imitation of the Romans) and aids to enable him to pay aids or reliefs to his fuperior lord; from which laft indeed the king's tenants *in capite* were, from the nature of their tenure, excufed, as they held immediately of the king who had no fuperior. To prevent this abufe, king John's *magna carta* [t] ordained, that no aids be taken by the king without confent of parliament, nor in any wife by inferior lords, fave only the three antient ones above-mentioned. But this provifion was omitted in Henry III's charter, and the fame oppreffions were continued till the 25 Edw. I; when the ftatute called *confirmatio chartarum* was enacted; which in this refpect revived king John's charter, by ordaining that none but the antient aids fhould be taken. But though the fpecies of aids was thus reftrained, yet the quantity

---

[r] Philips's life of Pole. I. 223.
[s] *Erat autem haec inter utrofque officiorum viciffitudo,—ut clientes ad collocandas fenatorum filias de fuo conferrent; in aeris alieni dif-* *folutionem gratuitam pecuniam erogarent; et ab hoftibus in bello captos redimerent.* Paul. Manutius *de fenatu Romano. c.* 1.
[t] *cap.* 12. 15.

of

of each aid remained arbitrary and uncertain. King John's charter indeed ordered, that all aids taken by inferior lords fhould be
reafonable [u]; and that the aids taken by the king of his tenants
in capite fhould be fettled by parliament [w]. But they were never
completely afcertained and adjufted till the ftatute Weftm. 1.
3 Edw. I. c. 36. which fixed the aids of inferior lords at twenty
fhillings, or the fuppofed twentieth part of every knight's fee,
for making the eldeft fon a knight, or marrying the eldeft daughter ; and the fame was done with regard to the king's tenants *in*
capite by ftatute 25 Edw. III. c. 11. The other aid, for ranfom
of the lord's perfon, being not in it's nature capable of any certainty, was therefore never afcertained.

2. RELIEF, *relevium*, was before mentioned as incident to
every feodal tenure, by way of fine or compofition with the lord
for taking up the eftate, which was lapfed or fallen in by the
death of the laft tenant. But, though reliefs had their original
while feuds were only life-eftates, yet they continued after feuds
became hereditary ; and were therefore looked upon, very juftly,
as one of the greateft grievances of tenure : efpecially when, at
the firft, they were merely arbitrary and at the will of the lord ;
fo that, if he pleafed to demand an exorbitant relief, it was in
effect to difinherit the heir [x]. The Englifh ill brooked this confequence of their new adopted policy ; and therefore William the
conqueror by his laws [y] *afcertained* the relief, by directing (in imitation of the Danifh heriots) that a certain quantity of arms and
habiliments of war fhould be paid by the earls, barons, and va-
vafours refpectively ; and, if the latter had no arms, they fhould
pay 100 *s.* William Rufus broke through this compofition, and
again demanded arbitrary uncertain reliefs, as due by the feodal
laws ; thereby in effect obliging every heir to new-purchafe or *re-*
deem his land [z]: but his brother Henry I by the charter before-
mentioned reftored his father's law ; and ordained, that the relief

---

[u] *cap.* 15.
[w] *Ibid.* 14.
[x] Wright. 99.

[y] c. 22, 23, 24.
[z] 2 Roll. Abr. 514.

to be paid fhould be according to the law fo eftablifhed, and not an arbitrary redemption[a]. But afterwards, when, by an ordinance in 27 Hen. II. called the affife of arms, it was provided that every man's armour fhould defcend to his heir, for defence of the realm; and it thereby became impracticable to pay thefe acknowlegements in arms, according to the laws of the conqueror, the compofition was univerfally accepted of 100*s*. for every knight's fee; as we find it ever after eftablifhed[b]. But it muft be remembered, that this relief was only then payable, if the heir at the death of his anceftor had attained his full age of one and twenty years.

3. PRIMER *feifin* was a feodal burthen, only incident to the king's tenants *in capite*, and not to thofe who held of inferior or mefne lords. It was a right which the king had, when any of his tenants *in capite* died feifed of a knight's fee, to receive of the heir (provided he were of full age) one whole year's profits of the lands, if they were in immediate poffeffion; and half a year's profits, if the lands were in reverfion expectant on an eftate for life[c]. This feems to be little more than an additional relief: but grounded upon this feodal reafon; that, by the antient law of feuds, immediately upon a death of a vafal the fuperior was intitled to enter and take feifin or poffeffion of the land, by way of protection againft intruders, till the heir appeared to claim it, and receive inveftiture: and, for the time the lord fo held it, he was entitled to take the profits; and, unlefs the heir claimed within a year and day, it was by the ftrict law a forfeiture[d]. This practice however feems not to have long obtained in England, if ever, with regard to tenures under inferior lords; but, as to the king's tenures *in capite*, this *prima feifina* was exprefsly declared, under Henry III and Edward II, to belong to the king by prerogative, in contradiftinction to other lords[e]. And the king was intitled to enter and receive the whole profits of the land, till livery was

---

[a] "*Hueres non redimet terram fuam, ficut* "*faciebat tempore fratris mei, fed legitima et* "*jufta relevatione relevabit eam.*" (*Text. Roffens. cap. 34.*)

[b] Glanv. *l.* 9. *c.* 4. Litt. §. 112.
[c] Co. Litt. 77.
[d] Feud. *l.* 2. *t.* 24.
[e] Stat. Marlbr. c. 16. 17 Edw. II. c. 3.

fued;

fued; which fuit being commonly within a year and day next after the death of the tenant, therefore the king ufed to take at an average the *firſt fruits*, that is to fay, one year's profits of the land [f]. And this afterwards gave a handle to the popes, who claimed to be feodal lords of the church, to claim in like manner from every clergyman in England the firſt year's profits of his benefice, by way of *primitiae*, or firſt fruits.

4. THESE payments were only due if the heir was of full age; but if he was under the age of twenty one, being a male, or fourteen, being a female [g], the lord was intitled to the *wardſhip* of the heir, and was called the guardian in chivalry. This wardſhip confiſted in having the cuſtody of the body and lands of fuch heir, without any account of the profits, till the age of twenty one in males, and fixteen in females. For the law fuppofed the heir-male unable to perform knight-fervice till twenty one; but as for the female, ſhe was fuppofed capable at fourteen to marry, and then her huſband might perform the fervice. The lord therefore had no wardſhip, if at the death of the anceſtor the heir-male was of the full age of twenty one, or the heir-female of fourteen: yet, if ſhe was then under fourteen, and the lord once had her in ward, he might keep her fo till fixteen, by virtue of the ſtatute of Weſtm. 1. 3 Edw. I. c. 22. the two additional years being given by the legiſlature for no other reafon but merely to benefit the lord [h].

THIS wardſhip, fo far as it related to land, though it was not nor could be part of the law of feuds, fo long as they were arbitrary, temporary, or for life only; yet, when they became hereditary, and did confequently often defcend upon infants, who by reafon of their age could neither perform nor ſtipulate for the fervices of the feud, does not feem upon feodal principles to have been unreafonable. For the wardſhip of the land, or cuſtody of the feud, was retained by the lord, that he might out of the profits thereof provide a fit perfon to fupply the infant's fervices,

[f] Staundf. Prerog. 12.   [h] *Ibid*.
[g] Litt. §. 103.

till

till he fhould be of age to perform them himfelf. And, if we confider a feud in it's original import, as a ftipend, fee, or reward for actual fervice, it could not be thought hard that the lord fhould withhold the ftipend, fo long as the fervice was fufpended. Though undoubtedly to our Englifh anceftors, where fuch ftipendiary donation was a mere fuppofition or figment, it carried abundance of hardfhip ; and accordingly it was relieved by the charter of Henry I before-mentioned, which took this cuftody from the lord, and ordained that the cuftody, both of the land and the children, fhould belong to the widow or next of kin. But this noble immunity did not continue many years.

THE wardfhip of the body was a confequence of the wardfhip of the land ; for he who enjoyed the infant's eftate was the propereft perfon to educate and maintain him in his infancy : and alfo, in a political view, the lord was moft concerned to give his tenant a fuitable education, in order to qualify him the better to perform thofe fervices which in his maturity he was bound to render.

WHEN the male heir arrived to the age of twenty one, or the heir-female to that of fixteen, they might fue out their livery or *oufterlemain*[i] ; that is, the delivery of their lands out of their guardian's hands. For this they were obliged to pay a fine, namely, half a year's profits of the land ; though this feems expreffly contrary to *magna carta*[k]. However, in confideration of their lands having been fo long in ward, they were excufed all reliefs, and the king's tenants alfo all primer feifins [l]. In order to afcertain the profits that arofe to the crown by thefe fruits of tenure, and to grant the heir his livery, the itinerant juftices, or juftices in eyre, had it formerly in charge to make inquifition concerning them by a jury of the county[m], commonly called an *inquifitio poft mortem* ; which was inftituted to enquire (at the death of any man of fortune) the value of his eftate, the tenure by which it

[i] Co. Litt. 77.
[k] 9 Hen. III. c. 3.
[l] Co. Litt. 77.
[m] Hoveden. *fub Ric. I.*

was

was holden, and who, and of what age, his heir was; thereby to afcertain the relief and value of the primer feifin, or the ward-fhip and livery accruing to the king thereupon. A manner of proceeding that came in procefs of time to be greatly abufed, and at length an intolerable grievance; it being one of the principal accufations againft Empfon and Dudley, the wicked engines of Henry VII, that by colour of falfe inquifitions they compelled many perfons to fue out livery from the crown, who by no means were tenants thereunto[n]. And, afterwards, a court of wards and liveries was erected[o], for conducting the fame enquiries in a more folemn and legal manner.

WHEN the heir thus came of full age, provided he held a knight's fee, he was to receive the order of knighthood, and was compellable to take it upon him, or elfe pay a fine to the king. For, in thofe heroical times, no perfon was qualified for deeds of arms and chivalry who had not received this order, which was conferred with much preparation and folemnity. We may plainly difcover the footfteps of a fimilar cuftom in what Tacitus relates of the Germans, who in order to qualify their young men to bear arms, prefented them in a full affembly with a fhield and lance; which ceremony, as was formerly hinted[p], is fuppofed to have been the original of the feodal knighthood[q]. This prerogative, of compelling the vafals to be knighted, or to pay a fine, was exprefsly recognized in parliament, by the ftatute *de militibus*, I Edw. II; was exerted as an expedient of raifing money by many of our beft princes, particularly by Edward VI and queen Eliza-beth; but yet was the occafion of heavy murmurs when exerted by Charles I: among whofe many misfortunes it was, that neither himfelf nor his people feemed able to diftinguifh between the ar-bitrary ftretch, and the legal exertion, of prerogative. However,

---

[n] 4 Inft. 198.
[o] Stat. 32 Hen. VIII. c. 46.
[p] Vol. I. pag. 392.
[q] " *In ipfo concilio vel principum aliquis,*
" *vel pater, vel propinquus, fcuto frameaque*

" *juvenem ornant. Haec apud illos toga, hic*
" *primus juventae honos: ante hoc domus pars*
" *videntur; mox reipublicae* " *de mor. Germ.*
cap. 13.

among the other conceſſions made by that unhappy prince, before the fatal recourſe to arms, he agreed to diveſt himſelf of this undoubted flower of his crown, and it was accordingly aboliſhed by ſtatute 16 Car. I. c. 20.

5. B U T, before they came of age, there was ſtill another piece of authority, which the guardian was at liberty to exerciſe over his infant wards; I mean the right of *marriage, (maritagium,* as contradiſtinguiſhed from *matrimonium)* which in it's feodal ſenſe ſignifies the power, which the lord or guardian in chivalry had of diſpoſing of his infant ward in matrimony. For, while the infant was in ward, the guardian had the power of tendering him or her a ſuitable match, without *diſparagement,* or inequality: which if the infants refuſed, they forfeited the value of the marriage, *valorem maritagii,* to their guardian [r]; that is, ſo much as a jury would aſſeſs, or any one would *bona fide* give to the guardian for ſuch an alliance [s]: and, if the infants married themſelves without the guardian's conſent, they forfeited double the value, *duplicem valorem maritagii* [t]. This ſeems to have been one of the greateſt hardſhips of our antient tenures. There are indeed ſubſtantial reaſons why the lord ſhould have the *reſtraint* and *controll* of the ward's marriage, eſpecially of his female ward; becauſe of their tender years, and the danger of ſuch female ward's intermarrying with the lord's enemy [u]. But no tolerable pretence could be aſſigned why the lord ſhould have the *ſale,* or *value,* of the marriage. Nor indeed is this claim of ſtrictly feodal original; the moſt probable account of it ſeeming to be this: that by the cuſtom of Normandy the lord's conſent was neceſſary to the marriage of his *female*-wards [w]; which was introduced into England, together with the reſt of the Norman doctrine of feuds: and it is likely that the lords uſually took money for ſuch their conſent, ſince in the often-cited charter of Henry the firſt, he engages for the future to take nothing for *his* conſent; which alſo he promiſes in general to give, provided ſuch

[r] Litt. §. 110.
[s] Stat. Mert. c. 6. Co. Litt. 82.
[t] Litt. §. 110.

[u] Bract. *l.* 2. *c.* 37. §. 6.
[w] Gr. Cuſt. 55.

female

female ward were not married to his enemy. But this, among other beneficial parts of that charter, being difregarded, and guardians ftill continuing to difpofe of their wards in a very arbitrary unequal manner, it was provided by king John's great charter, that heirs fhould be married without difparagement, the next of kin having previous notice of the contract[x]; or, as it was exprefled in the firft draught of that charter, *ita maritentur ne difparagentur, et per confilium propinquorum de confanguinitate fua*[y]. But thefe claufes in behalf of the relations were omitted in the charter of Henry III; wherein[z] the claufe ftands merely thus, " *haeredes maritentur abfque difparagatione;*" meaning certainly, by *haeredes*, heirs female, as there are no traces before this to be found of the lord's claiming the marriage of heirs male; and as Glanvil[a] exprefsly confines it to heirs female. But the king and his great lords thenceforward took a handle from the ambiguity of this expreffion to claim them both, *five fit mafculus five foemina*, as Bracton more than once expreffes it[b]; and alfo, as nothing but difparagement was reftrained by *magna carta*, they thought themfelves at liberty to make all other advantages that they could[c]. And afterwards this right, of felling the ward in marriage or elfe receiving the price or value of it, was exprefsly declared by the ftatute of Merton[d]; which is the firft direct mention of it that I have met with, in our own or in any other law.

6. ANOTHER attendant or confequence of tenure by knight-fervice was that of *fines* due to the lord for every *alienation*, whenever the tenant had occafion to make over his land to another. This depended on the nature of the feodal connexion; it not being reafonable nor allowed, as we have before feen, that a feudatory fhould transfer his lord's gift to another, and fubftitute a new tenant to do the fervice in his own ftead, without the confent of the lord: and, as the feodal obligation was confidered as

---

[x] *cap. 6. edit. Oxon.*
[y] *cap. 3. ibid.*
[z] *cap. 6.*
[a] *l. 9. c. 9. & 12. & l. 9. c. 4.*

[b] *l. 2. c. 38. §. 1.*
[c] Wright. 97.
[d] 20 Hen. III. c. 6.

reciprocal,

reciprocal, the lord alfo could not alienate his feignory without the confent of his tenant, which confent of his was called an *attornment.* This reftraint upon the lords foon wore away; that upon the tenants continued longer. For, when every thing came in procefs of time to be bought and fold, the lords would not grant a licence to their tenants to aliene, without a fine being paid; apprehending that, if it was reafonable for the heir to pay a fine or relief on the renovation of his paternal eftate, it was much more reafonable that a ftranger fhould make the fame acknowlegement on his admiffion to a newly purchafed feud. With us in England, thefe fines feem only to have been exacted from the king's tenants *in capite,* who were never able to aliene without a licence : but, as to common perfons, they were at liberty, by *magna carta*[e], and the ftatute of *quia emptores*[f], (if not earlier) to aliene the whole of their eftate, to be holden of the fame lord, as they themfelves held it of before. But the king's tenants *in capite,* not being included under the general words of thefe ftatutes, could not aliene without a licence : for if they did, it was in antient ftrictnefs an abfolute forfeiture of the lands[g]; though fome have imagined otherwife. But this feverity was mitigated by the ftatute 1 Edw. III. c. 12. which ordained, that in fuch cafe the lands fhould not be forfeited, but a reafonable fine be paid to the king. Upon which ftatute it was fettled, that one third of the yearly value fhould be paid for a licence of alienation; but, if the tenant prefumed to aliene without a licence, a full year's value fhould be paid[h].

7. THE laft confequence of tenure in chivalry was efcheat; which is the determination of the tenure, or diffolution of the mutual bond between the lord and tenant, from the extinction of the blood of the latter by either natural or civil means : if he died without heirs of his blood, or if his blood was corrupted and ftained by commiffion of treafon or felony; whereby every inheritable quality was intirely blotted out and abolifhed. In fuch

[e] *cap.* 32.
[f] 18 Edw. I. c. 1.
[g] 2 Inft. 66.
[h] *Ibid.* 67.

cafes

cafes the land efcheated, or fell back, to the lord of the fee[i] ; that is, the tenure was determined by breach of the original condition, expreffed or implied in the feodal donation. In the one cafe, there were no heirs fubfifting of the blood of the firft feudatory or purchafer, to which heirs alone the grant of the feud extended : in the other, the tenant, by perpetrating an atrocious crime, fhewed that he was no longer to be trufted as a vafal, having forgotten his duty as a fubject ; and therefore forfeited his feud, which he held under the implied condition that he fhould not be a traitor or a felon. The confequence of which in both cafes was, that the gift, being determined, refulted back to the lord who gave it[k].

THESE were the principal qualities, fruits, and confequences of the tenure by knight-fervice : a tenure, by which the greateft part of the lands in this kingdom were holden, and that principally of the king *in capite*, till the middle of the laft century ; and which was created, as fir Edward Coke exprefly teftifies[l], for a military purpofe ; *viz.* for defence of the realm by the king's own principal fubjects, which was judged to be much better than to truft to hirelings or foreigners. The defcription here given is that of knight-fervice proper ; which was to attend the king in his wars. There were alfo fome other fpecies of knight-fervice ; fo called, though improperly, becaufe the fervice or render was of a free and honourable nature, and equally uncertain as to the time of rendering as that of knight-fervice proper, and becaufe they were attended with fimilar fruits and confequences. Such was the tenure by *grand ferjeanty, per magnum fervitium*, whereby the tenant was bound, inftead of ferving the king *generally* in his wars, to do fome fpecial honorary fervice to the king in perfon; as to carry his banner, his fword, or the like; or to be his butler, champion, or other officer at his coronation[m]. It was in moft other refpects like knight-fervice[n] ; only he was

[i] Co. Litt. 13.   [m] Litt. §. 153.
[k] *Feud. l. 2. t.* 86. [n] *Ibid.* §. 158.
[l] 4 Inft. 192.

not bound to pay aid°, or efcuage ᵖ; and, when tenant by knight-
fervice paid five pounds for a relief on every knight's fee, tenant
by grand ferjeanty paid one year's value of his land, were it much
or little ᑫ. Tenure by *cornage*, which was, to wind a horn when
the Scots or other enemies entered the land, in order to warn the
king's fubjects, was (like other fervices of the fame nature) a
fpecies of grand ferjeanty ʳ.

THESE fervices, both of chivalry and grand ferjeanty, were
all perfonal, and uncertain as to their quantity or duration. But,
the perfonal attendance in knight-fervice growing troublefome
and inconvenient in many refpects, the tenants found means of
compounding for it; by firft fending others in their ftead, and in
procefs of time making a pecuniary fatisfaction to the lords in lieu
of it. This pecuniary fatisfaction at laft came to be levied by affeffments, at fo much for every knight's fee; and therefore this
kind of tenure was called *fcutagium* in Latin, or *fervitium fcuti*;
fcutum being then a well-known denomination of money : and,
in like manner it was called, in our Norman French, *efcuage* ;
being indeed a pecuniary, inftead of a military, fervice. The
firft time this appears to have been taken was in the 5 Hen. II.
on account of his expedition to Touloufe; but it foon came to
be fo univerfal, that perfonal attendance fell quite into difufe.
Hence we find in our antient hiftories that, from this period,
when our kings went to war, they levied fcutages on their tenants, that is, on all the landholders of the kingdom, to defray
their expenfes, and to hire troops : and thefe affeffments, in the
time of Henry II, feem to have been made arbitrarily and at the
king's pleafure. Which prerogative being greatly abufed by his
fucceffors, it became matter of national clamour, and king John
was obliged to confent, by his *magna carta*, that no fcutage fhould
be impofed without confent of parliament ˢ. But this claufe was
omitted in his fon Henry III's charter; where we only find ᵗ, that

---

° 2 Inft. 233.
ᵖ Litt. §. 158.
ᑫ Litt. §. 154.
ʳ Ibid. §. 156.

ˢ *Nullum fcutagium ponatur in regno noftro,*
nifi per commune confilium regni noftri. cap.12.
ᵗ *cap. 37.*

fcutages

scutages or escuage should be taken as they were used to be taken in the time of Henry II; that is, in a reasonable and moderate manner. Yet afterwards by statute 25 Edw. I. c. 5 & 6. and many subsequent statutes[u] it was enacted, that the king should take no aids or tasks but by the common assent of the realm. Hence it is held in our old books, that escuage or scutage could not be levied but by consent of parliament[w]; such scutages being indeed the groundwork of all succeeding subsidies, and the land-tax of later times.

SINCE therefore escuage differed from knight-service in nothing, but as a compensation differs from actual service, knight-service is frequently confounded with it. And thus Littleton[x] must be understood, when he tells us, that tenant by homage, fealty, and escuage was tenant by knight-service: that is, that this tenure (being subservient to the military policy of the nation) was respected[y] as a tenure in chivalry[z]. But as the actual service was uncertain, and depended upon emergences, so it was necessary that this pecuniary compensation should be equally uncertain, and depend on the assessments of the legislature suited to those emergences. For had the escuage been a settled invariable sum, payable at certain times, it had been neither more nor less than a mere pecuniary rent; and the tenure, instead of knight-service, would have then been of another kind, called socage[a], of which we shall speak in the next chapter.

FOR the present, I have only to observe, that by the degenerating of knight-service, or personal military duty, into escuage, or pecuniary assessments, all the advantages (either promised or real) of the feodal constitution were destroyed, and nothing but the hardships remained. Instead of forming a national militia composed of barons, knights, and gentlemen, bound by their interest, their honour, and their oaths, to defend their king and

---

[u] See Vol. I. pag. 136.
[w] Old Ten. *tit. Escuage.*
[x] §. 103.
[y] Wright. 122.

[z] *Pro feodo militari reputatur.* Flet. *l.* 2. c. 14. §. 7.
[a] Litt. §. 97. 120.

country,

country, the whole of this fyftem of tenures now tended to nothing elfe, but a wretched means of raifing money to pay an army of occafional mercenaries. In the mean time the families of all our nobility and gentry groaned under the intolerable burthens, which (in confequence of the fiction adopted after the conqueft) were introduced and laid upon them by the fubtlety and fineffe of the Norman lawyers. For, befides the fcutages they were liable to in defect of perfonal attendance, which however were affeffed by themfelves in parliament, they might be called upon by the king or lord paramount for *aids*, whenever his eldeft fon was to be knighted, or his eldeft daughter married; not to forget the ranfom of his own perfon. The heir, on the death of his anceftor, if of full age, was plundered of the firft emoluments arifing from his inheritance, by way of *relief* and *primer feifin*; and, if under age, of the whole of his eftate during infancy. And then, as fir Thomas Smith[b] very feelingly complains, "when "he came to his own, after he was out of *wardfhip*, his woods "decayed, houfes fallen down, ftock wafted and gone, lands let "forth and ploughed to be barren," to make amends he was yet to pay half a year's profits as a fine for fuing out his *livery*; and alfo the price or value of his *marriage*, if he refufed fuch wife as his lord and guardian had bartered for, and impofed upon him; or twice that value, if he married another woman. Add to this, the untimely and expenfive honour of *knighthood*, to make his poverty more completely fplendid. And when by thefe deductions his fortune was fo fhattered and ruined, that perhaps he was obliged to fell his patrimony, he had not even that poor privilege allowed him, without paying an exorbitant fine for a *licence* of *alienation*.

A s l a v e r y fo complicated, and fo extenfive as this, called aloud for a remedy in a nation that boafted of her freedom. Palliatives were from time to time applied by fucceffive acts of parliament, which affwaged fome temporary grievances. Till at length the humanity of king James I confented[c] for a proper

---

[b] Commonw. l. 3. c. 5. [c] 4 Inft. 202.

equivalent

equivalent to abolifh them all; though the plan then proceeded not to effect : in like manner as he had formed a fcheme, and began to put it in execution, for removing the feodal grievance of heretable jurifdictions in Scotland [d], which has fince been purfued and effected by the ftatute 20 Geo. II. c. 43. [e] King James's plan for exchanging our military tenures feems to have been nearly the fame as that which has been fince purfued; only with this difference, that, by way of compenfation for the lofs which the crown and other lords would fuftain, an annual feefarm rent fhould be fettled and infeparably annexed to the crown, and affured to the inferior lords, payable out of every knight's fee within their refpective fignories. An expedient, feemingly much better than the hereditary excife, which was afterwards made the principal equivalent for thefe conceffions. For at length the military tenures, with all their heavy appendages, were deftroyed at one blow by the ftatute 12 Car. II. c. 24. which enacts, " that the court of " wards and liveries, and all wardfhips, liveries, primer feifins, " and oufterlemains, values and forfeitures of marriages, by rea- " fon of any tenure of the king or others, be totally taken away. " And that all fines for alienations, tenures by homage, knights- " fervice, and efcuage, and alfo aids for marrying the daughter " or knighting the fon, and all tenures of the king *in capite*, be " likewife taken away. And that all forts of tenures, held of the " king or others, be turned into free and common focage; fave " only tenures in frankalmoign, copyholds, and the honorary fer- " vices (without the flavifh part) of grand ferjeanty." A ftatute, which was a greater acquifition to the civil property of this kingdom than even *magna carta* itfelf : fince that only pruned the luxuriances that had grown out of the military tenures, and thereby preferved them in vigour; but the ftatute of king Charles extirpated the whole, and demolifhed both root and branches.

---

[d] Dalrymp of feuds. 292.

[e] By another ftatute of the fame year (20 Geo. II. c.50.) the tenure of *wardhold-* ing (equivalent to the knight-fervice of England) is for ever abolifhed in Scotland.

CHAPTER THE SIXTH.

OF THE MODERN ENGLISH TENURES.

ALTHOUGH, by the means that were mentioned in
the preceding chapter, the oppreffive or military part of
the feodal conftitution was happily done away, yet we are not to
imagine that the conftitution itfelf was utterly laid afide, and a
new one introduced in it's room ; fince by the ftatute 12 Car. II.
the tenures of focage and frankalmoign, the honorary fervices of
grand ferjeanty, and the tenure by copy of court roll were referved ; nay all tenures in general, except frankalmoign, grand
ferjeanty, and copyhold, were reduced to one general fpecies of
tenure, then well known and fubfifting, called free and common
focage. And this, being fprung from the fame feodal original as
the reft, demonftrates the neceffity of fully contemplating that
antient fyftem ; fince it is that alone, to which we can recur to
explain any feeming, or real, difficulties, that may arife in our
prefent mode of tenure.

THE military tenure, or that by knight-fervice, confifted of
what were reputed the moft free and honourable fervices ; but
which in their nature were unavoidably uncertain in refpect to the
time of their performance. The fecond fpecies of tenure, or
free-focage, confifted alfo of free and honourable fervices ; but
fuch as were liquidated and reduced to an abfolute certainty. And
this tenure not only fubfifts to this day, but has in a manner ab-
forbed and fwallowed up (fince the ftatute of Charles the fecond)
almoft

almoſt every other ſpecies of tenure. And to this we are next
to proceed.

II. SOCAGE, in it's moſt general and extenſive ſignification,
ſeems to denote a tenure by any certain and determinate ſervice.
And in this ſenſe it is by our antient writers conſtantly put in op-
poſition to chivalry, or knight-ſervice, where the render was precarious and uncertain. Thus Braſton [a]; if a man holds by a rent
in money, without any eſcuage or ſerjeanty, " *id tenementum dici*
" *poteſt ſocagium:*" but if you add thereto any royal ſervice,
or eſcuage to any, the ſmalleſt, amount, " *illud dici poterit feodum*
" *militare.*" So too the author of Fleta [b]; " *ex donationibus ſer-*
" *vitia militaria vel magnae ſerjantiae non continentibus, oritur no-*
" *bis quoddam nomen generale, quod eſt ſocagium.*" Littleton alſo [c]
defines it to be, where the tenant holds his tenement of the lord
by any *certain* ſervice, in lieu of all other ſervices; ſo that they
be not ſervices of chivalry, or knight-ſervice. And therefore afterwards [d] he tells us, that whatſoever is not tenure in chivalry is
tenure in ſocage: in like manner as it is defined by Finch [e], a
tenure to be done out of war. The ſervice muſt therefore be certain, in order to denominate it ſocage; as to hold by fealty and
20 *s.* rent; or, by homage, fealty, and 20 *s.* rent; or, by homage
and fealty without rent; or, by fealty and certain corporal ſervice, as ploughing the lord's land for three days; or, by fealty
only without any other ſervice: for all theſe are tenures in ſocage [f].

BUT ſocage, as was hinted in the laſt chapter, is of two ſorts:
free-ſocage, where the ſervices are not only certain, but honourable; and *villein*-ſocage, where the ſervices, though certain, are
of a baſer nature. Such as hold by the former tenure are called
in Glanvil [g], and other ſubſequent authors, by the name of *liberi*
ſokemanni, or tenants in free-ſocage. Of this tenure we are firſt

[a] *l.* 2. *c.* 16. §. 9.
[b] *l.* 3. *c.* 14. § 9.
[c] §. 117.
[d] §. 118.
[e] L. 147.
[f] Litt. §. 117, 118, 119.
[g] *l.* 3. *c.* 7.

to fpeak ; and this, both in the nature of it's fervice, and the
fruits and confequences appertaining thereto, was always by much
the moft free and independent fpecies of any. And therefore I
cannot but affent to Mr Somner's etymology of the word [h] ; who
derives it from the Saxon appellation, *foc*, which fignifies liberty
or privilege, and, being joined to a ufual termination, is called
focage, in Latin *focagium* ; fignifying thereby a free or privileged
tenure [i]. This etymology feems to be much more juft than that
of our common lawyers in general, who derive it from *foca*, an
old Latin word denoting (as they tell us) a plough : for that in
antient time this focage tenure confifted in nothing elfe but fervices of hufbandry, which the tenant was bound to do to his lord,
as to plough, fow, or reap for him ; but that, in procefs of time,
this fervice was changed into an annual rent by confent of all
parties, and that, in memory of it's original, it ftill retains the
name of focage or plough-fervice [k]. But this by no means agrees
with what Littleton himfelf tells us [l], that to hold by fealty only,
without paying any rent, is tenure in focage ; for here is plainly
no commutation for plough-fervice. Befides, even fervices, confeffedly of a military nature and original, (as efcuage itfelf, which
while it remained uncertain was equivalent to knight-fervice) the
inftant they were reduced to a certainty changed both their name
and nature, and were called focage [m]. It was the certainty therefore that denominated it a focage tenure ; and nothing fure could
be a greater liberty or privilege, than to have the fervice afcertained, and not left to the arbitrary calls of the lord, as in the tenures of chivalry. Wherefore alfo Britton, who defcribes focage
tenure under the name of *fraunke ferme* [n], tells us, that they are
" lands and tenements, whereof the nature of the fee is changed
" by feoffment *out of chivalry* for *certain* yearly fervices, and in
" refpect whereof neither homage, ward, marriage, nor relief can
" be demanded." Which leads us alfo to another obfervation,

[h] Gavelk. 138.
[i] In like manner Skene in his expofition of the Scots' law, title *focage*, tells us that it is " anè kind of holding of lands, quhen " ony man is infeft *freely*," &c.

[k] Litt. §. 119.
[l] §. 118.
[m] Litt. §. 98. 120.
[n] c. 65.

that,

that, if focage tenures were of fuch bafe and fervile original, it is hard to account for the very great immunities which the tenants of them always enjoyed; fo highly fuperior to thofe of the tenants by chivalry, that it was thought, in the reigns of both Edward I and Charles II, a point of the utmoft importance and value to the tenants, to reduce the tenure by knight-fervice to *fraunk ferme* or tenure by focage. We may therefore, I think, fairly conclude in favour of Somner's etymology, and the liberal extraction of the tenure in free focage, againft the authority even of Littleton himfelf.

TAKING this then to be the meaning of the word, it feems probable that the focage tenures were the relicks of Saxon liberty, retained by fuch perfons, as had neither forfeited them to the king, nor been obliged to exchange their tenure for the more honourable, as it was called, but at the fame time more burthenfome, tenure of knight-fervice. This is peculiarly remarkable in the tenure which prevails in Kent, called gavelkind, which is generally acknowleged to be a fpecies of focage tenure°; the prefervation whereof inviolate from the innovations of the Norman conqueror is a fact univerfally known. And thofe who thus preferved their liberties were faid to hold in *free* and *common* focage.

AS therefore the grand criterion and diftinguifhing mark of this fpecies of tenure are the having it's renders or fervices afcertained, it will include under it all other methods of holding free lands by certain and invariable rents and duties: and, in particular, *petit ferjeanty*, tenure in *burgage*, and *gavelkind*.

WE may remember, that by the ftatute 12 Car. II. grand ferjeanty is not itfelf totally abolifhed, but only the flavifh appendages belonging to it; for the honorary fervices (fuch as carrying the king's fword or banner, officiating as his butler, carver, &c, at the coronation) are ftill referved. Now *petit ferjeanty* bears a great refemblance to grand ferjeanty; for as the one is a perfonal

* Wright. 211.

fervice, fo the other is a rent or render, both tending to fome purpofe relative to the king's perfon. Petit ferjeanty, as defined by Littleton[p], confifts in holding lands of the king by the fervice of rendering to him annually fome fmall implement of war, as a bow, a fword, a lance, an arrow, or the like. This, he fays[q], is but focage in effect; for it is no perfonal fervice, but a certain rent: and, we may add, it is clearly no predial fervice, or fervice of the plough, but in all refpects *liberum et commune focagium*; only, being held of the king, it is by way of eminence dignified with the title of *parvum fervitium regis*, or petit ferjeanty. And *magna carta* refpects it in this light, when it enacts[r], that no wardfhip of the lands or body fhall be claimed by the king in virtue of a tenure by petit ferjeanty.

TENURE in *burgage* is defcribed by Glanvil[s], and is expreffly faid by Littleton[t], to be but tenure in focage; and it is where the king or other perfon is lord of an antient borough, in which the tenements are held by a rent certain[u]. It is indeed only a kind of town focage; as common focage, by which other lands are holden, is ufually of a rural nature. A borough, as we have formerly feen, is diftinguifhed from other towns by the right of fending members to parliament; and, where the right of election is by burgage tenure, that alone is a proof of the antiquity of the borough. Tenure in burgage therefore, or burgage tenure, is where houfes, or lands which were formerly the fcite of houfes, in an antient borough, are held of fome lord in common focage, by a certain eftablifhed rent. And thefe feem to have withftood the fhock of the Norman encroachments principally on account of their infignificancy, which made it not worth while to compel them to an alteration of tenure; as an hundred of them put together would fcarce have amounted to a knight's fee. Befides, the owners of them, being chiefly artificers and perfons engaged in trade, could not with any tolerable propriety be put on fuch a

[p] §. 159.
[q] §. 160.
[r] *cap.* 27.
[s] *lib.* 7. *cap.* 3.
[t] §. 162.
[u] Litt. §. 162, 163.

military

military eftablifhment, as the tenure in chivalry was. And here
alfo we have again an inftance, where a tenure is confeffedly in
focage, and yet is impoffible ever to have been held by plough-
fervice; fince the tenants muft have been citizens or burghers,
the fituation frequently a walled town, the tenement a fingle
houfe; fo that none of the owners was probably mafter of a
plough, or was able to ufe one, if he had it. The free focage
therefore, in which thefe tenements are held, feems to be plainly
a remnant of Saxon liberty; which may alfo account for the great
variety of cuftoms, affecting thefe tenements fo held in antient
burgage: the principal and moft remarkable of which is that
called *Borough-Englifh*, fo named in contradiftinction as it were to
the Norman cuftoms, and which is taken notice of by Glanvil [w],
and by Littleton [x]; *viz.* that the youngeft fon, and not the eldeft,
fucceeds to the burgage tenement on the death of his father.
For which Littleton [y] gives this reafon; becaufe the youngeft fon,
by reafon of his tender age, is not fo capable as the reft of his
brethren to help himfelf. Other authors [z] have indeed given a
much ftranger reafon for this cuftom, as if the lord of the fee
had antiently a right to break the feventh commandment with his
tenant's wife on her wedding-night; and that therefore the tenement defcended not to the eldeft, but the youngeft, fon; who
was more certainly the offspring of the tenant. But I cannot
learn that ever this cuftom prevailed in England, though it certainly did in Scotland, (under the name of *mercheta* or *marcheta*)
till abolifhed by Malcolm III [a]. And perhaps a more rational account than either may be fetched (though at a fufficient diftance)
from the practice of the Tartars; among whom, according to
father Duhalde, this cuftom of defcent to the youngeft fon alfo
prevails. That nation is compofed totally of fhepherds and herdf-
men; and the elder fons, as foon as they are capable of leading
a paftoral life, migrate from their father with a certain allotment
of cattle; and go to feek a new habitation. The youngeft fon

[w] *ubi fupra.*
[x] §. 165.
[y] §. 211.

[z] 3 Mod. Pref.
[a] Seld. tit. of hon. *z.* 1. 47. *Reg. Mag.*
l. 4. *c.* 31.

therefore,

therefore, who continues lateſt with the father, is naturally the heir of his houſe, the reſt being already provided for. And thus we find that, among many other northern nations, it was the cuſtom for all the ſons but one to migrate from the father, which one became his heir [b]. So that poſſibly this cuſtom, wherever it prevails, may be the remnant of that paſtoral ſtate of our Britiſh and German anceſtors, which Caeſar and Tacitus deſcribe. Other ſpecial cuſtoms there are in burgage tenures; as that the wife ſhall be endowed of *all* her huſband's tenements [c], and not of the third part only, as at the common law: and that a man might diſpoſe of his tenements by will [d], which, in general, was not permitted after the conqueſt till the reign of Henry the eighth; though in the Saxon times it was allowable [e]. A pregnant proof that theſe liberties of ſocage tenure were fragments of Saxon liberty.

THE nature of the tenure in *gavelkind* affords us a ſtill ſtronger argument. It is univerſally known what ſtruggles the Kentiſhmen made to preſerve their antient liberties; and with how much ſucceſs thoſe ſtruggles were attended. And as it is principally here that we meet with the cuſtom of gavelkind, (though it was and is to be found in ſome other parts of the kingdom [f]) we may fairly conclude that this was a part of thoſe liberties; agreeably to Mr Selden's opinion, that gavelkind before the Norman conqueſt was the general cuſtom of the realm [g]. The diſtinguiſhing properties of this tenure are various: ſome of the principal are theſe; 1. The tenant is of age ſufficient to aliene his eſtate by feoffment at the age of fifteen [h]. 2. The eſtate does not eſcheat in caſe of an attainder and execution for felony; their maxim being, " the " father to the bough, the ſon to the plough [i]." 3. In moſt places

---

[b] *Pater cunctos filios adultos a ſe pellebat, praeter unum quem heredem ſui juris relinquebat. (Wallingh. Upodigm. Neuſtr. c. 1.)*

[c] Litt. §. 166.

[d] §. 167.

[e] Wright. 172.

[f] Stat. 32 Hen. VIII. c. 29. Kitch. of courts, 200.

[g] *In toto regno, ante ducis adventum, frequens et uſitata fuit: poſtea caeteris ademṭta, ſed privatis quorundam locorum conſuetudinibus alibi poſtea regerminans: Cantianis ſolum integra et inviolata remanſit. (Analect. l. 2. c. 7.)*

[h] Lamb. Peramb. 614.

[i] Lamb. 634.

he

he had a power of devifing lands by will, before the ftatute for that purpofe was made[k]. 4. The lands defcend, not to the eldeft, youngeft, or any one fon only, but to all the fons together[l]; which was indeed antiently the moft ufual courfe of defcent all over England[m], though in particular places particular cuftoms prevailed. Thefe, among other properties, diftinguifhed this tenure in a moft remarkable manner : and yet it is held to be only a fpecies of a focage tenure, modified by the cuftom of the country ; being holden by fuit of court and fealty, which is a fervice in it's nature certain[n]. Wherefore, by a charter of king John[o], Hubert arch-bifhop of Canterbury was authorized to *exchange* the gavelkind tenures holden of the fee of Canterbury into tenures by knight-fervice ; and by ftatute 31 Hen. VIII. c. 3. for difgavelling the lands of divers lords and gentlemen in the county of Kent, they are directed to be defcendible for the future *like other lands, which were never holden by fervice of focage.* Now the immunities which the tenants in gavelkind enjoyed were fuch, as we cannot conceive fhould be conferred upon mere ploughmen, or peafants : from all which I think it fufficiently clear, that tenures in free focage are in general of a nobler original than is affigned by Littleton, and after him by the bulk of our common lawyers.

HAVING thus diftributed and diftinguifhed the feveral fpecies of tenure in free focage, I proceed next to fhew that this alfo partakes very ftrongly of the feodal nature. Which may probably arife from it's antient Saxon original ; fince (as was before obferved[p]) feuds were not unknown among the Saxons, though they did not form a part of their military policy, nor were drawn out into fuch arbitrary confequences as among the Normans. It feems therefore reafonable to imagine, that focage tenure exifted in much the fame ftate before the conqueft as after ; that in Kent it was preferved with a high hand, as our hiftories inform us it was ;

---

[k] F. N. B. 198. Cro. Car. 561.
[l] Litt. §. 210.
[m] Glanv. *l.* 7. *c.* 3

[n] Wright. 211.
[o] Spelm. *cod. vet. leg.* 355.
[p] pag. 48.

an.l

and that the reſt of the ſocage tenures diſperſed through England eſcaped the general fate of other property, partly out of favour and affection to their particular owners, and partly from their own inſignificancy; ſince I do not apprehend the number of ſocage tenures ſoon after the conqueſt to have been very conſiderable, nor their value by any means large; till by ſucceſſive charters of enfranchiſement granted to the tenants, which are particularly mentioned by Britton ꝗ, their number and value began to ſwell ſo far, as to make a diſtinct, and juſtly envied, part of our Engliſh ſyſtem of tenures.

H o w e v e r this may be, the tokens of their feodal original will evidently appear from a ſhort compariſon of the incidents and conſequences of ſocage tenure with thoſe of tenure in chivalry; remarking their agreement or difference as we go along.

1. I n the firſt place, then, both were held of ſuperior lords; of the king as lord paramount, and ſometimes of a ſubject or meſne lord between the king and the tenant.

2. B o t h were ſubject to the feodal return, render, rent, or ſervice, of ſome ſort or other, which aroſe from a ſuppoſition of an original grant from the lord to the tenant. In the military tenure, or more proper feud, this was from it's nature uncertain; in ſocage, which was a feud of the improper kind, it was certain, fixed, and determinate, (though perhaps nothing more than bare fealty) and ſo continues to this day.

3. B o t h were, from their conſtitution, univerſally ſubject (over and above all other renders) to the oath of fealty, or mutual bond of obligation between the lord and tenant ʳ. Which oath of fealty uſually draws after it ſuit to the lord's court. And this oath every lord, of whom tenements are holden at this day, may and ought to call upon his tenants to take in his court baron; if it be only for the reaſon given by Littleton ˢ, that if it be ne-

ꝗ c. 66.　　　　　　　　　ˢ §. 130.
ʳ Litt. §. 117. 131.
　　　　　　　　　　　　　　　　　　glected,

glected, it will by long continuance of time grow out of memory (as doubtlefs it frequently has) whether the land be holden of the lord or not; and fo he may lofe his feignory, and the profit which may accrue to him by efcheats and other contingences[t].

4. THE tenure in focage was fubject, of common right, to aids for knighting the fon and marrying the eldeft daughter[u]: which were fixed by the ftatute Weftm.1. c.36. at 20 s. for every 20 l. *per annum* fo held; as in knight-fervice. Thefe aids, as in tenure by chivalry, were originally mere benevolences, though afterwards claimed as matter of right; but were all abolifhed by the ftatute 12 Car. II.

5. RELIEF is due upon focage tenure, as well as upon tenure in chivalry: but the manner of taking it is very different. The relief on a knight's fee was 5 l. or one quarter of the fuppofed value of the land; but a focage relief is one year's rent or render, payable by the tenant to the lord, be the fame either great or fmall[w]: and therefore Bracton[x] will not allow this to be properly a relief, but *quaedam praeftatio loco relevii in recognitionem domini*. So too the ftatute 28 Edw. I. c. 1. declares, that a free fokeman fhall give *no relief*, but fhall double his rent after the death of his anceftor, according to that which he hath ufed to pay his lord, and fhall not be grieved above meafure. Reliefs in knight-fervice were only payable, if the heir at the death of his anceftor was of full age: but in focage they were due, even though the heir was under age, becaufe the lord has no wardfhip over him[y]. The ftatute of Charles II referves the reliefs incident to focage tenures; and therefore, wherever lands in fee fimple are holden by a rent, relief is ftill due of common right upon the death of the tenant[z].

---

[t] *Eo maxime praeftandum eft, ne dubium reddatur jus domini et vetuftate temporis obfcuretur.* (Corvin. jus feud. l. 2, t. 7.)

[u] Co. Litt. 91.

[w] Litt. §. 126.

[x] l. 2. c. 37. §. 8.

[y] Litt. §. 127.

[z] 3 Lev. 145.

6. PRIMER

6. PRIMER feifin was incident to the king's focage tenants *in capite*, as well as to thofe by knight-fervice ª. But tenancy *in capite* as well as primer feifins, are alfo, among the other feodal burthens, intirely abolifhed by the ftatute.

7. WARDSHIP is alfo incident to tenure in focage; but of a nature very different from that incident to knight-fervice. For if the inheritance defcend to an infant under fourteen, the wardfhip of him fhall not belong to the lord of the fee; becaufe, in this tenure no military or other perfonal fervice being required, there is no occafion for the lord to take the profits, in order to provide a proper fubftitute for his infant tenant: but his neareft relation (to whom the inheritance cannot defcend) fhall be his guardian in focage, and have the cuftody of his land and body till he arrives at the age of fourteen. The guardian muft be fuch a one, to whom the inheritance by no poffibility can defcend; as was fully explained, together with the reafons for it, in the former book of thefe commentaries ᵇ. At fourteen this wardfhip in focage ceafes, and the heir may ouft the guardian, and call him to account for the rents and profits ᶜ: for at this age the law fuppofes him capable of chufing a guardian for himfelf. It was in this particular, of wardfhip, as alfo in that of marriage, and in the certainty of the render or fervice, that the focage tenures had fo much the advantage of the military ones. But as the wardfhip ceafed at fourteen, there was this difadvantage attending it; that young heirs, being left at fo tender an age to chufe their own guardians till twenty one, they might make an improvident choice. Therefore, when almoft all the lands of the kingdom were turned into focage tenures, the fame ftatute 12 Car. II. c. 24. enacted, that it fhould be in the power of any father by will to appoint a guardian, till his child fhould attain the age of twenty one. And, if no fuch appointment be made, the court of chancery will frequently interpofe, to prevent an infant heir from improvidently expofing himfelf to ruin.

ª Co. Litt. 77.
ᵇ page 449.

ᶜ Litt. §. 123. Co. Litt. 89.

8. MAR-

8. MARRIAGE, or the *valor maritagii*, was not in focage tenure any perquifite or advantage to the guardian, but rather the reverfe. For, if the guardian married his ward under the age of fourteen, he was bound to account to the ward for the value of the marriage, even though he took nothing for it, unlefs he married him to advantage [d]. For the law, in favour of infants, is always jealous of guardians, and therefore in this cafe it made them account, not only for what they *did*, but alfo for what they *might*, receive on the infant's behalf; left by fome collufion the guardian fhould have received the value, and not brought it to account : but, the ftatute having deftroyed all values of marriages, this doctrine of courfe is ceafed with them. At fourteen years of age the ward might have difpofed of himfelf in marriage, without any confent of his guardian, till the late act for preventing clandeftine marriages. Thefe doctrines of wardfhip and marriage in focage tenure were fo diametrically oppofite to thofe in knight-fervice, and fo entirely agree with thofe parts of king Edward's laws, that were reftored by Henry the firft's charter, as might alone convince us that focage was of a higher original than the Norman conqueft.

9. FINES for alienations were, I apprehend, due for lands holden of the king *in capite* by focage tenure, as well as in cafe of tenure by knight-fervice : for the ftatutes that relate to this point, and fir Edward Coke's comment on them [e], fpeak generally of all tenants *in capite*, without making any diftinction; though now all fines for alienation are demolifhed by the ftatute of Charles the fecond.

10. ESCHEATS are equally incident to tenure in focage, as they were to tenure by knight-fervice; except only in gavelkind lands, which are (as is before-mentioned) fubject to no efcheats for felony, though they are to efcheats for want of heirs [f].

---

[d] Litt. §. 123.
[e] 1 Inft. 43.   2 Inft. 65, 66, 67.

[f] Wright. 210.

THUS much for the two grand fpecies of tenure, under which almoft all the free lands of the kingdom were holden till the reftoration in 1660, when the former was abolifhed and funk into the latter: fo that lands of both forts are now holden by the one univerfal tenure of free and common focage.

THE other grand divifion of tenure, mentioned by Bracton as cited in the preceding chapter, is that of *villenage*, as contradiftinguifhed from *liberum tenementum*, or frank tenure. And this (we may remember) he fubdivides into two claffes, *pure*, and *privileged*, villenage: from whence have arifen two other fpecies of our modern tenures.

III. FROM the tenure of pure villenage have fprung our prefent *copyhold* tenures, or tenure by copy of court roll at the will of the lord; in order to obtain a clear idea of which, it will be previoufly neceffary to take a fhort view of the original and nature of manors.

MANORS are in fubftance as antient as the Saxon conftitution, though perhaps differing a little, in fome immaterial circumftances, from thofe that exift at this day [g]: juft as we obferved of feuds, that they were partly known to our anceftors, even before the Norman conqueft. A manor, *manerium, a manendo,* becaufe the ufual refidence of the owner, feems to have been a diftrict of ground, held by lords or great perfonages; who kept in their own hands fo much land as was neceffary for the ufe of their families, which were called *terrae dominicales*, or *demefne* lands; being occupied by the lord, or *dominus manerii*, and his fervants. The other *tenemental* lands they diftributed among their tenants; which from the different modes of tenure were called and diftinguifhed by two different names. Firft, *book-land*, or charter-land, which was held by deed under certain rents and free fervices, and in effect differed nothing from free focage lands [h]: and from

g Co. Cop. §. 2, & 10.   h Co. Cop. §. 3.

hence

hence have arifen all the freehold tenants which hold of particular manors, and owe fuit and fervice to the fame. The other fpecies was called *folk-land*, which was held by no affurance in writing, but diftributed among the common folk or people at the pleafure of the lord, and refumed at his difcretion; being indeed land held in villenage, which we fhall prefently defcribe more at large. The refidue of the manor, being uncultivated, was termed the lord's wafte, and ferved for public roads, and for common of pafture to the lord and his tenants. Manors were formerly called baronies, as they ftill are lordfhips : and each lord or baron was empowered to hold a domeftic court, called the court-baron, for redreffing mifdemefnors and nufances within the manor, and for fettling difputes of property among the tenants. This court is an infeparable ingredient of every manor; and if the number of fuitors fhould fo fail, as not to leave fufficient to make a jury or homage, that is, two tenants at the leaft, the manor itfelf is loft.

BEFORE the ftatute of *quia emptores*, 18 Edw. I. the king's greater barons, who had a large extent of territory held under the crown, granted out frequently fmaller manors to inferior perfons to be held of themfelves; which do therefore now continue to be held under a fuperior lord, who is called in fuch cafes the lord paramount over all thefe manors : and his feignory is frequently termed an honour, not a manor, efpecially if it hath belonged to an antient feodal baron, or hath been at any time in the hands of the crown. In imitation whereof, thefe inferior lords began to carve out and grant to others ftill more minute eftates, to be held as of themfelves, and were fo proceeding downwards *in infinitum*; till the fuperior lords obferved, that by this method of fubinfeudation they loft all their feodal profits, of wardfhips, marriages, and efcheats, which fell into the hands of thefe mefne or middle lords, who were the immediate fuperiors of the *terretenant*, or him who occupied the land. This occafioned the ftatute of Weftm. 3. or *quia emptores*, 18 Edw. I. to be made; which directs, that, upon all fales or feoffments of land, the feoffee

M 2   fhall

fhall hold the fame, not of his immediate feoffor, but of the chief lord of the fee, of whom fuch feoffor himfelf held it. And from hence it is held, that all manors exifting at this day, muft have exifted by immemorial prefcription; or at leaft ever fince the 18 Edw. I. when the ftatute of *quia emptores* was made. For no new manor can have been created fince that ftatute: becaufe it is effential to a manor, that there be tenants who hold of the lord, and that ftatute enacts, that for the future no fubject fhall create any new tenants to hold of himfelf.

N o w with regard to the folk-land, or eftates held in villenage, this was a fpecies of tenure neither ftrictly feodal, Norman, or Saxon; but mixed and compounded of them all[i]: and which alfo, on account of the heriots that ufually attend it, may feem to have fomewhat Danifh in it's compofition. Under the Saxon government there were, as fir William Temple fpeaks[k], a fort of people in a condition of downright fervitude, ufed and employed in the moft fervile works, and belonging, both they, their children, and effects, to the lord of the foil, like the reft of the cattle or ftock upon it. Thefe feem to have been thofe who held what was called the folk-land, from which they were removeable at the lord's pleafure. On the arrival of the Normans here, it feems not improbable, that they, who were ftrangers to any other than a feodal ftate, might give fome fparks of enfranchifement to fuch wretched perfons as fell to their fhare, by admitting them, as well as others, to the oath of fealty; which conferred a right of protection, and raifed the tenant to a kind of eftate fuperior to downright flavery, but inferior to every other condition[l]. This they called villenage, and the tenants villeins, either from the word *vilis*, or elfe, as fir Edward Coke tells us[m], *a villa*; becaufe they lived chiefly in villages, and were employed in ruftic works of the moft fordid kind: like the Spartan *helotes*, to whom alone the culture of the lands was configned; their rugged mafters, like our northern anceftors, efteeming war the only honourable employment of mankind.

---

[i] Wright. 215.
[k] Introd. Hift. Engl. 59.
[l] Wright. 217.
[m] 1 Inft. 116.

THESE villeins, belonging principally to lords of manors, were either villeins *regardant*, that is, annexed to the manor or land ; or elfe they were *in grofs*, or at large, that is, annexed to the perfon of the lord, and transferrable by deed from one owner to another [n]. They could not leave their lord without his permiffion ; but, if they ran away, or were purloined from him, might be claimed and recovered by action, like beafts or other chattels. They held indeed fmall portions of land by way of fuftaining themfelves and families ; but it was at the mere will of the lord, who might difpoffefs them whenever he pleafed ; and it was upon villein fervices, that is, to carry out dung, to hedge and ditch the lord's demefnes, and any other the meaneft offices [o] : and thefe fervices were not only bafe, but uncertain both as to their time and quantity [p]. A villein, in fhort, was in much the fame ftate with us, as lord Molefworth [q] defcribes to be that of the boors in Denmark, and Stiernhook [r] attributes alfo to the *traals* or flaves in Sweden ; which confirms the probability of their being in fome degree monuments of the Danifh tyranny. A villein could acquire no property either in lands or goods ; but, if he purchafed either, the lord might enter upon them, ouft the villein, and feife them to his own ufe, unlefs he contrived to difpofe of them again before the lord had feifed them ; for the lord had then loft his opportunity [s].

IN many places alfo a fine was payable to the lord, if the villein prefumed to marry his daughter to any one without leave from the lord [t] : and, by the common law, the lord might alfo bring an action againft the hufband for damages in thus purloining his property [u]. For the children of villeins were alfo in the fame ftate of bondage with their parents ; whence they were

---

[n] Litt. § 181.

[o] *Ibid.* §. 172.

[p] *Ille qui tenet in villenagio faciet quicquid ei praeceptum fuerit, nec fcire debet fero quid facere debet in craftino, et femper tenebitur ad incerta.* (Bracton. *l.* 4. *tr.* 1. *c.* 28.)

[q] c. 8.

[r] *de jure Sueonum. l. 2. c. 4.*

[s] Litt. §. 177.

[t] Co. Litt. 40.

[u] Litt. §. 202.

called

called in Latin, *nativi*, which gave rise to the female appellation of a villein, who was called a *neife* [w]. In case of a marriage between a freeman and a neife, or a villein and a freewoman, the issue followed the condition of the father, being free if he was free, and villein if he was villein ; contrary to the maxim of the civil law, that *partus sequitur ventrem*. But no bastard could be born a villein, because by another maxim of our law he is *nullius filius* ; and as he can *gain* nothing by inheritance, it were hard that he should *lose* his natural freedom by it [x]. The law however protected the persons of villeins, as the king's subjects, against atrocious injuries of the lord : for he might not kill, or maim his villein [y] ; though he might beat him with impunity, since the villein had no action or remedy at law against his lord, but in case of the murder of his ancestor or the maim of his own person. Niefes indeed had also an appeal of rape, in case the lord violated them by force [z].

VILLEINS might be enfranchised by manumission, which is either express or implied : express ; as where a man granted to the villein a deed of manumission [a] : implied ; as where a man bound himself in a bond to his villein for a sum of money, granted him an annuity by deed, or gave him an estate in fee, for life, or years [b] : for this was dealing with his villein on the footing of a freeman ; it was in some of the instances giving him an action against his lord, and in others vesting an ownership in him entirely inconsistent with his former state of bondage. So also if the lord brought an action against his villein, this enfranchised him [c] ; for, as the lord might have a short remedy against his villein, by seising his goods, (which was more than equivalent to any damages he could recover) the law, which is always ready to catch at any thing in favour of liberty, presumed that by bringing this action he meant to set his villein on the same footing

---

[w] Litt. §. 187.
[x] Ibid. §. 187, 188.
[y] Ibid. §. 189. 194.
[z] Ibid. §. 190.

[a] Ibid §. 204.
[b] §. 204, 5, 6.
[c] §. 208.

with

with himſelf, and therefore held it an implied manumiſſion. But, in caſe the lord indicted him for felony, it was otherwiſe; for the lord could not inflict a capital puniſhment on his villein, without calling in the aſſiſtance of the law.

VILLEINS, by this and many other means, in proceſs of time gained conſiderable ground on their lords; and in particular ſtrengthened the tenure of their eſtates to that degree, that they came to have in them an intereſt in many places full as good, in others better than their lords. For the goodnature and benevolence of many lords of manors having, time out of mind, permitted their villeins and their children to enjoy their poſſeſſions without interruption, in a regular couſe of deſcent, the common law, of which cuſtom is the life, now gave them title to preſcribe againſt their lords; and, on performance of the ſame ſervices, to hold their lands, in ſpight of any determination of the lord's will. For, though in general they are ſtill ſaid to hold their eſtates at the will of the lord, yet it is ſuch a will as is agreeable to the cuſtom of the manor; which cuſtoms are preſerved and evidenced by the rolls of the ſeveral courts baron in which they are entered, or kept on foot by the conſtant immemorial uſage of the ſeveral manors in which the lands lie. And, as ſuch tenants had nothing to ſhew for their eſtates but theſe cuſtoms, and admiſſions in purſuance of them, entered on thoſe rolls, or the copies of ſuch entries witneſſed by the ſteward, they now began to be called *tenants by copy of court roll*, and their tenure itſelf a *copyhold* [d].

THUS copyhold tenures, as ſir Edward Coke obſerves [e], although very meanly deſcended, yet come of an antient houſe; for, from what has been premiſed it appears, that copyholders are in truth no other but villeins, who, by a long ſeries of immemorial encroachments on the lord, have at laſt eſtabliſhed a cuſtomary right to thoſe eſtates, which before were held abſolutely at the lord's will. Which affords a very ſubſtantial reaſon for the great variety

[d] F. N. B. 12.   [e] Cop. §. 32.

of

of cuftoms that prevail in different manors, with regard both to the defcent of the eftates, and the privileges belonging to the tenants. And thefe encroachments grew to be fo univerfal, that when tenure in villenage was͜ abolifhed, (though copyholds were referved) by the ftatute of Charles II, there was hardly a pure villein left in the nation. For fir Thomas Smith [f] teftifies, that in all his time (and he was fecretary to Edward VI) he never knew any villein in grofs throughout the realm; and the few villeins regardant that were then remaining were fuch only as had belonged to bifhops, monafteries, or other ecclefiaftical corporations, in the preceding times of popery. For he tells us, that "the holy fathers, monks, and friars, had in their confeffions, "and fpecially in their extreme and deadly ficknefs, convinced the "laity how dangerous a practice it was, for one chriftian man to "hold another in bondage : fo that temporal men, by little and "little, by reafon of that terror in their confciences, were glad "to manumit all ,their villeins. But the faid holy fathers, with "the abbots and priors, did not in like fort by theirs; for they "alfo had a fcruple in confcience to empoverifh and defpoil the "church fo much, as to manumit fuch as were bond to their "churches, or to the manors which the church had gotten; and "fo kept their villeins ftill." By thefe feveral means the generality of villeins in the kingdom have long ago fprouted up into copyholders : their perfons being enfranchifed by manumiffion or long acquiefcence; but their eftates, in ftrictnefs, remaining fubject to the fame fervile conditions and forfeitures as before; though, in general, the villein fervices are ufually commuted for a fmall pecuniary quit-rent [g].

---

[f] Commonwealth. b. 3. c. 10.

[g] In fome manors the copyholders were bound to perform the moft fervile offices, as to hedge and ditch the lord's grounds, to lop his trees, to reap his corn, and the like; the lord ufually finding them meat and drink, and fometimes (as is ftill the ufe in the highlands of Scotland) a minftrell or piper for their diverfion. *(Rot. Maner. de Edgware Com. Midd.)* As in the kingdom of Whidah, on the flave coaft of Africa, the people are bound to cut and carry in the king's corn from off his demefne lands, and are attended by mufic during all the time of their labour. (Mod. Un. Hift. xvi. 429.)

A s

A s a farther confequence of what has been premifed, we may collect thefe two main principles, which are held[h] to be the fup-porters of a copyhold tenure, and without which it cannot exift ; 1. That the lands be parcel of, and fituate within, that manor, under which it is held. 2. That they have been demifed, or demifable, by copy of court roll immemorially. For immemor-ial cuftom is the life of all tenures by copy ; fo that no new copyhold can, ftrictly fpeaking, be granted at this day.

I n fome manors, where the cuftom hath been to permit the heir to fucceed the anceftor in his tenure, the eftates are ftiled copyholds of inheritance ; in others, where the lords have been more vigilant to maintain their rights, they remain copyholds for life only : for the cuftom of the manor has in both cafes fo far fuperfeded the will of the lord, that, provided the fervices be performed or ftipulated for by fealty, he cannot, in the firft in-ftance, refufe to admit the heir of his tenant upon his death ; nor, in the fecond, can he remove his prefent tenant fo long as he lives, though he holds nominally by the precarious tenure of his lord's will.

T h e fruits and appendages of a copyhold tenure, that it hath in common with free tenures, are fealty, fervices (as well in rents as otherwife) reliefs, and efcheats. The two latter belong only to copyholds of inheritance ; the former to thofe for life alfo. But, befides thefe, copyholds have alfo heriots, wardfhip, and fines. Heriots, which I think are agreed to be a Danifh cuftom, and of which we fhall fay more hereafter, are a render of the beft beaft or other good (as the cuftom may be) to the lord on the death of the tenant. This is plainly a relic of villein tenure ; there being originally lefs hardfhip in it, when all the goods and chattels belonged to the lord, and he might have feifed them even in the villein's lifetime. Thefe are incident to both fpecies of copyhold ; but wardfhip and fines to thofe of inheritance only.

[h] Co. Litt. 58.

Wardſhip, in copyhold eſtates, partakes both of that in chivalry and that in ſocage. Like that in chivalry, the lord is the legal guardian, who uſually aſſigns ſome relation of the infant tenant to act in his ſtead : and he, like guardian in ſocage, is accountable to his ward for the profits. Of fines, ſome are in the nature of primer ſeiſins, due on the death of each tenant, others are mere fines for alienation of the lands; in ſome manors only one of theſe ſorts can be demanded, in ſome both, and in others neither. They are ſometimes arbitrary and at the will of the lord, ſometimes fixed by cuſtom : but, even when arbitrary, the courts of law, in favour of the liberty of copyholders, have tied them down to be *reaſonable* in their extent; otherwiſe they might amount to a diſheriſon of the eſtate. No fine therefore is allowed to be taken upon deſcents and alienations, (unleſs in particular circumſtances) of more than two years improved value of the eſtate [1]. From this inſtance we may judge of the favourable diſpoſition, that the law of England (which is a law of liberty) hath always ſhewn to this ſpecies of tenants; by removing, as far as poſſible, every real badge of ſlavery from them, however ſome nominal ones may continue. It ſuffered cuſtom very early to get the better of the expreſs terms upon which they held their lands; by declaring, that the will of the lord was to be interpreted by the cuſtom of the manor : and, where no cuſtom has been ſuffered to grow up to the prejudice of the lord, as in this caſe of arbitrary fines, the law itſelf interpoſes in an equitable method, and will not ſuffer the lord to extend his power ſo far, as to diſinherit the tenant.

THUS much for the antient tenure of *pure* villenage, and the modern one of *copyhold at the will of the lord,* which is lineally deſcended from it.

IV. THERE is yet a fourth ſpecies of tenure, deſcribed by Bracton under the name ſometimes of *privileged* villenage, and ſometimes of *villein-ſocage.* This, he tells us [k], is ſuch as has been held of

[1] 2 Ch. Rep. 134.   [k] *l.* 4. *tr.* 1. *c.* 28.

the

the kings of England from the conqueſt downwards; that the
tenants herein "*villana faciunt ſervitia, ſed certa et determinata*;"
that they cannot aliene or transfer their tenements by grant or
feoffment, any more than pure villeins can; but muſt ſurrender
them to the lord or his ſteward, to be again granted out and held
in villenage. And from theſe circumſtances we may collect, that
what he here deſcribes is no other than an exalted ſpecies of copyhold, ſubſiſting at this day, *viz.* the tenure in *antient demeſne:*
to which, as partaking of the baſeneſs of villenage in the nature
of it's ſervices, and the freedom of ſocage in their certainty, he
has therefore given a name compounded out of both, and calls
it *villanum ſocagium.*

A N T I E N T demeſne conſiſts of thoſe lands or manors, which,
though now perhaps granted out to private ſubjects, were actually in the hands of the crown in the time of Edward the confeſſor, or William the conqueror; and ſo appear to have been by
the great ſurvey in the exchequer called domeſday book [l]. The
tenants of theſe lands, under the crown, were not all of the
ſame order or degree. Some of them, as Britton teſtifies [m], continued for a long time pure and abſolute villeins, dependent on
the will of the lord: and thoſe who have ſucceeded them in their
tenures now differ from common copyholders in only a few
points [n]. Others were in great meaſure enfranchiſed by the royal
favour: being only bound in reſpect of their lands to perform
ſome of the better ſort of villein ſervices, but thoſe determinate
and certain; as, to plough the king's land, to ſupply his court
with proviſions, and the like; all of which are now changed into
pecuniary rents: and in conſideration hereof they had many immunities and privileges granted to them [o]; as, to try the right of
their property in a peculiar court of their own, called a court of
antient demeſne, by a peculiar proceſs denominated a writ of *right
cloſe* [p]; not to pay toll or taxes; not to contribute to the expenſes
of knights of the ſhire; not to be put on juries, and the like [q].

---

[l] F. N. B. 14. 16.
[m] c. 66.
[n] F. N. B. 228.

[o] 4 Inſt. 269.
[p] F. N. B. 11.
[q] *Ibid.* 14.

T H E S E

T H E S E tenants therefore, though their *tenure* be abfolutely copyhold, yet have an *intereſt* equivalent to a freehold: for, though their ſervices were of a baſe and villenous original[r], yet the tenants were eſteemed in all other reſpects to be highly privileged villeins; and eſpecially in this, that their ſervices were fixed and determinate, and that they could not be compelled (like pure villeins) to relinquiſh theſe tenements at the lord's will, or to hold them againſt their own : " *et ideo,* ſays Bracton, *dicuntur liberi.*" Britton alſo, from ſuch their freedom, calls them abſolutely *ſokemans,* and their tenure *ſokemanries;* which he deſcribes[s] to be " lands and tenements, which are not held by knight-ſervice, nor " by grand ſerjeanty, nor by petit, but by ſimple ſervices, being " as it were lands enfranchiſed by the king or his predeceſſors " from their antient demeſne." And the ſame name is alſo given them in Fleta[t]. Hence Fitzherbert obſerves[u], that no lands are antient demeſne, but lands holden in ſocage : that is, not in free and common ſocage, but in this amphibious, ſubordinate claſs, of villein-ſocage. And it is poſſible, that as this ſpecies of ſocage tenure is plainly founded upon predial ſervices, or ſervices of the plough, it may have given cauſe to imagine that all ſocage tenures aroſe from the ſame original; for want of diſtinguiſhing, with Bracton, between free-ſocage or ſocage of frank-tenure, and villan-ſocage or ſocage of antient demeſne.

L A N D S held by this tenure are therefore a ſpecies of copyhold, and as ſuch preſerved and exempted from the operation of the ſtatute of Charles II. Yet they differ from common copyholds, principally in the privileges before-mentioned : as alſo they differ from freeholders by one eſpecial mark and tincture of villenage, noted by Bracton and remaining to this day; *viz.* that they cannot be conveyed from man to man by the general common law conveyances of feoffment, and the reſt; but muſt paſs by ſurrender to the lord or his ſteward, in the manner of common

---

[r] Gilb. hiſt. of the exch. 16. & 30.   [t] *l.* 1. *c.* 8.
[s] c. 66.   [u] N. B. 13.

copyholds : yet with this difference [w], that, in thefe furrenders of lands in antient demefne of frank tenure, it is not ufed to fay " *to* " *hold at the will of the lord*" in their copies, but only " *to hold* " *according to the cuftom of the manor.*"

THUS have we taken a compendious view of the principal and fundamental points of the doctrine of tenures, both antient and modern, in which we cannot but remark the mutual connexion and dependence that all of them have upon each other. And upon the whole it appears, that, whatever changes and alterations thefe tenures have in procefs of time undergone, from the Saxon aera to the 12 Car. II, all lay tenures are now in effect reduced to two fpecies ; *free* tenure in common focage ; and *bafe* tenure by copy of court roll.

I MENTIONED *lay* tenures only ; becaufe there is ftill behind one other fpecies of tenure, referved by the ftatute of Charles II, which is of a *fpiritual* nature, and called the tenure in frankalmoign.

V. TENURE in *frankalmoign, in libera eleemofyna,* or free alms, is that, whereby a religious corporation, aggregate or fole, holdeth lands of the donor to them and their fucceffors for ever [x]. The fervice, which they were bound to render for thefe lands was not certainly defined ; but only in general to pray for the fouls of the donor and his heirs, dead or alive ; and therefore they did no fealty, (which is incident to all other fervices but this [y]) becaufe this divine fervice was of a higher and more exalted nature [z]. This is the tenure, by which almoft all the antient monafteries and religious houfes held their lands ; and by which the parochial clergy, and very many ecclefiaftical and eleemofynary foundations, hold them at this day [a]; the nature of the fervice being upon the reformation altered, and made conformable to the purer doctrines

---

[w] Kitchen on courts. 194.
[x] Litt. §. 133.
[y] *Ibid.* 131.
[z] *Ibid.* 135.
[a] Bracton. *l.* 4. *tr.* 1. *c.* 28. §. 1.

of the church of England. It was an old Saxon tenure; and continued under the Norman revolution, through the great refpect that was fhewn to religion and religious men in antient times. Which is alfo the reafon that tenants in *frankalmoign* were difcharged of all other fervices, except the *trinoda neceffitas*, of repairing the highways, building caftles, and repelling invafions [b]: juft as the druids, among the antient Britons, had *omnium rerum immunitatem* [c]. And, even at prefent, this is a tenure of a nature very diftinct from all others; being not in the leaft feodal, but merely fpiritual. For if the fervice be neglected, the law gives no remedy by diftrefs or otherwife to the lord of whom the lands are holden; but merely a complaint to the ordinary or vifitor to correct it [d]. Wherein it materially differed from what was called *tenure by divine fervice*: in which the tenants were obliged to do fome fpecial divine fervices in certain; as to fing fo many maffes, to diftribute fuch a fum in alms, and the like; which, being expreffly defined and prefcribed, could with no kind of propriety be called *free* alms; efpecially as for this, if unperformed, the lord might diftrein, without any complaint to the vifitor [e]. All fuch donations are indeed now out of ufe: for, fince the ftatute of *quia emptores*, 18 Edw. I, none but the king can give lands to be holden by this tenure [f]. So that I only mention them, becaufe *frankalmoign* is excepted by name in the ftatute of Charles II, and therefore fubfifts in many inftances at this day. Which is all that fhall be remarked concerning it; herewith concluding our obfervations on the nature of tenures.

[b] Seld. *Jan.* 1. 42.
[c] Caefar *de bell. Gall. l.* 6. *c.* 13.
[d] Litt. §. 136.

[e] *Ibid.* 137.
[f] *Ibid.* 140.

CHAPTER THE SEVENTH.

OF FREEHOLD ESTATES, OF INHERITANCE.

THE next objects of our difquifitions are the nature and properties of *eftates*. An eftate in lands, tenements, and hereditaments, fignifies fuch intereft as the tenant hath therein : fo that if a man grants all *his eftate* to another, every thing that he can poffibly grant fhall pafs thereby [a]. It is called in Latin, *ftatus*; it fignifying the condition, or circumftance, in which the owner ftands, with regard to his property. And, to afcertain this with proper precifion and accuracy, eftates may be confidered in a threefold view: firft, with regard to the *quantity of intereft* which the tenant has in the tenement: fecondly, with regard to the *time* at which that quantity of intereft is to be enjoyed: and, thirdly, with regard to the *number* and *connexions* of the tenants.

FIRST, with regard to the *quantity of intereft* which the tenant has in the tenement, this is meafured by it's duration and extent. Thus, either his right of poffeffion is to fubfift for an uncertain period, during his own life, or the life of another man ; to determine at his own deceafe, or to remain to his defcendants after him : or it is circumfcribed within a certain number of years, months, or days : or, laftly, it is infinite and unlimited, being vefted in him and his reprefentatives for ever. And this

[a] Co. Litt. 345.

occafions

occafions the primary divifion of eftates, into fuch as are *free-hold*, and fuch as are *lefs than freehold*.

AN eftate of freehold, *liberum tenementum*, or franktenement, is defined by Britton [b] to be " the *poffeffion* of the foil by a free-" man." And St. Germyn [c] tells us, that " the *poffeffion* of the " land is called in the law of England the franktenement or free-" hold." Such eftate therefore, and no other, as requires actual poffeffion of the land, is legally fpeaking freehold : which actual poffeffion can, by the courfe of the common law, be only given by the ceremony called livery of feifin, which is the fame as the feodal inveftiture. And from thefe principles we may extract this defcription of a freehold; that it is fuch an eftate in lands as is conveyed by livery of feifin ; or, in tenements of an incorporeal nature, by what is equivalent thereto. And accordingly it is laid down by Littleton [d], that where a freehold fhall pafs, it behoveth to have livery of feifin. As therefore eftates of inheritance and eftates for life could not by common law be conveyed without livery of feifin, thefe are properly eftates of freehold ; and, as no other eftates were conveyed with the fame folemnity, therefore no others are properly freehold eftates.

ESTATES of freehold then are divifible into eftates *of inheritance*, and eftates *not of inheritance*. The former are again divided into inheritances *abfolute* or fee-fimple ; and inheritances *limited*, one fpecies of which we ufually call fee-tail.

I. TENANT in fee-fimple (or, as he is frequently ftiled, tenant in fee) is he that hath lands, tenements, or hereditaments, to hold to him and his heirs for ever [e] ; generally, abfolutely, and fimply ; without mentioning *what* heirs, but referring that to his own pleafure, or to the difpofition of the law. The true meaning of the word fee *(feodum)* is the fame with that of feud or fief, and in it's original fenfe it is taken in contradiftinction to

[b] c. 32.
[c] Dr & Stud. b. 2. d. 22.
[d] §. 59.
[e] Litt. §. 1.

allodium [f] ;

allodium [f]; which latter the writers on this subject define to be every man's own land, which he possesseth merely in his own right, without owing any rent or service to any superior. This is property in it's highest degree; and the owner thereof hath *absolutum et directum dominium,* and therefore it is said to be seised thereof absolutely *in dominico suo,* in his own demesne. But *feodum,* or fee, is that which is held of some superior, on condition of rendering him service; in which superior the ultimate property of the land resides. And therefore sir Henry Spelman [g] defines a feud or fee to be the right which the vasal or tenant hath in lands, to *use* the same, and take the profits thereof to him and his heirs, rendering to the lord his due services; the mere allodial *propriety* of the soil always remaining in the lord. This allodial property no subject in England has [h]; it being a received, and now undeniable, principle in the law, that all the lands in England are holden mediately or immediately of the king. The king therefore only hath *absolutum et directum dominium* [i]; but all subjects' lands are in the nature of *feodum* or fee; whether derived to them by descent from their ancestors, or purchased for a valuable consideration; for they cannot come to any man by either of those ways, unless accompanied with those feodal clogs, which were laid upon the first feudatory when it was originally granted. A subject therefore hath only the usufruct, and not the absolute property of the soil; or, as sir Edward Coke expresses it [k], he hath *dominium utile,* but not *dominium directum.* And hence it is that, in the most solemn acts of law, we express the strongest and highest estate, that any subject can have, by these words; " he is seised " thereof *in his demesne, as of fee."* It is a man's demesne, *dominicum,* or property, since it belongs to him and his heirs for ever: yet this *dominicum,* property, or demesne, is strictly not absolute or allodial, but qualified or feodal: it is his demesne, *as of fee;* that is, it is not purely and simply his own, since it is held of a superior lord, in whom the ultimate property resides.

---

[f] See pag. 45, 47.
[g] of feuds, c. 1.
[h] Co. Litt. 1.

[i] *Praedium domini regis est directum dominium, cujus nullus est author nisi Deus. Ibid.*
[k] *Ibid.*

THIS is the primary fenfe and acceptation of the word *fee*. But (as fir Martin Wright very juftly obferves[1]) the doctrine, "that all lands are holden," having been for fo many ages a fixed and undeniable axiom, our Englifh lawyers do very rarely (of late years efpecially) ufe the word *fee* in this it's primary original fenfe, in contradiftinction to *allodium* or abfolute property, with which they have no concern; but generally ufe it to exprefs the continuance or quantity of eftate. A *fee* therefore, in general, fignifies an eftate of inheritance; being the higheft and moft extenfive intereft that a man can have in a feud: and, when the term is ufed fimply, without any other adjunct, or has the adjunct of *fimple* annexed to it, (as, a fee, or, a fee-fimple) it is ufed in contradiftinction to a fee conditional at the common law, or a fee-tail by the ftatute; importing an abfolute inheritance, clear of any condition, limitation, or reftrictions to particular heirs, but defcendible to the heirs general, whether male or female, lineal or collateral. And in no other fenfe than this is the king faid to be feifed in fee, he being the feudatory of no man [m].

TAKING therefore *fee* for the future, unlefs where otherwife explained, in this it's fecondary fenfe, as a ftate of inheritance, it is applicable to, and may be had in, any kind of hereditaments either corporeal or incorporeal [n]. But there is this diftinction between the two fpecies of hereditaments; that, of a corporeal inheritance a man fhall be faid to be feifed *in his demefne, as of fee;* of an incorporeal one he fhall only be faid to be feifed *as of fee,* and not in his demefne [o]. For, as incorporeal hereditaments are in their nature collateral to, and iffue out of, lands and houfes [p], their owner hath no property, *dominicum,* or demefne, in the *thing* itfelf, but hath only fomething derived out of it; refembling the *fervitutes,* or fervices, of the civil law [q]. The *dominicum* or pro-

[1] pag. 148.
[m] Co. Litt. 1.
[n] *Feodum eft quod quis tenet fibi et heredibus fuis, five fit tenementum, five reditus, &c.* Flet. *l.* 5. *c.* 5. §. 7.

[o] Litt. §. 10.
[p] See pag. 20.
[q] *Servitus eft jus, quo res mea alterius rei vel perfonae fervit.* Ff. 8. 1. 1.

perty is frequently in one man, while the appendage or fervice is in another. Thus Gaius may be feifed *as of fee,* of a way going over the land, of which Titius is feifed *in his demefne as of fee.*

THE fee-fimple or inheritance of lands and tenements is generally vefted and refides in fome perfon or other; though divers inferior eftates may be carved out of it. As if one grants a leafe for twenty one years, or for one or two lives, the fee-fimple remains vefted in him and his heirs; and after the determination of thofe years or lives, the land reverts to the grantor or his heirs, who fhall hold it again in fee-fimple. Yet fometimes the fee may be in *abeyance,* that is (as the word fignifies) in expectation, remembrance, and contemplation of law; there being no perfon *in effe,* in whom it can veft and abide; though the law confiders it as always potentially exifting, and ready to veft whenever a proper owner appears. Thus, in a grant to John for life, and afterwards to the heirs of Richard, the inheritance is plainly neither granted to John nor Richard, nor can it veft in the heirs of Richard till his death, *nam nemo eft haeres viventis:* it remains therefore in waiting, or abeyance, during the life of Richard[r]. This is likewife always the cafe of a parfon of a church, who hath only an eftate therein for the term of his life: and the inheritance remains in abeyance[s]. And not only the fee, but the freehold alfo, may be in abeyance; as, when a parfon dies, the freehold of his glebe is in abeyance, until a fucceffor be named, and then it vefts in the fucceffor[t].

THE word, heirs, is neceffary in the grant or donation in order to make a fee, or inheritance. For if land be given to a man for ever, or to him and his affigns for ever, this vefts in him but an eftate for life[u]. This very great nicety about the infertion of the word "heirs" in all feoffments and grants, in order to veft a fee, is plainly a relic of the feodal ftrictnefs: by which we may remember[w] it was required, that the form of the donation fhould

[r] Co. Litt. 342.
[s] Litt. §. 646.
[t] Litt. §. 647.

[u] Litt. §. 1.
[w] See pag. 56.

O 2   be

be punctually purfued; or that, as Crag[x] expreffes it, in the words of Baldus, " *donationes fint ftricti juris, ne quis plus donaffe prae-* "*fumatur quam in donatione exprefferit.*" And therefore, as the perfonal abilities of the donee were originally fuppofed to be the only inducements to the gift, the donee's eftate in the land extended only to his own perfon, and fubfifted no longer than his life; unlefs the donor, by an exprefs provifion in the grant, gave it a longer continuance, and extended it alfo to his heirs. But this rule is now foftened by many exceptions[y].

FOR, 1. It does not extend to devifes by will; in which, as they were introduced at the time when the feodal rigor was apace wearing out, a more liberal conftruction is allowed : and therefore by a devife to a man for ever, or to one and his affigns for ever, or to one in fee-fimple, the devifee hath an eftate of inheritance; for the intention of the devifor is fufficiently plain from the words of perpetuity annexed, though he hath omitted the legal words of inheritance. But if the devife be to a man and his affigns, without annexing words of perpetuity, there the devifee fhall take only an eftate for life ; for it does not appear that the devifor intended any more. 2. Neither does this rule extend to fines or recoveries, confidered as a fpecies of conveyance; for thereby an eftate in fee paffes by act and operation of law without the word "heirs:" as it does alfo, for particular reafons, by certain other methods of conveyance, which have relation to a former grant or eftate, wherein the word "heirs" was expreffed[z]. 3. In creations of nobility by writ, the peer fo created hath an inheritance in his title, without expreffing the word, "heirs;" for they are implied in the creation, unlefs it be otherwife fpecially provided : but in creations by patent, which are *ftricti juris*, the word "heirs" muft be inferted, otherwife there is no inheritance. 4. In grants of lands to fole corporations and their fucceffors, the word "fucceffors" fupplies the place of "heirs;" for as heirs take from the anceftor, fo doth the fucceffor from

[x] *l.* 1. *t.* 9. §. 17.
[y] Co. Litt. 9, 10.
[z] *Ibid.* 9.

the

the predeceſſor. Nay, in a grant to a biſhop, or other ſole ſpiritual corporation, in *frankalmoign*, the word "*frankalmoign*" ſupplies the place of both "heirs" and "ſucceſſors," *ex vi termini*; and in all theſe caſes a fee-ſimple veſts in ſuch ſole corporation. But, in a grant of lands to a corporation aggregate, the word "ſucceſſors" is not neceſſary, though uſually inſerted: for, albeit ſuch ſimple grant be ſtrictly only an eſtate for life, yet, as that corporation never dies, ſuch eſtate for life is perpetual, or equivalent to a fee-ſimple, and therefore the law allows it to be one[a]. Laſtly, in the caſe of the king, a fee-ſimple will veſt in him, without the words "heirs" or "ſucceſſors" in the grant; partly from prerogative royal, and partly from a reaſon ſimilar to the laſt, becauſe the king in judgment of law never dies[b]. But the general rule is, that the word "heirs" is neceſſary to create an eſtate of inheritance.

II. WE are next to conſider limited fees, or ſuch eſtates of inheritance as are clogged and confined with conditions, or qualifications, of any ſort. And theſe we may divide into two ſorts: 1. *Qualified*, or *baſe* fees; and 2. Fees *conditional*, ſo called at the common law; and afterwards fees-*tail*, in conſequence of the ſtatute *de donis*.

1. A BASE, or qualified, fee is ſuch a one as has a qualification ſubjoined thereto, and which muſt be determined whenever the qualification annexed to it is at an end. As, in the caſe of a grant to A and his heirs, *tenants of the manor of Dale*; in this inſtance, whenever the heirs of A ceaſe to be tenants of that manor, the grant is intirely defeated. So, when Henry VI granted to John Talbot, lord of the manor of Kingſton-Liſle in Berks, that he and his heirs, lords of the ſaid manor, ſhould be peers of the realm, by the title of barons of Liſle; here John Talbot had a baſe or qualified fee in that dignity[c]; and the inſtant he or his heirs quitted the ſeignory of this manor, the dignity was at an

---

[a] See Vol. I. pag. 472.
[b] *Ibid*. 242.

[c] Co. Litt. 27.

end.

end. This eftate is a fee, becaufe by poffibility it may endure for ever in a man and his heirs; yet as that duration depends upon the concurrence of collateral circumftances, which qualify and debafe the purity of the donation, it is therefore a qualified or bafe fee.

2. A CONDITIONAL fee, at the common law, was a fee reftrained to fome particular heirs, exclufive of others: " *donatio* " *ftricta et coarctata* [d]; *ficut certis haeredibus, quibufdam a fucceffione* " *exclufis :*" as, to the heirs *of a man's body*, by which only his lineal defcendants were admitted, in exclufion of collateral heirs; or, to the heirs *male of his body*, in exclufion both of collaterals, and lineal females alfo. It was called a conditional fee, by reafon of the condition expreffed or implied in the donation of it, that if the donee died without fuch particular heirs, the land fhould revert to the donor. For this was a condition annexed by law to all grants whatfoever; that on failure of the heirs fpecified in the grant, the grant fhould be at an end, and the land return to it's antient proprietor [e]. Such conditional fees were ftrictly agreeable to the nature of feuds, when they firft ceafed to be mere eftates for life, and were not yet arrived to be abfolute eftates in fee-fimple. And we find ftrong traces of thefe limited, conditional fees, which could not be alienated from the lineage of the firft purchafor, in our earlieft Saxon laws [f].

Now, with regard to the condition annexed to thefe fees by the common law, our anceftors held, that fuch a gift (to a man and the heirs of his body) was a gift upon condition, that it fhould revert to the donor, if the donee had no heirs of his body; but, if he had, it fhould then remain to the donee. They therefore called it a fee-fimple, on condition that he had iffue. Now we muft obferve, that, when any condition is performed, it is thenceforth intirely gone; and the thing, to which it was before

[d] Flet. *l.* 3. *c.* 3. §. 5.
[e] Plowd. 241.
[f] *Si quis terram haereditariam habeat, eam non vendat a cognatis haeredibus fuis, fi illi viro prohibitum fit, qui eam ab initio acquifi-vit, ut ita facere nequeat.* LL. *Aelfred. c.*37.

annexed,

annexed, becomes abfolute, and wholly unconditional. So that, as foon as the grantee had any iffue born, his eftate was fuppofed to become abfolute, by the performance of the condition; at leaft, for thefe three purpofes: 1. To enable the tenant to aliene the land, and thereby to bar not only his own iffue, but alfo the donor of his intereft in the reverfion [s]. 2. To fubject him to forfeit it for treafon: which he could not do, till iffue born, longer than for his own life; left thereby the inheritance of the iffue, and reverfion of the donor, might have been defeated [h]. 3. To empower him to charge the land with rents, commons, and certain other incumbrances, fo as to bind his iffue [i]. And this was thought the more reafonable, becaufe, by the birth of iffue, the poffibility of the donor's reverfion was rendered more diftant and precarious: and *his* intereft feems to have been the only one which the law, as it then ftood, was folicitous to protect; without much regard to the right of fucceffion intended to be vefted in the iffue. However, if the tenant did not in fact aliene the land, the courfe of defcent was not altered by this performance of the condition: for if the iffue had afterwards died, and then the tenant, or original grantee, had died, without making any alienation; the land, by the terms of the donation, could defcend to none but the heirs *of his body*, and therefore, in default of them, muft have reverted to the donor. For which reafon, in order to fubject the lands to the ordinary courfe of defcent, the donees of thefe conditional fee-fimples took care to aliene as foon as they had performed the condition by having iffue; and afterwards re-purchafed the lands, which gave them a fee-fimple abfolute, that would defcend to the heirs general, according to the courfe of the common law. And thus ftood the old law with regard to conditional fees: which things, fays fir Edward Coke [k], though they feem antient, are yet neceffary to be known; as well for the declaring how the common law ftood in fuch cafes, as for the fake of annuities, and fuch like inheritances, as are not within the ftatutes of entail, and therefore remain as at the common law.

[s] Co. Litt. 19. 2 Inft. 233.   [i] Co. Litt. 19.
[h] Co. Litt. *Ibid.* 2 Inft. 234.   [k] 1 Inft. 19.

THE

T H E inconvenience, which attended thefe limited and fettered inheritances, were probably what induced the judges to give way to this fubtle fineffe, (for fuch it undoubtedly was) in order to fhorten the duration of thefe conditional eftates. But, on the other hand, the nobility, who were willing to perpetuate their poffeffions in their own families, to put a ftop to this practice, procured the ftatute of Weftminfter the fecond[1] (commonly called the ftatute *de donis conditionalibus*) to be made ; which pays a greater regard to the private will and intentions of the donor, than to the propriety of fuch intentions, or any public confiderations whatfoever. This ftatute revives in fome fort the antient feodal reftraints which were originally laid on alienations, by enacting, that from thenceforth the will of the donor be obferved ; and that the tenements fo given (to a man and the heirs of his body) fhould at all events go to the iffue, if there were any ; or, if none, fhould revert to the donor.

U p o n the conftruction of this act of parliament, the judges determined that the donee had no longer a conditional fee-fimple, which became abfolute and at his own difpofal, the inftant any iffue was born ; but they divided the eftate into two parts, leaving in the donee a new kind of particular eftate, which they denominated a *fee-tail*[m] ; and vefting in the donor the ultimate fee-fimple of the land, expectant on the failure of iffue ; which expectant eftate is what we now call a reverfion[n]. And hence it is that Littleton tells us[o], that tenant in fee-tail is by virtue of the ftatute of Weftminfter the fecond.

H a v i n g thus fhewn the *original* of eftates-tail, I now proceed to confider, *what things* may, or may not, be entailed under

---

[1] 13 Edw. I. c. 1.

[m] The expreffion *fee-tail*, or *feodum talliatum*, was borrowed from the feudifts ; (See Crag. *l.* 1. *t.* 10. §. 24, 25.) among whom it fignified any mutilated or truncated inheritance, from which the heirs general were *cut* off ; being derived from the barbarous verb *taliare*, to cut ; from which the French *tailler* and the Italian *tagliare* are formed. (Spelm. *Gloff.* 531.)

[n] 2 Inft. 335.

[o] §. 13.

the

the ſtatute *de donis*. Tenement is the only word uſed in the ſtatute : and this ſir Edward Coke [p] expounds to comprehend all
corporeal hereditaments whatſoever; and alſo all incorporeal hereditaments which favour of the realty, that is, which iſſue out
of corporeal ones, or which concern, or are annexed to, or may
be exerciſed within the ſame ; as, rents, eſtovers, commons, and
the like. Alſo offices and dignities, which concern lands, or have
relation to fixed and certain places, may be entailed [q]. But mere
perſonal chattels, which favour not at all of the realty, cannot
be entailed. Neither can an office, which merely relates to ſuch
perſonal chattels; nor an annuity, which charges only the perſon,
and not the lands, of the grantor. But in them, if granted to a
man and the heirs of his body, the grantee hath ſtill a fee conditional at common law, as before the ſtatute; and by his alienation may bar the heir or reverſioner [r]. An eſtate to a man and his
heirs for another's life cannot be entailed [s]; for this is ſtrictly no
eſtate of inheritance (as will appear hereafter) and therefore not
within the ſtatute *de donis*. Neither can a copyhold eſtate be entailed by virtue of the *ſtatute* ; for that would tend to encroach
upon and reſtrain the will of the lord : but, by the *ſpecial cuſtom*
of the manor, a copyhold may be limited to the heirs of the
body [t]; for here the cuſtom aſcertains and interprets the lord's will.

NEXT, as to the ſeveral *ſpecies* of eſtates-tail, and how they
are reſpectively created. Eſtates-tail are either *general*, or *ſpecial*.
Tail-general is where lands and tenements are given to one, and
the *heirs of his body begotten:* which is called tail-general, becauſe,
how often ſoever ſuch donee in tail be married, his iſſue in general by all and every ſuch marriage is, in ſucceſſive order, capable
of inheriting the eſtate-tail, *per formam doni* [u]. Tenant in tail-
ſpecial is where the gift is reſtrained to certain heirs of the donee's body, and does not go to all of them in general. And this

p 1 Inſt. 19, 20.　　　　　　　　s 2 Vern. 225.
q 7 Rep. 33.　　　　　　　　　　t 3 Rep. 8.
r Co. Litt. 19, 20.　　　　　　　u Litt. §. 14, 15.

may happen feveral ways [w]. I fhall inftance in only one : as where lands and tenements are given to a man and the *heirs of his body, on Mary his now wife to be begotten* ; here no iffue can inherit, but fuch fpecial iffue as is engendered between them two; not fuch as the hufband may have by another wife : and therefore it is called fpecial tail. And here we may obferve, that the words of inheritance (to him and his *heirs*) give him an eftate in fee ; but they being heirs *to be by him begotten,* this makes it a fee-tail ; and the perfon being alfo limited, on whom fuch heirs fhall be begotten, (viz. *Mary his prefent wife*) this makes it a fee-tail fpecial.

ESTATES, in general and fpecial tail, are farther diverfified by the diftinction of fexes in fuch entails ; for both of them may either be in tail *male* or tail *female.* As if lands be given to a man, and his *heirs male of his body begotten,* this is an eftate in tail male general ; but if to a man and the *heirs female of his body on his prefent wife begotten,* this is an eftate in tail female fpecial. And, in cafe of an entail male, the heirs female fhall never inherit, nor any derived from them; nor, *e converfo,* the heirs male, in cafe of a gift in tail female [x]. Thus, if the donee in tail male hath a daughter, who dies leaving a fon, fuch grandfon in this cafe cannot inherit the eftate-tail ; for he cannot deduce his defcent wholly by heirs male [y]. And as the heir male muft convey his defcent wholly by males, fo muft the heir female wholly by females. And therefore if a man hath two eftates-tail, the one in tail male, the other in tail female ; and he hath iffue a daughter, which daughter hath iffue a fon ; this grandfon can fucceed to neither of the eftates : for he cannot convey his defcent wholly either in the male or female line [z].

As the word *heirs* is neceffary to create a fee, fo, in farther imitation of the ftrictnefs of the feodal donation, the word *body,* or fome other words of procreation, are neceffary to make it a

[w] Litt. §. 16, 26, 27, 28, 29.
[x] *Ibid.* §. 21, 22.
[y] *Ibid.* §. 24.
[z] Co. Litt. 25.

fee-tail ;

fee-tail, and afcertain to what heirs in particular the fee is limited. If therefore either the words of inheritance or words of
procreation be omitted, albeit the others are inferted in the grant,
this will not make an eftate-tail. As, if the grant be to a man and
his *iffue of his body*, to a man and his *feed*, to a man and his
children, or *offspring*; all thefe are only eftates for life, there
wanting the words of inheritance, his heirs [a]. So, on the other
hand, a gift to a man, and his *heirs male*, or *female*, is an eftate
in fee-fimple, and not in fee-tail; for there are no words to afcertain the body out of which they fhall iffue [b]. Indeed, in laft wills
and teftaments, wherein greater indulgence is allowed, an eftate-
tail may be created by a devife to a man and his *feed*, or to a man
and his *heirs male*; or by other irregular modes of expreffion [c].

THERE is ftill another fpecies of entailed eftates, now indeed
grown out of ufe, yet ftill capable of fubfifting in law; which
are eftates *in libero maritagio*, or *frankmarriage*. Thefe are defined [d] to be, where tenements are given by one man to another,
together with a wife, who is the daughter or coufin of the donor,
to hold in frankmarriage. Now by fuch gift, though nothing
but the word *frankmarriage* is expreffed, the donees fhall have
the tenements to them, and the heirs of their two bodies begotten; that is, they are tenants in fpecial tail. For this one word,
frankmarriage, does *ex vi termini* not only create an inheritance,
like the word *frankalmoign*, but likewife limits that inheritance;
fupplying not only words of defcent, but of procreation alfo.
Such donees in frankmarriage are liable to no fervice but fealty;
for a rent referved thereon is void, until the fourth degree of confanguinity be paft between the iffues of the donor and donee [e].

THE *incidents* to a tenancy in tail, under the ftatute Weftm. 2.
are chiefly thefe [f]. 1. That a tenant in tail may commit *wafte* on
the eftate-tail, by felling timber, pulling down houfes, or the

[a] Co. Litt. 20.
[b] Litt. §. 31. Co. Litt. 27.
[c] Co. Litt. 9. 27.

[d] Litt. §. 17.
[e] Ibid. §. 19, 20.
[f] Co. Litt. 224.

like,

like, without being impeached, or called to account, for the fame.
2. That the wife of the tenant in tail fhall have her *dower*, or
thirds, of the eftate-tail. 3. That the hufband of a female tenant in tail may be tenant by the *curtefy* of the eftate-tail. 4. That
an eftate-tail may be *barred*, or deftroyed, by a fine, by a common recovery, or by lineal warranty defcending with affets to the
heir. All which will hereafter be explained at large.

THUS much for the nature of eftates-tail : the eftablifhment
of which family law (as it is properly ftiled by Pigott[g]) occafioned
infinite difficulties and difputes[h]. Children grew difobedient
when they knew they could not be fet afide: farmers were oufted
of their leafes made by tenants in tail; for, if fuch leafes had
been valid, then under colour of long leafes the iffue might have
been virtually difinherited : creditors were defrauded of their
debts; for, if tenant in tail could have charged his eftate with
their payment, he might alfo have defeated his iffue, by mort-
gaging it for as much as it was worth : innumerable latent entails were produced to deprive purchafers of the lands they had
fairly bought; of fuits in confequence of which our antient books
are full : and treafons were encouraged ; as eftates-tail were not
liable to forfeiture, longer than for the tenant's life. So that they
were juftly branded, as the fource of new contentions, and mifchiefs unknown to the common law; and almoft univerfally confidered as the common grievance of the realm[i]. But, as the nobility were always fond of this ftatute, becaufe it preferved their
family eftates from forfeiture, there was little hope of procuring
a repeal by the legiflature; and therefore, by the connivance of
an active and politic prince, a method was devifed to evade it.

ABOUT two hundred years intervened between the making of
the ftatute *de donis*, and the application of common recoveries to
this intent, in the twelfth year of Edward IV : which were then
openly declared by the judges to be a fufficient bar of an eftate-

[g] Com. Recov. 5.
[h] 1 Rep. 131.

[i] Co. Litt. 19. Moor. 156. 10 Rep. 38.

tail[k].

tail [k]. For though the courts had, fo long before as the reign of Edward III, very frequently hinted their opinion that a bar might be effected upon thefe principles [l], yet it never was carried into execution; till Edward IV obferving [m] (in the difputes between the houfes of York and Lancafter) how little effect attainders for treafon had on families, whofe eftates were protected by the fanctuary of entails, gave his countenance to this proceeding, and fuffered Taltarum's cafe to be brought before the court [n]: wherein, in confequence of the principles then laid down, it was in effect determined, that a common recovery fuffered by tenant in tail fhould be an effectual deftruction thereof. What common recoveries are, both in their nature and confequences, and why they are allowed to be a bar to the eftate-tail, muft be referved to a fubfequent enquiry. At prefent I fhall only fay, that they are fictitious proceedings, introduced by a kind of *pia fraus*, to elude the ftatute *de donis*, which was found fo intolerably mifchievous, and which yet one branch of the legiflature would not then confent to repeal: and, that thefe recoveries, however clandeftinely begun, are now become by long ufe and acquiefcence a moft common affurance of lands; and are looked upon as the legal mode of conveyance, by which tenant in tail may difpofe of his lands and tenements: fo that no court will fuffer them to be fhaken or reflected on, and even acts of parliament [o] have by a fidewind countenanced and eftablifhed them.

THIS expedient having greatly abridged eftates-tail with regard to their duration, others were foon invented to ftrip them of other privileges. The next that was attacked was their freedom from forfeitures for treafon. For, notwithftanding the large advances made by recoveries, in the compafs of about threefcore years, towards unfettering thefe inheritances, and thereby fubjecting the lands to forfeiture, the rapacious prince then reigning,

---

[k] 1 Rep. 131. 6 Rep. 40.
[l] 10 Rep. 37, 38.
[m] Pigott. 8.
[n] Year Book. 12 Edw. IV. 14. 19. Fitzh. *Abr. tit. faux recov.* 20. Bro. *Abr. ibid.* 30.

tit. recov. in value. 19. *tit. taile.* 36.
[o] 11 Hen. VII. c. 20.   7 Hen. VIII. c 4. 34 & 35 Hen. VIII. c. 20.   14 Eliz. c. 8. 4 & 5 Ann. c. 16.   14 Geo. II. c. 20.

finding them frequently re-setttled in a similar manner to suit the convenience of families, had addrefs enough to procure a ftatute ᵖ, whereby all eftates of inheritance (under which general words eftates-tail were covertly included) are declared to be forfeited to the king upon any conviction of high treason.

THE next attack which they fuffered, in order of time, was by the ftatute 32 Hen. VIII. c. 28. whereby certain leafes made by tenants in tail, which do not tend to the prejudice of the iffue, were allowed to be good in law, and to bind the iffue in tail. But they received a more violent blow, in the fame feffion of parliament, by the conftruction put upon the ftatute of fines �q, by the ftatute 32 Hen. VIII. c. 36. which declares a fine duly levied by tenant in tail to be a complete bar to him and his heirs, and all other perfons. claiming under fuch entail. This was evidently agreeable to the intention of Henry VII, whofe policy it was (before common recoveries had obtained their full ftrength and authority) to lay the road as open as poffible to the alienation of landed property, in order to weaken the overgrown power of his nobles. But as they, from the oppofite reafons, were not eafily brought to confent to fuch a provifion, it was therefore couched, in his act, under covert and obfcure expreffions. And the judges, though willing to conftrue that ftatute as favourably as poffible for the defeating of entailed eftates, yet hefitated at giving fines fo extenfive a power by mere implication, when the ftatute *de donis* had expreffly declared, that they fhould *not* be a bar to eftates-tail. But the ftatute of Henry VIII, when the doctrine of alienation was better received, and the will of the prince more implicitly obeyed than before, avowed and eftablifhed that intention. Yet, in order to preferve the property of the crown from any danger of infringement, all eftates-tail created by the crown, and of which the crown has the reverfion, are excepted out of this ftatute. And the fame was done with regard to common recoveries, by the ftatute 34 & 35 Hen. VIII. c. 20. which enacts, that no feigned recovery had againft tenants

ᵖ 26 Hen. VIII. c. 13.   �q 4 Hen. VII. c. 24.

in

in tail, where the eſtate was created by the crown [r], and the remainder or reverſion continues ſtill in the crown, ſhall be of any force or effect. Which is allowing, indirectly and collaterally, their full force and effect with reſpect to ordinary eſtates-tail, where the royal prerogative is not concerned.

LASTLY, by a ſtatute of the ſucceeding year [s], all eſtates-tail are rendered liable to be charged for payment of debts due to the king by record or ſpecial contract; as, ſince, by the bankrupt laws [t], they are alſo ſubjected to be ſold for the debts contracted by a bankrupt. And, by the conſtruction put on the ſtatute 43 Eliz. c. 4. an appointment [u] by tenant in tail of the lands entailed, to a charitable uſe, is good without fine or recovery.

ESTATES-TAIL, being thus by degrees unfettered, are now reduced again to almoſt the ſame ſtate, even before iſſue born, as conditional fees were in at common law, after the condition was performed, by the birth of iſſue. For, firſt, the tenant in tail is now enabled to aliene his lands and tenements by fine, by recovery, or by certain other means; and thereby to defeat the intereſt as well of his own iſſue, though unborn, as alſo of the reverſioner, except in the caſe of the crown : ſecondly, he is now liable to forfeit them for high treaſon: and, laſtly, he may charge them with reaſonable leaſes, and alſo with ſuch of his debts as are due to the crown on ſpecialties, or have been contracted with his fellow-ſubjects in a courſe of extenſive commerce.

[r] Co. Litt. 372.   [t] Stat. 21 Jac. I. c. 19.
[s] 33 Hen. VIII. c. 39. §. 75.   [u] 2 Vern. 453. Chan. Prec 16

C H A P T E R   T H E   E I G H T H.

OF FREEHOLDS, NOT OF INHERITANCE.

WE are next to difcourfe of fuch eftates of freehold, as are not of inheritance, but *for life* only. And, of thefe eftates for life, fome are *conventional*, or exprefïly created by the act of the parties; others merely *legal*, or created by conftruction and operation of law[a]. We will confider them both in their order.

I. E S T A T E S for life, exprefïly created by deed or grant, (which alone are properly conventional) are where a leafe is made of lands or tenements to a man, to hold for the term of his own life, or for that of any other perfon, or for more lives than one : in any of which cafes he is ftiled tenant for life ; only, when he holds the eftate by the life of another, he is ufually called tenant *pur auter vie*[b]. Thefe eftates for life are, like inheritances, of a feodal nature; and were, for fome time, the higheft eftate that any man could have in a feud, which (as we have before feen[c]) was not in it's original hereditary. They are given or conferred by the fame feodal rites and folemnities, the fame inveftiture or livery of feifin, as fees themfelves are; and they are held by fealty, if demanded, and fuch conventional rents and fervices as the lord or leffor, and his tenant or leffee, have agreed on.

[a] Wright. 190.   [c] pag. 55.
[b] Litt. §. 56.

E S T A T E S for life may be created, not only by the exprefs
words before-mentioned, but alfo by a general grant, without
defining or limiting any fpecifice ftate. As, if one grants to A. B.
the manor of Dale, this makes him tenant for life[d]. For though,
as there are no words of inheritance, or *heirs*, mentioned in the
grant, it cannot be conftrued to be a fee, it fhall however be conftrued to be as large an eftate as the words of the donation will
bear, and therefore an eftate for life. Alfo fuch a grant at large,
or a grant for term of life generally, fhall be conftrued to be an
eftate for the life *of the grantee*[e]; in cafe the grantor hath authority to make fuch a grant : for an eftate for a man's own life is
more beneficial and of a higher nature than for any other life ;
and the rule of law is, that all grants are to be taken moft ftrongly
againft the grantor[f], unlefs in the cafe of the king.

S u c h eftates for life will, generally fpeaking, endure as long
as the life for which they are granted : but there are fome eftates
for life, which may determine upon future contingencies, before
the life, for which they are created, expires. As, if an eftate be
granted to a woman during her widowhood, or to a man until he
be promoted to a benefice ; in thefe, and fimilar cafes, whenever
the contingency happens, when the widow marries, or when the
grantee obtains a benefice, the refpective eftates are abfolutely
determined and gone[g]. Yet, while they fubfift, they are reckoned
eftates for life ; becaufe, the time for which they will endure
being uncertain, they may by poffibility laft for life, if the contingencies upon which they are to determine do not fooner happen. And, moreover, in cafe an eftate be granted to a man for
his life, generally, it may alfo determine by his *civil* death ; as
if he enters into a monaftery, whereby he is dead in law[h] : for
which reafon in conveyances the grant is ufually made " for the
" term of a man's *natural* life ;" which can only determine by
his *natural* death[i].

[d] Co. Litt. 42.
[e] *Ibid.*
[f] *Ibid.* 36.

[g] Co. Litt. 42. 3 Rep. 20.
[h] 2 Rep. 48.
[i] See Vol. I. pag. 129.

THE *incidents* to an eftate for life, are principally the following; which are applicable not only to that fpecies of tenants for life, which are exprefily created by deed; but alfo to thofe, which are created by act and operation of law.

1. EVERY tenant for life, unlefs reftrained by covenant or agreement, may of common right take upon the land demifed to him reafonable *eftovers*[k] or *botes*[l]. For he hath a right to the full enjoyment and ufe of the land, and all it's profits, during his eftate therein. But he is not permitted to cut down timber or do other wafte upon the premifes[m]: for the deftruction of fuch things, as are not the temporary profits of the tenement, is not neceffary for the tenant's complete enjoyment of his eftate; but tends to the permanent and lafting lofs of the perfon entitled to the inheritance.

2. TENANT for life, or his reprefentatives, fhall not be prejudiced by any fudden determination of his eftate, becaufe fuch determination is contingent and uncertain[n]. Therefore if a tenant for his own life fows the lands, and dies before harveft, his executors fhall have the *emblements*, or profits of the crop: for the eftate was determined by the *act of God*; and it is a maxim in the law, that *actus Dei nemini facit injuriam*. The reprefentatives therefore of the tenant for life fhall have the emblements, to compenfate for the labour and expenfe of tilling, manuring, and fowing, the lands; and alfo for the encouragement of hufbandry, which being a public benefit, tending to the increafe and plenty of provifions, ought to have the utmoft fecurity and privilege that the law can give it. Wherefore, by the feodal law, if a tenant for life died between the beginning of September and the end of February, the lord, who was entitled to the reverfion, was alfo entitled to the profits of the whole year; but, if he died between the beginning of March and the end of Auguft, the

---

[k] See pag 35.
[l] Co. Litt. 41.

[m] *Ibid.* 53.
[n] *Ibid.* 55.

heirs

heirs of the tenant received the whole °. From hence our law of emblements feems to have been derived, but with very confiderable improvements. So it is alfo, if a man be tenant for the life of another, and *ceftuy que vie*, or he on whofe life the land is held, dies after the corn fown, the tenant *pur auter vie* fhall have the emblements. The fame is alfo the rule, if a life-eftate be determined by the *act of law*. Therefore, if a leafe be made to hufband and wife during coverture, (which gives them a determinable eftate for life) and the hufband fows the land, and afterwards they are divorced *a vinculo matrimonii*, the hufband fhall have the emblements in this cafe; for the fentence of divorce is the act of law ᴾ. But if an eftate for life be determined by the tenant's *own act*, (as, by forfeiture for wafte committed; or, if a tenant during widowhood thinks proper to marry) in thefe, and fimilar cafes, the tenants, having thus determined the eftate by their own acts, fhall not be entitled to take the emblements ��q. The doctrine of emblements extends not only to corn fown, but to roots planted, or other annual artificial profit: but it is otherwife of fruit-trees, grafs, and the like; which are not planted annually at the expenfe and labour of the tenant, but are either the permanent, or natural, profit of the earth ʳ. For even when a man plants a tree, he cannot be prefumed to plant it in contemplation of any prefent profit; but merely with a profpect of it's being ufeful to future fucceffions of tenants. The advantages alfo of emblements are particularly extended to the parochial clergy by the ftatute 28 Hen.VIII. c.11. For all perfons, who are prefented to any ecclefiaftical benefice, or to any civil office, are confidered as tenants for their own lives, unlefs the contrary be expreffed in the form of donation.

3. A THIRD incident to eftates for life relates to the under-tenants or leffees. For they have the fame, nay greater indulgences, than their leffors, the original tenants for life. The fame; for the law of eftovers and emblements, with regard to the tenant

---

° *Feud. l. 2. t. 28.*
ᴾ 5 Rep. 116.

�q Co. Litt. 55.
ʳ Co. Litt. 55, 56. 1 Roll. Abr. 728.

for life, is alſo law with regard to his under-tenant, who repreſents him and ſtands in his place[s]: and greater; for in thoſe caſes where tenant for life ſhall not have the emblements, becauſe the eſtate determines by his own act, the exception ſhall not reach his leſſee who is a third perſon. As in the caſe of a woman who holds *durante viduitate*; her taking huſband is her own act, and therefore deprives her of the emblements: but if ſhe leaſes her eſtate to an under-tenant, who ſows the land, and ſhe then marries, this her act ſhall not deprive the tenant of his emblements, who is a ſtranger and could not prevent her[t]. The leſſees of tenants for life had alſo at the common law another moſt unreaſonable advantage; for, at the death of their leſſors the tenants for life, theſe under-tenants might if they pleaſed quit the premiſes, and pay no rent to any body for the occupation of the land ſince the laſt quarter day, or other day aſſigned for payment of rent[u]. To remedy which it is now enacted[v], that the executors or adminiſtrators of tenant for life, on whoſe death any leaſe determined, ſhall recover of the leſſee a ratable proportion of rent, from the laſt day of payment to the death of ſuch leſſor.

II. THE next eſtate for life is of the legal kind, as contradiſtinguiſhed from conventional; *viz.* that of tenant *in tail after poſſibility of iſſue extinct*. This happens, where one is tenant in ſpecial tail, and a perſon, from whoſe body the iſſue was to ſpring, dies without iſſue; or, having left iſſue, that iſſue becomes extinct; in either of theſe caſes the ſurviving tenant in ſpecial tail becomes tenant in tail after poſſibility of iſſue extinct. As, where one has an eſtate to him and his heirs on the body of his preſent wife to be begotten, and the wife dies without iſſue[w]; in this caſe the man has an eſtate-tail, which cannot poſſibly deſcend to any one; and therefore the law makes uſe of this long periphraſis, as abſolutely neceſſary to give an adequate idea of his eſtate. For if it had called him barely *tenant in fee-tail ſpecial,* that would

---

[s] Co. Litt. 55.
[t] Cro. Eliz. 461. 1 Roll. Abr. 727.
[u] 10 Rep. 127.

[v] Stat. 11 Geo. II. c. 19. §. 15.
[w] Litt. §. 32.

not

not have diftinguifhed him from others ; and befides he has no longer an eftate of inheritance, or fee [x], for he can have no heirs, capable of taking *per formam doni.* Had it called him *tenant in tail without iffue,* this had only related to the prefent fact, and would not have excluded the poffibility of future iffue. Had he been ftiled *tenant in tail without poffibility of iffue,* this would exclude time paft as well as prefent, and he might under this defcription never have had any poffibility of iffue. No definition therefore could fo exactly mark him out, as this of tenant *in tail after poffibility of iffue extinct,* which (with a precifion peculiar to our own law) not only takes in the poffibility of iffue in tail which he once had, but alfo ftates that this poffibility is now extinguifhed and gone.

THIS eftate muft be created by the act of God, that is, by the death of that perfon out of whofe body the iffue was to fpring; for no limitation, conveyance, or other human act can make it. For, if land be given to a man and his wife, and the heirs of their two bodies begotten, and they are divorced *a vinculo matrimonii,* they fhall neither of them have this eftate, but be barely tenants for life, notwithftanding the inheritance once vefted in them [y]. A poffibility of iffue is always fuppofed to exift, in law, unlefs extinguifhed by the death of the parties ; even though the donees be each of them an hundred years old [z].

THIS eftate is of an amphibious nature, partaking partly of an eftate-tail, and partly of an eftate for life. The tenant is, in truth, only tenant for life, but with many of the privileges of a tenant in tail ; as, not to be punifhable for wafte, &c [a]: or, he is tenant in tail, with many of the reftrictions of a tenant for life ; as, to forfeit his eftate if he aliens it in fee-fimple [b]: whereas fuch alienation by tenant in tail, though voidable by the iffue, is no forfeiture of the eftate to the reverfioner ; who is not concerned in intereft, till all poffibility of iffue be extinct. But, in

---

[x] 1 Roll. Rep. 184. 11 Rep. 80.
[y] Co. Litt. 28.
[z] Litt. §. 34. Co. Litt. 28.

[a] Co. Litt. 27.
[b] *Ibid.* 28.

general, the law looks upon this estate as equivalent to an estate for life only; and, as such, will permit this tenant to exchange his estate with a tenant for life; which exchange can only be made, as we shall see hereafter, of estates that are equal in their nature.

III. TENANT *by the curtesy of England*, is where a man marries a woman seised of lands or tenements in fee-simple or fee-tail; that is, of any estate of inheritance; and has by her issue, born alive, which was capable of inheriting her estate. In this case, he shall, on the death of his wife, hold the lands for his life, as tenant by the curtesy of England [c].

THIS estate, according to Littleton, has it's denomination, because it is used within the realm of England only; and it is said in the mirrour [d] to have been introduced by king Henry the first: but it appears also to have been the established law of Scotland, wherein it was called *curialitas* [e]: so that probably our word *curtesy* was understood to signify rather an attendance upon the lord's *court* or *curtis*, (that is, being his vasal or tenant) than to denote any peculiar favour belonging to this island. And therefore it is laid down [f] that, by having issue, the husband shall be intitled to do homage to the lord, for the wife's lands, alone. It is likewise used in Ireland, by virtue of an ordinance of king Henry III [g]. It also appears [h] to have obtained in Normandy; and was likewise used among the antient Almains or Germans [i]. And yet it is not generally apprehended to have been a consequence of feodal tenure [k], though I think some substantial feodal reasons may be given for it's introduction. For, if a woman seised of lands hath issue by her husband, and dies, the husband is the natural guardian of the child, and as such is in reason entitled to the profits of the lands in order to maintain it: and therefore the

[c] Litt. §. 35, 52.

[d] c. 1. §. 3.

[e] Crag. *l.* 2. *t.* 19. §. 4.

[f] Litt. §. 90. Co. Litt. 30. 67.

[g] *Pat.* 11 *H.III. m.* 30. in 2 Bac. Abr. 659.

[h] *Grand Coustum. c.* 119.

[i] Lindenbrog. *LL. Alman. t.* 92.

[k] Wright. 294.

heir

heir apparent of a tenant by the curtefy could not be in ward to
the lord of the fee, during the life of fuch tenant [1]. As foon
therefore as any child was born, the father began to have a permanent intereft in the lands, he became one of the *pares curtis*, and
was called tenant by the curtefy *initiate*; and this eftate being
once vefted in him by the birth of the child, was not liable to
be determined by the fubfequent death or coming of age of the
infant.

THERE are four requifites neceffary to make a tenancy by the
curtefy; marriage, feifin of the wife, iffue, and death of the
wife [m]. 1. The marriage muft be canonical, and legal. 2. The
feifin of the wife muft be an actual feifin, or poffeffion of the
lands; not a bare right to poffefs, which is a feifin in law, but
an actual poffeffion, which is a feifin in deed. And therefore a
man fhall not be tenant by the curtefy of a remainder or reverfion.
But of fome incorporeal hereditaments a man may be tenant by
the curtefy, though there have been no actual feifin of the wife;
as in cafe of an advowfon, where the church has not become
void in the life time of the wife, which a man may hold by the
curtefy, becaufe it is impoffible to have had actual feifin of it;
and *impotentia excufat legem* [n]. If the wife be an idiot, the hufband
fhall not be tenant by the curtefy of her lands; for the king by
prerogative is entitled to them, the inftant fhe herfelf has any title:
and fince fhe could never be rightfully feifed of thefe lands, and
the hufband's title depends entirely upon her feifin, the hufband
can have no title as tenant by the curtefy [o]. 3. The iffue muft
be born alive. Some have had a notion that it muft be heard to
cry; but that is a miftake. Crying indeed is the *ftrongeft* evidence of it's being born alive; but it is not the *only* evidence [p].

ie iffue alfo muft be born during the life of the mother; for,
if the mother dies in labour, and the Caefarean operation is performed, the hufband in this cafe fhall not be tenant by the cur-

[1] F. N. B. 143.
[m] Co. Litt. 30.
[n] *Ibid.* 29.

[o] Co. Litt. 30. Plowd. 263.
[p] Dyer. 25. 8 Rep. 34.

tefy : becaufe, at the inftant of the mother's death, he was clearly not entitled, as having had no iffue born, but the land defcended to the child, while he was yet in his mother's womb ; and the eftate, being once fo vefted, fhall not afterwards be taken from him q. In gavelkind lands, a hufband may be tenant by the curtefy without having any iffue r. But in general there muft be iffue born ; and fuch iffue muft alfo be capable of inheriting the mother's eftate s. Therefore if a woman be tenant in tail *male*, and hath only a *daughter* born, the hufband is not thereby entitled to be tenant by the curtefy ; becaufe fuch iffue female can never inherit the eftate in tail male t. And this feems to be the true reafon, why the hufband cannot be tenant by the curtefy of any lands of which the wife was not actually feifed : becaufe, in order to intitle himfelf to fuch eftate, he muft have begotten iffue that may be heir to the wife ; but no one, by the ftanding rule of law, can be heir to the anceftor of any land, whereof the anceftor was not actually feifed ; and therefore, as the hufband hath never begotten any iffue that can be heir to thofe lands, he fhall not be tenant of them by the curtefy u. And hence we may obferve, with how much nicety and confideration the old rules of law were framed ; and how clofely they are connected and inter-woven together, fupporting, illuftrating, and demonftrating one another. The time when the iffue was born is immaterial, pro-vided it were during the coverture : for, whether it were born before or after the wife's feifin of the lands, whether it be living or dead at the time of the feifin, or at the time of the wife's deceafe, the hufband fhall be tenant by the curtefy w. The huf-band by the birth of the child becomes (as was before obferved) tenant by the curtefy *initiate* x, and may do many acts to charge the lands ; but his eftate is not *confummate* till the death of the wife ; which is the fourth and laft requifite to make a complete tenant by the curtefy y.

q Co. Litt. 29.   u *Ibid.* 40.
r *Ibid* 30.   w *Ibid.* 29.
s Litt. §. 56.   x *Ibid.* 30.
t Co. Litt. 29.   y *Ibid.*

IV. T E N A N T

IV. T E N A N T in *dower* is where the hufband of a woman is feifed of an eftate of inheritance, and dies; in this cafe, the wife fhall have the third part of all the lands and tenements whereof he was feifed during the coverture, to hold to herfelf for the term of her natural life [z].

D o w e r is called in Latin by the foreign jurifts *doarium*, but by Bracton and our Englifh writers *dos*; which among the Romans fignified the marriage portion, which the wife brought to her hufband; but with us is applied to fignify this kind of eftate, to which the civil law, in it's original ftate, had nothing that bore a refemblance : nor indeed is there any thing in general more different, than the regulation of landed property according to the Englifh, and Roman laws. Dower out of lands feems alfo to have been unknown in the early part of our Saxon conftitution ; for, in the laws of king Edmond [a], the wife is directed to be fupported wholly out of the perfonal eftate. Afterwards, as may be feen in gavelkind tenure, the widow became entitled to a conditional eftate in one half of the lands, with a provifo that fhe remained chafte and unmarried [b]; as is ufual alfo in copyhold dowers, or free bench. Yet fome [c] have afcribed the introduction of dower to the Normans, as a branch of *their* local tenures ; though we cannot expect any feodal reafon for it's invention, fince it was not a part of the pure, primitive, fimple law of feuds, but was firft of all introduced into that fyftem (wherein it was called *triens, tertia* [d], and *dotalitium)* by the emperor Frederick the fecond [e]; who was cotemporary with our king Henry III. It is poffible therefore that it might be with us the relic of a Danifh cuftom : fince, according to the hiftorians of that country, dower was introduced into Denmark by Swein, the father of our Canute the great, out of gratitude to the Danifh ladies, who fold all their

---

[z] Litt. §. 36.
[a] Wilk. 75.
[b] Somner. Gavelk. 51. Co. Litt. 33. Bro. *Dower*. 70.

[c] Wright. 192.
[d] Crag. *l.* 2. *t.* 22. §. 9.
[e] *Ibid.*

R   jewels

jewels to ranfom him when taken prifoner by the Vandals [f]. However this be, the reafon, which our law gives for adopting it, is
a very plain and a fenfible one ; for the fuftenance of the wife,
and the nurture and education of the younger children [g].

IN treating of this eftate, let us, firft, confider, *who* may be
endowed ; fecondly, of *what* fhe may be endowed ; thirdly, the
manner *how* fhe fhall be endowed ; and, fourthly, how dower
may be *barred* or prevented.

1. WHO may be endowed. She muft be the actual wife of
the party at the time of his deceafe. If fhe be divorced *a vinculo matrimonii,* fhe fhall not be endowed ; for *ubi nullum matrimonium, ibi nulla dos* [h]. But a divorce *a menfa et thoro* only doth
not deftroy the dower [i] ; no, not even for adultery itfelf, by the
common law [k]. Yet now by the ftatute Weftm. 2. [l] if a woman
elopes from her hufband, and lives with an adulterer, fhe fhall
lofe her dower, unlefs her hufband be voluntarily reconciled to
her. It was formerly held, that the wife of an idiot might be
endowed, though the hufband of an idiot could not be tenant by
the curtefy [m] : but as it feems to be at prefent agreed, upon principles of found fenfe and reafon, that an idiot cannot marry, being incapable of confenting to any contract, this doctrine cannot
now take place. By the antient law the wife of a perfon attainted
of treafon or felony could not be endowed ; to the intent, fays
Staunforde [n], that, if the love of a man's own life cannot reftrain
him from fuch atrocious acts, the love of his wife and children
may : though Britton [o] gives it another turn ; *viz.* that it is prefumed the wife was privy to her hufband's crime. However, the
ftatute 1 Edw. VI. c. 12. abated the rigor of the common law in

---

[f] Mod. Un. Hift. xxxii. 91.
[g] Bract. *l.* 2. *c.* 39. Co. Litt. 30.
[h] Bract. *l.* 2. *c.* 39. §. 4.
[i] Co. Litt. 32.
[k] Yet, among the antient Goths, an a-
dulterefs was punifhed by the lofs of her

dotalitii et trientis ex bonis mobilibus viri:
(Stiernh. *l.* 3. *c.* 2.)
[l] 13 Edw. I. c. 34.
[m] Co. Litt. 31.
[n] P. C. b. 3. c. 3.
[o] c. 110.

this

this particular, and allowed the wife her dower. But a fubfequent ftatute [p] revived this feverity againft the widows of traitors,
who are now barred of their dower, but not the widows of felons.
An alien alfo cannot be endowed, unlefs fhe be queen confort;
for no alien is capable of holding lands [q]. The wife muft be above
nine years old at her hufband's death, otherwife fhe fhall not be
endowed [r] : though in Bracton's time the age was indefinite, and
dower was then only due, "*fi uxor poffit dotem promereri, et vi-*
"*rum fuftinere* [s]."

2. W E are next to enquire, of what a wife may be endowed.
And fhe is now by law entitled to be endowed of all lands and
tenements, of which her hufband was feifed in fee-fimple or fee-
tail at any time during the coverture; and of which any iffue,
which fhe might have had, might by poffibility have been heir [t].
Therefore if a man, feifed in fee-fimple, hath a fon by his firft
wife, and after marries a fecond wife, fhe fhall be endowed of
his lands; for her iffue might by poffibility have been heir, on
the death of the fon by the former wife. But, if there be a
donee in fpecial tail, who holds lands to him and the heirs of his
body begotten on Jane his wife; though Jane may be endowed
of thefe lands, yet if Jane dies, and he marries a fecond wife,
that fecond wife fhall never be endowed of the lands entailed;
for no iffue, that fhe could have, could by any poffibility inherit
them [u]. A feifin in law of the hufband will be as effectual as a
feifin in deed, in order to render the wife dowable; for it is not
in the wife's power to bring the hufband's title to an actual feifin,
as it is in the hufband's power to do with regard to the wife's
lands : which is one reafon why he fhall not be tenant by the
curtefy, but of fuch lands whereof the wife, or he himfelf in
her right, was actually feifed in deed [w]. The feifin of the hufband, for a tranfitory inftant only, when the fame act which gives

[p] 5 & 6 Edw. VI. c. 11.
[q] Co. Litt. 31.
[r] Litt. §. 36.
[s] *l.* 2. *c.* 9. §. 3.

[t] Litt. §. 36. 53.
[u] *Ibid.* §. 53.
[w] Co. Litt. 31.

him

him the eftate conveys it alfo out of him again, (as where by a fine land is granted to a man, and he immediately renders it back by the fame fine) fuch a feifin will not intitle the wife to dower [x]: for the land was merely *in tranfitu*, and never refted in the hufband. But, if the land abides in him for a fingle moment, it feems that the wife fhall be endowed thereof [y]. And, in fhort, a widow may be endowed of all her hufband's lands, tenements, and hereditaments, corporeal or incorporeal, under the reftrictions before-mentioned; unlefs there be fome fpecial reafon to the contrary. Thus, a woman fhall not be endowed of a caftle, built for defence of the realm [z]: nor of a common without ftint; for, as the heir would then have one portion of this common, and the widow another, and both without ftint, the common would be doubly ftocked [a]. Copyhold eftates alfo are not liable to dower, being only eftates at the lord's will; unlefs by the fpecial cuftom of the manor, in which cafe it is ufually called the widow's freebench [b]. But, where dower is allowable, it matters not, though the hufband aliene the lands during the coverture; for he alienes them liable to dower [c].

3. NEXT, as to the manner in which a woman is to be endowed. There are now fubfifting four fpecies of dower; the fifth, mentioned by Littleton [d], *de la plus belle*, having been abolifhed together with the military tenures, of which it was a confequence. 1. Dower by the *common law*; or that which is before defcribed. 2. Dower by particular *cuftom* [e]; as that the wife fhall have half the hufband's lands, or in fome places the whole, and in fome only a quarter. 3. Dower *ad oftium ecclefiae* [f]: which is

---

[x] Cro. Jac. 615. 2 Rep. 67. Co. Litt. 31.

[y] This doctrine was extended very far by a jury in Wales, where the father and fon were both hanged in one cart, but the fon was fuppofed to have furvived the father, by appearing to ftruggle longeft; whereby he became feifed of an eftate by furvivorfhip, in confequence of which feifin his widow

had a verdict for her dower. (Cro. Eliz. 503.)

[z] Co. Litt. 31. 3 Lev. 401.

[a] Co. Litt. 32. 1 Jon. 315.

[b] 4 Rep. 22.

[c] Co. Litt. 32.

[d] §. 48, 49.

[e] Litt. §. 37.

[f] *Ibid*. §. 39.

where

where tenant in fee-fimple of full age, openly at the church door, where all marriages were formerly celebrated, after affiance made and (fir Edward Coke in his tranflation adds) troth plighted between them, doth endow his wife with the whole, or fuch quantity as he fhall pleafe, of his lands; at the fame time fpecifying and afcertaining the fame : on which the wife, after her hufband's death, may enter without farther ceremony. 4. Dower *ex affenfu patris*[g]; which is only a fpecies of dower *ad oftium ecclefiae*, made when the hufband's father is alive, and the fon by his confent, exprefsly given, endows his wife with parcel of his father's lands. In either of thefe cafes, they muft (to prevent frauds) be made[h] *in facie ecclefiae et ad oftium ecclefiae; non enim valent facta in lecto mortali, nec in camera, aut alibi ubi clandeftina fuere conjugia.*

IT is curious to obferve the feveral revolutions which the doctrine of dower has undergone, fince it's introduction into England. It feems firft to have been of the nature of the dower in gavelkind, before-mentioned ; *viz.* a moiety of the hufband's lands, but forfeitable by incontinency or a fecond marriage. By the famous charter of Henry I, this condition, of widowhood and chaftity, was only required in cafe the hufband left any iffue[i]: and afterwards we hear no more of it. Under Henry the fecond, according to Glanvil[k], the dower *ad oftium ecclefiae* was the moft ufual fpecies of dower; and here, as well as in Normandy[l], it was binding upon the wife, if by her confented to at the time of marriage. Neither, in thofe days of feodal rigour, was the hufband allowed to endow her *ad oftium ecclefiae* with more than the third part of the lands whereof he then was feifed, though he might endow her with lefs; left by fuch liberal endowments the lord fhould be defrauded of his wardfhips and other feodal profits[m]. But if no

[g] *Ibid.* §. 40.
[h] Bracton. *l.* 2. *c.* 39. §. 4.
[i] *Si mortuo viro uxor ejus remanferit, et fine liberis fuerit, dotem fuam habebit ;—fi vero uxor cum liberis remanferit, dotem quidem habebit, dum corpus fuum legitime fervaverit.*

(*Cart. Hen. I A. D.* 1101. Introd. to great charter, *edit. Oxon.* pag. iv.)
[k] *l.* 6. *c.* 1. & 2.
[l] *Gr. Couftum. c.* 101.
[m] Bract. *l.* 2. *c.* 39. §. 6.

fpecific

fpecific dotation was made at the church porch, then fhe was endowed *by the common law* of the third part (which was called her *dos rationabilis*) of fuch lands and tenements, as the hufband was feifed of at the time of the efpoufals, and no other ; unlefs he fpecially engaged before the prieft to endow her of his future acquifitions [n] : and, if the hufband had no lands, an endowment in goods, chattels, or money, at the time of efpoufals, was a bar of any dower [o] in lands which he afterwards acquired [p]. In king John's *magna carta*, and the firft charter of Henry III [q], no mention is made of any alteration of the common law, in refpect of the lands fubject to dower : but in thofe of 1217, and 1224, it is particularly provided, that a widow fhall be intitled for her dower to the third part of *all* fuch lands as the hufband had held in his life time [r] : yet, in cafe of a fpecific endowment of lefs *ad oftium ecclefiae*, the widow had ftill no power to waive it after her hufband's death. And this continued to be law, during the reigns of Henry III and Edward I [s]. In Henry IV's time it was denied to be law, that a woman can be endowed of her hufband's goods and chattels [t]: and, under Edward IV, Littleton lays it down ex-

---

[n] *De queftu fuo.* (Glanv. *ibid.*) *de terris acquifitis et acquirendis.* (Bract. *ibid.*)

[o] Glanv. *c.* 2.

[p] When fpecial endowments were made *ad oftium ecclefiae*, the hufband, after affiance made, and troth plighted, ufed to declare with what fpecific lands he meant to endow his wife, *(quod dotat eam de tali manerio cum pertinentiis, &c.* Bract. *ibid)* and therefore in the old York ritual (Seld. *Ux. Hebr. l.* 2. *c.* 27) there is, at this part of the matrimonial fervice, the following rubric; "*fa-* "*cerdos interroget dotem mulieris ; et, fi terra* "*ei in dotem detur, tunc dicatur pfalmus ifte,* "*&c.*" When the wife was endowed generally *(ubi quis uxorem fuam dotaverit in generali, de omnibus terris et tenementis* ; Bract. *ibid.)* the hufband feems to have faid, "with "all my lands and tenements I thee endow ;" and then they all became liable to her dower. When he endowed her with perfonalty only,

he ufed to fay, "with all my worldly goods "(or, as the Salifbury ritual has it, *with all* "*my worldly chatel)* I thee endow ;" which intitled the wife to her thirds, or *pars rationabilis*, of his perfonal eftate, which is provided for by *magna carta, cap.* 26. and will be farther treated of in the concluding chapter of this book : though the retaining this laft expreffion in our modern liturgy, if of any meaning at all, can now refer only to the right of maintenance, which fhe acquires during coverture, out of her hufband's perfonalty.

[q] *A. D.* 1216. *c.* 7. *edit. Oxon.*

[r] *Affignetur autem ei pro dote fua tertia pars totius terrae mariti fui quae fua fuit in vita fua, nifi de minori dotata fuerit ad oftium ecclefiae. c.* 7. *(Ibid.)*

[s] Bract. *ubi fupr.* Britton. *c.* 101, 102. Flet. *l.* 5. *c.* 23. §. 11, 12.

[t] *P.* 7 *Hen. IV.* 13, 14.

preffly,

preffly, that a woman may be endowed *ad oftium ecclefiae* with more than a third part [u]; and fhall have her election, after her hufband's death, to accept fuch dower, or refufe it and betake herfelf to her dower at common law [w]. Which ftate of uncertainty was probably the reafon, that thefe fpecific dowers, *ad oftium ec-clefiae* and *ex affenfu patris*, have fince fallen into total difufe.

I PROCEED therefore to confider the method of endowment, or affigning dower, by the common law, which is now the only ufual fpecies. By the old law, grounded on the feodal exactions, a woman could not be endowed without a fine paid to the lord: neither could fhe marry again without nis licence ; left fhe fhould contract herfelf, and fo convey part of the feud, to the lord's enemy [x]. This licence the lords took care to be well paid for ; and, as it feems, would fometimes force the dowager to a fecond marriage, in order to gain the fine. But, to remedy thefe op-preffions, it was provided, firft by the charter of Henry I [y], and afterwards by *magna carta* [z], that the widow fhall pay nothing for her marriage, nor fhall be diftreined to marry afrefh, if fhe choofes to live without a hufband ; but fhall not however marry againft the confent of the lord : and farther, that nothing fhall be taken for affignment of the widow's dower, but that fhe fhall remain in her hufband's capital manfion-houfe for forty days after his death, during which time her dower fhall be affigned. Thefe forty days are called the widow's *quarentine* ; a term made ufe of in law to fignify the number of forty days, whether applied to this occafion, or any other [a]. The particular lands to be held in dower, muft be affigned [b] by the heir of the hufband, or his guardian ; not only for the fake of notoriety, but alfo to entitle the lord of the fee to demand his fervices of the heir, in refpect of the lands fo held. For the heir by this entry becomes tenant

---

[u] §. 39 F. N. B. 150.
[w] §. 41.
[x] Mirr. c. 1. §. 3.
[y] *ubi fupra.*
[z] *cap.* 7.

[a] It fignifies, in particular, the forty days, which perfons coming from infected countries are obliged to wait, before they are permitted to land in England.
[b] Co. Litt. 34, 35.

thereof

thereof to the lord, and the widow is immediate tenant to the heir, by a kind of fubinfeudation or under-tenancy, completed by this inveftiture or affignment : which tenure may ftill be created, notwithftanding the ftatute of *quia emptores*, becaufe the heir parts not with the fee-fimple, but only with an eftate for life. If the heir or his guardian do not affign her dower within the term of quarentine, or do affign it unfairly, fhe has her remedy at law, and the fheriff is appointed to affign it[c]. If the thing of which fhe is endowed be divifible, her dower muft be fet out by metes and bounds ; but, if it be indivifible, fhe muft be endowed fpecially ; as, of the third prefentation to a church, the third toll-difh of a mill, the third part of the profits of an office, the third fheaf of tithe, and the like[d].

Upon preconcerted marriages, and in eftates of confiderable confequence, tenancy in dower happens very feldom : for, the claim of the wife to her dower at the common law diffufing itfelf fo extenfively, it became a great clog to alienations, and was otherwife inconvenient to families. Wherefore, fince the alteration of the antient law refpecting dower *ad oftium ecclefiae*, which hath occafioned the intire difufe of that fpecies of dower, jointures have been introduced in their ftead, as a bar to the claim at common law. Which leads me to enquire, laftly,

4. How dower may be *barred* or prevented. A widow may be barred of her dower not only by elopement, divorce, being an alien, the treafon of her hufband, and other difabilities beforementioned, but alfo by detaining the title deeds, or evidences of the eftate from the heir ; until fhe reftores them[e] : and, by the ftatute of Glocefter[f], if a dowager alienes the land affigned her for dower, fhe forfeits it *ipfo facto*, and the heir may recover it by action. A woman alfo may be barred of her dower, by levying a fine or fuffering a recovery of the lands, during her cover-

[c] Co. Litt. 34. 35.
[d] *Ibid.* 32.

[e] *Ibid.* 39.
[f] 6 Edw. I. c. 7.

ture[g].

ture [g]. But the moſt uſual method of barring dowers is by jointures, as regulated by the ſtatute 27 Hen. VIII. c. 10.

A JOINTURE, which ſtrictly ſpeaking ſignifies a joint eſtate,
limited to both huſband and wife, but in common acceptation
extends alſo to a ſole eſtate, limited to the wife only, is thus defined by ſir Edward Coke [h]; " a competent livelyhood of freehold
" for the wife, of lands and tenements; to take effect, in profit
" or poſſeſſion, preſently after the death of the huſband; for the
" life of the wife at leaſt." This deſcription is framed from the
purview of the ſtatute 27 Hen. VIII. c. 10. before-mentioned;
commonly called the ſtatute of *uſes*, of which we ſhall ſpeak
fully hereafter. At preſent I have only to obſerve, that, before
the making of that ſtatute, the greateſt part of the land of England was conveyed to uſes; the property or poſſeſſion of the ſoil
being veſted in one man, and the *uſe*, or profits thereof, in another; whoſe directions, with regard to the diſpoſition thereof,
the former was in conſcience obliged to follow, and might be
compelled by a court of equity to obſerve. Now, though a huſband had the *uſe* of lands in abſolute fee-ſimple, yet the wife was
not entitled to any dower therein; he not being *ſeiſed* thereof:
wherefore it became uſual, on marriage, to ſettle by expreſs deed
ſome ſpecial eſtate to the uſe of the huſband and his wife, for
their lives, in joint-tenancy or jointure; which ſettlement would
be a proviſion for the wife in caſe ſhe ſurvived her huſband. At
length the ſtatute of uſes ordained, that ſuch as had the *uſe* of
lands, ſhould, to all intents and purpoſes, be reputed and taken
to be abſolutely *ſeiſed* and poſſeſſed of the ſoil itſelf. In conſequence of which legal ſeiſin, all wives would have become dowable of ſuch lands as were held to the uſe of their huſbands, and
alſo entitled at the ſame time to any ſpecial lands that might be
ſettled in jointure; had not the ſame ſtatute provided, that upon
making ſuch an eſtate in jointure to the wife before marriage,
ſhe ſhall be for ever precluded from her dower [i]. But then theſe

g Pig. of recov. 66.   i 4 Rep. 1, 2.
h 1 Inſt. 36.

four requifites muft be punctually obferved. 1. The jointure muft take effect immediately on the death of the hufband. 2. It muft be for her own life at leaft, and not *pur auter vie*, or for any term of years, or other fmaller eftate. 3. It muft be made to herfelf, and no other in truft for her. 4. It muft be made, and fo in the deed particularly expreffed to be, in fatisfaction of her whole dower, and not of any particular part of it. If the jointure be made to her *after* marriage, fhe has her election after her hufband's death, as in dower *ad oftium ecclefiae*, and may either accept it, or refufe it and betake herfelf to her dower at common law; for fhe was not capable of confenting to it during coverture. And if, by any fraud or accident, a jointure made before marriage proves to be on a bad title, and the jointrefs is evicted, or turned out of poffeffion, fhe fhall then (by the provifions of the fame ftatue) have her dower *pro tanto* at the common law [k].

THERE are fome advantages attending tenants in dower that do not extend to jointreffes; and fo, *vice verfa*, jointreffes are in fome refpects more privileged than tenants in dower. Tenant in dower by the old common law is fubject to no tolls or taxes; and hers is almoft the only eftate on which, when derived from the king's debtor, the king cannot diftrain for his debt; if contracted during the coverture [l]. But, on the other hand, a widow may enter at once, without any formal procefs, on her jointure land; as fhe alfo might have done on dower *ad oftium ecclefiae*, which a

---

[k] Thefe fettlements, previous to marriage, feem to have been in ufe among the antient Germans, and their kindred nation the Gauls. Of the former Tacitus gives us this account. "*Dotem non uxor marito, fed* "*uxori maritus affert: interfunt parentes et* "*propinqui, et munera probant.*" *(de mer. Germ. c. 18.)* And Caefar, *(de bello Gallico, l. 6. c. 18.)* has given us the terms of a marriage fettlement among the Gauls, as nicely calculated as any modern jointure. "*Viri, quantas pecunias ab uxoribus dotis no-* "*mine acceperunt, tantas ex fuis bonis, aefti-*

"*matione facta, cum dotibus communicant.* "*Hujus omnis pecuniae conjunctim ratio habe-* "*tur, fructufque fervantur. Uter eorum vita* "*fuperarit, ad eum pars utriufque cum fruc-* "*tibus fuperiorum temporum pervenit.*" The dauphin's commentator on Caefar fuppofes that this Gaulifh cuftom was the ground of the new regulations made by Juftinian *(Nov. 97.)* with regard to the provifion for widows among the Romans: but furely there is as much reafon to fuppofe, that it gave the hint for our ftatutable jointures.

[l] Co. Litt. 31. a. F. N. B. 150.

jointure

jointure in many points refembles; and the refemblance was ftill greater, while that fpecies of dower continued in it's primitive ftate : whereas no fmall trouble, and a very tedious method of proceeding, is neceffary to compel a legal affignment of dower [m]. And, what is more, though dower be forfeited by the treafon of the hufband, yet lands fettled in jointure remain unimpeached to the widow [n]. Wherefore fir Edward Coke very juftly gives it the preference, as being more fure and fafe to the widow, than even dower *ad oftium ecclefiae*, the moft eligible fpecies of any.

[m] Co. Litt. 36.   [n] *Ibid.* 37.

CHAPTER THE NINTH.

OF ESTATES, LESS THAN FREEHOLD.

OF estates, that are lefs than freehold, there are three forts ; 1. Eftates for years : 2. Eftates at will : 3. Eftates by fufferance.

I. AN eftate for *years* is a contract for the poffeffion of lands or tenements, for fome determinate period : and it happens where a man letteth them to another for the term of a certain number of years, agreed upon between the leffor and the leffee[a], and the leffee enters thereon[b]. If the leafe be but for half a year, or a quarter, or any lefs time, this leffee is refpected as a tenant for years, and is ftiled fo in fome legal proceedings ; a year being the fhorteft term which the law in this cafe takes notice of[c]. And this may, not improperly, lead us into a fhort explanation of the divifion and calculation of time by the Englifh law.

THE fpace of a year is a determinate and well-known period, confifting commonly of 365 days : for, though in biffextile or

---

[a] We may here remark, once for all, that the terminations of " — or" and " — ee" obtain, in law, the one an active, the other a paffive fignification ; the former ufually denoting the doer of any act, the latter him to whom it is done. The feoffor is he that maketh a feoffment ; the feoffee is he to whom it is made : the donor is one that giveth lands in tail ; the donee is he who receiveth it : he that granteth a leafe is denominated the leffor ; and he to whom it is granted the leffee. (Litt. §. 57.)

[b] *Ibid.* 58.

[c] *Ibid.* 67.

leap-years

leap-years it confifts properly of 366, yet by the ftatute 21 Hen. III. the increafing day in the leap-year, together with the preceding day, fhall be accounted for one day only. That of a month is more ambiguous : there being, in common ufe, two ways of calculating months ; either as lunar, confifting of twenty eight days, the fuppofed revolution of the moon, thirteen of which make a year; or, as calendar months, of unequal lengths, according to the Julian divifion in our common almanacs, commencing at the calends of each month, whereof in a year there are only twelve. A month in law is a lunar month, or twenty eight days, unlefs otherwife expreffed ; not only becaufe it is always one uniform period, but becaufe it falls naturally into a quarterly divifion by weeks. Therefore a leafe for " twelve months" is only for forty eight weeks ; but if be for " *a* twelvemonth" in the fingular number, it is good for the whole year [d]. For herein the law recedes from it's ufual calculation, becaufe the ambiguity between the two methods of computation ceafes ; it being generally underftood that by the fpace of time called thus, in the fingular number, a twelvemonth, is meant the whole year, confifting of one folar revolution. In the fpace of a day all the twenty four hours are ufually reckoned ; the law generally rejecting all fractions of a day, in order to avoid difputes [e]. Therefore, if I am bound to pay money on any certain day, I difcharge the obligation if I pay it before twelve o' clock at night ; after which the following day commences. But to return to eftates for years.

THESE eftates were originally granted to mere farmers or hufbandmen, who every year rendered fome equivalent in money, provifions, or other rent, to the leffors or landlords ; but, in order to encourage them to manure and cultivate the ground, they had a permanent intereft granted them, not determinable at the will of the lord. And yet their poffeffion was efteemed of fo little confequence, that they were rather confidered as the bailiffs or fervants of the lord, who were to receive and account for the

[d] 6 Rep. 61.   [e] Co. Litt. 135.

profits,

profits at a fettled price, than as having any property of their own. And therefore they were not allowed to have a freehold eftate : but their intereft (fuch as it was) vefted after their deaths in their executors, who were to make up the accounts of their teftator with the lord, and his other creditors, and were intitled to the ftock upon the farm. The leffee's eftate might alfo, by the antient law, be at any time defeated, by a common recovery fuffered by the tenant of the freehold [f]; which annihilated all leafes for years then fubfifting, unlefs afterwards renewed by the recoveror, whofe title was fuppofed fuperior to his by whom thofe leafes were granted.

WHILE eftates for years were thus precarious, it is no wonder that they were ufually very fhort, like our modern leafes upon rack rent ; and indeed we are told [g] that by the antient law no leafes for more than forty years were allowable, becaufe any longer poffeffion (efpecially when given without any livery declaring the nature and duration of the eftate) might tend to defeat the inheritance. Yet this law, if it ever exifted, was foon antiquated : for we may obferve, in Madox's collection of antient inftruments, fome leafes for years of a pretty early date, which confiderably exceed that period [h]; and long terms, for three hundred years at leaft, were certainly in ufe in the time of Edward III [i], and probably of Edward I [k]. But certainly, when by the ftatute 21 Hen. VIII. c. 15. the termor (that is, he who is intitled to the term of years) was protected againft thefe fictitious recoveries, and his intereft rendered fecure and permanent, long terms began to be more frequent than before ; and were afterwards extenfively introduced, being found extremely convenient for family fettlements and mortgages : continuing fubject, however, to the fame rules of fucceffion, and with the fame inferiority to freeholds,

[f] Co. Litt. 46.

[g] Mirror. c. 2. §. 27. Co. Litt. 45, 46.

[h] Madox *Formulare Anglican.* n°. 239. *fol.* 140. Demife for eighty years, 21 Ric. II. .... *Ibid.* n°. 245. *fol.* 146: for the like

term, *A. D.* 1429. ..... *Ibid.* n°. 248. *fol.* 148. for fifty years, 7 Edw. IV.

[i] 32 Aff. pl. 6.

[k] Stat. of mortmain, 7 Edw. I.

as when they were little better than tenancies at the will of the landlord.

E V E R Y eftate which muft expire at a period certain and pre-fixed, by whatever words created, is an eftate for years.   And therefore this eftate is frequently called a term, *terminus*, becaufe it's duration or continuance is bounded, limited, and determined : for every fuch eftate muft have a certain beginning, and certain end[1].   But *id certum eft, quod certum reddi poteft :* therefore if a man make a leafe to another, for fo many years as J. S. fhall name, it is a good leafe for years[m] ; for though it is at prefent uncertain, yet when J. S. hath named the years, it is then re-duced to a certainty.   If no day of commencement is named in the creation of this eftate, it begins from the making, or delivery, of the leafe[n].   A leafe for fo many years as J. S. fhall live, is void from the beginning[o] ; for it is neither certain, nor can ever be reduced to a certainty, during the continuance of the leafe. And the fame doctrine holds, if a parfon make a leafe of his glebe for fo many years as he fhall continue parfon of Dale ; for this is ftill more uncertain.   But a leafe for twenty or more years, if J. S. fhall fo long live, or if he fhall fo long continue parfon, is good[p] : for there is a certain period fixed, beyond which it cannot laft ; though it may determine fooner, on the death of J. S. or his ceafing to be parfon there.

W E have before remarked, and endeavoured to affign the rea-fon of, the inferiority in which the law places an eftate for years, when compared with an eftate for life, or an inheritance : ob-ferving, that an eftate for life, even it be *pur auter vie*, is a free-hold ; but that an eftate for a thoufand years is only a chattel, and reckoned part of the perfonal eftate[q].   Hence it follows, that a leafe for years may be made to commence *in futuro*, though a leafe for life cannot.   As, if I grant lands to Titius to hold from

[1] Co. Litt. 45.
[m] 6 Rep. 35.
[n] Co. Litt. 46

[o] *Ibid.* 45.
[p] *Ibid.*
[q] *Ibid.* 46.

Michaelmas

Michaelmas next for twenty years, this is good; but to hold from Michaelmas next for the term of his natural life, is void. For no estate of freehold can commence *in futuro;* because it cannot be created at common law without livery of seisin, or corporal possession of the land : and corporal possession cannot be given of an estate now, which is not to commence now, but hereafter [r]. And, because no livery of seisin is necessary to a lease for years, such lessee is not said to be *seised,* or to have true legal seisin, of the lands. Nor indeed does the bare lease vest any estate in the lessee; but only gives him a right of entry on the tenement, which right is called his *interest in the term,* or *interesse termini :* but when he has actually so entered, and thereby accepted the grant, the estate is then and not before vested in him, and he is *possessed,* not properly of the land, but of the term of years [s] : the possession or seisin of the *land* remaining still in him who hath the freehold. Thus the word, *term,* does not merely signify the time specified in the lease, but the estate also and interest that passes by that lease : and therefore the *term* may expire, during the continuance of the *time;* as by surrender, forfeiture, and the like. For which reason, if I grant a lease to A for the term of three years, and after the expiration of the said *term* to B for six years, and A surrenders or forfeits his lease at the end of *one* year, B's interest shall immediately take effect : but if the remainder had been to B from and after the expiration of the said *three years,* or from and after the expiration of the said *time,* in this case B's interest will not commence till the time is fully elapsed, whatever may become of A's term [t].

TENANT for term of years hath incident to, and inseparable from his estate, unless by special agreement, the same estovers, which we formerly observed [u] that tenant for life was entitled to; that is to say, house-bote, fire-bote, plough-bote, and hay-bote [w] : terms which have been already explained [x].

[r] 5 Rep. 94.
[s] Co. Litt. 46.
[t] *Ibid.* 45.

[u] pag. 122.
[w] Co. Litt. 45.
[x] pag. 35.

WITH

WITH regard to emblements, or profits of land fowed by tenant for years, there is this difference between him, and tenant for life : that where the term of tenant for years depends upon a certainty, as if he holds from midfummer for ten years, and in the laft year he fows a crop of corn, and it is not ripe and cut before midfummer, the end of his term, the landlord fhall have it ; for the tenant knew the expiration of his term, and therefore it was his own folly to fow what he never could reap the profits of [y]. But where the leafe for years depends upon an uncertainty ; as, upon the death of the leffor, being himfelf only tenant for life, or being a hufband feifed in right of his wife ; or if the term of years be determinable upon a life or lives ; in all thefe cafes, the eftate for years not being certainly to expire at a time foreknown, but merely by the act of God, the tenant, or his executors, fhall have the emblements in the fame manner, that a tenant for life or his executors fhall be intitled thereto [z]. Not fo, if it determine by the act of the party himfelf ; as if tenant for years does any thing that amounts to a forfeiture : in which cafe the emblements fhall go to the leffor, and not to the leffee, who hath determined his eftate by his own default [a].

II. THE fecond fpecies of eftates not freehold are eftates at *will*. An eftate at will is where lands and tenements are let by one man to another, to have and to hold at the will of the leffor; and the tenant by force of this leafe obtains poffeffion [b]. Such tenant hath no certain indefeafible eftate, nothing that can be affigned by him to any other ; for that the leffor may determine his will, and put him out whenever he pleafes. But every eftate at will is at the will of both parties, landlord and tenant, fo that either of them may determine his will, and quit his connexions with the other at his own pleafure [c]. Yet this muft be underftood with fome reftriction. For, if the tenant at will fows his land,

[y] Litt. §. 68.
[z] Co. Litt. 56.
[a] Ibid. 55.

[b] Litt. §. 68.
[c] Co. Litt. 55.

and the landlord before the corn is ripe, or before it is reaped, puts him out, yet the tenant fhall have the emblements, and free ingrefs, egrefs, and regrefs, to cut and carry away the profits [d]. And this for the fame reafon, upon which all the cafes of emblements turn; *viz.* the point of uncertainty : fince the tenant could not poffibly know when his landlord would determine his will, and therefore could make no provifion againft it; and having fown the land, which is for the good of the public, upon a reafonable prefumption, the law will not fuffer him to be a lofer by it. But it is otherwife, and upon reafon equally good, where the tenant himfelf determines the will; for in this cafe the landlord fhall have the profits of the land [e].

WHAT act does, or does not, amount to a determination of the will on either fide, has formerly been matter of great debate in our courts. But it is now, I think, fettled, that (befides the exprefs determination of the leffor's will, by declaring that the leffee fhall hold no longer; which muft either be made upon the land [f], or notice muft be given to the leffee [g]) the exertion of any act of ownerfhip by the leffor, as entring upon the premifes and cutting timber [h], taking a diftrefs for rent and impounding them thereon [i], or making a feoffment, or leafe for years of the land to commence immediately [k]; any act of defertion by the leffee, as affigning his eftate to another, or committing wafte, which is an act inconfiftent with fuch a tenure [l]; or, which is *inftar omnium*, the death or outlawry, of either leffor or leffee [m]; puts an end to or determines the eftate at will.

THE law is however careful, that no fudden determination of the will by one party fhall tend to the manifeft and unforefeen prejudice of the other. This appears in the cafe of emblements

[d] Co. Litt. 56.
[e] *Ibid.* 55.
[f] *Ibid.*
[g] 1 Ventr. 248.
[h] Co. Litt. 55.

[i] *Ibid.* 57.
[k] 1 Roll. Abr. 860. 2 Lev. 88.
[l] Co. Litt. 57.
[m] 5 Rep. 116. Co. Litt. 57. 62.

before-

before-mentioned ; and, by a parity of reafon, the leffee after the determination of the leffor's will, fhall have reafonable ingrefs and egrefs to fetch away his goods and utenfils [n]. And, if rent be payable quarterly or half-yearly, and the leffee determines the will, the rent fhall be paid to the end of the current quarter or half-year [o]. And, upon the fame principle, courts of law have of late years leant as much as poffible againft conftruing demifes, where no certain term is mentioned, to be tenancies at will ; but have rather held them to be tenancies from year to year fo long as both parties pleafe, efpecially where an annual rent is referved : in which cafe they will not fuffer either party to determine the tenancy even at the end of the year, without reafonable notice to the other.

THERE is one fpecies of eftates at will, that deferves a more particular regard than any other ; and that is, an eftate held by copy of court roll ; or, as we ufually call it, a *copyhold* eftate. This, as was before obferved [p], was in it's original and foundation nothing better than a mere eftate at will. But, the kindnefs and indulgence of fucceffive lords of manors having permitted thefe eftates to be enjoyed by the tenants and their heirs, according to particular cuftoms eftablifhed in their refpective diftricts ; therefore, though they ftill are held at the will of the lord, and fo are in general expreffed in the court rolls to be, yet that will is qualified, reftrained, and limited, to be exerted according to the cuftom of the manor. This cuftom, being fuffered to grow up by the lord, is looked upon as the evidence and interpreter of his will : his will is no longer arbitrary and precarious ; but fixed and afcertained by the cuftom to be the fame, and no other, that has time out of mind been exercifed and declared by his anceftors. A copyhold tenant is therefore now full as properly a tenant by the cuftom, as a tenant at will, the cuftom having arifen from a feries of uniform wills. And therefore it is rightly obferved by Calthorpe [q], that " copyholders and cuftomary tenants differ not

[r] Litt. §. 69.   [p] pag. 93.
[o] Salk. 414. 1 Sid. 339.   [q] on copyholds. 51. 54.

T 2   " fo

" fo much in nature as in name : for although fome be called
" copyholders, fome cuftomary, fome tenants by the virge, fome
" bafe tenants, fome bond tenants, and fome by one name and
" fome by another, yet do they all agree in fubftance and kind of
" tenure : all the faid lands are holden in one general kind, that
" is, by cuftom and continuance of time ; and the diverfity of
" their names doth not alter the nature of their tenure."

A L M O S T every copyhold tenant being therefore thus tenant
at the will of the lord according to the cuftom of the manor;
which cuftoms differ as much as the humour and temper of the
refpective antient lords, (from whence we may account for their
great variety) fuch tenant, I fay, may have, fo far as the cuftom
warrants, any other of the eftates or quantities of intereft, which
we have hitherto confidered, or may hereafter confider, to hold
united with this cuftomary eftate at will. A copyholder may, in
many manors, be tenant in fee-fimple, in fee-tail, for life, by
the curtefy, in dower, for years, at fufferance, or on condition :
fubject however to be deprived of thefe eftates upon the concurrence of thofe circumftances which the will of the lord, promul-
ged by immemorial cuftom, has declared to be a forfeiture or abfolute determination of thofe interefts ; as in fome manors the
want of iffue male, in others the cutting down timber, the non-
payment of a fine, and the like. Yet none of thefe interefts
amount to freehold ; for the freehold of the whole manor abides
always in the lord only ', who hath granted out the ufe and occupation, but not the corporal feifin or true poffeffion, of certain parts and parcels thereof, to thefe his cuftomary tenants at
will.

T H E reafon of originally granting out this complicated kind
of intereft, fo that the fame man fhall, with regard to the fame
land, be at one and the fame time tenant in fee-fimple and alfo
tenant at the lord's will, feems to have arifen from the nature of
villenage tenure ; in which a grant of any eftate of freehold, or

' Litt. §. 81. 2 Inft. 325.

even

even for years abſolutely, was an immediate enfranchiſement of
the villein [s]. The lords therefore, though they were willing to
enlarge the intereſt of their villeins, by granting them eſtates
which might endure for their lives, or ſometimes be deſcendible
to their iſſue, yet did not care to manumit them entirely; and
for that reaſon it ſeems to have been contrived, that a power of
reſumption at the will of the lord ſhould be annexed to theſe
grants, whereby the tenants were ſtill kept in a ſtate of villenage,
and no freehold at all was conveyed to them in their reſpective
lands : and of courſe, as the freehold of all lands muſt neceſſa-
rily reſt and abide ſomewhere, the law ſuppoſes it to continue and
remain in the lord. Afterwards, when theſe villeins became
modern copyholders, and had acquired by cuſtom a ſure and in-
defeaſible eſtate in their lands, on performing the uſual ſervices,
but yet continued to be ſtiled in their admiſſions tenants at the
will of the lord, --- the law ſtill ſuppoſed it an abſurdity to allow,
that ſuch at were thus nominally tenants at will could have any
freehold intereſt : and therefore continued, and ſtill continues,
to determine, that the freehold of lands ſo holden abides in the
lord of the manor, and not in the tenant; for though he *really*
holds to him and his heirs for ever, yet he is alſo *ſaid* to hold at
another's will. But, with regard to certain other copyholders, of
free or privileged tenure, which are derived from the antient tenants in villein-ſocage [t], and are not ſaid to hold *at the will of the
lord*, but only *according to the cuſtom of the manor,* there is no
ſuch abſurdity in allowing them to be capable of enjoying a freehold intereſt; and therefore the law doth not ſuppoſe the freehold
of ſuch lands to reſt in the lord of whom they are holden, but in
the tenants themſelves [u]; who are allowed to have a freehold *intereſt,* though not a freehold *tenure.*

HOWEVER, in common caſes, copyhold eſtates are ſtill
ranked (for the reaſons above-mentioned) among tenancies at

---

[s] Mirr. c. 2. §. 28. Litt. §. 204, 5, 6.
[t] See page 98, &c.
[u] Fitzh. *Abr. tit. corone.* 310. *cuſtom.* 12.
Bro. *Abr. tit. cuſtom.* 2. 17. *tenant per copie.* 22.

9 Rep. 76. Co. Litt. 59. Co. Copyh. §. 32.
Cro. Car. 229. 1 Roll. Abr. 562. 2 Ventr.
143. Carth. 432. Lord Raym. 1225.

will; though custom, which is the life of the common law, has established a permanent property in the copyholders, who were formerly nothing better than bondmen, equal to that of the lord himself, in the tenements holden of the manor: nay sometimes even superior; for we may now look upon a copyholder of inheritance, with a fine certain, to be little inferior to an absolute freeholder in point of interest, and in other respects, particularly in the clearness and security of his title, to be frequently in a better situation.

III. AN estate at *sufferance*, is where one comes into possession of land by lawful title, but keeps it afterwards without any title at all. As if a man takes a lease for a year, and, after the year is expired, continues to hold the premises without any fresh leave from the owner of the estate. Or, if a man maketh a lease at will, and dies, the estate at will is thereby determined; but if the tenant continueth possession, he is tenant at sufferance [w]. But no man can be tenant at sufferance against the king, to whom no *laches*, or neglect, in not entering and ousting the tenant, is ever imputed by law: but his tenant, so holding over, is considered as an absolute intruder [x]. But, in the case of a subject, this estate may be destroyed whenever the true owner shall make an actual entry on the lands and oust the tenant; for, before entry, he cannot maintain an action of trespass against the tenant by sufferance, as he might against a stranger [y] : and the reason is, because the tenant being once in by a lawful title, the law (which presumes no wrong in any man) will suppose him to continue upon a title equally lawful; unless the owner of the land by some public and avowed act, such as entry is, will declare his continuance to be tortious, or, in common language, wrongful.

THUS stands the law, with regard to tenants by sufferance; and landlords are obliged in these cases to make formal entries upon their lands [z], and recover possession by the legal process of

[w] Co. Litt. 57.   [y] *Ibid.*
[x] *Ibid.*   [z] 5 Mod. 384.

ejectment:

ejectment: and at the utmoft, by the common law, the tenant was bound to account for the profits of the land fo by him detained. But now, by ftatute 4 Geo. II. c. 28. in cafe any tenant for life or years, or other perfon claiming under or by collufion with fuch tenant, fhall wilfully hold over after the determination of the term, and demand made in writing for recovering the poffeffion of the premifes, by him to whom the remainder or reverfion thereof fhall belong; fuch perfon, fo holding over, fhall pay, for the time he continues, at the rate of double the yearly value of the lands fo detained. This has almoft put an end to the practice of tenancy by fufferance, unlefs with the tacit confent of the owner of the tenement.

CHAPTER THE TENTH.

OF ESTATES UPON CONDITION.

BESIDES the feveral divifions of eftates, in point of intereft, which we have confidered in the three preceding
chapters, there is alfo another fpecies ftill remaining, which is
called an eftate *upon condition*; being fuch whofe exiftence depends upon the happening or not happening of fome uncertain
event, whereby the eftate may be either originally created, or enlarged, or finally defeated [a]. And thefe conditional eftates I have
chofen to referve till laft, becaufe they are indeed more properly
qualifications of other eftates, than a diftinct fpecies of themfelves; feeing that any quantity of intereft, a fee, a freehold, or
a term of years, may depend upon thefe provifional reftrictions.
Eftates then upon condition, thus underftood, are of two forts:
1. Eftates upon condition *implied*: 2. Eftates upon condition
expreffed: under which laft may be included, 3. Eftates held in
vadio, gage, or *pledge*: 4. Eftates by *ftatute merchant* or *ftatute
ftaple*: 5. Eftates held by *elegit*.

I. ESTATES upon condition implied in law, are where a
grant of an eftate has a condition annexed to it infeparably, from
it's effence and conftitution, although no condition be expreffed
in words. As if a grant be made to a man of an office, generally,
without adding other words; the law tacitly annexes hereto a
fecret condition, that the grantee fhall duly execute his office [b],

[a] Co. Litt. 201.   [b] Litt. §. 378.

on

on breach of which condition it is lawful for the grantor, or his heirs, to ouft him, and grant it to another perfon^c. For an office, either public or private, may be forfeited by *mif-ufer* or *non-ufer*; both of which are breaches of this implied condition. 1. By *mif-ufer*, or abufe; as if a judge takes a bribe, or a park-keeper kills deer without authority. 2. By *non-ufer*, or neglect; which in public offices, that concern the adminiftration of juftice, or the commonwealth, is of itfelf a direct and immediate caufe of forfeiture: but non-ufer of a private office is no caufe of forfeiture, unlefs fome fpecial damage is proved to be occafioned thereby^d. For in the one cafe delay muft neceffarily be occafioned in the affairs of the public, which require a conftant attention; but, private offices not requiring fo regular and unremitted a fervice, the temporary neglect of them is not neceffarily productive of mifchief; upon which account fome fpecial lofs muft be proved, in order to vacate thefe. Franchifes alfo, being regal privileges in the hands of a fubject, are held to be granted on the fame condition of making a proper ufe of them; and therefore they may be loft and forfeited, like offices, either by abufe or by neglect^e.

UPON the fame principle proceed all the forfeitures which are given by law of life eftates and others; for any acts done by the tenant himfelf, that are incompatible with the eftate which he holds. As if tenants for life or years enfeoff a ftranger in fee-fimple: this is, by the common law, a forfeiture of their feveral eftates; being a breach of the condition which the law annexes thereto, *viz.* that they fhall not attempt to create a greater eftate than they themfelves are entitled to^f. So if any tenants for years, for life, or in fee, commit a felony; the king or other lord of the fee is entitled to have their tenements, becaufe their eftate is determined by the breach of the condition, " that they fhall not " commit felony," which the law tacitly annexes to every feodal donation.

---

^c Litt. §. 379.		^e 9 Rep. 50.
^d Co. Litt. 233.		^f Co. Litt. 215.

II. A N estate on condition expressed in the grant itself, is where an estate is granted, either in fee-simple or otherwise, with an express qualification annexed, whereby the estate granted shall either commence, be enlarged, or be defeated, upon performance or breach of such qualification or condition[g]. These conditions are therefore either *precedent*, or *subsequent*. Precedent are such as must happen or be performed before the estate can vest or be enlarged; subsequent are such, by the failure or nonperformance of which an estate already vested may be defeated. Thus, if an estate for life be limited to A upon his marriage with B, the marriage is a precedent condition, and till that happens no estate[h] is vested in A. Or, if a man grant to his lessee for years, that upon payment of a hundred marks within the term he shall have the fee, this also is a condition precedent, and the fee-simple passeth not till the hundred marks be paid[i]. But if a man grant an estate in fee-simple, reserving to himself and his heirs a certain rent; and that, if such rent be not paid at the times limited, it shall be lawful for him and his heirs to re-enter, and avoid the estate; in this case the grantee and his heirs have an estate upon condition subsequent, which is defeasible if the condition be not strictly performed[k]. To this class may also be referred all base fees, and fee-simples conditional at the common law[l]. Thus an estate to a man and his heirs, *tenants of the manor of Dale*, is an estate on condition that he and his heirs continue tenants of that manor. And so, if a personal annuity be granted at this day to a man and the heirs of his body; as this is no tenement within the statute of Westminster the second, it remains, as at common law, a fee-simple on condition that the grantee has heirs of his body. Upon the same principle depend all the determinable estates of freehold, which we mentioned in the eighth chapter; as *durante viduitate*, *&c*: these are estates upon condition that the grantees do not marry, and the like. And, on the breach of any

[g] Co. Litt. 201.
[h] Show. Parl. Caf. 83, &c.
[i] Co. Litt. 217.

[k] Litt. §. 325.
[l] See pag. 109, 110, 111.

of

of thefe fubfequent conditions by the failure of thefe contingencies; by the grantee's not continuing tenant of the manor of Dale, by not having heirs of his body, or by not continuing fole; the eftates which were refpectively vefted in each grantee are wholly determined and void.

A DISTINCTION is however made between a *condition in deed* and a *limitation*, which Littleton [m] denominates alfo a *condition in law*. For when an eftate is fo expreffly confined and limited by the words of it's creation, that it cannot endure for any longer time than till the contingency happens upon which the eftate is to fail, this is denominated a *limitation :* as when land is granted to a man, *fo long as* he is parfon of Dale, or *while* he continues unmarried, or *until* out of the rents and profits he fhall have made 500 *l.* and the like [n]. In fuch cafes the eftate determines as foon as the contingency happens, (when he ceafes to be parfon, marries a wife, or has received the 500 *l.*) and the next fubfequent eftate, which depends upon fuch determination, becomes immediately vefted, without any act to be done by him who is next in expectancy. But when an eftate is, ftrictly fpeaking, upon *condition in deed* (as if granted expreffly *upon condition* to be void upon the payment of 40 *l.* by the grantor, or *fo that* the grantee continues unmarried, or *provided* he goes to York, *&c.* [o]) the law permits it to endure beyond the time when fuch contingency happens, unlefs the grantor or his heirs or affigns take advantage of the breach of the condition, and make either an entry or a claim in order to avoid the eftate [p]. But, though ftrict words of condition be ufed in the creation of the eftate, yet if on breach of the condition the eftate be limited over to a third perfon, and does not immediately revert to the grantor or his reprefentatives, (as if an eftate be granted by A to B, on condition that within two years B intermarry with C, and on failure thereof then to D and his heirs) this the law conftrues to be a limitation

---

[m] §. 380. 1 Inft. 234.
[n] 10 Rep. 41.

[o] *Ibid.* 42.
[p] Litt. §. 347. Stat. 32 Hen. VIII. c. 34.

and not a condition[q]: becaufe, if it were a condition, then, upon the breach thereof, only A or his reprefentatives could avoid the eftate by entry, and fo D's remainder might be defeated by their neglecting to enter; but, when it is a limitation, the eftate of B determines, and that of D commences, the inftant that the failure happens. So alfo, if a man by his will devifes land to his heir at law, on condition that he pays a fum of money, and for non-payment devifes it over, this fhall be confidered as a limitation; otherwife no advantage could be taken of the non-payment, for none but the heir himfelf could have entered for a breach of condition [r].

In all thefe inftances, of limitations or conditions fubfequent, it is to be obferved, that fo long as the condition, either exprefs or implied, either in deed or in law, remains unbroken, the grantee may have an eftate of freehold, provided the eftate upon which fuch condition is annexed be in itfelf of a freehold nature; as if the original grant exprefs either an eftate of inheritance, or for life, or no eftate at all, which is conftructively an eftate for life. For the breach of thefe conditions being contingent and uncertain, this uncertainty preferves the freehold [s]; becaufe the eftate is capable to laft for ever, or at leaft for the life of the tenant, fuppofing the condition to remain unbroken. But where the eftate is at the utmoft a chattel intereft, which muft determine at a time certain, and may determine fooner, (as a grant for ninety nine years, provided A, B, and C, and the furvivor of them, fhall fo long live) this ftill continues a mere chattel, and is not, by it's uncertainty, ranked among eftates of freehold.

These exprefs conditions, if they be *impoffible* at the time of their creation, or afterwards become impoffible by the act of God or the act of the feoffor himfelf, or if they be *contrary to law*, or *repugnant* to the nature of the eftate, are void. In any of which cafes, if they be conditions *fubfequent*, that is, to be per-

q 1 Ventr. 202. s Co. Litt. 42.
r Cro. Eliz. 205. 1 Roll. Abr. 411.

formed

formed after the eftate is vefted, the eftate fhall become abfolute
in the tenant.   As, if a feoffment be made to a man in fee-fimple,
on condition that unlefs he goes to Rome in twenty four hours;
or unlefs he marries with Jane S. by fuch a day; (within which
time the woman dies, or the feoffor marries her himfelf) or unlefs he
kills another; or in cafe he alienes in fee; then and in any of fuch
cafes the eftate fhall be vacated and determine: here the condition is void, and the eftate made abfolute in the feoffee.   For he
hath by the grant the eftate vefted in him, which fhall not be
defeated afterwards by a condition either impoffible, illegal, or
repugnant [t].   But if the condition be *precedent*, or to be performed
before the eftate vefts, as a grant to a man that, if he kills another or goes to Rome in a day, he fhall have an eftate in fee;
here, the void condition being precedent, the eftate which depends thereon is alfo void, and the grantee fhall take nothing by
the grant: for he hath no eftate until the condition be performed [u].

T H E R E are fome eftates defeafible upon condition fubfequent,
that require a more peculiar notice.   Such are

III.   E s t a t e s held *in vadio*, in *gage*, or pledge; which are
of two kinds, *vivum vadium*, or living pledge; and *mortuum vadium*, dead pledge, or *mortgage*.

V i v u m *vadium*, or living pledge, is when a man borrows a
fum (fuppofe 200 *l.*) of another; and grants him an eftate, as, of
20 *l. per annum*, to hold till the rents and profits fhall repay the
fum fo borrowed.   This is an eftate conditioned to be void, as foon
as fuch fum is raifed.   And in this cafe the land or pledge is faid
to be living: it fubfifts, and furvives the debt; and, immediately
on the difcharge of that, refults back to the borrower [w].   But
mortuum vadium, a dead pledge, or *mortgage*, (which is much
more common than the other) is where a man borrows of another

[t] Co. Litt. 206.   [w] *Ibid.* 205.
[u] *Ibid.*

a fpecific

a fpecific fum (*e. g.* 200 *l.*) and grants him an eftate in fee, on
condition that if he, the mortgagor, fhall repay the mortgagee
the faid fum of 200 *l.* on a certain day mentioned in the deed,
that then the mortgagor may re-enter on the eftate fo granted in
pledge ; or, as is now the more ufual way, that the mortgagee
fhall re-convey the eftate to the mortgagor : in this cafe the land,
which is fo put in pledge, is by law, in cafe of non-payment at
the time limited, for ever dead and gone from the mortgagor ;
and the mortgagee's eftate in the lands is then no longer conditional, but abfolute.   But, fo long as it continues conditional,
that is, between the time of lending the money, and the time
allotted for payment, the mortgagee is called tenant in mortgage[x].
But, as it was formerly a doubt[y], whether, by taking fuch e-
ftate in fee, it did not become liable to the wife's dower, and
other incumbrances of the mortgagee (though that doubt has
been long ago over-ruled by our courts of equity[z]) it therefore
became ufual to grant only a long term of years, by way of mortgage ; with condition to be void on re-payment of the mortgage-
money : which courfe has been fince continued, principally becaufe on the death of the mortgagee fuch term becomes vefted in
his perfonal reprefentatives, who alone are intitled in equity to
receive the money lent, of whatever nature the mortgage may
happen to be.

A s foon as the eftate is created, the mortgagee may immediately enter on the lands ; but is liable to be difpoffeffed, upon
performance of the condition by payment of the mortgage-money
at the day limited.   And therefore the ufual way is to agree that
the mortgagor fhall hold the land till the day affigned for payment ; when, in cafe of failure, whereby the eftate becomes
abfolute, the mortgagee may enter upon it and take poffeffion,
without any poffibility *at law* of being afterwards evicted by the
mortgagor, to whom the land is now for ever dead.   But here
again the courts of equity interpofe ; and, though a mortgage

[x] Litt. §. 332.   [z] Hardr. 466.
[y] *Ibid.* §. 357. Cro. Car. 191.

be

be thus forfeited, and the estate absolutely vested in the mortgagee at the common law, yet they will consider the real value of the tenements compared with the sum borrowed. And, if the estate be of greater value than the sum lent thereon, they will allow the mortgagor at any reasonable time to re-call or redeem his estate; paying to the mortgagee his principal, interest, and expenses: for otherwise, in strictness of law, an estate worth 1000 *l.* might be forfeited for non-payment of 100 *l.* or a less sum. This reasonable advantage, allowed to mortgagors, is called the *equity of redemption :* and this enables a mortgagor to call on the mortgagee, who has possession of his estate, to deliver it back and account for the rents and profits received, on payment of his whole debt and interest; thereby turning the *mortuum* into a kind of *vivum vadium.* But, on the other hand, the mortgagee may either compel the sale of the estate, in order to get the whole of his money immediately; or else call upon the mortgagor to redeem his estate presently, or, in default thereof, to be for ever *foreclosed* from redeeming the same; that is, to lose his equity of redemption without possibility of re-call. And also, in some cases of fraudulent mortgages[a], the fraudulent mortgagor forfeits all equity of redemption whatsoever. It is not therefore usual for mortgagees to take possession of the mortgaged estate, unless where the security is precarious, or small; or where the mortgagor neglects even the payment of interest: when the mortgagee is frequently obliged to bring an ejectment, and take the land into his own hands, in the nature of a pledge, or the *pignus* of the Roman law : whereas, while it remains in the hands of the mortgagor, it more resembles their *hypotheca,* which was where the possession of the thing pledged remained with the debtor[b]. But, by statute 7 Geo. II. c. 20. after payment or tender by the mortgagor of principal, interest, and costs, the mortgagee can maintain no ejectment; but may be compelled to re-assign his securities. In Glanvil's time, when the universal me-

---

[a] Stat. 4 & 5 W. & M. c. 16.

[b] *Pignoris appellatione eam proprie rem contineri dicimus, quae simul etiam traditur creditori. At eam, quae sine traditione nuda conventione tenetur, proprie hypothecae appellatione contineri dicimus. Inst. l. 4. t. 6. §. 7.*

thod of conveyance was by livery of feifin or corporal tradition of the lands, no gage or pledge of lands was good unlefs poffeffion was alfo delivered to the creditor; *"fi non fequatur ipfius va-* *" dii traditio, curia domini regis hujufmodi privatas conventiones tueri* *" non folet:"* for which the reafon given is, to prevent fubfequent and fraudulent pledges of the fame land; *" cum in tali cafu* *" poffit eadem res pluribus aliis creditoribus tum prius tum pofterius* *" invadiari*[c]. And the frauds which have arifen, fince the exchange of thefe public and notorious conveyances for more private and fecret bargains, have well evinced the wifdom of our antient law.

IV. A FOURTH fpecies of eftates, defeafible on condition fubfequent, are thofe held by *ftatute merchant*, and *ftatute ftaple*; which are very nearly related to the *vivum vadium* before-mentioned, or eftate held till the profits thereof fhall difcharge a debt liquidated or afcertained. For both the ftatute merchant and ftatute ftaple are fecurities for money; the one entered into purfuant to the ftatute 13 Edw. I. *de mercatoribus*, and thence called a ftatute merchant; the other purfuant to the ftatute 27 Edw. III. c. 9. before the mayor of the ftaple, that is to fay, the grand mart for the principal commodities or manufactures of the kingdom, formerly held by act of parliament in certain trading towns[d], and thence this fecurity is called a ftatute ftaple. They are both, I fay, fecurities for debts, originally permitted only among traders, for the benefit of commerce; whereby the lands of the debtor are conveyed to the creditor, till out of the rents and profits of them his debt may be fatisfied: and during fuch time as the creditor fo holds the lands, he is tenant by ftatute merchant or ftatute ftaple. There is alfo a fimilar fecurity, the recognizance in the nature of a ftatute ftaple, which extends the benefit of this mercantile tranfaction to all the king's fubjects in general, by virtue of the ftatute 23 Hen. VIII. c. 6.

V. ANOTHER fimilar conditional eftate, created by operation of law, for fecurity and fatisfaction of debts, is called an eftate

[c] *l.* 10. *c.* 8.   [d] See Book I. ch. 8.

by

by *elegit*. What an *elegit* is, and why so called, will be explained
in the third part of these commentaries. At present I need only
mention, that it is the name of a writ, founded on the statute[e]
of Westm. 2. by which, after a plaintiff has obtained judgment
for his debt at law, the sheriff gives him possession of one half
of the defendant's lands and tenements, to be held, occupied,
and enjoyed, until his debt and damages are fully paid : and,
during the time he so holds them, he is called tenant by *elegit*.
It is easy to observe, that this is also a mere conditional estate,
defeasible as soon as the debt is levied. But it is remarkable,
that the feodal restraints of alienating lands, and charging them
with the debts of the owner, were softened much earlier and
much more effectually for the benefit of trade and commerce, than
for any other consideration. Before the statute of *quia emptores*[f],
it is generally thought that the proprietor of lands was enabled
to alienate no more than a moiety of them : the statute therefore of Westm. 2. permits only so much of them to be affected
by the process of law, as a man was capable of alienating by his
own deed. But by the statute *de mercatoribus* (passed in the same
year[g]) the *whole* of a man's lands was liable to be pledged in a
statute merchant, for a debt contracted in trade ; though only *half*
of them was liable to be taken in execution for any other debt of
the owner.

I SHALL conclude what I had to remark of these estates,
by statute merchant, statute staple, and *elegit*, with the observa-
tion of sir Edward Coke[h]. "These tenants have uncertain interests
" in lands and tenements, and yet they have but chattels and no
" freeholds ;" (which makes them an exception to the general
rule) " because though they may hold an estate of inheritance,
" or for life, *ut liberum tenementum*, until their debt be paid ; yet
" it shall go to their executors : for *ut* is similitudinary ; and
" though, to recover their estates, they shall have the same remedy
" (by assise) as a tenant of the freehold shall have, yet it is but

[e] 13 Edw. I. c. 18.   [g] 13 Edw. I.
[f] 18 Edw. I.   [h] 1 Inst. 42, 43.

VOL. II.   W   " the

" the fimilitude of a freehold, and *nullum fimile eft idem.*" This
indeed only proves them to be chattel interefts, becaufe they go
to the executors, which is inconfiftent with the nature of a freehold : but it does not affign the reafon why thefe eftates, in contradiftinction to other uncertain interefts, fhall veft in the executors of the tenant and not the heir ; which is probably owing to
this : that, being a fecurity and remedy provided for perfonal
debts owing to the deceafed, to which debts the executor is intitled, the law has therefore thus directed their fucceffion ; as
judging it reafonable, from a principle of natural equity, that the
fecurity and remedy fhould be vefted in them, to whom the debts
if recovered would belong. And, upon the fame principle, if
lands be devifed to a man's executor, until out of their profits the
debts due from the teftator be difcharged, this intereft in the
lands fhall be a chattel intereft, and on the death of fuch executor fhall go to *his* executors[i] : becaufe they, being liable to
pay the original teftator's debts, fo far as his affets will extend,
are in reafon intitled to poffefs that fund, out of which he has
directed them to be paid.

[i] Co. Litt. 42.

CHAPTER THE ELEVENTH.

OF ESTATES IN POSSESSION, REMAINDER, AND REVERSION.

HITHERTO we have confidered eftates folely with regard to their duration, or the *quantity of intereft* which the
owners have therein. We are now to confider them in another
view; with regard to the *time of their enjoyment*, when the actual
pernancy of the profits (that is, the taking, perception, or receipt,
of the rents and other advantages arifing therefrom) begins. E-
ftates therefore, with refpect to this confideration, may either be
in *poffeffion*, or in *expectancy:* and of expectancies there are two
forts; one created by act of the parties, called a *remainder;* the
other by act of law, and called a *reverfion.*

I. OF eftates in *poffeffion*, (which are fometimes called eftates
executed, whereby a prefent intereft paffes to and refides in the
tenant, not depending on any fubfequent circumftance or contingency, as in the cafe of eftates *executory*) there is little or nothing
peculiar to be obferved. All the eftates we have hitherto fpoken
of are of this kind; for, in laying down general rules, we ufually
apply them to fuch eftates as are then actually in the tenant's
poffeffion. But the doctrine of eftates in expectancy contains
fome of the niceft and moft abftrufe learning in the Englifh law.
Thefe will therefore require a minute difcuffion, and demand
fome degree of attention.

II. AN

II. A n estate then in remainder may be defined to be, an estate limited to take effect and be enjoyed after another estate is determined. As if a man seised in fee-simple granteth lands to A for twenty years, and, after the determination of the said term, then to B and his heirs for ever : here A is tenant for years, remainder to B in fee. In the first place an estate for years is created or carved out of the fee, and given to A ; and the residue or remainder of it is given to B. But both these interests are in fact only one estate ; the present term of years and the remainder afterwards, when added together, being equal only to one estate in fee ᵃ. They are indeed different *parts*, but they constitute only one *whole* : they are carved out of one and the same inheritance : they are both created, and may both subsist, together ; the one in possession, the other in expectancy. So if land be granted to A for twenty years, and after the determination of the said term to B for life ; and, after the determination of B's estate for life, it be limited to C and his heirs for ever : this makes A tenant for years, with remainder to B for life, remainder over to C in fee. Now here the estate of inheritance undergoes a division into three portions : there is first A's estate for years carved out of it ; and after that B's estate for life ; and then the whole that remains is limited to C and his heirs. And here also the first estate, and both the remainders, for life and in fee, are one estate only ; being nothing but parts or portions of one entire inheritance : and if there were a hundred remainders, it would still be the same thing ; upon a principle grounded on mathematical truth, that all the parts are equal, and no more than equal, to the whole. And hence also it is easy to collect, that no remainder can be limited after the grant of an estate in fee-simple ᵇ: because a fee-simple is the highest and largest estate, that a subject is capable of enjoying ; and he that is tenant in fee hath in him the *whole* of the estate : a remainder therefore, which is only a portion, or residuary *part*, of the estate, cannot be reserved after the whole is disposed of. A particular estate, with all the remain-

ᵃ Co. Litt. 143.   ᵇ Plowd. 29.

ders

ders expectant thereon, is only one fee-fimple ; as 40 *l.* is part of
100 *l.* and 60 *l.* is the remainder of it : wherefore, after a fee-
fimple once vefted, there can no more be a remainder limited
thereon, than after the whole 100 *l.* is appropriated there can be
any refidue fubfifting.

THUS much being premifed, we fhall be the better enabled
to comprehend the rules that are laid down by law to be obferved
in the creation of remainders, and the reafons upon which thofe
rules are founded.

1. AND, firft, there muft neceffarily be fome particular eftate,
precedent to the eftate in remainder[c]. As, an eftate for years to
A, remainder to B for life ; or, an eftate for life to A, remainder to B in tail. This precedent eftate is called the *particular*
eftate, as being only a fmall part, or *particula*, of the inheritance ; the refidue or remainder of which is granted over to another. The neceffity of creating this preceding particular eftate,
in order to make a good remainder, arifes from this plain reafon ;
that *remainder* is a relative expreffion, and implies that fome part
of the thing is previoufly difpofed of : for, where the whole is
conveyed at once, there cannot poffibly exift a remainder ; but
the intereft granted, whatever it be, will be an eftate in poffeffion.

AN eftate created to commence at a diftant period of time,
without any intervening eftate, is therefore properly no remainder : it is the whole of the gift, and not a refiduary part. And
fuch future eftates can only be made of chattel interefts, which
were confidered in the light of mere contracts by the antient
law[d], to be executed either now or hereafter, as the contracting
parties fhould agree : but an eftate of freehold muft be created
to commence immediately. For it is an antient rule of the common law, that no eftate of freehold can be created to commence
in futuro ; but it ought to take effect prefently either in poffeffion
or remainder[e] : becaufe at common law no freehold in lands

[c] Co. Litt. 49. Plowd. 25.   [e] 5 Rep. 94.
[d] Raym. 151.

could

could pafs without livery of feifin; which muft operate either immediately, or not at all. It would therefore be contradictory, if an eftate, which is not to commence till hereafter, could be granted by a conveyance which imports an immediate poffeffion. Therefore, though a leafe to A for feven years, to commence from next Michaelmas, is good; yet a conveyance to B of lands, to hold to him and his heirs for ever from the end of three years next enfuing, is void. So that when it is intended to grant an eftate of freehold, whereof the enjoyment fhall be deferred till a future time, it is neceffary to create a previous particular eftate, which may fubfift till that period of time it completed; and for the grantor to deliver immediate poffeffion of the land to the tenant of this particular eftate, which is conftrued to be giving poffeffion to him in remainder, fince his eftate and that of the particular tenant are one and the fame eftate in law. As, where one leafes to A for three years, with remainder to B in fee, and makes livery of feifin to A; here by the livery the freehold is immediately created, and vefted in B, during the continuance of A's term of years. The whole eftate paffes at once from the grantor to the grantees, and the remainder-man is feifed of his remainder at the fame time that the termor is poffeffed of his term. The enjoyment of it muft indeed be deferred till hereafter; but it is to all intents and purpofes an eftate commencing *in praefenti*, though to be occupied and enjoyed *in futuro*.

A s no remainder can be created, without fuch a precedent particular eftate, therefore the particular eftate is faid to *fupport* the remainder. But a leafe at will is not held to be fuch a particular eftate, as will fupport a remainder over [f]. For an eftate at will is of a nature fo flender and precarious, that it is not looked upon as a portion of the inheritance; and a portion muft firft be taken out of it, in order to conftitute a remainder. Befides, if it be a freehold remainder, livery of feifin muft be given at the time of it's creation; and the entry of the grantor, to do this, determines the eftate at will in the very inftant in which it is

[f] 8 Rep. 75.

made [g].

made [g] : or, if it be a chattel interest, though perhaps it might operate as a *future contract*, if the tenant for years be a party to the deed of creation, yet it is void by way of *remainder :* for it is a feparate independent contract, diftinct from the precedent eftate at will ; and every remainder muft be part of one and the fame eftate, out of which the preceding particular eftate is taken [h]. And hence it is generally true, that if the particular eftate is void in it's creation, or by any means is defeated afterwards, the remainder fupported thereby fhall be defeated alfo [i]: as where the particular eftate is an eftate for the life of a perfon not *in effe* [k] ; or an eftate for life upon condition, on breach of which condition the grantor enters and avoids the eftate [l] ; in either of thefe cafes the remainder over is void.

2 A s e c o n d rule to be obferved is this ; that the remainder muft commence or pafs out of the grantor at the time of the creation of the particular eftate [m]. As, where there is an eftate to A for life, with remainder to B in fee : here B's remainder in fee paffes from the grantor at the fame time that feifin is delivered to A of his life eftate in poffeffion. And it is this, which induces the neceffity at common law of livery of feifin being made on the particular eftate, whenever a *freehold* remainder is created. For, if it be limited even on an eftate for years, it is neceffary that the leffee for years fhould have livery of feifin, in order to convey the freehold from and out of the grantor ; otherwife the remainder is void [n]. Not that the livery is neceffary to ftrengthen the eftate for years ; but, as livery of the land is requifite to convey the freehold, and yet cannot be given to him in remainder without infringing the poffeffion of the leffee for years, therefore the law allows fuch livery, made to the tenant of the particular eftate, to relate and enure to him in remainder, as both are but one eftate in law [o].

[g] Dyer. 18.

[h] Raym. 151.

[i] Co. Litt. 298.

[k] 2 Roll. Abr. 415.

[l] 1 Jon. 58.

[m] Litt. §. 671. Plowd. 25.

[n] Litt. §. 60.

[o] Co. Litt. 49.

3. A t h i r d

3. A THIRD rule refpecting remainders is this; that the remainder muft veft in the grantee during the continuance of the particular eftate, or *eo inftanti* that it determines [p]. As, if A be tenant for life, remainder to B in tail; here B's remainder is vefted in him, at the creation of the particular eftate to A for life: or, if A and B be tenants for their joint lives, remainder to the furvivor in fee; here, though during their joint lives the remainder is vefted in neither, yet on the death of either of them, the remainder vefts inftantly in the furvivor: wherefore both thefe are good remainders. But, if an eftate be limited to A for life, remainder to the eldeft fon of B in tail, and A dies before B hath any fon; here the remainder will be void, for it did not veft in any one during the continuance, nor at the determination, of the particular eftate: and, even fuppofing that B fhould afterwards have a fon, he fhall not take by this remainder; for, as it did not veft at or before the end of the particular eftate, it never can veft at all, but is gone for ever [q]. And this depends upon the principle before laid down, that the precedent particular eftate and the remainder are one eftate in law; they muft therefore fubfift and be *in effe* at one and the fame inftant of time, either during the continuance of the firft eftate or at the very inftant when that determines, fo that no other eftate can poffibly come between them. For there can be no intervening eftate between the particular eftate, and the remainder fupported thereby [r]: the thing fupported muft fall to the ground, if once it's fupport be fevered from it.

IT is upon thefe rules, but principally the laft; that the doctrine of *contingent* remainders depends. For remainders are either *vefted* or *contingent*. *Vefted* remainders (or remainders *executed*, whereby a prefent intereft paffes to the party, though to be enjoyed *in futuro*) are where the eftate is invariably fixed, to remain to a determinate perfon, after the particular eftate is fpent. As

[p] Plowd. 25. 1 Rep. 66. [r] 3 Rep. 21.
[q] 1 Rep. 138.

if

if A be tenant for twenty years, remainder to B in fee; here B's is a vefted remainder, which nothing can defeat, or fet afide.

CONTINGENT or *executory* remainders (whereby no prefent intereft paffes) are where the eftate in remainder is limited to take effect, either to a dubious and uncertain *perfon*, or upon a dubious and uncertain *event*; fo that the particular eftate may chance to be determined, and the remainder never take effect[s].

FIRST, they may be limited to a dubious and uncertain *perfon*. As if A be tenant for life, with remainder to B's eldeft fon (then unborn) in tail; this is a contingent remainder, for it is uncertain whether B will have a fon or no: but the inftant that a fon is born, the remainder is no longer contingent, but vefted. Though, if A had died before the contingency happened, that is, before B's fon was born, the remainder would have been abfo-lutely gone; for the particular eftate was determined before the remainder could veft. Nay, by the ftrict rule of law, if A were tenant for life, remainder to his own eldeft fon in tail, and A died without iffue born, but leaving his wife *enfeint* or big with child, and after his death a pofthumous fon was born, this fon could not take the land, by virtue of this remainder; for the particular eftate determined before there was any perfon *in effe*, in whom the remainder could veft[t]. But, to remedy this hardfhip, it is enacted by ftatute 10 & 11 W. III. c. 16. that pofthumous child-ren fhall be capable of taking in remainder, in the fame manner as if they had been born in their father's lifetime: that is, the remainder is allowed to veft in them, while yet in their mother's womb[u].

THIS fpecies of contingent remainders, to a perfon not in being, muft however be limited to fome one, that may by com-mon poffibility, or *potentia propinqua*, be *in effe* at or before the particular eftate determines[w]. As if an eftate be made to A for

---

[s] 3 Rep. 20.
[t] Salk. 228. 4 Mod. 282.

[u] See Vol. I. pag 126.
[w] 2 Rep. 51.

life, remainder to the heirs of B : now, if A dies before B, the remainder is at an end ; for during B's life he has no heir, *nema est haeres viventis :* but if B dies first, the remainder then immediately vests in his heir, who will be entitled to the land on the death of A. This is a good contingent remainder, for the possibility of B's dying before A is *potentia propinqua,* and therefore allowed in law.[x]. But a remainder to the right heirs of B (if there be no such person as B *in esse*) is void[y] For here there must two contingencies happen ; first, that such a person as B shall be born; and, secondly, that he shall also die during the continuance of the particular estate ; which make it *potentia remotissima,* a most improbable possibility. A remainder to a man's eldest son, who hath none, (we have seen) is good ; for by common possibility he may have one ; but if it be limited in particular to his son John, or Richard, it is bad, if he have no son of that name ; for it is too remote a possibility that he should not only have a son, but a son of a particular name[z]. A limitation of a remainder to a bastard before it is born, is not good[a] : for though the law allows the possibility of having bastards, it presumes it to be a very remote and improbable contingency. Thus may a remainder be contingent, on account of the uncertainty of the *person* who is to take it.

A REMAINDER may also be contingent, where the person to whom it is limited is fixed and certain, but the *event* upon which it is to take effect is vague and uncertain. As, where land is given to A for life, and in case B survives him, then with remainder to B in fee : here B is a certain person, but the remainder to him is a contingent remainder, depending upon a dubious event, the uncertainty of his surviving A. During the joint lives of A and B it is contingent ; and if B dies first, it never can vest in his heirs, but is for ever gone ; but if A dies first, the remainder to B becomes vested.

---

[x] Co. Litt. 378.   [z] 5 Rep. 51.
[y] Hob. 33.   [a] Cro. Eliz. 509.

CONTINGENT

CONTINGENT remainders of either kind, if they amount to a freehold, cannot be limited on an eftate for years, or any other particular eftate, lefs than a freehold. Thus if land be granted to A for ten years, with remainder in fee to the right heirs of B, this remainder is void [b] : but if granted to A for life, with a like remainder, it is good. For, unlefs the freehold paffes out of the grantor at the time when the remainder is created, fuch freehold remainder is void : it cannot pafs out of him, without vefting fomewhere; and in the cafe of a contingent remainder it muft veft in the particular tenant, elfe it can veft no where : unlefs therefore the eftate of fuch particular tenant be of a freehold nature, the freehold cannot veft in him, and confequently the remainder is void.

CONTINGENT remainders may be *defeated*, by deftroying or determining the particular eftate upon which they depend, before the contingency happens whereby they become vefted [c]. Therefore when there is tenant for life, with divers remainders in contingency, he may, not only by his death, but by alienation, furrender, or other methods, deftroy and determine his own life-eftate, before any of thofe remainders veft; the confequence of which is that he utterly defeats them all. As, if there be tenant for life, with remainder to his eldeft fon unborn in tail, and the tenant for life, before any fon is born, furrenders his life-eftate, he by that means defeats the remainder in tail to his fon : for his fon not being *in effe*, when the particular eftate determined, the remainder could not then veft; and, as it could not veft then, by the rules before laid down, it never can veft at all. In thefe cafes therefore it is neceffary to have truftees appointed to preferve the contingent remainders; in whom there is vefted an eftate in remainder for the life of the tenant for life, to commence when his determines. If therefore his eftate for life determines otherwife than by his death, their eftate, for the refidue of his natural life, will then take effect, and become a particu-

[b] 1 Rep. 130.   [c] *Ibid.* 66. 135.

lar

lar eftate in poffeffion, fufficient to fupport the remainders depending in contingency. This method is faid to have been invented by fir Orlando Bridgman, fir Geoffery Palmer, and other eminent council, who betook themfelves to conveyancing during the time of the civil wars; in order thereby to fecure in family fettlements a provifion for the future children of an intended marriage, who before were ufually left at the mercy of the particular tenant for life^d : and when, after the reftoration, thofe gentlemen came to fill the firft offices of the law, they fupported this invention within reafonable and proper bounds, and introduced it into general ufe.

Thus the ftudent will obferve how much nicety is required in creating and fecuring a remainder; and I truft he will in fome meafure fee the general reafons, upon which this nicety is founded. It were endlefs to attempt to enter upon the particular fubtilties and refinements, into which this doctrine, by the variety of cafes which have occurred in the courfe of many centuries, has been fpun out and fubdivided : neither are they confonant to the defign of thefe elementary difquifitions. I muft not however omit, that in devifes by laft will and teftament, (which, being often drawn up when the party is *inops concilii*, are always more favoured in conftruction than formal deeds, which are prefumed to be made with great caution, fore-thought, and advice) in thefe devifes, I fay, remainders may be created in fome meafure contrary to the rules before laid down : though our lawyers will not allow fuch difpofitions to be ftrictly remainders; but call them by another name, that of *executory devifes*, or devifes hereafter to be executed.

An executory devife of lands is fuch a difpofition of them by will, that thereby no eftate vefts at the death of the devifor, but only on fome future contingency. It differs from a remainder in three very material points : 1. That it needs not any particular

---

^d See Moor. 486. 2 Roll. Abr. 797. pl. 12. 2 Sid. 159. 2 Chan. Rep. 170.

eftate

eftate to fupport it. 2. That by it a fee-fimple or other lefs e-
ftate, may be limited after a fee-fimple. 3. That by this means
a remainder may be limited of a chattel intereft, after a particular eftate for life created in the fame.

1. THE firft cafe happens when a man devifes a future eftate,
to arife upon a contingency; and, till that contingency happens,
does not difpofe of the fee-fimple, but leaves it to defcend to his
heir at law. As if one devifes land to a feme-fole and her heirs,
upon her day of marriage: here is in effect a contingent remainder without any particular eftate to fupport it; a freehold commencing *in futuro*. This limitation, though it would be void
in a deed, yet is good in a will, by way of executory devife[e].
For, fince by a devife a freehold may pafs without corporal tradition or livery of feifin, (as it muft do, if it paffes at all) therefore it may commence *in futuro*; becaufe the principal reafon
why it cannot commence *in futuro* in other cafes, is the neceffity
of actual feifin, which always operates *in praefenti*. And, fince
it may thus commence *in futuro*, there is no need of a particular
eftate to fupport it; the only ufe of which is to make the remainder, by it's unity with the particular eftate, a prefent intereft.
And hence alfo it follows, that fuch an executory devife, not being a prefent intereft, cannot be barred by a recovery, fuffered
before it commences[f].

2. BY executory devife a fee, or other lefs eftate, may be limited
after a fee. And this happens where a devifor devifes his whole
eftate in fee, but limits a remainder thereon to commence on a
future contingency. As if a man devifes land to A and his heirs;
but, if he dies before the age of twenty one, then to B and his
heirs: this remainder, though void in a deed, is good by way of
executory devife[g]. But, in both thefe fpecies of executory devifes,
the contingencies ought to be fuch as may happen within a reafonable time; as within one or more life or lives in being, or within

[e] 1 Sid. 153.   [g] 2 Mod. 289.
[f] Cro. Jac. 593.

a moderate

a moderate term of years; for courts of juftice will not indulge even wills, fo as to create a perpetuity, which the law abhors[h]: becaufe by perpetuities, (or the fettlement of an intereft, which fhall go in the fucceffion prefcribed, without any power of alienation[i]) eftates are made incapable of anfwering thofe ends, of focial commerce, and providing for the fudden contingencies of private life, for which property was at firft eftablifhed. The utmoft length that has been hitherto allowed, for the contingency of an executory devife of either kind to happen in, is that of a life or lives in being, and one and twenty years afterwards. As when lands are devifed to fuch unborn fon of a feme-covert, as fhall firft attain the age of twenty one, and his heirs; the utmoft length of time that can happen before the eftate can veft, is the life of the mother and the fubfequent infancy of her fon: and this hath been decreed to be a good executory devife[k].

3. BY executory devife a term of years may be given to one man for his life, and afterwards limited over in remainder to another, which could not be done by deed: for by law the firft grant of it, to a man for life, was a total difpofition of the whole term; a life eftate being efteemed of a higher and larger nature than any term of years[l]. And, at firft, the courts were tender, even in the cafe of a will, of reftraining the devifee for life from aliening the term; but only held, that in cafe he died without exerting that act of ownerfhip, the remainder over fhould then take place[m]: for the reftraint of the power of alienation, efpecially in very long terms, was introducing a fpecies of perpetuity. But, foon afterwards, it was held[n], that the devifee for life hath no power of aliening the term, fo as to bar the remainder-man: yet in order to prevent the danger of perpetuities, it was fettled[o], that, though fuch remainders may be limited to as many perfons fucceffively as the devifor thinks proper, yet they muft all be *in effe*

[h] 12 Mod. 287.　1 Vern. 164.
[i] Salk. 229.
[k] Forr. 232.
[l] 8 Rep. 95.

[m] Bro. *tit. chatteles.* 23.　Dyer 74.
[n] Dyer. 358.　8 Rep. 96.
[o] 1 Sid. 451.

during

during the life of the firſt deviſee; for then all the candles are lighted and are confuming together, and the ultimate remainder is in reality only to that remainder-man who happens to ſurvive the reſt: or, that ſuch remainder may be limited to take effect upon ſuch contingency only, as muſt happen (if at all) during the life of the firſt deviſee [P].

THUS much for ſuch eſtates in expectancy, as are created by the expreſs words of the parties themſelves; the moſt intricate title in the law. There is yet another ſpecies, which is created by the act and operation of the law itſelf, and this is called a reverſion.

III. AN eſtate in *reverſion* is the reſidue of an eſtate left in the grantor, to commence in poſſeſſion after the determination of ſome particular eſtate granted out by him [q]. Sir Edward Coke [r] deſcribes a reverſion to be the returning of land to the grantor or his heirs after the grant is over. As, if there be a gift in tail, the reverſion of the fee is, without any ſpecial reſervation, veſted in the donor by act of law: and ſo alſo the reverſion, after an eſtate for life, years, or at will, continues in the leſſor. For the fee-ſimple of all lands muſt abide ſomewhere; and if he, who was before poſſeſſed of the whole, carves out of it any ſmaller eſtate, and grants it away, whatever is not ſo granted remains in him. A reverſion is therefore never created by deed or writing, but ariſes from conſtruction of law; a remainder can never be limited, unleſs by either deed or deviſe. But both are equally transferable, when actually veſted, being both eſtates *in praeſenti*, though taking effect *in futuro*.

THE doctrine of reverſions is plainly derived from the feodal conſtitution. For, when a feud was granted to a man for life, or to him and his iſſue male, rendering either rent, or other ſervices; then, on his death or the failure of iſſue male, the feud was de-

[P] Skinn. 341. 3 P. W[ms]. 258.
[q] Co. Litt. 22.
[r] 1 Inſt. 142.

terminied

termined and refulted back to the lord or proprietor, to be again difpofed of at his pleafure. And hence the ufual *incidents* to reverfions are faid to be *fealty* and *rent*. When no rent is referved on the particular eftate, fealty however refults of courfe, as an incident quite infeparable, and may be demanded as a badge of tenure, or acknowlegement of fuperiority ; being frequently the only evidence that the lands are holden at all. Where rent is referved, it is alfo incident, though not infeparably fo, to the reverfion[s]. The rent may be granted away, referving the reverfion ; and the reverfion may be granted away, referving the rent ; by *fpecial* words : but by a *general* grant of the reverfion, the rent will pafs with it, as incident thereunto ; though by the grant of the rent generally, the reverfion will not pafs. The incident paffes by the grant of the principal, but not *e converfo :* for the maxim of law is, " *accefforium non ducit, fed fequitur, fuum prin-* " *cipale*[t]."

THESE *incidental* rights of the reverfioner, and the refpective modes of defcent, in which remainders very frequently differ from reverfions, have occafioned the law to be careful in diftinguifhing the one from the other, however inaccurately the parties themfelves may defcribe them. For if one, feifed of a paternal eftate in fee, makes a leafe for life, with remainder to himfelf and his heirs, this is properly a mere reverfion[u], to which rent and fealty fhall be incident ; and which fhall only defcend to the heirs of his father's blood, and not to his heirs general, as a remainder limited to him by a third perfon would have done[w] : for it is the old eftate, which was originally in him, and never yet was out of him. And fo likewife, if a man grants a leafe for life to A, referving rent, with reverfion to B and his heirs, B hath a remainder defcendible to his heirs general, and not a reverfion to which the rent is incident ; but the grantor fhall be intitled to the rent, during the continuance of A's eftate[x].

[s] Co. Litt. 143.
[t] *Ibid.* 151, 152.
[u] Cro. Eliz. 321.

[w] 3 Lev. 407.
[x] 1 And. 23.

IN

IN order to affift fuch perfons as have any eftate in remainder, reverfion, or expectancy, after the death of others, againft fraudulent concealments of their deaths, it is enacted by the ftatute 6 Ann. c. 18. that all perfons on whofe lives any lands or tenements are holden, fhall (upon application to the court of chancery and order made thereupon) once in every year, if required, be produced to the court, or it's commiffioners; or, upon neglect or refufal, they fhall be taken to be actually dead, and the perfon entitled to fuch expectant eftate may enter upon and hold the lands and tenements, till the party fhall appear to be living.

BEFORE we conclude the doctrine of remainders and reverfions, it may be proper to obferve, that whenever a greater eftate and a lefs coincide and meet in one and the fame perfon, without any intermediate eftate ʸ, the lefs is immediately annihilated; or, in the law phrafe, is faid to be *merged*, that is, funk or drowned, in the greater. Thus, if there be tenant for years, and the reverfion in fee-fimple defcends to or is purchafed by him, the term of years is merged in the inheritance, and fhall never exift any more. But they muft come to one and the fame perfon in one and the fame right; elfe, if the freehold be in his own right, and he has a term in right of another *(en auter droit)* there is no merger. Therefore, if tenant for years dies, and makes him who hath the reverfion in fee his executor, whereby the term of years vefts alfo in him, the term fhall not merge; for he hath the fee in his own right, and the term of years in the right of the teftator, and fubject to his debts and legacies. So alfo, if he who hath the reverfion in fee marries the tenant for years, there is no merger; for he hath the inheritance in his own right, the leafe in the right of his wife ᶻ. An eftate-tail is an exception to this rule: for a man may have in his own right both an eftate-tail and a reverfion in fee; and the eftate-tail, though a lefs eftate, fhall not merge in the fee ᵃ. For eftates-tail are protected and preferved from

---

ʸ 3 Lev. 437.   ᵃ 2 Rep. 61. 8 Rep 74.
ᶻ Plow. 418. Cro. Jac. 275. Co. Litt. 338.

merger by the operation and conſtruction, though not by the expreſs words, of the ſtatute *de donis :* which operation and conſtruction have probably ariſen upon this conſideration ; that, in
the common caſes of *merger* of eſtates for life or years by uniting
with the inheritance, the particular tenant hath the ſole intereſt
in them, and hath full power at any time to defeat, deſtroy, or
ſurrender them to him that hath the reverſion ; therefore, when
ſuch an eſtate unites with the reverſion in fee, the law conſiders
it in the light of a virtual ſurrender of the inferior eſtate [b]. But,
in an eſtate-tail, the caſe is otherwiſe : the tenant for a long time
had no power at all over it, ſo as to bar or to deſtroy it ; and
now can only do it by certain ſpecial modes, by a fine, a recovery, and the like [c] : it would therefore have been ſtrangely improvident, to have permitted the tenant in tail, by purchaſing
the reverſion in fee, to merge his particular eſtate, and defeat the
inheritance of his iſſue : and hence it has become a maxim, that
a tenancy in tail, which cannot be ſurrendered, cannot alſo be
merged in the fee.

[b] Cro. Eliz. 302.   [c] See pag. 116.

CHAPTER THE TWELFTH.

OF ESTATES IN SEVERALTY, JOINT-TENANCY, COPARCENARY, AND COMMON.

WE come now to treat of estates, with respect to the number and connexions of their owners, the tenants who occupy and hold them. And, considered in this view, estates of any quantity or length of duration, and whether they be in actual possession or expectancy, may be held in four different ways; in severalty, in joint-tenancy, in coparcenary, and in common.

I. HE that holds lands or tenements in *severalty*, or is sole tenant thereof, is he that holds them in his own right only, without any other person being joined or connected with him in point of interest, during his estate therein. This is the most common and usual way of holding an estate; and therefore we may make the same observations here, that we did upon estates in possession, as contradistinguished from those in expectancy, in the preceding chapter: that there is little or nothing peculiar to be remarked concerning it, since all estates are supposed to be of this sort, unless where they are expressly declared to be otherwise; and that, in laying down general rules and doctrines, we usually apply them to such estates as are held in severalty. I shall therefore proceed to consider the other three species of estates, in which there are always a plurality of tenants.

Y 2 II. AN

II. An eftate in *joint-tenancy* is where lands or tenements are granted to two or more perfons, to hold in fee-fimple, fee-tail, for life, for years, or at will. In confequence of fuch grants the eftate is called an eftate in joint-tenancy[a], and fometimes an eftate in *jointure*, which word as well as the other fignifies a union or conjunction of intereft ; though in common fpeech the term, *jointure*, is now ufually confined to that joint eftate, which by virtue of the ftatute 27 Hen.VIII. c. 10. is frequently vefted in the hufband and wife before marriage, as a full fatisfaction and bar of the woman's dower[b].

In unfolding this title, and the two remaining ones in the prefent chapter, we will firft enquire, how thefe eftates may be *created*; next, their *properties* and refpective *incidents*; and laftly, how they may be *fevered* or *deftroyed*.

1. The *creation* of an eftate in joint-tenancy depends on the wording of the deed or devife, by which the tenants claim title ; for this eftate can only arife by purchafe or grant, that is, by the act of the parties, and never by the mere act of law. Now, if an eftate be given to a plurality of perfons, without adding any reftrictive, exclufive, or explanatory words, as if an eftate be granted to A and B and their heirs, this makes them immediately joint-tenants in fee of the lands. For the law interprets the grant fo as to make all parts of it take effect, which can only be done by creating an equal eftate in them both. As therefore the grantor has thus united their names, the law gives them a thorough union in all other refpects. For,

2. The *properties* of a joint eftate are derived from it's unity, which is fourfold ; the unity of *intereft*, the unity of *title*, the unity of *time*, and the unity of *poffeffion* : or, in other words, joint-tenants have one and the fame intereft, accruing by one and the fame conveyance, commencing at one and the fame time, and held by one and the fame undivided poffeffion.

[a] Litt. §. 277.   [b] See pag. 137.   First,

FIRST, they muft have one and the fame *intereft*. One joint-tenant cannot be entitled to one period of duration or quantity of interest in lands, and the other to a different : one cannot be tenant for life, and the other for years : one cannot be tenant in fee, and the other in tail [c]. But, if land be limited to A and B for their lives, this makes them joint-tenants of the freehold ; if to A and B and their heirs, it makes them joint-tenants of the inheritance [d]. If land be granted to A and B for their lives and to the heirs of A ; here A and B are joint-tenants of the freehold during their refpective lives, and A has the remainder of the fee in feveralty : or, if land be given to A and B, and the heirs of the body of A ; here both have a joint eftate for life, and A hath a feveral remainder in tail [e]. Secondly, joint-tenants muft alfo have an unity of *title :* their eftate muft be created by one and the fame act, whether legal or illegal ; as by one and the fame grant, or by one and the fame diffeifin [f]. Joint-tenancy cannot arife by defcent or act of law ; but merely by purchafe, or ac-quifition by the act of the party : and, unlefs that act be one and the fame, the two tenants would have different titles ; and if they had different titles, one might prove good, and the other bad, which would abfolutely deftroy the jointure. Thirdly, there muft alfo be an unity of *time :* their eftates muft be vefted at one and the fame period, as well as by one and the fame title. As in cafe of a prefent eftate made to A and B ; or a remainder in fee to A and B after a particular eftate ; in either cafe A and B are joint tenants of this prefent eftate, or this vefted remainder. But if, after a leafe for life, the remainder be limited to the heirs of A and B ; and during the continuance of the particular eftate A dies, which vefts the remainder of one moiety in his heir ; and then B dies, whereby the other moiety becomes vefted in the heir of B : now A's heir and B's heir are not joint-tenants of this remainder, but tenants in common ; for one moiety vefted at one time, and the other moiety vefted at another [g]. Yet, where

[c] Co. Litt. 188.
[d] Litt. §. 277.
[e] *Ibid.* §. 285.

[f] *Ibid.* §. 278.
[g] Co. Litt. 188.

a feoffment

a feoffment was made to the ufe of a man, and fuch wife as he fhould afterwards marry, for term of their lives, and he afterwards married; in this cafe it feems to have been held that the hufband and wife had a joint eftate, though vefted at different times [h] : becaufe the *ufe* of the wife's eftate was in abeyance and dormant till the intermarriage; and, being then awakened, had relation back, and took effect from the original time of creation. Laftly, in joint-tenancy, there muft be an unity of *poffeffion*. Joint-tenants are faid to be feifed *per my et per tout*, by the *half* or *moiety*, and by *all*; that is, they each of them have the entire poffeffion, as well of every *parcel* as of the *whole* [i]. They have not, one of them a feifin of one half or moiety, and the other of the other moiety; neither can one be exclufively feifed of one acre, and his companion of another; but each has an undivided moiety of the whole, and not the whole of an undivided moiety [k].

UPON thefe principles, of a thorough and intimate union of intereft and poffeffion, depend many other confequences and incidents to the joint-tenant's eftate. If two joint-tenants let a verbal leafe of their land, referving rent to be paid to one of them, it fhall enure to both, in refpect of the joint reverfion [l]. If their leffee furrenders his leafe to one of them, it fhall alfo enure to both, becaufe of the privity, or relation of their eftate [m]. On the fame reafon, livery of feifin, made to one joint-tenant, fhall enure to both of them [n]: and the entry, or re-entry, of one joint-tenant is as effectual in law as if it were the act of both [o]. In all actions alfo relating to their joint eftate, one joint-tenant cannot fue or be fued without joining the other [p]. But if two or more joint-tenants be feifed of an advowfon, and they prefent different clerks, the bifhop may refufe to admit either; becaufe neither joint-tenant hath a feveral right of patronage, but each is feifed of the

[h] Dyer. 340. 1 Rep. 101.
[i] Litt. §. 288. 5 Rep. 10.
[k] *Quilibet totum tenet et nihil tenet; fcilicet, iotum in communi, et nihil feparatim per fe.* Bract. *l.* 5. *tr.* 5. *c.* 26.

[l] Co. Litt. 214.
[m] *Ibid.* 192.
[n] *Ibid.* 49.
[o] *Ibid.* 319. 364.
[p] *Ibid.* 195.

whole :

whole : and, if they do not both agree within fix months, the right of prefentation fhall lapfe. But the ordinary may, if he pleafes, admit a clerk prefented by either, for the good of the church, that divine fervice may be regularly performed ; which is no more than he otherwife would be entitled to do, in cafe their difagreement continued, fo as to incur a lapfe : and, if the clerk of one joint-tenant be fo admitted, this fhall keep up the title in both of them ; in refpect of the privity and union of their eftate[q]. Upon the fame ground it is held, that one joint-tenant cannot have an action againft another for trefpafs, in refpect of his land[r]; for each has an equal right to enter on any part of it. But one joint-tenant is not capable by himfelf to do any act, which may tend to defeat or injure the eftate of the other ; as to let leafes, or to grant copyholds[s] : and, if any wafte be done, which tends to the deftruction of the inheritance, one joint-tenant may have an action of wafte againft the other, by conftruction of the ftatute Weftm. 2. c. 22[t]. So too, though at common law no action of account lay for one joint-tenant againft another, unlefs he had conftituted him his bailiff or receiver[u], yet now by the ftatute 4 Ann. c. 16. joint-tenants may have actions of account againft each other, for receiving more than their due fhare of the profits of the tenements held in joint-tenancy.

FROM the fame principle alfo arifes the remaining grand incident of joint eftates ; *viz.* the doctrine of *furvivorfhip :* by which, when two or more perfons are feifed of a joint eftate of inheritance, for their own lives, or *pur auter vie,* or are jointly poffeffed of any chattel intereft, the entire tenancy upon the deceafe of any of them remains to the furvivors, and at length to the laft furvivor ; and he fhall be entitled to the whole eftate, whatever it be, whether an inheritance or a common freehold only, or even a lefs eftate[w]. This is the natural and regular confequence of the union and entirety of their intereft. The intereft of two joint-

[q] Co. Litt. 185.
[r] 3 Leon. 262.
[s] 1 Leon. 234.

[t] 2 Inft. 403.
[u] Co. Litt. 200.
[w] Litt. §. 280, 281.

tenants is not only equal or fimilar, but alfo is one and the fame. One has not originally a diftinct moiety from the other; but, if by any fubfequent act (as by alienation or forfeiture of either) the intereft becomes feparate and diftinct, the joint-tenancy inftantly ceafes. But, while it continues, each of two joint-tenants has a concurrent intereft in the whole; and therefore, on the death of his companion, the fole intereft in the whole remains to the furvivor. For the intereft, which the furvivor originally had, is clearly not devefted by the death of his companion; and no other perfon can now claim to have a *joint* eftate with him, for no one can now have an intereft in the whole, accruing by the fame title, and taking effect at the fame time with his own; neither can any one claim a *feparate* intereft in any part of the tenements; for that would be to deprive the furvivor of the right which he has in all, and every part. As therefore the furvivor's original intereft in the whole ftill remains; and as no one can now be admitted, either jointly or feverally, to any fhare with him therein; it follows, that his own intereft muft now be entire and feveral, and that he fhall alone be entitled to the whole eftate (whatever it be) that was created by the original grant.

THIS right of furvivorfhip is called by our antient authors[x] the *jus accrefcendi*, becaufe the right, upon the death of one joint-tenant, accumulates and increafes to the furvivors; or, as they themfelves exprefs it, "*pars illa communis accrefcit fuperftitibus*, " *de perfona in perfonam, ufque ad ultimum fuperftitem.*" And this *jus accrefcendi* ought to be mutual; which I apprehend to be the reafon why neither the king[y], nor any corporation[z], can be a joint-tenant with a private perfon. For here is no mutuality: the private perfon has not even the remoteft chance of being feifed of the entirety, by benefit of furvivorfhip, for the king and the corporation can never die.

---

[x] Bracton, *l.* 4. *tr.* 3. *c.* 9. §. 3. Fleta.   [y] Co. Litt. 190. Finch L. 83.
l. 3. *c.* 4.   [z] 2 Lev. 12.

3. WE

3. WE are, laftly, to enquire, how an eftate in joint-tenancy may be *fevered* and *deftroyed*. And this may be done by deftroying any of it's conftituent unities. 1. That of *time*, which refpects only the original commencement of the joint eftate, cannot indeed (being now paft) by affected by any fubfequent tranfactions. But, 2. the joint-tenants' eftate may be deftroyed, without any alienation, by merely difuniting their *poffeffion*. For joint-tenants being feifed *per my et per tout*, every thing that tends to narrow that intereft, fo that they fhall not be feifed throughout the whole, and throughout every part, is a feverance or deftruction of the jointure. And therefore, if two joint-tenants agree to part their lands, and hold them in feveralty, they are no longer joint-tenants ; for they have now no joint intereft in the whole, but only a feveral intereft refpectively in the feveral parts. And, for that reafon alfo, the right of furvivorfhip is by fuch feparation deftroyed [a]. By common law all the joint-tenants might agree to make partition of the lands, but one of them could not compel the others fo to do [b] : for, this being an eftate originally created by the act and agreement of the parties, the law would not permit any one or more of them to deftroy the united poffeffion without a fimilar univerfal confent. But now by the ftatutes 31 Hen. VIII. c. 1. and 32 Hen. VIII. c. 32. joint-tenants, either of inheritances or other lefs eftates, are compellable by writ of partition to divide their lands. 3. The jointure may be deftroyed, by deftroying the unity of *title*. As if one joint-tenant alienes and conveys his eftate to a third perfon : here the joint-tenancy is fevered, and turned into tenancy in common [d]; for the grantee and the remaining joint-tenant hold by different titles, (one derived from the original, the other from the fubfequent, grantor) though, till partition made, the unity of poffeffion conti-

---

[a] Co. Litt. 188. 193.
[b] Litt. §. 290.
[c] Thus, by the civil law, *nemo invitus compellitur ad communionem. (Ff.* 12. 6. 26. §. 4.) And again : *fi non omnes qui rem*

communem habent, fed certi ex his, dividere defiderant ; hoc judicium inter eos accipi poteft. (Ff. 10. 3. 8.)
[d] Litt. §. 292.

nues.

nues. But a devife of one's fhare by will is no feverance of the
jointure : for no teftament takes effect till after the death of the
teftator, and by fuch death the right of the furvivor (which accrued at the original creation of the eftate, and has therefore a
priority to the other [e]) is already vefted [f]. 4. It may alfo be deftroyed, by deftroying the unity of *intereft*. And therefore, if
there be two joint-tenants for life, and the inheritance is purchafed by or defcends upon either, it is a feverance of the jointure [g]: though, if an eftate is originally limited to two for life, and
after to the heirs of one of them, the freehold fhall remain in jointure, without merging in the inheritance; becaufe, being created
by one and the fame conveyance, they are not feparate eftates,
(which is requifite in order to a merger) but branches of one intire eftate [h]. In like manner, if a joint-tenant in fee makes a
leafe for life of his fhare, this defeats the jointure [i]; for it deftroys the unity both of title and of intereft. And, whenever or
by whatever means the jointure ceafes or is fevered, the right of
furvivorfhip or *jus accrefcendi* the fame inftant ceafes with it [k]. Yet,
if one of three joint-tenants alienes his fhare, the two remaining
tenants ftill hold their parts by joint-tenancy and furvivorfhip [l]:
and, if one of three joint-tenants releafes his fhare to one of his
companions, though the joint-tenancy is deftroyed with regard
to that part, yet the two remaining parts are ftill held in jointure [m]; for they ftill preferve their original conftituent unities.
But when, by any act or event, different interefts are created in
the feveral parts of the eftate, or they are held by different titles,
or if merely the poffeffion is feparated; fo that the tenants have
no longer thefe four indifpenfable properties, a famenefs of intereft, an undivided poffeffion, a title vefting at one and the fame
time, and by one and the fame act or grant; the jointure is inftantly diffolved.

---

[e] *Jus accrefcendi praefertur ultimae voluntati.*
Co. Litt. 185.
[f] Litt. §. 287.
[g] Cro. Eliz. 470.
[h] 2 Rep. 60. Co. Litt. 182.

[i] Litt. §. 302, 303.
[k] *Nihil de re accrefcit ei, qui nihil in re
quando jus accrefceret habet.* Co. Litt. 188.
[l] Litt. §. 294.
[m] *Ibid.* §. 304.

I N

IN general it is advantageous for the joint-tenants to diffolve the jointure; fince thereby the right of furvivorfhip is taken away, and each may tranfmit his own part to his own heirs. Sometimes however it is difadvantageous to diffolve the joint eftate : as if there be joint-tenants for life, and they make partition, this dif-folves the jointure; and, though before they each of them had an eftate in the whole for their own lives and the life of their companion, now they have an eftate in a moiety only for their own lives merely; and, on the death of either, the reverfioner fhall enter on his moiety[n]. And therefore, if there be two joint-tenants for life, and one grants away his part for the life of his companion, it is a forfeiture[o] : for, in the firft place, by the fe-verance of the jointure he has given himfelf in his own moiety only an eftate for his own life; and then he grants the fame land for the life of another : which grant, by a tenant for his own life merely, is a forfeiture of his eftate[p]; for it is creating an eftate which may by poffibility laft longer than that which he is legally entitled to.

III. AN eftate held in *coparcenary* is where lands of inherit-ance defcend from the anceftor to two or more perfons. It *arifes* either by common law, or particular cuftom. By common law : as where a perfon feifed in fee-fimple or in fee-tail dies, and his next heirs are two or more females, his daughters, fifters, aunts, coufins, or their reprefentatives; in this cafe they fhall all in-herit, as will be more fully fhewn, when we treat of defcents hereafter : and thefe co-heirs are then called *coparceners*; or, for brevity, *parceners* only[q]. Parceners by particular cuftom are where lands defcend, as in gavelkind, to all the males in equal degree, as fons, brothers, uncles, &c[r]. And, in either of thefe cafes, all the parceners put together make but one heir; and have but one eftate among them[s].

---

[n] 1 Jones. 55.
[o] 4 Leon. 237.
[p] Co. Litt. 252.

[q] Litt. §. 241, 242.
[r] *Ibid.* §. 265.
[s] Co. Litt. 163.

THE *properties* of parceners are in fome refpects like thofe of joint-tenants; they having the fame unities of *intereſt, title,* and *poſſeſſion.* They may fue and be fued jointly for matters relating to their own lands[t]: and the entry of one of them fhall in fome cafes enure as the entry of them all[u]. They cannot have an action of trefpafs againſt each other : but herein they differ from joint-tenants, that they are alfo excluded from maintaining an action of waſte[w]; for coparceners could at all times put a ſtop to any waſte by a writ of partition, but till the ſtatute of Henry the eighth joint-tenants had no fuch power. Parceners alfo differ materially from joint-tenants in four other points : 1. They always claim by defcent, whereas joint-tenants always claim by purchafe. Therefore if two fiſters purchafe lands, to hold to them and their heirs, they are not parceners, but joint-tenants[x]: and hence it likewife follows, that no lands can be held in coparcenary, but eſtates of inheritance, which are of a defcendible nature ; whereas not only eſtates in fee and in tail, but for life or years, may be held in joint-tenancy. 2. There is no unity of *time* neceſſary to an eſtate in coparcenary. For if a man hath two daughters, to whom his eſtate defcends in coparcenary, and one dies before the other ; the furviving daughter and the heir of the other, or, when both are dead, their two heirs, are ſtill parceners[y]; the eſtates veſting in each of them at different times, though it be the fame quantity of intereſt, and held by the fame title. 3. Parceners, though they have a *unity,* have not an *entirety,* of intereſt. They are properly intitled each to the whole of a diſtinct moiety[z]; and of courfe there is no *jus accrefcendi,* or furvivorfhip between them : for each part defcends feverally to their refpective heirs, though the unity of poſſeſſion continues. And as long as the lands continue in a courfe of defcent, and united in poſſeſſion, fo long are the tenants thereof, whether male or female, called parceners. But if the poſſeſſion be once fevered

[t] Co. Litt. 164.
[u] *Ibid.* 188.
[w] 2 Inſt. 403.

[x] Litt. §. 254.
[y] Co. Litt. 164. 174.
[z] *Ibid.* 163, 164.

by

by partition, they are no longer parceners, but tenants in feveralty; or if one parcener aliens her fhare, though no partition
be made, then are the lands no longer held in *coparcenary*, but
in *common* [a].

PARCENERS are fo called, faith Littleton [b], becaufe they
may be conftrained to make *partition*. And he mentions many
methods of making it [c]; four of which are by confent, and one
by compulfion. The firft is, where they agree to divide the lands
into equal parts in feveralty, and that each fhall have fuch a determinate part. The fecond is, when they agree to chufe fome
friend to make partition for them, and then the fifters fhall chufe
each of them her part according to feniority of age; or otherwife, as fhall be agreed. But this privilege of feniority is then
perfonal; for if the eldeft fifter be dead, her iffue fhall not chufe
firft, but the next fifter. But, if an advowfon defcend in coparcenary, and the fifters cannot agree in the prefentation, the eldeft
and her iffue, nay her hufband, or her affigns, fhall prefent alone,
before the younger [d]. And the reafon given is that the former
privilege, of priority in choice upon a divifion, arifes from an act
of her own, the agreement to make partition; and therefore is
merely perfonal: the latter, of prefenting to the living, arifes
from the act of the law, and is annexed not only to her perfon,
but to her eftate alfo. A third method of partition is, where the
eldeft divides, and then fhe fhall chufe laft; for the rule of law
is, *cujus eft divifio, alterius eft electio.* The fourth method is where
the fifters agree to caft lots for their fhares. And thefe are the
methods by confent. That by compulfion is, where one or more
fue out a writ of partition againft the others, whereupon the
fheriff fhall go to the lands, and make partition thereof by the
verdict of a jury there impanneled, and affign to each of the parceners her part in feveralty [e]. But there are fome things which

[a] Litt. §. 309.
[b] §. 241.
[c] §. 243 to 264.
[d] Co. Litt. 166. 3 Rep. 22.
[e] By ftatute 8 & 9 W. III. c.3. An eafier

method of carrying on the proceedings on
a writ of partition, of lands held either in
joint-tenancy, parcenary, or common, than
was ufed at the common law, is chalked
out and provided.

are

are in their nature impartible. The manfion-houfe, common of eftovers, common of pifcary uncertain, or any other common without ftint, fhall not be divided; but the eldeft fifter, if fhe pleafes, fhall have them, and make the others a reafonable fatis- faction in other parts of the inheritance; or, if that cannot be, then they fhall have the profits of the thing by turns, in the fame manner as they take the advowfon [f].

THERE is yet another confideration attending the eftate in coparcenary; that if one of the daughters has had an eftate given with her in *frankmarriage* by her anceftor (which we may re- member was a fpecies of eftates-tail, freely given by a relation for advancement of his kinfwoman in marriage [g]) in this cafe, if lands defcend from the *fame* anceftor to her and her fifters in fee-fimple, fhe or her heirs fhall have no fhare of them, unlefs they will agree to divide the lands fo given in frankmarriage in equal proportion with the reft of the lands defcending [h]. This general divifion was known in the law of the Lombards [i], which direct the woman fo preferred in marriage, and claiming her fhare of the inheritance, *mittere in confufum cum fororibus, quan- tum pater aut frater ei dederit, quando ambulaverit ad maritum.* With us it is denominated bringing thofe lands into *hotchpot* [k]; which term I fhall explain in the very words of Littleton [l]: "it "feemeth that this word, hotchpot, is in Englifh, a pudding; "for in a pudding is not commonly put one thing alone, but one "thing with other things together." By this houfewifely meta- phor our anceftors meant to inform us [m], that the lands, both thofe given in frankmarriage and thofe defcending in fee-fimple, fhould be mixed and blended together, and then divided in equal portions among all the daughters. But this was left to the choice of the donee in frankmarriage, and if fhe did not chufe to put her lands in hotchpot, fhe was prefumed to be fufficiently provi-

[f] Co. Litt. 164, 165.
[g] See pag. 115.
[h] Bracton. *l.* 2. *c.* 34. Litt. §. 266 to 273.
[i] *l.* 2. *t.* 14. *c.* 15.
[k] Britton. *c.* 72.
[l] §. 267.
[m] Litt. §. 268.

ded

ded for, and the reft of the inheritance was divided among her other fifters. The law of hotchpot took place then only, when the other lands defcending from the anceftor were fee-fimple; for, if they defcended in tail, the donee in frankmarriage was entitled to her fhare, without bringing her lands fo given into hotchpot [n]. And the reafon is, becaufe lands defcending in fee-fimple are diftributed by the policy of law, for the maintenance of all the daughters; and, if one has a fufficient provifion out of the fame inheritance, equal to the reft, it is not reafonable that fhe fhould have more: but lands, defcending in tail, are not diftributed by the operation of law, fo properly as *per formam doni*; it matters not therefore how unequal this diftribution may be. Alfo no lands, but fuch as are given in frankmarriage, fhall be brought into hotchpot; for no others are looked upon in law as given for the advancement of the woman, or by way of marriage-portion [o]. And therefore, as gifts in frankmarriage are fallen into difufe, I fhould hardly have mentioned the law of hotchpot, had not this method of divifion been revived and copied by the ftatute for diftribution of perfonal eftates, which we fhall hereafter confider at large.

THE eftate in coparcenary may be *diffolved*, either by partition; which difunites the poffeffion; by alienation of one parcener, which difunites the title, and may difunite the intereft; or by the whole at laft defcending to and vefting in one fingle perfon, which brings it to an eftate in feveralty.

IV. TENANTS in *common* are fuch as hold by feveral and diftinct titles, but by unity of poffeffion; becaufe none knoweth his own feveralty, and therefore they all occupy promifcuoufly [p]. This tenancy therefore happens, where there is an unity of poffeffion merely, but perhaps an entire difunion of intereft, of title, and of time. For, if there be two tenants in common of lands, one may hold his part in fee-fimple, the other in tail, or for life;

[n] Litt. §. 274.   [p] *Ibid.* 292.
[o] *Ibid.* 275.

fo that there is no neceffary unity of intereft : one may hold by defcent, the other by purchafe; or the one by purchafe from A, the other by purchafe from B; fo that there is no unity of title : one's eftate may have been vefted fifty years, the other's but yefterday; fo there is no unity of time. The only unity there is, is that of poffeffion; and for this Littleton gives the true reafon, becaufe no man can certainly tell which part is his own : otherwife even this would be foon deftroyed.

TENANCY in common may be created, either by the deftruction of the two other eftates, in joint-tenancy and coparcenary, or by fpecial limitation in a deed. By the deftruction of the two other eftates, I mean fuch deftruction as does not fever the unity of poffeffion, but only the unity of title or intereft. As, if one of two joint-tenants in fee alienes his eftate for the life of the alienee, the alienee and the other joint-tenant are tenants in common : for they now have feveral titles, the other joint-tenant by the original grant, the alienee by the new alienation ⁹; and they alfo have feveral interefts, the former joint-tenant in fee-fimple, the alienee for his own life only. So, if one joint-tenant give his part to A in tail, and the other gives his to B in tail, the donees are tenants in common, as holding by different titles and conveyances ʳ. If one of two parceners alienes, the alienee and the remaining parcener are tenants in common ˢ; becaufe they hold by different titles, the parcener by defcent, the alienee by purchafe. So likewife, if there be a grant to two *men,* or two *women,* and the heirs of their bodies, here the grantees fhall be joint-tenants of the life-eftate, but they fhall have feveral inheritances; becaufe they cannot poffibly have one heir of their two bodies, as might have been the cafe had the limitation been to *a man and woman,* and the heirs of their bodies begottenᵗ: and in this, and the like cafes, their iffues fhall be tenants in common; becaufe they muft claim by different titles, one as heir of A, and the other as heir of B; and thofe too not titles by

⁹ Litt. §. 293.
ʳ *Ibid.* 295.
ˢ *Ibid.* 309.
ᵗ *Ibid.* 283.

purchafe,

purchafe, but defcent. In fhort, whenever an eftate in joint-tenancy or coparcenary is diffolved, fo that there be no partition made, but the unity of poffeffion continues, it is turned into a tenancy in common.

A T E N A N C Y in common may alfo be created by exprefs limitation in a deed : but here care muft be taken not to infert words which imply a joint eftate; and then if lands be given to two or more, and it be not joint-tenancy, it muft be a tenancy in common. But the law is apt in it's conftructions to favour joint-tenancy rather than tenancy in common [u]; becaufe the divifible fervices iffuing from land (as rent, *&c*) are not divided, nor the entire fervices (as fealty) multiplied, by joint-tenancy, as they muft neceffarily be upon a tenancy in common. Land given to two, to be holden the one moiety to one, and the other moiety to the other, is an eftate in common [w]; and, if one grants to another *half* his land, the grantor and grantee are alfo tenants in common [x] : becaufe, as has been before [y] obferved, joint-tenants do not take by diftinct halves or moieties ; and by fuch grants the divifion and feveralty of the eftate is fo plainly expreffed, that it is impoffible they fhould take a joint intereft in the whole of the tenements. But a *devife* to two perfons, to hold *jointly and feverally*, is a joint-tenancy ; becaufe that is implied in the word "jointly," even though the word "feverally" feems to imply the direct reverfe [z] : and an eftate given to A and B, *equally to be divided* between them, though in *deeds* it hath been faid to be a joint-tenancy [a], (for it implies no more than the law has annexed to that eftate, *viz.* divifibility [b]) yet in *wills* it is certainly a tenancy in common [c]; becaufe the devifor may be prefumed to have meant what is moft beneficial to both the devifees, though his meaning is imperfectly expreffed. And this nicety in the wording of grants makes it the moft ufual as well as the fafeft

[u] Salk. 392.
[w] Litt. §. 298.
[x] *Ibid.* 299.
[y] See pag. 182.

[z] Poph. 52.
[a] 1 Equ. Caf. abr. 291.
[b] 1 P. W^ms. 17.
[c] 3 Rep. 39. 1 Ventr. 32.

way, when a tenancy in common is meant to be created, to add exprefs words of exclufion as well as defcription, and limit the eftate to A and B, to hold *as tenants in common, and not as joint-tenants.*

A s to the *incidents* attending a tenancy in common : tenants in common (like joint-tenants) are compellable by the ftatutes of Henry VIII and William III, before-mentioned[d], to make partition of their lands ; which they were not at common law. They properly take by diftinct moieties, and have no entirety of intereft ; and therefore there is no furvivorfhip between tenants in common. Their other incidents are fuch as merely arife from the unity of poffeffion ; and are therefore the fame as appertain to joint-tenants merely upon that account : fuch as being liable to reciprocal actions of wafte, and of account, by the ftatutes of Weftm. 2. c. 22. and 4 Ann. c. 16. For by the common law no tenant in common was liable to account to his companion for embezzling the profits of the eftate[e] ; though, if one actually turns the other out of poffeffion, an action of ejectment will lie againft him[f]. But, as for other incidents of joint-tenants, which arife from the privity of title, or the union and entirety of intereft, (fuch as joining or being joined in actions[g], unlefs in the cafe where fome intire or indivifible thing is to be recovered[h]) thefe are not applicable to tenants in common, whofe interefts are diftinct, and whofe titles are not joint but feveral.

E s t a t e s in common can only be *diffolved* two ways : 1. By uniting all the titles and interefts in one tenant, by purchafe or otherwife ; which brings the whole to one feveralty : 2. By making partition between the feveral tenants in common, which gives them all refpective feveralties. For indeed tenancies in common differ in nothing from fole eftates, but merely in the blending and unity of poffeffion. And this finifhes our enquiries with refpect to the nature of *eftates.*

[d] pag. 185, & 186.
[e] Co. Litt. 199.
[f] *Ibid.* 200.

[g] Litt. §. 311.
[h] Co. Litt. 197.

CHAPTER THE THIRTEENTH.

)F THE TITLE TO THINGS REAL,

IN GENERAL.

THE foregoing chapters having been principally employed in defining the *nature* of things real, in defcribing the *tenures* by which they may be holden, and in diftinguifhing the feveral kinds of *eftate* or intereft that may be had therein, I come now to confider, laftly, the *title* to things real, with the manner of acquiring and lofing it. A title is thus defined by fir Edward Coke[a], *titulus eft jufta caufa poffidendi id quod noftrum eft*; or, it is the means whereby the owner of lands hath the juft poffeffion of his property.

THERE are feveral ftages or degrees requifite to form a complete title to lands and tenements. We will confider them in a progreffive order.

I. THE loweft and moft imperfect degree of title confifts in the mere *naked poffeffion*, or actual occupation of the eftate; without any apparent right, or any fhadow or pretence of right, to hold and continue fuch poffeffion. This may happen, when one man invades the poffeffion of another, and by force or furprize turns him out of the occupation of his lands; which is termed a *diffeifin*, being a deprivation of that actual feifin, or corporal

[a] 1 Inft. 345.

A a 2 freehold

freehold of the lands, which the tenant before enjoyed. Or it may happen, that after the death of the anceftor and before the entry of the heir, or after the death of a particular tenant and before the entry of him in remainder or reverfion, a ftranger may contrive to get poffeffion of the vacant land, and hold out him that had a right to enter. In all which cafes, and many others that might be here fuggefted, the wrongdoer has only a mere naked poffeffion, which the rightful owner may put an end to, by a variety of legal remedies, as will more fully appear in the third book of thefe commentaries. But in the mean time, till fome act be done by the rightful owner to deveft this poffeffion and affert his title, fuch actual poffeffion is, *prima facie*, evidence of a legal title in the poffeffor; and it may, by length of time, and negligence of him who hath the right, by degrees ripen into a perfect and indefeafible title. And, at all events, without fuch actual poffeffion no title can be completely good.

II. THE next ftep to a good and perfect title is the *right of poffeffion*, which may refide in one man, while the actual poffeffion is either in himfelf or in another. For if a man be diffeifed, or otherwife kept out of poffeffion, by any of the means beforementioned, though the *actual* poffeffion be loft, yet he has ftill remaining in him the *right* of poffeffion; and may exert it whenever he thinks proper, by entering upon the diffeifor, and turning him out of that occupancy which he has fo illegally gained. But this right of poffeffion is of two forts: an *apparent* right of poffeffion, which may be defeated by proving a better; and an *actual* right of poffeffion, which will ftand the teft againft all opponents. Thus if the diffeifor, or other wrongdoer, dies poffeffed of the land whereof he fo became feifed by his own unlawful act, and the fame defcends to his heir; now the heir hath obtained an *apparent* right, though the *actual* right of poffeffion refides in the perfon diffeifed; and it fhall not be lawful for the perfon diffeifed to deveft this apparent right by mere entry or other act of his own, but only by an action at law [b]. For, until

[b] Litt. §. 386.

the

the contrary be proved by legal demonstration, the law will rather presume the right to reside in the heir, whose ancestor died seised, than in one who has no such presumptive evidence to urge in his own behalf. Which doctrine in some measure arose from the principles of the feodal law, which, after feuds became hereditary, much favoured the right of descent; in order that there might be a person always on the spot to perform the feodal duties and services[c]: and therefore, when a feudatory died in battle, or otherwise, it presumed always that his children were entitled to the feud, till the right was otherwise determined by his fellow-soldiers and fellow-tenants, the peers of the feodal court. But if he, who has the actual right of possession, puts in his claim and brings his action within a reasonable time, and can prove by what unlawful means the ancestor became seised, he will then by sentence of law recover that possession, to which he hath such actual right. Yet, if he omits to bring this his possessory action within a competent time, his adversary may imperceptibly gain an actual right of possession, in consequence of the other's negligence. And by this, and certain other means, the party kept out of possession may have nothing left in him, but what we are next to speak of; *viz.*

III. THE mere *right of property*, the *jus proprietatis*, without either possession or even the right of possession. This is frequently spoken of in our books under the name of the *mere right*, *jus merum*; and the estate of the owner is in such cases said to be totally devested, and *put to a right*[d]. A person in this situation may have the true ultimate property of the lands in himself: but by the intervention of certain circumstances, either by his own negligence, the solemn act of his ancestor, or the determination of a court of justice, the presumptive evidence of that right is strongly in favour of his antagonist; who has thereby obtained the absolute right of possession. As, in the first place, if a person disseised, or turned out of possession of his estate, neglects to pursue his remedy within the time limited by law; by this means

[c] Gilb. Ten. 18.   [d] Co. Litt. 345.

the

the diffeifor or his heirs gain the actual right of poffeffion : for the law prefumes that either he had a good right originally, in virtue of which he entered on the lands on queftion, or that fince fuch his entry he has procured a fufficient title ; and therefore, after fo long an acquiefcence, the law will not fuffer his poffeffion to be difturbed without enquiring into the abfolute right of property. Yet, ftill, if the perfon diffeifed or his heir hath the true right of property remaining in himfelf, his eftate is indeed faid to be turned into a mere right ; but, by proving fuch his better right, he may at length recover the lands. Again; if a tenant in tail difcontinues his eftate-tail, by alienating the lands to a ftranger in fee, and dies ; here the iffue in tail hath no right of *pof-feffion*, independent of the right of *property* : for the law prefumes *prima facie* that the anceftor would not difinherit, or attempt to difinherit, his heir, unlefs he had power fo to do; and therefore, as the anceftor had in himfelf the right of poffeffion, and has transferred the fame to a ftranger, the law will not permit that poffeffion now to be difturbed, unlefs by fhewing the abfolute right of property to refide in another perfon. The heir therefore in this cafe has only a *mere right*, and muft be ftrictly held to the proof of it, in order to recover the lands. Laftly, if by accident, neglect, or otherwife, judgment is given for either party in any *poffeffory* action, (that is, fuch wherein the right of poffeffion only, and not that of property, is contefted) and the other party hath indeed in himfelf the right of property, this is now turned to a *mere right* ; and upon proof thereof in a fubfequent action, denominated a writ of right, he fhall recover his feifin of the lands.

Thus, if a diffeifor turns me out of poffeffion of my lands, he thereby gains a *mere naked poffeffion*, and I ftill retain the *right of poffeffion*, and *right of property*. If the diffeifor dies, and the lands defcend to his fon, the fon gains an *apparent* right of *poffeffion* ; but I ftill retain the *actual* right both of *poffeffion* and *property*. If I acquiefce for thirty years, without bringing any action to recover poffeffion of the lands, the fon gains the *actual right*

right of poffeffion, and I retain nothing but the *mere right of property.* And even this right of property will fail, or at leaſt it will
be without a remedy, unlefs I purfue it within the ſpace of ſixty
years.　So alfo if the father be tenant in tail, and alienes the
eftate-tail to a ſtranger in fee, the alienee thereby gains the *right
of poffeffion,* and the fon hath only the *mere right* or *right of property.*
And hence it will follow, that one man may have the *poffeffion,*
another the *right of poffeffion,* and a third the *right of property.*
For if tenant in tail alienes to A in fee-fimple, and dies, and B
diffeifes A ; now B will have the *poffeffion,* A the *right of poffeffion,* and the iffue in tail the *right of property :* A may recover
the poffeffion againſt B; and afterwards the iffue in tail may evict
A, and unite in himfelf the poffeffion, the right of poffeffion,
and alfo the right of property.　In which union confifts,

IV.　A COMPLETE title to lands, tenements, and hereditaments.　For it is an antient maxim of the law[e], that no title is
completely good, unlefs the right of poffeffion be joined with the
right of property ; which right is then denominated a double
right, *jus duplicatum,* or *droit droit*[f].　And when to this double
right the actual poffeffion is alſo united, when there is, according
to the expreffion of Fleta[g], *juris et feifinae conjunctio,* then, and
then only, is the title completely legal.

---

[e] Mirr. *l.* 2. *c.* 27.

[f] Co. Litt. 266. Bract. *l.* 5. *tr.* 3. *c.* 5

[g] *l.* 3. *c.* 15. §. 5.

Of TITLE by DESCENT.

THE feveral gradations and ftages, requifite to form a complete title to lands, tenements, and hereditaments, having
been briefly ftated in the preceding chapter, we are next to confider the feveral manners, in which this complete title (and therein
principally the right of *propriety*) may be reciprocally loft and acquired : whereby the dominion of things real is either continued,
or transferred from one man to another. And here we muft firft
of all obferve, that (as gain and lofs are terms of relation, and
of a reciprocal nature) by whatever method one man gains an
eftate, by that fame method or it's correlative fome other man
has loft it. As where the heir acquires by defcent, the anceftor
has firft loft or abandoned the eftate by his death : where the
lord gains land by efcheat, the eftate of the tenant is firft of all
loft by the natural or legal extinction of all his hereditary blood :
where a man gains an intereft by occupancy, the former owner
has previoufly relinquifhed his right of poffeffion : where one
man claims by prefcription or immemorial ufage, another man
has either parted with his right by an antient and now forgotten
grant, or has forfeited it by the fupinenefs or neglect of himfelf
and his anceftors for ages : and fo, in cafe of forfeiture, the tenant
by his own mifbehaviour or neglect has renounced his intereft in
the eftate ; whereupon it devolves to that perfon who by law may
take advantage of fuch default : and, in alienation by common
affurances, the two confiderations of lofs and acquifition are fo

interwoven,

interwoven, and fo conftantly contemplated together, that we never hear of a conveyance, without at once receiving the idea as well of the grantor as the grantee.

THE methods therefore of acquiring on the one hand, and of lofing on the other, a title to eftates in things real, are reduced by our law to two : *defcent*, where the title is vefted in a man by the fingle operation of law ; and *purchafe*, where the title is vefted in him by his own act or agreement[a].

DESCENT, or hereditary fucceffion, is the title whereby a man on the death of his anceftor acquires his eftate by right of reprefentation, as his heir at law. An heir therefore is he upon whom the law cafts the eftate immediately on the death of the anceftor : and an eftate, fo defcending to the heir, is in law called the inheritance.

THE doctrine of defcents, or law of inheritances in fee-fimple, is a point of the higheft importance ; and is indeed the principal object of the laws of real property in England. All the rules relating to purchafes, whereby the legal courfe of defcents is broken and altered, perpetually refer to this fettled law of inheritance, as a *datum* or firft principle univerfally known, and upon which their fubfequent limitations are to work. Thus a gift in tail, or to a man and the heirs of his body, is a limitation that cannot be perfectly underftood without a previous knowlege of the law of defcents in fee-fimple. One may well perceive, that this is an eftate confined in it's defcent to fuch heirs only of the donee, as have fprung or fhall fpring from his body ; but who thofe heirs are, whether all his children both male and female, or the male only, and (among the males) whether the eldeft, youngeft, or other fon alone, or all the fons together, fhall be his heir ; this is a point, that we muft refult back to the ftanding law of defcents in fee-fimple to be informed of.

[a] Co. Litt. 18.

IN

I N order therefore to treat a matter of this univerfal confequence the more clearly, I fhall endeavour to lay afide fuch matters as will only tend to breed embaraffment and confufion in our
enquiries, and fhall confine myfelf entirely to this one object. I
fhall therefore decline confidering at prefent who are, and who
are not, capable of being heirs; referving that for the chapter of
efcheats. I fhall alfo pafs over the frequent divifion of defcents,
into thofe by *cuftom, ftatute,* and *common law:* for defcents by
particular cuftom, as to all the fons in gavelkind, and to the youngeft
in borough-englifh, have already been often[b] hinted at, and may
alfo be incidentally touched upon again; but will not make a feparate confideration by themfelves, in a fyftem fo general as the
prefent: and defcents by *ftatute,* or fee-tail *per formam doni,* in
purfuance of the ftatute of Weftminfter the fecond, have alfo been
already[c] copioufly handled; and it has been feen that the defcent
in tail is reftrained and regulated according to the words of the
original donation, and does not intirely purfue the common law
doctrine of inheritance; which, and which only, it will now be
our bufinefs to explain.

A N D, as this depends not a little on the nature of kindred,
and the feveral degrees of confanguinity, it will be previoufly neceffary to ftate, as briefly as poffible, the true notion of this kindred or alliance in blood[d].

C O N S A N G U I N I T Y, or kindred, is defined by the writers on
thefe fubjects to be " *vinculum perfonarum ab eodem ftipite defcen-*
" *dentium;*" the connexion or relation of perfons defcended from
the fame ftock or common anceftor. This confanguinity is either
lineal, or collateral.

---

[b] See Vol. I. pag. 74, 75. Vol. II.
pag. 83, 85.
[c] See pag. 112, &c.
[d] For a fuller explanation of the doctrine
of confanguinity, and the confequences refulting from a right apprehenfion of it's nature, fee *an effay on collateral confanguinity,* in
the firft volume of law tracts. *Oxon.*1762. 8°.

Table of Consanguinity

LINEAL confanguinity is that which fubfifts between perfons, of whom one is defcended in a direct line from the other:
as between John Stiles (the *propofitus* in the table of confanguinity) and his father, grandfather, great-grandfather, and fo upwards in the direct afcending line; or between John Stiles and
his fon, grandfon, great-grandfon, and fo downwards in the direct defcending line. Every generation, in this lineal direct confanguinity, conftitutes a different degree, reckoning either upwards or downwards: the father of John Stiles is related to him
in the firft degree, and fo likewife is his fon; his grandfire and
grandfon in the fecond; his great-grandfire, and great-grandfon
in the third. This is the only natural way of reckoning the degrees in the direct line, and therefore univerfally obtains, as well
in the civil [e], and canon [f], as in the common law [g].

THE doctrine of lineal confanguinity is fufficiently plain and
obvious; but it is at the firft view aftonifhing to confider the number of lineal anceftors which every man has, within no very great
number of degrees: and fo many different bloods [h] is a man faid
to contain in his veins, as he hath lineal anceftors. Of thefe he
hath two in the firft afcending degree, his own parents; he hath
four in the fecond, the parents of his father and the parents of
his mother; he hath eight in the third, the parents of his two
grandfathers and two grandmothers; and, by the fame rule of
progreffion, he hath an hundred and twenty eight in the feventh;
a thoufand and twenty four in the tenth; and at the twentieth
degree, or the diftance of twenty generations, every man hath
above a million of anceftors, as common arithmetic will demonftrate [i]. This lineal confanguinity, we may obferve, falls ftrictly
within the definition of *vinculum perfonarum ab eodem ftipite def-*

---

[e] *Ff.* 38. 10. 10.
[f] *Decretal. l.* 4. *tit.* 14.
[g] Co. Litt. 23.
[h] *Ibid.* 12.
[i] This will feem furprizing to thofe who
are unacquainted with the encreafing power
of progreffive numbers; but is palpably
evident from the following table of a geometrical progreffion, in which the firft term
is 2, and the denominator alfo 2: or, to

cendentium; fince lineal relations are fuch as defcend one from the other, and both of courfe from the fame common anceftor.

COLLATERAL kindred anfwers to the fame defcription: collateral relations agreeing with the lineal in this, that they defcend from the fame ftock or anceftor; but differing in this, that they do not defcend from each other. Collateral kinfmen as fuch then as lineally fpring from one and the fame anceftor, who is the *ftirps,* or root, the *ftipes,* trunk, or common ftock, from whence thefe relations are branched out. As if John Stiles hath

fpeak more intelligibly, it is evident, that each of us has two anceftors in the firft degree; the number of whom is doubled at every remove, becaufe each of our anceftors has alfo two immediate anceftors of his own.

Lineal Degrees.	Number of Anceftors.
1	2
2	4
3	8
4	16
5	32
6	64
7	128
8	256
9	512
10	1024
11	2048
12	4096
13	8192
14	16384
15	32768
16	65536
17	131072
18	262144
19	524288
20	1048576

A fhorter method of finding the number of anceftors at any even degree is by fquaring the number of anceftors at half that number of degrees. Thus 16 (the number of anceftors at four degrees) is the fquare of 4, the number of anceftors at two; 256 is the fquare of 16; 65536 of 256; and the number of anceftors at 40 degrees would be the fquare of 1048576, or upwards of a million millions.

two fons, who have each a numerous iffue; both thefe iffues are lineally defcended from John Stiles as their common anceitor; and they are collateral kinfmen to each other, becaufe they are all defcended from this common anceftor, and all have a portion of his blood in their veins, which denominates them *confanguineos.*

WE muft be careful to remember, that the very being of col-lateral confanguinity confifts in this defcent from one and the fame common anceftor. Thus *Titius* and his brother are related; why? becaufe both are derived from one father: *Titius* and his firft coufin are related; why? becaufe both defcend from the fame grandfather: and his fecond coufin's claim to confanguinity is this, that they both are derived from one and the fame great-grandfather. In fhort, as many anceftors as a man has, fo many common ftocks he has, from which collateral kinfmen may be derived. And as we are taught by holy writ, that there is one couple of anceftors belonging to us all, from whom the whole race of mankind is defcended, the obvious and undeniable confe-quence is, that all men are in fome degree related to each other. For indeed, if we only only fuppofe each couple of our anceftors to have left, one with another, two children; and each of thofe children on an average to have left two more; (and, without fuch a fuppofition, the human fpecies muft be daily diminifhing) we fhall find that all of us have now fubfifting near two hundred and feventy millions of kindred in the fifteenth degree, at the fame diftance from the feveral common anceftors as ourfelves are; be-fides thofe that are one or two defcents nearer to or farther from the common ftock, who may amount to as many more[k]. And, if this calculation fhould appear incompatible with the number of inhabitants on the earth, it is becaufe, by intermarriages among the feveral defcendants from the fame anceftor, a hundred or a thoufand modes of confanguinity may be confolidated in one perfon, or he may be related to us a hundred or a thoufand different ways.

[k] This will fwell more confiderably than the former calculation: for here, though the firft term is but 1, the denominator is 4; that is, there is *one* kinfman (a brother) in the firft degree, who makes, together with the *propofitus*, the two defcendants from the firft couple of anceftors; and in every other degree the number of kindred men

b.

TH E method of computing thefe degrees in the canon law[1], which our law has adopted[m], is as follows. We begin at the common anceftor, and reckon downwards; and in whatfoever degree the two perfons, or the moft remote of them, is diftant

be the *quadruple* of thofe in the degree which immediately precedes it. For, fince each couple of anceftors has two defcendants, who encreafe in a duplicate *ratio*, it will follow that the *ratio*, in which all the defcendants encreafe downwards, muft be double to that in which the anceftors encreafe upwards: but we have feen that the anceftors encreafe in a duplicate *ratio*: therefore the defcendants muft encreafe in a double duplicate, that is, in a quadruple, *ratio*.

Collateral Degrees.	*Number of Kindred.*
1	1
2	4
3	16
4	64
5	256
6	1024
7	4096
8	16384
9	65536
10	262144
11	1048576
12	4194304
13	16777216
14	67108864
15	268435456
16	1073741824
17	4294967296
18	17179869184
19	68719476736
20	274877906944

This calculation may alfo be formed by a more compendious procefs, *viz.* by fquaring the couples, or half the number, of ancef- tors at any given degree; which will fur- nifh us w th the number of kindred we have in the fame degree, at equal diftance with ourfelves from the common ftock, befides thofe at unequal diftances. Thus, in the tenth lineal degree, the number of anceftors is 1024; it's half, or the couples, amount to 512; the number of kindred in the tenth collateral degree amounts therefore to 262144, or the fquare of 512. And if we will be at the trouble to recollect the ftate of the feveral families within our own knowlege, and obferve how far they agree with this account; that is, whether, on an average, eveiy man has not one brother or fifter, four firft coufins, fixteen fecond con- fins, and fo on; we fhall find that the pre- fent calculation is very far from being over- charged.

[1] *Decretal.* 4. 14. 3 *&* 9.
[m] Co. Litt. 23.   from

from the common anceftor, that is the degree in which they are related to each other. Thus *Titius* and his brother are related in the firft degree; for from the father to each of them is counted only one: *Titius* and his nephew are related in the fecond degree; for the nephew is two degrees removed from the common anceftor; *viz.* his own grandfather, the father of *Titius*. Or, (to give a more illuftrious inftance from our Englifh annals) king Henry the feventh, who flew Richard the third in the battle of Bofworth, was related to that prince in the fifth degree. Let the *propofitus* therefore in the table of confanguinity reprefent king Richard the third, and the clafs marked (e) king Henry the feventh. Now their common ftock or anceftor was king Edward the third, the *abavus* in the fame table: from him to Edmond duke of York, the *proavus*, is one degree; to Richard earl of Cambridge, the *avus*, two; to Richard duke of York, the *pater*, three; to king Richard the third, the *propofitus*, four: and from king Edward the third to John of Gant (a) is one degree; to John earl of Somerfet (b) two; to John duke of Somerfet (c) three; to Margaret countefs of Richmond (d) four; to king Henry the feventh (e) five. Which laft mentioned prince, being the fartheft removed from the common ftock, gives the denomination to the degree of kindred in the canon and municipal law. Though according to the computation of the civilians, (who count upwards, from either of the perfons related, to the common ftock, and then downwards again to the other; reckoning a degree for each perfon both afcending and defcending) thefe two princes were related in the ninth degree: for from king Richard the third to Richard duke of York is one degree; to Richard earl of Cambridge, two; to Edmond duke of York, three; to king Edward the third, the common anceftor, four; to John of Gant, five; to John earl of Somerfet, fix; to John duke of Somerfet, feven; to Margaret countefs of Richmond, eight; to king Henry the feventh, nine[n].

---

[n] See the table of confanguinity annexed; wherein all the degrees of collateral kindred to the *propofitus* are computed, fo far as the tenth of the civilians and the feventh of the canonifts inclufive; the former being diftinguifhed by the numeral letters, the latter by the common ciphers.

THE

TH E nature and degrees of kindred being thus in some measure explained, I shall next proceed to lay down a series of rules, or canons of inheritance, according to which estates are transmitted from the ancestor to the heir ; together with an explanatory comment, remarking their original and progress, the reasons upon which they are founded, and in some cases their agreement with the laws of other nations.

I. TH E first rule is, that inheritances shall lineally descend to the issue of the person last actually seised, *in infinitum;* but shall never lineally ascend.

TO explain the more clearly both this and the subsequent rules, it must first be observed, that by law no inheritance can vest, nor can any person be the actual complete heir of another, till the ancestor is previously dead. *Nemo est haeres viventis.* Before that time the person who is next in the line of succession is called an heir apparent, or heir presumptive. Heirs apparent are such, whose right of inheritance is indefeasible, provided they outlive the ancestor ; as the eldest son or his issue, who must by the course of the common law be heirs to the father whenever he happens to die. Heirs presumptive are such, who, if the ancestor should die immediately, would in the present circumstances of things be his heirs ; but whose right of inheritance may be defeated by the contingency of some nearer heir being born : as a brother, or nephew, whose presumptive succession may be destroyed by the birth of a child ; or a daughter, whose present hopes may be hereafter cut off by the birth of a son. Nay, even if the estate hath descended, by the death of the owner, to such brother, or nephew, or daughter ; in the former cases the estate shall be devested and taken away by the birth of a posthumous child ; and, in the latter, it shall also be totally devested by the birth of a posthumous son [o].

---

[o] Bro. *tit. descent.* 58.

WE muft alfo remember, that no perfon can be properly fuch an anceftor, as that an inheritance in lands or tenements can be derived from him, unlefs he hath had actual feifin of fuch lands, either by his own entry, or by the poffeffion of his own or his anceftor's leffee for years, or by receiving rent from a leffee of the freehold P : or unlefs he hath had what is equivalent to corporal feifin in hereditaments that are incorporeal ; fuch as the receipt of rent, a prefentation to the church in cafe of an advowfon q, and the like. But he fhall not be accounted an anceftor, who hath had only a bare right or title to enter or be otherwife feifed. And therefore all the cafes, which will be mentioned in the prefent chapter, are upon the fuppofition that the deceafed (whofe inheritance is now claimed) was the laft perfon actually feifed thereof. For the law requires this notoriety of poffeffion, as evidence that the anceftor had that property in himfelf, which is now to be tranfmitted to his heir. Which notoriety hath fucceeded in the place of the antient feodal inveftiture, whereby, while feuds were precarious, the vafal on the defcent of lands was formerly admitted in the lord's court (as is ftill the practice in Scotland) and there received his feifin, in the nature of a renewal of his anceftors grant, in the prefence of the feodal peers : till at length, when the right of fucceffion became indefeafible, an entry on any part of the lands within the county (which if difputed was afterwards to be tried by thofe peers) or other notorious poffeffion, was admitted as equivalent to the formal grant of feifin, and made the tenant capable of tranfmitting his eftate by defcent. The feifin therefore of any perfon, thus underftood, makes him the root or ftock, from which all future inheritance by right of blood muft be derived : which is very briefly expreffed in this maxim, *feifina facit ftipitem* r.

P Co. Litt. 15.   r Flet. *l.* 6. *c.* 2. §. 2.
q *Ibid.* 11.

WHEN therefore a person dies so seised, the inheritance first goes to his issue : as if there be Geoffrey, John, and Matthew, grandfather, father, and son ; and John purchases land and dies; his son Matthew shall succeed him as heir, and not the grandfather Geoffrey; to whom the land shall never ascend, but shall rather escheat to the lord[.]

THIS rule, so far as it is affirmative and relates to lineal descents, is almost universally adopted by all nations ; and it seems founded on a principle of natural reason, that (whenever a right of property transmissible to representatives is admitted) the possessions of the parents should go, upon their decease, in the first place to their children, as those to whom they have given being, and for whom they are therefore bound to provide. But the negative branch, or total exclusion of parents and all lineal ancestors from succeeding to the inheritance of their offspring, is peculiar to our own laws, and such as have been deduced from the same original. For, by the Jewish law, on failure of issue the father succeeded to the son, in exclusion of brethren, unless one of them married the widow and raised up seed to his brother[.] And, by the laws of Rome, in the first place the children or lineal descendants were preferred ; and, on failure of these, the father and mother or lineal ascendants succeeded together with the brethren and sisters[;] though by the law of the twelve tables the mother was originally, on account of her sex, excluded[.] Hence this rule of our laws has been censured and declaimed against, as absurd and derogating from the maxims of equity and natural justice[.] Yet that there is nothing unjust or absurd in it, but that on the contrary it is founded upon very good reason, may appear from considering as well the nature of the rule itself, as the occasion of introducing it into our laws.

[.] Litt. §. 3.
[.] Selden. *de succiff. Ebraeor. c.* 12.
[.] *Ff.* 38. 15. 1. *Nov.* 118. 127.

[.] *Inst.* 3. 3. 1.
[.] Craig. *de jur. feud. l.* 2. *t.* 13. §. 15.
Locke on gov. part. 1. §. 90.

WE

WE are to reflect, in the firſt place, that all rules of ſucceſſion to eſtates are creatures of the civil polity, and *juris poſitivi* merely. The right of property, which is gained by occupancy, extends naturally no farther than the life of the preſent poſſeſſor; after which the land by the law of nature would again become common, and liable to be ſeiſed by the next occupant: but ſociety, to prevent the miſchiefs that might enſue from a doctrine ſo productive of contention, has eſtabliſhed conveyances, wills, and ſucceſſions; whereby the property originally gained by poſſeſſion is continued, and tranſmitted from one man to another, according to the rules which each ſtate has reſpectively thought proper to preſcribe. There is certainly therefore no injuſtice done to individuals, whatever be the path of deſcent marked out by the municipal law.

IF we next conſider the time and occaſion of introducing this rule into our law, we ſhall find it to have been grounded upon very ſubſtantial reaſons. I think there is no doubt to be made, but that it was introduced at the ſame time with, and in conſequence of, the feodal tenures. For it was an expreſs rule of the feodal law [x], that *ſucceſſionis feudi talis eſt natura, quod aſcendentes non ſuccedunt;* and therefore the ſame maxim obtains alſo in the French law to this day [y]. Our Henry the firſt indeed, among other reſtorations of the old Saxon laws, reſtored the right of ſucceſſion in the aſcending line [z]: but this ſoon fell again into diſuſe; for ſo early as Glanvil's time, who wrote under Henry the ſecond, we find it laid down as eſtabliſhed law [a], that *haereditas nunquam aſcendit;* which has remained an invariable maxim ever ſince. Theſe circumſtances evidently ſhew this rule to be of feodal original; and, taken in that light, there are ſome arguments in it's favour, beſides thoſe which are drawn merely from the reaſon of the thing. For if the feud, of which the ſon died

---

[x] 2 *Feud.* 50.

[y] Domat. *p.* 2. *l.* 2. *t.* 2. Monteſqu. *Eſp.*
L. *l.* 31. *c.* 33.

[z] *LL. Hen. I. c.* 70.

[a] *l.* 7. *c.* 1.

ſeiſed,

feifed, was really *feudum antiquum,* or one defcended to him from his anceftors, the father could not poffibly fucceed to it, becaufe it muft have paffed him in the courfe of defcent, before it could come to the fon ; unlefs it were *feudum maternum,* or one de-fcended from his mother, and then for other reafons (which will appear hereafter) the father could in no wife inherit it. And if it were *feudum novum,* or one newly acquired by the fon, then only the defcendants from the body of the feudatory himfelf could fucceed, by the known maxim of the early feodal confti-tutions[b]; which was founded as well upon the perfonal merit of the vafal, which might be tranfmitted to his children but could not afcend to his progenitors, as alfo upon this confideration of military policy, that the decrepit grandfire of a vigorous vafal would be but indifferently qualified to fucceed him in his feodal fervices. Nay, even if this *feudum novum* were held by the fon *ut feudum antiquum,* or with all the qualities annexed of a feud defcended from his anceftors, fuch feud muft in all refpects have defcended as if it had been really an antient feud ; and therefore could not go to the father, becaufe, if it had been an antient feud, the father muft have been dead before it could have come to the fon. Thus whether the feud was ftrictly *novum,* or ftrictly *antiquum,* or whether it was *novum* held *ut antiquum,* in none of thefe cafes the father could poffibly fucceed. Thefe reafons, drawn from the hiftory of the rule itfelf, feem to be more fatisfactory than that quaint one of Bracton[c], adopted by fir Edward Coke[d], which regulates the defcent of lands acccording to the laws of gravitation.

II. A s e c o n d general rule or canon is, that the male iffue fhall be admitted before the female.

[b] 1 *Feud.* 20.

[c] *Defcendit itaque jus, quafi ponderofum quid,*　　*cadens deorfum recta linea, et nunquam reafcen-dit. l. 2. c.* 29.

[d] 1 Inft. 11.

T h u s

THUS fons fhall be admitted before daughters; or, as our male lawgivers have fomewhat uncomplaifantly expreffed it, the worthieft of blood fhall be preferred[e]. As if John Stiles hath two fons, Matthew and Gilbert, and two daughters, Margaret and Charlotte, and dies; firft Matthew, and (in cafe of his death without iffue) then Gilbert, fhall be admitted to the fucceffion in preference to both the daughters.

THIS preference of males to females is entirely agreeable to the law of fucceffion among the Jews[f], and alfo among the ftates of Greece, or at leaft among the Athenians[g]; but was totally unknown to the laws of Rome[h], (fuch of them, I mean, as are at prefent extant) wherein brethren and fifters were allowed to fucceed to equal portions of the inheritance. I fhall not here enter into the comparative merit of the Roman and the other conftitutions in this particular, nor examine into the greater dignity of blood in the male or female fex; but fhall only obferve, that our prefent preference of males to females feems to have arifen entirely from the feodal law. For though our Britifh anceftors, the Welfh, appear to have given a preference to males[i], yet our fubfequent Danifh predeceffors feem to have made no diftinction of fexes, but to have admitted all the children at once to the inheritance[k]. But the feodal law of the Saxons on the continent (which was probably brought over hither, and firft altered by the law of king Canute) gives an evident preference of the male to the female fex. " *Pater aut mater, defuncti, filio non* " *filiae haereditatem relinquent. . . . . Qui defunctus non filios fed* " *filias reliquerit, ad eas omnis haereditas pertineat*[l]." It is poffible therefore that this preference might be a branch of that imperfect fyftem of feuds, which obtained here before the conqueft; efpe-

[e] Hal. H. C. L. 235.
[f] Numb. c. 27.
[g] Petit. *LL. Attic. l.* 6. *t.* 6.
[h] *Inft.* 3. 1. 6.

[i] *Stat. Wall.* 12 Edw. 1.
[k] *LL. Canut. c.* 68.
[l] *tit.* 7. §. 1 & 4.

cially as it subsists among the customs of gavelkind, and as, in the charter or laws of king Henry the first, it is not (like many Norman innovations) given up, but rather enforced [m]. The true reason of preferring the males must be deduced from feodal principles: for, by the genuine and original policy of that constitution, no female could ever succeed to a proper feud [n], inasmuch as they were incapable of performing those military services, for the sake of which that system was established. But our law does not extend to a total exclusion of females, as the Salic law, and others, where feuds were most strictly retained: it only postpones them to males; for, though daughters are excluded by sons, yet they succeed before any collateral relations: our law, like that of the Saxon feudists before-mentioned, thus steering a middle course, between the absolute rejection of females, and the putting them on a footing with males.

III. A THIRD rule, or canon of descent, is this; that, where there are two or more males in equal degree, the eldest only shall inherit; but the females all together.

As if a man hath two sons, Matthew and Gilbert, and two daughters, Margaret and Charlotte, and dies; Matthew his eldest son shall alone succeed to his estate, in exclusion of Gilbert the second son and both the daughters: but, if both the sons die without issue before the father, the daughters Margaret and Charlotte shall both inherit the estate as coparceners [o].

THIS right of primogeniture in males seems antiently to have only obtained among the Jews, in whose constitution the eldest son had a double portion of the inheritance [p]; in the same manner as with us, by the laws of king Henry the first [q], the eldest son had the capital fee or principal feud of his father's possessions,

[m] *c.* 70.
[n] 1 *Feud.* 8.
[o] Litt. §. 5. Hale. H. C. L. 238.
[p] Selden. *de succ. Ebr. c.* 5.
[q] *c.* 70.

and

and no other pre-eminence; and as the eldeſt daughter had afterwards the principal manſion, when the eſtate deſcended in coparcenary[r]. The Greeks, the Romans, the Britons, the Saxons, and
even originally the feudiſts, divided the lands equally; ſome
among all the children at large, ſome among the males only.
This is certainly the moſt obvious and natural way; and has the
appearance, at leaſt in the opinion of younger brothers, of the
greateſt impartiality and juſtice. But when the emperors began
to create honorary feuds, or titles of nobility, it was found neceſſary (in order to preſerve their dignity) to make them impartible[s], or (as they ſtiled them) *feuda individua*, and in conſequence
deſcendible to the eldeſt ſon alone. This example was farther enforced by the inconveniences that attended the ſplitting of eſtates;
namely, the diviſion of the military ſervices, the multitude of
infant tenants incapable of performing any duty, the conſequen-
tial weakening of the ſtrength of the kingdom, and the inducing
younger ſons to take up with the buſineſs and idleneſs of a country life, inſtead of being ſerviceable to themſelves and the public,
by engaging in mercantile, in military, in civil, or in eccleſiaſtical employments[t]. Theſe reaſons occaſioned an almoſt total change
in the method of feodal inheritances abroad; ſo that the eldeſt
male began univerſally to ſucceed to the whole of the lands in all
military tenures: and in this condition the feodal conſtitution was
eſtabliſhed in England by William the conqueror.

YET we find, that ſocage eſtates frequently deſcended to all
the ſons equally, ſo lately as when Glanvil[u] wrote, in the reign
of Henry the ſecond; and it is mentioned in the mirror[w] as a
part of our antient conſtitution, that knights' fees ſhould deſcend
to the eldeſt ſon, and ſocage fees ſhould be partible among the
male children. However in Henry the third's time we find by
Bracton[x] that ſocage lands, in imitation of lands in chivalry, had

[r] Glanvil. *l*. 7. *c*. 3.
[s] 2 *Feud.* 55.
[t] Hale. H. C. L. 221.

[u] *l*. 7. *c*. 3.
[w] *c*. 1. §. 3.
[x] *l*. 2. *c*. 30, 31

almoſt

almoſt entirely fallen into the right of ſucceſſion by primogeniture, as the law now ſtands : except in Kent, where they gloried
in the preſervation of their antient gavelkind tenure, of which a
principal branch was the joint inheritance of all the ſons [y] ; and
except in ſome particular manors and townſhips, where their local cuſtoms continued the deſcent, ſometimes to all, ſometimes
to the youngeſt ſon only, or in other more ſingular methods of
ſucceſſion.

As to the females, they are ſtill left as they were by the antient law : for they were all equally incapable of performing any
perſonal ſervice ; and therefore, one main reaſon of preferring
the eldeſt ceaſing, ſuch preference would have been injurious to
the reſt : and the other principal purpoſe, the prevention of the
too minute ſubdiviſion of eſtates, was left to be conſidered and
provided for by the lords, who had the diſpoſal of theſe female
heireſſes in marriage. However, the ſucceſſion by primogeniture,
even among females, took place as to the inheritance of the
crown [z] ; wherein the neceſſity of a ſole and determinate ſucceſſion is as great in the one ſex as the other. And the right of ſole
ſucceſſion, though not of primogeniture, was alſo eſtabliſhed with
reſpect to female dignities and titles of honour. For if a man
holds an earldom to him and the heirs of his body, and dies,
leaving only daughters ; the eldeſt ſhall not of courſe be counteſs,
but the dignity is in ſuſpenſe or abeyance till the king ſhall declare his pleaſure ; for he, being the fountain of honour, may
confer it on which of them he pleaſes [a]. In which diſpoſition is
preſerved a ſtrong trace of the antient law of feuds, before their
deſcent by primogeniture even among the males was eſtabliſhed ;
namely, that the lord might beſtow them on which of the ſons
he thought proper : --- " *progreſſum eſt, ut ad filios deveniret, in*
" *quem ſcilicet dominus hoc vellet beneficium confirmare* [b]."

[y] Somner. Gavelk. 7.　　　　　　　[a] *Ibid.*
[z] C . Litt. 165.　　　　　　　　　　[b] 1 *Feud.* 1.

IV. A FOURTH

IV. A FOURTH rule, or canon of defcents, is this; that the lineal defcendants, *in infinitum*, of any perfon deceafed fhall reprefent their anceftor; that is, fhall ftand in the fame place as the perfon himfelf would have done, had he been living.

THUS the child, grandchild, or great-grandchild (either male or female) of the eldeft fon fucceeds before the younger fon, and fo *in infinitum*[c]. And thefe reprefentatives fhall take neither more nor lefs, but juft fo much as their principals would have done. As if there be two fifters, Margaret and Charlotte; and Margaret dies, leaving fix daughters; and then John Stiles the father of the two fifters dies, without other iffue: thefe fix daughters fhall take among them exactly the fame as their mother Margaret would have done, had fhe been living; that is, a moiety of the lands of John Stiles in coparcenary: fo that, upon partition made, if the land be divided into twelve parts, thereof Charlotte the furviving fifter fhall have fix, and her fix neices, the daughters of Margaret, one apiece.

THIS taking by reprefentation is called a fucceffion *in ftirpes*, according to the roots; fince all the branches inherit the fame fhare that their root, whom they reprefent, would have done. And in this manner alfo was the Jewifh fucceffion directed[d]; but the Roman fomewhat differed from it. In the defcending line the right of reprefentation continued *in infinitum*, and the inheritance ftill defcended *in ftirpes*: as if one of three daughters died, leaving ten children, and then the father died; the two furviving daughters had each one third of his effects, and the ten grandchildren had the remaining third divided between them. And fo among collaterals, if any perfons of equal degree with the perfons reprefented were ftill fubfifting, (as if the deceafed left one brother, and two nephews the fons of another brother) the fucceffion was ftill guided by the *roots*: but, if both the brethren were dead leaving iffue, then (I apprehend) their repre-

---

[c] Hale. H. C. L. 236, 237.   [d] Selden *de fucc. Ebr. c.* 1.

fentatives in equal degree became themfelves principals, and fhared the inheritance *per capita*, that is, fhare and fhare alike; they being themfelves now the next in degree to the anceftor, in their own right, and not by right of reprefentation^e. So, if the next heirs of *Titius* be fix nieces, three by one fifter, two by another, and one by a third; his inheritance by the Roman law was divided into fix parts, and one given to each of the nieces: whereas the law of England in this cafe would ftill divide it only into three parts, and diftribute it *per ftirpes*, thus; one third to the three children who reprefent one fifter, another third to the two who reprefent the fecond, and the remaining third to the one child who is the fole reprefentative of her mother.

THIS mode of reprefentation is a neceffary confequence of the double preference given by our law, firft to the male iffue, and next to the firftborn among the males, to both which the Roman law is a ftranger. For if all the children of three fifters were in England to claim *per capita*, in their own rights as next of kin to the anceftor, without any refpect to the ftocks from whence they fprung, and thofe children were partly male and partly female; then the eldeft male among them would exclude not only his own brethren and fifters, but all the iffue of the other two daughters; or elfe the law in this inftance muft be inconfiftent with itfelf, and depart from the preference which it conftantly gives to the males, and the firftborn, among perfons in equal degree. Whereas, by dividing the inheritance according to the roots or *ftirpes*, the rule of defcent is kept uniform and fteady: the iffue of the eldeft fon excludes all other pretenders, as the fon himfelf (if living) would have done; but the iffue of two daughters divide the inheritance between them, provided their mothers (if living) would have done the fame: and among thefe feveral iffues, or reprefentatives of the refpective roots, the fame preference to males and the fame right of primogeniture obtain, as would have obtained at the firft among the roots themfelves, the fons or daughters of the deceafed. As if a man hath

e Nov. 118. *c.* 3. *Inft.* 3. 1. 6.

two

two fons, A and B, and A dies leaving two fons, and then the grandfather dies; now the eldeft fon of A fhall fucceed to the whole of his grandfather's eftate: and if A had left only two daughters, they fhould have fucceeded alfo to equal moieties of the whole, in exclufion of B and his iffue. But if a man hath only three daughters, C, D, and E; and C dies leaving two fons, D leaving two daughters, and E leaving a daughter and a fon who is younger than his fifter: here, when the grandfather dies, the eldeft fon of C fhall fucceed to one third, in exclufion of the younger; the two daughters of D to another third in partnerfhip; and the fon of E to the remaining third, in exclufion of his elder fifter. And the fame right of reprefentation, guided and reftrained by the fame rules of defcent, prevails downwards *in infinitum*.

YET this right does not appear to have been thoroughly eftablifhed in the time of Henry the fecond, when Glanvil wrote; and therefore, in the title to the crown efpecially, we find frequent contefts between the younger (but furviving) brother, and his nephew (being the fon and reprefentative of the elder deceafed) in regard to the inheritance of their common anceftor: for the uncle is certainly nearer of kin to the common ftock, by one degree, than the nephew; though the nephew, by reprefenting his father, has in him the right of primogeniture. The uncle alfo was ufually better able to perform the fervices of the fief; and befides had frequently fuperior intereft and ftrength, to back his pretenfions and crufh the right of his nephew. And even to this day, in the lower Saxony, proximity of blood takes place of reprefentative primogeniture; that is, the younger furviving brother is admitted to the inheritance before the fon of an elder deceafed: which occafioned the difputes between the two houfes of Mecklenburg, Schwerin and Strelitz, in 1692[f]. Yet Glanvil, with us, even in the twelfth century, feems[g] to declare for the right of the nephew by reprefentation; provided the eldeft fon had not received a provifion in lands from his father, (or as the

---

[f] Mod. Un. Hift. xlii. 334.   [g] *l.* 7. *c.* 3.

civil

civil law would call it) had not been forisfamiliated, in his lifetime. King John, however, who kept his nephew Arthur from
the throne, by difputing this right of reprefentation, did all in
his power to abolifh it throughout the realm [h] : but in the time
of his fon, king Henry the third, we find the rule indifputably
fettled in the manner we have here laid it down [i], and fo it has
continued ever fince. And thus much for lineal defcents.

V. A FIFTH rule is, that, on failure of lineal defcendants, or
iffue, of the perfon laft feifed, the inheritance fhall defcend to the
blood of the firft purchafor; fubjeft to the three preceding rules.

THUS if Geoffrey Stiles purchafes land, and it defcends to
John Stiles his fon, and John dies feifed thereof without iffue;
whoever fucceeds to this inheritance muft be of the blood of
Geoffrey the firft purchafor of this family [k]. The firft purchafor,
perquifitor, is he who firft acquired the eftate to his family,
whether the fame was transferred to him by fale, or by gift, or
by any other method, except only that of defcent.

THIS is a rule almoft peculiar to our own laws, and thofe of
a fimilar original. For it was entirely unknown among the Jews,
Greeks, and Romans : none of whofe laws looked any farther
than the perfon himfelf who died feifed of the eftate; but affigned him an heir, without confidering by what title he gained
it, or from what anceftor he derived it. But the law of Normandy [l] agrees with our law in this refpeft : nor indeed is that
agreement to be wondered at, fince the law of defcents in both
is of feodal original ; and this rule or canon cannot otherwife be
accounted for than by recurring to feodal principles.

WHEN feuds firft began to be hereditary, it was made a neceffary qualification of the heir, who would fucceed to a feud,
that he fhould be of the blood of, that is lineally defcended from,

[h] Hale. H. C. L. 217, 229.
[i] Braƈton. *l. 2. c.* 30. §. 2.

[k] Co. Litt. 12.
[l] *Gr. Couftum. c.* 25.

the

the firft feudatory or purchafor. In confequence whereof, if a
vafal died poffeffed of a feud of his own acquiring, or *feudum
novum*, it could not defcend to any but his own offspring; no,
not even to his brother, becaufe he was not defcended, nor derived his blood, from the firft acquirer. But if it was *feudum
antiquum*, that is, one defcended to the vafal from his anceftors,
then his brother, or fuch other collateral relation as was defcended
and derived his blood from the firft feudatory, might fucceed to
fuch inheritance. To this purpofe fpeaks the following rule;
"*frater fratri fine legitimo haerede defuncto, in beneficio quod eorum
"patris fuit, fuccedat : fin autem unus e fratribus a domino feu-
"dum acceperit, eo defuncto fine legitimo haerede, frater ejus in feu-
"dum non fuccedit* [m]." The true feodal reafon for which rule was
this; that what was given to a man, for his perfonal fervice and
perfonal merit, ought not to defcend to any but the heirs of his
perfon. And therefore, as in eftates-tail, (which a proper feud
very much refembled) fo in the feodal donation, "*nomen haeredis,
"in prima inveftitura expreffum, tantum ad defcendentes ex corpore
"primi vafalli extenditur; et non ad collaterales, nifi ex corpore
"primi vafalli five ftipitis defcendant* [n] :" the will of the donor, or
original lord, (when feuds were turned from life eftates into inheritances) not being to make them abfolutely hereditary, like
the Roman *allodium*, but hereditary only *fub modo*; not hereditary to the collateral relations, or lineal anceftors, or hufband, or
wife of the feudatory, but to the iffue defcended from his body
only.

HOWEVER, in procefs of time, when the feodal rigour was
in part abated, a method was invented to let in the collateral relations of the grantee to the inheritance, by granting him a *feudum novum* to hold *ut feudum antiquum*; that is, with all the
qualities annexed of a feud derived from his anceftors; and then
the collateral relations were admitted to fucceed even *in infinitum*,
becaufe they might have been of the blood of, that is defcended
from, the firft imaginary purchafor. For fince it is not afcertained

---

[m] 1 *Feud.* 1. §. 2.   [n] Crag. *l.* 1. *t.* 9. §. 36.

in fuch general grants, whether this feud fhall be held *ut feudum paternum*, or *feudum avitum*, but *ut feudum antiquum* merely, as a feud of indefinite antiquity; that is, fince it is not afcertained from which of the anceftors of the grantee this feud fhall be fuppofed to have defcended; the law will not afcertain it, but will fuppofe *any* of his anceftors, *pro re nata*, to have been the firft purchafor : and therefore it admits *any* of his collateral kindred (who have the other neceffary requifites) to the inheritance, becaufe every collateral kinfman muft be defcended from fome one of his lineal anceftors.

O f this nature are all the grants of fee-fimple eftates of this kingdom; for there is now in the law of England no fuch thing as a grant of a *feudum novum*, to be held *ut novum* ; unlefs in the cafe of a fee-tail, and there we fee that this rule is ftrictly obferved, and none but the lineal defcendants of the firft donee (or purchafor) are admitted : but every grant of lands in fee-fimple is with us a *feudum novum* to be held *ut antiquum*, as a feud whofe antiquity is indefinite ; and therefore the collateral kindred of the grantee, or defcendants from any of his lineal anceftors, by whom the lands might have poffibly been purchafed, are capable of being called to the inheritance.

Y e t, when an eftate hath really defcended in a courfe of inheritance to the perfon laft feifed, the ftrict rule of the feodal law is ftill obferved ; and none are admitted, but the heirs of thofe through whom the inheritance hath paffed : for all others have demonftrably none of the blood of the firft purchafor in them, and therefore fhall never fucceed. As, if lands come to John Stiles by defcent from his mother Lucy Baker, no relation of his father (as fuch) fhall ever be his heir of thefe lands ; and, *vice verfa*, if they defcended from his father Geoffrey Stiles, no relation of his mother (as fuch) fhall ever be admitted thereto ; for his father's kindred have none of his mother's blood, nor have his mother's relations any fhare of his father's blood. And fo, if the eftate defcended from his father's father, George Stiles ;

the

the relations of his father's mother, Cecilia Kempe, fhall for the fame reafon never be admitted, but only thofe of his father's father. This is alfo the rule of the French law°, which is derived from the fame feodal fountain.

HERE we may obferve, that, fo far as the feud is really *antiquum*, the law traces it back, and will not fuffer any to inherit but the blood of thofe anceftors, from whom the feud was conveyed to the late proprietor. But when, through length of time, it can trace it no farther; as if it be not known whether his grandfather, George Stiles, inherited it from his father Walter Stiles, or his mother Chriftian Smith ; or if it appear that his grandfather was the firft grantee, and fo took it (by the general law) as a feud of indefinite antiquity; in either of thefe cafes the law admits the defcendants of any anceftor of George Stiles, either paternal or maternal, to be in their due order the heirs to John Stiles of this eftate : becaufe in the firft cafe it is really uncertain, and in the fecond cafe it is fuppofed to be uncertain, whether the grandfather derived his title from the part of his father or his mother.

THIS then is the great and general principle, upon which the law of collateral inheritances depends; that, upon failure of iffue in the laft proprietor, the eftate fhall defcend to the blood of the firft purchafor; or, that it fhall refult back to the heirs of the body of that anceftor, from whom it either really has, or is fuppofed by fiction of law to have, originally defcended : according to the rule laid down in the yearbooks ᵖ, Fitzherbert �q, Brook ʳ, and Hale ˢ; " that he who would have been heir to the " father of the deceafed" (and, of courfe, to the mother, or any other purchafing anceftor) " fhall alfo be heir to the fon."

THE remaining rules are only rules of evidence, calculated to inveftigate who that purchafing anceftor was ; which, *in feudis*

° Domat. *part.* 2. *pr.*

ᵖ M. 12 *Edw. IV.* 14.

q *Abr. t. difcent.* 2.

ʳ *Ibid.* 38.

ˢ H. C. L. 243.

vere

vere antiquis, has in procefs of time been forgotten, and is fup-pofed fo to be in feuds that are held *ut antiquis*.

VI. A s i x t h rule or canon therefore is, that the collateral heir of the perfon laft feifed muft be his next collateral kinfman, of the whole blood.

F i r s t, he muft be his next collateral kinfman, either perfo-nally or *jure reprefentationis;* which proximity is reckoned ac-cording to the canonical degrees of confanguinity before-mentioned. Therefore, the brother being in the firft degree, he and his defcend-ants fhall exclude the uncle and his iffue, who is only in the fecond. And herein confifts the true reafon of the different methods of computing the degrees of confanguinity, in the civil law on the one hand, and in the canon and common laws on the other. The civil law regards confanguinity principally with refpect to fuccef-fions, and therein very naturally confiders only the perfon decea-fed, to whom the relation is claimed : it therefore counts the de-grees of kindred according to the number of perfons through whom the claim muft be derived from him; and makes not only his great-nephew but alfo his firft-coufin to be both related to him in the fourth degree; becaufe there are three perfons between him and each of them. The canon law regards confanguinity principally with a view to prevent inceftuous marriages, between thofe who have a large portion of the fame blood running in their refpective veins; and therefore looks up to the author of that blood, or the common anceftor, reckoning the degrees from him : fo that the great-nephew is related in the third canonical degree to the perfon propofed, and the firft-coufin in the fecond; the former being diftant three degrees from the common anceftor, and therefore deriving only one fourth of his blood from the fame fountain with the *propofitus;* the latter, and alfo the *propofitus,* being each of them diftant only two degrees from the common anceftor, and therefore having one half of each of their bloods the fame. The common law regards confanguinity principally with refpect to defcents; and, having therein the fame object in

view

view as the civil, it may feem as if it ought to proceed according
to the civil computation. But as it alfo refpects the purchafing
anceftor, from whom the eftate was derived, it therein refembles
the canon law, and therefore counts it's degrees in the fame
manner. Indeed the defignation of perfon (in feeking for the next
of kin) will come to exactly the fame end (though the degrees
will be differently numbered) whichever method of computation
we fuppofe the law of England to ufe; fince the right of reprefentation (of the father by the fon, &c) is allowed to prevail *in*
infinitum. This allowance was abfolutely neceffary, elfe there
would have frequently been many claimants in exactly the fame
degree of kindred, as (for inftance) uncles and nephews of the
deceafed; which multiplicity, though no inconvenience in the
Roman law of partible inheritances, yet would have been productive of endlefs confufion where the right of fole fucceffion, as
with us, is eftablifhed. The iffue or defcendants therefore of
John Stiles's brother are all of them in the firft degree of kindred
with refpect to inheritances, as their father alfo, when living,
was; thofe of his uncle in the fecond; and fo on; and are feverally called to the fucceffion in right of fuch their reprefentative
proximity.

THE right of reprefentation being thus eftablifhed, the former
part of the prefent rule amounts to this; that, on failure of iffue
of the perfon laft feifed, the inheritance fhall defcend to the iffue
of his next immediate anceftor. Thus if John Stiles dies without iffue, his eftate fhall defcend to Francis his brother, who is
lineally defcended from Geoffrey Stiles his next immediate anceftor, or father. On failure of brethren, or fifters, and their iffue,
it fhall defcend to the uncle of John Stiles, the lineal defcendant
of his grandfather George, and fo on *in infinitum.* Very fimilar
to which was the law of inheritance among the antient Germans,
our progenitors: "*haeredes fucceffórefque fui cuique liberi, et nullum*
"*teftamentum: fi liberi non funt, proximus gradus in poffeffione,*
"*fratres, patrui, avunculi*[t]."

<hr>

[t] Tacitus *de mor. Germ.* 21.

Now here it muft be obferved, that the lineal anceftors, though (according to the firft rule) incapable themfelves of fucceeding to the eftate, becaufe it is fuppofed to have already paffed them, are yet the common ftocks from which the next fucceffor muft fpring. And therefore in the Jewifh law, which in this refpect entirely correfponds with ours ", the father or other lineal anceftor is himfelf faid to be the heir, though long fince dead, as being reprefented by the perfons of his iffue; who are held to fucceed not in their own rights, as brethren, uncles, *&c*, but in right of reprefentation, as the fons of the father, grandfather, *&c*, of the deceafed ᵛ. But, though the common anceftor be thus the root of the inheritance, yet with us it is not neceffary to *name* him in making out the pedigree or defcent. For the defcent between two brothers is held to be an *immediate* defcent; and therefore title may be made by one brother or his reprefentatives *to* or *through* another, without mentioning their common father ᵂ. If Geoffrey Stiles hath two fons, John and Francis, Francis may claim as heir to John, without naming their father Geoffrey: and fo the fon of Francis may claim as coufin and heir to Matthew the fon of John, without naming the grandfather; viz. as fon of Francis, who was the brother of John, who was the father of Matthew. But though the common anceftors are not named in deducing the pedigree, yet the law ftill refpects them as the fountains of inheritable blood: and therefore in order to afcertain the collateral heir of John Stiles, it is in the firft place neceffary to recur to his anceftors in the firft degree; and if they have left any other iffue befides John, that iffue will be his heir. On default of fuch, we muft afcend one ftep higher to the anceftors in the fecond degree, and then to thofe in the third, and fourth, and fo upwards *in infinitum*; till fome anceftors be found, who have other iffue defcending from them befides the deceafed, in a parallel or collateral line. From thefe anceftors the heir of John Stiles muft derive his defcent; and in fuch derivation the fame rules muft

ᵘ Numb. c. 27. ᵂ 1 Sid. 193. 1 Lev. 60. 12 Mod. 619.
ᵛ Selden. *de fucc. Ebr. c.* 12.

be

be obferved, with regard to fex, primogeniture, and reprefentation, that have juft been laid down with regard to lineal defcents
from the perfon of the laft proprietor.

BUT, fecondly, the heir need not be the neareft kinfman abfolutely, but only *fub modo*; that is, he muft be the neareft kinfman of the whole blood; for, if there be a much nearer kinfman of the half blood, a diftant kinfman of the whole blood
fhall be admitted, and the other entirely excluded.

A KINSMAN of the whole blood is he that is derived, not
only from the fame anceftor, but from the fame couple of anceftors. For, as every man's own blood is compounded of the bloods
of his refpective anceftors, he only is properly of the whole or
entire blood with another, who hath (fo far as the diftance of degrees will permit) all the fame ingredients in the compofition of
his blood that the other hath. Thus, the blood of John Stiles
being compofed of thofe of Geoffrey Stiles his father and Lucy
Baker his mother, therefore his brother Francis, being defcended
from both the fame parents, hath entirely the fame blood with
John Stiles; or, he is his brother of the whole blood. But if,
after the death of Geoffrey, Lucy Baker the mother marries a
fecond hufband, Lewis Gay, and hath iffue by him; the blood
of this iffue, being compounded of the blood of Lucy Baker (it
is true) on the one part, but of that of Lewis Gay (inftead of
Geoffrey Stiles) on the other part, it hath therefore only half the
fame ingredients with that of John Stiles; fo that he is only his
brother of the half blood, and for that reafon they fhall never
inherit to each other. So alfo, if the father has two fons, A and
B, by different venters or wives; now thefe two brethren are
not brethren of the whole blood, and therefore fhall never inherit to each other, but the eftate fhall rather efcheat to the lord.
Nay, even if the father dies, and his lands defcend to his eldeft
fon A, who enters thereon, and dies feifed without iffue; ftill B
fhall not be heir to this eftate, becaufe he is only of the half
blood to A, the perfon laft feifed: but, had A died without en-

try

try, then B might have inherited ; not as heir to A his half-bro-
ther, but as heir to their common father, who was the perfon
laft actually feifed[x].

THIS total exclufion of the half blood from the inheritance,
being almoft peculiar to our own law, is looked upon as a ftrange
hardfhip by fuch as are unacquainted with the reafons on which
it is grounded. But thefe cenfures arife from a mifapprehenfion
of the rule ; which is not fo much to be confidered in the light
of a rule of defcent, as of a rule of evidence ; an auxiliary rule,
to carry a former into execution. And here we muft again remember, that the great and moft univerfal principle of collateral
inheritances being this, that an heir to a *feudum antiquum* muft
be of the blood of the firft feudatory or purchafor, that is, derived in a lineal defcent from him ; it was originally requifite, as
upon gifts in tail it ftill is, to make out the pedigree of the heir
from the firft donee or purchafor, and to fhew that fuch heir was
his lineal reprefentative. But when, by length of time and a long
courfe of defcents, it came (in thofe rude and unlettered ages) to
be forgotten who was really the firft feudatory or purchafor, and
thereby the proof of an actual defcent from him became impoffible ; then the law fubftituted what fir Martin Wright[y] calls a
reafonable, in the ftead of an *impoffible*, proof : for it remits the
proof of an actual defcent from the firft purchafor ; and only requires, in lieu of it, that the claimant be next of the whole blood
to the perfon laft in poffeffion ; (or derived from the fame couple
of anceftors) which will probably anfwer the fame end as if he
could trace his pedigree in a direct line from the firft purchafor.
For he who is my kinfman of the whole blood can have no anceftors beyond or higher than the common ftock, but what are
equally my anceftors alfo ; and mine are *vice verfa* his : he therefore is very likely to be derived from that unknown anceftor of
mine, from whom the inheritance defcended. But a kinfman
of the half blood has but one half of his anceftors above the
common ftock the fame as mine ; and therefore there is not the

[x] Hale. H. C. L. 238.   [y] Tenures. 186.

fame

fame probability of that ftanding requifite in the law, that he be derived from the blood of the firft purchafor.

To illuftrate this by example. Let there be John Stiles, and Francis, brothers by the fame father and mother, and another fon of the fame mother by Lewis Gay a fecond hufband. Now, if John dies feifed of lands, but it is uncertain whether they defcended to him from his father or mother; in this cafe his brother Francis, of the whole blood, is qualified to be his heir; for he is fure to be in the line of defcent from the firft purchafor, whether it were the line of the father or the mother. But if Francis fhould die before John, without iffue, the mother's fon by Lewis Gay (or brother of the half blood) is utterly incapable of being heir; for he cannot prove his defcent from the firft purchafor, who is unknown, nor has he that fair probability which the law admits as prefumptive evidence, fince he is to the full as likely *not to be* defcended from the line of the firft purchafor, as *to be* defcended: and therefore the inheritance fhall go to the neareft relation poffeffed of this prefumptive proof, the whole blood.

AND, as this is the cafe *in feudis antiquis,* where there really did once exift a purchafing anceftor, who is forgotten; it is alfo the cafe *in feudis novis* held *ut antiquis,* where the purchafing anceftor is merely ideal, and never exifted but only in fiction of law. Of this nature are all grants of lands in fee-fimple at this day, which are inheritable as if they defcended from fome uncertain indefinite anceftor, and therefore any of the collateral kindred of the real modern purchafor (and not his own offspring only) may inherit them, provided they be of the whole blood; for all fuch are, in judgment of law, likely enough to be derived from this indefinite anceftor: but thofe of the half blood are excluded, for want of the fame probability. Nor fhould this be thought hard, that a brother of the purchafor, though only of the half blood, muft thus be difinherited, and a more remote relation of the whole blood admitted, merely upon a fuppofition and

fiction

fiction of law; fince it is only upon a like fuppofition and fiction, that brethren of purchafors (whether of the whole or half blood) are entitled to inherit at all: for we have feen that in *feudis ſtriƈte novis* neither brethren nor any other collaterals were admitted. As therefore *in feudis antiquis* we have feen the reafonablenefs of excluding the half blood, if by a fiction of law a *feudum novum* be made defcendible to collaterals as if it was *feudum antiquum,* it is juſt and equitable that it fhould be fubjeƈt to the fame re-ſtriƈtions as well as the fame latitude of defcent.

Perhaps by this time the exclufion of the half blood does not appear altogether fo unreafonable, as at firſt fight it is apt to do. It is certainly a very fine-fpun and fubtile nicety: but, con-fidering the principles upon which our law is founded, it is nei-ther an injuſtice nor a hardſhip; fince even the fucceffion of the whole blood was originally a beneficial indulgence, rather than the ſtriƈt right of collaterals: and, though that indulgence is not extended to the demi-kindred, yet they are rarely abridged of any right which they could poffibly have enjoyed before. The doƈtrine of whole blood was calculated to fupply the frequent impoffibility of proving a defcent from the firſt purchafor, with-out fome proof of which (according to our fundamental maxim) there can be no inheritance allowed of. And this purpofe it an-fwers, for the moſt part, effeƈtually enough. I fpeak with thefe reſtriƈtions, becaufe it does not, neither can any other method, anfwer this purpofe entirely. For though all the anceſtors of John Stiles, above the common ſtock, are alfo the anceſtors of his col-lateral kinfman of the whole blood; yet, unlefs that common ſtock be in the firſt degree, (that is, unlefs they have the fame father and mother) there will be intermediate anceſtors below the common ſtock, that may belong to either of them refpeƈtively, from which the other is not defcended, and therefore can have none of their blood. Thus, though John Stiles and his brother of the whole blood can each have no other anceſtors, than what are in common to them both; yet with regard to his uncle, where the common ſtock is removed one degree higher, (that is,

the

the grandfather and grandmother) one half of John's anceftors will not be the anceftors of his uncle: his *patruus*, or father's brother, derives not his defcent from John's maternal anceftors; nor his *avunculus*, or mother's brother, from thofe in the paternal line. Here then the fupply of proof is deficient, and by no means amounts to a certainty: and, the higher the common ftock is removed, the more will even the probability decreafe. But it muft be obferved, that (upon the fame principles of calculation) the half blood have always a much lefs chance to be defcended from an unknown indefinite anceftor of the deceafed, than the whole blood in the fame degree. As, in the firft degree, the whole brother of John Stiles is fure to be defcended from that unknown anceftor; his half brother has only an even chance, for half John's anceftors are not his. So, in the fecond degree, John's uncle of the whole blood has an even chance; but the chances are three to one againft his uncle of the half blood, for three fourths of John's anceftors are not his. In like manner, in the third degree, the chances are only three to one againft John's great uncle of the whole blood, but they are feven to one againft his great uncle of the half blood, for feven eighths of John's anceftors have no connexion in blood with him. Therefore the much lefs probability of the half blood's defcent from the firft purchafor, compared with that of the whole blood, in the feveral degrees, has occafioned a general exclufion of the half blood in all.

BUT, while I thus illuftrate the reafon of excluding the half blood in general, I muft be impartial enough to own, that, in fome inftances, the practice is carried farther than the principle upon which it goes will warrant. Particularly, when a man has two fons by different venters, and the eftate on his death defcends from him to the eldeft, who enters, and dies without iffue: now the younger fon cannot inherit this eftate, becaufe he is not of the whole blood to the laft proprietor. This, it muft be owned, carries a hardfhip with it, even upon feodal principles: for the rule was introduced only to fupply the proof of a defcent from the firft purchafor; but here, as this eftate notorioufly defcended from

the

the father, and as both the brothers confeſſedly ſprung from him, it is demonſtrable that the half brother muſt be of the blood of the firſt purchaſor, who was either the father or ſome of the father's anceſtors. When therefore there is actual demonſtration of the thing to be proved, it is hard to exclude a man by a rule ſubſtituted to ſupply that proof when deficient. So far as the inheritance can be evidently traced back, there ſeems no need of calling in this preſumptive proof, this rule of probability, to inveſtigate what is already certain. Had the elder brother indeed been a purchaſor, there would have been no hardſhip at all, for the reaſons already given : or had the *frater uterinus* only, or brother by the mother's ſide, been excluded from an inheritance which deſcended from the father, it had been highly reaſonable.

I N D E E D it is this very inſtance, of excluding a *frater conſanguineus*, or brother by the father's ſide, from an inheritance which deſcended *a patre*, that Craig[z] has ſingled out, on which to ground his ſtrictures on the Engliſh law of half blood. And, really, it ſhould ſeem, as if the cuſtom of excluding the half blood in Normandy[a] extended only to exclude a *frater uterinus*, when the inheritance deſcended *a patre*, and *vice verſa :* as even with us it remained a doubt, in the time of Bracton[b], and of Fleta[c], whether the half blood on the father's ſide were excluded from the inheritance which originally deſcended from the common father, or only from ſuch as deſcended from the reſpective mothers, and from newly purchaſed lands. And the rule of law, as laid down by our Forteſcue[d], extends no farther than this ; *frater fratri uterino non ſuccedet in haereditate paterna.* It is moreover worthy of obſervation, that by our law, as it now ſtands, the crown (which is the higheſt inheritance in the nation) may deſcend to the half blood of the preceding ſovereign[e], ſo as it be the blood of the firſt monarch, purchaſor, or (in the feodal language) conqueror, of the reigning family. Thus it actually

[z] *l. 2. t.* 15. §. 14.
[a] Gr. *Couſtum. c.* 25.
[b] *l. 2. c.* 30. §. 3.

[c] *l. 6. c.* 1. §. 14.
[d] *de laud. LL. Angl.* 5.
[e] Plowd. 245. Co. Litt. 15.

did

did defcend from king Edward the fixth to queen Mary, and from her to queen Elizabeth, who were refpectively of the half blood to each other. For, the royal pedigree being always a matter of fufficient notoriety, there is no occafion to call in the aid of this prefumptive rule of evidence, to render probable the defcent from the royal ftock; which was formerly king William the Norman, and is now (by act of parliament[f]) the princefs Sophia of Hanover. Hence alfo it is, that in eftates-tail, where the pedigree from the firft donee muft be ftrictly proved, half blood is no impediment to the defcent[g]: becaufe, when the lineage is clearly made out, there is no need of this auxiliary proof. How far it might be defirable for the legiflature to give relief, by amending the law of defcents in this fingle inftance, and ordaining that the half blood might inherit, where the eftate notorioufly defcended from it's own proper anceftor, but not otherwife; or how far a private inconvenience fhould be fubmitted to, rather than a long eftablifhed rule fhould be fhaken; it is not for me to determine.

THE rule then, together with it's illuftration, amounts to this: that, in order to keep the eftate of John Stiles as nearly as poffible in the line of his purchafing anceftor, it muft defcend to the iffue of the neareft couple of anceftors that have left defcendants behind them; becaufe the defcendants of one anceftor only are not fo likely to be in the line of that purchafing anceftor, as thofe who are defcended from two.

BUT here another difficulty arifes. In the fecond, third, fourth, and every fuperior degree, every man has many couples of anceftors, increafing according to the diftances in a geometrical progreffion upwards[h], the defcendants of all which refpective couples are (reprefentatively) related to him in the fame degree. Thus in the fecond degree, the iffue of George and Cecilia Stiles and of Andrew and Efther Baker, the two grandfires and grand-

---

[f] 12 Will. III. c. 2.
[g] Litt. §. 14, 15.
[h] See pag. 204.

mothers of John Stiles, are each in the fame degree of propinquity; in the third degree, the refpective iffues of Walter and Chriftian Stiles, of Luke and Frances Kempe, of Herbert and Hannah Baker, and of James and Emma Thorpe, are (upon the extinction of the two inferior degrees) all equally entitled to call themfelves the next kindred of the whole blood to John Stiles. To which therefore of thefe anceftors muft we firft refort, in order to find out defcendants to be preferably called to the inheritance? In anfwer to this, and to avoid the confufion and uncertainty that muft arife between the feveral ftocks, wherein the purchafing anceftor may be fought for,

VII. T H E feventh and laft rule or canon is, that in collateral inheritances the male ftocks fhall be preferred to the female; (that is, kindred derived from the blood of the male anceftors fhall be admitted before thofe from the blood of the female) --- unlefs where the lands have, in fact, defcended from a female.

T H U S the relations on the father's fide are admitted *in infinitum,* before thofe on the mother's fide are admitted at all[i]; and the relations of the father's father, before thofe of the father's mother; and fo on. And in this the Englifh law is not fingular, but warranted by the examples of the Hebrew and Athenian laws, as ftated by Selden[k], and Petit[l]; though among the Greeks, in the time of Hefiod[m], when a man died without wife or children, all his kindred (without any diftinction) divided his eftate among them. It is likewife warranted by the example of the Roman laws; wherein the *agnati,* or relations by the father, were preferred to the *cognati,* or relations by the mother, till the edict of the emperor Juftinian[n] abolifhed all diftinction between them. It is alfo conformable to the cuftomary law of Normandy[o], which indeed in moft refpects agrees with our law of inheritance.

[i] Litt. §. 4.
[k] *de fucc. Ebraeor. c.* 12.
[l] *LL. Attic. l.* 1. *t.* 6.

[m] Θεογον. 606.
[n] *Nov.* 118.
[o] *Gr. Couftum. c.* 25.

H O W E V E R

HOWEVER, I am inclined to think, that this rule of our laws does not owe it's immediate original to any view of conformity to thofe which I have juft now mentioned; but was eftablifhed in order to effectuate and carry into execution the fifth rule or canon before laid down; that every heir muft be of the blood of the firft purchafor. For, when fuch firft purchafor was not eafily to be difcovered after a long courfe of defcents, the lawyers not only endeavoured to inveftigate him by taking the next relation of the whole blood to the perfon laft in poffeffion; but alfo, confidering that a preference had been given to males (by virtue of the fecond canon) through the whole courfe of lineal defcent from the firft purchafor to the prefent time, they judged it more likely that the lands fhould have defcended to the laft tenant from his male than from his female anceftors; from the father (for inftance) rather than from the mother; from the father's father, rather than the father's mother: and therefore they hunted back the inheritance (if I may be allowed the expreffion) through the male line; and gave it to the next relations on the fide of the father, the father's father, and fo upwards; imagining with reafon that this was the moft probable way of continuing it in the line of the firft purchafor. A conduct much more rational than the preference of the *agnati* by the Roman laws: which, as they gave no advantage to the males in the firft inftance or direct lineal fucceffion, had no reafon for preferring them in the tranfverfe collateral one: upon which account this preference was very wifely abolifhed by Juftinian.

THAT this was the true foundation of the preference of the *agnati* or male ftocks, in our law, will farther appear if we confider, that, whenever the lands have notorioufly defcended to a man from his mother's fide, this rule is totally reverfed, and no relation of his by the father's fide, as fuch, can ever be admitted to them; becaufe he cannot poffibly be of the blood of the firft purchafor. And fo, *e converfo*, if the lands defcended from the father's fide, no relation of the mother, as fuch, fhall ever in-

herit

herit. So alſo, if they in faċt deſcended to John Stiles from his father's mother Cecilia Kempe; here not only the blood of Lucy Baker his mother, but alſo of George Stiles his father's father, is perpetually excluded. And, in like manner, if they be known to have deſcended from Frances Holland the mother of Cecilia Kempe, the line not only of Lucy Baker, and of George Stiles, but alſo of Luke Kempe the father of Cecilia, is excluded. Whereas when the ſide from which they deſcended is forgotten, or never known, (as in the caſe of an eſtate newly purchaſed to be holden *ut feudum antiquum*) here the right of inheritance firſt runs up all the father's ſide, with a preference to the male ſtocks in every inſtance; and, if it finds no heirs there, it then, and then only, reſorts to the mother's ſide; leaving no place untried, in order to find heirs that may by poſſibility be derived from the original purchaſor. The greateſt probability of finding ſuch was among thoſe deſcended from the male anceſtors; but, upon failure of iſſue there, they may poſſibly be found among thoſe derived from the females.

THIS I take to be the true reaſon of the conſtant preference of the agnatic ſucceſſion, or iſſue derived from the male anceſtors, through all the ſtages of collateral inheritance; as the ability for perſonal ſervice was the reaſon for preferring the males at firſt in the direċt lineal ſucceſſion. We ſee clearly, that, if males had been perpetually admitted, in utter excluſion of females, the tracing the inheritance back through the male line of anceſtors muſt at laſt have inevitably brought us up to the firſt purchaſor : but, as males have not been *perpetually admitted*, but only *generally preferred*; as females have not been *utterly excluded*, but only *generally poſtponed* to males; the tracing the inheritance up through the male ſtocks will not give us abſolute demonſtration, but only a ſtrong probability, of arriving at the firſt purchaſor; which, joined with the other probability, of the wholeneſs or entirety of blood, will fall little ſhort of a certainty.

BEFORE

BEFORE we conclude this branch of our enquiries, it may not be amifs to exemplify thefe rules by a fhort fketch of the manner in which we muft fearch for the heir of a perfon, as *John Stiles,* who dies feifed of land which he acquired, and which therefore he held as a feud of indefinite antiquity [P].

IN the firft place fucceeds the eldeft fon, Matthew Stiles, or his iffue: (n° 1.) --- if his line be extinct, then Gilbert Stiles and the other fons, refpectively, in order of birth, or their iffue: (n° 2.) --- in default of thefe, all the daughters together, Margaret and Charlotte Stiles, or their iffue. (n° 3.) --- On failure of the defcendants of *John Stiles* himfelf, the iffue of Geoffrey and Lucy Stiles, his parents, is called in: *viz.* firft, Francis Stiles, the eldeft brother of the whole blood, or his iffue: (n° 4.) --- then Oliver Stiles, and the other whole brothers, refpectively, in order of birth, or their iffue: (n° 5.) --- then the fifters of the whole blood, all together, Bridget and Alice Stiles, or their iffue. (n° 6.) --- In defect of thefe, the iffue of George and Cecilia Stiles, his father's parents; refpect being ftill had to their age and fex: (n° 7.) --- then the iffue of Walter and Chriftian Stiles, the parents of his paternal grandfather: (n° 8.) --- then the iffue of Richard and Anne Stiles, the parents of his paternal grandfather's father: (n° 9.) --- and fo on in the paternal grandfather's paternal line, or blood of Walter Stiles, *in infinitum.* In defect of thefe, the iffue of William and Jane Smith, the parents of his paternal grandfather's mother: (n° 10.) --- and fo on in the paternal grandfather's maternal line, or blood of Chriftian Smith, *in infinitum*; till both the immediate bloods of George Stiles, the paternal grandfather, are fpent. --- Then we muft refort to the iffue of Luke and Frances Kempe, the parents of *John Stiles's* paternal grandmother: (n° 11.) --- then to the iffue of Thomas and Sarah Kempe, the parents of his paternal grandmother's father: (n° 12.) --- and fo on in the paternal grandmother's paternal line, or blood of Luke Kempe, *in infinitum.* ---

[P] See the table of defcents annexed.

In

In default of which, we muſt call in the iſſue of Charles and
Mary Holland, the parents of his paternal grandmother's mother:
(n° 13.) --- and ſo on in the paternal grandmother's maternal
line, or blood of Frances Holland, *in infinitum*; till both the
immediate bloods of Cecilia Kempe, the paternal grandmother,
are alſo ſpent. --- Whereby the paternal blood of *John Stiles* entirely failing, recourſe muſt then, and not before, be had to his
maternal relations; or the blood of the Bakers, (n° 14, 15, 16.)
Willis's, (n° 17.) Thorpes, (n° 18, 19.) and Whites; (n° 20.)
in the ſame regular ſucceſſive order as in the paternal line.

T H E ſtudent ſhould however be informed, that the claſs, n° 10,
would be poſtponed to n° 11, in conſequence of the doctrine laid
down, *arguendo*, by juſtice Manwoode, in the caſe of Clere and
Brooke [q]; from whence it is adopted by lord Bacon [r], and ſir Matthew Hale [s]. And yet, notwithſtanding theſe reſpectable authorities, the compiler of this table hath ventured to give the preference therein to n° 10 before n° 11; for the following reaſons:
1. Becauſe this point was not the principal queſtion in the caſe of
Clere and Brooke; but the law concerning it is delivered *obiter*
only, and in the courſe of argument, by juſtice Manwoode;
though afterwards ſaid to be confirmed by the three other juſti-
ces in ſeparate, extrajudicial, conferences with the reporter.
2. Becauſe the chief-juſtice, ſir James Dyer, in reporting the reſolution of the court in what ſeems to be the ſame caſe [t], takes
no notice of this doctrine. 3. Becauſe it appears, from Plowden's
report, that very many gentlemen of the law were diſſatisfied
with this poſition of juſtice Manwoode. 4. Becauſe the poſition
itſelf deſtroys the otherwiſe entire and regular ſymmetry of our
legal courſe of deſcents, as is manifeſt by inſpecting the table;
and deſtroys alſo that conſtant preference of the male ſtocks in
the law of inheritance, for which an additional reaſon is before
given, beſides the mere dignity of blood. 5. Becauſe it introduces all that uncertainty and contradiction, which is pointed

q Plowd. 450.   s H. C. L. 240, 244.
r Elem. c. 1.   t Dyer. 314.

out by an ingenious author[u]; and eſtabliſhes a collateral doctrine, incompatible with the principal point reſolved in the caſe of Clere and Brooke, viz. the preference of n° 11 to n° 14. And, though that learned writer propoſes to reſcind the principal point then reſolved, in order to clear this difficulty; it is apprehended, that the difficulty may be better cleared, by rejecting the collateral doctrine, which was never yet reſolved at all. 6. Becauſe by the reaſon that is given for this doctrine, in Plowden, Bacon, and Hale, (viz. that in any degree, paramount the firſt, the law reſpecteth proximity, and not dignity of blood) n° 18 ought alſo to be preferred to n° 16; which is directly contrary to the eighth rule laid down by Hale himſelf[w]. 7. Becauſe this poſition ſeems to contradict the allowed doctrine of ſir Edward Coke[x]; who lays it down (under different names) that the blood of the Kempes (*alias* Sandies) ſhall not inherit till the blood of the Stiles's (*alias* Fairfields) fail. Now the blood of the Stiles's does certainly not fail, till both n° 9 and n° 10 are extinct. Wherefore n° 11 (being the blood of the Kempes) ought not to inherit till then. 8. Becauſe in the caſe, Mich. 12 Edw. IV. 14[y]. (much relied on in that of Clere and Brooke) it is laid down as a rule, that "*ceſtuy, que doit inheriter al pere, doit inheriter al fits.*" And ſo ſir Matthew Hale[z] ſays, "that though the law excludes the father from in-"heriting, yet it ſubſtitutes and directs the deſcent, as it ſhould "have been, had the father inherited." Now it is ſettled, by the reſolution in Clere and Brooke, that n° 10 ſhould have inherited to Geoffrey Stiles, the father, before n° 11; and therefore n° 10 ought alſo to be preferred in inheriting to *John Stiles,* the ſon.

IN caſe *John Stiles* was not himſelf the purchaſor, but the eſtate in fact came to him by deſcent from his father, mother, or any higher anceſtor, there is this difference; that the blood of that line of anceſtors, from which it did not deſcend, can never

[u] Law of inheritances. 2ᵈ edit. pag. 30, 38, 61, 62, 66.

[w] Hiſt. C. L. 247.

[x] Co. Litt. 12. Hawk. abr. *in loc.*

[y] Fitzh. abr. tit. *diſcent.* 2. Bro. abr. t. *diſcent.* 3.

[z] Hiſt. C. L. 243.

inherit

inherit. Thus, if it defcended from Geoffrey Stiles, the father, the blood of Lucy Baker, the mother, is perpetually excluded : and fo, *vice verfa*, if it defcended from Lucy Baker, it cannot defcend to the blood of Geoffrey Stiles. This, in either cafe, cuts off one half of the table from any poffible fucceffion. And farther, if it can be fhewn to have defcended from George Stiles, this cuts off three fourths ; for now the blood, not only of Lucy Baker, but alfo of Cecilia Kempe, is excluded. If, laftly, it defcended from Walter Stiles, this narrows the fucceffion ftill more, and cuts off feven eighths of the table ; for now, neither the blood of Lucy Baker, nor of Cecilia Kempe, nor of Chrif-tian Smith, can ever fucceed to the inheritance. And the like rule will hold upon defcents from any other anceftors.

THE ftudent fhould bear in mind, that, during this whole procefs, *John Stiles* is the perfon fuppofed to have been laft ac-tually feifed of the eftate. For if ever it comes to veft in any other perfon, as heir to *John Stiles*, a new order of fucceffion muft be obferved upon the death of fuch heir ; fince he, by his own feifin, now becomes himfelf an anceftor, or *ftipes*, and muft be put in the place of *John Stiles*. The figures therefore denote the order, in which the feveral claffes would fucceed to *John Stiles*, and not to each other : and, before we fearch for an heir in any of the higher figures, (as n° 8.) we muft be firft affured that all the lower claffes (from n° 1 to 7.) were extinct, at *John Stiles's* deceafe.

CHAPTER THE FIFTEENTH.

OF TITLE BY PURCHASE, AND FIRST
BY ESCHEAT.

PURCHASE, *perquifitio*, taken in it's largeſt and moſt extenſive ſenſe, is thus defined by Littleton[a]; the poſſeſſion of
lands and tenements, which a man hath by his own act or agreement; and not by deſcent from any of his anceſtors or kindred.
In this ſenſe it is contradiſtinguiſhed from acquiſition by right of
blood, and includes every other method of coming to an eſtate,
but merely that by inheritance; wherein the title is veſted in a
perſon, not by his own act or agreement, but by the ſingle operation of law[b].

PURCHASE, indeed, in it's vulgar and confined acceptation,
is applied only to ſuch acquiſitions of land, as are obtained by
way of bargain and ſale, for money, or ſome other valuable conſideration. But this falls far ſhort of the legal idea of purchaſe:
for, if I *give* land freely to another, he is in the eye of the law
a purchaſor[c]; and falls within Littleton's definition, for he comes
to the eſtate by his own agreement, that is, he conſents to the
gift. A man who has his father's eſtate ſettled upon him in tail,
before he is born, is alſo a purchaſor; for he takes quite another
eſtate than the law of deſcents would have given him. Nay even
if the anceſtor deviſes his eſtate to his heir at law by will, with
other limitations or in any other ſhape than the courſe of deſcents
would direct, ſuch heir ſhall take by purchaſe[d]. But if a man,
ſeiſed in fee, deviſes his whole eſtate to his heir at law, ſo that
the heir takes neither a greater nor a leſs eſtate by the deviſe than

a §. 12.
b Co. Litt. 18.
c *Ibid.*
d Lord Raym. 728.

PATERNAL LINE

MATERNAL LINE

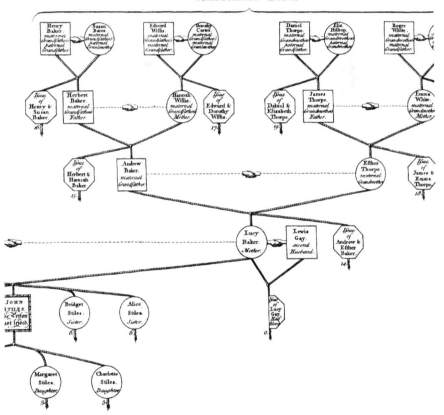

he would have done without it, he fhall be adjudged to take by
defcent[e], even though it be charged with incumbrances[f]; for the
benefit of creditors, and others, who have demands on the eftate
of the anceftor. If a remainder be limited to *the heirs* of Sempronius, here Sempronius himfelf takes nothing; but, if he dies
during the continuance of the particular eftate, his heirs fhall take
as purchafors[g]. But, if an eftate be made to A for life, remainder to his right heirs in fee, his heirs fhall take by defcent : for
it is an antient rule of law, that wherever the anceftor takes an
eftate for life, the heir cannot by the fame conveyance take an
eftate in fee by *purchafe*, but only by *defcent*[h]. And, if A dies
before entry, ftill his heir fhall take by defcent, and not by purchafe ; for, where the heir takes any thing that might have vefted
in the anceftor, he takes by way of defcent[i]. The anceftor, during his life, beareth in himfelf all his heirs[k]; and therefore,
when once he is or might have been feifed of the land, the
inheritance fo limited to his heirs vefts in the anceftor himfelf : and the word " heirs" in this cafe is not efteemed a word
of *purchafe*, but a word of *limitation*, enuring fo as to encreafe
the eftate of the anceftor from a tenancy for life to a fee-fimple.
And, had it been otherwife, had the heir (who is uncertain till
the death of the anceftor) been allowed to take as a purchafor o-
riginally nominated in the deed, as muft have been the cafe if the
remainder had been exprefsly limited to Matthew or Thomas by
name ; then, in the times of ftrict feodal tenure, the lord would
have been defrauded by fuch a limitation of the fruits of his figniory, arifing from a defcent to the heir.

WH A T we call *purchafe*, *perquifitio*, the feudifts call *conqueſt*,
conquaeſtus, or *conquifitio*[l] : both denoting any means of acquiring
an eftate out of the common courfe of inheritance. And this is
ftill the proper phrafe in the law of Scotland[m]; as it was, among

[e] 1 Roll. Abr. 626.
[f] Salk. 241. Lord Raym. 728.
[g] 1 Roll. Abr. 627.
[h] 1 Rep. 104. 2 Lev. 60. Raym. 334.
[i] 1 Rep. 98.
[k] Co. Litt. 23.
[l] Crag. *l.* 1. *t.* 10. §. 18.
[m] Dalrymple of feuds. 210.

the

the Norman jurifts, who ftiled the firft purchafor (that is, he who firft brought the eftate into the family which at prefent owns it) the conqueror or *conquereur*[n]. Which feems to be all that was meant by the appellation which was given to William the Norman, when his manner of afcending the throne of England was, in his own and his fucceffors' charters, and by the hiftorians of the times, entitled *conquaeftus*, and himfelf *conquaeftor* or *conquifitor*[o]; fignifying, that he was the firft of his family who acquired the crown of England, and from whom therefore all future claims by defcent muft be derived : though now, from our difufe of the feodal fenfe of the word, together with the reflexion on his forcible method of acquifition, we are apt to annex the idea of *victory* to this name of *conqueft* or *conquifition*; a title which, however juft with regard to the *crown*, the conqueror never pretended with regard to the *realm* of England, nor, in fact, ever had[p].

THE difference in effect, between the acquifition of an eftate by defcent and by purchafe, confifts principally in thefe two points : 1. That by purchafe the eftate acquires a new inheritable quality, and is defcendible to the owner's blood in general, and not the blood only of fome particular anceftor. For, when a man takes an eftate by purchafe, he takes it not *ut feudum paternum* or *maternum*, which would defcend only to the heirs by the father's or the mother's fide : but he takes it *ut feudum antiquum*, as a feud of indefinite antiquity; whereby it becomes inheritable to his heirs general, firft of the paternal, and then of the maternal line[q]. 2. An eftate taken by purchafe will not make the heir anfwerable for the acts of the anceftor, as an eftate by defcent will. For, if the anceftor by any deed, obligation, covenant, or the like, bindeth himfelf and his heirs, and dieth; this deed, obligation, or covenant, fhall be binding upon the heir, fo far forth only as he had any eftate of inheritance vefted in him (or in fome other in truft for him[r]) by defcent from that

[n] *Gr. Couftum. Gloff. c. 25. pag.* 40.
[o] Spelm. *Gloff.* 145.
[p] See Book I. ch. 3.

[q] See pag 236.
[r] Stat. 29 Car. II. c. 3.

G g 2 anceftor,

anceftor, fufficient to anfwer the charge'; whether he remains in poffeffion, or hath aliened it before action brought ': which fufficient eftate is in law called *affets*; from the French word, *affez*, enough ". Therefore if a man covenants, for himfelf and his heirs, to keep my houfe in repair, I can then (and then only) compel his heir to perform this covenant, when he has an eftate fufficient for this purpofe, or *affets*, by defcent from the cove-nantor : for though the covenant defcends to the heir, whether he inherits any eftate or no, it lies dormant, and is not compul-fory, until he has affets by defcent ᵛ.

THIS is the legal fignification of the word *perquifitio*, or pur-chafe ; and in this fenfe it includes the five following methods of acquiring a title to eftates : 1. Efcheat. 2. Occupancy. 3 Pre-fcription. 4. Forfeiture. 5. Alienation. Of all thefe in their order.

I. ESCHEAT, we may remember ʷ, was one of the fruits and confequences of feodal tenure. The word itfelf is originally French or Norman ˣ, in which language it fignifies chance or ac-cident ; and with us denotes an obftruction of the courfe of de-fcent, and a confequent determination of the tenure, by fome unforefeen contingency : in which cafe the land naturally refults back, by a kind of reverfion, to the original grantor or lord of the fee ʸ.

ESCHEAT therefore being a title frequently vefted in the lord by inheritance, as being the fruit of a figniory to which he was intitled by defcent, (for which reafon the lands efcheating fhall attend the figniory, and be inheritable by fuch only of his heirs as are capable of inheriting the other ᶻ) it may feem in fuch cafes to fall more properly under the former general head of acquiring title to eftates, *viz.* by defcent, (being vefted in him by act of

---

ˢ 1 P. Wᵐˢ. 777.

ᵗ Stat. 3 & 4 W. & M. c. 14.

ᵘ Finch. law. 119.

ᵛ Finch. Rep. 86.

ʷ See pag. 72.

ˣ *Efchet* or *échet*, formed from the verb *efchoir* or *échoir*, to happen.

ʸ 1 *Feud.* 86. Co. Litt. 13.

ᶻ Co. Litt. 13.

law,

law, and not by his own act or agreement) than under the present, by purchase. But it must be remembered that in order to
complete this title by escheat, it is necessary that the lord perform
an act of his own, by *entering* on the lands and tenements so es-
cheated, or suing out a *writ of escheat*[a] *:* on failure of which,
or by doing any act that amounts to an implied waiver of his
right, as by accepting homage or rent of a stranger who usurps
the possession, his title by escheat is barred[b]. It is therefore in
some respect a title acquired by his own act, as well as by act of
law. Indeed this may also be said of descents themselves, in
which an entry or other seisin is required, in order to make a
complete title; and therefore this distribution by our legal writers seems in this respect rather inaccurate : for, as escheats must
follow the nature of the signiory to which they belong, they may
vest by either purchase or descent, according as the signiory is
vested. And, though sir Edward Coke considers the lord by escheat as in some respects the assignee of the last tenant[c], and
therefore taking by purchase; yet, on the other hand, the lord
is more frequently considered as being *ultimus haeres*, and therefore taking by descent in a kind of caducary succession.

THE law of escheats is founded upon this single principle,
that the blood of the person last seised in fee-simple is, by some
means or other, utterly extinct and gone : and, since none can
inherit his estate but such as are of his blood and consanguinity,
it follows as a regular consequence, that when such blood is extinct, the inheritance itself must fail; the land must become
what the feodal writers denominate *feudum apertum*; and must
result back again to the lord of the fee, by whom, or by those
whose estate he hath, it was given.

ESCHEATS are frequently divided into those *propter defectum
sanguinis* and those *propter delictum tenentis :* the one sort, if the
tenant dies without heirs; the other, if his blood be attainted[d].

[a] Bro. *Abr. tit. escheat.* 26.   [c] 1 Inst. 215.
[b] *Ibid. tit. acceptance.* 25. Co. Litt. 268.   [d] Co. Litt. 13. 92.

But both thefe fpecies may well be comprehended under the firft denomination only; for he that is attainted fuffers an extinction of his blood, as well as he that dies without relations. The inheritable quality is expunged in one inftance, and expires in the other; or, as the doctrine of efcheats is very fully expreffed in Fleta.[c], "*dominus capitalis feodi loco haeredis habetur, quoties per* "*defectum vel delictum extinguitur fanguis tenentis.*"

ESCHEATS therefore arifing merely upon the deficiency of the blood, whereby the defcent is impeded, their doctrine will be better illuftrated by confidering the feveral cafes wherein hereditary blood may be deficient, than by any other method whatfoever.

1, 2, 3. THE firft three cafes, wherein inheritable blood is wanting, may be collected from the rules of defcent laid down and explained in the preceding chapter, and therefore will need very little illuftration or comment. Firft, when the tenant dies without any relations on the part of any of his anceftors: fecondly, when he dies without any relations on the part of thofe anceftors from whom his eftate defcended: thirdly, when he dies without any relations of the whole blood. In two of thefe cafes the blood of the firft purchafor is certainly, in the other it is probably, at an end; and therefore in all of them the law directs, that the land fhall efcheat to the lord of the fee: for the lord would be manifeftly prejudiced, if, contrary to the inherent condition tacitly annexed to all feuds, any perfon fhould be fuffered to fucceed to lands, who is not of the blood of the firft feudatory, to whom for his perfonal merit the eftate is fuppofed to have been granted.

4. A MONSTER, which hath not the fhape of mankind, but in any part evidently bears the refemblance of the brute creation, hath no inheritable blood, and cannot be heir to any land, albeit it be brought forth in marriage: but, although it hath deformity

[c] *l.* 6. *c.* 1.

in any part of it's body, yet if it hath human fhape, it may be heir[f]. This is a very antient rule in the law of England[g]; and it's reafon is too obvious, and too fhocking, to bear a minute difcuffion. The Roman law agrees with our own in excluding fuch births from fucceffions[h] : yet accounts them, however, children in fome refpects, where the parents, or at leaft the father, could reap any advantage thereby[i]; (as the *jus trium liberorum*, and the like) efteeming them the misfortune, rather than the fault, of that parent. But our law will not admit a birth of this kind to be fuch an iffue, as fhall intitle the hufband to be tenant by the curtefy[k]; becaufe it is not capable of inheriting. And therefore, if there appears no other heir than fuch a prodigious birth, the land fhall efcheat to the lord.

5. B A S T A R D S are incapable of being heirs. Baftards, by our law, are fuch children as are not born either in lawful wedlock, or within a competent time after it's determination[l]. Such are held to be *nullius filii*, the fons of nobody ; for the maxim of law is, *qui ex damnato coitu nafcuntur, inter liberos non computantur*[m]. Being thus the fons of nobody, they have no blood in them, at leaft no inheritable blood ; confequently, none of the blood of the firft purchafor : and therefore, if there be no other claimant than fuch illegitimate children, the land fhall efcheat to the lord[n]. The civil law differs from ours in this point, and allows a baftard to fucceed to an inheritance, if after it's birth the mother was married to the father[o] : and alfo, if the father had no lawful wife or child, then, even if the concubine was never married to the father, yet fhe and her baftard fon were admitted each to one twelfth of the inheritance[p], and a baftard was like-

[f] Co. Litt. 7, 8.

[g] *Qui contra formam humani generis converfo more procreantur, ut fi mulier monftrofum vel prodigiofum enixa fit, inter liberos non. computentur. Partus tamen, cui natura aliquantulum addiderit vel diminuerit, ut fi fex vel tantum quatuor digitos habuerit, bene debet inter liberos connumerari : et, fi membra fint inutilia aut tortuofa, non tamen eft partus monftrofus.* Bracton. *l.*1. *c.*6. *& l.*5. *tr.*5. *c.*30.

[h] *Ff.* 1. 5. 14.

[i] *Ff.* 50. 16. 135. Paul. 4 *fent.* 9. §. 63.

[k] Co. Litt. 29.

[l] See Book I. ch. 16.

[m] Co. Litt. 8.

[n] Finch. law. 117.

[n] *Nov.* 89. *c.* 8.

[o] *Ibid. c.* 12.

wife

wife capable of fucceeding to the whole of his mother's eftate, although fhe was never married; the mother being fufficiently certain, though the father is not [q]. But our law, in favour of marriage, is much lefs indulgent to baftards.

THERE is indeed one inftance, in which our law has fhewn them fome little regard; and that is ufually termed the cafe of *baftard eignè* and *mulier puifnè*. This happens when a man has a baftard fon, and afterwards marries the mother, and by her has a legitimate fon, who in the language of the law is called a *mulier*, or as Glanvil [r] expreffes it in his Latin, *filius mulieratus*; the woman before marriage being *concubina*, and afterwards *mulier*. Now here the eldeft fon is baftard, or *baftard eignè*; and the younger fon is legitimate, or *mulier puifnè*. If then the father dies, and the *baftard eignè* enters upon his land, and enjoys it to his death, and dies feifed thereof, whereby the inheritance defcends to his iffue; in this cafe the *mulier puifnè*, and all other heirs, (though minors, feme-coverts, or under any incapacity whatfoever) are totally barred of their right [s]. And this, 1. As a punifhment on the *mulier* for his negligence, in not entering during the *baftard*'s life, and evicting him. 2. Becaufe the law will not fuffer a man to be baftardized after his death, who entered as heir and died feifed, and fo paffed for legitimate in his lifetime. 3. Becaufe the canon law (following the civil) did allow fuch *baftard eignè* to be legitimate, on the fubfequent marriage of his mother: and therefore the laws of England (though they would not admit either the civil or canon law to rule the inheritances of this kingdom, yet) paid fuch a regard to a perfon thus peculiarly circumftanced, that, after the land had defcended to his iffue, they would not unravel the matter again, and fuffer his eftate to be fhaken. But this indulgence was fhewn to no other kind of baftard; for, if the mother was never married to the father, fuch baftard could have no colourable title at all [t].

[q] *Cod.* 6. 57. 5.
[r] *l.* 7. *c.* 1.
[s] Litt. §. 399. Co. Litt. 244.
[t] Litt. §. 400.

As

As baftards cannot be heirs themfelves, fo neither can they have any heirs but thofe of their own bodies. For, as all collateral kindred confifts in being derived from the fame common anceftor, and as a baftard has no legal anceftors, he can have no collateral kindred; and, confequently, can have no legal heirs, but fuch as claim by a lineal defcent from himfelf. And therefore if a baftard purchafes land, and dies feifed thereof without iffue, and inteftate, the land fhall efcheat to the lord of the fee[u].

6. Aliens alfo are incapable of taking by defcent, or inheriting[w]: for they are not allowed to have any inheritable blood in them; rather indeed upon a principle of national or civil policy, than upon reafons ftrictly feodal. Though, if lands had been fuffered to fall into their hands who owe no allegiance to the crown of England, the defign of introducing our feuds, the defence of the kingdom, would have been defeated. Wherefore if a man leaves no other relations but aliens, his land fhall efcheat to the lord.

As aliens cannot inherit, fo far they are on a level with baftards; but, as they are alfo difabled to hold by purchafe[x], they are under ftill greater difabilities. And, as they can neither hold by purchafe, nor by inheritance, it is almoft fuperfluous to fay that they can have no heirs, fince they can have nothing for an heir to inherit: but fo it is exprefly holden[y], becaufe they have not in them any inheritable blood.

And farther, if an alien be made a denizen by the king's letters patent, and then purchafes lands, (which the law allows fuch a one to do) his fon, born before his denization, fhall not (by the common law) inherit thofe lands; but a fon born afterwards may, even though his elder brother be living; for the father, before denization, had no inheritable blood to communicate

<hr />

[u] Braƈt. *l.* 2. *c.* 7. Co. Litt. 244.   [x] *Ibid.* 2.
[w] Co. Litt. 8.   [y] *Ibid.* 1 Lev. 59.

to his eldeft fon; but by denization it acquires an hereditary quality, which will be tranfmitted to his fubfequent pofterity. Yet, if he had been naturalized by act of parliament, fuch eldeft fon might then have inherited; for that cancels all defects, and is allowed to have a retrofpective energy, which fimple denization has not [z].

S I R Edward Coke [a] alfo holds, that if an alien cometh into England, and there hath iffue two fons, who are thereby natural born fubjects; and one of them purchafes land, and dies; yet neither of thefe brethren can be heir to the other. For the *commune vinculum,* or common ftock of their confanguinity, is the father; and, as he had no inheritable blood in him, he could communicate none to his fons; and, when the fons can by no poffibility be heirs to the father, the one of them fhall not be heir to the other. And this opinion of his feems founded upon folid principles of the antient law; not only from the rule before cited [b], that *ceftuy, que doit inheriter al pere, doit inheriter al fits;* but alfo becaufe we have feen that the only feodal foundation upon which newly purchafed land can poffibly defcend to a brother, is the fuppofition and fiction of law, that it defcended from fome one of his anceftors: but in this cafe as the immediate anceftor was an alien, from whom it could by no poffibility defcend, this fhould deftroy the fuppofition, and impede the defcent, and the land fhould be inherited *ut feudum ftricte novum;* that is, by none but the lineal defcendants of the purchafing brother; and, on failure of them, fhould efcheat to the lord of the fee. But this opinion hath been fince overruled [c]: and it is now held for law, that the fons of an alien, born here, may inherit to each other. And reafonably enough upon the whole: for, as (in common purchafes) the whole of the fuppofed defcent from indefinite anceftors is but fictitious, the law may as well fuppofe the requifite anceftor as fuppofe the requifite defcent.

---

[z] Co. Litt. 129.   [b] See pag. 223 and 239.
[a] 1 Inft. 8.   [c] 1 Ventr. 473. 1 Lev. 59. 1 Sid. 193.

I T

IT is alfo enacted, by the ftatute 11 & 12 W. III. c. 6. that all perfons, being natural-born fubjects of the king, may inherit and make their titles by defcent from any of their anceftors lineal or collateral; although their father, or mother, or other anceftor, by, from, through, or under whom they derive their pedigrees, were born out of the king's allegiance. But inconveniences were afterwards apprehended, in cafe perfons fhould thereby gain a future capacity to inherit, who did not exift at the death of the perfon laft feifed. As, if Francis the elder brother of John Stiles be an alien, and Oliver the younger be a natural-born fubject, upon John's death without iffue his lands will defcend to Oliver the younger brother : now, if afterwards Francis hath a child, it was feared that, under the ftatute of king William, this new-born child might defeat the eftate of his uncle Oliver. Where-fore it is provided, by the ftatute 25 Geo. II. c. 39. that no right of inheritance fhall accrue by virtue of the former ftatute to any perfons whatfoever, unlefs they are in being and capable to take as heirs at the death of the perfon laft feifed : --- with an excep-tion however to the cafe, where lands fhall defcend to the daugh-ter of an alien; which daughter fhall refign fuch inheritance to her after-born brother, or divide it with her after-born fifters, according to the ufual rule ᵈ of defcents by the common law.

7. BY attainder alfo, for treafon or other felony, the blood of the perfon attainted is fo corrupted, as to be rendered no longer inheritable.

GREAT care muft be taken to diftinguifh between forfeiture of lands to the king, and this fpecies of efcheat to the lord; which, by reafon of their fimilitude in fome circumftances, and becaufe the crown is very frequently the immediate lord of the fee and therefore entitled to both, have been often confounded together. Forfeiture of lands, and of whatever elfe the offender poffeffed, was the doctrine of the old Saxon law ᵉ, as a part of

---

ᵈ See pag. 208 and 214.			ᵉ *LL. Aelfred. c.* 4. *LL. Canut. c.* 54.

punifhment for the offence ; and does not at all relate to the feodal fyftem, nor is the confequence of any figniory or lordfhip paramount [f] : but, being a prerogative vefted in the crown, was neither fuperfeded nor diminifhed by the introduction of the Norman tenures ; a fruit and confequence of which efcheat muft undoubtedly be reckoned. Efcheat therefore operates in fubordination to this more antient and fuperior law of forfeiture.

THE doctrine of efcheat upon attainder, taken fingly, is this : that the blood of the tenant, by the commiffion of any felony, (under which denomination all treafons were formerly comprized [g]) is corrupted and ftained, and the original donation of the feud is thereby determined, it being always granted to the vafal on the implied condition of *dum bene fe gefferit*. Upon the thorough demonftration of which guilt, by legal attainder, the feodal covenant and mutual bond of fealty are held to be broken, the eftate inftantly falls back from the offender to the lord of the fee, and the inheritable quality of his blood is extinguifhed and blotted out for ever. In this fituation the law of feodal efcheat was brought into England at the conqueft ; and in general fuperadded to the antient law of forfeiture. In confequence of which corruption and extinction of hereditary blood, the land of all felons would immediately reveft in the lord, but that the fuperior law of forfeiture intervenes, and intercepts it in it's paffage ; in cafe of treafon, for ever ; in cafe of other felony, for only a year and a day, after which time it goes to the lord in a regular courfe of efcheat [h], as it would have done to the heir of the felon in cafe the feodal tenures had never been introduced. And that this is the true operation and genuine hiftory of efcheats will moft evidently appear from this incident to gavelkind lands, (which feem to be the old Saxon tenure) that they are in no cafe fubject to efcheat for felony, though they are liable to forfeiture for treafon [i].

---

[f] 2 Inft. 64. Salk. 85.
[g] 3 Inft. 15. Stat. 25 Edw. III. c. 2. § 12.
[h] 2 Inft. 36.
[i] Somner. 53. Wright. Ten. 118.

As

As a confequence of this doctrine of efcheat, all lands of inheritance immediately revefting in the lord, the wife of the felon
was liable to lofe her dower, till the ftatute 1 Edw. VI. c. 12.
enacted, that albeit any perfon be attainted of mifprifion of treafon, murder, or felony, yet his wife fhall enjoy her dower. But
fhe has not this indulgence where the antient law of forfeiture
operates, for it is expreffly provided by the ftatute 5 & 6 Edw. VI.
c. 11. that the wife of one attaint of high treafon fhall not be
endowed at all.

HITHERTO we have only fpoken of eftates vefted in the offender, at the time of his offence, or attainder. And here the
law of forfeiture ftops ; but the law of efcheat purfues the matter ftill farther. For, the blood of the tenant being utterly corrupted and extinguifhed, it follows, not only that all he now has
fhould efcheat from him, but alfo that he fhould be incapable of
inheriting any thing for the future. This may farther illuftrate
the diftinction between forfeiture and efcheat. If therefore a father be feifed in fee, and the fon commits treafon and is attainted,
and then the father dies : here the land fhall efcheat to the lord ;
becaufe the fon, by the corruption of his blood, is incapable to
be heir, and there can be no other heir during his life : but nothing fhall be forfeited to the king, for the fon never had any intereft in the lands to forfeit [k]. In this cafe the efcheat operates,
and not the forfeiture ; but in the following inftance the forfeiture works, and not the efcheat. As where a new felony is created by act of parliament, and it is provided (as is frequently the
cafe) that it fhall not extend to corruption of blood : here the
lands of the felon fhall not efcheat to the lord, but yet the profits of them fhall be forfeited to the king fo long as the offender
lives [l].

THERE is yet a farther confequence of the corruption and
extinction of hereditary blood, which is this : that the perfon

[k] Co. Litt. 13.   [l] 3 Inft. 47.

attainted

attainted fhall not only be incapable himfelf of inheriting, or transmitting his own property by heirfhip, but fhall alfo obftruct the defcent of lands or tenements to his pofterity, in all cafes where they are obliged to derive their title through him from any remoter anceftor. The chanel, which conveyed the hereditary blood from his anceftors to him, is not only exhaufted for the prefent, but totally dammed up and rendered impervious for the future. This is a refinement upon the antient law of feuds, which allowed that the grandfon might be heir to his grandfather, though the fon in the intermediate generation was guilty of felony [m]. But, by the law of England, a man's blood is fo univerfally corrupted by attainder, that his fons can neither inherit to him nor to any other anceftor [n], at leaft on the part of their attainted father.

Th i s corruption of blood cannot be abfolutely removed but by authority of parliament. The king may excufe the public punifhment of an offender; but cannot abolifh the private right, which has accrued or may accrue to individuals as a confequence of the criminal's attainder. He may remit a forfeiture, in which the intereft of the crown is alone concerned: but he cannot wipe away the corruption of blood; for therein a third perfon hath an intereft, the lord who claims by efcheat. If therefore a man hath a fon, and is attainted, and afterwards pardoned by the king; this fon can never inherit to his father, or father's anceftors; becaufe his paternal blood, being once throughly corrupted by his father's attainder, muft continue fo: but if the fon had been born after the pardon, he might inherit; becaufe by the pardon the father is made a new man, and may convey new inheritable blood to his after-born children [o].

H e r e i n there is however a difference between aliens and perfons attainted. Of aliens, who could never by any poffibility be heirs, the law takes no notice: and therefore we have feen,

[m] Van Leeuwen *in* 2 *Feud.* 31.   [o] *Ibid.* 392.
[n] Co. Litt. 391.

that

that an alien elder brother fhall not impede the defcent to a natural-born younger brother. But in attainders it is otherwife : for
if a man hath iffue a fon, and is attainted, and afterwards pardoned, and then hath iffue a fecond fon, and dies ; here the corruption of blood is not removed from the eldeft, and therefore
he cannot be heir : neither can the youngeft be heir, for he hath
an elder brother living, of whom the law takes notice, as he
once had a poffibility of being heir; and therefore the younger
brother fhall not inherit, but the land fhall efcheat to the lord :
though, had the elder died without iffue in the life of the father,
the younger fon born after the pardon might well have inherited,
for he hath no corruption of blood [p]. So if a man hath iffue two
fons, and the elder in the lifetime of the father hath iffue, and
then is attainted and executed, and afterwards the father dies,
the lands of the father fhall not defcend to the younger fon : for
the iffue of the elder, which had once a poffibility to inherit,
fhall impede the defcent to the younger, and the land fhall efcheat
to the lord [q]. Sir Edward Coke in this cafe allows [r], that if the
anceftor be attainted, his fons born before the attainder may be
heirs to each other; and diftinguifhes it from the cafe of the
fons of an alien, becaufe in this cafe the blood was inheritable
when imparted to them from the father : but he makes a doubt
(upon the fame principles, which are now overruled [s]) whether
fons, born after the attainder, can inherit to each other; for they
never had any inheritable blood in them.

UPON the whole it appears, that a perfon attainted is neither
allowed to retain his former eftate, nor to inherit any future one,
nor to tranfmit any inheritance to his iffue, either immediately
from himfelf, or mediately through himfelf from any remoter
anceftor; for his inheritable blood, which is neceffary either to
hold, to take, or to tranfmit any feodal property, is blotted out,
corrupted, and extinguifhed for ever : the confequence of which
is, that eftates, thus impeded in their defcent, refult back and
efcheat to the lord.

[p] Co. Litt. 8.   [r] Co. Litt. 8.
[q] Dyer. 48.   [s] 1 Hal. P. C. 357.

THIS

T H I S corruption of blood, thus arifing from feodal principles, but perhaps extended farther than even thofe principles will warrant, has been long looked upon as a peculiar hardfhip : becaufe, the oppreffive parts of the feodal tenures being now in general abolifhed, it feems unreafonable to referve one of their moſt inequitable confequences; namely, that the children fhould not only be reduced to prefent poverty, (which, however fevere, is fufficiently juſtified upon reafons of public policy) but alſo be laid under future difficulties of inheritance, on account of the guilt of their anceſtors.   And therefore in moſt (if not all) of the new felonies, created by parliament fince the reign of Henry the eighth, it is declared that they fhall not extend to any corruption of blood : and by the ſtatute 7 Ann. c. 21. (the operation of which is poſtponed by the ſtatute 17 Geo. II. c. 39.) it is enacted, that, after the death of the pretender, and his fons, no attainder for treafon fhall extend to the difinheriting any heir, nor the prejudice of any perfon, other than the offender himfelf : which provifions have indeed carried the remedy farther, than was required by the hardfhip above complained of; which is only the future obſtruction of defcents, where the pedigree happens to be deduced through the blood of an attainted anceſtor.

B E FO R E I conclude this head, of efcheat, I muſt mention one fingular inſtance in which lands held in fee-fimple are not liable to efcheat to the lord, even when their owner is no more, and hath left no heirs to inherit them.   And this is the cafe of a corporation : for if that comes by any accident to be diffolved, the donor or his heirs fhall have the land again in reverfion, and not the lord by efcheat : which is perhaps the only inſtance where a reverfion can be expectant on a grant in fee-fimple abfolute. But the law, we are told[t], doth tacitly annex a condition to every fuch gift or grant, that if the corporation be diffolved, the donor or grantor fhall re-enter ; for the caufe of the gift or grant

[t] Co. Litt. 13.

faileth.

faileth. This is indeed founded upon the felf-fame principle as the law of efcheat; the heirs of the donor being only fubftituted inftead of the chief lord of the fee: which was formerly very frequently the cafe in fubinfeudations, or alienations of lands by a vafal to be holden as of himfelf; till that practice was reftrained by the ftatute of *quia emptores*, 18 Edw. I. ft. 1. to which this very fingular inftance ftill in fome degree remains an exception.

THERE is one more incapacity of taking by defcent, which, not being productive of any efcheat, is not properly reducible to this head, and yet muft not be paffed over in filence. It is enacted by the ftatute 11 & 12 Will. III. c. 4. that every papift who fhall not abjure the errors of his religion by taking the oaths to the government, and making the declaration againft tranfubftantia-tion, within fix months after he has attained the age of eighteen years, fhall be incapable of inheriting, or taking, by defcent as well as purchafe, any real eftates whatfoever; and his next of kin, being a proteftant, fhall hold them to his own ufe till fuch time as he complies with the terms impofed by the act. This in-capacity is merely perfonal; it affects himfelf only, and does not deftroy the inheritable quality of his blood, fo as to impede the defcent to others of his kindred. In like manner as, even in the times of popery, one who entered into religion and became a monk profeffed was incapable of inheriting lands, both in our own[u] and the feodal law; *eo quod defiit effe miles feculi qui factus eft miles Chrifti; nec beneficium pertinet ad eum qui non debet gerere officium*[w]. But yet he was accounted only *civiliter mortuus*; he did not impede the defcent to others, but the next heir was entitled to his or his anceftor's eftate.

THESE are the feveral deficiencies of hereditary blood, re-cognized by the law of England; which, fo often as they hap-pen, occafion lands to efcheat to the original proprietary or lord.

[u] Co. Litt. 132.   [w] 2 *Feud.* 21.

CHAPTER THE SIXTEENTH.

OF TITLE BY OCCUPANCY.

OCCUPANCY is the taking poſſeſſion of thoſe things, which before belonged to nobody. This, as we have ſeen[a], is the true ground and foundation of all property, or of holding thoſe things in ſeveralty, which by the law of nature, unqualified by that of ſociety, were common to all mankind. But, when once it was agreed that every thing capable of ownerſhip ſhould have an owner, natural reaſon ſuggeſted, that he who could firſt declare his intention of appropriating any thing to his own uſe, and, in conſequence of ſuch intention, actually took it into poſ-ſeſſion, ſhould thereby gain the abſolute property of it; accord-ing to that rule of the law of nations, recognized by the laws of Rome[b], *quod nullius eſt, id ratione naturali occupanti conceditur.*

THIS right of occupancy, ſo far as it concerns real property, (for of perſonal chattels I am not in this place to ſpeak) hath been confined by the laws of England within a very narrow com-paſs; and was extended only to a ſingle inſtance: namely, where a man was tenant *pur auter vie,* or had an eſtate granted to him-ſelf only (without mentioning his heirs) for the life of another man, and died during the life of *ceſtuy que vie,* or him by whoſe life it was holden: in this caſe he, that could firſt enter on the land, might lawfully retain the poſſeſſion ſo long as *ceſtuy que vie* lived, by right of occupancy[c].

[a] See pag. 3 & 8.   [c] Co. Litt. 41.
[b] *Ff.* 41. 1. 3.   THIS

THIS feems to have been recurring to firft principles, and calling in the law of nature to afcertain the property of the land, when left without a legal owner. For it did not revert to the grantor; who had parted with all his intereft, fo long as *ceftuy que vie* lived: it did not efcheat to the lord of the fee; for all efcheats muft be of the abfolute entire fee, and not of any particular eftate carved out of it; much lefs of fo minute a remnant as this: it did not belong to the grantee; for he was dead: it did not defcend to his heirs; for there were no words of inheritance in the grant: nor could it veft in his executors; for no executors could fucceed to a free-hold. Belonging therefore to nobody, like the *haereditas jacens* of the Romans, the law left it open to be feifed and appropriated by the firft perfon that could enter upon it, during the life of *ceftuy que vie*, under the name of an occupant. But there was no right of occupancy allowed, where the king had the reverfion of the lands; for the reverfioner hath an equal right with any other man to enter upon the vacant poffeffion, and where the king's title and a fubject's concur, the king's fhall be always preferred: againft the king therefore there could be no prior occupant, be-caufe *nullum tempus occurrit regi*[d]. And, even in the cafe of a fub-ject, had the eftate *pur auter vie* been granted to a man *and his heirs* during the life of *ceftuy que vie*, there the heir might, and ftill may, enter and hold poffeffion, and is called in law a *fpecial occupant*; as having a fpecial exclufive right, by the terms of the original grant, to enter upon and occupy this *haereditas jacens*, during the refidue of the eftate granted: though fome have thought him fo called with no very great propriety[e]; and that fuch eftate is rather a defcendible freehold. But the title of com-mon occupancy is now reduced almoft to nothing by two ftatutes; the one, 29 Car. II. c. 3. which enacts, that where there is no fpecial occupant, in whom the eftate may veft, the tenant *pur auter vie* may devife it by will, or it fhall go to the executors and be affets in their hands for payment of debts: the other that of 14 Geo. II. c. 20. which enacts, that it fhall veft not only in the

[d] *Ibid.*   [e] Vaugh. 201.

I i 2   executors,

executors, but, in cafe the tenant dies inteftate, in the adminiftrators alfo; and go in a courfe of diftribution like a chattel
intereft.

B Y thefe two ftatutes the title of *common* occupancy is utterly
extinct and abolifhed : though that of *fpecial* occupancy, by the
heir at law, continues to this day; fuch heir being held to fucceed to the anceftor's eftate, not by defcent, for then he muft
take an eftate of inheritance, but as an occupant, fpecially marked
out and appointed by the original grant. The doctrine of common occupancy may however be ufefully remembered on the following account, among others : that, as by the common law no
occupancy could be of incorporeal hereditaments, as of rents,
tithes, advowfons, commons, or the like [f], (becaufe, with refpect
to them, there could be no actual entry made, or corporal feifin
had; and therefore by the death of the grantee *pur auter vie* a
grant of fuch hereditaments was entirely determined [g]) fo now,
I apprehend, notwithftanding thefe ftatutes, fuch grant would be
determined likewife; and the hereditaments would not be devifable, nor veft in the executors, nor go in a courfe of diftribution.
For the ftatutes muft not be conftrued fo as to create any new e-
ftate, or to keep that alive which by the common law was determined, and thereby to defer the grantor's reverfion; but merely
to difpofe of an intereft in being, to which by law there was no
owner, and which therefore was left open to the firft occupant.
When there is a refidue left, the ftatutes give it to the executors,
&c, inftead of the firft occupant; but they will not *create* a refidue, on purpofe to give it the executors. They only meant to
provide an appointed inftead of a cafual, a certain inftead of an
uncertain, owner, of lands which before were nobody's; and
thereby to fupply this *cafus omiffus*, and render the difpofition of
law in all refpects entirely uniform : this being the only inftance
wherein a title to a real eftate could ever be acquired by occupancy.

[f] Co. Litt. 41.   [g] Vaugh. 201.

THIS, I fay, was the only inftance; for I think there can be no other cafe devifed, wherein there is not fome owner of the land appointed by the law. In the cafe of a fole corporation, as a parfon of a church, when he dies or refigns, though there is no *actual* owner of the land till a fucceffor be appointed, yet there is a *legal, potential* ownerfhip, fubfifting in contemplation of law; and when the fucceffor is appointed, his appointment fhall have a retrofpect and relation backwards, fo as to entitle him to all the profits from the inftant that the vacancy commenced. And, in all other inftances, when the tenant dies inteftate, and no other owner of the lands is to be found in the common courfe of defcents, there the law vefts an ownerfhip in the king, or in the fubordinate lord of the fee, by efcheat.

So alfo in fome cafes, where the laws of other nations give a right by occupancy, as in lands newly created, by the rifing of an ifland in a river, or by the alluvion or dereliction of the fea; in thefe inftances the law of England affigns them an immediate owner. For Bracton tells us[h], that if an ifland arife in the *middle* of a *river*, it belongs in common to thofe who have lands on each fide thereof; but if it be nearer to one bank than the other, it belongs only to him who is proprietor of the neareft fhore: which is agreeable to, and probably copied from, the civil law[i]. Yet this feems only to be reafonable, where the foil of the river is equally divided between the owners of the oppofite fhores: for if the whole foil is the freehold of any one man, as it muft be whenever a feveral fifhery is claimed[k], there it feems juft (and fo is the ufual practice) that the eyotts or little iflands, arifing in any part of the river, fhall be the property of him who owneth the pifcary and the foil. However, in cafe a new ifland rife in the *fea*, though the civil law gives it to the firft occupant[l], yet ours gives it to the king[m]. And as to lands gained from the fea, either by *allu-*

---

[h] *l. 2. c. 2.*
[i] *Inft. 2. 1. 22.*
[k] Salk. 637.

[l] *Inft.* 2. 1. 18.
[m] Bract. *l. 2. c. 2.* Callis of fewers. 22.

vion, by the wafhing up of fand and earth, fo as in time to make *terra firma*; or by *dereliction*, as when the fea fhrinks back below the ufual watermark; in thefe cafes the law is held to be, that if this gain be by little and little, by fmall and imperceptible degrees, it fhall go to the owner of the land adjoining. For *de minimis non curat lex*: and, befides, thefe owners being often lofers by the breaking in of the fea, or at charges to keep it out, this poffible gain is therefore a reciprocal confideration for fuch poffible charge or lofs. But, if the alluvion or dereliction be fudden and confiderable, in this cafe it belongs to the king: for, as the king is lord of the fea, and fo owner of the foil while it is covered with water, it is but reafonable he fhould have the foil, when the water has left it dry [n]. So that the quantity of ground gained, and the time during which it is gaining, are what make it either the king's, or the fubject's property. In the fame manner if a river, running between two lordfhips, by degrees gains upon the one, and thereby leaves the other dry; the owner who lofes his ground thus imperceptibly has no remedy: but if the courfe of the river be changed by a fudden and violent flood, or other hafty means, and thereby a man lofes his ground, he fhall have what the river has left in any other place, as a recompence for this fudden lofs [o]. And this law of alluvions and derelictions, with regard to *rivers*, is nearly the fame in the imperial law [p]; from whence indeed thofe our determinations feem to have been drawn and adopted: but we ourfelves, as iflanders, have applied them to *marine* increafes; and have given our fovereign the prerogative he enjoys, as well upon the particular reafons before-mentioned, as upon this other general ground of prerogative, which was formerly remarked [q], that whatever hath no other owner is vefted by law in the king.

[n] Callis. 24. 28.
[o] Callis. 28.

[p] *Inft.* 2. 1. 20, 21, 22, 23, 24.
[q] See Vol. I. pag. 289.

CHAPTER THE SEVENTEENTH.

OF TITLE BY PRESCRIPTION.

A THIRD method of acquiring real property by purchafe is
that by *prefcription*; as when a man can fhew no other
title to what he claims, than that he, and thofe under whom he
claims, have immemorially ufed to enjoy it. Concerning cuftoms,
or immemorial ufages, in general, with the feveral requifites and
rules to be obferved, in order to prove their exiftence and validity, we enquired at large in the preceding part of thefe commentaries [a]. At prefent therefore I fhall only, firft, diftinguifh
between *cuftom*, ftrictly taken, and *prefcription*; and then fhew,
what fort of things may be prefcribed for.

AND, firft, the diftinction between cuftom and prefcription is
this; that cuftom is properly a *local* ufage, and not annexed to
any *perfon*; fuch as, a cuftom in the manor of Dale that lands
fhall defcend to the youngeft fon: prefcription is merely a *perfonal*
ufage; as, that Sempronius, and his anceftors, or thofe whofe eftate
he hath, have ufed time out of mind to have fuch an advantage
or privilege [b]. As for example: if there be a ufage in the parifh of
Dale, that all the inhabitants of that parifh may dance on a certain clofe, at all times, for their recreation; (which is held [c] to
be a lawful ufage) this is ftrictly a cuftom, for it is applied to
the *place* in general, and not to any particular *perfons*: but if the

---

[a] See Vol. I. pag. 75, &c.   [c] 1 Lev. 176.
[b] Co. Litt. 113.

tenant,

tenant, who is feifed of the manor of Dale in fee, alleges that he and his anceftors, or all thofe whofe eftate he hath in the faid manor, have ufed time out of mind to have common of pafture in fuch a clofe, this is properly called a prefcription; for this is a ufage annexed to the *perfon* of the owner of this eftate. All prefcription muft be either in a man and his anceftors, or in a man and thofe whofe eftate he hath[d]; which laft is called prefcribing in a *que eftate*. And formerly a man might, by the common law, have prefcribed for a right which had been enjoyed by his anceftors or predeceffors at any diftance of time, though his or their enjoyment of it had been fufpended[e] for an indefinite feries of years. But by the ftatute of limitations, 32 Hen. VIII. c. 2. it is enacted, that no perfon fhall make any prefcription by the feifin or poffeffion of his anceftor or predeceffor, unlefs fuch feifin or poffeffion hath been within threefcore years next before fuch prefcription made[f].

SECONDLY, as to the feveral fpecies of things which may, or may not, be prefcribed for: we may in the firft place, obferve, that nothing but incorporeal hereditaments can be claimed by prefcription; as a right of way, a common, &c; but that no prefcription can give a title to lands, and other corporeal fubftances, of which more certain evidence may be had[g]. For no man can be faid to prefcribe, that he and his anceftors have immemorially ufed to hold the caftle of Arundel: for this is clearly another fort of title; a title by corporal feifin and inheritance, which is more permanent, and therefore more capable of proof, than that of prefcription. But, as to a right of way, a common, or the like, a man may be allowed to prefcribe; for of thefe there is no corporal feifin, the enjoyment will be frequently by intervals, and therefore the right to enjoy them can depend on nothing elfe but immemorial ufage. 2. A prefcription muft

---

[d] 4 Rep. 32.

[e] Co. Litt. 113.

[f] This title, of prefcription, was well known in the Roman law by the name of *ufucapio*; (*Ff*. 41. 3. 3.) fo called, becaufe a man, that gains a title by prefcription, may be faid *ufu rem capere*.

[g] Dr & St. dial. 1. c. 8. Finch. 132.

always

always be laid in him that is tenant of the fee. A tenant for life, for years, at will, or a copyholder, cannot prescribe, by reason of the imbecillity of their estates [h]. For, as prescription is usage beyond time of memory, it is absurd that they should pretend to prescribe, whose estates commenced within the remembrance of man. And therefore the copyholder must prescribe under cover of his lord's estate, and the tenant for life under cover of the tenant in fee-simple. As, if tenant for life of a manor would prescribe for a right of common as appurtenant to the same, he must prescribe under cover of the tenant in fee-simple; and must plead, that John Stiles and his ancestors had immemorially used to have this right of common, appurtenant to the said manor, and that John Stiles demised the said manor, with it's appurtenances, to him the said tenant for life. 3. A prescription cannot be for a thing which cannot be raised by grant. For the law allows prescription only in supply of the loss of a grant, and therefore every prescription presupposes a grant to have existed. Thus a lord of a manor cannot prescribe to raise a tax or toll upon strangers; for, as such claim could never have been good by any grant, it shall not be good by prescription [i]. 4. A fourth rule is, that what is to arise by matter of record cannot be prescribed for, but must be claimed by grant, entered on record: such as, for instance, the royal franchises of deodands, felons' goods, and the like. These, not being forfeited till the matter on which they arise is found by the inquisition of a jury, and so made a matter of record, the forfeiture itself cannot be claimed by any inferior title. But the franchises of treasure-trove, waifs, estrays, and the like, may be claimed by prescription; for they arise from private contingencies, and not from any matter of record [k]. 5. Among things incorporeal, which may be claimed by prescription, a distinction must be made with regard to the manner of prescribing; that is, whether a man shall prescribe in a *que estate*, or in himself and his ancestors. For, if a man prescribes in a *que estate*, (that is, in himself and those whose estate he holds) nothing is claim-

---

[h] 4 Rep. 31, 32.　　　　[k] Co. Litt. 114.
[i] 1 Ventr. 387.

able by this prefcription, but fuch things as are incident, appendant, or appurtenant to lands; for it would be abfurd to claim
any thing as the confequence, or appendix, of an eftate, with
which the thing claimed has no connexion : but, if he prefcribes
in himfelf and his anceftors, he may prefcribe for any thing whatfoever that lies in grant; not only things that are appurtenant,
but alfo fuch as may be in grofs[1]. Therefore a man may prefcribe,
that he, and thofe whofe eftate he hath in the manor of Dale, have
ufed to hold the advowfon of Dale, as *appendant* to that manor :
but, if the advowfon be a diftinct inheritance, and not appendant,
then he can only prefcribe in his anceftors. So alfo a man may
prefcribe in a *que eftate* for a common *appurtenant* to a manor ;
but, if he would prefcribe for a common *in grofs*, he muft prefcribe in himfelf and his anceftors. 6. Laftly, we may obferve,
that eftates gained by prefcription are not, of courfe, defcendible
to the heirs general, like other purchafed eftates, but are an exception to the rule. For, properly fpeaking, the prefcription is
rather to be confidered as an evidence of a former acquifition,
than as an acquifition *de novo :* and therefore, if a man prefcribes for a right of way in himfelf and his anceftors, it will
defcend only to the blood of that line of anceftors in whom he fo
prefcribes; the prefcription in this cafe being indeed a fpecies of
defcent. But, if he prefcribes for it in a *que eftate*, it will follow
the nature of that eftate in which the prefcription is laid, and be
inheritable in the fame manner, whether that were acquired by
defcent or purchafe : for every acceffory followeth the nature of
it's principal.

[1] Litt. §. 183. Finch. L. 104.

CHAPTER THE EIGHTEENTH.

OF TITLE BY FORFEITURE.

FORFEITURE is a punifhment annexed by law to fome illegal act, or negligence, in the owner of lands, tenements, or hereditaments; whereby he lofes all his intereft therein, and they go to the party injured, as a recompenfe for the wrong which either he alone, or the public together with himfelf, hath fuftained.

LANDS, tenements, and hereditaments, may be forfeited in various degrees and by various means: 1. By crimes and mifdemefnors. 2. By alienation contrary to law. 3. By non-prefentation to a benefice, when the forfeiture is denominated a *lapfe*. 4. By fimony. 5. By non-performance of conditions. 6. By wafte. 7. By breach of copyhold cuftoms. 8. By bankruptcy.

I. THE foundation and juftice of forfeitures for *crimes and mifdemefnors,* and the feveral degrees of thofe forfeitures, proportioned to the feveral offences, have been hinted at in the preceding volume[a]; but will be more properly confidered, and more at large, in the fourth book of thefe commentaries. At prefent I fhall only obferve in general, that the offences which induce a forfeiture of lands and tenements to the crown are principally the following fix; 1. Treafon. 2. Felony. 3. Mifprifion of

---

[a] Vol. I. pag. 289.

treafon.

treafon. 4. Praemunire. 5. Drawing a weapon on a judge, or ftriking any one in the prefence of the king's principal courts of juftice. 6. Popifh recufancy, or non-obfervance of certain laws enacted in reftraint of papifts. But at what time they feverally commence, how far they extend, and how long they endure, will with greater propriety be referved as the object of our future enquiries.

II. LANDS and tenements may be forfeited by *alienation*, or conveying them to another, contrary to law. This is either alienation in *mortmain*, alienation to an *alien*, or alienation by *particular tenants*; in the two former of which cafes the forfeiture arifes from the incapacity of the alienee to take, in the latter from the incapacity of the alienor to grant.

1. ALIENATION in *mortmain, in mortua manu,* is an alienation of lands or tenements to any corporation, fole or aggregate, ecclefiaftical or temporal. But thefe purchafes having been chiefly made by religious houfes, in confequence whereof the lands became perpetually inherent in one dead hand, this hath occafioned the general appellation of mortmain to be applied to fuch alienations[b], and the religious houfes themfelves to be principally confidered in forming the ftatutes of mortmain : in deducing the hiftory of which ftatutes, it will be matter of curiofity to obferve the great addrefs and fubtil contrivance of the ecclefiaftics in eluding from time to time the laws in being, and the zeal with which fucceffive parliaments have purfued them through all their fineffes; how new remedies were ftill the parents of new evafions; till the legiflature at laft, though with difficulty, hath obtained a decifive victory.

BY the common law any man might difpofe of his lands to any other private man at his own difcretion, efpecially when the feodal reftraints of alienation were worn away. Yet in confequence of thefe it was always, and is ftill, neceffary[c], for corporations to have a licence of mortmain from the crown, to enable them to purchase lands : for as the king is the ultimate lord of every fee, he ought not, unless by his own consent, to lose his privilege of escheats and other feodal profits, by the vesting of lands in tenants that can never be attainted or die. And such licences of mortmain seem to have been necessary among the Saxons, above sixty years before the Norman conquest[d]. But, besides this general licence from the king, as lord paramount of the kingdom, it was also requisite, whenever there was a mesne or intermediate lord between the king and the alienor, to obtain his licence also (upon the same feodal principles) for the alienation of the specific land. And if no such licence was obtained, the king or other lord might respectively enter on the lands so aliened in mortmain, as a forfeiture. The necessity of this licence from the crown was acknowleged by the constitutions of Clarendon[e], in respect of advowsons, which the monks always greatly coveted, as being the groundwork of subsequent appropriations[f]. Yet such were the influence and ingenuity of the clergy, that (notwithstanding this fundamental principle) we find that the largest and most considerable dotations of religious houses happened within less than two centuries after the conquest. And (when a licence could not be obtained) their contrivance seems to have been this : that, as the forfeiture for such alienations accrued in the first place to the immediate lord of the fee, the tenant who meant to alienate first conveyed his lands to the religious house, and instantly took them back again, to hold as tenant to the monastery ; which kind of instantaneous seisin was probably held not to occasion any forfeiture : and then, by pretext of some other forfeiture, surrender, or escheat, the society entered into those lands in right of such their newly acquired signiory, as immediate lords of the fee. But, when these dotations began to grow numerous, it was observed that the feodal services, ordained for the defence of the kingdom, were every day visibly withdrawn ; that the circulation of landed property from man to man began to

---

[d] Selden. Jan. Angl. l. 2. §. 45.

[e] *Ecclesiae de feudo domini regis non possunt in perpetuum dari, absque assensu et consensione* *ipsius. c. 2. A. D. 1164.*

[f] See Vol. I. pag. 373.

stagnate ;

ftagnate ; and that the lords were curtailed of the fruits of their figniories, their efcheats, wardfhips, reliefs, and the like : and therefore, in order to prevent this, it was ordained by the fecond of king Henry III's great charters[g], and afterwards by that printed in our common ftatute-books, that all fuch attempts fhould be void, and the land forfeited to the lord of the fee[h].

BUT, as this prohibition extended only to religious *houfes*, bifhops and other fole corporations were not included therein ; and the aggregate ecclefiaftical bodies (who, fir Edward Coke obferves[i], in this were to be commended, that they ever had of their counfel the beft learned men that they could get) found many means to creep out of this ftatute, by buying in lands that were *bona fide* holden of themfelves as lords of the fee, and thereby evading the forfeiture ; or by taking long leafes for years, which firft introduced thofe extenfive terms, for a thoufand or more years, which are now fo frequent in conveyances. This produced the ftatute *de religiofis*, 7 Edw. I ; which provided, that no *perfon*, religious or other whatfoever, fhould buy, or fell, or receive, under pretence of a gift, or term of years, or any other title whatfoever, nor fhould by any art or ingenuity appropriate to himfelf, any lands or tenements in mortmain ; upon pain that the immediate lord of the fee, or, on his default for one year, the lords paramount, and, in default of all of them, the king, might enter thereon as a forfeiture.

THIS feemed to be a fufficient fecurity againft all alienations in mortmain : but, as thefe ftatutes extended only to gifts and conveyances between the parties, the religious houfes now began to fet up a fictitious title to the land, which it was intended they fhould have, and to bring an action to recover it againft the tenant ;

g *A. D.* 1217. *cap.* 43. *edit. Oxon.*
h *Non licet alicui de caetero dare terram fuam alicui domui religiofae, ita quod illam refumat tenendum de eadem domo ; nec liceat alicui domui religiofae terram alicujus fic accipere, quod tradat illam ei a quo ipfam recepit tenendam :*
fi quis autem autem de caetero terram fuam domui religiofae fic dederit, et fuper hoc convincatur, donum fuum penitus caffetur, et terra illa domino fuo illius feodi incurratur. Mag. Cart. 9 *Hen. III. c.* 36.
i 2 Inft. 75.

who,

who, by fraud and collusion, made no defence, and thereby judgment was given for the religious house, which then *recovered* the
land by sentence of law upon a supposed prior title. And thus
they had the honour of inventing those fictitious adjudications of
right, which are since become the great assurance of the kingdom, under the name of *common recoveries*. But upon this the
statute of Westminster the second, 1 3 Edw. I. c. 32. enacted,
that in such cases a jury shall try the true right of the demand-
ants or plaintiffs to the land, and if the religious house or corporation be found to have it, they shall still recover seisin; otherwise
it shall be forfeited to the immediate lord of the fee, or else to the
next lord, and finally to the king, upon the immediate or other
lord's default. And the like provision was made by the succeeding chapter [k], in case the tenants set up crosses upon their lands
(the badges of knights templars and hospitallers) in order to protect them from the feodal demands of their lords, by virtue of
the privileges of those religious and military orders. And so careful was this provident prince to prevent any future evasions, that
when the statute of *quia emptores*, 18 Edw. I. abolished all sub-
infeudations, and gave liberty for all men to alienate their lands
to be holden of the next immediate lord [l], a proviso was inserted [m]
that this should not extend to authorize any kind of alienation in
mortmain. And when afterwards the method of obtaining the
king's licence by writ of *ad quod damnum* was marked out, by
the statute 27 Edw. I. st. 2. it was farther provided by statute
34 Edw. I. st. 3. that no such licence should be effectual, without the consent of the mesne or intermediate lords.

YET still it was found difficult to set bounds to ecclesiastical
ingenuity: for when they were driven out of all their former
holds, they devised a new method of conveyance, by which the
lands were granted, not to themselves directly, but to nominal
feoffees *to the use of* the religious houses; thus distinguishing between the *possession* and the *use*, and receiving the actual profits,

[k] *cap.* 33.   [m] *cap.* 3.
[l] 2 Inst. 501.

while the feifin of the land remained in the nominal feoffee: who was held by the courts of equity (then under the direction of the clergy) to be bound in confcience to account to his *ceftuy que ufe* for the rents and emoluments of the eftate. And it is to thefe inventions that our practifers are indebted for the introduction of ufes and trufts, the foundation of modern conveyancing. But, unfortunately for the inventors themfelves, they did not long enjoy the advantage of their new device, for the ftatute 15 Ric. II. c. 5. enacts, that the lands which had been fo purchafed to ufes fhould be amortifed by licence from the crown, or elfe be fold to private perfons; and that, for the future, ufes fhall be fubject to the ftatutes of mortmain, and forfeitable like the lands themfelves. And whereas the ftatutes had been eluded by purchafing large tracts of land, adjoining to churches, and confecrating them by the name of church-yards, fuch fubtile imagination is alfo declared to be within the compafs of the ftatutes of mortmain. And civil or lay corporations, as well as ecclefiaftical, are alfo declared to be within the mifchief, and of courfe within the remedy provided by thofe falutary laws. And, laftly, as during the times of popery lands were frequently given to fuperftitious ufes, though not to any corporate bodies; or were made liable in the hands of heirs and devifees to the charge of obits, chaunteries, and the like, which were equally pernicious in a well-governed ftate as actual alienations in mortmain; therefore, at the dawn of the reformation, the ftatute 32 Hen. VIII. c. 10. declares, that all future grants of lands for any of the purpofes aforefaid, if granted for any longer term than twenty years, fhall be void.

BUT, during all this time, it was in the power of the crown, by granting a licence of mortmain, to remit the forfeiture, fo far as related to it's own rights; and to enable any fpiritual or other corporation to purchafe and hold any lands or tenements in perpetuity: which prerogative is declared and confirmed by the ftatute 18 Edw. III. ft. 3. c. 3. But, as doubts were conceived at the time of the revolution how far fuch licence was valid[n], fince

[n] 2 Hawk. P. C. 391.

the

the king had no power to difpenfe with the ftatutes of mortmain
by a claufe of *non obftante* [o], which was the ufual courfe, though
it feems to have been unneceffary [p]; and as, by the gradual de-
clenfion of mefne figniories through the long operation of the
ftatute of *quia emptores*, the rights of intermediate lords were reduced to a very fmall compafs; it was therefore provided by the
ftatute 7 & 8 W. III. c. 37. that the crown for the future at it's
own difcretion may grant licences to aliene or take in mortmain,
of whomfoever the tenements may be holden.

AFTER the diffolution of monafteries under Henry VIII,
though the policy of the next popifh fucceffor affected to grant a
fecurity to the poffeffors of abbey lands, yet, in order to regain
fo much of them as either the zeal or timidity of their owners
might induce them to part with, the ftatutes of mortmain were
fufpended for twenty years by the ftatute 1 & 2 P. & M. c. 8.
and, during that time, any lands or tenements were allowed to
be granted to any fpiritual corporation without any licence whatfoever.   And, long afterwards, for a much better purpofe, the
augmentation of poor livings, it was enacted by the ftatute
17 Car. II. c. 3. that appropriators may annex the great tithes
to the vicarages; and that all benefices under 100 *l. per annum*
may be augmented by the purchafe of lands, without licence of
mortmain in either cafe : and the like provifion hath been fince
made, in favour of the governors of queen Anne's bounty [q].   It
hath alfo been held [r], that the ftatute 23 Hen. VIII. before-mentioned did not extend to any thing but *fuperftitious* ufes; and that
therefore a man may give lands for the maintenance of a fchool,
an hofpital, or any other *charitable* ufes.   But as it was apprehended from recent experience, that perfons on their deathbeds
might make large and improvident difpofitions even for thefe
good purpofes, and defeat the political ends of the ftatutes of
mortmain; it is therefore enacted by the ftatute 9 Geo. II. c. 36.
that no lands or tenements, or money to be laid out thereon,

---

[o] Stat. 1. W. & M. ft. 2. c. 2.   [q] Stat. 2 & 3 Ann. c. 11.
[p] Co. Litt. 99.   [r] 1 Rep. 24.

fhall be given for or charged with any *charitable* ufes whatfoever, unlefs by deed indented, executed in the prefence of two witneffes twelve calendar months before the death of the donor, and enrolled in the court of chancery within fix months after it's execution, (except ftocks in the public funds, which may be transferred within fix months previous to the donor's death) and unlefs fuch gift be made to take effect immediately, and be without power of revocation : and that all other gifts fhall be void. The two univerfities, their colleges, and the fcholars upon the foundation of the colleges of Eaton, Winchefter, and Weftminfter, are excepted out of this act : but fuch exemption was granted with this provifo, that no college fhall be at liberty to purchafe more advowfons, than are equal in number to one moiety of the fellows or ftudents, upon the refpective foundations.

2. SECONDLY, alienation *to an alien* is alfo a caufe of forfeiture to the crown of the lands fo alienated, not only on account of his incapacity to hold them, which occafions him to be paffed by in defcents of land', but likewife on account of his prefumption in attempting, by an act of his own, to acquire any real property; as was obferved in the preceding volume'.

3. LASTLY, alienations *by particular tenants*, when they are greater than the law entitles them to make, and deveft the remainder or reverfion', are alfo forfeitures to him whofe right is attacked thereby. As, if tenant for his own life alienes by feoffment or fine for the life of another, or in tail, or in fee ; thefe being eftates, which either muft or may laft longer than his own, the creating them is not only beyond his power, and inconfiftent with the nature of his intereft, but is alfo a forfeiture of his own particular eftate to him in remainder or reverfion". For which there feem to be two reafons. Firft, becaufe fuch alienation amounts to a renuntiation of the feodal connexion and dependence ; it implies a refufal to perform the due renders and fervices to the lord

' See pag. 249, 250.
' Book I. ch. 10.

, Co. Litt. 251.
" Litt. §. 415.

of

of the fee, of which fealty is conftantly one; and it tends in it's
confequences to defeat and deveft the remainder or reverfion expectant : as therefore that is put in jeopardy, by fuch act of the
particular tenant, it is but juft that, upon difcovery, the particular eftate fhould be forfeited and taken from him, who has
fhewn fo manifeft an inclination to make an improper ufe of it.
The other reafon is, becaufe the particular tenant, by granting a
larger eftate than his own, has by his own act determined and put
an entire end to his own original intereft; and on fuch determination the next taker is intitled to enter regularly, as in his remainder or reverfion. The fame law, which is thus laid down
with regard to tenants for life, holds alfo with refpect to all tenants of the mere freehold, or of chattel interefts; but if tenant
in tail alienes in fee, this is no immediate forfeiture to the remainder-man, but a mere *difcontinuance* (as it is called ^w) of the
eftate-tail, which the iffue may afterwards avoid by due courfe
of law ^x : for he in remainder or reverfion hath only a very remote and barely poffible intereft therein, until the iffue in tail is
extinct. But, in cafe of fuch forfeitures by particular tenants, all
legal eftates by them before created, as if tenant for twenty years
grants a leafe for fifteen, and all charges by him lawfully made on
the lands, fhall be good and available in law ^y. For the law will
not hurt an innocent leffee for the fault of his leffor; nor permit
the leffor, after he has granted a good and lawful eftate, by his
own act to avoid it, and defeat the intereft which he himfelf has
created.

EQUIVALENT, both in it's nature and it's confequences, to
an illegal alienation by the particular tenant, is the civil crime of
difclaimer; as where a tenant, who holds of any lord, neglects
to render him the due fervices, and, upon an action brought to
recover them, difclaims to hold of his lord. Which difclaimer
of tenure in any court of record is a forfeiture of the lands to the
lord ^z, upon reafons moft apparently feodal. And fo likewife, if

---

w See Book III.

x Litt. §. 595, 6, 7.

y Co. Litt. 233.

z Finch. 270, 271.

in any court of record the particular tenant does any act which amounts to a virtual difclaimer; if he claims any greater eftate than was granted him at the firft infeodation, or takes upon himfelf thofe rights which belong only to tenants of a fuperior clafs[a]; if he affirms the reverfion to be in a ftranger, by accepting his fine, attorning as his tenant, collufive pleading, and the like[b]; fuch behaviour amounts to a forfeiture of his particular eftate.

III. LAPSE is a fpecies of forfeiture, whereby the right of prefentation to a church accrues to the ordinary by neglect of the patron to prefent, to the metropolitan by neglect of the ordinary, and to the king by neglect of the metropolitan. For it being for the intereft of religion, and the good of the public, that the church fhould be provided with an officiating minifter, the law has therefore given this right of lapfe, in order to quicken the patron; who might otherwife, by fuffering the church to remain vacant, avoid paying his ecclefiaftical dues, and fruftrate the pious intentions of his anceftors. This right of lapfe was firft eftablifhed about the time (though not by the authority[c]) of the council of Lateran[d], which was in the reign of our Henry the fecond, when the bifhops firft began to exercife univerfally the right of inftitution to churches[e]. And therefore, where there is no right of inftitution, there is no right of lapfe: fo that no donative can lapfe to the ordinary[f], unlefs it hath been augmented by the queen's bounty[g]. But no right of lapfe can accrue, when the original prefentation is in the crown[h].

THE term, in which the title to prefent by lapfe accrues from the one to the other fucceffively, is fix calendar months[i]; (following in this cafe the computation of the church, and not the ufual one of the common law) and this exclufive of the day of

---

[a] Co. Litt. 152.
[b] *Ibid.* 153.
[c] 2 Roll. Abr. 336. pl. 10.
[d] Bracton. *l.* 4. *tr.* 2. *c.* 3.
[e] See pag. 23.

[f] Bro. *Abr. tit. Quar. Imped.* 131. Cro. Jac. 518.
[g] Stat. 1 Geo. I. ft. 2. c. 10.
[h] Stat. 17 Edw. II. c. 8. 2 Inft. 273.
[i] 6 Rep. 62. Regiftr. 42.

the

the avoidance[k]. But, if the bifhop be both patron and ordinary, he fhall not have a double time allowed him to collate in[l]; for the forfeiture accrues by law, whenever the negligence has continued fix months in the fame perfon. And alfo, if the bifhop doth not collate his own clerk immediately to the living, and the patron prefents, though after the fix months are lapfed, yet his prefentation is good, and the bifhop is bound to inftitute the patron's clerk[m]. For as the law only gives the bifhop this title by lapfe, to punifh the patron's negligence, there is no reafon that, if the bifhop himfelf be guilty of equal or greater negligence, the patron fhould be deprived of his turn. If the bifhop fuffer the prefentation to lapfe to the metropolitan, the patron alfo has the fame advantage if he prefents before the arch-bifhop has filled up the benefice; and that for the fame reafon. Yet the ordinary cannot, after lapfe to the metropolitan, collate his own clerk to the prejudice of the arch-bifhop[n]. For he had no permanent right and intereft in the advowfon, as the patron hath, but merely a temporary one; which having neglected to make ufe of during the time, he cannot afterwards retrieve it. But if the prefentation lapfes to the king, prerogative here intervenes and makes a difference; and the patron fhall never recover his right, till the king has fatisfied his turn by prefentation : for *nullum tempus occurrit regi*[o]. And therefore it may feem, as if the church might continue void for ever, unlefs the king fhall be pleafed to prefent; and a patron thereby be abfolutely defeated of his advowfon. But to prevent this inconvenience, the law has lodged a power in the patron's hands, of as it were compelling the king to prefent. For if, during the delay of the crown, the patron himfelf prefents, and his clerk is inftituted, the king indeed by prefenting another may turn out the patron's clerk; but if he does not, and the patron's clerk dies incumbent, or is canonically deprived, the king hath loft his right, which was only to the next or firft prefentation[p].

---

[k] 2 Inft. 361.
[l] Gibf. Cod. 769.
[m] 2 Inft. 273.

[n] 2 Roll. Abr. 368.
[o] Dr & St. d. 2. c. 36. Cro. Car. 355.
[p] 7 Rep. 28. Cro. Eliz. 44.

IN

IN cafe the benefice becomes void by death, or ceffion through plurality of benefices, there the patron is bound to take notice of the vacancy at his own peril; for thefe are matters of equal notoriety to the patron and ordinary : but in cafe of a vacancy by refignation, or canonical deprivation, or if a clerk prefented be refufed for infufficiency, thefe being matters of which the bi-fhop alone is prefumed to be cognizant, here the law requires him to give notice thereof to the patron, otherwife he can take no advantage by way of lapfe [q]. Neither fhall any lapfe thereby accrue to the metropolitan or to the king; for it is univerfally true, that neither the arch-bifhop or the king fhall ever prefent by lapfe, but where the immediate ordinary might have collated by lapfe, within the fix months, and hath exceeded his time : for the firft ftep or beginning faileth, *et quod non habet principium, non habet finem* [r]. If the bifhop refufe or neglect to examine and admit the patron's clerk, without good reafon affigned or notice given, he is ftiled a difturber by the law, and fhall not have any title to prefent by lapfe; for no man fhall take advantage of his own wrong [s]. Alfo if the right of prefentation be litigious or contefted, and an action be brought againft the bifhop to try the title, no lapfe fhall incur till the queftion of right be decided [t].

IV. BY *fimony*, the right of prefentation to a living is for-feited, and vefted *pro hac vice* in the crown. Simony is the cor-rupt prefentation of any one to an ecclefiaftical benefice for mo-ney, gift, or reward. It is fo called from the refemblance it is faid to bear to the fin of Simon Magus, though the purchafing of holy orders feems to approach nearer to his offence. It was by the canon law a very grievous crime : and is fo much the more odious, becaufe, as fir Edward Coke obferves [u], it is ever accom-panied with perjury; for the prefentee is fworn to have commit-ted no fimony. However it is not an offence punifhable in a cri-

[q] 4 Rep. 75. 2 Inft. 632.
[r] Co. Litt. 344, 345.
[s] 2 Roll. Abr. 369.

[t] Co. Litt. 344.
[u] 3 Inft. 156.

minal

minal way at the common law [w]; it being thought sufficient to leave the clerk to ecclesiastical censures. But as these did not affect the simoniacal patron, nor were efficacious enough to repel the notorious practice of the thing, divers acts of parliament have been made to restrain it by means of civil forfeitures; which the modern prevailing usage, with regard to spiritual preferments, calls aloud to be put in execution. I shall briefly confider them in this place, because they divest the corrupt patron of the right of presentation, and vest a new right in the crown.

B Y the statute 31 Eliz. c. 6. it is for avoiding of simony enacted, that if any patron for any corrupt consideration, by gift or promise, directly or indirectly, shall present or collate any person to an ecclesiastical benefice or dignity; such presentation shall be void, and the presentee be rendered incapable of ever enjoying the same benefice: and the crown shall present to it for that turn only [x]. Also by the statute 12 Ann. stat. 2. c. 12. if any person for money or profit shall procure, in his own name or the name of any other, the next presentation to any living ecclesiastical, and shall be presented thereupon, this is declared to be a simoniacal contract; and the party is subjected to all the ecclesiastical penalties of simony, is disabled from holding the benefice, and the presentation devolves to the crown.

U P O N these statutes many questions have arisen, with regard to what is, and what is not simony. And, among others, these points seem to be clearly settled: 1. That to purchase a presentation, the living being actually vacant, is open and notorious simony [y]; this being expressly in the face of the statute. 2. That for a clerk to bargain for the next presentation, the incumbent being sick and about to die, was simony, even before the statute of queen Anne [z]: and now, by that statute, to purchase, either in his own name or another's, the next presentation, and be

[w] Moor. 564.
[x] For other penalties inflicted by this statute, see Book IV.

[y] Cro. Eliz. 788.   Moor. 914.
[z] Hob. 165.

thereupon

thereupon prefented at any future time to the living, is direct and palpable fimony. But, 3. It is held that for a father to pur-chafe fuch a prefentation, in order to provide for his fon, is not fimony : for the fon is not concerned in the bargain, and the fa-ther is by nature bound to make a provifion for him [a]. 4. That if a fimoniacal contract be made with the patron, the clerk not being privy thereto, the prefentation for that turn fhall indeed devolve to the crown, as a punifhment of the guilty patron; but the clerk, who is innocent, does not incur any difability or for-feiture [b]. 5. That bonds given to pay money to charitable ufes, on receiving a prefentation to a living, are not fimoniacal [c], pro-vided the patron or his relations be not benefited thereby [d]; for this is no corrupt confideration, moving to the patron. 6. That bonds of refignation, in cafe of non-refidence or taking any other living, are not fimoniacal [e]; there being no corrupt confideration herein, but fuch only as is for the good of the public. So alfo bonds to refign, when the patron's fon comes to canonical age, are legal; upon the reafon before given, that the father is bound to provide for his fon [f]. 7. Laftly, general bonds to refign at the patron's requeft are held to be legal [g] : for they may poffibly be given for one of the legal confiderations before-mentioned; and where there is a poffibility that a tranfaction may be fair, the law will not fuppofe it iniquitous without proof. But, if the party can prove the contract to have been a corrupt one, fuch proof will be admitted, in order to fhew the bond fimoniacal, and therefore void. Neither will the patron be fuffered to make an ill ufe of fuch a general bond of refignation; as by extorting a compofition for tithes, procuring an annuity for his relation, or by demanding a refignation wantonly and without good caufe, fuch as is approved by the law; as, for the benefit of his own fon, or on account of non-refidence, plurality of livings, or grofs immorality in the incumbent [h].

[a] Cro Eliz. 686. Moor. 916.
[b] 3 Inft. 154. Cro. Jac. 385.
[c] Noy 142.
[d] Stra. 534.
[e] Cro. Car. 180.

[f] Cro. Jac. 248. 274
[g] Cro. Car. 180. Stra. 227.
[h] 1 Vern. 411. 1 Equ. Caf. abr. 86, 87. Stra. 534.

V. THE

V. THE next kind of forfeitures are thofe by *breach* or non-performance of a *condition* annexed to the eftate, either expreſſly by deed at it's original creation, or impliedly by law from a principle of natural reafon. Both which we confidered at large in a former chapter [i].

VI. I THEREFORE now proceed to another fpecies of forfeiture, viz. by *wafte*. Wafte, *vaftum*, is a fpoil or deftruction in houfes, gardens, trees, or other corporeal hereditaments, to the difherifon of him that hath the remainder or reverfion in fee-fimple or fee-tail [k].

WASTE is either *voluntary*, which is a crime of commiffion, as by pulling down a houfe; or it is *permiffive*, which is a matter of omiffion only, as by fuffering it to fall for want of necef-fary reparations. Whatever does a lafting damage to the freehold or inheritance is wafte [l]. Therefore removing wainfcot, floors, or other things once fixed to the freehold of a houfe, is wafte [m]. If a houfe be deftroyed by tempeft, lightening, or the like, which is the act of providence, it is no wafte: but otherwife, if the houfe be burnt by the careleffnefs or negligence of the leffee; though now by the ftatute 6 Ann. c. 3. no action will lie againft a tenant for an accident of this kind, left misfortune be added to misfortune. Wafte may alfo be committed in ponds, dove-houfes, warrens, and the like; by fo reducing the number of the creatures therein, that there will not be fufficient for the reverfioner when he comes to the inheritance [n]. Timber alfo is part of the inheritance [o]. Such are oak, afh, and elm in all places: and in fome particular countries, by local cuftom, where other trees are generally ufed for building, they are thereupon confidered as timber; and to cut down fuch trees, or top them, or do any other act whereby the timber may decay, is wafte [p]. But underwood

---

[i] See chap. 10. pag. 152.
[k] Co. Litt. 53.
[l] Hetl. 35.
[m] 4 Rep. 64.

[n] Co Litt. 53.
[o] 4 Rep. 62.
[p] Co. Litt. 53.

the tenant may cut down at any feafonable time that he pleafes[q];
and may take fufficient eftovers of common right for houfe-bote
and cart-bote ; unlefs reftrained (which is ufual) by particular covenants or exceptions[r]. The converfion of land from one fpecies
to another is wafte. To convert wood, meadow, or pafture, into
arable ; to turn arable, meadow, or pafture into woodland ; or
to turn arable or woodland into meadow or pafture ; are all of them
wafte[s]. For, as fir Edward Coke obferves[t], it not only changes
the courfe of hufbandry, but the evidence of the eftate ; when
fuch a clofe, which is conveyed and defcribed as pafture, is found
to be arable, and *e converfo.* And the fame rule is obferved, for
the fame reafon, with regard to converting one fpecies of edifice
into another, even though it is improved in it's value[u]. To open
the land to fearch for mines of metal, coal, &c, is wafte ; for
that is a detriment to the inheritance[w]: but, if the pits or mines
were open before, it is no wafte for the tenant to continue digging them for his own ufe[x]; for it is now become the mere annual profit of the land. Thefe three are the general heads of
wafte, viz. in houfes, in timber, and in land. Though, as was
before faid, whatever tends to the deftruction, or depreciating the
value, of the inheritance, is confidered by the law as wafte.

LET us next fee, who are liable to be punifhed for committing wafte. And by the feodal law, feuds being originally granted
for life only, we find that the rule was general for all vafals or
feudatories ; "*fi vafallus feudum diffipaverit, aut infigni detrimento*
"*deterius fecerit, privabitur*[y]." But in our antient common law
the rule was by no means fo large ; for not only he that was feifed of an eftate of inheritance might do as he pleafed with it,
but alfo wafte was not punifhable in any tenant, fave only in three
perfons ; guardian in chivalry, tenant in dower, and tenant by

[q] 2 Roll. Abr. 817.   [u] 1 Lev. 309.
[r] Co. Litt. 41.   [w] 5 Rep. 12.
[s] Hob. 296.   [x] Hob. 295.
[t] 1 Inft. 53.   [y] Wright. 44.

the

the curtefy [z]; and not in tenant for life or years [a]. And the reafon of the diverfity was, that the eftate of the three former was
created by the act of the law itfelf, which therefore gave a remedy againft them: but tenant for life, or for years, came in
by the demife and leafe of the owner of the fee, and therefore
he might have provided againft the committing of wafte by his
leffee; and if he did not, it was his own default. But, in favour
of the owners of the inheritance, the ftatutes of Marlbridge [b] and
Glocefter [c] provided, that the writ of wafte fhall not only lie
againft tenants by the law of England, (or curtefy) and thofe in
dower, but againft any farmer or other that holds in any manner for
life or years. So that, for above five hundred years paft, all tenants
for life or for any lefs eftate, have been punifhable or liable to be
impeached for wafte, both voluntary and permiffive; unlefs their
leafes be made, as fometimes they are, without impeachment of
wafte, *abfque impetitione vafti*; that is, with a provifion or protection
that no man fhall *impetere*, or fue him, for wafte committed.

THE punifhment for wafte committed was, by common law and
the ftatute of Marlbridge, only fingle damages [d]; except in the cafe
of a guardian, who alfo forfeited his wardfhip [e] by the provifions
of the great charter [f]: but the ftatute of Glocefter directs, that the
other four fpecies of tenants fhall lofe and forfeit the place wherein
the wafte is committed, and alfo treble damages, to him that
hath the inheritance. The expreffion of the ftatute is, " he fhall
" forfeit the *thing* which he hath wafted;" and it hath been determined, that under thefe words the *place* is alfo included [g].
And if wafte be done *fparfim*, or here and there, all over a wood,
the whole wood fhall be recovered; or if in feveral rooms of a
houfe, the whole houfe fhall be forfeited [h]; becaufe it is impracticable for the reverfioner to enjoy only the identical places wafted,

[z] It was however a doubt whether wafte
was punifhable at the common law in tenant by the curtefy. Regift. 72. Bro. Abr.
tit. wafte. 88. 2 Inft. 301.

[a] 2 Inft. 299.

[b] 52 Hen. III. c. 24.

[c] 6 Edw. I. c. 5.

[d] 2 Inft. 146.

[e] *Ibid.* 300.

[f] 9 Hen. III. c. 4.

[g] 2 Inft. 303.

[h] Co. Litt. 51.

when

when lying interfperfed with the other. But if wafte be done only
in one end of a wood (or perhaps in one room of a houfe) if
that can be conveniently feparated from the reft, that part only
is the *locus vaftatus*, or thing wafted, and that only fhall be forfeited to the reverfioner [i].

VII. A SEVENTH fpecies of forfeiture is that of *copyhold*
eftates, by *breach* of the *cuftoms* of the manor. Copyhold eftates
are not only liable to the fame forfeitures as thofe which are held
in focage, for treafon, felony, alienation, and wafte ; whereupon
the lord may feife them without any prefentment by the homage [k];
but alfo to peculiar forfeitures, annexed to this fpecies of tenure,
which are incurred by the breach of either the general cuftoms
of all copyholds, or the peculiar local cuftoms of certain particular manors. And we may obferve that, as thefe tenements were
originally holden by the loweft and moft abject vafals, the marks
of feodal dominion continue much the ftrongeft upon this mode
of property. Moft of the offences, which occafioned a refump-
tion of the fief by the feodal law, and were denominated *felo-
niae, per quas vafallus amitteret feudum* [l], ftill continue to be
caufes of forfeiture in many of our modern copyholds. As, by
fubtraction of fuit and fervice [m]; *fi dominum defervire noluerit* [n] :
by difclaiming to hold of the lord, or fwearing himfelf not his
copyholder [o]; *fi dominum ejuravit, i. e. negavit fe a domino feudum habere* [p] : by neglect to be admitted tenant within a year and
a day [q]; *fi per annum et diem ceffaverit in petenda inveftitura* [r] : by
contumacy in not appearing in court after three proclamations [s];
fi a domino ter citatus non comparuerit [t] : or by refufing, when
fworn of the homage, to prefent the truth according to his oath [u];
fi pares veritatem noverint, et dicant fe nefcire, cum fciant [w]. In

[i] 2 Inft. 304.
[k] 2 Ventr. 38. Cro. Eliz. 499.
[l] *Feud. l. 2. t. 26. in calc.*
[m] 3 Leon. 108. Dyer. 211.
[n] *Feud. l. 1. t. 21.*
[o] Co. Copyh. §. 57.
[p] *Feud. l. 2. t. 34. & t. 26. §. 3.*

[q] Plowd. 372.
[r] *Feud. l. 2. t. 24.*
[s] 8 Rep. 99. Co. Copyh. §. 57.
[t] *Feud. l. 2. t. 22.*
[u] Co. Copyh. §. 57.
[w] *Feud. l. 2. t. 58.*

thefe,

thefe, and a variety of other cafes, which it is impoffible here to enumerate, the forfeiture does not accrue to the lord till after the offences are prefented by the homage, or jury of the lord's court baron[x]; *per laudamentum parium fuorum*[y]: or, as it is more fully expreffed in another place[z], *nemo miles adimatur de poffeffione fui beneficii, nifi convicta culpa, quae fit laudanda*[a] *per judicium parium fuorum.*

VIII. The eighth and laft method, whereby lands and tenements may become forfeited, is that of *bankruptcy*, or the act of becoming a bankrupt : which unfortunate perfon may, from the feveral defcriptions given of him in our ftatute law, be thus defined; a trader, who fecretes himfelf, or does certain other acts, tending to defraud his creditors.

Who fhall be fuch a trader, or what acts are fufficient to denominate him a bankrupt, with the feveral connected confequences refulting from that unhappy fituation, will be better confidered in a fubfequent chapter; when we fhall endeavour more fully to explain it's nature, as it moft immediately relates to perfonal goods and chattels. I fhall only here obferve the manner in which the property of lands and tenements are transferred, upon the fuppofition that the owner of them is clearly and indifputably a bankrupt, and that a commiffion of bankrupt is awarded and iffued againft him.

By the ftatute 13 Eliz. c.7. the commiffioners for that purpofe, when a man is declared a bankrupt, fhall have full power to difpofe of all his lands and tenements, which he had in his own right at the time when he became a bankrupt, or which fhall defcend or come to him at any time afterwards, before his debts are fatisfied or agreed for; and all lands and tenements which were purchafed by him jointly with his wife or children to his own

---

[x] Co. Copyh. §. 58.
[y] *Feud. l. 1. t.* 21.
[z] *Ibid. t.* 22.

[a] *i. e. arbitranda, definienda.* Du Frefne. IV. 79.

ufe, (or fuch intereft therein as he may lawfully part with) or purchafed with any other perfon upon fecret truft for his own ufe; and to caufe them to be appraifed to their full value, and to fell the fame by deed indented and inrolled, or divide them proportionably among the creditors. The ftatute expreffly includes not only free, but copyhold, lands: but did not extend to eftates-tail, farther than for the bankrupt's life; nor to equities of redemption on a mortgaged eftate, wherein the bankrupt has no legal intereft, but only an equitable reverfion. Whereupon the ftatute 21 Jac. I. c. 19. enacts, that the commiffioners fhall be impowered to fell or convey, by deed indented and inrolled, any lands or tenements of the bankrupt, wherein he fhall be feifed of an eftate-tail in poffeffion, remainder, or reverfion, unlefs the remainder or reverfion thereof fhall be in the crown; and that fuch fale fhall be good againft all fuch iffues in tail, remaindermen, and reverfioners, whom the bankrupt himfelf might have barred by a common recovery, or other means: and that all equities of redemption upon mortgaged eftates, fhall be at the difpofal of the commiffioners; for they fhall have power to redeem the fame, as the bankrupt himfelf might have done, and after redemption to fell them. And alfo, by this and a former act[b], all fraudulent conveyances to defeat the intent of thefe ftatutes are declared void; but that no purchafer *bona fide*, for a good or valuable confideration, fhall be affected by the bankrupt laws, unlefs the commiffion be fued forth within five years after the act of bankruptcy committed.

By virtue of thefe ftatutes a bankrupt may lofe all his real eftates; which may at once be transferred by his commiffioners to their affignees, without his participation or confent.

[b] 1 Jac. I. c. 15.

CHAPTER THE NINETEENTH.

OF TITLE BY ALIENATION.

THE moft ufual and univerfal method of acquiring a title
to real eftates is that of alienation, conveyance, or purchafe in it's limited fenfe : under which may be comprized any
method wherein eftates are voluntarily refigned by one man, and
accepted by another ; whether that be effected by fale, gift, marriage fettlement, devife, or other tranfmiffion of property by the
mutual confent of the parties.

THIS means of taking eftates, by alienation, is not of equal
antiquity in the law of England with that of taking them by
defcent. For we may remember that, by the feodal law[a], a pure
and genuine feud could not be transferred from one feudatory
to another without the confent of the lord ; left thereby a feeble
or fufpicious tenant might have been fubftituted and impofed upon
him, to perform the feodal fervices, inftead of one on whofe abilities and fidelity he could depend. Neither could the feudatory
then fubject the land to his debts ; for, if he might, the feodal
reftraint of alienation would have been eafily fruftrated and eva-
ded[b]. And, as he could not aliene it in his lifetime, fo neither
could he by will defeat the fucceffion, by devifing his feud to another family ; nor even alter the courfe of it, by impofing particular limitations, or prefcribing an unufual path of defcent. Nor,
in fhort, could he aliene the eftate, even with the confent of the
lord, unlefs he had alfo obtained the confent of his own next apparent, or prefumptive, heir[c]. And therefore it was very ufual in
antient feoffments to exprefs, that the alienation was made by con-

---

[a] See pag. 57.
[b] *Feud. l. 1. t. 27.*

[c] Co. Litt. 94. Wright. 168.

fent

fent of the heirs of the feoffor; or fometimes for the heir apparent himfelf to join with the feoffor in the grant[d]. And, on the other hand, as the feodal obligation was looked upon to be reciprocal, the lord could not aliene or transfer his figniory without the confent of his vafal : for it was efteemed unreafonable to fubjedt a feudatory to a new fuperior, with whom he might have a deadly enmity, without his own approbation; or even to transfer his fealty, without his being thoroughly apprized of it, that he might know with certainty to whom his renders and fervices were due, and be able to diftinguifh a lawful diftrefs for rent from a hoftile feifing of his cattle by the lord of a neighbouring clan[e]. This confent of the vafal was expreffed by what was called *attorning*[f], or profeffing to become the tenant of the new lord; which dodtrine of attornment was afterwards extended to all leffees for life or years. For if one bought an eftate with any leafe for life or years ftanding out thereon, and the leffee or tenant refufed to attorn to the purchafor, and to become his tenant, the grant or contradt was in moft cafes void, or at leaft incomplete[g] : which was alfo an additional clog upon alienations.

B u t by degrees this feodal feverity is worn off; and experience hath fhewn, that property beft anfwers the purpofes of civil life, efpecially in commercial countries, when it's transfer and circulation are totally free and unreftrained. The road was cleared in the firft place by a law of king Henry the firft, which allowed a man to fell and difpofe of lands which he himfelf had purchafed; for over thefe he was thought to have a more extenfive power, than over what had been tranfmitted to him in a courfe of defcent from his anceftors[h] : a dodtrine, which is coun-

---

[d] Madox, *Formul. Angl.* n°. 316.319.427.
[e] Gilb. Ten. 75.
[f] The fame dodtrine and the fame denomination prevailed in Bretagne. —— *poffeffiones in jurifdidtionalibus non aliter apprehendi poffe, quam per attournances et avirances, ut loqui folent ; cum vafallus, ejurato prioris domini obfequio et fide, novo fe facramento novo*

item domino acquirenti obftringebat ; idque juffu audtoris. D' Argentre *Antiq. Confuet. Brit. apud* Dufrefne. i. 819, 820.
[g] Litt. §. 551.
[h] *Emptiones vel acquifitiones fuas det cui magis velit. Terram autem quam ei parentes dederunt, non mittat extra cognationem fuam.* LL. Hen. I. c. 70.

tenanced

tenanced by the feodal conftitutions themfelves j : but he was not
allowed to fell the whole of his own acquirements, fo as totally to
difinherit his children, any more than he was at liberty to aliene
his paternal eftate [i]. Afterwards a man feems to have been at liberty to part with all his own acquifitions, if he had previoufly
purchafed to him and his *affigns* by name ; but, if his *affigns* were
not fpecified in the purchafe deed, he was not empowered to
aliene [k] : and alfo he might part with one fourth of the inheritance of his anceftors without the confent of his heir [l]. By the
great charter of Henry III [m], no fubinfeudation was permitted of
part of the land, unlefs fufficient was left to anfwer the fervices
due to the fuperior lord, which fufficiency was probably interpreted to be one half or moiety of the land [n]. But thefe reftrictions were in general removed by the ftatute of *quia emptores* [o],
whereby all perfons, except the king's tenants *in capite*, were left
at liberty to aliene all or any part of their lands at their own difcretion [p]. And even thefe tenants *in capite* were by the ftatute
1 Edw. III. c. 12. permitted to aliene, on paying a fine to the
king [q]. By the temporary ftatutes 11 Hen. VII. c. 3. and
3 Hen. VIII. c. 4. all perfons attending the king in his wars were
allowed to aliene their lands without licence, and were relieved
from other feodal burdens. And, laftly, thefe very fines for alienations were, in all cafes of freehold tenure, entirely abolifhed by
the ftatute 12 Car. II. c. 24. As to the power of *charging* lands
with the debts of the owner, this was introduced fo early as ftatute Weftm. 2. which [r] fubjefted a *moiety* of the tenant's lands
to executions, for debts recovered by law ; as the *whole* of them
was likewife fubjefted to be pawned in a ftatute merchant by the
ftatute *de mercatoribus*, made the fame year, and in a ftatute ftaple
by ftatute 27 Edw. III. c. 9. and in other fimilar recognizances

---

j *Feud. l. 2. t.* 39.

[i] *Si queftum tantum habuerit is, qui partem
terrae fuae donare voluerit, tunc quidem hoc ei
licet; fed non totum queftum, quia non poteft filium
fuum haeredem exhaeredare.* Glanv. *l.* 7. *c.* 1.

[k] Mirr. c.1. §.3. This is alfo borrowed
from the feodal law. *Feud. l. 2. t.* 48.

[l] Mirr. *ibid.*

[m] 9 Hen. III. c. 32.

[n] Dalrymple of feuds. 95.

[o] 18 Edw. I. c. 1.

[p] See pag. 72.

[q] 2 Inft. 67.

[r] 13 Edw. I. c. 18.

by

by ftatute 23 Hen.VIII. c. 6. And, now, the whole of them is
not only fubject to be *pawned* for the debts of the owner, but
likewife to be abfolutely *fold* for the benefit of trade and commerce by the feveral ftatutes of bankruptcy. The reftraint of *de-*
vifing lands by will, except in fome places by particular cuftom,
lafted longer; that not being totally removed, till the abolition
of the military tenures. The doctrine of *attornments* continued
ftill later than any of the reft, and became extremely troublefome, though many methods were invented to evade them; till,
at laft, they were made no longer neceffary, by ftatutes 4 & 5 Ann.
c. 16. and 11 Geo. II. c. 19.

I n examining the nature of alienation, let us firft enquire,
briefly, *who* may aliene and to *whom*; and then, more largely,
how a man may aliene, or the feveral modes of conveyance.

I. W h o may aliene, and to whom; or, in other words, who
is capable of conveying and who of purchafing. And herein we
muft confider rather the incapacity, than capacity, of the feveral
parties: for all perfons in *poffeffion* are, *prima facie*, capable both
of conveying and purchafing, unlefs the law has laid them under
any particular difabilites. But, if a man has only in him the *right*
of either poffeffion or property, he cannot convey it to any other,
left pretended titles might be granted to great men, whereby juftice might be trodden down, and the weak oppreffed'. Yet reverfions and vefted remainders may be granted; becaufe the poffeffion of the particular tenant is the poffeffion of him in reverfion
or remainder: but *contingencies*, and mere *poffibilities*, though they
may be releafed, or devifed by will, or may pafs to the heir or
executor, yet cannot (it hath been faid) be affigned to a ftranger,
unlefs coupled with fome prefent intereft f.

P e r s o n s attainted of treafon, felony, and *praemunire*, are
incapable of conveying, from the time of the offence committed,

---

' Co. Litt. 214.

f Sheppard's touchftone. 238, 239, 322.
11 Mod. 152. 1 P. W^m. 574. Stra. 1 32.

provided

provided attainder follows[t]: for fuch conveyance by them may tend to defeat the king of his forfeiture, or the lord of his efcheat. But they may *purchafe* for the benefit of the crown, or the lord of the fee, though they are difabled to *hold:* the lands fo purchafed, if after attainder, being fubject to immediate forfeiture; if before, to efcheat as well as forfeiture, according to the nature of the crime[u]. So alfo corporations, religious or others, may purchafe lands; yet, unlefs they have a licence to hold in mortmain, they cannot retain fuch purchafe; but it fhall be forfeited to the lord of the fee.

IDIOTS and perfons of nonfane memory, infants, and perfons under durefs, are not totally difabled either to convey or purchafe, but *fub modo* only. For their conveyances and purchafes are voidable, but not actually void. The king indeed, on behalf of an idiot, may avoid his grants or other acts[w]. But it hath been faid, that a *non compos* himfelf, though he be afterwards brought to a right mind, fhall not be permitted to allege his own infanity in order to avoid fuch grant: for that no man fhall be allowed to ftultify himfelf, or plead his own difability. The progrefs of this notion is fomewhat curious. In the time of Edward I, *non compos* was a fufficient plea to avoid a man's own bond[x]: and there is a writ in the regifter[y] for the alienor himfelf to recover lands aliened by him during his infanity; *dum fuit non compos mentis fuae, ut dicit, &c.* But under Edward III a fcruple began to arife, whether a man fhould be permitted to *blemifh* himfelf, by pleading his own infanity[z]: and, afterwards, a defendant in affife having pleaded a releafe by the plaintiff fince the laft continuance, to which the plaintiff replied (*ore tenus*, as the manner then was) that he was out of his mind when he gave it, the court adjourned the affife; doubting, whether as the plaintiff was fane both then and at the commencement of the fuit, he fhould be permitted to plead an intermediate deprivation of reafon; and the queftion

---

[t] Co. Litt. 42.
[u] *Ibid.* 2.
[w] *Ibid.* 247.

[x] Britton, *c.* 28. *fol.* 66.
[y] *fol.* 228.
[z] 5 *Edw. III.* 70.

was afked, how he came to remember the releafe, if out of his fenfes when he gave it [a]. Under Henry VI this way of reafoning (that a man fhall not be allowed to difable himfelf, by pleading his own incapacity, becaufe he cannot know what he did under fuch a fituation) was ferioufly adopted by the judges in argument [b]; upon a queftion, whether the heir was barred of his right of entry by the feoffment of his infane anceftor. And from thefe loofe authorities, which Fitzherbert does not fcruple to reject as being contrary to reafon [c], the maxim that a man fhall not ftultify himfelf hath been handed down as fettled law [d]: though later opinions, feeling the inconvenience of the rule, have in many points endeavoured to reftrain it [e]. And, clearly, the next heir, or other perfon interefted, may, after the death of the idiot or *non compos*, take advantage of his incapacity and avoid the grant [f]. And fo too, if he purchafes under this difability, and does not afterwards upon recovering his fenfes agree to the purchafe, his heir may either waive or accept the eftate at his option [g]. In like manner, an infant may waive fuch purchafe or conveyance, when he comes to full age; or, if he does not then actually agree to it, his heirs may waive it after him [h]. Perfons alfo, who purchafe or convey under durefs, may affirm or avoid fuch tranfaction, whenever the durefs is ceafed [i]. For all thefe are under the protection of the law; which will not fuffer them to be impofed upon, through the imbecillity of their prefent condition; fo that their acts are only binding, in cafe they be afterwards agreed to, when fuch imbecillity ceafes.

THE cafe of a feme-covert is fomewhat different. She may *purchafe* an eftate without the confent of her hufband, and the conveyance is good during the coverture, till he avoids it by fome act declaring his diffent [k]. And, though he does nothing to avoid

[a] 35 *Aff.* *pl.* 10.
[b] 39 *Hen. VI.* 42.
[c] F. N. B. 202.
[d] Litt. §. 405. Cro. Eliz. 398. 4 Rep. 123.
[e] Comb. 469. 3 Mod. 310, 311. 1 Equ. caf. abr. 279.

[f] Perkins. §. 21.
[g] Co. Litt. 2.
[h] *Ibid.*
[i] 2 Inft. 483. 5 Rep. 119.
[k] Co. Litt. 3.

it,

it, or even if he actually confents, the feme-covert herfelf may, after the death of her hufband, waive or difagree to the fame: nay, even her heirs may waive it after her, if fhe dies before her hufband, or if in her widowhood fhe does nothing to exprefs her confent or agreement[l]. But the *conveyance* or other contract of a feme-covert (except by fome matter of record) is abfolutely void, and not merely voidable[m]; and therefore cannot be affirmed or made good by any fubfequent agreement.

THE cafe of an alien born is alfo peculiar. For he may purchafe any thing; but after purchafe he can *hold* nothing, except a leafe for years of a houfe for convenience of merchandize, in cafe he be an alien-friend: all other purchafes (when found by an inqueft of office) being immediately forfeited to the king[n].

PAPISTS, laftly, and perfons profeffing the popifh religion, are by ftatute 11 & 12 W. III. c. 4. difabled to purchafe any lands, rents, or hereditaments; and all eftates made to their ufe, or in truft for them, are void. But this ftatute is conftrued to extend only to papifts above the age of eighteen; fuch only being abfolutely difabled to purchafe: yet the next proteftant heir of a papift under eighteen fhall have the profits, during his life; unlefs he renounces his errors within the time limited by law[o].

II. WE are next, but principally, to enquire, *how* a man may aliene or convey; which will lead us to confider the feveral modes of conveyance.

IN confequence of the admiffion of property, or the giving a feparate right by the law of fociety to thofe things which by the law of nature were in common, there was neceffarily fome means to be devifed, whereby that feparate right or exclufive property fhould be originally acquired; which, we have more than once obferved, was that of occupancy or firft poffeffion. But this pof-

[l] *Ibid.*
[m] Perkins. §. 154. 1 Sid. 120.
[n] Co. Litt. 2.
[o] 1 P. W^{ms}. 354.

feffion,

feffion, when once gained, was alfo neceffarily to be continued ;
or elfe, upon one man's dereliction of the thing he had feifed, it
would again become common, and all thofe mifchiefs and contentions would enfue, which property was introduced to prevent.
For this purpofe therefore, of continuing the poffeffion, the municipal law has eftablifhed *defcents* and *alienations :* the former to
continue the poffeffion in the heirs of the proprietor, after his
involuntary dereliction of it by his death ; the latter to continue
it in thofe perfons, to whom the proprietor, by his own *voluntary*
act, fhall choofe to relinquifh it in his lifetime. A tranflation,
or transfer, of property being thus admitted by law, it became
neceffary that this transfer fhould be properly evidenced : in order to prevent difputes, either about the fact, as whether there
was any transfer at all ; or concerning the perfons, by whom and
to whom it was transferred ; or with regard to the fubjectmatter,
as what the thing transferred confifted of ; or, laftly, with relation to the mode and quality of the transfer, as for what period
of time (or, in other words, for what eftate and intereft) the
conveyance was made. The legal evidences of this tranflation of
property are called the *common affurances* of the kingdom; whereby every man's eftate is affured to him, and all controverfies,
doubts, and difficulties are either prevented or removed.

T H E S E common affurances are of four kinds : 1. By matter
in pais, or deed ; which is an affurance tranfacted between two
or more private perfons *in pais*, in the country ; that is (according to the old common law) upon the very fpot to be transferred.
2. By matter of *record*, or an affurance tranfacted only in the
king's public courts of record. 3. By fpecial *cuftom*, obtaining
in fome particular places, and relating only to fome particular
fpecies of property. Which three are fuch as take effect during
the life of the party conveying or affuring. 4. The fourth takes
no effect, till after his death ; and that is by *devife*, contained in
his laft will and teftament. We fhall treat of each in it's order.

CHAPTER THE TWENTIETH.

OF ALIENATION BY DEED.

IN treating of deeds I shall consider, first, their general nature; and, next, the several sorts or kinds of deeds, with their respective incidents. And in explaining the former, I shall examine, first, what a deed is; secondly, it's requisites; and, thirdly, how it may be avoided.

I. FIRST then, a deed is a writing sealed and delivered by the parties [a]. It is sometimes called a charter, *carta*, from it's materials; but most usually, when applied to the transactions of private subjects, it is called a deed, in Latin *factum*, κατ᾽ ἐξοχην, because it is the most solemn and authentic act that a man can possibly perform, with relation to the disposal of his property; and therefore a man shall always be *estopped* by his own deed, or not permitted to aver or prove any thing in contradiction to what he has once so solemnly and deliberately avowed [b]. If a deed be made by more parties than one, there ought to be regularly as many copies of it as there are parties, and each should be cut or indented (formerly in acute angles *instar dentium*, but at present in a waving line) on the top or side, to tally or correspond with the other; which deed, so made, is called an indenture. Formerly, when deeds were more concise than at present, it was usual to write both parts on the same piece of parchment, with some word or letters of the alphabet written between them; through which the parchment was cut, either in a strait or indented line, in such

[a] Co. Litt. 171. [b] Plowd. 434.

a man-a manner as to leave half the word on one part and half on the other. Deeds thus made were denominated *syngrapha* by the canonists [c]; and with us *chirographa*, or hand-writings [d]; the word *cirographum* or *cyrographum* being usually that which was divided in making the indenture: and this custom is still preserved in making out the indentures of a fine, whereof hereafter. But at length indenting only has come into use, without cutting through any letters at all; and it seems at present to serve for little other purpose, than to give name to the species of the deed. When the several parts of an indenture are interchangeably executed by the several parties, that part or copy which is executed by the grantor is usually called the *original*, and the rest are *counterparts:* though of late it is most frequent for all the parties to execute every part; which renders them all originals. A deed made by one party only is not indented, but *polled* or shaved quite even; and is therefore called a *deed-poll*, or a single deed [e].

II. WE are in the next place to consider the *requisites* of a deed. The first of which is, that there be persons able to contract and be contracted with, for the purposes intended by the deed; and also a thing, or subject matter to be contracted for; all which must be expressed by sufficient names [f]. So as in every grant there must be a grantor, a grantee, and a thing granted; in every lease a lessor, a lessee, and a thing demised.

SECONDLY; the deed must be founded upon good and sufficient *consideration*. Not upon an usurious contract [g]; nor upon fraud or collusion, either to deceive purchasors *bona fide* [h], or just and lawful creditors [i]; any of which bad considerations will vacate the deed. A deed also, or other grant, made without any consideration, is, as it were, of no effect; for it is construed to enure, or to be effectual, only to the use of the grantor himself [k].

[c] Lyndew. *l.* 1. *t.* 10. *c.* 1.
[d] Mirror. c. 2. §. 27.
[e] *Ibid.* Litt. §. 371, 372.
[f] Co. Litt. 35.
[g] Stat. 13 Eliz. c. 8.
[h] Stat. 27 Eliz. c. 4.
[i] Stat. 13 Eliz. c. 5.
[k] Perk. §. 533.

The

The confideration may be either a *good*, or a *valuable* one. A good confideration is fuch as that of blood, or of natural love and af-fection, when a man grants an eftate to a near relation; being founded in motives of generofity, prudence, and natural duty: a valuable confideration is fuch as money, marriage, or the like, which the law efteems an equivalent given for the grant[1]; and is therefore founded in motives of juftice. Deeds, made upon good confideration only, are confidered as merely voluntary, and are fre-quently fet afide in favour of creditors, and *bona fide* purchafors.

THIRDLY; the deed muft be *written*, or I prefume *printed*; for it may be in any character or any language; but it muft be upon paper, or parchment. For if it be written on ftone, board, linen, leather, or the like, it is no deed[m]. Wood or ftone may be more durable, and linen lefs liable to rafures; but writing on paper or parchment unites in itfelf, more perfectly than any other way, both thofe defirable qualities: for there is nothing elfe fo durable, and at the fame time fo little liable to alteration; nothing fo fecure from alteration, that is at the fame time fo durable. It muft alfo have the regular ftamps, impofed on it by the feveral ftatutes for the increafe of the public revenue; elfe it cannot be given in evidence. Formerly many conveyances were made by parol, or word of mouth only, without writing; but this giving a handle to a variety of frauds, the ftatute 29 Car. II. c. 3. enacts, that no leafe or eftate in lands, tenements, or hereditaments, (ex-cept leafes, not exceeding three years from the making, and whereon the referved rent is at leaft two thirds of the real value) fhall be looked upon as of greater force than a leafe or eftate at will; unlefs put in writing, and figned by the party granting, or his agent lawfully authorized in writing.

FOURTHLY; the matter written muft be *legally* and *orderly* fet forth: that is, there muft be words fufficient to fpecify the agreement and bind the parties: which fufficiency muft be left to

---

[1] 3 Rep. 83.   [m] Co. Litt. 229. F. N. B. 122.

the courts of law to determine [n]. For it is not abfolutely neceffary in law, to have all the formal parts that are ufually drawn
out in deeds, fo as there be fufficient words to declare clearly and
legally the party's meaning. But, as thefe formal and orderly
parts are calculated to convey that meaning in the cleareft, dif-
tincteft, and moft effectual manner, and have been well confidered
and fettled by the wifdom of fucceffive ages, it is prudent not to
depart from them without good reafon or urgent neceffity ; and
therefore I will here mention them in their ufual [o] order.

1. THE *premifes* may be ufed to fet forth the number and
names of the parties, with their additions or titles. They alfo contain the recital, if any, of fuch deeds, agreements, or matters
of fact, as are neceffary to explain the reafons upon which the
prefent tranfaction is founded : and herein alfo is fet down the
confideration upon which the deed is made. And then follows
the certainty of the grantor, grantee, and thing granted [p].

2. 3. NEXT come the *habendum* and *tenendum* [q]. The office
of the *habendum* is properly to determine what eftate or intereft is
granted by the deed : though this may be performed, and fometimes is performed, in the premifes. In which cafe the *habendum*
cannot *leffen*, but it may *enlarge*, the eftate granted in the premifes ; as if a grant be " to A and the heirs of his body" in the
premifes, *habendum* " to him and his heirs for ever," here A has
an eftate-tail, and a fee-fimple expectant thereon [r]. But had it
been in the premifes " to him and his heirs," *habendum* " to him
" and the heirs of his body," the *habendum* would be utterly
void [s]; for the larger and more beneficial eftate is vefted in him
before the *habendum* comes, and fhall not afterwards be narrowed,
or devefted, by it. The *tenendum*, " and to hold," is now of very
little ufe, and is only kept in by cuftom. It was fometimes formerly ufed to fignify the tenure, by which the eftate granted was

[n] Co. Litt. 225. [q] *Ibid.*
[o] *Ibid.* 6. [r] Co. Litt. 21.
[p] See appendix, N°. 2. §. 2. pag. v. [s] 8 Rep. 154.

to

to be holden; viz. "*tenendum per servitium militare, in burgagio,* "*in libero socagio, &c.*" But, all these being now reduced to free and common socage, the tenure is never specified. Before the statute of *quia emptores,* 18 Edw. I. it was also sometimes used to denote the lord of whom the land should be holden; but that statute directing all future purchasers to hold, not of the immediate grantor, but of the chief lord of the fee, this use of the *tenendum* hath been also antiquated; though for a long time after we find it mentioned in antient charters, that the tenements shall be holden *de capitalibus dominis feodi*[t]: but, as this expressed nothing more than the statute had already provided for, it gradually grew out of use.

4. NEXT follow the terms or stipulations, if any, upon which the grant is made: the first of which is the *reddendum* or reservation, whereby the grantor doth create or reserve some new thing to himself out of what he had before granted. As "rendering "therefore yearly the sum of ten shillings, or a pepper corn, or "two days ploughing, or the like[u]." This render, *reditus,* return, or rent, under the pure feodal system consisted, in chivalry, principally of military services; in villenage, of the most slavish offices; and, in socage, it usually consists of money, though it may consist of services still, or of any other certain profit[w]. To make a *reddendum* good, if it be of any thing newly created by the deed, the reservation must be to the grantors, or some, or one of them, and not to any stranger to the deed[x]. But if it be of antient services or the like, annexed to the land, then the reservation may be to the lord of the fee[y].

5. ANOTHER of the terms upon which a grant may be made is a *condition;* which is a clause of contingency, on the happening of which the estate granted may be defeated; as "provided "always, that if the mortgagor shall pay the mortgagee 500 *l.*

[t] Append. N°. I. Madox. *Formul. passim.*
[u] Append. N°. II. §. 1. pag. iii.
[w] See pag. 41.

[x] Plowd. 13. 8 Rep. 71.
[y] Append. N°. I. pag. i.

"upon

" upon fuch a day, the whole eftate granted fhall determine ;"
and the like [z].

6. N E X T may follow the claufe of *warranty*; whereby the
grantor doth, for himfelf and his heirs, warrant and fecure to the
grantee the eftate fo granted [a]. By the feodal conftitution, if the
vafal's title to enjoy the feud was difputed, he might vouch, or
call, the lord or donor to warrant or infure his gift; which if he
failed to do, and the vafal was evicted, the lord was bound to
give him another feud of equal value in recompenfe [b]. And fo,
by our antient law, if before the ftatute of *quia emptores* a man
enfeoffed another in fee, by the feodal verb *dedi*, to hold of himfelf and his heirs by certain fervices; the law annexed a warranty to this grant, which bound the feoffor and his heirs, to
whom the fervices (which were the confideration and equivalent
for the gift) were originally ftipulated to be rendered [c]. Or if a
man and his anceftors had immemorially holden land of another
and his anceftors by the fervice of homage (which was called
homage aunceftrel) this alfo bound the lord to warranty [d]; the
homage being an evidence of fuch a feodal grant. And, upon a
fimilar principle, in cafe, after a partition or exchange of lands
of inheritance, either party or his heirs be evicted of his fhare,
the other and his heirs are bound to warranty [e], becaufe they
enjoy the equivalent. And fo, even at this day, upon a gift in
tail or leafe for life, rendering rent, the donor or leffor and his
heirs (to whom the rent is payable) are bound to warrant the
title [f]. But in a feoffment in fee by the verb *dedi*, fince the ftatute of *quia emptores,* the feoffor only is bound to the implied
warranty, and not his heirs [g]; becaufe it is a mere perfonal contract on the part of the feoffor, the tenure (and of courfe the antient fervices) refulting back to the fuperior lord of the fee. And
in other forms of alienation, gradually introduced fince that fta-

[z] Append. N°. II. §. 2. pag. viii.
[a] *Ibid.* N°. I. pag. i.
[b] *Feud. l* 2. *t.* 8, & 25.
[c] Co. Litt. 384.

[d] Litt. §. 143.
[e] Co. Litt. 174.
[f] *Ibid.* 384.
[g] *Ibid.*

tute,

tute, no warranty whatſoever is implied[h]; they bearing no ſort of analogy to the original feodal donation. And therefore in ſuch caſes it became neceſſary to add an expreſs clauſe of warranty, to bind the grantor and his heirs; which is a kind of covenant real, and can only be created by the verb *warrantizo* or *warrant*[i].

THESE expreſs warranties were introduced, even prior to the ſtatute of *quia emptores*, in order to evade the ſtrictneſs of the feodal doctrine of non-alienation without the conſent of the heir. For, though he, at the death of his anceſtor, might have entered on any tenements that were aliened without his concurrence, yet, if a clauſe of warranty was added to the anceſtor's grant, this covenant deſcending upon the heir inſured the grantee; not ſo much by confirming his title, as by obliging ſuch heir to yield him a recompenſe in lands of equal value: the law, in favour of alienations, ſuppoſing that no anceſtor would wantonly diſinherit his next of blood[k]; and therefore preſuming that he had received a valuable conſideration, either in land, or in money which had purchaſed land, and that this equivalent deſcended to the heir together with the anceſtor's warranty. So that when either an anceſtor, being the rightful tenant of the freehold, conveyed the land to a ſtranger and his heirs, or releaſed the right in fee-ſimple to one who was already in poſſeſſion, and ſuperadded a warranty to his deed, it was held that ſuch warranty not only bound the warrantor himſelf to protect and aſſure the title of the warrantee, but it alſo bound his heir: and this, whether that warranty was *lineal*, or *collateral* to the title of the land. *Lineal* warranty was where the heir derived, or might by poſſibility have derived, his title to the land warranted, either from or through the anceſtor who made the warranty; as, where a father, or an elder ſon in the life of the father, releaſed to the diſſeiſor of either themſelves or the grandfather, with warranty, this was lineal to the younger ſon[l]. *Collateral* warranty was where the heir's title to the land neither was, nor could have been, derived from

[h] Co. Litt. 102.
[i] Litt. §. 733.

[k] Co. Litt. 373.
[l] Litt. §. 703. 706. 707.

the

the warranting anceftor; as, where a younger brother releafed to his father's diffeifor, with warranty, this was collateral to the elder brother [m]. But where the very conveyance, to which the warranty was annexed, immediately followed a diffeifin, or operated itfelf as fuch (as, where a father tenant for years, with remainder to his fon in fee, aliened in fee-fimple with warranty) this, being in it's original manifeftly founded on the *tort* or wrong of the warrantor himfelf, was called a warranty *commencing by diffeifin*; and, being too palpably injurious to be fupported, was not binding upon any heir of fuch tortious warrantor [n].

I n both lineal and collateral warranty, the obligation of the heir (in cafe the warrantee was evicted, to yield him other lands in their ftead) was only on condition that he had other fufficient lands by defcent from the warranting anceftor [o]. But though, without affets, he was not bound to infure the title of *another*, yet, in cafe of lineal warranty, whether affets defcended or not, the heir was perpetually barred from claiming the land *himfelf*; for, if he could fucceed in fuch claim, he would then gain affets by defcent (if he had them not before) and muft fulfil the warranty of his anceftor : and the fame rule [p] was with lefs juftice adopted alfo in refpect of collateral warranties, which likewife (though no affets defcended) barred the heir of the warrantor from claiming the land by any collateral title; upon the prefumption of law that he might hereafter have affets by defcent either from or through the fame anceftor. The inconvenience of this latter branch of the rule was felt very early, when tenants by the curtefy took upon them to aliene their lands with warranty ; which collateral warranty of the father defcending upon his fon (who was the heir of both his parents) barred him from claiming his maternal inheritance : to remedy which the ftatute of Glocefter, 6 Edw. I. c. 3. declared, that fuch warranty fhould be no bar to the fon, unlefs affets defcended from the father. It was afterwards attempted in 50 Edw. III. to make the fame pro-

[m] Litt. §. 705. 707.　　　[o] Co. Litt. 102.
[n] *Ibid.* §. 698. 702.　　　[p] Litt. §. 711. 712.

vifion

vifion univerfal, by enacting that no collateral warranty fhould
be a bar, unlefs where affets defcended from the fame anceftor[q],
but it then proceeded not to effect. However, by the ftatute
11 Hen.VII. c. 20. notwithftanding any alienation with warranty
by tenant in dower, the heir of the hufband is not barred, though
he be alfo heir to the wife. And by ftatute 4 & 5 Ann. c. 16.
all warranties by any tenant for life fhall be void againft thofe in
remainder or reverfion ; and all collateral warranties by any anceftor who has no eftate of inheritance in poffeffion fhall be void
againft his heir. By the wording of which laft ftatute it fhould
feem, that the legiflature meant to allow, that the collateral warranty of tenant in tail, defcending (though without affets) upon
a remainder-man or reverfioner, fhould ftill bar the remainder or
reverfion. For though the judges, in expounding the ftatute *de
donis*, held that, by analogy to the ftatute of Glocefter, a lineal
warranty by the tenant in tail without affets fhould not bar the
iffue in tail, yet they held fuch warranty with affets to be a fufficient bar[r] : which was therefore formerly mentioned[s] as one of
the ways whereby an eftate tail might be deftroyed ; it being indeed nothing more in effect, than exchanging the lands entailed
for others of equal value. They alfo held that collateral warranty
was not within the ftatute *de donis* ; as that act was principally
intended to prevent the tenant in tail from difinheriting his own
iffue : and therefore collateral warranty (though without affets)
was allowed to be, as at common law, a fufficient bar of the
eftate-tail and all remainders and reverfions expectant thereon[t].
And fo it ftill continues to be, notwithftanding the ftatute of
queen Anne, if made by tenant in tail in poffeffion : who therefore may now, without the forms of a fine or recovery, in fome
cafes make a good conveyance in fee-fimple, by fuperadding a
warranty to his grant ; which, if accompanied with affets, bars
his own iffue, and without them bars fuch of his heirs as may be
in remainder or reverfion.

[q] Co. Litt. 373.   [s] pag. 116.
[r] Litt. §. 712. 2 Inft. 293.   [t] Co. Litt. 374. 2 Inft. 335.

7 A F T E R

7. A F T E R warranty ufually follow *covenants*, or conventions; which are claufes of agreement contained in a deed,
whereby either party may ftipulate for the truth of certain facts,
or may bind himfelf to perform, or give, fomething to the other.
Thus the grantor may covenant that he hath a right to convey;
or for the grantee's quiet enjoyment; or the like: the grantee
may covenant to pay his rent, to repair the premifes, &c ᵘ. If
the covenantor covenants for himfelf and his *heirs*, it is then a
covenant real, and defcends upon the heirs; who are bound to
perform it, provided they have affets by defcent, but not otherwife: if he covenants alfo for his *executors* and *adminiftrators*, his
perfonal affets, as well as his real, are likewife pledged for the
performance of the covenant; which makes fuch covenant a better fecurity than any warranty, and it has therefore in modern
practice totally fuperfeded the other.

8. L A S T L Y, comes the *conclufion*, which mentions the execution and date of the deed, or the time of it's being given or
executed, either exprefsly, or by reference to fome day and year
before-mentioned ʷ. Not but a deed is good, although it mention
no date; or hath a falfe date; or even if it hath an impoffible
date, as the thirtieth of February; provided the real day of it's
being dated or given, that is, delivered, can be proved ˣ.

I P R O C E E D now to the *fifth* requifite for making a good deed;
the *reading* of it. This is neceffary, wherever any of the parties
defire it; and, if it be not done on his requeft, the deed is void
as to him. If he can, he fhould read it himfelf: if he be blind
or illiterate, another muft read it to him. If it be read falfely,
it will be void; at leaft for fo much as is mifrecited: unlefs it
be agreed by collufion that the deed fhall be read falfe, on purpofe to make it void; for in fuch cafe it fhall bind the fraudulent
party ʸ.

ᵘ Append. Nº. II. §. 2. pag. viii.   ˣ Co. Litt. 46. Dyer. 28.
ʷ *Ibid*. pag. xii.   ʸ 2 Rep. 3. 9. 11 Rep. 27.

S I X T H L Y,

SIXTHLY, it is requisite that the party, whose deed it is, should *seal*, and in most cases I apprehend should *sign* it also. The use of seals, as a mark of authenticity to letters and other instruments in writing, is extremely antient. We read of it among the Jews and Persians in the earliest and most sacred records of history[z]. And in the book of Jeremiah there is a very remarkable instance, not only of an attestation by seal, but also of the other usual formalities attending a Jewish purchase[a]. In the civil law also[b], seals were the evidence of truth; and were required, on the part of the witnesses at least, at the attestation of every testament. But in the times of our Saxon ancestors, they were not much in use here. For though sir Edward Coke[c] relies on an instance of king Edwyn's making use of a seal about an hundred years before the conquest, yet it does not follow that this was the usage among the whole nation : and perhaps the charter he mentions may be of doubtful authority, from this very circumstance, of being sealed; since we are assured by all our antient historians, that sealing was not then in common use. The method of the Saxons was for such as could write to subscribe their names, and, whether they could write or not, to affix the sign of the cross : which custom our illiterate vulgar do, for the most part, to this day keep up; by signing a cross for their mark, when unable to write their names. And indeed this inability to write, and therefore making a cross in it's stead, is honestly avowed by Caedwalla, a Saxon king, at the end of one of his charters[d]. In like manner, and for the same unsurmountable reason, the Normans, a brave but

---

[z] 1 Kings. c. 21. Daniel. c. 6. Esther. c. 8.

[a] " And I bought the field of Hanameel, " and weighed him the money, even seven- " teen shekels of silver. And I subscribed " the evidence, and sealed it, and took wit- " nesses, and weighed him the money in the " ballances. And I took the evidence of " the purchase, both that which was sealed " according to the law and custom, and " also that which was open." c. 32.

[b] *Inst.* 2. 10. 2 & 3.

[c] 1 Inst. 7.

[d] " *Propria manu pro ignorantia literarum.* " *signum sanctae crucis expressi et subscripsi.*" Seld. *Jan Angl. l.* 1. §. 42. And this (according to Procopius) the emperor Justin in the east, and Theodoric king of the Goths in Italy, had before authorized by their example, on account of their inability to write.

illiterate

illiterate nation, at their firſt ſettlement in France, uſed the practice of ſealing only, without writing their names : which cuſtom
continued, when learning made it's way among them, though
the reaſon for doing it had ceaſed ; and hence the charter of Edward the confeſſor to Weſtminſter abbey, himſelf being brought
up in Normandy, was witneſſed only by his ſeal, and is generally
thought to be the oldeſt ſealed charter of any authenticity in
England [e]. At the conqueſt, the Norman lords brought over
into this kingdom their own faſhions; and introduced waxen ſeals
only, inſtead of the Engliſh method of writing their names, and
ſigning with the ſign of the croſs [f]. The impreſſions of theſe
ſeals were ſometimes a knight on horſeback, ſometimes other
deviſes : but coats of arms were not introduced into ſeals, nor
indeed into any other uſe, till about the reign of Richard the
firſt, who brought them from the croiſade in the holy land;
where they were firſt invented and painted on the ſhields of the
knights, to diſtinguiſh the variety of perſons of every chriſtian
nation who reſorted thither, and who could not, when clad in
complete ſteel, be otherwiſe known or aſcertained.

THIS neglect of ſigning, and reſting only upon the authenticity of ſeals, remained very long among us ; for it was held in
all our books that ſealing alone was ſufficient to authenticate a
deed : and ſo the common form of atteſting deeds, --- "*ſealed*
and delivered," continues to this day; notwithſtanding the ſtatute 29 Car. II. c. 3. before-mentioned revives the Saxon cuſtom, and expreſſly directs the ſigning, in all grants of lands, and
many other ſpecies of deeds ; in which therefore ſigning ſeems
to be now as neceſſary as ſealing, though it hath been ſometimes
held, that the one includes the other [g].

A SEVENTH requiſite to a good deed is that it be *delivered*,
by the party himſelf or his certain attorney : which therefore is

---

[e] Lamb. *Archeion.* 51.

[f] " *Normanni chirographorum confectionem,*
" *cum crucibus aureis, aliiſque ſignaculis ſacris,*
" *in Anglia firmari ſolitam, in ſacram impreſ-*
" *ſam mutant, modumque ſcribendi Anglicum*
" *rejiciunt.*" Ingulph.

[g] 3 Lev. 1. Stra. 764.

alſo

alſo expreſſed in the atteſtation; "ſealed and *delivered*." A deed
takes effect only from this tradition or delivery; for, if the date
be falſe or impoſſible, the delivery aſcertains the time of it. And
if another perſon ſeals the deed, yet if the party delivers it himſelf, he thereby adopts the ſealing [h], and by a parity of reaſon the
ſigning alſo, and makes them both his own. A delivery may
be either abſolute, that is, to the party or grantee himſelf; or to
a third perſon, to hold till ſome conditions be performed on the
part of the grantee : in which laſt caſe it is not delivered as a
deed, but as an *eſcrow*; that is, as a ſcrowl or writing, which is
not to take effect as a deed till the conditions be performed; and
then it is a deed to all intents and purpoſes [i].

T H E *laſt* requiſite to the validity of a deed is the *atteſtation*, or
execution of it *in the preſence of witneſſes:* though this is neceſſary,
rather for preſerving the evidence, than for conſtituting the eſſence,
of the deed. Our modern deeds are in reality nothing more than
an improvement or amplification of the *brevia teſtata* mentioned
by the feodal writers [k]; which were written memorandums, introduced to perpetuate the tenor of the conveyance and inveſtiture,
when grants by parol only became the foundation of frequent diſpute and uncertainty. To this end they regiſtered in the deed the
perſons who attended as witneſſes, which was formerly done
without their ſigning their names (that not being always in their
power) but they only heard the deed read; and then the clerk
or ſcribe added their names, in a ſort of memorandum; thus;
" *hijs teſtibus, Johanne Moore, Jacobo Smith, et aliis ad hanc rem*
" *convocatis* [l]." This, like all other ſolemn tranſactions, was originally done only *coram paribus* [m], and frequently when aſſembled
in the court baron, hundred, or county court; which was then
expreſſed in the atteſtation, *teſte comitatu, hundredo, &c* [n]. Afterwards the atteſtation of other witneſſes was allowed, the trial in

[h] Perk. §. 130.
[i] Co. Litt. 36.
[k] *Feud. l.* 1. *t.* 4.
[l] Co. Litt. 7.

[m] *Feud. l.* 2. *t.* 32.
[n] Spelm. *Gloſſ.* 228. Madox. *Formul.*
n°. 221. 322. 660.

caſe

cafe of a difpute being ftill referved to the *pares;* with whom the witneffes (if more than one) were affociated, and joined in the verdict[o]: till that alfo was abrogated by the ftatute of York, 12 Edw. II. ft. 1. c. 2. And in this manner, with fome fuch claufe of *hijs teftibus,* are all old deeds and charters, particularly *magna carta,* witneffed. And, in the time of fir Edward Coke, creations of nobility were ftill witneffed in the fame manner[p]. But in the king's common charters, writs, or letters patent, the ftile is now altered : for, at prefent, the king is his own witnefs, and attefts his letters patent thus ; " *tefte meipfo,* witnefs ourfelf at Weftminfter, &c :" a form which was introduced by Richard the firft[q], but not commonly ufed till about the beginning of the fifteenth century ; nor the claufe of *hijs teftibus* intirely difconti- nued till the reign of Henry the eighth[r] : which was alfo the aera of difcontinuing it in the deeds of fubjects, learning being then revived, and the faculty of writing more general: and there- fore ever fince that time the witneffes have fubfcribed their at- teftation, either at the bottom, or on the back, of the deed[s].

III. WE are next to confider, how a deed may be *avoided,* or rendered of no effect. And from what has been before laid down it will follow, that if a deed wants any of the effential re- quifites before-mentioned; either, 1. Proper parties, and a pro- per fubject matter : 2. A good and fufficient confideration : 3. Writing, on paper or parchment, duly ftamped : 4. Sufficient and legal words, properly difpofed : 5. Reading, if defired, be- fore the execution : 6. Sealing ; and, by the ftatute, in many cafes figning alfo : or, 7. Delivery : it is a void deed *ab initio.* It may alfo be avoided by matter *ex poft facto :* as, 1. By rafure, interlining, or other alteration in any material part ; unlefs a memorandum be made thereof at the time of the execution and atteftation[t]. 2. By breaking off, or defacing, the feal[u]. 3. By

[o] Co. Litt. 6.
[p] 2 Inft. 77.
[q] Madox, *Formul.* n[o]. 515.
[r] *Ibid.* Differt. fol. 32.

[s] 2 Inft. 78.
[t] 11 Rep. 27.
[u] 5 Rep. 23.

delivering

delivering it up to be cancelled; that is to have lines drawn over it, in the form of lattice work or *cancelli*; though the phrase is now used figuratively for any manner of obliteration or defacing it. 4. By the difagreement of fuch, whofe concurrence is neceffary, in order for the deed to ftand: as, the hufband, where a feme covert is concerned; an infant, or perfon under durefs, when thofe difabilities are removed; and the like. 6. By the judgment or decree of a court of judicature. This was antiently the province of the court of ftar chamber, and now of the chancery: when it appears that the deed was obtained by fraud, force, or other foul practice; or is proved to be an abfolute forgery ʷ. In any of thefe cafes the deed may be voided, either in part or totally, according as the caufe of avoidance is more or lefs extenfive.

AND, having thus explained the general nature of deeds, we are next to confider their feveral fpecies, together with their refpective incidents. And herein I fhall only examine the particulars of thofe, which, from long practice and experience of their efficacy, are generally ufed in the alienation of *real* eftates: for it would be tedious, nay infinite, to defcant upon all the feveral inftruments made ufe of in *perfonal* concerns, but which fall under our general definition of a deed; that is, a writing fealed and delivered. The former, being principally fuch as ferve to *convey* the property of lands and tenements from man to man, are commonly denominated *conveyances:* which are either conveyances at *common law,* or fuch as receive their force and efficacy by virtue of the *ftatute of ufes.*

I. OF conveyances by the common law, fome may be called *original,* or *primary* conveyances; which are thofe by means whereof the benefit or eftate is created or firft arifes: others are *derivative* or *fecondary;* whereby the benefit or eftate, originally created, is enlarged, reftrained, transferred, or extinguifhed.

ʷ Toth. 90.

ORIGINAL

O R I G I N A L conveyances are the following; 1. Feoffment: 2. Gift; 3. Grant; 4. Leafe; 5. Exchange; 6. Partition: *derivative* are, 7. Releafe; 8. Confirmation; 9. Surrender; 10. Aflignment; 11. Defeazance.

1. A FEOFFMENT, *feoffamentum*, is a fubftantive derived from the verb, to enfeoff, *feoffare* or *infeudare*, to give one a feud; and therefore feoffment is properly *donatio feudi*[x]. It is the moft antient method of conveyance, the moft folemn and public, and therefore the moft eafily remembered and proved. And it may properly be defined, the gift of any corporeal hereditament to another. He that fo gives, or enfeoffs, is called the *feoffor*; and the perfon enfeoffed is denominated the *feoffee*.

T H I S is plainly derived from, or is indeed itfelf the very mode of the antient feodal donation; for though it may be performed by the word "enfeoff" or "grant," yet the apteft word of feoffment is "*do* or *dedi*[y]." And it is ftill directed and governed by the fame feodal rules; infomuch that the principal rule relating to the extent and effect of a feodal grant, "*tenor eft* "*qui legem dat feudo*," is in other words become the maxim of our law with relation to feoffments, "*modus legem dat donationi*[z]." And therefore as in pure feodal donations the lord, from whom the feud moved, muft expreflly limit and declare the continuance or quantity of eftate he meant to confer, "*ne quis plus donaffe* "*praefumatur, quam in donatione exprefferit*[a];" fo, if one grants by feoffment lands or tenements to another, and limits or expreffes no eftate, the grantee (due ceremonies of law being performed) hath barely an eftate for life[b]. For, as the perfonal abilities of the feoffee were originally prefumed to be the immediate or principal inducements to the feoffment, the feoffee's eftate ought to be confined to his perfon, and fubfift only for his

---

[x] Co. Litt. 9.
[y] *Ibid*.
[z] Wright. 21.

[a] pag. 108.
[b] Co. Litt. 42.

life;

life; unlefs the feoffor, by exprefs provifion in the creation and conftitution of the eftate, hath given it a longer continuance. Thefe exprefs provifions are indeed generally made; for this was for ages the only conveyance, whereby our anceftors were wont to create an eftate in fee-fimple [c], by giving the land to the feoffee, to hold to him and his heirs for ever; though it ferves equally well to convey any other eftate of freehold [d].

BUT by the mere words of the deed the feoffment is by no means perfected. There remains a very material ceremony to be performed, called *livery of feifin*; without which the feoffee has but a mere eftate at will [e]. This livery of feifin is no other than the pure feodal inveftiture, or delivery of corporal poffeffion of the land or tenement; which was held abfolutely neceffary to complete the donation. " *Nam feudum fine inveftitura nullo modo* " *conftitui potuit* [f] :" and an eftate was then only perfect, when, as Fleta expreffes it in our law, " *fit juris et feifinae conjunctio* [g]."

INVESTITURES, in their original rife, were probably intended to demonftrate in conquered countries the actual poffeffion of the *lord*; and that he did not grant a bare litigious right, which the foldier was ill qualified to profecute, but a peaceable and firm poffeffion. And, at a time when writing was feldom practifed, a mere oral gift, at a diftance from the fpot that was given, was not likely to be either long or accurately retained in the memory of by-ftanders, who were very little interefted in the grant. Afterwards they were retained as a public and notorious act, that the country might take notice of and teftify the transfer of the eftate; and that fuch as claimed title by other means might know againft whom to bring their actions.

IN all well-governed nations, fome notoriety of this kind has been ever held requifite, in order to acquire and afcertain the

[c] See Appendix. N°. I.
[d] Co. Litt. 9.
[e] Litt. §. 66.
[f] Wright. 37.
[g] *l.* 3. *c.* 15. §. 5.

property of lands. In the Roman law *plenum dominium* was not
faid to fubfift, unlefs where a man hath both the *right*, and the
corporal poffeffion; which poffeffion could not be acquired without both an actual intention to poffefs, and an actual feifin, or
entry into the premifes, or part of them in the name of the
whole [h]. And even in ecclefiaftical promotions, where the freehold paffes to the perfon promoted, corporal poffeffion is required at this day, to veft the property completely in the new proprietor; who, according to the diftinction of the canonifts [i], acquires the *jus ad rem*, or inchoate and imperfect right, by nomination and inftitution; but not the *jus in re*, or complete and
full right, unlefs by corporal poffeffion. Therefore in dignities
poffeffion is given by inftallment; in rectories and vicarages by
induction, without which no temporal rights accrue to the minifter, though every ecclefiaftical power is vefted in him by inftitution. So alfo even in defcents of lands, by our law, which
are caft on the heir by act of the law itfelf, the heir has not *plenum dominium*, or full and complete ownerfhip, till he has made
an actual corporal entry into the lands : for if he dies before *entry*
made, *his* heir fhall not be intitled to take the poffeffion, but the
heir of the perfon who was laft actually feifed [k]. It is not therefore only a mere right to enter, but the actual entry, that makes
a man complete owner ; fo as to tranfmit the inheritance to his
own heirs : *non jus, fed feifina, facit ftipitem* [l].

YET, the corporal tradition of lands being fometimes inconvenient, a fymbolical delivery of poffeffion was in many cafes
antiently allowed; by transferring fomething near at hand, in the
prefence of credible witneffes, which by agreement fhould ferve
to reprefent the very thing defigned to be conveyed ; and an oc-

[h] *Nam apifcimur poffeffionem corpore et animo : neque per fe corpore ; neque per fe animo.
Non autem ita accipiendum eft, ut qui fundum
poffidere velit, omnes glebas circumambulet ; fed
fufficit quamlibet partem ejus fundi introire.*
(*Ff.* 41. 2. 3.) And again : *traditionibus do-*
minia rerum, non nudis pactis, transferuntur.
(Cod. 2. 3. 20.)

[i] Decretal. *l.* 3. *t.* 4. *c.* 40.
[k] See pag. 209. 227, 228.
[l] Flet. *l.* 6. *c.* 2. §. 2.

cupancy

cupancy of this sign or symbol was permitted as equivalent to occupancy of the land itself. Among the Jews we find the evidence of a purchase thus defined in the book of Ruth [m] : " now " this was the manner in former time in Israel, concerning re- " deeming and concerning changing, for to confirm all things : " a man plucked off his shoe, and gave it to his neighbour ; and " this was a testimony in Israel." Among the antient Goths and Swedes, contracts for the sale of lands were made in the presence of witnesses, who extended the cloak of the buyer, while the seller cast a clod of the land into it, in order to give possession : and a staff or wand was also delivered from the vendor to the vendee, which passed through the hands of the witnesses [n]. With our Saxon ancestors the delivery of a turf was a necessary solemnity, to establish the conveyance of lands [o]. And, to this day, the conveyance of our copyhold estates is usually made from the seller to the lord or his steward by delivery of a rod or virge, and then from the lord to the purchasor by re-delivery of the same, in the presence of a jury of tenants.

CONVEYANCES in writing were the last and most refined improvement. The mere delivery of possession, either actual or symbolical, depending on the ocular testimony and remembrance of the witnesses, was liable to be forgotten or misrepresented, and became frequently incapable of proof. Besides, the new occasions and necessities, introduced by the advancement of commerce, required means to be devised of charging and incumbering estates, and of making them liable to a multitude of conditions and minute designations for the purposes of raising money, without an absolute sale of the land; and sometimes the like proceedings were found useful in order to make a decent and competent provision for the numerous branches of a family, and for other domestic views. None of which could be effected by a mere, simple, corporal transfer of the soil from one man to another, which was principally calculated for conveying an absolute

<hr />

[m] ch. 4. v. 7.
[n] Stiernhook. *de jure Sueon. l. 2. c. 4.*
[o] Hickes. *Differt. epiftolar.* 85.

unli-

unlimited dominion. Written deeds were therefore introduced, in order to ſpecify and perpetuate the peculiar purpoſes of the party who conveyed : yet ſtill, for a very long ſeries of years, they were never made uſe of, but in company with the more an- tient and notorious method of transfer, by delivery of corporal poſſeſſion.

Livery of feifin, by the common law, is neceſſary to be made upon every grant of an eſtate of freehold in hereditaments corporeal, whether of inheritance or for life only. In heredita- ments incorporeal it is impoſſible to be made ; for they are not the object of the ſenſes : and in leaſes for years, or other chattel intereſts, it is not neceſſary. In leaſes for years indeed an actual *entry* is neceſſary, to veſt the eſtate in the leſſee : for the bare leaſe gives him only a right to enter, which is called his intereſt in the term, or *intereſſe termini*; and, when he enters in purſuance of that right, he is then and not before in poſſeſſion of his term, and complete tenant for years [p]. This entry by the tenant him- ſelf ſerves the purpoſe of notoriety, as well as livery of feifin from the grantor could have done ; which it would have been improper to have given in this caſe, becauſe that ſolemnity is appropriated to the conveyance of a freehold. And this is one reaſon why freeholds cannot be made to commence *in futuro,* be- cauſe they cannot be made but by livery of feifin ; which livery, being an actual manual tradition of the land, muſt take effect *in praeſenti,* or not at all [q].

On the creation of a *freehold* remainder, at one and the ſame time with a particular eſtate for years, we have before ſeen that at the common law livery muſt be made to the particular tenant [r]. But if ſuch a remainder be created afterwards, expectant on a leaſe for years now in being, the livery muſt not be made to the leſſee for years, for then it operates nothing ; " *nam quod ſemel* " *meum eſt, amplius meum eſſe non poteſt* [s] :" but it muſt be made

[p] Co. Litt. 46.   [r] pag. 167.
[q] See pag. 165.   [s] Co. Litt. 49.

to the remainder-man himself, by consent of the lessee for years :
for without his consent no livery of the possession can be given[t];
partly because such forcible livery would be an ejectment of the
tenant from his term, and partly for the reasons before given[u] for
introducing the doctrine of attornments.

LIVERY of seisin is either in *deed*, or in *law*. Livery in *deed*
is thus performed. The feoffor, lessor, or his attorney, together
with the feoffee, lessee, or his attorney, (for this may as effectually
be done by deputy or attorney, as by the principals themselves in
person) come to the land, or to the house; and there, in the presence of witnesses, declare the contents of the feoffment or lease,
on which livery is to be made. And then the feoffor, if it be of
land, doth deliver to the feoffee, all other persons being out of
the ground, a clod or turf, or a twig or bough there growing,
with words to this effect. " I deliver these to you in the name
" of seisin of all the lands and tenements contained in this deed."
But, if it be of a house, the feoffor must take the ring, or latch
of the door, the house being quite empty, and deliver it to the
feoffee in the same form ; and then the feoffee must enter alone,
and shut to the door, and then open it, and let in the others[w].
If the conveyance or feoffment be of divers lands, lying scattered
in one and the same county, then in the feoffor's possession, livery
of seisin of any parcel, in the name of the rest, sufficeth for all[x];
but, if they be in several counties, there must be as many liveries
as there are counties. For, if the title to these lands comes to be
disputed, there must be as many trials as there are counties, and
the jury of one county are no judges of the notoriety of a fact
in another. Besides, antiently this seisin was obliged to be delivered *coram paribus de vicineto*, before the peers or freeholders
of the neighbourhood, who attested such delivery in the body or
on the back of the deed ; according to the rule of the feodal
law[y], *pares debent interesse investiturae feudi, et non alii :* for which

---

[t] Co. Litt. 48.
[u] pag. 288.
[w] Co. Litt. 48. West. Symb. 251.

[x] Litt. §. 414.
[y] *Feud. l. 2. t. 58.*

this reafon is exprefily given; becaufe the peers or vafals of the
lord, being bound by their oath of fealty, will take care that no
fraud be committed to his prejudice, which ftrangers might be
apt to connive at. And though, afterwards, the ocular atteftation of the *pares* was held unneceffary, and livery might be made
before any credible witneffes, yet the trial, in cafe it was difputed, (like that of all other atteftations[a]) was ftill referved to the
pares or jury of the county[a]. Alfo, if the lands be out on leafe,
though all lie in the fame county, there muft be as many liveries
as there are tenants: becaufe no livery can be made in this cafe,
but by the confent of the particular tenant; and the confent of
one will not bind the reft[b]. And in all thefe cafes it is prudent,
and ufual, to endorfe the livery of feifin on the back of the deed,
fpecifying the manner, place, and time of making it; together
with the names of the witneffes[c]. And thus much for livery in
deed.

L I V E R Y in *law* is where the fame is not made *on* the land,
but *in fight of it* only; the feoffor faying to the feoffee, " I give
" you yonder land, enter and take poffeffion." Here, if the feoffee
enters during the life of the feoffor, it is a good livery, but not
otherwife; unlefs he dares not enter, through fear of his life or
bodily harm: and then his continual claim, made yearly, in due
form of law, as near as poffible to the lands[d], will fuffice without an entry[e]. This livery in law cannot however be given or
received by attorney, but only by the parties themfelves[f].

2. T H E conveyance by *gift, donatio,* is properly applied to
the creation of an eftate-tail, as feoffment is to that of an eftate
in fee, and leafe to that of an eftate for life or years. It differs
in nothing from a feoffment, but in the nature of the eftate paffing by it: for the operative words of conveyance in this cafe are
do or *dedi*[g]; and gifts in tail are equally imperfect without livery

---

[a] See pag. 307.
[a] Gilb. Ten. 35.
[b] Dyer. 18.
[c] See appendix. Nº. I.

[d] Litt. §. 421, &c.
[e] Co. Litt. 48.
[f] *Ibid.* 52.
[g] Weft's Symbol. 256.

of

of feifin, as feoffments in fee-fimple [h]. And this is the only diftinction that Littleton feems to take, when he fays [i], "it is to be
"underftood that there is feoffor and feoffee, donor and donee,
"leffor and leffee;" viz. feoffor is applied to a feoffment in fee-
fimple, donor to a gift in tail, and leffor to a leafe for life, or for
years, or at will. In common acceptation gifts are frequently
confounded with the next fpecies of deeds : which are,

3. GRANTS, *conceffiones*; the regular method by the common law of transferring the property of *incorporeal* hereditaments, or, fuch things whereof no livery can be had [k]. For
which reafon all corporeal hereditaments, as lands and houfes,
are faid to lie *in livery*; and the others, as advowfons, commons,
rents, reverfions, &c, to lie *in grant* [l]. And the reafon is given
by Bracton [m] : "*traditio*, or livery, *nihil aliud eft quam rei corpo-
"ralis de perfona in perfonam, de manu in manum, tranflatio aut in
"poffeffionem inductio; fed res incorporales, quae funt ipfum jus rei
"vel corpori inhaerens, traditionem non patiuntur.*" Thefe therefore pafs merely by the delivery of the deed. And in figniories,
or reverfions of lands, fuch grant, together with the attornment
of the tenant (while attornments were requifite) were held to be
of equal notoriety with, and therefore equivalent to, a feoffment
and livery of lands in immediate poffeffion. It therefore differs
but little from a feoffment, except in it's fubject matter : for the
operative words therein commonly ufed are *dedi et conceffi*, "have
given and granted."

4. A LEASE is properly a conveyance of any lands or tenements, (ufually in confideration of rent or other annual recompenfe) made for life, for years, or at will, but always for
a *lefs* time than the leffor hath in the premifes : for if it be
for the *whole* intereft, it is more properly an affignment than
a leafe. The ufual words of operation in it are, "demife, grant,

h Litt. §. 59.   l *Ibid.* 172.
i §. 57.   m *l.* 2. *c.* 18.
k Co. Litt. 9.

"and

" and to farm let; *dimifi, conceffi, et ad firmam tradidi.*" *Farm,* or *feorme,* is an old Saxon word fignifying provifions[n] : and it came to be ufed inftead of rent or render, becaufe antiently the greater part of rents were referved in provifions; in corn, in poultry, and the like; till the ufe of money became more frequent. So that a farmer, *firmarius,* was one who held his lands upon payment of a rent or *feorme:* though at prefent, by a gradual departure from the original fenfe, the word *farm* is brought to fignify the very eftate or lands fo held upon farm or rent. By this conveyance an eftate for life, for years, or at will, may be created, either in corporeal or incorporeal hereditaments : though livery of feifin is indeed incident and neceffary to one fpecies of leafes, *viz.* leafes for life of corporeal hereditaments; but to no other.

WHATEVER reftrictions, by the feverity of the feodal law, might in times of very high antiquity be obferved with regard to leafes; yet by the common law, as it has ftood for many centuries, all perfons feifed of any eftate might let leafes to endure fo long as their own intereft lafted, but no longer. Therefore tenant in fee-fimple might let leafes of any duration; for he hath the whole intereft : but tenant in tail, or tenant for life, could make no leafes which fhould bind the iffue in tail or reverfioner; nor could a hufband, feifed *jure uxoris,* make a firm or valid leafe for any longer term than the joint lives of himfelf and his wife, for then his intereft expired. Yet fome tenants for life, where the fee-fimple was in abeyance, might (with the concurrence of fuch as have the guardianfhip of the fee) make leafes of equal duration with thofe granted by tenants in fee-fimple : fuch as parfons and vicars with confent of the patron and ordinary[o]. So alfo bifhops, and deans, and fuch other fole ecclefiaftical corporations as are feifed of the fee-fimple of lands in their corporate right, might, with the concurrence and confirmation of fuch perfons as the law requires, have made leafes for years, or for life, eftates in tail, or in fee, without any limitation or controll.

[n] Spelm. *Gl.* 229.　　　　　[o] Co. Litt. 44.

And

And corporations aggregate might have made what estates they pleased, without the confirmation of any other person whatsoever. Whereas now, by several statutes, this power where it was un-reasonable, and might be made an ill use of, is restrained; and, where in the other cases the restraint by the common law seemed too hard, it is in some measure removed. The former statutes are called the *restraining*, the latter the *enabling* statute. We will take a view of them all, in order of time.

AND, first, the *enabling* statute, 32 Hen. VIII. c. 28. em-powers three manner of persons to make leases, to endure for three lives or one and twenty years, which could not do so be-fore. As, first, tenant in tail, may by such leases bind his issue in tail, but not those in remainder or reversion. Secondly, a hus-band seised in right of his wife, in fee-simple or fee-tail, provi-ded the wife joins in such lease, may bind her and her heirs thereby. Lastly, all persons seised of an estate of fee-simple in right of their churches, except parsons and vicars, may (without the concurrence of any other person) bind their successors. But then there must many requisites be observed, which the statute specifies, otherwise such leases are not binding [p]. 1. The lease must be by indenture; and not by deed poll, or by parol. 2. It must begin from the making, or day of the making, and not at any greater distance of time. 3. If there be any old lease in being, it must be first absolutely surrendered, or be within a year of ex-piring. 4. It must be *either* for twenty one years, *or* three lives; and not for both. 5. It must not exceed the term of three lives, or twenty one years, but may be for a shorter term. 6. It must be of corporeal hereditaments, and not of such things as lie merely in grant; for no rent can be reserved thereout by the common law, as the lessor cannot resort to them to distrein [q]. 7. It must be of

---

[p] Co. Litt. 44.

[q] But now by the statute 5 Geo. III. c. 17. a lease of tithes or other incorporeal here-ditaments, alone, may be granted by any bishop or ecclesiastical or eleemosynary cor-poration, and the successor shall be intitled to recover the rent by an action of debt, which (in case of a freehold lease) he could not have brought at the common law.

lands

lands and tenements moſt commonly letten for twenty years paſt; ſo that if they have been let for above half the time (or eleven years out of the twenty) either for life, for years, at will, or by copy of court roll, it is ſufficient. 8. The moſt uſual and cuſtomary feorm or rent, for twenty years paſt, muſt be reſerved yearly on ſuch leaſe. 9. Such leaſes muſt not be made without impeachment of waſte. Theſe are the guards, impoſed by the ſtatute (which was avowedly made for the ſecurity of farmers and the conſequent improvement of tillage) to prevent unreaſonable abuſes, in prejudice of the iſſue, the wife, or the ſucceſſor, of the reaſonable indulgence here given.

NEXT follows, in order of time, the *diſabling* or *reſtraining* ſtatute, 1 Eliz. c. 19. (made entirely for the benefit of the ſucceſſor) which enacts, that all grants by archbiſhops and biſhops (which include even thoſe confirmed by the dean and chapter; the which, however long or unreaſonable, were good at common law) other than for the term of one and twenty years or three lives from the making, or without reſerving the uſual rent, ſhall be void. Concurrent leaſes, if confirmed by the dean and chapter, are held to be within the exception of this ſtatute, and therefore valid; provided they do not exceed (together with the leaſe in being) the term permitted by the act[r]. But, by a ſaving expreſſly made, this ſtatute of 1 Eliz. did not extend to grants made by any biſhop to the crown; by which means queen Elizabeth procured many fair poſſeſſions to be made over to her by the prelates, either for her own uſe, or with intent to be granted out again to her favourites, whom ſhe thus gratified without any expenſe to herſelf. To prevent which[s] for the future, the ſtatute 1 Jac. I. c. 3. extends the prohibition to grants and leaſes made to the king, as well as to any of his ſubjects.

NEXT comes the ſtatute 13 Eliz. c. 10. explained and enforced by the ſtatutes 14 Eliz. c. 11 & 14. 18 Eliz. c. 11. and 43 Eliz. c. 29. which extend the reſtrictions, laid by the laſt

[r] Co. Litt. 45.   [s] 11 Rep. 71.

mentioned

mentioned ſtatute on biſhops, to certain other inferior corporations, both ſole and aggregate. From laying all which together
we may collect, that all colleges, cathedrals, and other eccleſiaſtical, or eleemoſynary corporations, and all parſons and vicars,
are reſtrained from making any leaſes of their lands, unleſs under
the following regulations : 1. They muſt not exceed twenty one
years, or three lives, from the making. 2. The accuſtomed
rent, or more, muſt be yearly reſerved thereon. 3. Houſes in
corporations, or market towns, may be let for forty years ; provided they be not the manſion-houſes of the leſſors, nor have
above ten acres of ground belonging to them ; and provided the
leſſee be bound to keep them in repair : and they may alſo be
aliened in fee-ſimple for lands of equal value in recompenſe.
4. Where there is an old leaſe in being, no concurrent leaſe ſhall
be made, unleſs where the old one will expire within three
years. 5. No leaſe (by the equity of the ſtatute) ſhall be made
without impeachment of waſte[t]. 6. All bonds and covenants
tending to fruſtrate the proviſions of the ſtatutes 13 & 18 Eliz.
ſhall be void.

CONCERNING theſe reſtrictive ſtatutes there are two obſervations to be made. Firſt, that they do not, by any conſtruction,
enable any perſons to make ſuch leaſes as they were by common
law diſabled to make. Therefore a parſon, or vicar, though he
is reſtrained from making longer leaſes than for twenty one years
or three lives, even *with* the conſent of patron and ordinary, yet
is not enabled to make any leaſe at all, ſo as to bind his ſucceſſor, *without* obtaining ſuch conſent[u]. Secondly, that though
leaſes contrary to theſe acts are declared void, yet they are good
againſt the *leſſor* during his life, if he be a ſole corporation ;
and are alſo good againſt an aggregate corporation ſo long as the
head of it lives, who is preſumed to be the moſt concerned in
intereſt. For the act was intended for the benefit of the ſucceſſor only ; and no man ſhall make an advantage of his own wrong[w].

[t] Co. Litt. 45.   [w] *Ibid.* 45.
[u] *Ibid.* 44.

TH E R E is yet another reſtriction with regard to college leaſes, by ſtatute 18 Eliz. c. 6. which directs, that one third of the old rent, then paid, ſhould for the future be reſerved in wheat or malt, reſerving a quarter of wheat for each 6 *s* 8 *d*, or a quarter of malt for every 5 *s*; or that the leſſees ſhould pay for the ſame according to the price that wheat and malt ſhould be ſold for, in the market next adjoining to the reſpective colleges, on the market-day before the rent becomes due. This is ſaid[x] to have been an invention of lord treaſurer Burleigh, and ſir Thomas Smith, then principal ſecretary of ſtate; who, obſerving how greatly the value of money had ſunk, and the price of all proviſions riſen, by the quantity of bullion imported from the newfound Indies, (which effects were likely to increaſe to a greater degree) deviſed this method for upholding the revenues of colleges. Their foreſight and penetration has in this reſpect been very apparent: for, though the rent ſo reſerved in corn was at firſt but one third of the old rent, or half of what was ſtill reſerved in money, yet now the proportion is nearly inverted; and the money ariſing from corn rents is, *communibus annis*, almoſt double to the rents reſerved in money.

TH E leaſes of beneficed clergymen are farther reſtrained, in caſe of their non-reſidence, by ſtatutes 13 Eliz. c. 20. 14 Eliz. c. 11. and 18 Eliz. c. 11. which direct, that, if any beneficed clergyman be abſent from his cure above fourſcore days in any one year, he ſhall not only forfeit one year's profit of his benefice, to be diſtributed among the poor of the pariſh; but that all leaſes made by him, of the profits of ſuch benefice, and all covenants and agreements of like nature, ſhall ceaſe and be void: except in the caſe of licenſed pluraliſts, who are allowed to demiſe the living, on which they are non-reſident, to their curates only; provided ſuch curates do not abſent themſelves above forty days in any one year. And thus much for leaſes, with their ſeveral enlargements and reſtrictions[y].

---

[x] Strype's annals of Eliz.
[y] For the other learning relating to leaſes, which is very curious and diffuſive, I muſt refer the ſtudent to 3 Bac. abridg. 295. (title, *leaſes*

5. AN *exchange* is a mutual grant of equal interefts, the one in confideration of the other. The word " exchange" is fo individually requifite and appropriated by law to this cafe, that it cannot be fupplied by any other word or expreffed by any circumlocution[z]. The eftates exchanged muft be equal in quantity[a]; not of *value*, for that is immaterial, but of *intereft*; as fee-fimple for fee-fimple, a leafe for twenty years for a leafe for twenty years, and the like. And the exchange may be of things that lie either in grant or in livery[b]. But no livery of feifin, even in exchanges of freehold, is neceffary to perfect the conveyance[c]: for each party ftands in the place of the other and occupies his right, and each of them hath already had corporal poffeffion of his own land. But entry muft be made on both fides; for, if either party die before entry, the exchange is void, for want of fufficient notoriety[d]. And fo alfo, if two parfons, by confent of patron and ordinary, exchange their preferments; and the one is prefented, inftituted, and inducted, and the other is prefented, and inftituted, but dies before induction; the former fhall not keep his new benefice, becaufe the exchange was not completed, and therefore he fhall return back to his own . For if, after an exchange of lands or other hereditaments, either party be evicted of thofe which were taken by him in exchange, through defect of the other's title; he fhall return back to the poffeffion of his own, by virtue of the implied warranty contained in all exchanges[f].

6. A PARTITION, is when two or more joint-tenants, co-parceners, or tenants in common, agree to divide the lands fo held among them in feveralty, each taking a diftinct part. Here, as in fome inftances there is a unity of intereft, and in all a unity

---

leafes and terms for years) where the fubject is treated in a perfpicuous and mafterly manner; being fuppofed to be extracted from a manufcript of fir Geoffrey Gilbert.
  [z] Co. Litt. 50, 51.
  [a] Litt. §. 64, 65.

[b] Co Litt. 51.
[c] Litt. §. 62.
[d] Co. Litt. 50.
[e] Perk. §. 288.
[f] pag. 301.

of

of poſſeſſion, it is neceſſary that they all mutually convey and aſſure to each other the ſeveral eſtates, which they are to take and enjoy ſeparately. By the common law coparceners, being compellable to make partition, might have made it by parol only; but joint-tenants and tenants in common muſt have done it by deed: and in both caſes the conveyance muſt have been perfected by livery of ſeiſin [g]. And the ſtatutes of 31 Hen. VIII. c. 1. and 32 Hen. VIII. c. 32. made no alteration in this point. But the ſtatute of frauds 29 Car. II. c. 3. hath now aboliſhed this diſtinction, and made a deed in all caſes neceſſary.

THESE are the ſeveral ſpecies of *primary*, or *original* conveyances. Thoſe which remain are of the *ſecondary*, or *derivative* ſort; which preſuppoſe ſome other conveyance precedent, and only ſerve to enlarge, confirm, alter, reſtrain, reſtore, or transfer the intereſt granted by ſuch original conveyance. As,

7. RELEASES; which are a diſcharge or conveyance of a man's right in lands or tenements, to another that hath ſome former eſtate in poſſeſſion. The words generally uſed therein are "remiſed, releaſed, and for ever quit-claimed [h]." And theſe releaſes may enure either, 1. By way of *enlarging an eſtate*, or *enlarger l'eſtate:* as, if there be tenant for life or years, remainder to another in fee, and he in remainder releaſes all his right to the particular tenant and his heirs, this gives him the eſtate in fee [i]. But in this caſe the releſſee muſt be in *poſſeſſion* of ſome eſtate, for the releaſe to work upon; for if there be leſſee for years, and, before he enters and is in poſſeſſion, the leſſor releaſes to him all his right in the reverſion, ſuch releaſe is void for want of poſſeſſion in the releſſee [k]. 2. By way of *paſſing an eſtate*, or *mitter l'eſtate:* as when one of two coparceners releaſeth all her right to the other, this paſſeth the fee-ſimple of the whole [l]. And in both theſe caſes there muſt be a privity of eſtate between the releſſor and releſſee [m]; that is, one of their eſtates muſt be

[g] Litt. §. 250. Co. Litt. 169.
[h] Litt. §. 445.
[i] *Ibid.* §. 465.
[k] *Ibid.* §. 459.
[l] Co. Litt. 273.
[m] *Ibid.* 272, 273.

fo related to the other, as to make but one and the fame eftate
in law. 3. By way of *paffing a right*, or *mitter le droit :* as if a
man be diffeifed, and releafeth to his diffeifor all his right; hereby
the diffeifor acquires a new right, which changes the quality of
his eftate, and renders that lawful which before was tortious[n].
4. By way of *extinguifhment :* as if my tenant for life makes a
leafe to A for life, remainder to B and his heirs, and I releafe to
A; this extinguifhes my right to the reverfion, and fhall enure
to the advantage of B's remainder as well as of A's particular
eftate[o]. 5. By way of *entry and feoffment :* as if there be two
joint diffeifors, and the diffeifee releafes to one of them, he fhall
be fole feifed, and fhall keep out his former companion ; which
is the fame in effect as if the diffeifee had entered, and thereby
put an end to the diffeifin, and afterwards had enfeoffed one of
the diffeifors in fee[p]. And hereupon we may obferve, that when
a man has in himfelf the poffeffion of lands, he muft at the common law convey the freehold by feoffment and livery ; which
makes a notoriety in the country : but if a man has only a right
or a future intereft, he may convey that right or intereft by a
mere releafe to him that is in poffeffion of the land : for the occupancy of the releffee is a matter of fufficient notoriety already.

8. A C O N F I R M A T I O N is of a nature nearly allied to a releafe. Sir Edward Coke defines it[q] to be a conveyance of an
eftate or right *in effe*, whereby a voidable eftate is made fure and
unavoidable, or whereby a particular eftate is encreafed : and
the words of making it are thefe, " have given, granted, rati-
" fied, approved, and confirmed[r]." An inftance of the firft branch
of the definition is, if tenant for life leafeth for forty years, and
dieth during that term ; here the leafe for years is voidable by
him in reverfion : yet, if he hath confirmed the eftate of the
leffee for years, before the death of tenant for life, it is no longer voidable but fure[s]. The latter branch, or that which tends

[n] Litt. §. 466.
[o] *Ibid.* §. 470.
[p] Co. Litt. 278.

[q] 1 Inft. 295.
[r] Litt. §. 515. 531.
[s] *Ibid.* §. 516.

to the encreafe of a particular eftate, is the fame in all refpects with that fpecies of releafe, which operates by way of enlargement.

9. A SURRENDER, *furfumredditio,* or rendering up, is of a nature directly oppofite to a releafe; for, as that operates by the greater eftate's defcending upon the lefs, a furrender is the falling of a lefs eftate into a greater by deed. It is defined[t], a yielding up of an eftate for life or years to him that hath the immediate reverfion or remainder, wherein the particular eftate may merge or drown, by mutual agreement between them. It is done by thefe words, "hath furrendered, granted, and yielded up." The furrenderor muft be in poffeffion[u]; and the furrenderee muft have a higher eftate, in which the eftate furrendered may merge: therefore tenant for life cannot furrender to him in remainder for years[w]. In a furrender there is no occafion for livery of feifin[x]; for there is a privity of eftate between the furrenderor, and the furrenderee; the one's particular eftate, and the other's remainder are one and the fame eftate; and livery having been once made at the creation of it, there is no neceffity for having it afterwards. And, for the fame reafon, no livery is required on a releafe or confirmation in fee to tenant for years or at will, though a freehold thereby paffes; fince the reverfion of the releffor, or confirmor, and the particular eftate of the releffee, or confirmee, are one and the fame eftate; and where there is already a poffeffion, derived from fuch a privity of eftate, any farther delivery of poffeffion would be vain and nugatory[y].

10. AN *affignment* is properly a transfer, or making over to another, of the right one has in *any* eftate; but it is ufually applied to an eftate for life or years. And it differs from a leafe only in this: that by a leafe one grants an intereft lefs than his own, referving to himfelf a reverfion; in affignments he parts with the whole

[t] Co. Litt. 337.
[u] *Ibid.* 338.
[w] Perk. §. 589.

[x] Co. Litt. 50.
[y] Litt. §. 460.

property,

property, and the affignee ftands to all intents and purpofes in the place of the affignor.

11. A DEFEAZANCE is a collateral deed, made at the fame time with a feoffment or other conveyance, containing certain conditions, upon the performance of which the eftate then created may be *defeated*[z] or totally undone. And in this manner mortgages were in former times ufually made; the mortgagor enfeoffing the mortgagee, and he at the fame time executing a deed of defeazance, whereby the feoffment was rendered void on re-payment of the money borrowed at a certain day. And this, when executed at the fame time with the original feoffment, was confidered as part of it by the antient law[a]; and, therefore only, indulged: no fubfequent fecret revocation of a folemn conveyance, executed by livery of feifin, being allowed in thofe days of fimplicity and truth; though, when ufes were afterwards introduced, a revocation of fuch ufes was permitted by the courts of equity. But things that were merely executory, or to be completed by matter fubfequent, (as rents, of which no feifin could be had till the time of payment; and fo alfo annuities, conditions, warranties, and the like) were always liable to be recalled by defeazances made fubfequent to the time of their creation[b].

II. THERE yet remain to be fpoken of fome few conveyances, which have their force and operation by virtue of the *ftatute of ufes.*

USES and *trufts* are in their original of a nature very fimilar, or rather exactly the fame: anfwering more to the *fidei-commiffum* than the *ufus-fructus,* of the civil law; which latter was the temporary right of ufing a thing, without having the ultimate property, or full dominion of the fubftance[c]. But the *fidei-commiffum,* which ufually was created by will, was the difpofal of an inheritance to one, in confidence that he fhould convey it or dif-

[z] From the French verb *defaire, infectum reddere.*

[a] Co. Litt. 236.

[b] *Ibid.* 237.

[c] *Ff.* 7. 1. 1.

pofe of the profits at the will of another. And it was the bufinefs of a particular magiftrate, the *praetor fidei-commiffarius*, inftituted by Auguftus, to enforce the obfervance of this confidence[d].
So that the right thereby given was looked upon as a vefted right,
and entitled to a remedy from a court of juftice : which occafioned that known divifion of rights by the Roman law, into *jus
legitimum*, a legal right, which was remedied by the ordinary
courfe of law; *jus fiduciarium*, a right in truft, for which there
was a remedy in confcience; and *jus precarium*, a right in cour-
tefy, for which the remedy was only by intreaty or requeft[e]. In
our law, a ufe might be ranked under the rights of the fecond
kind; being a confidence repofed in another who was tenant of
the land, or *terre-tenant*, that he fhould difpofe of the land according to the intentions of *ceftuy que ufe*, or him to whofe ufe it
was granted, and fuffer him to take the profits[f]. As, if a feoffment was made to A and his heirs, to the ufe of (or in truft for) B
and his heirs; here at the common law A the *terre-tenant* had the
legal property and poffeffion of the land, but B the *ceftuy que ufe*
was in confcience and equity to have the profits and difpofal of it.

THIS notion was tranfplanted into England from the civil law,
about the clofe of the reign of Edward III[g], by means of the
foreign ecclefiaftics; who introduced it to evade the ftatutes of
mortmain, by obtaining grants of lands, not to their religious houfes
directly, but to *the ufe of* the religious houfes[h]: which the cleri-
cal chancellors of thofe times held to be *fidei-commiffa*, and binding in confcience; and therefore affumed the jurifdiction, which
Auguftus had vefted in his *praetor*, of compelling the execution
of fuch trufts in the court of chancery. And, as it was moft
eafy to obtain fuch grants from dying perfons, a maxim was eftablifhed, that though by law the lands themfelves were not devifable, yet if a teftator had enfeoffed another to his own ufe,
and fo was poffeffed of the ufe only, fuch ufe was devifable by

[d] *Inft.* 2. *tit.* 23.
[e] *Ff.* 43. 26. 1. Bacon on ufes. 8°. 306.
[f] Plowd. 352.

[g] Stat. 50 Edw. III. c.6.   1 Ric. II. c.9.
[h] See pag. 271.

will.

will. But we have seen [i] how this evasion was crushed in it's infancy, by statute 15 Ric. II. c. 5. with respect to religious houses.

YET, the idea being once introduced, however fraudulently, it afterwards continued to be often innocently, and sometimes very laudably, applied to a number of civil purposes : particularly as it removed the restraint of alienations by will, and permitted the owner of lands in his lifetime to make various designations of their profits, as prudence, or justice, or family convenience, might from time to time require. Till at length, during our long wars in France and the subsequent civil commotions between the houses of York and Lancaster, uses grew almost universal : through the desire that men had (when their lives were continually in hazard) of providing for their children by will, and of securing their estates from forfeitures; when each of the contending parties, as they became uppermost, alternately attainted the other. Wherefore about the reign of Edward IV, (before whose time, lord Bacon remarks [k], there are not six cases to be found relating to the doctrine of uses) the courts of equity began to reduce them to something of a regular system.

ORIGINALLY it was held that the chancery could give no relief, but against the very person himself intrusted for *cestuy que use*, and not against his heir or alienee. This was altered in the reign of Henry VI, with respect to the heir [l]; and afterwards the same rule, by a parity of reason, was extended to such alienees as had purchased either without a valuable consideration, or with an express notice of the use [m]. But a purchasor for a valuable consideration, without notice, might hold the land discharged of any trust or confidence. And also it was held, that neither the king or queen, on account of their dignity royal [n], nor any corporation aggregate, on account of it's limited capacity [o], could be seised to any use but their own ; that is, they

[i] pag. 272.
[k] on uses. 313.
[l] Keilw. 42. Yearbook 22 Edw. IV. 6.
[m] Keilw. 46. Bacon of uses. 312.

[n] Bro. *Abr. tit. Feoffm. al uses.* 31. Bacon of uses. 346, 347.
[o] Bro. *Abr. tit. Feoffm. al uses.* 40. Bacon. 347.

might

might hold the lands, but were not compellable to execute the truſt. And, if the feoffee to uſes died without heir, or committed a forfeiture, or married, neither the lord who entered for his eſcheat or forfeiture, nor the huſband who retained the poſſeſſion as tenant by the curteſy, nor the wife who was aſſigned her dower, were liable to perform the uſe[p]; becauſe they were not parties to the truſt, but came in by act of law : though doubtleſs their title in reaſon was no better than that of the heir.

ON the other hand the uſe itſelf, or intereſt of *ceſtuy que uſe,* was learnedly refined upon with many elaborate diſtinctions. And, 1. It was held that nothing could be granted to a uſe, whereof the uſe is inſeparable from the poſſeſſion ; as annuities, ways, commons, and authorities, *quae ipſo uſu conſumuntur*[q]*:* or whereof the ſeiſin could not be inſtantly given[r]. 2. A uſe could not be raiſed without a ſufficient conſideration. For where a man makes a feoffment to another without any conſideration, equity preſumes that he meant it to the uſe of himſelf[s] : unleſs he expreſſly declares it to be to the uſe of another, and then nothing ſhall be preſumed contrary to his own expreſſions[t]. But, if either a good or a valuable conſideration appears, equity will immediately raiſe a uſe correſpondent to ſuch conſideration[u]. 3. Uſes were deſcendible according to the rules of the common law, in the caſe of inheritances in poſſeſſion[w]; for in this and many other reſpects *aequitas ſequitur legem,* and cannot eſtabliſh a different rule of property from that which the law has eſtabliſhed. 4. Uſes might be aſſigned by ſecret deeds between the parties[x], or be deviſed by laſt will and teſtament[y] : for, as the legal eſtate in the ſoil was not transferred by theſe tranſactions, no livery of ſeiſin was neceſſary; and, as the intention of the parties was the leading principle in this ſpecies of property, any inſtrument declaring that intention was allowed to be binding in

[p] 1 Rep. 122.
[q] 1 Jon. 127.
[r] Cro. Eliz. 401.
[s] See pag 296.
[t] 1 And. 37.

[u] Moor. 684.
[w] 2 Roll. Abr. 780.
[x] Bacon of uſes. 312.
[y] *Ibid.* 308.

equity.

equity. But *ceſtuy que uſe* could not at common law aliene the legal intereſt of the lands, without the concurrence of his feoffee[z]; to whom he was accounted by law to be only tenant at ſufferance[a]. 5. Uſes were not liable to any of the feodal burthens; and particularly did not eſcheat for felony or other defect of blood; for eſcheats, &c, are the conſequence of *tenure*, and uſes are *held* of nobody: but the land itſelf was liable to eſcheat, whenever the blood of the feoffee to uſes was extinguiſhed by crime or by defect; and the lord (as was before obſerved) might hold it diſcharged of the uſe[b]. 6. No wife could be endowed, or huſband have his curteſy, of a uſe[c]: for no truſt was declared for their benefit, at the original grant of the eſtate. And therefore it became cuſtomary, when moſt eſtates were put in uſe, to ſettle before marriage ſome joint eſtate to the uſe of the huſband and wife for their lives; which was the original of modern jointures[d]. 7. A uſe could not be extended by writ of *elegit*, or other legal proceſs, for the debts of *ceſtuy que uſe*[e]. For, being merely a creature of equity, the common law, which looked no farther than to the perſon actually ſeiſed of the land, could award no proceſs againſt it.

IT is impracticable, upon our preſent plan, to purſue the doctrine of uſes through all the refinements and niceties, which the ingenuity of the times (abounding in ſubtile diſquiſitions) deduced from this child of the imagination; when once a departure was permitted from the plain ſimple rules of property eſtabliſhed by the antient law. Theſe principal outlines will be fully ſufficient to ſhew the ground of lord Bacon's complaint[f], that this courſe of proceeding "was turned to deceive many of their juſt and "reaſonable rights. A man, that had cauſe to ſue for land, knew "not againſt whom to bring his action, or who was the owner "of it. The wife was defrauded of her thirds; the huſband of

[z] Stat. 1 Ric. III. c. 1.
[a] Bro. *Abr. ibid.* 23.
[b] Jenk. 190.
[c] 4 Rep. 1. 2 And. 75.
[d] See pag. 137.
[e] Bro. *Abr. tit. executions.* 90.
[f] Uſe of the law. 153.

"his

" his curtefy; the lord of his wardfhip, relief, heriot, and ef-
" cheat; the creditor of his extent for debt; and the poor te-
" nant of his leafe." To remedy thefe inconveniences abundance
of ftatutes were provided, which made the lands liable to be extended by the creditors of *ceftuy que ufe*[g]; allowed actions for
the freehold to be brought againft him, if in the actual pernancy
or enjoyment of the profits[h]; made him liable to actions of
wafte[i]; eftablifhed his conveyances and leafes made without the
concurrence of his feoffees[k]; and gave the lord the wardfhip
of his heir, with certain other feodal perquifites[l].

THESE provifions all tended to confider *ceftuy que ufe* as the
real owner of the eftate; and at length that idea was carried into
full effect by the ftatute 27 Hen. VIII. c. 10. which is ufually
called the *ftatute of ufes*, or, in conveyances and pleadings, the
ftatute *for transferring ufes into poffeffion*. The hint feems to have
been derived from what was done at the acceffion of king Richard III; who having, when duke of Glocefter, been frequently
made a feoffee to ufes, would upon the affumption of the crown (as
the law was then underftood) have been intitled to hold the lands
difcharged of the ufe. But, to obviate fo notorious an injuftice,
an act of parliament was immediately paffed[m], which ordained
that, where he had been fo infeoffed jointly with other perfons,
the land fhould veft in the other feoffees, as if he had never been
named; and that, where he ftood folely infeoffed, the eftate
itfelf fhould veft in *ceftuy que ufe* in like manner as he had the
ufe. And fo the ftatute of Henry VIII, after reciting the various
inconveniences before-mentioned and many others, enacts, that
" when any perfon fhall be *feifed* of lands, &c, to the ufe, confi-
" dence, or truft, of any other perfon or body politick, the perfon
" or corporation intitled to the ufe in fee-fimple, fee-tail, for life,

---

g Stat. 50 Edw III. c. 6. 2 Ric. II. feff. 2.
c. 3. 19 Hen V 1 c. 15.
h Stat 1 Ric. II. c 9. 4 Hen. IV. c. 7.
11 Hen VI. c. 3. 1 Hen. VII. c. 1.
i Stat. 11 Hen. VI. c. 5.

k Stat. 1 Ric. III. c. 1.
l Stat. 4 Hen. VII. c. 17. 19 Hen. VII.
c. 15.
m 1 Ric. III. c. 5.

" or

" or years, or otherwife, fhall from thenceforth ftand and be feifed
" or poffeffed of the land, *&c,* of and in the like eftates as they
" have in the ufe, truft, or confidence; and that the eftate of
" the perfon fo feifed to ufes fhall be deemed to be in him or
" them that have the ufe, in fuch quality, manner, form, and
" condition, as they had before in the ufe." The ftatute thus
executes the ufe, as our lawyers term it; that is, it conveys the
poffeffion to the ufe, and transfers the ufe into poffeffion : thereby
making *ceftuy que ufe* complete owner of the lands and tenements,
as well at law as in equity.

THE ftatute having thus, not abolifhed the conveyance to
ufes, but only annihilated the intervening eftate of the feoffee,
and turned the intereft of *ceftuy que ufe* into a legal inftead of an
equitable ownerfhip; the courts of common law began to take
cognizance of ufes, inftead of fending the party to feek his relief in chancery. And, confidering them now as merely a mode
of conveyance, very many of the rules before eftablifhed in equity
were adopted with improvements by the judges of the common
law. The fame perfons only were held capable of being feifed
to a ufe, the fame confiderations were neceffary for raifing it,
and it could only be raifed of the fame hereditaments, as formerly. But as the ftatute, the inftant it was raifed, converted it
into an actual poffeffion of the land, a great number of the incidents, that formerly attended it in it's fiduciary ftate, were now
at an end. The land could not efcheat or be forfeited by the act
or defect of the feoffee, nor be aliened to any purchafor difcharged of the ufe, nor be liable to dower or curtefy on account of
the feifin of fuch feoffee; becaufe the legal eftate never refts in
him for a moment, but is inftantaneoufly transferred to *ceftuy que
ufe,* as foon as the ufe is declared. And, as the ufe and the land
were now convertible terms, they became liable to dower, curtefy,
and efcheat, in confequence of the feifin of *ceftuy que ufe,* who
was now become the *terre-tenant* alfo; and they likewife were
no longer devifable by will.

THE various neceffities of mankind induced alfo the judges very foon to depart from the rigour and fimplicity of the rules of the common law, and to allow a more minute and complex conftruction upon conveyances to ufes than upon others. Hence it was adjudged, that the ufe need not always be executed the inftant the conveyance is made : but, if it cannot take effect at that time, the operation of the ftatute may wait till the ufe fhall arife upon fome future contingency, to happen within a reafonable period of time; and in the mean while the antient ufe fhall remain in the original grantor : as, when lands are conveyed to the ufe of A and B, after a marriage fhall be had between them[n], or to the ufe of A and his heirs till B fhall pay him a fum of money, and then to the ufe of B and his heirs[o]. Which doctrine, when devifes by will were again introduced, and confidered as equivalent in point of conftruction to declarations of ufes, was alfo adopted in favour of *executory devifes*[p]. But herein thefe, which are called *contingent* or *fpringing*, ufes differ from an executory devife; in that there muft be a perfon feifed to fuch ufes at the time when the contingency happens, elfe they can never be executed by the ftatute; and therefore, if the eftate of the feoffee to fuch ufe be deftroyed by alienation or otherwife, before the contingency arifes, the ufe is deftroyed for ever[q] : whereas by an executory devife the freehold itfelf is transferred to the future devifee. And, in both thefe cafes, a fee may be limited to take effect after a fee[r]; becaufe, though that was forbidden by the common law in favour of the lord's efcheat, yet, when the legal eftate was not extended beyond one fee-fimple, fuch fubfequent ufes (after a ufe in fee) were before the ftatute permitted to be limited in equity; and then the ftatute executed the legal eftate in the fame manner as the ufe before fubfifted. It was alfo held that a ufe, though executed, may change from one to another by circumftances *ex poft facto*[s] ; as, if A makes a feoffment

---

[n] 2 Roll. Abr. 791. Cro. Eliz. 439.
[o] Bro. *Abr. tit. Feoffm. al ufes.* 30.
[p] See pag. 173.

[q] 1 Rep. 134. 138. Cro. Eliz. 439.
[r] Pollexf. 78. 10 Mod. 423.
[s] Bro. *Abr. tit. Feoffm. al ufes.* 30.

to

to the ufe of his intended wife and her eldeft fon for their
lives, upon the marriage the wife takes the whole ufe in feveralty; and, upon the birth of a fon, the ufe is executed jointly
in them both[t]. This is fometimes called a *fecondary*, fometimes
a *fhifting*, ufe. And, whenever the ufe limited by the deed expires,
or cannot veft, it returns back to him who raifed it, after fuch
expiration or during fuch impoffibility, and is ftiled a *refulting*
ufe. As, if a man makes a feoffment to the ufe of his intended
wife for life, with remainder to the ufe of her firft-born fon in
tail: here, till he marries the ufe refults back to himfelf; after
marriage, it is executed in the wife for life; and, if fhe dies without iffue, the whole refults back to him in fee[u]. It was likewife
held, that the ufes originally declared may be revoked at any future time, and new ufes be declared of the land, provided the
grantor referved to himfelf fuch a power at the creation of the
eftate; whereas the utmoft that the common law would allow,
was a deed of defeazance coeval with the grant itfelf (and therefore efteemed a part of it) upon events fpecifically mentioned[w].
And, in cafe of fuch a revocation, the old ufes were held inftantly
to ceafe, and the new ones to become executed in their ftead[x].
And this was permitted, partly to indulge the convenience, and
partly the caprice of mankind; who (as lord Bacon obferves[y])
have always affected to have the difpofition of their property revocable in their own time, and irrevocable ever afterwards.

By this equitable train of decifions in the courts of law, the
power of the court of chancery over landed property was greatly
curtailed and diminifhed. But one or two technical fcruples, which
the judges found it hard to get over, reftored it with tenfold increafe. They held in the firft place, that "no ufe could be li-
"mited on a ufe[z]," and that when a man bargains and fells his
land for money, which raifes a ufe by implication to the bargainee, the limitation of a farther ufe to another perfon is re-

---

[t] Bacon of ufes. 351.
[u] *Ibid.* 350. 1 Rep. 120.
[w] See pag. 327.
[x] Co. Litt. 237.
[y] on ufes. 316.
[z] Dyer. 155.

pugnant and therefore void ³. And therefore, on a feoffment to A and his heirs, to the ufe of B and his heirs, in truft for C and his heirs, they held that the ftatute executed only the firft ufe, and that the fecond was a mere nullity : not adverting, that the inftant the firft ufe was executed in B, he became feifed to the ufe of C, which fecond ufe the ftatute might as well be permitted to execute as it did the firft; and fo the legal eftate might be in-ftantaneoufly tranfmitted down, through a hundred ufes upon ufes, till finally executed in the laft *ceftuy que ufe.* Again; as the ftatute mentions only fuch perfons as were *feifed* to the ufe of o-thers, this was held not to extend to terms of years, or other chattel interefts, whereof the termor is not *feifed,* but only *poffeffed* ᵇ; and therefore, if a term of one thoufand years be limited to A, to the ufe of (or in truft for) B, the ftatute does not execute this ufe, but leaves it as at common law ᶜ. And laftly, (by more modern refolutions) where lands are given to one and his heirs, in truft to receive and pay over the profits to another, this ufe is not executed by the ftatute : for the land muft remain in the truftee to enable him to perform the truft ᵈ.

O F the two more antient diftinctions the courts of equity quickly availed themfelves. In the firft cafe it was evident, that B was never intended by the parties to have any beneficial inte-reft; and, in the fecond, the *ceftuy que ufe* of the term was ex-preffly driven into the court of chancery to feek his remedy : and therefore that court determined, that though thefe were not *ufes,* which the ftatute could execute, yet ftill they were *trufts* in e-quity, which in confcience ought to be performed. To this the reafon of mankind affented, and the doctrine of ufes was revived, under the denomination of *trufts :* and thus, by this ftrict con-ftruction of the courts of law, a ftatute made upon great delibe-ration, and introduced in the moft folemn manner, has had little other effect than to make a flight alteration in the formal words of a conveyance ᵉ.

ᵃ 1 And. 37. 136.
ᵇ Bacon law of ufes. 335. Jenk. 244.
ᶜ Poph. 76. Dyer. 369.
ᵈ 1 Equ. Caf. abr. 383, 384.
ᵉ Vaugh. 50. Atk. 591

H O W E V E R,

HOWEVER, the courts of equity, in the exercife of this new jurifdiction, have wifely avoided in a great degree thofe milchiefs which made ufes intolerable. They now confider a truft-eftate (either when exprefly declared or refulting by neceffary implica-tion) as equivalent to the legal ownerfhip, governed by the fame rules of property, and liable to every charge in equity, which the other is fubject to in law: and, by a long feries of uniform determinations, for now near a century paft, with fome affiftance from the legiflature, they have raifed a new fyftem of rational jurifprudence, by which trufts are made to anfwer in general all the beneficial ends of ufes, without their inconvenience or frauds. The truftee is confidered as merely the inftrument of conveyance, and can in no fhape affect the eftate, unlefs by alienation for a valuable confideration to a purchafor without notice [f]; which, as *ceftuy que ufe* is generally in poffeffion of the land, is a thing that can rarely happen. The truft will defcend, may be aliened, is liable to debts, to forfeiture, to leafes and other incumbrances, nay even to the curtefy of the hufband, as if it was an eftate at law. It has not yet indeed been fubjected to dower, more from a cautious adherence to fome hafty precedents [g], than from any well-grounded principle. It hath alfo been held not liable to efcheat to the lord, in confequence of attainder or want of heirs [h]: becaufe the truft could never be intended for his benefit. But let us now return to the ftatute of ufes.

THE only fervice, as was before obferved, to which this fta-tute is now configned, is in giving efficacy to certain new and fecret fpecies of conveyances; introduced in order to render tranf-actions of this fort as private as poffible, and to fave the trouble of making livery of feifin, the only antient conveyance of corpo-real freeholds: the fecurity and notoriety of which public invef-titure abundantly overpaid the labour of going to the land, or of fending an attorney in one's ftead. But this now has given way to

[f] 2 Freem. 43.
[g] 1 Chanc. Rep. 254. 2 P. W^ms. 640.
[h] Hardr. 494. Burgefs & Wheate. Hil. 32 Geo. II. in Canc.

12. A TWELFTH fpecies of conveyance, called a *covenant to
ſtand ſeiſed to uſes:* by which a man, ſeiſed of lands, covenants
in conſideration of blood or marriage that he will ſtand ſeiſed of
the ſame to the uſe of his child, wife, or kinſman ; for life, in
tail, or in fee. Here the ſtatute executes at once the eſtate ; for
the party intended to be benefited, having thus acquired the uſe,
is thereby put at once into corporal poſſeſſion of the land[i], without ever ſeeing it, by a kind of parliamentary magic. But this
conveyance can only operate, when made upon ſuch weighty and
intereſting conſiderations as thoſe of blood or marriage.

13. A THIRTEENTH fpecies of conveyance, introduced by
this ſtatute, is that of a *bargain and ſale* of lands; which is a
kind of a real contract, whereby the bargainor for ſome pecuniary conſideration bargains and ſells, that is, contracts to convey, the land to the bargainee; and becomes by ſuch bargain a
truſtee for, or ſeiſed to the uſe of, the bargainee; and then the
ſtatute of uſes completes the purchaſe[j] : or, as it hath been well
expreſſed[k], the bargain firſt veſts the uſe, and then the ſtatute
veſts the poſſeſſion. But as it was foreſeen that conveyances, thus
made, would want all thoſe benefits of notoriety, which the old
common law aſſurances were calculated to give; to prevent therefore clandeſtine conveyances of freeholds, it was enacted in the
ſame ſeſſion of parliament by ſtatute 27 Hen. VIII. c. 16. that
ſuch bargains and ſales ſhould not enure to paſs a freehold, unleſs the ſame be made by indenture, and *enrolled* within ſix months
in one of the courts of Weſtminſter-hall or with the *cuſtos ro-
tulorum* of the county. Clandeſtine bargains and ſales of chattel
intereſts, or leaſes for years, were thought not worth regarding,
as ſuch intereſts were very precarious till about ſix years before[l];
which alſo occaſioned them to be overlooked in framing the ſtatute of uſes : and therefore ſuch bargains and ſales are not directed to be enrolled. But how impoſſible is it to foreſee, and

---

[i] Bacon. Uſe of the law. 151.   [k] Cro. Jac. 696.
     Ibid. 150.   [l] See pag. 142.

provide againft, *all* the confequences of innovations! This omiffion has given rife to

14. A FOURTEENTH fpecies of conveyance, *viz.* by *leafe
and releafe;* firft invented by ferjeant Moore, foon after the ftatute of ufes, and now the moft common of any, and therefore
not to be fhaken; though very great lawyers (as, particularly,
Mr Noy) have formerly doubted it's validity[m]. It is thus contrived. A leafe, or rather bargain and fale, upon fome pecuniary
confideration, for one year, is made by the tenant of the freehold
to the leffee or bargainee. Now this, without any enrollment,
makes the bargainor ftand feifed to the ufe of the bargainee, and
vefts in the bargainee the *ufe* of the term for a year; and then
the ftatute immediately annexes the *poffeffion.* He therefore, being thus in poffeffion, is capable of receiving a releafe of the freehold and reverfion; which, we have feen before[n], muft be made
to a tenant in poffeffion: and accordingly, the next day, a releafe
is granted to him[o]. This is held to fupply the place of livery of
feifin; and fo a conveyance by leafe and releafe is faid to amount
to a feoffment[p].

15. To thefe may be added deeds to *lead* or *declare the ufes* of
other more direct conveyances, as feoffments, fines, and recoveries; of which we fhall fpeak in the next chapter: and,

16. DEEDS of *revocation of ufes;* hinted at in a former page[q],
and founded in a previous power, referved at the raifing of the
ufes[r], to revoke fuch as were then declared; and to appoint others
in their ftead, which is incident to the power of revocation[s].
And this may fuffice for a fpecimen of conveyances founded upon
the ftatute of ufes; and will finifh our obfervations upon fuch
deeds as ferve to *transfer* real property.

---

[m] 2 Mod. 252.   [q] *pag.* 335.
[n] pag. 324.   [r] See Appendix. Nᵒ. II. pag. xi.
[o] See Appendix. Nᵒ. II. §. 1, 2.   [s] Co. Litt. 237.
[p] Co. Litt. 270. Cro. Jac. 604.

BEFORE we conclude, it will not be improper to fubjoin a few remarks upon fuch deeds as are ufed not to *convey*, but to *charge* or incumber, lands, and *difcharge* them again : of which nature are, *obligations* or bonds, *recognizances*, and *defeazances* upon them both.

1. AN *obligation*, or bond, is a deed' whereby the obligor obliges himfelf, his heirs, executors, and adminiftrators, to pay a certain fum of money to another at a day appointed. If this be all, the bond is called a fingle one, *fimplex obligatio*; but there is generally a condition added, that if the obligor does fome particular act, the obligation fhall be void, or elfe fhall remain in full force : as, payment of rent ; performance of covenants in a deed ; or repayment of a principal fum of money borrowed of the obligee, with intereft, which principal fum is ufually one half of the penal fum fpecified in the bond. In cafe this condition is not performed, the bond becomes forfeited, or abfolute at law, and charges the obligor while living ; and after his death the obligation defcends upon his heir, who (on defect of perfonal affets) is bound to difcharge it, provided he has real affets by defcent as a recompenfe. So that it may be called, though not a *direct*, yet a *collateral*, charge upon the lands. How it affects the perfonal property of the obligor, will be more properly confidered hereafter.

IF the condition of a bond be impoffible at the time of making it, or be to do a thing contrary to fome rule of law that is merely pofitive, or be uncertain, or infenfible, the condition alone is void, and the bond fhall ftand fingle and unconditional : for it is the folly of the obligor to enter into fuch an obligation, from which he can never be releafed. If it be to do a thing that is *malum in fe*, the obligation itfelf is void : for the whole is an unlawful contract, and the obligee fhall take no advantage from fuch a tranfaction. And if the condition be poffible at the time

᠎   ' See Appendix. N°. III. pag. xiii.

of

of making it, and afterwards becomes impoſſible by the act of
God, the act of law, or the act of the obligee himſelf, there the
penalty of the obligation is ſaved : for no prudence or foreſight
of the obligor could guard againſt ſuch a contingency [u]. On the
forfeiture of a bond, or it's becoming ſingle, the whole penalty
was recoverable at law : but here the courts of equity interpoſed,
and would not permit a man to take more than in conſcience he
ought ; *viz.* his principal, intereſt, and expenſes, in caſe the forfeiture accrued by non-payment of money borrowed ; the damages ſuſtained, upon non-performance of covenants ; and the like.
And the ſtatute 4 & 5 Ann. c. 16. hath alſo enacted, in the ſame
ſpirit of equity, that in caſe of a bond, conditioned for the payment of money, the payment or tender of the principal ſum
due, with intereſt, and coſts, even though the bond be forfeited
and a ſuit commenced thereon, ſhall be a full ſatisfaction and
diſcharge.

2. A *recognizance* is an obligation of record, which a man enters into before ſome court of record or magiſtrate duly authorized [w], with condition to do ſome particular act ; as to appear at
the aſſiſes, to keep the peace, to pay a debt, or the like. It is
in moſt reſpects like another bond : the difference being chiefly
this ; that the bond is the creation of a freſh debt or obligation
de novo, the recognizance is an acknowlegement of a former debt
upon record ; the form whereof is, " that A. B. doth acknow-
" lege to owe to our lord the king, to the plaintiff, to C. D. or
" the like, the ſum of ten pounds," with condition to be void on
performance of the thing ſtipulated : in which caſe the king,
the plaintiff, C. D. *&c*, is called the cognizee, " *is cui cognoſci-*
" *tur*;" as he that enters into the recognizance is called the cognizor, " *is qui cognoſcit.*" This, being either certified to, or taken
by the officer of ſome court, is witneſſed only by the record of
that court, and not by the party's ſeal : ſo that it is not in ſtrict
propriety a deed, though the effects of it are greater than a common obligation ; being allowed a priority in point of payment,

[u] Co. Litt. 206.   [w] Bro. *Abr. tit. recognizance.* 24.

and

and binding the lands of the cognizor, from the time of enrollment on record[x]. There are alfo other recognizances, of a private kind, *in nature of a ftatute ftaple*, by virtue of the ftatute 23 Hen. VIII. c. 6. which have been already explained[y], and fhewn to be a charge upon real property.

3. A DEFEAZANCE, on a bond, or recognizance, or judgment recovered, is a condition which, when performed, defeats or undoes it, in the fame manner as a defeazance of an eftate before-mentioned. It differs only from the common condition of a bond, in that the one is always inferted in the deed or bond itfelf, the other is made between the fame parties by a feparate and frequently a fubfequent deed[z]. This, like the condition of a bond, when performed, difcharges and difincumbers the eftate of the obligor.

THESE are the principal fpecies of deeds or matter *in pais*, by which eftates may be either conveyed, or at leaft affected. Among which the conveyances to ufes are by much the moft frequent of any; though in thefe there is certainly one palpable defect, the want of fufficient notoriety: fo that purchafors or creditors cannot know with any abfolute certainty, what the eftate, and the title to it, in reality are, upon which they are to lay out or to lend their money. In the antient feodal method of conveyance (by giving corporal feifin of the lands) this notoriety was in fome meafure anfwered ; but all the advantages refulting from thence are now totally defeated by the introduction of death-bed devifes and fecret conveyances : and there has never been yet any fufficient guard provided againft fraudulent charges and incumbrances; fince the difufe of the old Saxon cuftom of tranfacting all conveyances at the county court, and entering a memorial of them in the chartulary or leger-book of fome adjacent monaftery[a]; and the failure of the general regifter eftablifhed by king Richard the firft, for mortgages made to Jews, in the *capitula de Judaeis*,

---

[x] Stat. 29 Car. II. c. 3. §. 18.
[y] See pag. 160.

[z] Co. Litt. 237. 2 Saund. 47.
[a] Hickes *Differtat. epiftolar.* 9.

of

of which Hoveden has preferved a copy. How far the eftablifhment of a like general regifter, for deeds, and wills, and other
acts affecting real property, would remedy this inconvenience,
deferves to be well confidered. In Scotland every act and event,
regarding the tranfmiffion of property, is regularly entered on
record[b]. And fome of our own provincial divifions, particularly
the extended county of York, and the populous county of Middlefex, have prevailed with the legiflature[c] to erect fuch regifters
in their feveral diftricts. But, however plaufible thefe provifions
may appear in theory, it hath been doubted by very competent
judges, whether more difputes have not arifen in thofe counties
by the inattention and omiffions of parties, than prevented by
the ufe of regifters.

[b] Dalrymple on feodal property. 262, &c.   [c] Stat. 2 & 3 Ann. c. 4.   6 Ann. c. 35.
7 Ann. c. 20.   8 Geo. II. c. 6.

C H A P T E R   T H E   T W E N T Y   F I R S T.

O F ALIENATION B Y M A T T E R O F RECORD.

A S S U R A N C E S by *matter of record* are fuch as do not
entirely depend on the act or confent of the parties themfelves: but the fanction of a court of record is called in, to fub-
ftantiate, preferve, and be a perpetual teftimony of, the transfer
of property from one man to another; or of it's eftablifhment,
when already transferred. Of this nature are, 1. Private acts of
parliament. 2. The king's grants. 3. Fines. 4. Common recoveries.

I. P R I V A T E *acts of parliament* are, efpecially of late years,
become a very common mode of affurance. For it may fometimes happen, that, by the ingenuity of fome, and the blunders
of other practitioners, an eftate is moft grievoufly entangled by
a multitude of contingent remainders, refulting trufts, fpringing
ufes, executory devifes, and the like artificial contrivances; (a
confufion unknown to the fimple conveyances of the common
law) fo that it is out of the power of either the courts of law
or equity to relieve the owner. Or it may fometimes happen,
that, by the ftrictnefs or omiffions of family fettlements, the tenant of the eftate is abridged of fome reafonable power, (as letting leafes, making a jointure for a wife, or the like) which
power cannot be given him by the ordinary judges either in common law or equity. Or it may be neceffary, in fettling an e-
ftate, to fecure it againft the claims of infants or other perfons
                                                              under

under legal difabilities; who are not bound by any judgments or decrees of the ordinary courts of juftice. In thefe, or other cafes of the like kind, the tranfcendent power of parliament is called in, to cut the Gordian knot; and by a particular law, enacted for this very purpofe, to unfetter an eftate; to give it's tenant reafonable powers; or to affure it to a purchafor, againft the remote or latent claims of infants or difabled perfons, by fettling a proper equivalent in proportion to the intereft fo barred. This practice was carried to a great length in the year fucceeding the reftoration; by fetting afide many conveyances alleged to have been made by conftraint, or in order to fcreen the eftates from being forfeited during the ufurpation. And at laft it proceeded fo far, that, as the noble hiftorian expreffes it [a], every man had raifed an equity in his own imagination, that he thought ought to prevail againft any defcent, teftament, or act of law, and to find relief in parliament : which occafioned the king at the clofe of the feffion to remark [b], that the good old rules of law are the beft fecurity; and to wifh, that men might not have too much caufe to fear, that the fettlements which they make of their eftates fhall be too eafily unfettled when they are dead, by the power of parliament.

ACTS of this kind are however at prefent carried on, in both houfes, with great deliberation and caution; particularly in the houfe of lords they are ufually referred to two judges, to examine and report the facts alleged, and to fettle all technical forms. Nothing alfo is done without the confent, expreffly given, of all parties in being and capable of confent, that have the remoteft intereft in the matter; unlefs fuch confent fhall appear to be perverfely and without any reafon withheld. And, as was before hinted, an equivalent in money or other eftate is ufually fettled upon infants, or perfons not *in effe*, or not of capacity to act for themfelves, who are to be concluded by this act. And a general faving is conftantly added, at the clofe of the bill, of the right and intereft of all perfons whatfoever; except thofe whofe con-

[a] Lord Clar. Contin. 162. [b] *Ibid.* 163.

fent is fo given or purchafed, and who are therein particularly named.

A LAW, thus made, though it binds all parties to the bill, is yet looked upon rather as a private conveyance, than as the folemn act of the legiflature. It is not therefore allowed to be a *public*, but a mere *private* ftatute ; it is not printed or publifhed among the other laws of the feffion ; and no judge or jury is bound to take notice of it, unlefs the fame be fpecially fet forth and pleaded to them. It remains however enrolled among the public records of the nation, to be for ever preferved as a perpetual teftimony of the conveyance or affurance fo made or eftablifhed.

II. THE *king's grants* are alfo matter of public record. For, as St. Germyn fays [c], the king's excellency is fo high in the law, that no freehold may be given to the king, nor derived from him, but by matter of record. And to this end a variety of offices are erected, communicating in a regular fubordination one with another, through which all the king's grants muft pafs, and be tranfcribed, and enrolled ; that the fame may be narrowly infpected by his officers, who will inform him if any thing contained therein is improper, or unlawful to be granted. Thefe grants, whether of lands, honours, liberties, franchifes, or ought befides, are contained in charters, or letters *patent*, that is, open letters, *literae patentes :* fo called becaufe they are not fealed up, but expofed to open view, with the great feal pendant at the bottom ; and are ufually directed or addreffed by the king to all his fubjects at large. And therein they differ from certain other letters of the king, fealed alfo with his great feal, but directed to particular perfons, and for particular purpofes : which therefore, not being proper for public infpection, are clofed up and fealed on the outfide, and are thereupon called writs *clofe*, *literae claufae ;* and are recorded in the *clofe-rolls,* in the fame manner as the others are in the *patent-rolls.*

[c] Dr & Stud. l. 1. d. 8.

GRANTS

GRANTS or letters patent muſt firſt paſs by *bill:* which is prepared by the attorney and ſolicitor general, in conſequence of a warrant from the crown; and is then ſigned, that is, ſuper-ſcribed at the top, with the king's own *ſign manual,* and ſealed with his *privy ſignet,* which is always in the cuſtody of the prin-cipal ſecretary of ſtate; and then ſometimes it immediately paſſes under the great ſeal, in which caſe the patent is ſubſcribed in theſe words, "*per ipſum regem,* by the king himſelf[d]." Otherwiſe the courſe is to carry an extract of the bill to the keeper of the *privy ſeal,* who makes out a writ or warrant thereupon to the chancery; ſo that the ſign manual is the warrant to the privy ſeal, and the privy ſeal is the warrant to the great ſeal: and in this laſt caſe the patent is ſubſcribed, "*per breve de privato ſigillo,* by writ of privy "ſeal[e]." But there are ſome grants, which only paſs through certain offices, as the admiralty or treaſury, in conſequence of a *ſign manual,* without the confirmation of either the *ſignet,* the *great,* or the *privy* ſeal.

THE *manner* of granting by the king, does not more differ from that by a ſubject, than the *conſtruction* of his grants, when made. 1. A grant made by the king, *at the ſuit of the grantee,* ſhall be taken moſt beneficially *for* the king, and *againſt* the par-ty: whereas the grant of a ſubject is conſtrued moſt ſtrongly *a-gainſt the grantor.* Wherefore is is uſual to inſert in the king's grants, that they are made, not at the ſuit of the grantee, but "*ex ſpeciali gratia, certa ſcientia, et mero motu regis*;" and then they have a more liberal conſtruction[f]. 2. A ſubject's grant ſhall be conſtrued to include many things, beſides what are expreſſed, if neceſſary for the operation of the grant. Therefore, in a pri-vate grant of the profits of land for one year, free ingreſs, egreſs, and regreſs, to cut and carry away thoſe profits, are alſo inclu-ſively granted[g]: and if a feoffment of land was made by a lord

9 Rep. 18.   [f] Finch. L. 100. 10 Rep. 112.
[e] *Ibid* 2 Inſt. 555   [g] Co. Litt. 56.

to his villein, this operated as a manumiffion [h]; for he was other-wife unable to hold it. But the king's grant fhall not enure to any other intent, than that which is precifely expreffed in the grant. As, if he grants land to an alien, it operates nothing; for fuch grant fhall not alfo enure to make him a denizen, that fo he may be capable of taking by grant [i]. 3. When it appears, from the face of the grant, that the king is miftaken, or deceived, either in matter of fact or matter of law, as in cafe of falfe fug-geftion, mifinformation, or mifrecital of former grants; or if his own title to the thing granted be different from what he fuppofes; or if the grant be informal; or if he grants an eftate contrary to the rules of law; in any of thefe cafes the grant is abfolutely void [k]. For inftance; if the king grants lands to one and his *heirs male*, this is merely void: for it fhall not be an eftate-tail, becaufe there want words of procreation, to afcertain the body, out of which the heirs fhall iffue: neither is it a fee-fimple, as in common grants it would be; becaufe it may reafonably be fuppofed, that the king meant to give no more than an eftate-tail [l]: the grantee is therefore (if any thing) nothing more than tenant at will [m]. And, to prevent deceits of the king, with re-gard to the value of the eftate granted, it is particularly provided by the ftatute 1 Hen. IV. c. 6. that no grant of his fhall be good, unlefs, in the grantee's petition for them, exprefs mention be made of the real value of the lands.

III. WE are next to confider a very ufual fpecies of affurance, which is alfo of record; viz. a *fine* of lands and tenements. In which it will be neceffary to explain, 1. The *nature* of a fine; 2. It's feveral *kinds*; and 3. It's *force* and *effect*.

1. A FINE is fometimes faid to be a feoffment of record [n]: though it might with more accuracy be called, an acknowledge-ment of a feoffment on record. By which is to be underftood,

[h] Litt. §. 206.
[i] Bro. *Abr. tit* Patent. 62. Finch. L. 110.
[k] Freem. 172.
[l] Finch. 101, 102.

[m] Bro. *Abr. tit. Eftates.* 34. *tit. Patents.* 104. Dyer 270. Dav. 45.
[n] Co. Litt. 50.

that

that it has at leaft the fame force and effect with a feoffment, in the conveying and affuring of lands : though it is one of thofe methods of transferring eftates of freehold by the common law, in which livery of feifin is not neceffary to be actually given; the fuppofition and acknowlegement thereof in a court of record, however fictitious, inducing an equal notoriety. But, more particularly, a fine may be defcribed to be an amicable compofition or agreement of a fuit, either actual or fictitious, by leave of the king or his juftices; whereby the lands in queftion become, or are acknowleged to be, the right of one of the parties°. In it's original it was founded on an actual fuit, commenced at law for recovery of the poffeffion of land; and the poffeffion thus gained by fuch compofition was found to be fo fure and effectual, that fictitious actions were, and continue to be, every day commenced, for the fake of obtaining the fame fecurity.

A FINE is fo called becaufe it puts an *end*, not only to the fuit thus commenced, but alfo to all other fuits and controverfies concerning the fame matter. Or, as it is expreffed in an antient record of parliament P, 18 Edw. I. " *non in regno Angliae provide-*" *tur, vel eft, aliqua fecuritas major vel folennior, per quam aliquis* " *ftatum certiorem habere poffit, neque ad ftatum fuum verificandum* " *aliquod folennius teftimonium producere, quam finem in curia domini* " *regis levatum: qui quidem finis fic vocatur, eo quod finis et con-*" *fummatio omnium placitorum effe debet, et hac de caufa provideba-*" *tur.*" Fines indeed are of equal antiquity with the firft rudiments of the law itfelf; are fpoken of by Glanvil �q and Bracton ʳ in the reigns of Henry II, and Henry III, as things then well known and long eftablifhed; and inftances have been produced of them even before the Norman invafion ˢ. So that the ftatute 18 Edw. I. called *modus levandi fines*, did not give them original, but only declared and regulated the manner in which they fhould be levied, or carried on. And that is as follows :

° Co. Litt. 120.			ʳ *l.* 5. *t.* 5. *c.* 28.
P 2 Roll. Abr. 13.		ˢ Plowd. 369.
�q *l.* 8. *c.* 1.

I. THE

1. T H E party, to whom the land is to be conveyed or affured, commences an action or fuit at law againft the other, generally an action of covenant, by fuing out a writ or *praecipe*, called a writ of covenant [t] : the foundation of which is a fuppofed agreement or covenant, that the one fhall convey the lands to the other ; on the breach of which agreement the action is brought. On this writ there is due to the king, by antient prerogative, a *primer fine*, or a noble for every five marks of land fued for; that is, one tenth of the annual value [u]. The fuit being thus commenced, then follows,

2. T H E *licentia concordandi*, or leave to agree the fuit [w]. For, as foon as the action is brought, the defendant, knowing himfelf to be in the wrong, is fuppofed to make overtures of peace and accommodation to the plaintiff. Who, accepting them, but having, upon fuing out the writ, given pledges to profecute his fuit, which he endangers if he now deferts it without licence, he therefore applies to the court for leave to make the matter up. This leave is readily granted, but for it there is alfo another fine due to the king by his prerogative ; which is an antient revenue of the crown, and is called the *king's filver*, or fometimes the *poft fine*, with refpect to the *primer fine* before-mentioned. And it is as much as the *primer fine*, and half as much more, or ten fhillings for every five marks of land ; that is, three twentieths of the fuppofed annual value [x].

3. N E X T comes the *concord*, or agreement itfelf [y], after leave obtained from the court; which is ufually an acknowlegement from the deforciants (or thofe who keep the other out of poffeffion) that the lands in queftion are the right of the complainant. And from this acknowlegement, or recognition of right, the party levying the fine is called the *cognizor*, and he to whom it is levied

---

[t] See Appendix, N°. IV. §. 1.
[u] 2 Inft. 511.
[w] Append. N°. IV. §. 2.

[x] 5 Rep. 39. 2 Inft. 511.
[y] Append. N°. IV. §. 3.

the *cognizee*. This acknowlegement muſt be made either openly in the court of common pleas, or before one of the judges of that court, or elſe before commiſſioners in the country, empowered by a ſpecial authority called a writ of *dedimus poteſtatem*; which judges and commiſſioners are bound by ſtatute 18 Edw. I. ſt. 4. to take care that the cognizors be of full age, found memory, and out of priſon. If there be any feme-covert among the cognizors, ſhe is privately examined whether ſhe does it willingly and freely, or by compulſion of her huſband.

B y theſe acts all the eſſential parts of a fine are completed ; and, if the cognizor dies the next moment after the fine is acknowleged, provided it be ſubſequent to the day on which the writ is made returnable [z], ſtill the fine ſhall be carried on in all it's remaining parts : of which the next is

4. T h e *note* of the fine [a] : which is only an abſtract of the writ of covenant, and the concord ; naming the parties, the parcels of land, and the agreement. This muſt be enrolled of record in the proper office, by direction of the ſtatute 5 Hen. IV. c. 14.

5. T h e fifth part is the *foot* of the fine, or concluſion of it : which includes the whole matter, reciting the parties, day, year, and place, and before whom it was acknowleged or levied [b]. Of this there are indentures made, or engroſſed, at the chirographer's office, and delivered to the cognizor and the cognizee ; uſually beginning thus, " *haec eſt finalis concordia,* this is the final agree-" ment," and then reciting the whole proceeding at length. And thus the fine is completely levied at common law.

B y ſeveral ſtatutes ſtill more ſolemnities are ſuperadded, in order to render the fine more univerſally public, and leſs liable to be levied by fraud or covin. And, firſt, by 27 Edw. I. c. 1. the

[z] Comb. 71.
[a] Append. Nº. IV. §. 4.
[b] *Ibid.* § 5.

note of the fine fhall be openly read in the court of common pleas, at two feveral days in one week, and during fuch reading all pleas fhall ceafe. By 5 Hen. IV. c. 14. and 23 Eliz. c. 3. all the proceedings on fines either at the time of acknowlegement, or previous, or fubfequent thereto, fhall be enrolled of record in the court of common pleas. By 1 Ric. III. c. 7. confirmed and enforced by 4 Hen. VII. c. 24. the fine, after engroffment, fhall be openly read and proclaimed in court fixteen times ; viz. four times in the term in which it is made, and four times in each of the three fucceeding terms ; during which time all pleas fhall ceafe : but this is reduced to once in each term by 31 Eliz. c. 2. and thefe proclamations are endorfed on the back of the record [c]. It is alfo enacted by 23 Eliz. c. 3. that the chirographer of fines fhall every term write out a table of the fines levied in each county in that term, and fhall affix them in fome open part of the court of common pleas all the next term : and fhall alfo deliver the contents of fuch table to the fheriff of every county, who fhall at the next affifes fix the fame in fome open place in the court, for the more public notoriety of the fine.

2. F i n e s, thus levied, are of four kinds. 1. What in our law French is called a fine "*fur cognizance de droit, come ceo que il ad de fon done ;*" or, a fine upon acknowlegement of the right of the cognizee, as that which he hath of the gift of the cognizor [d]. This is the beft and fureft kind of fine ; for thereby the deforciant, in order to keep his covenant with the plaintiff, of conveying to him the lands in queftion, and at the fame time to avoid the formality of an actual feoffment and livery, acknowleges in court a former feoffment, or gift in poffeffion, to have been made by him to the plaintiff. This fine is therefore faid to be a feoffment of record ; the livery thus acknowleged in court, being equivalent to an actual livery : fo that this affurance is rather a confeffion of a former conveyance, than a conveyance now originally made ; for the deforciant, or cognizor, acknowleges,

---

[c] Append. Nᵒ. IV. §. 6.

[d] This is that fort, of which an example is given in the appendix, Nᵒ. IV.

cognofcit,

cognofcit, the right to be in the plaintiff, or cognizee, as that which he hath *de fon done*, of the proper gift of himfelf, the cognizor. 2. A fine "*fur cognizance de droit tantum*," or, upon acknowlegement of the right merely; not with the circumftance of a preceding gift from the cognizor. This is commonly ufed to pafs a *reverfionary* intereft, which is in the cognizor. For of fuch reverfions there can be no feoffment, or donation with livery, fuppofed; as the poffeffion during the particular eftate belongs to a third perfon[e]. It is worded in this manner; "that "the cognizor acknowleges the right to be in the cognizee; and "grants for himfelf and his heirs, that the reverfion, after the "particular eftate determines, fhall go to the cognizee[f]. 3. A fine "*fur conceffit*" is where the cognizor, in order to make an end of difputes, though he acknowleges no precedent right, yet grants to the cognizee an eftate *de novo*, ufually for life or years, by way of fuppofed compofition. And this may be done referving a rent, or the like: for it operates as a new grant[g]. 4. A fine "*fur done, grant, et render*," is a double fine, comprehending the fine *fur cognizance de droit come ceo, &c*, and the fine *fur conceffit*; and may be ufed to create particular limitations of eftate: whereas the fine *fur cognizance de droit come ceo, &c*, conveys nothing but an abfolute eftate, either of inheritance or at leaft of freehold[h]. In this laft fpecies of fine, the cognizee, after the right is acknowleged to be in him, grants back again, or renders to the cognizor, or perhaps to a ftranger, fome other eftate in the premifes. But, in general, the firft fpecies of fine, "*fur cogni-* "*zance de droit come ceo, &c*," is the moft ufed, as it conveys a clean and abfolute freehold, and gives the cognizee a feifin in law, without any actual livery; and is therefore called a fine executed, whereas the others are but executory.

3. WE are next to confider the *force* and *effect* of a fine. Thefe principally depend, at this day, on the common law, and the two ftatutes, 4 Hen. VII. c. 24. and 32 Hen. VIII. c. 36. The

[e] Moor. 629.   [g] Weft. p. 2. §. 66.
[f] Weft. Symb. p. 2. §. 95. [h] Salk. 340.

VOL. II.   W w   antient

antient common law, with respect to this point, is very forcibly
declared by the statute 18 Edw. I. in these words. "And the
"reason, why such solemnity is required in the passing of a fine,
"is this; because the fine is so high a bar, and of so great force,
"and of a nature so powerful in itself, that it precludes not only
"those which are parties and privies to the fine, and their heirs,
"but all other persons in the world, who are of full age, out of
"prison, of sound memory, and within the four seas the day of
"the fine levied; unless they put in their claim within a year
"and a day." But this doctrine, of barring the right by *non-claim*,
was abolished for a time by a statute made in 34 Edw. I. c. 16.
which admitted persons to claim, and falsify a fine, at any indefinite distance[i]: whereby, as sir Edward Coke observes[k], great
contention arose, and few men were sure of their possessions, till
the parliament held 4 Hen. VII reformed that mischief, and ex-
cellently moderated between the latitude given by the statute and
the rigour of the common law. For the statute, then made[l], restored the doctrine of non claim; but extended the time of claim.
So that now, by that statute, the right of all strangers whatsoever
is bound, unless they make claim, not within *one* year and a day,
as by the common law, but within *five* years after proclamations
made : except *feme-coverts*, infants, prisoners, persons beyond
the seas, and such as are not of whole mind; who have five years
allowed to them and their heirs, after the death of their husbands,
their attaining full age, recovering their liberty, returning into
England, or being restored to their right mind.

I T seems to have been the intention of that politic prince,
king Henry VII, to have covertly by this statute extended fines
to have been a bar of estates-tail, in order to unfetter the more
easily the estates of his powerful nobility, and lay them more
open to alienations; being well aware that power will always accompany property. But doubts having arisen whether they could,
by mere implication, be adjudged a sufficient bar, (which they

[i] Litt. §. 441.
[k] 2 Inst. 518.

[l] 4 Hen.V' 24.

were

were expreſſly declared *not* to be by the ſtatute *de donis*) the ſtatute 32 Hen.VIII. c. 36. was thereupon made; which removes
all difficulties, by declaring that a fine levied by any perſon of
full age, to whom or to whoſe anceſtors lands have been entailed,
ſhall be a perpetual bar to them and their heirs claiming by force
of ſuch entail: unleſs the fine be levied by a woman after the
death of her huſband, of lands which were, by the gift of him
or his anceſtor, aſſigned to her in tail for her jointure[m]; or unleſs it be of lands entailed by act of parliament or letters patent,
and whereof the reverſion belongs to the crown.

FROM this view of the common law, regulated by theſe ſtatutes, it appears, that a fine is a ſolemn conveyance on record from
the cognizor to the cognizee, and that the perſons bound by a
fine are *parties, privies,* and *ſtrangers.*

THE *parties* are either the cognizors, or cognizees; and theſe
are immediately concluded by the fine, and barred of any latent
right they might have, even though under the legal impediment
of coverture. And indeed, as this is almoſt the only act that a
feme-covert, or married woman, is permitted by law to do, (and
that becauſe ſhe is privately examined as to her voluntary conſent, which removes the general ſuſpicion of compulſion by her
huſband) it is therefore the uſual and almoſt the only ſafe method, whereby ſhe can join in the ſale, ſettlement, or incumbrance, of any eſtate.

PRIVIES to a fine are ſuch as are any way related to the
parties who levy the fine, and claim under them by any right of
blood, or other right of repreſentation. Such as are the heirs
general of the cognizor, the iſſue in tail ſince the ſtatute of Henry
the eighth, the vendee, the deviſee, and all others who muſt
make title by the perſons who levied the fine. For the act of the
anceſtor ſhall bind the heir, and the act of the principal his ſub-

---

[m] See ſtatute 11 Hen.VII. c. 20.

ftitute, or fuch as claim under any conveyance made by him fubfequent to the fine fo levied ⁿ.

STRANGERS to a fine are all other perfons in the world,
except only parties and privies. And thefe are alfo bound by a
fine, unlefs, within five years after proclamations made, they
interpofe their claim; provided they are under no legal impediments, and have then a prefent intereft in the eftate. The impediments, as hath before been faid, are coverture, infancy, imprifonment, infanity, and abfence beyond fea: and perfons, who
are thus incapacitated to profecute their rights, have five years
allowed them to put in their claims after fuch impediments are
removed. Perfons alfo that have not a prefent, but a future intereft only, as thofe in remainder or reverfion, have five years allowed them to claim in, from the time that fuch right accrues °.
And if within that time they neglect to claim, or (by the ftatute
4 Ann. c. 16.) if they do not bring an action to try the right,
within one year after making fuch claim, and profecute the fame
with effect, all perfons whatfoever are barred of whatever right
they may have, by force of the ftatute of non-claim.

BUT, in order to make a fine of any avail at all, it is neceffary that the parties fhould have fome intereft or eftate in the
lands to be affected by it. Elfe it were poffible that two ftrangers, by a mere confederacy, might without any rifque defraud
the owners by levying fines of their lands; for if the attempt be
difcovered, they can be no fufferers, but muft only remain *in ftatu
quo:* whereas if a tenant for life or years levies a fine, it is an
abfolute forfeiture of his eftate to the remainder-man or reverfioner ᵖ, if claimed in proper time. It is not therefore to be
fuppofed that fuch tenants will frequently run fo great a hazard;
but if they do, and the claim is not duly made within five years
after their refpective terms expire �۹, the eftate is for ever barred

ⁿ 3 Rep. 87.
° Co. Litt. 372.
ᵖ *Ibid.* 251.
۹ 2 Lev. 52.

by

by it. Yet where a ſtranger, whoſe preſumption cannot thus be
puniſhed, officiouſly interferes in an eſtate which in no wiſe belongs to him, his fine is of no effect; and may at any time be
ſet aſide (unleſs by ſuch as are parties or privies thereunto ʳ) by
pleading that "*partes finis nihil habuerunt*." And thus much for
the conveyance or aſſurance by fine: which not only like other
conveyances binds the grantor himſelf, and his heirs; but alſo
all mankind, whether concerned in the transfer or no, if they
fail to put in their claims within the time allotted by law.

IV. THE fourth ſpecies of aſſurance, by matter of record, is
a *common recovery*. Concerning the original of which, it was formerly obſerved ˢ, that common recoveries were invented by the
eccleſiaſtics to elude the ſtatutes of mortmain; and afterwards
encouraged by the fineſſe of the courts of law in 12 Edw. IV.
in order to put an end to all fettered inheritances, and bar not
only eſtates-tail, but alſo all remainders and reverſions expectant
thereon. I am now therefore only to conſider, firſt, the *nature*
of a common recovery; and, ſecondly, it's *force* and *effect*.

1. AND, firſt, the *nature* of it; or what a common recovery
is. A common recovery is ſo far like a fine, that it is a ſuit or
action, either actual or fictitious: and in it the lands are *recovered*
againſt the tenant of the freehold; which recovery, being a ſuppoſed adjudication of the right, binds all perſons, and veſts a free
and abſolute fee-ſimple in the recoveror. A recovery therefore
being in the nature of an action at law, not immediately com-
promiſed like a fine, but carried on through every regular ſtage
of proceeding, I am greatly apprehenſive that it's form and method will not be eaſily underſtood by the ſtudent, who is not yet
acquainted with the courſe of judicial proceedings; which cannot be thoroughly explained, till treated of at large in the third
book of theſe commentaries. However I ſhall endeavour to ſtate
it's nature and progreſs, as clearly and conciſely as I can; avoid-

ʳ Hob. 334.   ˢ pag. 117. 271.

ing

ing, as far as poffible, all technical terms, and phrafes not hitherto interpreted.

LET us, in the firft place, fuppofe David Edwards[t] to be tenant of the freehold, and defirous to fuffer a common recovery, in order to bar all entails, remainders, and reverfions, and to convey the fame in fee-fimple to Francis Golding. To effect this, Golding is to bring an action againft him for the lands; and he accordingly fues out a writ, called a *praecipe quod reddat*, becaufe thofe were it's initial or moft operative words, when the law proceedings were in Latin. In this writ the demandant Golding alleges, that the defendant Edwards (here called the tenant) has no legal title to the land; but that he came into poffeffion of it after one Hugh Hunt had turned the demandant out of it[v]. The fubfequent proceedings are made up into a record or recovery roll[u], in which the writ and complaint of the demandant are firft recited: whereupon the tenant appears, and calls upon one Jacob Morland, who is fuppofed, at the original purchafe, to have warranted the title to the tenant; and thereupon he prays, that the faid Jacob Morland may be called in to defend the title which he fo warranted. This is called the *voucher, vocatio*, or calling of Jacob Morland to warranty; and Morland is called the *vouchee*. Upon this, Jacob Morland, the vouchee, appears, is impleaded, and defends the title. Whereupon Golding, the demandant, defires leave of the court to *imparl*, or confer with the vouchee in private; which is (as ufual) allowed him. And foon afterwards the demandant, Golding, returns to court, but Morland the vouchee difappears, or makes default. Whereupon judgment is given for the demandant, Golding, now called the recoveror, to recover the lands in queftion againft the tenant, Edwards, who is now the recoveree: and Edwards has judgment to recover of Jacob Morland lands of equal value, in recompenfe for the lands fo warranted by him, and now loft by his default; which is agreeable to the doctrine of warranty mentioned in the preceding

[t] See appendix, N°. V. [u] §. 2.
[v] §. 1.

chapter[w].

chapter ᵂ. This is called the recompenfe, or *recovery in value*. But Jacob Morland having no lands of his own, being ufually the cryer of the court (who, from being frequently thus vouched, is called the *common vouchee*) it is plain that Edwards has only a nominal recompenfe for the lands fo recovered againft him by Golding; which lands are now abfolutely vefted in the faid recoveror by judgment of law, and feifin thereof is delivered by the fheriff of the county. So that this collufive recovery operates merely in the nature of a conveyance in fee-fimple, from Edwards the tenant in tail, to Golding the purchafor.

THE recovery, here defcribed, is with a *fingle* voucher only; but fometimes it is with *double, treble,* or farther voucher, as the exigency of the cafe may require. And indeed it is now ufual always to have a recovery with double voucher at the leaft; by firft conveying an eftate of freehold to any indifferent perfon, againft whom the *praecipe* is brought; and then he vouches the tenant in tail, who vouches over the common vouchee ˣ. For, if a recovery be had immediately againft tenant in tail, it bars only fuch eftate in the premifes of which he is then actually feifed; whereas if the recovery be had againft another perfon, and the tenant in tail be vouched, it bars every latent right and intereft which he may have in the lands recovered ʸ. If Edwards therefore be tenant of the freehold in poffeffion, and John Barker be tenant in tail in remainder, here Edwards doth firft vouch Barker, and then Barker vouches Jacob Morland the common vouchee; who is always the laft perfon vouched, and always makes default: whereby the demandant Golding recovers the land againft the tenant Edwards, and Edwards recovers a recompenfe of equal value againft Barker the firft vouchee; who recovers the like againft Morland the common vouchee, againft whom fuch ideal recovery in value is always ultimately awarded.

ᵂ pag. 301.
ˣ See appendix, pag. xviii.   ʸ Bro. *Abr. tit. Taile* 32. Plowd. 8.

THIS

T H I S suppofed recompenfe in value is the reafon why the iffue
in tail is held to be barred by a common recovery. For, if the
recoveree fhould ever obtain a recompenfe in lands from the common vouchee (which there is a poffibility in contemplation of
law, though a very improbable one, of his doing) thefe lands
would fupply the place of thofe fo recovered from him by collufion, and would defcend to the iffue in tail [z]. This reafon will
alfo hold, with equal force, as to *moft* remainder-men and reverfioners; to whom the poffibility will remain and revert, as a full
recompenfe for the reality, which they were otherwife entitled
to: but it will not *always* hold; and therefore, as Pigott fays [a],
the judges have been even *aftuti*, in inventing other reafons to
maintain the authority of recoveries. And, in particular, it hath
been faid, that, though the eftate-tail is gone from the recoveree,
yet it is not *deftroyed*, but only *transferred*; and ftill fubfifts, and
will ever continue to fubfift (by conftruction of law) in the recoveror, his heirs, and affigns: and, as the eftate-tail fo continues
to fubfift for ever, the remainders or reverfions expectant on the
determination of fuch eftate-tail can never take place.

To fuch awkward fhifts, fuch fubtile refinements, and fuch
ftrange reafoning, were our anceftors obliged to have recourfe, in
order to get the better of that ftubborn ftatute *de donis*. The defign, for which thefe contrivances were fet on foot, was certainly
laudable; the unrivetting the fetters of eftates-tail, which were
attended with a legion of mifchiefs to the commonwealth: but,
while we applaud the end, we cannot but admire the means. Our
modern courts of juftice have indeed adopted a more manly way
of treating the fubject; by confidering common recoveries in no
other light, than as the formal mode of conveyance, by which
tenant in tail is enabled to aliene his lands. But, fince the ill confequences of fettered inheritances are now generally feen and allowed, and of courfe the utility and expedience of fetting them
at liberty are apparent; it hath often been wifhed, that the pro-

---

[z] Dr & St. l. 1. dial. 26.   [a] of com. recov. 13, 14.

cefs

cefs of this conveyance was fhortened, and rendered lefs fubject
to niceties, by either totally repealing the ftatute *de donis*, which
perhaps, by reviving the old doctrine of conditional fees, might
give birth to many litigations : or by vefting in every tenant in
tail of full age the fame abfolute fee-fimple at once, which now
he may obtain whenever he pleafes, by the collufive fiction of a
common recovery; though this might poffibly bear hard upon
thofe in remainder or reverfion, by abridging the chances they
would otherwife frequently have, as no recovery can be fuffered
in the intervals between term and term, which fometimes continue for near five months together : or, laftly, by empowering
the tenant in tail to bar the eftate-tail by a folemn deed, to be
made in term time and enrolled in fome court of record ; which
is liable to neither of the other objections, and is warranted not
only by the ufage of our American colonies, but by the precedent of the ftatute[b] 21 Jac. I. c. 19. which, in cafe of a bankrupt
tenant in tail, empowers his commiffioners to fell the eftate at any
time, by deed indented and enrolled. And if, in fo national a
concern, the emoluments of the officers, concerned in paffing recoveries, are thought to be worthy attention, thofe might be
provided for in the fees to be paid upon each enrollment.

2. The *force* and *effect* of common recoveries may appear,
from what has been faid, to be an abfolute bar not only of all
eftates-tail, but of remainders and reverfions expectant on the
determination of fuch eftates. So that a tenant in tail may, by
this method of affurance, convey the lands held in tail to the recoveror his heirs and affigns, abfolutely free and difcharged of all
conditions and limitations in tail, and of all remainders and reverfions. But, by ftatute 34 & 35 Hen.VIII. c. 20. no recovery
had againft tenant in tail, of the king's gift, whereof the remainder or reverfion is in the king, fhall bar fuch eftate-tail, or
the remainder or reverfion of the crown. And by the ftatute
11 Hen.VII. c. 20. no woman, after her hufband's death, fhall
fuffer a recovery of lands fettled on her in tail by way of jointure

[b] See pag. 286.

by her hufband or any of his anceftors. And by ftatute 14 Eliz.
c. 8. no tenant for life, of any fort, can fuffer a recovery, fo as
to bind them in remainder or reverfion. For which reafon, if
there be tenant for life, with remainder in tail, and other remainders over, and the tenant for life is defirous to fuffer a valid recovery; either he, or the tenant to the *praecipe* by him made,
muft *vouch* the remainder-man in tail, otherwife the recovery is
void : but if he does vouch fuch remainder-man, and he appears
and vouches the common vouchee, it is then good ; for if a man
be vouched and appears, and fuffers the recovery to be had, it is
as effectual to bar the eftate-tail as if he himfelf were the recoveree [c].

IN all recoveries it is neceffary that the recoveree, or tenant
to the *praecipe*, as he is ufually called, be actually feifed of the
freehold, elfe the recovery is void [d]. For all actions, to recover
the feifin of lands, muft be brought againft the actual tenant of
the freehold, elfe the fuit will lofe it's effect ; fince the freehold
cannot be recovered of him who has it not. And, though thefe
recoveries are in themfelves fabulous and fictitious, yet it is neceffary that there be *actores fabulae*, properly qualified. But the
nicety thought by fome modern practitioners to be requifite in
conveying the legal freehold, in order to make a good tenant to the
praecipe, is removed by the provifions of the ftatute 14 Geo. II.
c. 20. which enacts, with a retrofpect and conformity to the antient rule of law [e], that, though the legal freehold be vefted in
leffees, yet thofe who are intitled to the next freehold eftate in
remainder or reverfion may make a good tenant to the *praecipe* :
and that, though the deed or fine which creates fuch tenant be
fubfequent to the judgment of recovery, yet, if it be in the fame
term, the recovery fhall be valid in law : and that, though the recovery itfelf do not appear to be entered, or be not regularly entered, on record, yet the deed to make a tenant to the *praecipe*,
and declare the ufes of the recovery, fhall after a poffeffion of

[c] Salk. 571.
[d] Pigott. 28.

[e] Pigott. 41, &c. 4 Burr. I. 115.

twenty

twenty years be sufficient evidence, on behalf of a purchasor for valuable consideration, that such recovery was duly suffered. And this may suffice to give the student a general idea of common recoveries, the last species of assurances by matter of record.

BEFORE I conclude this head, I must add a word concerning deeds to *lead*, or to *declare*, the *uses* of fines, and of recoveries. For if they be levied or suffered without any good consideration, and without any uses declared, they, like other conveyances, enure only to the use of him who levies or suffers them [f]. And if a consideration appears, yet as the most usual fine, *" sur cog-*" nizance de droit come ceo, &c,"* conveys an absolute estate, without any limitations, to the cognizee ; and as common recoveries do the same to the recoveror ; these assurances could not be made to answer the purpose of family settlements, (wherein a variety of uses and designations is very often expedient) unless their force and effect were subjected to the direction of other more complicated deeds, wherein particular uses can be more particularly expressed. The fine or recovery itself, like a power once gained in mechanics, may be applied and directed to give efficacy to an infinite variety of movements, in the vast and intricate machine of a voluminous family settlement. And, if these deeds are made previous to the fine or recovery, they are called deeds to *lead* the uses ; if subsequent, deeds to *declare* them. As, if A tenant in tail, with remainder to himself in fee, would settle his estate on B for life, remainder to C in tail, remainder to D in fee ; this is what by law he has no power of doing effectually, while his own estate-tail is in being. He therefore usually covenants to levy a fine (or, if there be any remainders over, to suffer a recovery) to E, and that the same shall enure to the uses in such settlement mentioned. This is now a deed to *lead* the uses of the fine or recovery ; and the fine when levied, or recovery when suffered, shall enure to the uses so specified and no other. For though E, the conusee or recoveree, hath a fee-simple vested in himself by the fine or recovery ; yet, by the operation of this deed, he be-

[f] Dyer. 18.

X x 2   comes

comes a mere inftrument or conduit-pipe, feifed only *to the ufe* of B, C, and D, in fucceffive order : which ufe is executed immediately, by force of the ftatute of ufes[g]. Or, if a fine or recovery be had without any previous fettlement, and a deed be *afterwards* made between the parties, *declaring* the ufes to which the fame fhall be applied, this will be equally good, as if it had been exprefly levied or fuffered, in confequence of a deed directing it's operation to thofe particular ufes. For by ftatute 4 & 5 Ann. c. 16. indentures to *declare* the ufes of fines and recoveries, made *after* the fines and recoveries had and fuffered, fhall be good and effectual in law, and the fine and recovery fhall enure to fuch ufes, and be efteemed to be only in truft, notwithftanding the ftatute of frauds 29 Car. II. c. 3. enacts, that all trufts fhall be declared in writing, *at* (and not *after*) the time when fuch trufts are created.

[g] This doctrine may perhaps be more clearly illuftrated by example. In the deed or marriage fettlement in the appendix, N°. II. §. 2. we may fuppofe the lands to have been originally fettled on Abraham and Cecilia Barker for life, remainder to John Barker in tail, with divers other remainders over, reverfion to Cecilia Barker in fee ; and now intended to be fettled to the feveral ufes therein expreffed, viz of Abraham and Cecilia Barker till the marriage; remainder to John Barker for life ; remainder to truftees to preferve the contingent remainders ; remainder to his widow for life, for her jointure ; remainder to other truftees, for a term of five hundred years ; remainder to their firft and other fons in tail; remainder to their daughters in tail ; remainder to John Barker in tail ; remainder to Cecilia Barker in fee. Now it is neceffary, in order to bar the eftate-tail of John Barker, and the remainders expectant thereon, that a recovery be fuffered of the premifes ; and it is thought proper (for though ufual, it is by no means neceffary : fee Forrefter.167.) that in order to make a good tenant of the frehold, or tenant to the *praecipe*, during the coverture, a fine fhould be levied by Abraham, Cecilia, and John Barker ; and it is agreed that the recovery itfelf be fuffered againft this tenant to the *praecipe,* who fhall vouch John Barker, and thereby bar his eftate-tail ; and become tenant of the fee-fimple by virtue of fuch recovery : the ufes of which eftate, fo acquired, are declred to be thofe expreffed in this deed. Accordingly the parties covenant to do thefe feveral acts, (fee pag. viii.) And in confequence thereof the fine and recovery are had and fuffered (N°. IV. and N°. V.) of which this conveyance is a deed to *lead the* ufes.

C H A P T E R   T H E   T W E N T Y   S E C O N D.

O F ALIENATION B Y SPECIAL CUSTOM.

W E are next to confider affurances by fpecial cuftom, obtaining only in particular places, and relative only to a
particular fpecies of real property. This therefore is a very narrow title ; being confined to copyhold lands, and fuch cuftomary
eftates, as are holden in antient demefne, or in manors of a fimilar nature : which, being of a very peculiar kind, and originally no more than tenancies in pure or privileged villenage, were
never alienable by deed ; for, as that might tend to defeat the
lord of his figniory, it is therefore a forfeiture of a copyhold [a].
Nor are they transferrable by matter of record, even in the king's
courts, but only in the court baron of the lord. The method
of doing this is generally by *furrender*; though in fome manors,
by fpecial cuftom, recoveries may be fuffered of copyholds [b]: but
thefe differing in nothing material from recoveries of free land,
fave only that they are not fuffered in the king's courts, but in
the court baron of the manor, I fhall confine myfelf to conveyances by furrender, and their confequences.

S U R R E N D E R, *furfumredditio*, is the yielding up of the eftate
by the tenant into the hands of the lord, for fuch purpofes as in
the furrender are expreffed. As, it may be, to the ufe and behoof of A and his heirs ; to the ufe of his own will ; and the
like. The procefs, in moft manors, is, that the tenant comes to

---

[a] Litt. §. 74.   [b] Moor. 637.

the

the fteward, either in court, (or, if the cuftom permits, out of court) or elfe to two cuftomary tenants of the fame manor, provided that alfo have a cuftom to warrant it; and there by delivering up a rod, a glove, or other fymbol, as the cuftom directs, refigns into the hands of the lord, by the hands and acceptance of his faid fteward, or of the faid two tenants, all his intereft and title to the eftate; in truft to be again granted out by the lord, to fuch perfons and for fuch ufes as are named in the furrender, and the cuftom of the manor will warrant. If the furrender be made out of court, then, at the next or fome fubfequent court, the jury or homage muft prefent and find it upon their oaths; which prefentment is an information to the lord or his fteward of what has been tranfacted out of court. Immediately upon fuch furrender in court, or upon prefentment of a furrender made out of court, the lord by his fteward grants the fame land again to *ceftuy que ufe*, (who is fometimes, though rather improperly, called the furrenderee) to hold by the antient rents and cuftomary fervices; and thereupon admits him tenant to the copyhold, according to the form and effect of the furrender, which muft be exactly purfued. And this is done by delivering up to the new tenant the rod, or glove, or the like, in the name, and as the fymbol, of corporal feifin of the lands and tenements. Upon which admiffion he pays a fine to the lord, according to the cuftom of the manor, and takes the oath of fealty.

In this brief abftract, of the manner of transferring copyhold eftates, we may plainly trace the vifible footfteps of the feodal inftitutions. The fief, being of a bafe nature and tenure, is unalienable without the knowlege and confent of the lord. For this purpofe it is refigned up, or furrendered into his hands. Cuftom, and the indulgence of the law, which favours liberty, has now given the tenant a right to name his fucceffor; but formerly it was far otherwife. And I am apt to fufpect that this right is of much the fame antiquity with the introduction of ufes with refpect to freehold lands: for the alienee of a copyhold had merely *jus fiduciarium*, for which there was no remedy at law, but only by *fubpoena* in chancery[c]. When therefore the lord had accepted a furrender of his tenant's intereft, upon confidence to re-grant the eftate to another perfon, either then exprefly named or to be afterwards named in the tenant's will, the chancery inforced this truft as a matter of confcience ; which jurifdiction, though feemingly new in the time of Edward IV[d], was generally acquiefced in, as it opened the way for the alienation of copyholds, as well as of freehold eftates, and as it rendered the *ufe* of them both equally devifable by teftament. Yet, even to this day, the new tenant cannot be admitted but by compofition with the lord, and paying him a fine by way of acknowlegement for the licence of alienation. Add to this the plain feodal inveftiture, by delivering the fymbol of feifin in prefence of the other tenants in open court ; " *quando hafta vel aliud corporeum quidlibet porrigitur a domino fe in-* " *veftituram facere dicente ; quae faltem coram duobus vafallis fo-* " *lenniter fieri debet*[e] :" and, to crown the whole, the oath of fealty annexed, the very bond of feodal fubjection. From all which we may fairly conclude, that, had there been no other evidence of the fact in the reft of our tenures and eftates, the very exiftence of copyholds, and the manner in which they are transferred, would inconteftably prove the very univerfal reception, which this northern fyftem of property for a long time obtained in this ifland ; and which communicated itfelf, or at leaft it's fimilitude, even to our very villeins and bondmen.

THIS method of conveyance is fo effential to the nature of a copyhold eftate, that it cannot poffibly be transferred by any other affurance. No feoffment, fine, or recovery (in the king's courts) has any operation thereupon. If I would exchange a copyhold eftate with another, I cannot do it by an ordinary deed of exchange at the common law; but we muft furrender to each other's ufe, and the lord will admit us accordingly. If I would devife a copyhold, I muft furrender it to the ufe of my laft will

[c] Cro. Jac. 568.
[d] Bro. *Abr. tit. Tenant per copie.* 10.
[e] *Feud. l. 2. t. 2.*

and

and teftament; and in my will I muft declare my intentions, and name a devifee, who will then be entitled to admiffion [f].

I N order the more clearly to apprehend the nature of this peculiar affurance, let us take a feparate view of it's feveral parts; the furrender, the prefentment, and the admittance.

1. A s u r r e n d e r, by an admittance fubfequent whereto the conveyance is to receive it's perfection and confirmation, is rather a manifeftation of the alienor's intention, than a transfer of any intereft in poffeffion. For, till admittance of *ceftuy que ufe*, the lord taketh notice of the furrenderor as his tenant; and he fhall receive the profits of the land to his own ufe, and fhall difcharge all fervices due to the lord. Yet the intereft remains in him not abfolutely, but *fub modo*; for he cannot pafs away the land to any other, or make it fubject to any other incumbrance than it was fubject to at the time of the furrender. But no manner of legal intereft is vefted in the nominee before admittance. If he enters, he is a trefpaffer and punifhable in an action of trefpafs: and if he furrenders to the ufe of another, fuch furrender is merely void, and by no matter *ex poft facto* can be confirmed. For though he be admitted in purfuance of the original furrender, and thereby acquires afterwards a fufficient and plenary intereft as abfolute owner, yet his fecond furrender previous to his own admittance is abfolutely void *ab initio*; becaufe at the time of fuch furrender he had but a poffibility of an intereft, and could therefore transfer nothing: and no fubfequent admittance can make an act good, which was *ab initio* void. Yet, though upon the original furrender the nominee hath but a poffibility, it is however fuch a poffibility, as may whenever he pleafes be reduced to a certainty: for he cannot either by force or fraud be deprived or deluded of the effect and fruits of the furrender; but if the lord refufe to admit him, he is compellable to do it by a bill in chancery or a *mandamus* [g]: and the furrenderor can in no wife defeat his grant; his hands being for ever bound from difpofing of the land

[f] Co. Copyh. §. 36.   [g] 2 Roll. Rep. 107.

in

in any other way, and his mouth for ever ſtopped from revoking or countermanding his own deliberate aɛt[h]; except in the caſe of a ſurrender to the uſe of his will, which is always revocable[j].

2. As to the *preſentment :* that, by the *general* cuſtom of manors, is to be made at the next court baron immediately after the ſurrender ; but by *ſpecial* cuſtom in ſome places it will be good, though made at the ſecond or other ſubſequent court. And it is to be brought into court by the *ſame* perſons that took the ſurrender, and then preſented by the homage ; and in all points material muſt correſpond with the true tenor of the ſurrender itſelf. And therefore, if the ſurrender be conditional, and the preſentment be abſolute, both the ſurrender, preſentment, and admittance thereupon are wholly void[i] : the ſurrender, as being never truly preſented ; the preſentment, as being falſe ; and the admittance, as being founded on ſuch untrue preſentment. If a man ſurrenders out of court, and dies before preſentment, and preſentment be made after his death, according to the cuſtom, this is ſufficient[k]. So too, if *ceſtuy que uſe* dies before preſentment, yet, upon preſentment made after his death, his heir according to the cuſtom ſhall be admitted. The ſame law is, if thoſe, into whoſe hands the ſurrender is made, die before preſentment ; for, upon ſufficient proof in court that ſuch a ſurrender was made, the lord ſhall be compelled to admit accordingly. And if the ſteward, the tenants, or others into whoſe hands ſuch ſurrender is made, do refuſe or negleɛt to bring it in to be preſented, upon a petition preferred to the lord in his court baron the party grieved ſhall find remedy. But if the lord will not do him right and juſtice, he may ſue both the lord, and them that took the ſurrender, in chancery, and ſhall there find relief[l].

[h] Co. Copyh. §. 39.
[j] 4 Rep. 23.
[i] Co. Copyh. 40.

[k] Co. Litt. 62.
[l] Co. Copyh. §. 40.

3. A D M I T T A N C E is the laſt ſtage, or perfection, of copy-hold aſſurances. And this is of three ſorts : firſt, an admittance upon a voluntary grant from the lord ; ſecondly, an admittance upon ſurrender by the former tenant; and thirdly, an admittance upon a deſcent from the anceſtor.

I N admittances, even upon a *voluntary grant* from the lord, when copyhold lands have eſcheated or reverted to him, the lord is conſidered as an inſtrument. For, though it is in his power to keep the lands in his own hands, or to diſpoſe of them at his pleaſure, by granting an abſolute fee-ſimple, a freehold, or a chattel intereſt therein ; and quite to change their nature from copyhold to ſocage tenure, ſo that he may well be reputed their abſolute owner and lord ; yet, if he will ſtill continue to diſpoſe of them as copyhold, he is bound to obſerve the antient cuſtom preciſely in every point, and can neither in tenure nor eſtate in-troduce any kind of alteration ; for that were to create a new copyhold : wherefore in this reſpect the law accounts him cuſ-tom's inſtrument. For if a copyhold for life falls into the lord's hands, by the tenant's death, though the lord may deſtroy the tenure and enfranchiſe the land, yet if he grants it out again by copy, he can neither add to nor diminiſh the antient rent, nor make any the minuteſt variation in other reſpects [m] : nor is the tenant's eſtate, ſo granted, ſubject to any charges or incumbran-ces by the lord [n].

I N admittances upon *ſurrender* of another, the lord is to no intent reputed as owner, but wholly as an inſtrument : and the tenant admitted ſhall likewiſe be ſubject to no charges or incum-brances of the lord ; for his claim to the eſtate is ſolely under him that made the ſurrender .

[m] Co. Cop. §. 41.   [n] 4 Rep. 27. Co. Litt. 59.
[n] 8 Rep. 63.

A N D,

AND, as in admittances upon furrenders, fo in admittances *upon defcents* by the death of the anceftor, the lord is ufed as a mere inftrument; and, as no manner of intereft paffes into him by the furrender or the death of his tenant, fo no intereft paffes out of him by the act of admittance. And therefore neither in the one cafe, nor the other, is any refpect had to the quantity or quality of the lord's eftate in the manor. For whether he be tenant in fee or for years, whether he be in poffeffion by right or by wrong, it is not material; fince the admittances made by him fhall not be impeached on account of his title, becaufe they are judicial, or rather minifterial, acts, which every lord in poffeffion is bound to perform P.

ADMITTANCES, however, upon furrender differ from admittances upon defcent in this; that by furrender nothing is vefted in *ceftuy que ufe* before admittance, no more than in voluntary admittances; but upon defcent the heir is tenant by copy immediately upon the death of his anceftor: not indeed to all intents and purpofes, for he cannot be fworn on the homage nor maintain an action in the lord's court as tenant; but to moft intents the law taketh notice of him as of a perfect tenant of the land inftantly upon the death of his anceftor, efpecially where he is concerned with any ftranger. He may enter into the land before admittance; may take the profits; may punifh any trefpafs done upon the ground q; nay, upon fatisfying the lord for his fine due upon the defcent, may furrender into the hands of the lord to whatever ufe he pleafes. For which reafons we may conclude, that the admittance of an heir is principally for the benefit of the lord, to intitle him to his fine, and not fo much neceffary for the ftrengthening and compleating the heir's title. Hence indeed an obfervation might arife, that if the benefit, which the heir is to receive by the admittance, is not equal to the charges of the fine, he will never come in and be admitted

P 4 Rep. 27. 1 Rep. 140. q 4 Rep. 23.

to his copyhold in court; and fo the lord may be defrauded of his fine. But to this we may reply in the words of fir Edward Coke ᶜ, "I affure myfelf, if it were in the election of " the heir to be admitted or not to be admitted, he would be " beft contented without admittance; but the cuftom in every " manor is in this point compulfory. For, either upon pain of " forfeiture of their copyhold, or of incurring fome great pe- " nalty, the heirs of copyholders are inforced, in every manor, " to come into court and be admitted according to the cuftom, " within a fhort time after notice given of their anceftor's de- " ceafe."

ᶜ Copyh. §.41.

CHAPTER THE TWENTY THIRD.

OF ALIENATION BY DEVISE.

THE laſt method of conveying real property, is by *deviſe*, or diſpoſition contained in a man's laſt will and teſtament. And, in conſidering this ſubject, I ſhall not at preſent enquire into the nature of wills and teſtaments, which are more properly the inſtruments to convey perſonal eſtates; but only into the original and antiquity of deviſing real eſtates by will, and the conſtruction of the ſeveral ſtatutes upon which that power is now founded.

IT ſeems ſufficiently clear, that, before the conqueſt, lands were deviſable by will[a]. But, upon the introduction of the military tenures, the reſtraint of deviſing lands naturally took place, as a branch of the feodal doctrine of non-alienation without the conſent of the lord[b]. And ſome have queſtioned, whether this reſtraint (which we may trace even from the antient Germans[c]) was not founded upon truer principles of policy, than the power of wantonly diſinheriting the heir by will, and transferring the eſtate, through the dotage or caprice of the anceſtor, from thoſe of his blood to utter ſtrangers. For this, it is alleged, maintained the ballance of property, and prevented one man from growing too big or powerful for his neighbours; ſince it rarely happens,

[a] Wright of tenures. 172.
[b] See pag. 57.
[c] *Tacit. de mcr. Germ. c.* 21.

that

that the fame man is heir to many others, though by art and management he may frequently become their devifee. Thus the antient law of the Athenians directed that the eftate of the deceafed fhould always defcend to his children ; or, on failure of lineal defcendants, fhould go to the collateral relations : which had an admirable effect in keeping up equality and preventing the accumulation of eftates. But when Solon [d] made a flight alteration, by permitting them (though only on failure of iffue) to difpofe of their lands by teftament, and devife away eftates from the collateral heir, this foon produced an excefs of wealth in fome, and of poverty in others : which, by a natural progreffion, firft produced popular tumults and diffentions ; and thefe at length ended in tyranny, and the utter extinction of liberty; which was quickly followed by a total fubverfion of their ftate and nation. On the other hand, it would now feem hard, on account of fome abufes, (which are the natural confequence of free agency, when coupled with human infirmity) to debar the owner of lands from diftributing them after his death, as the exigence of his family affairs, or the juftice due to his creditors, may perhaps require. And this power, if prudently managed, has with us a peculiar propriety ; by preventing the very evil which refulted from Solon's inftitution, the too great accumulation of property : which is the natural confequence of our doctrine of fucceffion by primogeniture, to which the Athenians were ftrangers. Of this accumulation the ill effects were feverely felt even in the feodal times ; but it fhould always be ftrongly difcouraged in a commercial country, whofe welfare depends on the number of moderate fortunes engaged in the extenfion of trade.

However this be, we find that, by the common law of England fince the conqueft, no eftate, greater than for term of years, could be difpofed of by teftament [e]; except only in Kent, and in fome antient burghs, and a few particular manors, where their Saxon immunities by fpecial indulgence fubfifted [f]. And

[d] Plutarch. *in vita Solon.*
[e] 2 Inft. 7.
[f] Litt. §. 167. 1 Inft. 111.

though

though the feodal reſtraint on alienations by deed vaniſhed very early, yet this on wills continued for ſome centuries after; from an apprehenſion of infirmity and impoſition on the teſtator *in extremis,* which made ſuch deviſes ſuſpicious. Beſides, in deviſes there was wanting that general notoriety, and public deſignation of the ſuc-ceſſor, which in deſcents is apparent to the neighbourhood, and which the ſimplicity of the common law always required in every transfer and new acquiſition of property.

B u t when eccleſiaſtical ingenuity had invented the doctrine of uſes, as a thing diſtinct from the land, uſes began to be de-viſed very frequently [g], and the deviſee of the uſe could in chan-cery compel it's execution. For it is obſerved by Gilbert [h], that, as the popiſh clergy then generally ſate in the court of chancery, they conſidered that men are moſt liberal when they can enjoy their poſſeſſions no longer ; and therefore at their death would chooſe to diſpoſe of them to thoſe, who, according to the ſuper-ſtition of the times, could intercede for their happineſs in an-other world. But, when the ſtatute of uſes [i] had annexed the poſſeſſion to the uſe, theſe uſes, being now the very land itſelf, became no longer deviſable : which might have occaſioned a great revolution in the law of deviſes, had not the ſtatute of wills been made about five years after, viz. 32 Hen. VIII. c. 1. explained by 34 Hen. VIII. c. 5. which enacted, that all perſons being ſeiſed in fee-ſimple (except feme-coverts, infants, idiots, and perſons of nonſane memory) might by will and teſtament in writing de-viſe to any other perſon, but not to bodies corporate, two thirds of their lands, tenements, and hereditaments, held in chivalry, and the whole of thoſe held in ſocage : which now, through the alteration of tenures by the ſtatute of Charles the ſecond, a-mounts to the whole of their landed property, except their copy-hold tenements.

C o r p o r a t i o n s were excepted in theſe ſtatutes, to pre-vent the extenſion of gifts in mortmain ; but now, by conſtruc-

g Plowd. 414.　　　　　　　i 27 Hen. VIII. c. 10.
h on deviſes, 7.

tion.

tion of the ſtatute 43 Eliz. c. 4. it is held, that a deviſe to a corporation for a charitable uſe is valid, as operating in the nature
of an *appointment*, rather than of a *bequeſt*. And indeed the piety
of the judges hath formerly carried them great lengths in ſup-
porting ſuch charitable uſes [k]; it being held that the ſtatute of
Elizabeth, which favours appointments to charities, ſuperſedes
and repeals all former ſtatutes [l], and ſupplies all defects of aſſurances [m]: and therefore not only a deviſe to a corporation, but a
deviſe by a copyhold tenant without ſurrendering to the uſe of
his will [n], and a deviſe (nay even a ſettlement) by tenant in tail
without either fine or recovery, if made to a charitable uſe, are
good by way of appointment [o].

WITH regard to deviſes in general, experience ſoon ſhewed
how difficult and hazardous a thing it is, even in matters of public utility, to depart from the rules of the common law; which
are ſo nicely conſtructed and ſo artificially connected together,
that the leaſt breach in any one of them diſorders for a time the
texture of the whole. Innumerable frauds and perjuries were
quickly introduced by this parliamentary method of inheritance:
for ſo looſe was the conſtruction made upon this act by the courts
of law, that bare notes in the hand writing of another perſon
were allowed to be good wills within the ſtatute [p]. To remedy
which, the ſtatute of frauds and perjuries, 29 Car. II. c. 3. directs, that all deviſes of lands and tenements ſhall not only be in
writing, but ſigned by the teſtator, or ſome other perſon in his
preſence, and by his expreſs direction; and be ſubſcribed, in
his preſence, by three or four credible witneſſes. And a ſimilar
ſolemnity is requiſite for revoking a deviſe.

IN the conſtruction of this laſt ſtatute, it has been adjudged
that the teſtator's name, written with his own hand, at the beginning of his will, as, " I John Mills do make this my laſt will

[k] Ch. Prec. 272.
[l] Gilb. Rep. 45. 1 P. Wms. 248.
[m] Duke's charit. uſes. 84.

[n] Moor. 890.
[o] 2 Vern. 453. Ch. Prec. 16.
[p] Dyer. 72. Cro. Eliz. 100.

" and

"and teſtament," is a ſufficient ſigning, without any name at the bottom ᑫ; though the other is the ſafer way. It has alſo been determined, that though the witneſſes muſt all ſee the teſtator ſign, or at leaſt acknowlege the ſigning, yet they may do it at different times ʳ. But they muſt all ſubſcribe their names as wit-neſſes *in his preſence*, left by any poſſibility they ſhould miſtake the inſtrument ˢ. And, in a caſe determined about twenty years ago ᵗ, the judges were extremely ſtrict in regard to the credibility, or rather the competency, of the witneſſes : for they would not allow any legatee, nor by conſequence a creditor, where the legacies and debts were charged on the real eſtate, to be a competent witneſs to the deviſe, as being too deeply con-cerned in intereſt not to wiſh the eſtabliſhment of the will ; for, if it were eſtabliſhed, he gained a ſecurity for his legacy or debt from the real eſtate, whereas otherwiſe he had no claim but on the perſonal aſſets. This determination however alarm-ed many purchaſors and creditors, and threatened to ſhake moſt of the titles in the kingdom, that depended on deviſes by will. For, if the will was atteſted by a ſervant to whom wages were due, by the apothecary or attorney whoſe very attendance made them creditors, or by the miniſter of the pariſh who had any demand for tithes or eccleſiaſtical dues, (and theſe are the per-ſons moſt likely to be preſent in the teſtator's laſt illneſs) and if in ſuch caſe the teſtator had charged his real eſtate with the payment of his debts, the whole will, and every diſpoſition there-in, ſo far as related to real property, were held to be utterly void. This occaſioned the ſtatute 25 Geo. II. c. 6. which reſto-red both the competency and the credit of ſuch *legatees*, by de-claring void all legacies given to witneſſes, and thereby removing all poſſibility of their intereſt affecting their teſtimony. The ſame ſtatute likewiſe eſtabliſhed the competency of *creditors*, by di-recting the teſtimony of all ſuch creditors to be admitted, but leaving their credit (as well as that of all other witneſſes) to be conſidered, on a view of all the circumſtances, by the court and

ᑫ 3 Lev. 1.
ʳ Freem. 486. 2Ch. Caſ. 109. Pr. Ch. 185.
ˢ 1 P. Wᵐˢ. 740.
ᵗ St a. 1253.

jury before whom fuch will fhall be contefted. And in a much later cafe ᵘ the teftimony of three witneffes, who were creditors, was held to be fufficiently credible, though the land was charged with the payment of debts; and the reafons of the former determination were adjudged to be infufficient.

A n o t h e r inconvenience was found to attend this new method of conveyance by devife; in that creditors by bond and other fpecialties, which affected the heir provided he had affets by defcent, were now defrauded of their fecurities, not having the fame remedy againft the devifee of their debtor. To obviate which, the ftatute 3 & 4 W. & M. c. 14. hath provided, that all wills, and teftaments, limitations, difpofitions, and appointments of real eftates, by tenants in fee-fimple or having power to difpofe by will, fhall (as againft fuch creditors only) be deemed to be fraudulent and void : and that fuch creditors may maintain their actions jointly againft both the heir and the devifee.

A w i l l of lands, made by the permiffion and under the controll of thefe ftatutes, is confidered by the courts of law not fo much in the nature of a teftament, as of a conveyance declaring the ufes to which the land fhall be fubject : with this difference, that in other conveyances the actual *fubfcription* of the witneffes is not required by law ʷ, though it is prudent for them fo to do, in order to affift their memory when living and to fupply their evidence when dead; but in devifes of lands fuch fubfcription is now abfolutely neceffary by ftatute, in order to identify a conveyance, which in it's nature can never be fet up till after the death of the devifor. And upon this notion, that a devife affecting lands is merely a fpecies of conveyance, is founded this diftinction between fuch devifes and teftaments of perfonal chattels; that the latter will operate upon whatever the teftator dies poffeffed of, the former only upon fuch real eftates as were his at the time of executing and publifhing his will ˣ. Wherefore no after-

---

ᵘ M. 31 Geo. II. 4 Burr. I. 430.   ˣ 1 P. Wᵐˢ. 575.
ʷ See pag. 307.

purchafed

purchafed lands will pafs under fuch devife[y], unlefs, fubfequent to the purchafe or contract[z], the devifor re-publifhes his will[a].

WE have now confidered the feveral fpecies of common af-furances, whereby a title to lands and tenements may be tranf-ferred and conveyed from one man to another. But, before we conclude this head, it may not be improper to take notice of a few general rules and maxims, which have been laid down by courts of juftice, for the conftruction and expofition of them all. Thefe are

1. THAT the conftruction be *favourable*, and as near the minds and apparent intents of the parties, as the rules of law will admit[b]. For the maxims of law are, that "*verba inten-*" *tioni debent infervire ;*" and, "*benigne interpretamur chartas* "*propter fimplicitatem laicorum.*" And therefore the conftruc-tion muft alfo be *reafonable*, and agreeable to common under-ftanding[c].

2. THAT *quoties in verbis nulla eft ambiguitas, ibi nulla expo-fitio contra verba fienda eft*[d]*:* but that, where the *intention* is clear, too minute a ftrefs be not laid on the ftrict and precife fignification of *words ; nam qui haeret in litera, haeret in cortice.* Therefore, by a grant of a remainder a reverfion may well pafs, and *e con-verfo*[e]. And another maxim of law is, that "*mala grammatica* "*non vitiat chartam ;*" neither falfe Englifh nor bad Latin will deftroy a deed[f]. Which perhaps a claffical critic may think to be no unneceffary caution.

3. THAT the conftruction be made upon the entire deed, and not merely upon difjointed parts of it. "*Nam ex antecedentibus*

[y] Moor. 255. 11 Mod. 127.
[z] 1 Ch. Caf. 39. 2 Ch. Caf. 144.
[a] Salk. 238.
[b] And. 60.

[c] 1 Bulftr. 175. Hob. 304.
[d] 2 Saund. 157.
[e] Hob. 27.
[f] 10 Rep. 133. Co. Litt. 223. 2 Show. 334.

"*et*

" *et confequentibus fit optima interpretatio* [g]." And therefore that every part of it, be (if poffible) made to take effect; and no word but what may operate in fome fhape or other [h]. " *Nam* " *verba debent intelligi cum effectu, ut res magis valeat quem pe-* " *reat* [i]."

4. T H A T the deed be taken moft ftrongly againft him that is the agent or contractor, and in favour of the other party. " *Verba* " *fortius accipiuntur contra proferentem.*" For the principle of felf-prefervation will make men fufficiently careful, not to prejudice their own intereft by the too extenfive meaning of their words: and hereby all manner of deceit in any grant is avoided; for men would always affect ambiguous and intricate expreffions, provided they were afterwards at liberty to put their own conftruction upon them. But here a diftinction muft be taken between an indenture and a deed poll: for the words of an indenture, executed by both parties, are to be confidered as the words of them both; for, though delivered as the words of one party, yet they are not his words only, but the other party hath given his confent to every one of them. But in a deed poll, executed only by the gran-tor, they are the words of the grantor only, and fhall be taken moft ftrongly againft him [k]. However, this, being a rule of fome ftrictnefs and rigor, is the laft to be reforted to, and is never to be relied upon, but where all other rules of expofition fail [l].

5. T H A T, if the words will bear two fenfes, one agreeable to, and another againft, law; that fenfe be preferred, which is moft agreeable thereto [m]. As if tenant in tail lets a leafe for life generally, it fhall be conftrued for his own life only, for that ftands with the law; and not for the life of the leffee, which is beyond his power to grant.

[g] 1 Bulftr. 101.
[h] 1 P. W[m]. 457.
[i] Plowd. 156.

[k] Plowd. 134.
[l] Bacon's Elem. c. 3.
[m] Co. Litt. 42.

6. T H A T

6. THAT, in a deed, if there be two claufes fo totally repugnant to each other, that they cannot ftand together, the firft fhall
be received and the latter rejected[n] : wherein it differs from a
will; for there, of two fuch repugnant claufes the latter fhall
ftand[o]. Which is owing to the different natures of the two inftruments; for the firft deed, and the laft will are always moft
available in law. Yet in both cafes we fhould rather attempt to
reconcile them[p].

7. THAT a devife be moft favourably expounded, to purfue
if poffible the will of the devifor, who for want of advice or
learning may have omitted the legal and proper phrafes. And
therefore many times the law difpenfes with the want of words
in devifes, that are abfolutely requifite in all other inftruments.
Thus a fee may be conveyed without words of inheritance[q]; and
an eftate-tail without words of procreation[r]. By a will alfo an
eftate may pafs by mere implication, without any exprefs words
to direct it's courfe. As, where A devifes lands to his heir at law,
after the death of his wife : here, though no eftate is given to
the wife in exprefs terms, yet fhe fhall have an eftate for life by
implication[s]; for the intent of the teftator is clearly to poftpone
the heir till after her death; and, if fhe does not take it, nobody
elfe can. So alfo, where a devife is of black-acre to A and of
white-acre to B in tail, and if they both die without iffue, then
to C in fee : here A and B have *crofs remainders* by implication,
and on the failure of either's iffue, the other or his iffue fhall
take the whole; and C's remainder over fhall be poftponed till
the iffue of both fhall fail[t]. But, to avoid confufion, no crofs
remainders are allowed between more than two devifees[u]: and,
in general, where any implications are allowed, they muft be
fuch as are *neceffary* (or at leaft highly *probable*) and not merely

---

[n] Hardr. 94.
[o] Co. Litt. 112.
[p] Cro. Eliz. 420. 1 Vern. 30.
[q] See pag. 108.

[r] See pag. 115.
[s] 1 Ventr. 376.
[t] Freem. 484.
[u] Cro. Jac. 655. 1 Ventr. 224. 2 Show 139.

poffible

poſſible implications[w]. And herein there is no diſtinction between the rules of law and of equity; for the will, being conſidered in both courts in the light of a limitation to uſes[x], is conſtrued in each with equal favour and benignity, and expounded rather on it's own particular circumſtances, than by any general rules of poſitive law.

AND thus we have taken a tranſient view, in this and the three preceding chapters, of a very large and diffuſive ſubject, the doctrine of common aſſurances : which concludes our obſervations on the *title* to things real, or the means by which they may be reciprocally loſt and acquired. We have before conſidered the *eſtates* which may be had in them, with regard to their duration or quantity of intereſt, the time of their enjoyment, and the number and connexions of the perſons entitled to hold them : we have examined the *tenures*, both antient and modern, whereby thoſe eſtates have been, and are now, holden : and have diſtinguiſhed the object of all theſe enquiries, namely, things real, into the corporeal or ſubſtantial, and incorporeal or ideal *kind*; and have thus conſidered the rights of real property in every light wherein they are contemplated by the laws of England. A ſyſtem of laws, that differs much from every other ſyſtem, except thoſe of the ſame feodal origin, in it's notions and regulations of landed eſtates; and which therefore could in this particular be very ſeldom compared with any other.

THE ſubject, which has thus employed our attention, is of very extenſive uſe, and of as extenſive variety. And yet, I am afraid, it has afforded the ſtudent leſs amuſement and pleaſure in the purſuit, than the matters diſcuſſed in the preceding volume. To ſay the truth, the vaſt alterations which the doctrine of real property has undergone from the conqueſt to the preſent time; the infinite determinations upon points that continually ariſe, and which have been heaped one upon another for a courſe

---

[w] Vaugh. 262.　　　　　　　[x] Fitzg. 236. 11 Mod. 153.

of

of feven centuries, without any order or method; and the multiplicity of acts of parliament which have amended, or fometimes only altered, the common law; thefe cafes have made
the ftudy of this branch of our national jurifprudence a little
perplexed and intricate. It hath been my endeavour principally
to felect fuch parts of it, as were of the moft general ufe, where
the principles were the moft fimple, the reafons of them the
moft obvious, and the practice the leaft embarraffed. Yet I cannot prefume that I have always been thoroughly intelligible to
fuch of my readers, as were before ftrangers even to the very
terms of art, which I have been obliged to make ufe of: though,
whenever thofe have firft occurred, I have generally attempted a
fhort explication of their meaning. Thefe are indeed the more
numerous, on account of the different languages which our law
has at different periods been taught to fpeak; the difficulty arifing from which will infenfibly diminifh by ufe and familiar ac-
quaintance. And therefore I fhall clofe this branch of our enquiries with the words of fir Edward Coke[y]: "albeit the ftu-
"dent fhall not at any one day, do what he can, reach to the
"full meaning of all that is here laid down, yet let him no way
"difcourage himfelf, but proceed; for on fome other day, in
"fome other place," (or perhaps upon a fecond perufal of the
fame) "his doubts will be probably removed."

[y] Proeme to 1 Inft.

CHAPTER THE TWENTY FOURTH.

Of THINGS PERSONAL.

UNDER the name of things *perfonal* are included all forts
of things *moveable*, which may attend a man's perfon
wherever he goes ; and therefore, being only the objects of the
law while they remain within the limits of it's jurifdiction, and
being alfo of a perifhable quality, are not efteemed of fo high a
nature, nor paid fo much regard to by the law, as things that are
in their nature more permanent and *immoveable*, as lands, and
houfes, and the profits iffuing thereout. Thefe being conftantly
within the reach, and under the protection of the law, were the
principal favourites of our firft legiflators : who took all imagin-
able care in afcertaining the rights, and directing the difpofition,
of fuch property as they imagined to be lafting, and which would
anfwer to pofterity the trouble and pains that their anceftors employed about them ; but at the fame time entertained a very low
and contemptuous opinion of all perfonal eftate, which they regarded only as a tranfient commodity. The amount of it indeed
was, comparatively, very trifling, during the fcarcity of money
and the ignorance of luxurious refinements, which prevailed in
the feodal ages. Hence it was, that a tax of the *fifteenth, tenth,*
or fometimes a much larger proportion, of all the moveables of
the fubject, was frequently laid without fcruple, and is mentioned
with much unconcern by our antient hiftorians, though now it
would juftly alarm our opulent merchants and ftockholders. And
hence likewife may be derived the frequent forfeitures inflicted
by

by the common law, of all a man's goods and chattels, for mif-
behaviours and inadvertencies that at prefent hardly feem to deferve fo fevere a punifhment. Our antient law-books, which are
founded upon the feodal provifions, do not therefore often con-
defcend to regulate this fpecies of property. There is not a chapter in Britton or the mirroir, that can fairly be referred to this
head ; and the little that is to be found in Glanvil, Bracton, and
Fleta, feems principally borrowed from the civilians. But of
later years, fince the introduction and extenfion of trade and commerce, which are entirely occupied in this fpecies of property,
and have greatly augmented it's quantity and of courfe it's value,
we have learned to conceive different ideas of it. Our courts
now regard a man's perfonalty in a light nearly, if not quite,
equal to his realty : and have adopted a more enlarged and lefs
technical mode of confidering the one than the other ; frequently drawn from the rules which they found already eftablifhed by
the Roman law, wherever thofe rules appeared to be well-grounded and appofite to the cafe in queftion, but principally from reafon and convenience, adapted to the circumftances of the times ;
preferving withal a due regard to antient ufages, and a certain
feodal tincture, which is ftill to be found in fome branches of
perfonal property.

B u t things perfonal, by our law, do not only include things
moveable, but alfo fomething more. The whole of which is comprehended under the general name of *chattels, catalla* ; which,
fir Edward Coke fays [a], is a French word fignifying goods. And
this is true, if underftood of the Norman dialect ; for in the
grand couftumier [b], we find the word *chattels* ufed and fet in oppofition to a fief or feud : fo that not only goods, but whatever
was not a feud, were accounted chattels. And it is, I apprehend, in the fame large, extended, negative fenfe, that our law
adopts it ; the idea of goods, or moveables only, being not fufficiently comprehenfive to take in every thing that our law con-

[a] 1 Inft. 118.   [b] c. 87.

fiders as a chattel intereft. For fince, as the commentator on the *couſtumier* obferves, there are two requifites to make a fief or heritage, duration as to time, and immobility with regard to place; whatever wants either of thefe qualities is not, according to the Normans, an heritage or fief ᶜ; or, according to us, is not a *real* eftate : the confequence of which in both laws is, that it muft be a perfonal eftate, or chattel.

C h a t t e l s therefore are diftributed by the law into two kinds; chattels *real,* and chattels *perſonal.*

1. C h a t t e l s *real,* faith fir Edward Coke ᵈ, are fuch as concern, or favour of, the realty; as terms for years of land, wardſhips in chivalry (while the military tenures fubfifted) the next prefentation to a church, eftates by ftatute-merchant, ftatute-ftaple, *elegit,* or the like; of all which we have already fpoken. And thefe are called real chattels, as being interefts iffuing out of, or annexed to real eftates : of which they have one quality, viz. immobility, which denominates them *real*; but want the other, viz. a fufficient, legal, indeterminate duration : and this want it is, that conftitutes them *chattels.* The utmoft period for which they can laft is fixed and determinate, either for fuch a fpace of time certain, or till fuch a particular fum of money be raifed out of fuch a particular income; fo that they are not equal in the eye of the law to the loweft eftate of freehold, a leafe for another's life : their tenants were confidered, upon feodal principles, as merely bailiffs or farmers; and the tenant of the freehold might at any time have deftroyed their intereft, till the reign of Henry VIII ᵉ. A freehold, which alone is a real eftate, and feems (as has been faid) to anfwer to the fief in Normandy, is conveyed by corporal inveftiture and livery of feifin; which gives the tenant fo ftrong a hold of the land, that it never after can

---

ᶜ *Cateux ſont meubles et immeubles : ſicomme vrais meubls ſont qui tranſporter ſe peuvent, et enſuivir le corps ; immeubles ſont choſes qui ne peuvent enſuivir le corps, nieſtre tranſportees,* et tout ce qui n' eſt point en heritage. *LL.* Will. Nothi, c 4. *apud* Du refne. II. 409.
ᵈ 1 Inft. 118.
ᵉ See pag. 141, 142.

be

be wrefted from him during his life, but by his own act, of voluntary transfer or of forfeiture ; or elfe by the happening of fome future contingency, as in eftates *pur auter vie,* and the determinable freeholds mentioned in a former chapter [f]. And even thefe, being of an uncertain duration, may by poffibility laft for the owner's life ; for the law will not prefuppofe the contingency to happen before it actually does, and till then the eftate is to all intents and purpofes a life eftate, and therefore a freehold intereft. On the other hand, a chattel intereft in lands, which the Normans put in oppofition to fief, and we to freehold, is conveyed by no feifin or corporal inveftiture, but ·the poffeffion is gained by the mere entry of the tenant himfelf; and it is fure to expire at a time prefixed and determined, if not fooner. Thus a leafe for years muft neceffarily fail at the end and completion of the term ; the next prefentation to a church is fatisfied and gone the inftant it comes into poffeffion, that is, by the firft avoidance and prefentation to the living ; the conditional eftates by ftatutes and *elegit* are determined as foon as the debt is paid ; and fo guardianfhips in chivalry were fure to expire the moment that the heir came of age. And if there be any other chattel real, it will be found to correfpond with the reft in this effential quality, that it's duration is limited to a time certain, beyond which it cannot fubfift.

2. C H A T T E L S perfonal are, properly and ftrictly fpeaking, things *moveable*; which may be annexed to or attendant on the perfon of the owner, and carried about with him from one part of the world to another. Such are animals, houfehold-ftuft, money, jewels, corn, garments, and every thing elfe that can properly be put in motion, and transferred from place to place. And of this kind of chattels it is, that we are principally to fpeak in the remainder of this book ; having been unavoidably led to confider the nature of chattels real, and their incidents, in the former chapters which were employed upon real eftates : that

[f] pag. 121.

kind

kind of property being of a mongrel amphibious nature, originally endowed with one only of the characteriſtics of each ſpecies of things; the immobility of things real, and the precarious
duration of things perſonal.

C H A T T E L intereſts being thus diſtinguiſhed and diſtributed,
it will be proper to conſider, firſt, the nature of that *property*,
or dominion, to which they are liable; which muſt be principally, nay ſolely, referred to perſonal chattels: and, ſecondly,
the *title* to that property, or how it may be loſt and acquired.
Of each of theſe in it's order.

CHAPTER THE TWENTY FIFTH.

OF PROPERTY IN THINGS PERSONAL.

PROPERTY, in chattels perfonal, may be either in *poffef-fion*; which is where a man hath not only the right to enjoy, but hath the actual enjoyment of, the thing: or elfe it is in *action*; where a man hath only a bare right, without any occupation or enjoyment. And of thefe the former, or property in *poffeffion*, is divided into two forts, an *abfolute* and a *qualified* property.

I. FIRST then of property in *poffeffion abfolute*; which is where a man hath, folely and exclufively, the right, and alfo the occupation, of any moveable chattels; fo that they cannot be transferred from him, or ceafe to be his, without his own act or default. Such may be all *inanimate* things, as goods, plate, money, jewels, implements of war, garments, and the like : fuch alfo may be all *vegetable* productions, as the fruit or other parts, when fevered from the plant, or the whole plant itfelf, when fevered from the ground ; none of which can be moved out of the owner's poffeffion without his own act or confent, or at leaft without doing him an injury, which it is the bufinefs of the law to prevent or remedy. Of thefe therefore there remains little to be faid.

BUT with regard to *animals*, which have in themfelves a principle and power of motion, and (unlefs particularly confined) can convey themfelves from one part of the world to another, there

there is a great difference made with refpect to their feveral claffes, not only in our law, but in the law of nature and of all civilized nations. They are diftinguifhed into fuch as are *domitae*,
and fuch as are *ferae naturae*; fome being of a *tame*, and others
of a *wild* difpofition. In fuch as are of a nature tame and domeftic, (as horfes, kine, fheep, poultry, and the like) a man
may have as abfolute a property as in any inanimate beings; becaufe thefe continue perpetually in his occupation, and will not
ftray from his houfe or perfon, unlefs by accident or fraudulent
enticement, in either of which cafes the owner does not lofe
his property[a]: in which our law agrees with the laws of France
and Holland[b]. The ftealing, or forcible abduction, of fuch property as this, is alfo felony; for thefe are things of intrinfic value, ferving for the food of man, or elfe for the ufes of hufbandry[c]. But in animals *ferae naturae* a man can have no abfolute
property.

O F all tame and domeftic animals, the brood belongs to the
owner of the dam or mother; the Englifh law agreeing with the
civil, that *"partus fequitur ventrem"* in the brute creation, though
for the moft part in the human fpecies it difallows that maxim.
And therefore in the laws of England[d], as well as Rome[e], *" fi
" equam meam equus tuus praegnantem fecerit, non eft tuum fed
" meum quod natum eft."* And, for this, Puffendorf[f] gives a fenfible reafon : not only becaufe the male is frequently unknown ;
but alfo becaufe the dam, during the time of her pregnancy, is
almoft ufelefs to the proprietor, and muft be maintained with
greater expence and care: wherefore as her owner is the lofer by
her pregnancy, he ought to be the gainer by her brood. An exception to this rule is in the cafe of young cygnets ; which belong equally to the owner of the cock and hen, and fhall be divided between them[g]. But here the reafons of the general rule

---

[a] 2 Mod. 319.
[b] *Vinn. in Inft. l. 2. tit. 1. §. 15.*
[c] 1 Hal. P. C. 511, 512.
[d] Bro. *Abr. tit. Propertie.* 29.

[e] *Ff.* 6. 1. 5.
[f] L. of N. l. 4. c. 7.
[g] 7 Rep. 17.

ceafe,

ceafe, and " *ceffante ratione ceffat et ipfa lex:*" for the male is well
known, by his conftant affociation with the female ; and for the
fame reafon the owner of the one doth not fuffer more difadvantage, during the time of pregnancy and nurture, than the owner
of the other.

II. O T H E R animals, that are not of a tame and domeftic
nature, are either not the objects of property at all, or elfe fall
under our other divifion, namely, that of *qualified, limited*, or
fpecial property : which is fuch as is not in it's nature permanent,
but may fometimes fubfift, and at other times not fubfift. In dif-
cuffing which fubject, I fhall in the firft place fhew, how this
fpecies of property may fubfift in fuch animals, as are *ferae naturae,* or of a wild nature ; and then, how it may fubfift in any
other things, when under particular circumftances.

F I R S T then, a man may be invefted with a qualified, but not
an abfolute, property in all creatures that are *ferae naturae,* either
per induftriam, propter impotentiam, or *propter privilegium.*

1. A QUALIFIED property may fubfift in animals *ferae
naturae, per induftriam hominis :* by a man's *reclaiming* and making them tame by art, induftry, and education ; or by fo con-
fining them within his own immediate power, that they cannot
efcape and ufe their natural liberty. And under this head fome
writers have ranked all the former fpecies of animals we have
mentioned, apprehending none to be originally and naturally
tame, but only made fo by art and cuftom : as, horfes, fwine,
and other cattle ; which, if originally left to themfelves, would
have chofen to rove up and down, feeking their food at large, and
are only made domeftic by ufe and familiarity, and are therefore,
fay they, called *manfueta, quafi manui affueta.* But however well
this notion may be founded, abftractedly confidered, our law apprehends the moft obvious diftinction to be, between fuch animals
as we generally fee tame, and are therefore feldom, if ever, found
wandering at large, which it calls *domitae naturae;* and fuch creatures

tures as are ufually found at liberty, which are therefore fuppofed to be more emphatically *ferae naturae*, though it may happen that the latter fhall be fometimes tamed and confined by the art and induftry of man. Such as are deer in a park, hares or rabbets in an enclofed warren, doves in a dovehoufe, pheafants or partridges in a mew, hawks that are fed and commanded by their owner, and fifh in a private pond or in trunks. Thefe are no longer the property of a man, than while they continue in his keeping or actual poffeffion : but, if at any time they regain their natural liberty, his property inftantly ceafes ; unlefs they have *animum revertendi*, which is only to be known by their ufual cuftom of returning [h]. A maxim which is borrowed from the civil law [i]; " *revertendi animum videntur definere habere tunc, cum revertendi* " *confuetudinem deferuerint.*" The law therefore extends this poffeffion farther than the mere manual occupation ; for my tame hawk that is purfuing his quarry in my prefence, though he is at liberty to go where he pleafes, is neverthelefs my property ; for he hath *animum revertendi*. So are my pigeons, that are flying at a diftance from their home (efpecially thofe of the carrier kind) and likewife the deer that is chafed out of my park or foreft, and is inftantly purfued by the keeper or forefter : all which remain ftill in my poffeffion, and I ftill preferve my qualified property in them. But if they ftray without my knowlege, and do not return in the ufual manner, it is then lawful for any ftranger to take them [k]. But if a deer, or any wild animal reclaimed, hath a collar or other mark put upon him, and goes and returns at his pleafure ; or if a wild fwan is taken, and marked and turned loofe in the river, the owner's property in him ftill continues, and it is not lawful for any one elfe to take him [l] : but otherwife, if the deer has been long abfent without returning, or the fwan leaves the neighbourhood. Bees alfo are *ferae naturae* ; but, when hived and reclaimed, a man may have a qualified property in them, by the law of nature, as well as by the civil law [m]. And to the fame purpofe, not to fay in the fame

h Bracton. *l.* 2. *c.* 1.　7 Rep. 17.　　　i Crompt. of courts. 167.　7 Rep. 16.
i *Inft.* 2. 1. 15.　　　　　　　　　m Puff. *l.* 4. *c.* 6. §. 5. *Inft.* 2. 1. 14.
k Finch. L. 177.

words,

words, with the civil law, fpeaks Bracton[a] : occupation, that is, hiving or including them, gives the property in bees; for, though a fwarm lights upon my tree, I have no more property in them till I have hived them, than I have in the birds which make their nefts thereon; and therefore if another hives them, he fhall be their proprietor : but a fwarm, which flie from and out of my hive, are mine fo long as I can keep them in fight, and have power to purfue them; and in thefe circumftances no one elfe is intitled to take them. But it hath been alfo faid[o], that with us the only ownerfhip in bees is *ratione foli*; and the charter of the foreft[p], which allows every freeman to be entitled to the honey found within his own woods, affords great countenance to this doctrine, that a qualified property may be had in bees, in confideration of the property of the foil whereon they are found.

In all thefe creatures, reclaimed from the wildnefs of their nature, the property is not abfolute, but defeafible : a property, that may be deftroyed if they refume their antient wildnefs, and are found at large. For if the pheafants efcape from the mew, or the fifhes from the trunk, and are feen wandering at large in their proper element, they become *ferae naturae* again; and are free and open to the firft occupant that has ability to feife them. But while they thus continue my qualified or defeafible property, they are as much under the protection of the law, as if they were abfolutely and indefeafibly mine : and an action will lie againft any man that detains them from me, or unlawfully deftroys them. It is alfo as much felony by common law to fteal fuch of them as are fit for food, as it is to fteal tame animals[q] : but not fo, if they are only kept for pleafure, curiofity, or whim, as dogs, bears, cats, apes, parrots, and finging birds[r]; becaufe their value is not intrinfic, but depending only on the caprice of the owner[s] : though it is fuch an invafion of property as may

---

[a] *l.* 2. *c.* 1. §. 3.
[o] Bro. *Abr. tit. Propertie.* 37. cites
43 Edw. III. 24.
[p] 9 Hen. III. c. 13.

[q] 1 Hal. P. C. 512.
[r] Lamb. Eiren. 275.
[s] 7 Rep. 18.   3 Inft. 109.

amount to a civil injury, and be redreſſed by a civil action[t]. Yet to ſteal a reclaimed hawk is felony both by common law and ſtatute[u]; which ſeems to be a relick of the tyranny of our antient ſportſmen. And, among our elder anceſtors the antient Britons, another ſpecies of reclaimed animals, *viz.* cats, were looked upon as creatures of intrinſic value; and the killing or ſtealing one was a grievous crime, and ſubjected the offender to a fine; eſpecially if it belonged to the king's houſhold, and were the *cuſtos horrei regii,* for which there was a very peculiar forfeiture[w]. And thus much of qualified property in wild animals, reclaimed *per induſtriam.*

2. A QUALIFIED property may alſo ſubſiſt with relation to animals *ferae naturae, ratione impotentiae,* on account of their own inability. As when hawks, herons, or other birds build in my trees, or coneys or other creatures make their neſts or burrows in my land, and have young ones there; I have a qualified property in thoſe young ones, till ſuch time as they can fly, or run away, and then my property expires[x]: but, till then, it is in ſome caſes treſpaſs, and in others felony, for a ſtranger to take them away[y]. For here, as the owner of the land has it in his power to do what he pleaſes with them, the law therefore veſts a property in him of the young ones, in the ſame manner as it does of the old ones if reclaimed and confined: for theſe cannot through weakneſs, any more than the others through reſtraint, uſe their natural liberty and forſake him.

3. A MAN may, laſtly, have a qualified property in animals *ferae naturae, propter privilegium:* that is, he may have the privilege of hunting, taking, and killing them, in excluſion of other

---

[t] Bro. *Abr. tit. Treſpaſs.* 407.

[u] 1 Hal. P. C. 512. 1 Hawk. P. C. c. 33.

[w] "*Si quis felem, horrei regii cuſtodem, oc-*
"*ciderit vel furto abſtulerit, felis ſumma cau-*
"*da ſuſpendatur, capite aream attingente, et in*
"*eam grana tritici effundantur, uſquedum ſum-*
"*mitas caudae tritico co-operiatur.*" Wotton.

LL. Wall. l. 3. *c.* 5. §. 5. An amercement ſimilar to which, ſir Edward Coke tells us (7 Rep. 18.) there antiently was for ſtealing ſwans; only ſuſpending them by the beak, inſtead of the tail.

[x] *Carta de foreſt.* 9 Hen. III. c. 13.

[y] 7 Rep. 17. Lamb. Eiren. 274.

perſons.

perſons. Here he has a tranſient property in theſe animals, uſually called game, ſo long as they continue within his liberty [r]; and may reſtrain any ſtranger from taking them therein : but the inſtant they depart into another liberty, this qualified property ceaſes. The manner, in which this privilege is acquired, will be ſhewn in a ſubſequent chapter.

T H E qualified property which we have hitherto conſidered, extends only to animals *ferae naturae*, when either reclaimed, impotent, or privileged. Many other things may alſo be the objects of qualified property. It may ſubſiſt in the very elements, of fire or light, of air, and of water. A man can have no abſolute permanent property in theſe, as he may in the earth or land ; ſince theſe are of a vague and fugitive nature, and therefore can admit only of a precarious and qualified ownerſhip, which laſts ſo long as they are in actual uſe and occupation, but no longer. If a man diſturbs another, and deprives him of the lawful enjoyment of theſe ; if one obſtructs another's antient windows [a], corrupts the air of his houſe or gardens [b], fouls his water [c], or unpens and lets it out, or if he diverts an antient watercourſe that uſed to run to the other's mill or meadow [d]; the law will animadvert hereon as an injury, and protect the party injured in his poſſeſſion. But the property in them ceaſes the inſtant they are out of poſſeſſion : for, when no man is engaged in their actual occupation, they become again common, and every man has an equal right to appropriate them to his own uſe.

T H E S E kinds of qualification in property depend upon the peculiar circumſtances of the ſubject matter, which is not capable of being under the abſolute dominion of any proprietor. But property may alſo be of a qualified or ſpecial nature, on account of the peculiar circumſtances of the owner, when the thing itſelf is very capable of abſolute ownerſhip. As in caſe of *bail-*

<hr/>

[z] Cro. Car. 554. Mar. 48. 5 Mod. 376.
1 2 Mod. 144.
[a] 9 Rep. 58.
[b] *Ibid.* 59 Lutw. 92.
[c] 9 Rep. 59.
[d] 1 Leon. 273. Skinn. 389.

ment,

ment, or delivery, of goods to another perfon for a particular ufe; as to a carrier to convey to London, to an innkeeper to fecure in his inn, or the like. Here there is no abfolute property in either the bailor or the bailee, the perfon delivering, or him to whom it is delivered : for the bailor hath only the right, and not the immediate poffeffion ; the bailee hath the poffeffion, and only a temporary right. But it is a qualified property in them both ; and each of them is entitled to an action, in cafe the goods be damaged or taken away : the bailee on account of his immediate poffeffion ; the bailor, becaufe the poffeffion of the bailee is, mediately, his poffeffion alfo[e]. So alfo in cafe of goods pledged or pawned upon condition, either to repay money or otherwife; both the pledgor and pledgee have a qualified, but neither of them an abfolute, property therein: the pledgor's property is conditional, and depends upon the performance of the condition of re-payment, &c; and fo too is that of the pledgee, which depends upon it's non-performance[f]. The fame may be faid of goods diftreined for rent, or other caufe of diftrefs : which are in the nature of a pledge, and are not, at the firft taking, the abfolute property of either the diftreinor, or party diftreined; but may be redeemed, or elfe forfeited, by the fubfequent conduct of the latter. But a fervant, who hath the care of his mafter's goods or chattels, as a butler of plate, a fhepherd of fheep, and the like, hath not any property or poffeffion either abfolute or qualified, but only a mere charge or overfight[g].

HAVING thus confidered the feveral divifions of property in *poffeffion*, which fubfifts there only, where a man hath both the right and alfo the occupation of the thing; we will proceed next to take a fhort view of the nature of property in *action*, or fuch where a man hath not the occupation, but merely a bare right to occupy the thing in queftion ; the poffeffion whereof may however be recovered by a fuit or action at law : from whence

[e] 1 Roll. Abr. 607.
[f] Cro. Jac. 245.

[g] 3 Inft. 108.

the

the thing fo recoverable is called a thing or *chofe, in action*[h]. Thus money due on a bond is a *chofe* in action; for a property in the debt vefts at the time of forfeiture mentioned in the obligation, but there is no poffeffion till recovered by courfe of law. If a man promifes, or covenants with me, to do any act, and fails in it, whereby I fuffer damage; the recompenfe for this damage is a *chofe* in action : for though a right to fome recompenfe vefts in me, at the time of the damage done, yet what and how large fuch recompenfe fhall be, can only be afcertained by verdict; and the poffeffion can only be given me by legal judgment and execution. In the former of thefe cafes the ftudent will obferve, that the property, or right of action, depends upon an *exprefs* contract or obligation to pay a ftated fum : and in the latter it depends upon an *implied* contract, that if the covenantor does not perform the act he engaged to do, he fhall pay me the damages I fuftain by his breach of covenant. And hence it may be collected, that all property in action depends entirely upon contracts, either exprefs or implied; which are the only regular means of acquiring a *chofe* in action, and of the nature of which we fhall difcourfe at large in a fubfequent chapter.

AT prefent we have only to remark, that upon all contracts or promifes, either exprefs or implied, and the infinite variety of cafes into which they are and may be fpun out, the law gives an action of fome fort or other to the party injured in cafe of nonperformance ; to compel the wrongdoer to do juftice to the party with whom he has contracted, and, on failure of performing the identical thing he engaged to do, to render a fatisfaction equivalent to the damage fuftained. But while the thing, or it's equivalent, remains in fufpenfe, and the injured party has only the right and not the occupation, it is called a *chofe* in action ; being a thing rather *in potentia* than *in effe :* though the owner may

---

[h] The fame idea, and the fame denomination, of property prevailed in the civil law. "*Rem in bon.: noftris habere intelligimur,* " quotiens ad reciperandam eam actionem habe- "*amus.*" (*Ff.* 41.1.52.) And again ; "*ae- " que bonis adnumerabitur etiam, fi quid eft in- " actionibus, petitionibus, perfecutionibus. Nam. " et haec in bonis effe videntur.*" (*Ff.* 50.16.49.)

have as abfolute a property of fuch things in action, as of things in poffeffion.

AND, having thus diftinguifhed the different *degree* or *quantity* of *dominion* or *property* to which things perfonal are fubject, we may add a word or two concerning the *time* of their *enjoyment*, and the *number* of their *owners*; in conformity to the method before obferved in treating of the property of things real.

FIRST, as to the *time* of *enjoyment*. By the rules of the antient common law, there could be no future property, to take place in expectancy, created in perfonal goods and chattels; becaufe, being things tranfitory, and by many accidents fubject to be loft, deftroyed, or otherwife impaired, and the exigencies of trade requiring alfo a frequent circulation thereof, it would occafion perpetual fuits and quarrels, and put a ftop to the freedom of commerce, if fuch limitations in remainder were *generally* tolerated and allowed. But yet in laft wills and teftaments fuch limitations of perfonal goods and chattels, in remainder after a bequeft for life, were permitted [i] : though originally that indulgence was only fhewn, when merely the *ufe* of the goods, and not the goods themfelves, was given to the firft legatee [k]; the property being fuppofed to continue all the time in the executor of the devifor. But now that diftinction is difregarded : and therefore if a man either by deed or will limits his books or furniture to A for life, with remainder over to B, this remainder is good. But, where an eftate-tail in things perfonal is given to the firft or any fubfequent poffeffor, it vefts in him the total property, and no remainder over fhall be permitted on fuch a limitation [m]. For this, if allowed, would tend to a perpetuity, as the devifee or grantee in tail of a chattel has no method of barring the entail ; and therefore the law vefts in him at once the entire dominion of the goods, being analogous to the fee-fimple which a tenant in tail may acquire in a real eftate.

[i] 1 Equ. Caf. abr. 360.
[k] Mar. 106.

[l] 2 Freem. 206.
[m] 1 P. Wms. 290.

NEXT,

NEXT, as to the *number* of *owners*. Things perfonal may belong to their owners, not only in feveralty, but alfo in joint-tenancy, and in common, as well as real eftates. They cannot indeed be vefted in coparcenary; becaufe they do not defcend from the anceftor to the heir, which is neceffary to conftitute coparceners. But if a horfe, or other perfonal chattel, be given to two or more, abfolutely, they are joint-tenants hereof; and, unlefs the jointure be fevered, the fame doctrine of furvivorfhip fhall take place as in eftates of lands and tenements [n]. And, in like manner, if the jointure be fevered, as by either of them felling his fhare, the vendee and the remaining part-owner fhall be tenants in common, without any *jus accrefcendi* or furvivorfhip [o]. So alfo if 100*l.* be given by will to two or more, *equally to be divided* between them, this makes them tenants in common [p]; as, we have formerly feen [p], the fame words would have done, in regard to real eftates. But, for the encouragement of hufbandry and trade, it is held that a ftock on a farm, though occupied jointly, and alfo a ftock ufed in a joint undertaking, by way of partnerfhip in trade, fhall always be confidered as common and not as joint property; and there fhall be no furvivorfhip therein [r].

---

[n] Litt. §. 282. 1 Vern. 482.
[o] Litt. §. 321.
[p] 1 Equ. Caf. abr. 292.

[q] pag. 193.
[r] 1 Vern. 217. Co. Litt. 182.

CHAPTER THE TWENTY SIXTH.

OF TITLE TO THINGS PERSONAL
BY OCCUPANCY.

WE are next to confider the *title* to things perfonal, or the various means of *acquiring*, and of *lofing*, fuch property as may be had therein: both which confiderations of gain and lofs fhall be blended together in one and the fame view, as was done in our obfervations upon real property; fince it is for the moft part impoffible to contemplate the one, without contemplating the other alfo. And thefe methods of acquifition or lofs are principally twelve: 1. By occupancy. 2. By prerogative. 3. By forfeiture. 4. By cuftom. 5. By fucceffion. 6. By marriage. 7. By judgment. 8. By gift. 9. By contract. 10. By bankruptcy. 11. By teftament. 12. By adminiftration.

AND, firft, a property in goods and chattels may be acquired by *occupancy:* which, we have more than once [a] remarked, was the original and only primitive method of acquiring any property at all; but which has fince been reftrained and abridged, by the pofitive laws of fociety, in order to maintain peace and harmony among mankind. For this purpofe, by the laws of England, gifts, and contracts, teftaments, legacies, and adminiftrations have been introduced and countenanced, in order to transfer and continue that property and poffeffion in things perfonal, which

[a] See pag. 3. 8. 258.

has

has once been acquired by the owner. And, where fuch things are found without any other owner, they for the moſt part belong to the king by virtue of his prerogative; except in fome few in- ſtances, wherein the original and natural right of occupancy is ſtill permitted to fubfiſt, and which we are now to confider.

1. THUS, in the firſt place, it hath been faid, that any body may feife to his own ufe fuch goods as belong to an alien enemy[b]. For fuch enemies, not being looked upon as members of our fo- ciety, are not entitled during their ſtate of enmity to the benefit or protection of the laws; and therefore every man that has op- portunity is permitted to feife upon their chattels, without being compelled as in other cafes to make reſtitution or fatisfaction to the owner. But this, however generally laid down by fome of our writers, muſt in reafon and juſtice be reſtrained to fuch cap- tors as are authorized by the public authority of the ſtate, refi- ding in the crown[c]; and to fuch goods as are brought into this country by an alien enemy, after a declaration of war, without a fafe-conduct or paſſport. And therefore it hath been held[d], that where a foreigner is refident in England, and afterwards a war breaks out between his country and ours, his goods are not liable to be feifed. It hath alfo been adjudged, that if an enemy take the goods of an Engliſhman, which are afterwards retaken by another fubject of this kingdom, the former owner ſhall lofe his property therein, and it ſhall be indefeafibly veſted in the fe- cond taker; unlefs they were retaken the fame day, and the owner before fun-fet puts in his claim of property[e]. Which is agree- able to the law of nations, as underſtood in the time of Grotius[f], even with regard to captures made at fea; which were held to be the property of the captors after a poſſeſſion of twenty four hours: though the modern authorities[g] require, that before the property can be changed, the goods muſt have been brought into

[b] Finch. L. 178.
[c] Freem. 40.
[d] Bro. *Abr. tit. propertie.* 38. *forfeiture.* 57.
[e] *Ibid.*

[f] *de j. b. & p. l.* 3. *c.* 6. § 3.
[g] Bynkerſh. *quaeſt. jur. publ. I.* 4. Rccc. *de. Aſſecur. not.* 66.

VOL. II.   C c c   port,

port, and have continued a night *intra praefidia*, in a place of safe cuftody, fo that all hope of recovering them is loft.

AND, as in the *goods* of an enemy, fo alfo in his *perfon*, a man may acquire a fort of qualified property, by taking him a prifoner in war[h]; at leaft till his ranfom be paid[j]. And this doctrine feems to have been extended to negro-fervants[i], who are purchafed, when captives, of the nations with whom they are at war, and continue therefore in fome degree the property of their mafters who buy them : though, accurately fpeaking, that property confifts rather in the perpetual *fervice*, than in the *body* or *perfon*, of the captive[k].

2. THUS again, whatever moveables are found upon the furface of the earth, or in the fea, and are unclaimed by any owner, are fuppofed to be abandoned by the laft proprietor ; and, as fuch, are returned into the common ftock and mafs of things : and therefore they belong, as in a ftate of nature, to the firft occupant or fortunate finder, unlefs they fall within the defcription of waifs, or eftrays, or wreck, or hidden treafure ; for thefe, we have formerly feen[l], are vefted by law in the king, and form a part of the ordinary revenue of the crown.

3. THUS too the benefit of the elements, the light, the air, and the water, can only be *appropriated* by occupancy. If I have an antient window overlooking my neighbour's ground, he may not erect any blind to obftruct the light : but if I build my houfe clofe to his wall, which darkens it, I cannot compel him to demolifh his wall ; for there the firft occupancy is rather in him, than in me. If my neighbour makes a tan-yard, fo as to annoy

---

[h] Bro. *Abr. tit. propertie.* 18.

[i] We meet with a curious writ of trefpafs in the regifter (102.) for breaking a man's houfe, and fetting fuch a prifoner at large. "*Quare domum ipfius A. apud W. (in* "*qua idem A. quendam H. Scotum per ipfum* "*A. de guerra captum tanquam prifonem fuum,* "*quoufque fibi de centum libris, per quas idem*

"*H. redemptionem fuam cum praefato A. pro* "*vita fua falvanda fecerat, fatisfactum foret,* "*detinuit) fregit, et ipfum H. cepit et abduxit,* "*vel quo voluit abire permifit, &c.*"

[l] 2 Lev. 201.

[k] Carth. 396. L[d] Raym. 147. Salk. 667.

[l] Book I. ch. 8.

and

and render lefs falubrious the air of my houfe or gardens, the law will furnifh me with a remedy; but if he is firft in poffeffion of the air, and I fix my habitation near him, the nufance is of my own feeking, and muft continue. If a ftream be unoccupied, I may erect a mill thereon, and detain the water; yet not fo as to injure my neighbour's prior mill, or his meadow : for he hath by the firft occupancy acquired a property in the current.

4. WITH regard likewife to animals *ferae naturae*, all mankind had by the original grant of the creator a right to purfue and take any fowl or infect of the air, any fifh or inhabitant of the waters, and any beaft or reptile of the field : and this natural right ftill continues in every individual, unlefs where it is reftrained by the civil laws of the country. And when a man has once fo feifed them, they become while living his *qualified* property, or, if dead, are *abfolutely* his own : fo that to fteal them, or otherwife invade this property, is, according to the refpective values, fometimes a criminal offence, fometimes only a civil injury. The reftrictions which are laid upon this right, by the laws of England, relate principally to royal fifh, as whale and fturgeon, and fuch terreftrial, aërial, or aquatic animals as go under the denomination of *game*; the taking of which is made the exclufive right of the prince, and fuch of his fubjects to whom he has granted the fame royal privilege. But thofe animals, which are not exprefsly fo referved, are ftill liable to be taken and appropriated by any of the king's fubjects, upon their own territories; in the fame manner as they might have taken even game itfelf, till thefe civil prohibitions were iffued: there being in nature no diftinction between one fpecies of wild animals and another, between the right of acquiring property in a hare or a fquirrel, in a partridge or a butterfly; but the difference, at prefent made, arifes merely from the pofitive municipal law.

5. TO this principle of occupancy alfo muft be referred the method of acquiring a fpecial perfonal property in corn growing on the ground, or other *emblements*, by any *poffeffor* of the land

who

who hath fown or planted it, whether he be owner of the inheritance in fee or in tail, or be tenant for life, for years, or at will : which emblements are diftinct from the real eftate in the land, and fubject to many, though not all, the incidents attending perfonal chattels. They were devifable by teftament before the ftatute of wills[m], and at the death of the owner fhall veft in his executor and not his heir : they are forfeitable by outlawry in a perfonal action[n] : and by the ftatute 11 Geo. II. c. 19. though not by the common law[o], they may be diftreined for rent arrere. The reafon for admitting the acquifition of this fpecial property, by tenants who have temporary interefts, was formerly given[p]; and it was extended to tenants in fee, principally for the benefit of their creditors : and therefore, though the emblements are affets in the hands of the executor, are forfeitable upon outlawry, and diftreinable for rent, they are not in other refpects confidered as perfonal chattels; and, particularly, they are not the object of larciny, before they are fevered from the ground[q].

6. T H E doctrine of property arifing from *acceffion* is alfo grounded on the right of occupancy. By the Roman law, if any given corporeal fubftance received afterwards an acceffion by natural or by artificial means, as by the growth of vegetables, the pregnancy of animals, the embroidering of cloth, or the converfion of wood or metal into veffels and utenfils, the original owner of the thing was intitled by his right of poffeffion to the property of it under fuch it's ftate of improvement[r] : but if the thing itfelf, by fuch operation, was changed into a different fpecies, as by making wine, oil, or bread, out of another's grapes, olives, or wheat, it belonged to the new operator; who was only to make a fatisfaction to the former proprietor for the materials, which he had fo converted[s]. And thefe doctrines are implicitly copied and adopted by our Bracton[t], in the reign of king Henry III; and have fince been confirmed by many refolutions of the

---

[m] Perk. §. 512.

[n] Bro. *Abr. tit. emblements.*21. 5 Rep. 116.

[o] 1 Roll. Abr. 666.

[p] pag. 122. 146.

[q] 3 Inft. 109.

[r] *Inft.* 2. 1. 25, 26, 31.   *Ff.* 6. 1. 5.

[s] *Inft.* 2. 1. 25, 34.

[t] *l.* 2. *c.* 2 & 3.

courts[u]. It hath even been held, that if one takes away another's wife or fon, and cloaths them, and afterwards the hufband or father retakes them back, the garments fhall ceafe to be the property of him who provided them, being now annexed to the perfon of the child or woman[w].

7. B u t in the cafe of *confufion* of goods, where thofe of two perfons are fo intermixed, that the feveral portions can be no longer diftinguifhed, the Englifh law partly agrees with, and partly differs from, the civil. If the intermixture be by confent, I apprehend that in both laws the proprietors have an intereft in common, in proportion to their refpective fhares[x]. But, if one wilfully intermixes his money, corn, or hay, with that of another man, without his approbation or knowlege, or cafts gold in like manner into another's melting-pot or crucible, the civil law, though it gives the fole property of the whole to him who has not interfered in the mixture, yet allows a fatisfaction to the other for what he has fo improvidently loft[y]. But our law, to guard againft fraud, allows no remedy in fuch a cafe; but gives the intire property, without any account, to him, whofe original dominion is invaded, and endeavoured to be rendered uncertain, without his own confent[z].

8. Th e r e is ftill another fpecies of property, which, being grounded on labour and invention, is more properly reducible to the head of occupancy than any other; fince the right of occupancy itfelf is fuppofed by Mr Locke[a], and many others[b], to be founded on the perfonal labour of the occupant. And this is the right, which an author may be fuppofed to have in his own original literary compofitions: fo that no other perfon without his leave may publifh or make profit of the copies. When a man by the exertion of his rational powers has produced an original work, he has clearly a right to difpofe of that identical work as

[u] Bro. *Abr. tit. propertie.* 23.   Moor. 20.
Poph. 38.
   [w] Moor. 214.
   [x] *Inft.* 2. 1. 27, 28.   1Vern. 217.

[y] *Inft.* 2. 1. 28.
[z] Poph. 38.   2 Bulftr. 325.   2Vern. 516.
[a] on Gov. part 2. ch. 5.
[b] See pag. 8.

he

he pleafes, and any attempt to take it from him, or vary the difpofition he has made of it, is an invafion of his right of property.
Now the identity of a literary compofition confifts intirely in the
fentiment and the *language*; the fame conceptions, cloathed in the
fame words, muft neceffarily be the fame compofition : and whatever method be taken of conveying that compofition to the ear
or the eye of another, by recital, by writing, or by printing, in
any number of copies or at any period of time, it is always the
identical work of the author which is fo conveyed; and no other
man can have a right to convey or transfer it without his confent,
either tacitly or expreflly given. This confent may perhaps be
tacitly given, when an author permits his work to be publifhed,
without any referve of right, and without ftamping on it any
marks of ownerfhip : it is then a prefent to the public, like the
building of a church, or the laying out a new highway : but,
in cafe of a bargain for a fingle impreffion, or a fale or gift of the
copyright, the reverfion is plainly continued in the original proprietor, or the whole property transferred to another.

T H E Roman law adjudged, that if one man wrote any thing,
though never fo elegantly, on the paper or parchment of another, the writing fhould belong to the original owner of the
materials on which it was written[c] : meaning certainly nothing
more thereby, than the mere mechanical operation of writing,
for which it directed the fcribe to receive a fatisfaction ; efpecially as, in works of genius and invention, fuch as a picture painted on another man's canvas, the fame law[d] gave the canvas to
the painter. We find no other mention in the civil law of any
property in the works of the underftanding, though the fale of
literary copies, for the purpofes of recital or multiplication, is
certainly as antient as the times of Terence[e], Martial[f], and
Statius[g]. Neither with us in England hath there been any direct
determination upon the right of authors at the common law.

---

[c] *Si in chartis membranifve tuis carmen vel*
hiftoriam vel orationem Titius fcripferit, hujus
corporis non Titius fed tu dominus effe videris.
Inft. 2. 1. 33.

[d] *Ibid.* §. 34.
[e] *Prol. in Eunuch.* 20.
[f] *Epigr.* i. 67. iv. 72. xiii. 3. xiv. 194.
[g] *Juv.* vii. 83.

But

But much may be gathered from the frequent injunctions of the court of chancery, prohibiting the invasion of this property: especially where either the injunctions have been *perpetual*[h], or have related to unpublished manuscripts[i], or to such antient books, as were not within the provisions of the statute of queen Anne[k]. Much may also be collected from the several legislative recognitions of copyrights[l]; and from those adjudged cases at common law, wherein the crown hath been considered as invested with certain prerogative copyrights[m]; for, if the crown is capable of an exclusive right in any one book, the subject seems also capable of having the same right in another.

BUT, exclusive of such copyright as may subsist by the rules of the common law, the statute 8 Ann. c. 19. hath protected by additional penalties the property of authors and their assigns for the term of fourteen years; and hath directed that if, at the end of that term, the author himself be living, the right shall then return to him for another term of the same duration: and a similar privilege is extended to the inventors of prints and engravings, for the term of fourteen years, by the statute 8 Geo. II. c. 13. Both which appear to have been copied from the exception in the statute of monopolies, 21 Jac. I. c. 3. which allows a royal patent of privilege to be granted for fourteen years to any inventor of a new manufacture, for the sole working or making of the same; by virtue whereof a temporary property becomes vested in the patentee[n].

[h] Knaplock v. Curl. 9 Nov. 1722. Viner Abr. *tit. Books.* pl. 3. — Baller v. Watson. 6 Dec. 1737.

[i] Webb v. Rose. 24 May 1732. — Pope v. Curl. 5 Jun. 1741.—Forrester v. Waller. 13 Jun 1741. — Duke of Queensberry v. Sheboeare. 31 July 1758.

[k] Knaplock v. Curl. before cited.—Eyre v. Walker. 9 Jun. 1735.—Motte v. Faulk-

ner. 28 Nov. 1735. —Walthoe v. Walker. 27 Jan. 1736.—Tonson v. Walker. 12 May 1739. and 30 Apr. 1752.

[l] *A. D.* 1649. c. 60. Scobell. 92. 13 & 14 Car. II. c. 33. 10 Ann. c. 19. §. 112. 5 Geo. III. c. 12. §. 26.

[m] Cart. 89. 1 Mod. 257. 4 Burr. 661.

[n] 1 Vern. 62.

CHAPTER THE TWENTY SEVENTH.

OF TITLE BY PREROGATIVE, AND FORFEITURE.

A SECOND method of acquiring property in perfonal chattels is by the *king's prerogative*: whereby a right may accrue either to the crown itfelf, or to fuch as claim under the title of the crown, as by grant or by prefcription.

SUCH in the firft place are all *tributes, taxes,* and *cuftoms;* whether conftitutionally inherent in the crown, as flowers of the prerogative and branches of the *cenfus regalis* or antient royal revenue, or whether they be occafionally created by authority of parliament; of both which fpecies of revenue we treated largely in the former volume. In thefe the king acquires and the fubject lofes a property the inftant they become due : if paid, they are a *chofe* in poffeffion ; if unpaid, a *chofe* in action. Hither alfo may be referred all forfeitures, fines, and amercements due to the king, which accrue by virtue of his antient prerogative, or by particular modern ftatutes : which revenues created by ftatute do always affimilate, or take the fame nature, with the antient revenues ; and may therefore be looked upon as arifing from a kind of artificial or fecondary prerogative. And, in either cafe, the owner of the thing forfeited, and the perfon fined or amerced, do lofe and part with the property of the forfeiture, fine, or amercement, the inftant the king or his grantee acquires it.

IN

I N thefe feveral methods of acquiring property by prerogative there is alfo this peculiar quality, that the king cannot have a *joint* property with any perfon in one entire chattel, or fuch a one as is not capable of divifion or feparation; but where the titles of the king and a fubject concur, the king fhall have the whole : in like manner as the king can, neither by grant nor contract, become a joint-tenant of a chattel real with another perfon[a]; but by fuch grant or contract fhall become intitled to the whole in feveralty. Thus, if a horfe be given to the king and a private perfon, the king fhall have the fole property : if a bond be made to the king and a fubject, the king fhall have the whole penalty; the debt or duty being one fingle chattel[b] : and fo, if two perfons have the property of a horfe between them, or have a joint debt owing them on bond, and one of them affigns his part to the king, or is attainted, whereby his moiety is forfeited to the crown; the king fhall have the entire horfe, and entire debt[c]. For, as it is not confiftent with the dignity of the crown to be partner with a fubject, fo neither does the king ever lofe his right in any inftance; but, where they interfere, his is always preferred to that of another perfon[d] : from which two principles it is a neceffary confequence, that the innocent, though unfortunate, partner muft lofe his fhare in both the debt and the horfe, or in any other chattel in the fame circumftances.

T H I S doctrine has no opportunity to take place in certain other inftances of title by prerogative, that remain to be mentioned; as the chattels thereby vefted are originally and folely vefted in the crown, without any transfer or derivative affignment either by deed or law from any former proprietor. Such is the acquifition of property in wreck, in treafure-trove, in waifs, in eftrays, in royal fifh, in fwans, and the like; which are not *transferred* to the fovereign from any former owner, but are ori-

---

[a] See pag. 184.
[b] Fitzh. *Abr. t. dette.* 38. Plowd. 243.
[c] Cro. Eliz. 263. Plowd. 323. Finch. Law. 178. 10 Mod. 245.
[d] Co. Litt. 30.

ginally *inherent* in him by the rules of law, and are derived to particular fubjects, as royal franchifes, by his bounty. Thefe are afcribed to him, partly upon the particular reafons mentioned in the eighth chapter of the former book; and partly upon the general principle of their being *bona vacantia,* and therefore vefted in the king, as well to preferve the peace of the public, as in truft to employ them for the fafety and ornament of the commonwealth.

WITH regard to the prerogative *copyrights,* which were mentioned in the preceding chapter, they are held to be vefted in the crown upon different reafons. Thus, 1. The king, as the executive magiftrate, has the right of promulging to the people all acts of ftate and government. This gives him the exclufive privilege of printing, at his own prefs, or that of his grantees, all *acts of parliament, proclamations,* and *orders of council.* 2. As fupreme head of the church, he hath a right to the publication of all *liturgies* and books of *divine fervice.* 3. He hath a right by purchafe to the copies of fuch *lawbooks, grammars,* and other compofitions, as were compiled or tranflated at the expenfe of the crown. And upon thefe two laft principles the exclufive right of printing the tranflation of the *bible* is founded. 4. *Almanacks* have been faid to be prerogative-copies, either as things derelict, or elfe as being fubftantially nothing more than the calendar prefixed to our liturgy[e]. And indeed the regulation of time has been often confidered as a matter of ftate. The Roman *fafti* were under the care of the pontifical college : and Romulus, Numa, and Julius Caefar, fucceffively regulated the Roman calendar.

THERE ftill remains another fpecies of prerogative property, founded upon a very different principle from any that have been mentioned before ; the property of fuch animals *ferae naturae,* as are known by the denomination of *game,* with the right of purfuing, taking, and deftroying them : which is vefted in the king alone, and from him derived to fuch of his fubjects as have

[e] 1 Mod. 257.

received

received the grants of a chafe, a park, a free warren, or free fifh-ery. This may lead us into an enquiry concerning the original of thefe franchifes, or royalties, on which we touched a little in a former chapter[f]; the right itfelf being an incorporeal hereditament, though the fruits and profits of it are of a perfonal nature.

I N the firft place then we have already fhewn, and indeed it cannot be denied, that by the law of nature every man, from the prince to the peafant, has an equal right of purfuing, and taking to his own ufe, all fuch creatures as are *ferae naturae,* and therefore the property of nobody, but liable to be feifed by the firft occupant. And fo it was held by the imperial law, even fo late as Juftinian's time : *" ferae igitur beftiae, et volucres, et " omnia animalia quae mari, coelo, et terra nafcuntur, fimul atque " ab aliquo capta fuerint, jure gentium ftatim illius effe incipiunt. " Quod enim nullius eft, id naturali ratione occupanti conceditur* [g]." But it follows from the very end and conftitution of fociety, that this natural right, as well as many others belonging to man as an individual, may be reftrained by pofitive laws enacted for reafons of ftate, or for the fuppofed benefit of the community. This reftriction may be either with refpect to the *place* in which this right may, or may not, be exercifed ; with refpect to the *animals* that are the fubject of this right ; or with refpect to the *perfons* allowed or forbidden to exercife it. And, in confequence of this authority, we find that the municipal laws of many nations have exerted fuch power of reftraint ; have in general forbidden the entering on another man's grounds, for any caufe, without the owner's leave ; have extended their protection to fuch particular animals as are ufually the objects of purfuit ; and have invefted the prerogative of hunting and taking fuch animals in the fovereign of the ftate only, and fuch as he fhall autho-rize [h]. Many reafons have concurred for making thefe conftitu-tions : as, 1. For the encouragement of agriculture and improve-ment of lands, by giving every man an exclufive dominion over

[f] pag. 38, 39.
[g] *Inft.* 2. 1. 12.
[h] Puff. L. N. l. 4. c. 6. §. 5.

his own foil. 2. For prefervation of the feveral fpecies of thefe animals, which would foon be extirpated by a general liberty. 3. For prevention of idlenefs and diffipation in hufbandmen, artificcrs, and others of lower rank; which would be the unavoidable confequence of univerfal licence. 4. For preventing of popular infurrections and refiftance to the government, by difarming the bulk of the people[i]: which laft is a reafon oftener meant, than avowed, by the makers of foreft or game laws. Nor, certainly, in thefe prohibitions is there any *natural* injuftice, as fome have weakly enough fuppofed: fince, as Puffendorf obferves, the law does not hereby take from any man his prefent property, or what was already his own, but barely abridges him of one means of acquiring a future property, that of occupancy; which indeed the law of nature would allow him, but of which the laws of fociety have in moft inftances very juftly and reafonably deprived him.

YET, however defenfible thefe provifions in general may be, on the footing of reafon, or juftice, or civil policy, we muft notwithftanding acknowlege that, in their prefent fhape, they owe their immediate original to flavery. It is not till after the irruption of the northern nations into the Roman empire, that we read of any other prohibitions, than that natural one of not fporting on any private grounds without the owner's leave; and another of a more fpiritual nature, which was rather a rule of ecclefiaftical difcipline, than a branch of municipal law. The Roman or civil law, though it knew no reftriction as to *perfons* or *animals*, fo far regarded the article of *place*, that it allowed no man to hunt or fport upon another's ground, but by confent of the owner of the foil. " *Qui alienum fundum ingreditur, venandi aut aucu-* " *pandi gratia, poteft a domino prohiberi ne ingrediatur*[k]." For if there can, by the law of nature, be any inchoate imperfect property fuppofed in wild animals before they are taken, it feems moft reafonable to fix it in him upon whofe land they are found. And as to the other reftriction, which relates to *perfons* and not

[i] Warburton's alliance. 324.   [k] *Inft.* 2. 1. §. 12.

to

to *place*, the pontificial or canon law[1] interdicts "*venationes, et* "*fylvaticas vagationes cum canibus, et accipitribus*" to all *clergymen* without diftinction ; grounded on a faying of St. Jerom[m], that it never is recorded that thefe diverfions were ufed by the faints, or primitive fathers. And the canons of our Saxon church, pub-lifhed in the reign of king Edgar[n], concur in the fame pro-hibition : though our fecular laws, at leaft after the conqueft, did even in the times of popery difpenfe with this canonical im-pediment ; and fpiritual perfons were allowed by the common law to hunt for their recreation, in order to render them fitter for the performance of their duty : as a confirmation whereof we may obferve, that it is to this day a branch of the king's prerogative, at the death of every bifhop, to have his kennel of hounds, or a compofition in lieu thereof[o].

BUT, with regard to the rife and original of our prefent civil prohibitions, it will be found that all foreft and game laws were introduced into Europe at the fame time, and by the fame po-licy, as gave birth to the feodal fyftem ; when thofe fwarms of barbarians iffued from their northern hive, and laid the founda-tion of moft of the prefent kingdoms of Europe, on the ruins of the weftern empire. For when a conquering general came to fettle the oeconomy of a vanquifhed country, and to part it out among his foldiers or feudatories, who were to render him mili-tary fervice for fuch donations ; it behoved him, in order to fe-cure his new acquifitions, to keep the *ruftici* or natives of the country, and all who were not his military tenants, in as low a condition as poffible, and efpecially to prohibit them the ufe of arms. Nothing could do this more effectually than a prohibition of hunting and fporting : and therefore it was the policy of the conqueror to referve this right to himfelf, and fuch on whom he fhould beftow it ; which were only his capital feudatories, or greater barons. And accordingly we find, in the feudal conftitu-tions[p], one and the fame law prohibiting the *ruftici* in general

---

[1] *Decretal. l.* 5. *tit.* 24. *c.* 2.
[m] *Decret. part.* 1. *dift.* 34. *l.* 1.
[a] *cap.* 64.

[o] 4 Inft. 309.
[p] *Feud. l.* 2. *tit.* 27. §. 5.

from

from carrying arms, and alſo proſcribing the uſe of nets, ſnares, or other engines for deſtroying the game. This excluſive privilege well ſuited the martial genius of the conquering troops, who delighted in a ſport[q] which in it's purſuit and ſlaughter bore ſome reſemblance to war. *Vita omnis,* (ſays Caeſar, ſpeaking of the antient Germans) *in venationibus atque in ſtudiis rei militaris conſiſtit*[r]. And Tacitus in like manner obſerves, that *quotiens bella non ineunt, multum venatibus, plus per otium tranſigunt*[s]. And indeed, like ſome of their modern ſucceſſors, they had no other amuſement to entertain their vacant hours ; they deſpiſing all arts as effeminate, and having no other learning, than was couched in ſuch rude ditties, as were ſung at the ſolemn carouſals which ſucceeded theſe antient huntings. And it is remarkable that, in thoſe nations where the feodal policy remains the moſt uncorrupted, the foreſt or game laws continue in their higheſt rigor. In France all game is properly the king's ; and in ſome parts of Germany it is death for a peaſant to be found hunting in the woods of the nobility[t].

WITH us in England alſo, hunting has ever been eſteemed a moſt princely diverſion and exerciſe. The whole iſland was repleniſhed with all ſorts of game in the times of the Britons ; who lived in a wild and paſtoral manner, without incloſing or improving their grounds, and derived much of their ſubſiſtence from the chaſe, which they all enjoyed in common. But when huſbandry took place under the Saxon government, and lands began to be cultivated, improved, and encloſed, the beaſts naturally fled into the woody and deſart tracts ; which were called the foreſts, and, having never been diſpoſed of in the firſt diſtribution of lands, were therefore held to belong to the crown. Theſe were filled with great plenty of game, which our royal ſportſ-

---

^q In the laws of Jenghiz Khan, founder of the Mogul and Tartarian empire, publiſhed *A. D.* 1205. there is one which prohibits the killing of all game from March to October ; that the court and ſoldiery might find plenty enough in the winter, during their receſs from war. (Mod. Univ. Hiſt. iv. 468.)

^r *De bell. Gall. l.* 6. *c.* 20.

^s *c.* 15.

^t Mattheus *de Crimin. c.* 3. *tit.* 1. Carpzov. *Practic. Saxonic. p.* 2. *c.* 84.

men

men referved for their own diverfion, on pain of a pecuniary forfeiture for fuch as interfered wtih their fovereign. But every
freeholder had the full liberty of fporting upon his own territories, provided he abftained from the king's forefts : as is fully
expreffed in the laws of Canute[v], and of Edward the confeffor[u];
" *fit quilibet homo dignus venatione fua, in fylva, et in agris, fibi*
" *propriis, et in dominio fuo : et abftineat omnis homo a venariis re-*
" *gis, ubicunque pacem eis habere voluerit :*" which indeed was the
antient law of the Scandinavian continent, from whence Canute
probably derived it. " *Cuique enim in proprio fundo quamlibet fe-*
" *ram quoquo modo venari permiffum[w].*"

HOWEVER, upon the Norman conqueft, a new doctrine took
place ; and the right of purfuing and taking all beafts of chafe
or *venary*, and fuch other animals as were accounted *game*, was
then held to belong to the king, or to fuch only as were authorized under him. And this, as well upon the principles of the
feodal law, that the king is the ultimate proprietor of all the
lands in the kingdom, they being all held of him as the chief
lord, or lord paramount of the fee ; and that therefore he has
the right of the univerfal foil, to enter thereon, and to chafe
and take fuch creatures at his pleafure : as alfo upon another
maxim of the common law, which we have frequently cited and
illuftrated, that thefe animals are *bona vacantia*, and, having no
other owner, belong to the king by his prerogative. As therefore the former reafon was held to veft in the king a *right* to
purfue and take them any where ; the latter was fuppofed to
give the king, and fuch as he fhould authorize, a *fole* and *ex-*
clufive right.

THIS right, thus newly vefted in the crown, was exerted
with the utmoft rigor, at and after the time of the Norman eftablifhment ; not only in the antient forefts, but in the new ones
which the conqueror made, by laying together vaft tracts of

[v] c. 77.   [w] Stiernhook. *de jure Sueon. l.* 2. *c.* 8.
[u] c. 36.

country,

country, depopulated for that purpofe, and referved folely for the king's royal diverfion ; in which were exercifed the moft horrid tyrannies and oppreffions, under colour of foreft law, for the fake of preferving the beafts of chafe; to kill any of which, within the limits of the foreft, was as penal as the death of a man. And, in purfuance of the fame principle, king John laid a total interdict upon the *winged* as well as the *fourfooted* creation: " *capturam avium per totam Angliam interdixit*[x]." The cruel and infupportable hardfhips, which thefe foreft laws created to the fubject, occafioned our anceftors to be as zealous for their refor-mation, as for the relaxation of the feodal rigors and the other exactions introduced by the Norman family; and accordingly we find the immunities of *carta de forefta* as warmly contended for, and extorted from the king with as much difficulty, as thofe of *magna carta* itfelf. By this charter, confirmed in parliament[y], many forefts were difafforefted, or ftripped of their oppreffive privileges, and regulations were made in the regimen of fuch as remained ; particularly[z] killing the king's deer was made no lon-ger a capital offence, but only punifhed by fine, imprifonment, or abjuration of the realm. And by a variety of fubfequent fta-tutes, together with the long acquiefcence of the crown without exerting the foreft laws, this prerogative is now become no lon-ger a grievance to the fubject.

BUT, as the king referved to himfelf the *forefts* for his own exclufive diverfion, fo he granted out from time to time other tracts of land to his fubjects under the names of *chafes* or *parks*[a]; or gave them licence to make fuch in their own grounds; which indeed are fmaller forefts, in the hands of a fubject, but not go-verned by the foreft laws : and by the common law no perfon is at liberty to take or kill any beafts of chafe, but fuch as hath an antient chafe or park ; unlefs they be alfo beafts of prey.

[x] M. Paris. 303.
[y] 9 *Hen. III.*
[z] *cap.* 10.
[a] See pag. 38.

As

As to all inferior fpecies of game, called beafts and fowls of warren, the liberty of taking or killing them is another franchife or royalty, derived likewife from the crown, and called *free warren*; a word, which fignifies prefervation or cuftody : as the exclufive liberty of taking and killing fifh in a public ftream or river is called a *free fifhery*; of which however no new franchife can at prefent be granted, by the exprefs provifion of *magna carta, c.* 16 [b]. The principal intention of granting a man thefe franchifes or liberties was in order to protect the game, by giving him a fole and exclufive power of killing it himfelf, provided he prevented other perfons. And no man, but he who has a chafe or free warren, by grant from the crown, or prefcription which fuppofes one, can juftify hunting or fporting upon another man's foil; nor indeed, in thorough ftrictnefs of common law, either hunting or fporting at all.

However novel this doctrine may feem, it is a regular confequence from what has been before delivered; that the fole right of taking and deftroying game belongs exclufively to the king. This appears, as well from the hiftorical deduction here made, as becaufe he may grant to his fubjects an exclufive right of taking them; which he could not do, unlefs fuch a right was firft inherent in himfelf. And hence it will follow, that no perfon whatever, but he who has fuch derivative right from the crown, is by common law entitled to take or kill any beafts of chafe, or other game whatfover. It is true, that by the acquiefcence of the crown, the frequent grants of free warren in antient times, and the introduction of new penalties of late by certain ftatutes for preferving the game, this exclufive prerogative of the king is little known or confidered; every man, that is exempted from thefe modern penalties, looking upon himfelf as at liberty to do what he pleafes with the game : whereas the contrary is ftrictly true, that no man, however well *qualified* he may vulgarly be efteemed, has a right to encroach on the royal

[b] Mirr. c. 5. §. 2. See pag. 39.

prerogative by the killing of game, unlefs he can fhew a particular grant of free warren ; or a prefcription, which prefumes a grant; or fome authority under an act of parliament. As for the latter, I know but of two inftances wherein an exprefs permiffion to kill game was ever given by ftatute ; the one by 1 Jac. I. c. 27. altered by 7 Jac. I. c. 11. and virtually repealed by 22 & 23 Car. II. c. 25. which gave authority, fo long as they remained in force, to the owners of free warren, to lords of manors, and to all freeholders having 40 *l. per annum* in lands of inheritance, or 80 *l.* for life or lives, or 400 *l.* perfonal eftate, (and their fervants) to take partridges and pheafants upon their own, or their mafter's, free warren, inheritance, or freehold : the other by 5 Ann. c. 14. which empowers lords and ladies of manors to appoint gamekeepers to kill game for the ufe of fuch lord or lady ; which with fome alterations ftill fubfifts, and plainly fuppofes fuch power not to have been in them before. The truth of the matter is, that thefe game laws (of which we fhall have occafion to fpeak again in the fourth book of thefe commentaries) do indeed *qualify* nobody, except in the inftance of a gamekeeper, to kill game : but only, to fave the trouble and formal procefs of an action by the perfon injured, who perhaps too might remit the offence, thefe ftatutes inflict *additional* penalties, to be recovered either in a regular or fummary way, by any of the king's fubjects, from certain perfons of inferior rank who may be found offending in this particular. But it does not follow that perfons, excufed from thefe additional penalties, are therefore *authorifed* to kill game. The circumftances, of having 100 *l. per annum,* and the reft, are not properly qualifications, but exemptions. And thefe perfons, fo exempted from the penalties of the game ftatutes, are not only liable to actions of trefpafs by the owners of the land ; but alfo, if they kill game within the limits of any royal franchife, they are liable to the actions of fuch who may have the right of chafe or free warren therein.

UPON

UPON the whole it appears, that the king, by his prerogative, and such persons as have, under his authority, the royal franchises of chase, park, free warren, or free fishery, are the *only* persons, who may acquire any property, however fugitive and transitory, in these animals *ferae naturae*, while living; which is said to be vested in them, as was observed in a former chapter, *propter privilegium*. And it must also be remembered, that such persons as may thus lawfully hunt, fish, or fowl, *ratione privilegii*, have (as has been said) only a qualified property in these animals; it not being absolute or permanent, but lasting only so long as the creatures remain within the limits of such respective franchise or liberty, and ceasing the instant they voluntarily pass out of it. It is held indeed, that if a man starts any game within his own grounds, and follows it into another's, and kills it there, the property remains in himself[c]. And this is grounded on reason and natural justice[d]: for the property consists in the possession; which possession commences by the finding it in his own liberty, and is continued by the immediate pursuit. And so, if a stranger starts game in one man's chase or free warren, and hunts it into another liberty, the property continues in the owner of the chase or warren; this property arising from privilege[e], and not being changed by the act of a mere stranger. Or if a man starts game on another's private grounds and kills it there, the property belongs to him in whose ground it was killed, because it was also started there[f]; this property arising *ratione soli*. Whereas if, after being started there, it is killed in the grounds of a third person, the property belongs not to the owner of the first ground, because the property is local; nor yet to the owner of the second, because it was not started in his soil; but it vests in the person who started and killed it[g], though guilty of a trespass against both the owners.

<hr />

[c] 11 Mod. 75.
[d] Puff. L. N. l. 4. c. 6.
[e] Lord Raym. 251.

[f] *Ibid.*
[g] Farr. 18. Lord Raym. *ibid.*

III. I PROCEED now to a third method, whereby a title to goods and chattels may be acquired and loft, *viz.* by *forfeiture;* as a punifhment for fome crime or mifdemefnor in the party forfeiting, and as a compenfation for the offence and injury committed againft him to whom they are forfeited. Of forfeitures, confidered as the means whereby *real* property might be loft and acquired, we treated in a former chapter [h]. It remains therefore in this place only to mention, by what means or for what offences goods and chattels become liable to forfeiture.

IN the variety of penal laws with which the fubject is at prefent incumbered, it were a tedious and impracticable tafk to reckon up the various forfeitures, inflicted by fpecial ftatutes, for particular crimes and mifdemefnors : fome of which are *mala in fe,* or offences againft the divine law, either natural or revealed; but by far the greateft part are *mala prohibita,* or fuch as derive their guilt merely from their prohibition by the laws of the land : fuch as is the forfeiture of 40 *s. per* month by the ftatute 5 Eliz. c. 4. for exercifing a trade without having ferved feven years as an apprentice thereto; and the forfeiture of 10 *l.* by 9 Ann. c. 23. for printing an almanac without a ftamp. I fhall therefore confine myfelf to thofe offences only, by which *all* the goods and chattels of the offender are forfeited : referring the ftudent for fuch, where pecuniary mulcts of different quantities are inflicted, to their feveral proper heads, under which very many of them have been or will be mentioned; or elfe to the collections of Hawkins and Burn, and other laborious compilers. Indeed, as moft of thefe forfeitures belong to the crown, they may feem as if they ought to have been referred to the preceding method of acquiring perfonal property, namely, by prerogative. But as, in the inftance of partial forfeitures, a moiety often goes to the informer, the poor, or fometimes to other perfons; and as one total forfeiture, namely that by a bankrupt who is guilty of felony by

[h] See pag. 267.

concealing

concealing his effects, accrues entirely to his creditors, I have therefore made it a diftinct head of transferring property.

Goods and chattels then are totally forfeited by conviction of *high treafon,* or *mifprifion* of treafon; of *petit treafon;* of *felony* in general, and particularly of *felony de fe,* and of *manflaughter;* nay even by conviction of *excufable homicide*[1]; by *outlawry* for treafon or felony; by conviction of *petit larceny;* by *flight* in treafon or felony, even though the party be acquitted of the fact; by *flanding mute,* when arraigned of felony; by *drawing a weapon on a judge,* or *ftriking* any one *in the prefence of the king's courts;* by *praemunire;* by *pretended prophecies,* upon a fecond conviction; by *owling;* by the *refiding abroad* of artificers; and by *challenging to fight* on account of money won at gaming. All thefe offences, as will more fully appear in the fourth book of thefe commentaries, induce a total forfeiture of goods and chattels.

And this forfeiture commences from the time of *conviction,* not the time of committing the fact, as in forfeitures of real property. For chattels are of fo vague and fluctuating a nature, that to affect them, by any relation back, would be attended with more inconvenience than in the cafe of landed eftates : and part, if not the whole of them, muft be expended in maintaining the delinquent, between the time of committing the fact and his conviction. Yet a fraudulent conveyance of them, to defeat the intereft of the crown, is made void by ftatute 13 Eliz. c. 5.

[1] Co. Litt. 391   2 Inft. 316.   3 Inft. 320.

C H A P T E R   T H E   T W E N T Y   E I G H T H.

O F   T I T L E   B Y   CUSTOM.

A FOURTH method of acquiring property in things perfonal, or chattels, is by *cuſtom :* whereby a right veſts in ſome particular perſons, either by the local uſage of ſome particular place, or by the almoſt general and univerſal uſage of the kingdom. It were endleſs, ſhould I attempt to enumerate all the ſeveral kinds of ſpecial cuſtoms, which may entitle a man to a chattel intereſt in different parts of the kingdom : I ſhall therefore content myſelf with making ſome obſervations on three ſorts of cuſtomary intereſts, which obtain pretty generally throughout moſt parts of the nation, and are therefore of more univerſal concern ; viz. *heriots, mortuaries,* and *heir-looms.*

1. H E R I O T S, which were ſlightly touched upon in a former chapter[a], are uſually divided into two ſorts, heriot-*ſervice,* and heriot-*cuſtom.* The former are ſuch as are due upon a ſpecial reſervation in a grant or leaſe of lands, and therefore amount to little more than a mere rent[b] : the latter ariſe upon no ſpecial reſervation whatſoever, but depend merely upon immemorial uſage and cuſtom[c]. Of theſe therefore we are here principally to ſpeak : and they are defined to be a cuſtomary tribute of goods and chattels, payable to the lord of the fee on the deceaſe of the owner of the land.

[a] pag. 97.
[b] 2 Saund. 166.
[c] Co. Cop. §. 24.

T H E

THE firſt eſtabliſhment, if not introduction, of compulſory heriots into England, was by the Danes : and we find in the laws of king Canute[d] the ſeveral *heregeates* or heriots ſpecified, which were then exacted by the king on the death of divers of his ſubjects, according to their reſpective dignities ; from the higheſt *eorle* down to the moſt inferior *thegne* or landholder. Theſe, for the moſt part, conſiſted in arms, horſes, and habiliments of war ; which the word itſelf, according to ſir Henry Spelman[e], ſignifies. Theſe were delivered up to the ſovereign on the death of the vaſal, who could no longer uſe them, to be put into other hands for the ſervice and defence of the country. And upon the plan of this Daniſh eſtabliſhment did William the conqueror faſhion his law of reliefs, as was formerly obſerved[f] ; when he aſcertained the preciſe relief to be taken of every tenant in chivalry, and, contrary to the feodal cuſtom and the uſage of his own duchy of Normany, required arms and implements of war to be paid inſtead of money[g].

THE Daniſh compulſive heriots, being thus tranſmuted into reliefs, underwent the ſame ſeveral viciſſitudes as the feodal tenures, and in ſocage eſtates do frequently remain to this day, in the ſhape of a double rent payable at the death of the tenant : the heriots which now continue among us, and preſerve that name, ſeeming rather to be of Saxon parentage, and at firſt to have been merely diſcretionary[h]. Theſe are now for the moſt part confined to copyhold tenures, and are due by cuſtom only, which is the life of all eſtates by copy ; and perhaps are the only inſtance where cuſtom has favoured the lord. For this payment was originally a voluntary donation, or gratuitous legacy of the tenant ; perhaps in acknowlegement of his having been raiſed a degree above villenage, when all his goods and chattels were quite at the mercy of the lord : and cuſtom, which has on the

[d] *c.* 69.
[e] of feuds. c. 18.
[f] pag. 65.

[g] *LL. Guil. Conqu. c* 22, 23, 24.
[h] Lambard. Peramb. of Kent. 492.

one hand confirmed the tenant's intereſt in excluſion of the lord's will, has on the other hand eſtabliſhed this diſcretional piece of gratitude into a permanent duty. An heriot may alſo appertain to free land, that is held by ſervice and ſuit of court; in which caſe it is moſt commonly a copyhold enfranchiſed, whereupon the heriot is ſtill due by cuſtom. Braćton[1] ſpeaks of heriots as frequently due on the death of both ſpecies of tenants : " *eſt* " *quidem alia praeſtatio quae nominatur heriettum; ubi tenens, liber* " *vel ſervus, in morte ſua dominum ſuum, de quo tenuerit, reſpicit* " *de meliori averio ſuo, vel de ſecundo meliori, ſecundum diverſam lo-* " *corum conſuetudinem."* And this, he adds, " *magis fit de gratia* " *quam de jure;"* in which Fleta[k] and Britton[l] agree : thereby plainly intimating the original of this cuſtom to have been merely voluntary, as a legacy from the tenant ; though now the immemorial uſage has eſtabliſhed it as of right in the lord.

T H I S heriot is ſometimes the beſt live beaſt, or *averium*, which the tenant dies poſſeſſed of, (which is particularly denominated the villein's relief in the twenty ninth law of king William the conqueror) ſometimes the beſt inanimate good, under which a jewel or piece of plate may be included : but it is always a *perſonal* chattel, which, immediately on the death of the tenant who was the owner of it, being aſcertained by the option of the lord[m], becomes veſted in him as his property ; and is no charge upon the lands, but merely on the goods and chattels. The tenant muſt be the owner of it, elſe it cannot be due ; and therefore on the death of a feme-covert no heriot can be taken ; for ſhe can have no ownerſhip in things perſonal[n]. In ſome places there is a cuſtomary compoſition in money, as ten or twenty ſhillings in lieu of a heriot, by which the lord and tenant are both bound, if it be an indiſputably antient cuſtom : but a new compoſition of this ſort will not bind the repreſentatives of either party ; for that amounts to the creation of a new cuſtom, which is now impoſſible[o].

[l] *l. 2. c. 36. §. 9.*
[k] *l 3. c. 18.*
[l] *c. 69.*

[m] Hob. 60.
[n] Keilw. 84. 4 Leon. 239.
[o] Co. Cop. §. 31.

2. Mor-

2. MORTUARIES are a fort of ecclefiaftical heriots, being
a cuftomary gift claimed by and due to the minifter in very many
parifhes on the death of his parifhioners. They feem originally
to have been, like lay heriots, only a voluntary bequeft to the
church; being intended, as Lyndewode informs us from a conftitution of archbifhop Langham, as a kind of expiation and
amends to the clergy for the perfonal tithes, and other ecclefiaftical duties, which the laity in their life-time might have neglected or forgotten to pay. For this purpofe, *after* [p] the lord's
heriot or beft good was taken out, the fecond beft chattel was
referved to the church as a mortuary : "*fi decedens plura habuerit*
"*animalia, optimo cui de jure fuerit debitum refervato, ecclefiae fuae*
"*fine dolo, fraude, feu contradictione qualibet, pro recompenfatione*
"*fubtractionis decimarum perfonalium, necnon et oblationum, fecun-*
"*dum melius animal refervetur, poft obitum, pro falute animae fuae* [q]."
And therefore in the laws of king Canute [r] this mortuary is called
foul-fcot (ᵹaplᵹceaꞇ) or *fymbolum animae*. And, in purfuance of
the fame principle, by the laws of Venice, where no perfonal
tithes have been paid during the life of the party, they are paid
at his death out of his merchandize, jewels, and other moveables [s]. So alfo, by a fimilar policy, in France, every man that
died without bequeathing a part of his eftate to the church,
which was called *dying without confeffion*, was formerly deprived
of chriftian burial : or, if he died inteftate, the relations of the
deceafed, jointly with the bifhop, named proper arbitrators to
determine what he ought to have given to the church, in cafe
he had made a will. But the parliament, in 1409, redreffed
this grievance [t].

IT was antiently ufual in this kingdom to bring the mortuary
to church along with the corpfe when it came to be buried; and
thence [u] it is fometimes called a *corfe-prefent :* a term, which

---

[p] Co. Litt. 185. [s] Panormitan. *ad Decretal. l.*3. *t.*20. *c.*32.
[q] *Provinc. l* 1. *tit.*3. [t] Sp. L. b.28. c. 41.
[r] c. 13. [u] Selden. hift. of tithes. c. 10.

befpeaks it to have been once a voluntary donation. However in Bracton's time, fo early as Henry III, we find it rivetted into an eftablifhed cuftom : infomuch that the bequefts of heriots and mortuaries were held to be neceffary ingredients in every teftament of chattels. *" Imprimis autem debet quilibet, qui teftamentum " fecerit, dominum fuum de meliori re quam habuerit recognofcere ; " et poftea ecclefiam de alia meliori :"* the lord muft have the beft good left him as an heriot ; and the church the fecond beft as a mortuary. But yet this cuftom was different in different places : *" in quibufdam locis habet ecclefia melius animal de confuetudine ; in " quibufdam fecundum, vel tertium melius ; et in quibufdam nihil : " et ideo confideranda eft confuetudo loci* [w].*"* This cuftom ftill varies in different places, not only as to the mortuary to be paid, but the perfon to whom it is payable. In Wales, a mortuary or corfeprefent was due upon the death of every clergyman to the bifhop of the diocefe ; till abolifhed, upon a recompenfe given to the bifhop, by the ftatute 12 Ann. ft. 2. c. 6. And in the archdeaconry of Chefter a cuftom alfo prevailed, that the bifhop, who is alfo archdeacon, fhould have at the death of every clergyman dying therein, his beft horfe or mare, bridle, faddle, and fpurs, his beft gown or cloak, hat, upper garment under his gown, and tippet, and alfo his beft fignet or ring [x]. But by ftatute 28 Geo. II. c. 6. this mortuary is directed to ceafe, and the act has fettled upon the bifhop an equivalent in it's room. The king's claim to many goods, on the death of all prelates in England, feems to be of the fame nature; though fir Edward Coke [y] apprehends, that this is a *duty due upon death* and not a *mortuary :* a diftinction which feems to be without a difference. For not only the king's ecclefiaftical character, as fupreme ordinary, but alfo the fpecies of the goods claimed, which bear fo near a refemblance to thofe in the archdeaconry of Chefter, which was an acknowleged mortuary, puts the matter out of difpute. The king, according to the record vouched by fir Edward Coke, is entitled to fix things ; the bifhop's beft horfe or palfrey, with his furniture : his cloak,

---

[w] Bracton. *l.* 2. *c.* 26. Flet. *l.* 2. *c.* 57.   [y] 2 Inft. 491.
[x] Cro. Car. 237.

or

or gown, and tippet : his cup, and cover : his baſon, and ewer :
his gold ring : and, laſtly, his *muta canum*, his mew or kennel
of hounds; as was mentioned in the preceding chapter[z].

THIS variety of cuſtoms, with regard to mortuaries, giving
frequently a handle to exactions on the one ſide, and frauds or
expenſive litigations on the other; it was thought proper by ſtatute 21 Hen. VIII. c. 6. to reduce them to ſome kind of certainty.
For this purpoſe it is enacted, that all mortuaries, or corſe-preſents
to parſons of any pariſh, ſhall be taken in the following manner;
unleſs where by cuſtom leſs or none at all is due : viz. for every
perſon who does not leave goods to the value of ten marks, nothing : for every perſon who leaves goods to the value of ten
marks, and under thirty pounds, 3*s*. 4*d*. if above thirty pounds,
and under forty pounds, 6*s*. 8*d*. if above forty pounds, of what
value ſoever they may be, 10*s*. and no more. And no mortuary
ſhall throughout the kingdom be paid for the death of any feme-
covert; nor any child; nor for any one of full age, that is not
a houſekeeper; nor for any wayfaring man; but ſuch wayfaring
man's mortuary ſhall be paid in the pariſh to which he belongs.
And upon this ſtatute ſtands the law of mortuaries to this day.

3. HEIR-LOOMS are ſuch goods and perſonal chattels, as, contrary to the nature of chattels, ſhall go by ſpecial cuſtom to the
heir along with the inheritance, and not to the executor of the
laſt proprietor. The termination, *loom*, is of Saxon original; in
which language it ſignifies a limb or member[a]; ſo that an heir-
loom is nothing elſe, but a limb or member of the inheritance.
They are generally ſuch things as cannot be taken away without
damaging or diſmembering the freehold; otherwiſe the general
rule is, that no chattel intereſt whatſoever ſhall go to the heir,
notwithſtanding it be expreſſly limited to a man and his heirs,
but ſhall veſt in the executor[b]. But deer in a real authorized
park, fiſhes in a pond, doves in a dove-houſe, *&c*, though in

[z] pag. 413.   [b] Co. Litt. 388.
[a] Spelm. *Gloſſ.* 277.

them-

themfelves perfonal chattels, yet they are fo annexed to and fo neceffary to the well-being of the inheritance, that they fhall accompany the land wherever it vefts, by either defcent or pur-chafe[c]. For this reafon alfo I apprehend it is, that the antient jewels of the crown are held to be heir-looms[d] : for they are neceffary to maintain the ftate, and fupport the dignity, of the fovereign for the time being. Charters likewife, and deeds, court-rolls, and other evidences of the land, together with the chefts in which they are contained, fhall pafs together with the land to the heir, in the nature of heir-looms, and fhall not go to the executor[e]. By fpecial cuftom alfo, in fome places, carriages, utenfils, and other houfehold implements may be heir-looms[f]; but fuch cuftom muft be ftrictly proved. On the other hand, by almoft general cuftom, whatever is ftrongly affixed to the free-hold or inheritance, and cannot be fevered from thence without violence or damage, " *quod ab aedibus non facile revellitur*[g]," is become a member of the inheritance, and fhall thereupon pafs to the heir; as marble chimney-pieces, pumps, old fixed or dor-mant tables, benches, and the like[h]. A very fimilar notion to which prevails in the duchy of Brabant ; where they rank cer-tain things moveable among thofe of the immoveable kind, call-ing them, by a very peculiar appellation, *praedia volantia*, or vo-latile eftates : fuch as beds, tables, and other heavy implements of furniture, which (as an author of their own obferves) " *dig-*
" *nitatem iftam nacta funt, ut villis, fylvis, et aedibus, aliifque prae-*
" *diis, comparentur ; quod folidiora mobilia ipfis aedibus ex deftina-*
" *tione patrisfamilias cohaerere videantur, et pro parte ipfarum ae-*
" *dium aeftimentur*[i]."

OTHER perfonal chattels there are, which alfo defcend to the heir in the nature of heir-looms, as a monument or tombftone in a church, or the coat-armor of his anceftor there hung up,

[c] Co Litt. 8.
[d] *Ibid.* 18.
[e] Bro. *Abr. tit. chatteles.* 18.
[f] Co. Litt. 18. 185.
[g] Spelm. *Gloff.* 277.
[h] 12 Mod. 520.
[i] Stockmans *de jure devolutionis. c.* 3. §. 16.

with

with the pennons and other enfigns of honor, fuited to his degree. In this cafe, albeit the freehold of the church is in the
parfon, and thefe are annexed to that freehold, yet cannot the
parfon or any other take them away or deface them, but is liable
to an action from the heir [k]. Pews in the church are fomewhat
of the fame nature, which may defcend by cuftom immemorial
(without any ecclefiaftical concurrence) from the anceftor to the
heir [l]. But though the heir has a property in the monuments
and efcutcheons of his anceftors, yet he has none in their bodies
or afhes ; nor can he bring any civil action againft fuch as inde-
cently at leaft, if not impioufly, violate and difturb their remains,
when dead and buried. The parfon indeed, who has the freehold of the foil, may bring an action of trefpafs againft fuch as
dig and difturb it : and, if any one in taking up a dead body
fteals the fhrowd or other apparel, it will be felony [m]; for the
property thereof remains in the executor, or whoever was at the
charge of the funeral.

BUT to return to heir-looms : thefe, though they be mere
chattels, yet cannot be devifed away from the heir by will; but
fuch a devife is void [n], even by a tenant in fee-fimple. For, though
the owner might during his life have fold or difpofed of them, as
he might of the timber of the eftate, fince as the inheritance
was his own, he might mangle or difmember it as he pleafed ;
yet, they being at his death inftantly vefted in the heir, the devife (which is fubfequent, and not to take effect till *after* his
death) fhall be poftponed to the cuftom, whereby they have already defcended.

---

[k] 12 Rep. 105. Co. Litt. 18.
[l] 3 Inft. 202. 12 Rep. 105.

[m] 3 Inft. 110. 12 Rep. 113. 1 Hal. P. C.
515.
[n] Co. Litt. 185.

CHAPTER THE TWENTY NINTH.

Of TITLE by SUCCESSION, MARRIAGE, and JUDGMENT.

I N the prefent chapter we fhall take into confideration three
other fpecies of title to goods and chattels.

V. T H E fifth method therefore of gaining a property in chattels, either perfonal or real, is by *fucceffion:* which is, in ftrictnefs of law, only applicable to corporations aggregate of many,
as dean and chapter, mayor and commonalty, mafter and fellows,
and the like; in which one fet of men may, by fucceeding another fet, acquire a property in all the goods, moveables, and
other chattels of the corporation. The true reafon whereof is,
becaufe in judgment of law a corporation never dies; and
therefore the predeceffors, who lived a century ago, and their
fucceffors now in being, are one and the fame body corporate ª.
Which identity is a property fo inherent in the nature of a body
politic, that, even when it is meant to give any thing to be taken
in fucceffion by fuch a body, that fucceffion need not be expreffed; but the law will of itfelf imply it. So that a gift to fuch a
corporation, either of lands or of chattels, without naming their
fucceffors, vefts an abfolute property in them fo long as the corporation fubfifts ᵇ. And thus a leafe for years, an obligation, a

ª 4 Rep. 65.   ᵇ Bro. *Abr. t. eftates.* 90. Cro. Eliz. 464.

jewel,

jewel, a flock of fheep, or other chattel intereft, will veft in the fucceffors, by fucceffion, as well as in the identical members, to whom it was originally given.

But, with regard to fole corporations, a confiderable diftinction muft be made. For if fuch fole corporation be the reprefentative of a number of perfons; as the mafter of an hofpital, who is a corporation for the benefit of the poor brethren; an abbot, or prior, by the old law before the reformation, who reprefented the whole convent; or the dean of fome antient cathedrals, who ftands in the place of, and reprefents in his corporate capacity, the chapter; fuch fole corporations as thefe have in this refpect the fame powers, as corporations aggregate have, to take perfonal property or chattels in fucceffion. And therefore a bond to fuch a mafter, abbot, or dean, and his fucceffors, is good in law; and the fucceffor fhall have the advantage of it, for the benefit of the aggregate fociety, of which he is in law the reprefentative[c]. Whereas in the cafe of fole corporations, which reprefent no others but themfelves, as bifhops, parfons, and the like, no chattel intereft can regularly go in fucceffion : and therefore, if a leafe for years be made to the bifhop of Oxford and his fucceffors, in fuch cafe his executors or adminiftrators, and not his fucceffors, fhall have it[d]. For the word *fucceffors*, when applied to a perfon in his politic capacity, is equivalent to the word *heirs* in his natural : and as fuch a leafe for years, if made to John and his heirs, would not veft in his heirs, but his executors; fo, if it be made to John bifhop of Oxford and his fucceffors, who are the heirs of his body politic, it fhall ftill veft in his executors and not in fuch his fucceffors. The reafon of this is obvious : for, befides that the law looks upon goods and chattels as of too low and perifhable a nature to be limited either to heirs, or fuch fucceffors as are equivalent to heirs; it would alfo follow, that if any fuch chattel intereft (granted to a fole corporation and his fucceffors) were allowed to defcend to fuch fucceffor, the property thereof muft be in abeyance from the death of the prefent owner

---

[c] Dyer. 48. Cro. Eliz. 464.   [d] Co. Litt. 46.

until

until the fucceffor be appointed : and this is contrary to the nature of a chattel intereft, which can never be in abeyance or without an owner ᶜ ; but a man's right therein, when once fufpended, is gone for ever. This is not the cafe in corporations aggregate, where the right is never in fufpence ; nor in the other fole corporations before-mentioned, who are rather to be confidered as heads of an aggregate body, than fubfifting merely in their own right : the chattel intereft therefore, in fuch a cafe, is really and fubftantially vefted in the hofpital, convent, chapter, or other aggregate body; though the head is the vifible perfon in whofe name every act is carried on, and in whom every intereft is therefore faid (in point of form) to veft. But the general rule, with regard to corporations merely fole, is this, that no chattel can go or be acquired by right of fucceffion ᶠ.

YE T to this rule there are two exceptions. One in the cafe of the king, in whom a chattel may veft by a grant of it formerly made to a preceding king and his fucceffors ᵍ. The other exception is, where, by a *particular* cuftom, fome *particular* corporations fole have acquired a power of taking *particular* chattel interefts in fucceffion. And this cuftom, being againft the general tenor of the common law, muft be ftrictly interpreted, and not extended to any other chattel interefts than fuch immemorial ufage will ftrictly warrant. Thus the chamberlain of London, who is a corporation fole, may by the cuftom of London take *bonds* and *recognizances* to himfelf and his fucceffors, for the benefit of the orphan's fund ʰ : but it will not follow from thence, that he has a capacity to take a *leafe for years* to himfelf and his fucceffors for the fame purpofe ; for the cuftom extends not to that : nor that he may take a *bond* to himfelf and his fucceffors, for any other purpofe than the benefit of the orphan's fund ; for that alfo is not warranted by the cuftom. Wherefore, upon the whole, we may clofe this head with laying down this general rule ; that fuch right of fucceffion to chattels is univerfally inhe-

ᶜ Brownl. 132.
ᶠ Co. Litt. 46.

ᵍ *Ibid.* 90.
ʰ 4 Rep. 65. Cro. Eliz. 682.

rent

rent by the common law in all aggregate corporations, in the king, and in such single corporations as represent a number of persons; and may, by special custom, belong to certain other sole corporations for some particular purposes: although, generally, in sole corporations no such right can exist.

VI. A s i x t h method of acquiring property in goods and and chattels is by *marriage*; whereby those chattels, which belonged formerly to the wife, are by act of law vested in the husband, with the same degree of property and with the same powers, as the wife, when sole, had over them.

Th i s depends entirely on the notion of an unity of person between the husband and wife; it being held that they are one person in law [i], so that the very being and existence of the woman is suspended during the coverture, or entirely merged and incorporated in that of the husband. And hence it follows, that whatever personal property belonged to the wife, before marriage, is by marriage absolutely vested in the husband. In a real estate he only gains a title to the rents and profits during coverture: for that, depending upon feodal principles, remains entire to the wife after the death of her husband, or to her heirs, if she dies before him; unless, by the birth of a child, he becomes tenant for life by the curtesy. But, in chattel interests, the sole and absolute property vests in the husband, to be disposed of at his pleasure, if he chuses to take possession of them: for, unless he reduces them to possession, by exercising some act of ownership upon them, no property vests in him, but they shall remain to the wife, or to her representatives, after the coverture is determined.

Th e r e is therefore a very considerable difference in the acquisition of this species of property by the husband, according to the subject-matter; viz. whether it be a chattel *real*, or a

i See Book I. c. 15.

chattel *perſonal*; and, of chattels perſonal, whether it be in *poſſeſſion*, or in *aɛɛion* only. A *chattel real* veſts in the huſband, not abſolutely, but *ſub modo*. As, in caſe of a leaſe for years; the huſband ſhall receive all the rents and profits of it, and may, if he pleaſes, ſell, ſurrender, or diſpoſe of it during the coverture[k] : if he be outlawed or attainted, it ſhall be forfeited to the king[l]: it is liable to execution for his debts[m] : and, if he ſurvives his wife, it is to all intents and purpoſes his own[n]. Yet if he has made no diſpoſition thereof in his lifetime, and dies before his wife, he cannot diſpoſe of it by will[o] : for, the huſband having made no alteration in the property during his life, it never was transferred from the wife; but after his death ſhe ſhall remain in her antient poſſeſſion, and it ſhall not go to his executors. So it is alſo of chattels perſonal (or *choſes*) in *aɛɛion*; as debts upon bond, contraɛts, and the like : theſe the huſband may have if he pleaſes; that is, if he reduces them into poſſeſſion by receiving or recovering them at law. And, upon ſuch receipt or recovery, they are abſolutely and entirely his own; and ſhall go to his executors or adminiſtrators, or as he ſhall bequeath them by will, and ſhall not reveſt in the wife. But, if he dies before he has recovered or reduced them into poſſeſſion, ſo that at his death they ſtill continue *choſes in aɛɛion*, they ſhall ſurvive to the wife; for the huſband never exerted the power he had of obtaining an excluſive property in them[p]. And ſo, if an eſtray comes into he wife's franchiſe, and the huſband ſeiſes it, it is abſolutely his property : but, if he dies without ſeiſing it, his executors are not now at liberty to ſeiſe it, but the wife or her heirs[q]; for the huſband never exerted the right he had, which right determined with the coverture. Thus in both theſe ſpecies of property the law is the ſame, in caſe the wife ſurvives the huſband ; but, in caſe the huſband ſurvives the wife, the law is very different with reſpeɛ to *chattels real* and *choſes in aɛɛion* :

k Co. Litt. 46.
l Plowd. 263.
m Co. Litt. 351.
n Ibid. 300.

o Poph. 5. Co. Litt. 351.
p Co. Litt. 351.
q Ibid.

for

for he fhall have the *chattel real* by furvivorfhip, but not the
chofe in action[r]; except in the cafe of arrears of rent, due to the
wife before her coverture, which in cafe of her death are given
to the hufband by ftatute 32 Hen.VIII. c. 37. And the reafon
for the general law is this : that the hufband is in abfolute poffeffion of the *chattel real* during the coverture, by a kind of
joint-tenancy with his wife; wherefore the law will not wreft it
out of his hands, and give it to her reprefentatives : though in
cafe he had died firft, it would have furvived to the wife, unlefs
he thought proper in his lifetime to alter the poffeffion. But a
chofe in action fhall not furvive to him, becaufe he never was in
poffeffion of it at all, during the coverture; and the only method
he had to gain poffeffion of it, was by fuing in his wife's right :
but as, after her death, he cannot (as hufband) bring an action
in her right, becaufe they are no longer one and the fame perfon
in law, therefore he can never (as fuch) recover the poffeffion.
But he ftill will be intitled to be her adminiftrator; and may, in
that capacity, recover fuch things in action as became due to
her before or during the coverture.

THUS, and upon thefe reafons, ftands the law between hufband and wife, with regard to *chattels real,* and *chofes in action:*
but, as to *chattels perfonal* (or *chofes*) *in poffeffion,* which the wife
hath in her own right, as ready money, jewels, houfehold goods,
and the like, the hufband hath therein an immediate and abfolute property, devolved to him by the marriage, not only potentially but in fact, which never can again reveft in the wife or her
reprefentative[s].

AND, as the hufband may thus, generally, acquire a property
in all the perfonal fubftance of the wife, fo in one particular inftance the wife may acquire a property in fome of her hufband's
goods; which fhall remain to her after his death, and fhall not go
to his executors. Thefe are called her *paraphernalia*; which is

[r] 3 Mod. 186.   [s] Co. Litt. 351.

a term

a term borrowed from the civil law [t], and is derived from the Greek language, fignifying fomething over and above her dower. Our law ufes it to fignify the apparel and ornaments of the wife, fuitable to her rank and degree; which fhe becomes entitled to at the death of her hufband over and above her jointure or dower, and preferably to all other reprefentatives : and the jewels of a peerefs, ufually worn by her, have been held to be *parapherna-lia* [w]. Neither can the hufband devife by his will fuch ornaments and jewels of his wife; though during his life perhaps he hath the power (if unkindly inclined to exert it) to fell them or give them away [x]. But if fhe continues in the ufe of them till his death, fhe fhall afterwards retain them againft his executors and adminiftrators, and all other perfons, except creditors where there is a deficiency of affets [y]. And her neceffary apparel is protected even againft the claim of creditors [z].

VII. A JUDGMENT, in confequence of fome fuit or action in a court of juftice, is frequently the means of vefting the right and property of chattel interefts in the prevailing party. And here we muft be careful to diftinguifh between property, the *right* of which is before vefted in the party, and of which only *poffef-fion* is recovered by fuit or action; and property, to which a man before had no determinate title or certain claim, but he gains as well the right as the poffeffion by the procefs and judgment of the law. Of the former fort are all debts and *chofes in action*; as if a man gives bond for 20 *l*, or agrees to buy a horfe at a ftated fum, or takes up goods of a tradefman upon an implied contract to pay as much as they are reafonably worth : in all thefe cafes the right accrues to the creditor, and is completely vefted in him at the time of the bond being fealed, and the contract or agreement made; and the law only gives him a remedy to reco-

[t] *Ff*. 23. 3. 9. §. 3.
[s] Cro. Car. 343.   1 Roll. Abr. 911.
2 Leon. 166.
[w] Moor. 213.

[x] Noy's Max. c. 49. — Grahme v. Lord Londonderry. 24 Nov. 1746. Canc.
[y] 1 P. W[m]. 730.
[z] Noy. *ibid*.

ver

ver the poffeffion of that right, which already in juftice belongs to him.   But there is alfo a fpecies of property to which a man has not any claim or title whatfoever, till after fuit commenced and judgment obtained in a court of law :   where the right and the remedy do not follow each other, as in common cafes, but accrue at one and the fame time ; and where, before judgment had, no man can fay that he has any abfolute property, either in poffeffion or in action.   Of this nature are,

1. S u c h penalties as are given by particular ftatutes, to be recovered on an action *popular*; or, in other words, to be recovered by him or them that will fue for the fame.   Such as the penalty of 500 *l*, which thofe perfons are by feveral acts of parliament made liable to forfeit, that, being in particular offices or fituations in life, neglect to take the oaths to the government; which penalty is given to him or them that will fue for the fame.   Now here it is clear that no particular perfon, A or B, has any right, claim, or demand, in or upon this penal fum, till after action brought[a]; for he that brings his action and can *bona fide* obtain judgment firft, will undoubtedly fecure a title to it, in exclufion of every body elfe.   He obtains an inchoate imperfect degree of property, by commencing his fuit ; but it is not confummated till judgment, for if any collufion appears, he lofes the priority he had gained[b].   But, otherwife, the right fo attaches in the firft informer, that the king (who before action brought may grant a pardon which fhall be a bar to all the world) cannot after fuit commenced remit any thing but his own part of the penalty[c].   For by commencing the fuit the informer has made the popular action his own private action, and it is not in the power of the crown, or of any thing but parliament, to releafe the informer's intereft.   This therefore is one inftance, where a fuit and judgment at law are not only the means of re-

[a] 2 Lev. 141. Stra. 1169. Combe v.   [b] Stat. 4 Hen. VII. c. 20.
Pitt. B. R. T. 3 Geo. III.   [c] Cro. Eliz. 138. 11 Rep. 65.

covering,

covering, but alfo of acquiring, property. And what is faid of this one penalty is equally true of all others, that are given thus at large to a common informer, or to any perfon that will fue for the fame. They are placed as it were in a ftate of nature, acceffible by all the king's fubjects,. but the acquired right of none of them : open therefore to the firft occupant, who declares his intention to poffefs them by bringing his action ; and who carries that intention into execution, by obtaining judgment to recover them.

2. A N O T H E R fpecies of property, that is acquired and loft by fuit and judgment at law, is that of *damages* given to a man by a jury, as a compenfation and fatisfaction for fome injury fuftained ; as for a battery, for imprifonment, for flander, or for trefpafs. Here the plaintiff has no certain demand till after verdict ; but, when the jury has affeffed his damages, and judgment is given thereupon, whether they amount to twenty pounds or twenty fhillings, he inftantly acquires, and the defendant lofes at the fame time, a right to that fpecific fum. It is true, that this is not an acquifition fo perfectly original as in the former inftance : for here the injured party has unqueftionably a vague and indeterminate right to fome damages or other, the inftant he receives the injury ; and the verdict of the jurors, and judgment of the court thereupon, do not in this cafe fo properly veft a *new* title in him, as fix and afcertain the *old* one ; they do not *give*, but *define*, the right. But however, though ftrictly fpeaking the primary right to a fatisfaction for injuries is given by the law of nature, and the fuit is only the means of afcertaining and recovering that fatisfaction ; yet, as the legal proceedings are the only vifible means of this acquifition of property, we may fairly enough rank fuch damages, or fatisfaction affeffed, under the head of property acquired by fuit and judgment at law.

3. H I T H E R

3. HITHER alfo may be referred, upon the fame principle, all title to cofts and expenfes of fuit; which are often arbitrary, and reft entirely in the determination of the court, upon weighing all circumftances, both as to the *quantum*, and alfo (in the courts of equity efpecially, and upon motions in the courts of law) whether there fhall be any cofts at all. Thefe cofts therefore, when given by the court to either party, may be looked upon as an acquifition made by the judgment of law.

CHAPTER THE THIRTIETH.

Of TITLE by GIFT, GRANT, and CONTRACT.

W E are now to proceed, according to the order marked out, to the difcuffion of two of the remaining methods of acquiring a title to property in things perfonal, which are much connected together, and anfwer in fome meafure to the conveyances of real eftates; being thofe by *gift* or *grant*, and by *contract*: whereof the former vefts a property in *poffeffion*, the latter a property in *action*.

VIII. G I F T S then, or *grants*, which are the eighth method of transferring perfonal property, are thus to be diftinguifhed from each other, that *gifts* are always gratuitous, *grants* are upon fome confideration or equivalent: and they may be divided, with regard to their fubject-matter, into gifts or grants of chattels *real*, and gifts or grants of chattels *perfonal*. Under the head of gifts or grants of chattels *real* may be included all leafes for years of land, affignments, and furrenders of thofe leafes; and all the other methods of conveying an eftate lefs than freehold, which were confidered in the twentieth chapter of the prefent book, and therefore need not be here again repeated: though thefe very feldom carry the outward appearance of a gift, however freely beftowed; being ufually expreffed to be made in confideration of blood, or natural affection, or of five or ten fhillings nominally paid to the grantor; and, in cafe of leafes, always referving a rent, though it be but a peppercorn: any of which confiderations will, in the eye of the law, convert the gift, if executed, into a grant; if not executed, into a contract.

G R A N T S

GRANTS or gifts, of chattels *perfonal*, are the act of tranf-
ferring the right and the poffeffion of them; whereby one man
renounces, and another man immediately acquires, all title and
intereft therein : which may be done either in writing, or by
word of mouth [a] attefted by fufficient evidence, of which the
delivery of poffeffion is the ftrongeft and moft effential. But this
conveyance, when merely voluntary, is fomewhat fufpicious : and
is ufually conftrued to be fraudulent, if creditors or others become
fufferers thereby. And, particularly, by ftatute 3 Hen.VII. c. 4.
all deeds of gift of goods, made in truft to the ufe of the donor,
fhall be void; becaufe otherwife perfons might be tempted to
commit treafon or felony, without danger of forfeiture; and the
creditors of the donor might alfo be defrauded of their rights.
And by ftatute 13 Eliz. c. 5. every grant or gift of chattels, as
well as lands, with intent to defraud creditors or others [b], fhall
be void as againft fuch perfons to whom fuch fraud would be prejudicial; but, as againft the grantor himfelf, fhall ftand good and
effectual : and all perfons partakers in, or privy to, fuch fraudulent grants, fhall forfeit the whole value of the goods, one moiety
to the king, and another moiety to the party grieved; and alfo on
conviction fhall fuffer imprifonment for half a year.

A TRUE and proper gift or grant is always accompanied with
delivery of poffeffion, and takes effect immediately; as if A gives
to B 100*l*, or a flock of fheep, and puts him in poffeffion of them
directly, it is then a gift executed in the donee; and it is not in
the donor's power to retract it; though he did it without any
confideration or recompenfe [c] : unlefs it be prejudicial to creditors; or the donor were under any legal incapacity, as infancy,
coverture, durefs, or the like; or if he were drawn in, circum-
vented, or impofed upon, by falfe pretences, ebriety, or furprize.
But if the gift does not take effect, by delivery of immediate
poffeffion, it is then not properly a gift, but a contract : and this

[a] Perk. §. 57.
[b] See 3 Rep. 82.
[c] Jenk. 109.

a man cannot be compelled to perform, but upon good and fufficient confideration; as we fhall fee under our next divifion.

IX. A CONTRACT, which ufually conveys an intereft merely in action, is thus defined : " an agreement, upon fufficient con- " fideration, to do or not to do a particular thing." From which definition there arife three points to be contemplated in all contracts ; 1. The *agreement:* 2. The *confideration:* and 3. The *thing* to be done or omitted, or the different fpecies of contracts.

FIRST then it is an *agreement,* a mutual bargain or convention ; and therefore there muft at leaft be two contracting parties, of fufficient ability to make a contract : as where A contracts with B to pay him 100 *l.* and thereby transfers a property in fuch fum to B. Which property is however not in poffeffion, but in action merely, and recoverable by fuit at law ; wherefore it could not be transferred to another perfon by the ftrict rules of the antient common law : for no *chofe* in action could be affigned or granted over [d], becaufe it was thought to be a great encouragement to litigioufnefs, if a man were allowed to make over to a ftranger his right of going to law. But this nicety is now difregarded : though, in compliance with the antient principle, the form of affigning a *chofe* in action is in the nature of a declaration of truft, and an agreement to permit the affignee to make ufe of the name of the affignor, in order to recover the poffeffion. And therefore, when in common acceptation a debt or bond is faid to be affigned over, it muft ftill be fued in the original creditor's name ; the perfon, to whom it is transferred, being rather an attorney than an affignee. But the king is an exception to this general rule; for he might always either grant or receive a *chofe* in action by affignment [e]: and our courts of equity, confidering that in a commercial country almoft all perfonal property muft neceffarily lie in contract, will protect the affignment of a *chofe* in action, as much as the law will that of a *chofe* in poffeffion [f].

[d] Co. Litt. 214.

[e] Dyer. 30. Bro. *Abr. tit. chofe in action.*

1 & 4.

[f] 3 P. W^mʳ. 199.

THIS

THIS contract or agreement may be either exprefs or implied. *Exprefs* contracts are where the terms of the agreement are openly uttered and avowed at the time of the making, as to deliver an ox, or ten load of timber, or to pay a ftated price for certain goods. *Implied* are fuch as reafon and juftice dictate, and which therefore the law prefumes that every man undertakes to perform. As, if I employ a perfon to do any bufinefs for me, or perform any work; the law implies that I undertook, or contracted, to pay him as much as his labour deferves. If I take up wares from a tradefman, without any agreement of price, the law concludes that I contracted to pay their real value. And there is alfo one fpecies of implied contracts, which runs through and is annexed to all other contracts, conditions, and covenants; *viz.* that if I fail in my part of the agreement, I fhall pay the other party fuch damages as he has fuftained by fuch my neglect or refufal. In fhort, almoft all the rights of perfonal property (when not in actual poffeffion) do in great meafure depend upon contracts of one kind or other, or at leaft might be reduced under fome of them: which indeed is the method taken by the civil law; it having referred the greateft part of the duties and rights, which it treats of, to the head of obligations *ex contractu* and *quafi ex contractu*[s].

A CONTRACT may alfo be either *executed*, as if A agrees to change horfes with B, and they do it immediately; in which cafe the poffeffion and the right are transferred together: or it may be *executory*, as if they agree to change next week; here the right only vefts, and their reciprocal property in each other's horfe is not in poffeffion but in action: for a contract *executed* (which differs nothing from a grant) conveys a *chofe in poffeffion*; a contract *executory* conveys only a *chofe in action*.

HAVING thus fhewn the general nature of a contract, we are, *fecondly*, to proceed to the *confideration* upon which it is founded; or the reafon which moves the party contracting to enter into

[s] *Inft.* 3. 14. 2.

the

the contract. "It is an agreement, upon *fufficient confideration*." The civilians hold, that in all contracts, either exprefs or implied, there muft be fomething given in exchange, fomething that is mutual or reciprocal [h]. This thing, which is the price or motive of the contract, we call the confideration: and it muft be a thing lawful in itfelf, or elfe the contract is void. A *good* confideration, we have before feen [i], is that of blood or natural affection between near relations; the fatisfaction accruing from which the law efteems an equivalent for whatever benefit may move from one relation to another [j]. This confideration may fometimes however be fet afide, and the contract become void, when it tends in it's confequences to defraud creditors or other third perfons of their juft rights. But a contract for *any valuable* confideration, as for marriage, for money, for work done, or for other reciprocal contracts, can never be impeached at law; and, if it be of a fufficient adequate value, is never fet afide in equity: for the perfon contracted with has then given an equivalent in recompenfe, and is therefore as much an owner, or a creditor, as any other perfon.

THESE valuable confiderations are divided by the civilians [k] into four fpecies. 1. *Do, ut des:* as when I give money or goods, on a contract that I fhall be repaid money or goods for them again. Of this kind are all loans of money upon bond, or promife of repayment; and all fales of goods, in which there is either an exprefs contract to pay fo much for them, or elfe the law implies a contract to pay fo much as they are worth. 2. The fecond fpecies is, *facio, ut facias:* as when I agree with a man to do his work for him, if he will do mine for me; or if two perfons agree to marry together; or to do any other pofitive acts on both fides. Or, it may be to forbear on one fide in confideration of fomething done on the other; as, that in confideration A, the tenant, will repair his houfe, B, the landlord, will not fue him for wafte. Or, it may be for mutual forbearance on both

[h] *In omnibus contractibus, five nominatis five innominatis, permutatio continetur.* Gravin. *l.* 2. §. 12.

[i] pag. 297.
[j] 3 Rep. 83.
[k] *Ff.* 19. 5. 5.

fides;

fides; as, that in confideration that A will not trade to Lifbon, B will not trade to Marfeilles; fo as to avoid interfering with each other. 3. The third fpecies of confiderations is, *facio, ut des*: when a man agrees to perform any thing for a price, either fpecifically mentioned, or left to the determination of the law to fet a value on it. As when a fervant hires himfelf to his mafter, for certain wages or an agreed fum of money: here the fervant contracts to do his mafter's fervice, in order to earn that fpecific fum. Otherwife, if he be hired generally; for then he is under an implied contract to perform this fervice for what it fhall be reafonably worth. 4. The fourth fpecies is, *do, ut facias*: which is the direct counterpart of the other. As when I agree with a fervant to give him fuch wages upon his performing fuch work: which, we fee, is nothing elfe but the laft fpecies inverted; for *fervus facit, ut herus det*, and *herus dat, ut fervus faciat.*

A CONSIDERATION of fome fort or other is fo abfolutely ne-ceffary to the forming of a contract, that a *nudum pactum* or a-greement to do or pay any thing on one fide, without any com-penfation on the other, is totally void in law; and a man cannot be compelled to perform it[1]. As if one man promifes to give another 100 *l.* here there is nothing contracted for or given on the one fide, and therefore there is nothing binding on the other. And, however a man may or may not be bound to perform it, in honor or confcience, which the municipal laws do not take upon them to decide; certainly thofe municipal laws will not compel the execution of what he had no vifible inducement to engage for: and therefore our law has adopted [m] the maxim of the civil law [n], that *ex nudo pacto non oritur actio.* But any degree of reciprocity will prevent the pact from being nude: nay, even if the thing be founded on a prior moral obligation, (as a promife to pay a juft debt, though barred by the ftatute of limitations) it is no longer *nudum pactum.* And as this rule was principally eftablifhed, to avoid the inconvenience that would arife from fet-ting up mere verbal promifes, for which no good reafon could

[1] D. & t. d. 2 c. 24.   [n] *Cod.* 2. 3. 10. & 5. 14. 1.
[m] Bro. *Abr. tit. uette.* 79. Salk. 129.

be

be affigned°, it therefore does not hold in fome cafes, where fuch promife is authentically proved by written documents. For if a man enters into a voluntary bond, or gives a promiffory note, he fhall not be allowed to aver the want of a confideration in order to evade the payment: for every bond from the folemnity of the inftrument[p], and every note from the fubfcription of the drawer[q], carries with it an internal evidence of a good confideration. Courts of juftice will therefore fupport them both, as againft the contractor himfelf; but not to the prejudice of creditors, or ftrangers to the contract.

We are next to confider, *thirdly*, the thing agreed to be done or omitted. " A contract is an agreement, upon fufficient confi-" deration, *to do or not to do a particular thing*." The moft ufual contracts, whereby the right of chattels perfonal may be acquired in the laws of England, are, 1. That of *fale* or *exchange*. 2. That of *bailment*. 3. That of *hiring* and *borrowing*. 4. That of *debt*.

1. SALE or *exchange* is a tranfmutation of property from one man to another, in confideration of fome recompenfe in value: for there is no fale without a recompenfe; there muft be *quid pro quo*[r]. If it be a commutation of goods for goods, it is more properly an *exchange*; but, if it be a transferring of goods for money, it is called a *fale:* which is a method of exchange introduced for the convenience of mankind, by eftablifhing an univerfal medium, which may be exchanged for all forts of other property; whereas if goods were only to be exchanged for goods, by way of barter, it would be difficult to adjuft the refpective values, and the carriage would be intolerably cumberfome. All civilized nations adopted therefore very early the ufe of money; for we find Abraham giving " four hundred fhekels of filver, cur-" rent money with the merchant," for the field of Machpelah[s]; though the practice of exchanges ftill fubfifts among feveral of the favage nations. But with regard to the *law* of fales and exchanges,

° Plowd. 308, 309.
[p] Hardr 200. 1 Ch. Rep. 157.
[q] Lord Raym. 760.

[r] Noy's Max. c. 42.
[s] Gen. c. 23. v. 16.

there

there is no difference. I fhall therefore treat of them both under the denomination of fales only; and fhall confider their force and effect, in the firft place where the vendor *hath* in himfelf, and fecondly where he *hath not*, the property of the thing fold.

WHERE the vendor *hath* in himfelf the property of the goods fold, he hath the liberty of difpofing of them to whomever he pleafes, at any time, and in any manner: unlefs judgment has been obtained againft him for a debt or damages, and the writ of execution is actually delivered to the fheriff. For then, by the ftatute of frauds[f], the fale fhall be looked upon as fraudulent, and the property of the goods fhall be bound to anfwer the debt, from the time of delivering the writ. Formerly it was bound from the *tefte*, or iffuing, of the writ[t], and any fubfequent fale was fraudulent; but the law was thus altered in favour of *pur-chafors*, though it ftill remains the fame between the *parties*: and therefore, if a defendant dies after the awarding and before the delivery of the writ, his goods are bound by it in the hands of his executors[v].

IF a man agrees with another for goods at a certain price, he may not carry them away before he hath paid for them; for it is no fale without payment, unlefs the contrary be exprefsly agreed. And therefore, if the vendor fays, the price of a beaft is four pounds, and the vendee fays he will give four pounds, the bargain is ftruck; and they neither of them are at liberty to be off, provided immediate poffeffion be tendered by the other fide. But if neither the money be paid, nor the goods delivered, nor tender made, nor any fubfequent agreement be entered into, it is no contract, and the owner may difpofe of the goods as he pleafes[u]. But if any part of the price is paid down, if it be but a penny, or any portion of the goods delivered by way of *earneft* (which the civil law calls *arrha*, and interprets to be " *emptionis-vendi-*

---

29 Car. II. c. 3.
[t] 8 Rep. 171. 1 Mod. 188.

[v] Comb. 33. 12 Mod. 5. 7 Mod. 95.
[u] Hob 41. Noy's Max. c. 42.

" *tionis*

" *tionis contractae argumentum* [w]," the property of the goods is abfolutely bound by it: and the vendee may recover the goods by action, as well as the vendor may the price of them [x]. And fuch regard does the law pay to earneft as an evidence of a contract, that, by the fame ftatute 29 Car. II. c. 3. no contract for the fale of goods, to the value of 10 *l.* or more, fhall be valid, unlefs the buyer actually receives part of the goods fold, by way of earneft on his part; or unlefs he gives part of the price to the vendor by way of earneft to bind the bargain, or in part of payment; or unlefs fome note in writting be made and figned by the party, or his agent, who is to be charged with the contract. And, with regard to goods under the value of 10 *l,* no contract or agreement for the fale of them fhall be valid, unlefs the goods are to be delivered within one year, or unlefs the contract be made in writing, and figned by the party who is to be charged therewith. Antiently, among all the northern nations, fhaking of hands was held neceffary to bind the bargain; a cuftom which we ftill retain in many verbal contracts. A fale thus made was called *handfale,* " *venditio per mutuam manuum complexionem* [y];" till in procefs of time the fame word was ufed to fignify the price or earneft, which was given immediately after the fhaking of hands, or inftead thereof.

A s foon as the bargain is ftruck, the property of the goods is transferred to the vendee, and that of the price to the vendor; but the vendee cannot take the goods, until he renders the price agreed on [z]. But if he tenders the money to the vendor, and he refufes it, the vendee may feife the goods, or have an action againft the vendor for detaining them. And by a regular fale, without delivery, the property is fo abfolutely vefted in the vendee; that if A fells a horfe to B for 10 *l,* and B pays him earneft, or figns a note in writing of the bargain; and afterwards, before the delivery of the horfe or money paid, the horfe dies in the vendor's cuftody; ftill he is entitled to the money, becaufe by

---

[w] *Inft.* 3. *tit.* 24.
[x] Noy, *ibid.*

[y] Stiernhook *de jure Goth. l.* 2. *c.* 5.
[z] Hob. 41.

the

the contract, the property was in the vendee[a]. Thus may property in goods be transferred by fale, where the vendor *hath* fuch property in himfelf.

B U T property may alfo in fome cafes be transferred by fale, though the vendor *hath none at all* in the goods: for it is expedient that the buyer, by taking proper precautions, may at all events be fecure of his purchafe; otherwife all commerce between man and man muft foon be at an end. And therefore the general rule of law is[b], that all fales and contracts of any thing vendible, in fairs or markets *overt*, (that is, open) fhall not only be good between the parties, but alfo be binding on all thofe that have any right or property therein. And for this purpofe, the mirroir informs us[c], were tolls eftablifhed in markets, viz. to teftify the making of contracts; for every private contract was difcountenanced by law. Wherefore our Saxon anceftors prohibited the fale of any thing above the value of twenty pence, unlefs in open market, and directed every bargain and fale to be contracted in the prefence of credible witneffes[d]. Market overt in the country is only held on the fpecial days, provided for particular towns by charter or prefcription; but in London every day, except Sunday, is market day[e]. The market place, or fpot of ground fet apart by cuftom for the fale of particular goods, is alfo in the country the only market overt[f]; but in London every fhop in which goods are expofed publicly to fale, is market overt, for fuch things only as the owner profeffes to trade in[g]. But if my goods are ftolen from me, and fold, out of market overt, my property is not altered, and I may take them wherever I find them. And it is exprefsly provided by ftatute 1 Jac. I. c. 21. that the fale of any goods wrongfully taken, to any pawnbroker in London or within two miles thereof, fhall not alter the property. For this, being ufually a clandeftine trade, is therefore made an

[a] Noy, c. 42.
[b] 2 Inft. 713.
[c] c. 1. §. 3.
[d] LL. *Ethel.*10,12. LL. *Eadg.* Wilk. 80.
[e] Cro. Jac. 68.
[f] Godb. 131.
[g] 5 Rep. 83. 12 Mod. 521.

excep-

exception to the general rule. And, even in market overt, if the goods be the property of the king, fuch fale (though regular in all other refpects) will in no cafe bind him; though it binds infants, feme coverts, ideots or lunatics, and men beyond fea or in prifon : or if the goods be ftolen from a common perfon, and then taken by the king's officer from the felon, and fold in open market; ftill, if the owner has ufed due diligence in profecuting the thief to conviction, he lofes not his property in the goods [h]. So likewife, if the buyer knoweth the property not to be in the feller ; or there be any other fraud in the tranfaction; if he knoweth the feller to be an infant, or feme covert, not ufually trading for herfelf; if the fale be not originally and wholly made in the fair or market, or not at the ufual hours ; the owner's property is not bound thereby [i]. If a man buys his own goods in a fair or market, the contract of fale fhall not bind him fo as that he fhall render the price, unlefs the property had been previoufly altered by a former fale [k]. And, notwithftanding any number of intervening fales, if the original vendor, who fold without having the property, comes again into poffeffion of the goods, the original owner may take them, when found in his hands who was guilty of the firft breach of juftice [l]. By which wife regulations the common law has fecured the right of the proprietor in perfonal chattels from being devefted, fo far as was confiftent with that other neceffary policy, that purchafors, *bona fide*, in a fair, open, and regular manner, fhould not be afterwards put to difficulties by reafon of the previous knavery of the feller.

B u t there is one fpecies of perfonal chattels, in which the property is not eafily altered by fale, without the exprefs confent of the owner, and thofe are horfes ; the fale of which, even in fairs or markets overt, is void in many inftances, where that of other property is valid : becaufe a horfe is fo fleet an animal, that the ftealers of them may flee far off in a fhort fpace [m], and

[h] Bacon's ufe of the law. 158. [l] 2 Inft. 713.
[i] 2 Inft. 713, 714.   [m] *Ibid.* 714.
[k] Perk. §. 93.

be

be out of the reach of the moſt induſtrious owner. All perſons therefore that have occaſion to deal in horſes, and are therefore liable ſometimes to buy ſtolen ones, would do well to obſerve, that whatever price they may give, or how long ſoever they may keep poſſeſſion before it be claimed, they gain no property in a horſe that has been ſtolen, unleſs it be bought in a fair or market overt : nor even then, unleſs the directions be purſued that are laid down in the ſtatutes 2 P. & M. c. 7. and 31 Eliz. c. 12. By which it is enacted, that every horſe, ſo to be ſold, ſhall be openly expoſed, in the time of ſuch fair or market, for one whole hour together, between ten in the morning and ſunſet, in the open and public place uſed for ſuch ſales, and not in any private yard or ſtable : that the horſe ſhall be brought by both the vendor and vendee to the tollgatherer or bookkeeper of ſuch fair or market : that toll be paid, if any be due ; and if not, one penny to the bookkeeper, who ſhall enter down the price, colour, and marks of the horſe, with the names, additions, and abode of the vendee and the vendor ; the latter either upon his own knowlege, or the teſtimony of ſome credible witneſs. And, even if all theſe points be fully complied with, yet ſuch ſale ſhall not take away the property of the owner, if within ſix months after the horſe is ſtolen he puts in his claim before the mayor, or ſome juſtice, of the diſtrict in which the horſe ſhall be found ; and within forty days after that, proves ſuch his property by the oath of two witneſſes before ſuch mayor or juſtice ; and alſo tenders to the perſon in poſſeſſion ſuch price as he *bona fide* paid for him in market overt. But in caſe any one of the points beforementioned be omitted, or not obſerved in the ſale, ſuch ſale is utterly void ; and the owner ſhall not loſe his property, but at any diſtance of time may ſeiſe or bring an action for his horſe, wherever he happens to find him. Wherefore ſir Edward Coke obſerves [n], that, both by the common law and theſe two ſtatutes, the property of horſes is ſo well preſerved, that if the owner be of capacity to underſtand them, and be vigilant and induſtrious to purſue the ſame, it is almoſt impoſſible that the property of any horſe, either

[n] 2 Inſt. 719.

ſtolen

ftolen or not ftolen, fhould be altered by any fale in market overt
by him that is *malae fidei poffeffor*.

B y the civil law ° an implied warranty was annexed to every
fale, in refpect to the title of the vendor : and fo too, in our
law, a purchafor of goods and chattels may have a fatisfaction
from the feller, if he fells them as his own, and the title proves
deficient, without any exprefs warranty for that purpofe ᴾ. But,
with regard to the goodnefs of the wares fo purchafed, the vendor is not bound to anfwer; unlefs he expreffly warrants them
to be found and good �۹, or unlefs he knew them to be otherwife
and hath ufed any art to difguife them ʳ, or unlefs they turn out
to be different from what he reprefented to the buyer.

2. B a i l m e n t, from the French *bailler*, to deliver, is a delivery of goods in truft, upon a contract expreffed or implied,
that the truft fhall be faithfully executed on the part of the
bailee. As if cloth be delivered, or (in our legal dialect) bailed,
to a taylor to make a fuit of cloaths, he has it upon an implied
contract to render it again when made, and that in a workmanly
manner ˢ. If money or goods be delivered to a common carrier,
to convey from Oxford to London, he is under a contract in law
to pay, or carry, them to the perfon appointed ᵗ. If a horfe, or
other goods, be delivered to an inn-keeper or his fervants, he is
bound to keep them fafely, and reftore them when his gueft
leaves the houfe ᵘ. If a man takes in a horfe, or other cattle,
to graze and depafture in his grounds, which the law calls *agift-
ment*, he takes them upon an implied contract to return them
fafe to the owner ʷ. If a pawnbroker receives plate or jewels as
a pledge, or fecurity, for the repayment of money lent thereon
at a day certain, he has them upon an exprefs contract or condition to reftore them, if the pledgor performs his part by redeeming them in due time ˣ: for the due execution of which

---

° *Ff.* 21. 2. 1.
ᴾ Cro. Jac. 474. 1 Roll. Abr. 90.
۹ F. N. B. 94.
ʳ 2 Roll. Rep. 5.
ˢ 1 Vern. 268.

ᵗ 12 Mod. 482.
ᵘ Cro. Eliz. 622.
ʷ Cro. Car. 271.
ˣ Cro. Jac. 245. Yelv. 178.

contract

contract many ufeful regulations are made by ſtatute 30 Geo. II.
c. 24. And ſo if a landlord diſtreins goods for rent, or a pariſh
officer for taxes, theſe for a time are only a pledge in the hands
of the diſtreinors, and they are bound by an implied contract in
law to reſtore them on payment of the debt, duty, and expenſes,
before the time of ſale; or, when ſold, to render back the overplus.
If a friend delivers any thing to his friend to keep for him, the
receiver is bound to reſtore it on demand : and it was formerly
held that in the mean time he was anſwerable for any damage or
loſs it might ſuſtain, whether by accident or otherwiſe[y]; unleſs
he expreſſly undertook[z] to keep it only with the ſame care as his
own goods, and then he ſhould not be anſwerable for theft or
other accidents. But now the law ſeems to be ſettled upon a
much more rational footing[a]; that ſuch a general bailment will
not charge the bailee with any loſs, unleſs it happens by groſs
neglect, which is conſtrued to be an evidence of fraud : but, if
the bailee undertakes ſpecially to keep the goods ſafely and ſe-
curely, he is bound to anſwer all perils and damages, that may
befal them for want of the ſame care with which a prudent
man would keep his own[b].

I N all theſe inſtances there is a ſpecial qualified property tranſ-
ferred from the bailor to the bailee, together with the poſſeſſion.
It is not an abſolute property in the bailee, becauſe of his contract for reſtitution; and the bailor hath nothing left in him but
the right to a *choſe* in action, grounded upon ſuch contract, the
poſſeſſion being delivered to the bailee. And, on account of this
qualified property of the bailee, he may (as well as the bailor)
maintain an action againſt ſuch as injure or take away theſe chattels. The taylor, the carrier, the innkeeper, the agiſting farmer,
the pawnbroker, the diſtreinor, and the general bailee, may all

---

[y] Co. Litt. 89.
[z] 4 Rep. 84.
[a] Lord Raym. 909. 12 Mod. 487.
[b] By the laws of Sweden, the depoſitary
or bailee of goods is not bound to reſtitution, in caſe of accident by fire or theft:
provided his own goods periſhed in the ſame
manner: "*jura enim noſtra,* ſays Stiernhook,
"*dolum praeſumunt, ſi una non pereant.*" (*De
jure Sueon. l. 2. c. 5.*)

of them vindicate, in their own right, this their poffeffory intereft, againft any ftranger or third perfon[c]. For, as fuch bailee
is refponfible to the bailor, if the goods are loft or damaged by
his wilful default or grofs negligence, or if he do not deliver up
the chattels on lawful demand, it is therefore reafonable that he
fhould have a right to recover either the fpecific goods, or elfe a
fatisfaction in damages, againft all other perfons, who may have
purloined or injured them ; that he may always be ready to anfwer the call of the bailor.

3. HIRING and *borrowing* are alfo contracts by which a
qualified property may be transferred to the hirer or borrower :
in which there is only this difference, that hiring is always for
a price, a ftipend, or additional recompenfe; borrowing is
merely gratuitous. But the law in both cafes is the fame.
They are both contracts, whereby the poffeffion and a tranfient
property is transferred for a particular time or ufe, on condition and agreement to reftore the goods fo hired or borrowed,
as foon as the time is expired or ufe performed; together with
the price or ftipend (in cafe of hiring) either expreffly agreed
on by the parties, or left to be implied by law according to the
value of the fervice. By this mutual contract, the hirer or borrower gains a temporary property in the thing hired, accompanied with an implied condition to ufe it with moderation and
not abufe it ; and the owner or lender retains a reverfionary intereft in the fame, and acquires a new property in the price or
reward. Thus if a man hires or borrows a horfe for a month,
he has the poffeffion and a qualified property therein during that
period ; on the expiration of which his qualified property determines, and the owner becomes (in cafe of hiring) intitled to
the premium or price, for which the horfe was hired[d].

THERE is one fpecies of this price or reward, the moft ufual
of any, but concerning which many good and learned men have

[c] 13 Rep. 69.   [d] Yelv. 172. Cro. Jac. 236.

in

in former times very much perplexed themfelves and other people, by raiſing doubts about it's legality *in foro conſcientiae*. That
is, when money is lent on a contract to receive not only the
principal ſum again, but alſo an increaſe by way of compenſation
for the uſe; which is generally called *intereſt* by thoſe who think
it lawful, and *uſury* by thoſe who do not ſo. It may not be
amiſs therefore to enter into a ſhort enquiry, upon what footing this matter of intereſt or uſury does really ſtand.

THE enemies to intereſt in general make no diſtinction between that and uſury, holding any increaſe of money to be in-
defenſibly uſurious. And this they ground as well on the prohibition of it by the law of Moſes among the Jews, as alſo upon
what is laid down by Ariſtotle [e], that money is naturally barren,
and to make it breed money is prepoſterous, and a perverſion of
the end of it's inſtitution, which was only to ſerve the purpoſes of exchange, and not of increaſe. Hence the ſchool di-
vines have branded the practice of taking intereſt, as being contrary to the divine law both natural and revealed; and the canon
law [f], has proſcribed the taking any, the leaſt, increaſe for the
loan of money as a mortal ſin.

BUT, in anſwer to this, it may be obſerved, that the moſai-
cal precept was clearly a political, and not a moral precept. It
only prohibited the Jews from taking uſury from their brethren
the Jews; but in expreſs words permitted them to take it of a
ſtranger [g]: which proves that the taking of moderate uſury, or
a reward for the uſe, for ſo the word ſignifies, is not *malum in
ſe*, ſince it was allowed where any but an Iſraelite was concerned.
And as to Ariſtotle's reaſon, deduced from the natural barrenneſs
of money, the ſame may with equal force be alleged of houſes,
which never breed houſes; and twenty other things, which nobody doubts it is lawful to make profit of, by letting them to

[e] *Polit. l. 1. c. 10.*
[f] *Decretal. l. 5. tit. 19.*

[g] "Unto a ſtranger thou mayeſt lend up-
"on uſury, but unto thy brother thou ſhalt
"not lend upon uſury." Deut. xxiii. 20.

hire.

hire. And though money was originally ufed only for the purpofes of exchange, yet the laws of any ftate may be well jufti-
fied in permitting it to be turned to the purpofes of profit, if the
convenience of fociety (the great end for which money was invented) fhall require it. And that the allowance of moderate intereft tends greatly to the benefit of the public, efpecially in a
trading country, will appear from that generally acknowleged
principle, that commerce cannot fubfift without mutual and extenfive credit. Unlefs money therefore can be borrowed, trade
cannot be carried on : and if no premium were allowed for the
hire of money, few perfons would care to lend it; or at leaft the
eafe of borrowing at a fhort warning (which is the life of commerce) would be entirely at an end. Thus, in the dark ages of
monkifh fuperftition and civil tyranny, when intereft was laid under a total interdict, commerce was alfo at it's loweft ebb, and
fell entirely into the hands of the Jews and Lombards : but when
men's minds began to be more enlarged, when true religion and
real liberty revived, commerce grew again into credit; and again
introduced with itfelf it's infeparable companion, the doctrine of
loans upon intereft.

A N D, really, confidered abftractedly from this it's ufe, fince
all other conveniences of life may either be bought or hired, but
money can only be hired, there feems no greater impropriety in
taking a recompenfe or price for the hire of this, than of any
other convenience. If I borrow 100 *l.* to employ in a beneficial
trade, it is but equitable that the lender fhould have a proportion
of my gains. To demand an exorbitant price is equally contrary to confcience, for the loan of a horfe, or the loan of a fum
of money : but a reafonable equivalent for the temporary inconvenience the owner may feel by the want of it, and for the hazard
of his lofing it entirely, is not more immoral in one cafe than it
is in the other. And indeed the abfolute prohibition of lending
upon any, even moderate intereft, introduces the very inconvenience
which it feems meant to remedy. The neceffity of individuals
will make borrowing unavoidable. Without fome profit allowed

by

by law there will be but few lenders : and thofe principally bad men, who will break through the law, and take a profit ; and then will endeavour to indemnify themfelves from the danger of the penalty, by making that profit exorbitant. Thus, while all degrees of profit were difcountenanced, we find more complaints of ufury, and more flagrant inftances of oppreffion, than in modern times, when money may be eafily had at a low intereft. A capital diftinction muft therefore be made between a moderate and exorbitant profit ; to the former of which we ufually give the name of intereft, to the latter the truly odious appellation of ufury : the former is neceffary in every civil ftate, if it were but to exclude the latter, which ought never to be tolerated in any well-regulated fociety. For, as the whole of this matter is well fummed up by Grotius[h], " if the compenfation allowed by law does " not exceed the proportion of the hazard run, or the want felt, " by the loan, it's allowance is neither repugnant to the revealed " nor the natural law : but if it exceeds thofe bounds, it is then " oppreffive ufury ; and though the municipal laws may give it " impunity, they never can make it juft."

WE fee, that the exorbitance or moderation of intereft, for money lent, depends upon two circumftances ; the inconvenience of parting with it for the prefent, and the hazard of lofing it entirely. The inconvenience to individual lenders can never be eftimated by laws ; the rate therefore of general intereft muft depend upon the ufual or general inconvenience. This refults entirely from the quantity of fpecie or current money in the kingdom : for, the more fpecie there is circulating in any nation, the greater fuperfluity there will be, beyond what is neceffary to carry on the bufinefs of exchange and the common concerns of life. In every nation or public community there is a certain quantity of money thus neceffary ; which a perfon well fkilled in political arithmetic might perhaps calculate as exactly, as a private banker can the demand for running cafh in his own fhop : all above this necef-

h de j. b. & p. l. 2. c. 12. §. 22.

fary

fary quantity may be fpared, or lent, without much inconvenience to the refpective lenders; and the greater this national fuperfluity is, the more numerous will be the lenders, and the lower ought the rate of the national intereft to be : but where there is not enough, or barely enough, circulating cafh, to anfwer the ordinary ufes of the public, intereft will be proportionably high; for lenders will be but few, as few can fubmit to the inconvenience of lending.

So alfo the hazard of an entire lofs has it's weight in the regulation of intereft : hence, the better the fecurity, the lower will the intereft be; the rate of intereft being generally in a compound *ratio*, formed out of the inconvenience and the hazard. And as, if there were no inconvenience, there fhould be no intereft, but what is equivalent to the hazard; fo, if there were no hazard, there ought to be no intereft, fave only what arifes from the mere inconvenience of lending. Thus, if the quantity of fpecie in a nation be fuch, that the general inconvenience of lending for a year is computed to amount to *three per cent :* a man that has money by him will perhaps lend it upon good perfonal fecurity at *five per cent,* allowing two for the hazard run; he will lend it upon landed fecurity, or mortgage, at *four per cent,* the hazard being proportionably lefs; but he will lend it to the ftate, on the maintenance of which all his property depends, at *three per cent,* the hazard being none at all.

But fometimes the hazard may be greater, than the rate of intereft allowed by law will compenfate. And this gives rife to the practice, 1. Of bottomry, or *refpondentia.* 2. Of policies of infurance.

And firft, *bottomry* (which originally arofe from permitting the mafter of a fhip, in a foreign country, to hypothecate the fhip in order to raife money to refit) is in the nature of a mortgage of a fhip; when the owner takes up money to enable him to carry on his voyage, and pledges the keel or *bottom* of the fhip

(pars

(pars pro toto) as a fecurity for the repayment. In which cafe it is underftood, that, if the fhip be loft, the lender lofes alfo his whole money; but, if it returns in fafety, then he fhall receive back his principal, and alfo the premium or intereft agreed upon, however it may exceed the legal rate of intereft. And this is allowed to be a valid contract in all trading nations, for the benefit of commerce, and by reafon of the extraordinary hazard run by the lender [i]. And in this cafe the fhip and tackle, if brought home, are anfwerable (as well as the perfon of the borrower) for the money lent. But if the loan is not upon the veffel, but upon the goods and merchandize, which muft neceffarily be fold or exchanged in the courfe of the voyage, then only the borrower, perfonally, is bound to anfwer the contract; who therefore in this cafe is faid to take up money at *refpondentia*. Thefe terms are alfo applied to contracts for the repayment of money borrowed, not on the fhip and goods only, but on the mere hazard of the voyage itfelf; when a man lends a merchant 1000*l.* to be employed in a beneficial trade, with condition to be repaid with extraordinary intereft, in cafe fuch a voyage be fafely performed [k]: which kind of agreement is fometimes called *foenus nauticum*, and fometimes *ufura maritima* [l]. But, as this gave an opening for ufurious and gaming contracts, efpecially upon long voyages, it was enacted by the ftatute 19 Geo. II. c. 37. that all monies lent on bottomry or at *refpondentia*, on veffels bound to or from the Eaft Indies, fhall be exprefsly lent only upon the fhip or upon the merchandize; that the lender fhall have the benefit of falvage; and that, if the borrower has not on board effects to the value of the fum borrowed, he fhall be refponfible to the lender for fo much of the principal as hath not been laid out, with legal intereft and all other charges, though the fhip and merchandize be totally loft.

---

[i] Moll. *de jur. mar.* 361. Malyne *lex mercat.* b. 1. c. 31. Cro. Jac. 208. Bynkerfh. *quaeft. jur. privat. l.* 3. *c.* 16.

[k] 1 Sid. 27.
[l] Molloy *ibid.* Malyne *ibid.*

SECONDLY, a policy of *infurance* is a contract between A and B, that, upon A's paying a premium equivalent to the hazard run, B will indemnify or infure him againft a particular event. This is founded upon one of the fame principles as the doctrine of intereft upon loans, that of hazard; but not that of inconvenience. For if I infure a fhip to the levant, and back again, at *five per cent*; here I calculate the chance that fhe performs her voyage to be twenty to one againft her being loft: and, if fhe be loft, I lofe 100 *l.* and get 5 *l.* Now this is much the fame as if I lend the merchant, whofe whole fortunes are embarked in this veffel, 100 *l.* at the rate of *eight per cent*. For by a loan I fhould be immediately out of my money, the inconvenience of which we have computed equal to *three per cent*: if therefore I had actually lent him 100 *l*, I muft have added 3 *l.* on the fcore of inconvenience, to the 5 *l.* allowed for the hazard; which together would have made 8 *l.* But as, upon an infurance, I am never out of my money till the lofs actually happens, nothing is therein allowed upon the principle of inconvenience, but all upon the principle of hazard. Thus too, in a loan, if the chance of repayment depends upon the borrower's life, it is frequent (befides the ufual rate of intereft) for the borrower to have his life infured till the time of repayment; for which he is loaded with an additional premium, fuited to his age and conftitution. Thus, if Sempronius has only an annuity for his life, and would borrow 100 *l.* of Titius for a year; the inconvenience and general hazard of this loan, we have feen, are equivalent to 5 *l.* which is therefore the legal intereft: but there is alfo a fpecial hazard in this cafe; for, if Sempronius dies within the year, Titius muft lofe the whole of his 100 *l.* Suppofe this chance to be as one to ten: it will follow that the extraordinary hazard is worth 10 *l.* more; and therefore that the reafonable rate of intereft in this cafe would be *fifteen per cent*. But this the law, to avoid abufes, will not permit to be taken: Sempronius therefore gives Titius the lender only 5 *l*, the legal intereft; but applies to Gaius an infurer, and gives him the other 10 *l.* to indemnify Titius againft

the

the extraordinary hazard. And in this manner may any extraordinary or particular hazard be provided againft, which the eftablifhed rate of intereft will not reach; that being calculated by the ftate to anfwer only the ordinary and general hazard, together with the lender's inconvenience in parting with his fpecie for the time.

THE learning relating to marine infurances hath of late years been greatly improved by a feries of judicial decifions, which have now eftablifhed the law in fuch a variety of cafes, that (if well and judicioufly collected) they would form a very complete title in a code of commercial jurifprudence. But, being founded on equitable principles, which chiefly refult from the fpecial circumftances of the cafe, it is not eafy to reduce them to any general heads in mere elementary inftitutes. Thus much may however be faid; that, being contracts, the very effence of which confifts in obferving the pureft good faith and integrity, they are vacated by any the leaft fhadow of fraud or undue concealment: and, on the other hand, being much for the benefit and extenfion of trade, by diftributing the lofs or gain among a number of adventurers, they are greatly encouraged and protected both by common law and acts of parliament. But, as a practice had obtained of infuring large fums without having any property on board, which were called infurances, *intereft or no intereft*; and alfo of infuring the fame goods feveral times over; both of which were a fpecies of gaming, without any advantage to commerce, and were denominated *wagering* policies: it is therefore enacted by the ftatute 19 Geo. II. c. 37. that all infurances, intereft or no intereft, or without farther proof of intereft than the policy itfelf, or by way of gaming or wagering, or without benefit of falvage to the infurer, (all which had the fame pernicious tendency) fhall be totally null and void, except upon privateers, or fhips in the Spanifh and Portuguefe trade, for reafons fufficiently obvious; and that no re-affurance fhall be lawful, except the former infurer fhall be infolvent, a bankrupt, or dead; and laftly that, in the Eaft India trade, the lender of money on bottomry, or at *refpondentia*, fhall

alone

alone have a right to be infured for the money lent, and the borrower fhall (in cafe of a lofs) recover no more upon any infurance than the furplus of his property, above the value of his bottomry or *refpondentia* bond. But, to return to the doctrine of common intereft on loans:

U P O N the two principles of inconvenience and hazard, compared together, different nations have at different times eftablifhed different rates of intereft. The Romans at one time allowed *centefimae*, or *twelve per cent*, to be taken for common loans; but Juftinian[m] reduced it to *trientes*, or one third of the *as* or *centefimae*, that is, *four per cent*; but allowed higher intereft to be taken of merchants, becaufe there the hazard was greater[n]. So too Gro-

---

[m] *Cod.* 4. 32. 26. *Nov.* 33, 34, 35.

[n] A fhort explication of thefe terms, and of the divifion of the Roman *as*, will be ufeful to the ftudent, not only for underftanding the civilians, but alfo the more claffical writers, who perpetually refer to this diftribution. Thus Horace, *ad Pifones.* 325.

> Romani *pueri longis rationibus* affem
> Difcunt in partes centum diducere. Dicat
> Filius Albini, fi de quincunce remota eft
> Uncia, quid fuperet? poterat dixiffe, triens : eu,
> Rem poteris fervare tuam! redit uncia, quid fit?
> Semis. ———

It is therefore to be obferved, that, in calculating the rate of intereft, the Romans divided the principal fum into an *hundred* parts; one of which they allowed to be taken monthly : and this, which was the higheft rate of intereft permitted, they called *ufurae centefimae*, amounting yearly to twelve *per cent*. Now as the *as*, or Roman pound, was commonly ufed to exprefs any integral fum, and was divifible into twelve parts or *unciae*, therefore thefe twelve monthly payments or *unciae* were held to amount annually to one pound, or *as ufurarius*; and fo the *ufurae affes* were fynonymous to the *ufurae centefimae*. And all lower rates of intereft were denominated according to the relation they bore to this centefimal ufury, or *ufurae affes* : for the feveral multiples of the *unciae*, or duodecimal parts of the *as*, were known by different names according to their different combinations; *fextans, quadrans, triens, quincunx, femis, feptunx, bes, dodrans, dextrans, deunx,* containing refpectively 2, 3, 4, 5, 6, 7, 8, 9, 10, 11 *unciae* or duodecimal parts of an *as*. (*Ff.* 28. 5. 50. §. 2. Gravin. *orig. jur. civ. l.* 2. §. 47.) This being premifed, the following table will clearly exhibit at once the fubdivifions of the *as*, and the denominations of the rate of intereft.

U s u r æ

tius informs us°, that in Holland the rate of intereſt was then eight *per cent* in common loans, but twelve to merchants. Our law eſtabliſhes one ſtandard for all alike, where the pledge or ſecurity itſelf is not put in jeopardy; left, under the general pretence of vague and indeterminate hazards, a door ſhould be opened to fraud and uſury : leaving ſpecific hazards to be provided againſt by ſpecific inſurances, or by loans upon *reſpondentia*, or bottomry. But as to the rate of legal intereſt, it has varied and decreaſed for two hundred years paſt, according as the quantity of ſpecie in the kingdom has encreaſed by acceſſions of trade, the introduction of paper credit, and other circumſtances. The ſtatute 37 Hen.VIII. c.9. confined intereſt to ten *per cent,* and ſo did the ſtatute 13 Eliz. c. 8. But as, through the encouragements given in her reign to commerce, the nation grew more wealthy, ſo under her ſucceſſor the ſtatute 21 Jac. I. c. 17. reduced it to eight *per cent ;* as did the ſtatute 12 Car. II. c. 13. to fix : and laſtly by the ſtatute 12 Ann. ſt. 2. c. 16. it was brought down to five *per cent* yearly, which is now the extremity of legal intereſt that can be taken. But yet, if a contract, which carries intereſt, be made in a foreign country, our courts will direct the payment of intereſt according to the law of that country in which the contract was made ᴾ. Thus Iriſh, American,

USURAE.	PARTES ASSIS.	PER ANNUM.
Aſſes, ſive centeſimae ———— integer ——————		12 *per cent.*
Deunces ——————————— $\frac{11}{12}$ —————		11
Dextances, vel decunces —— $\frac{5}{6}$ —————		10
Dodrantes ——————— $\frac{3}{4}$ —————		9
Beſſes ————————— $\frac{2}{3}$ —————		8
Septunces ——————— $\frac{7}{12}$ ————		7
Semiſſes ———————— $\frac{1}{2}$ —————		6
Quincunces —————— $\frac{5}{12}$ —————		5
Trientes ————————— $\frac{1}{3}$ —————		4
Quadrantes —————— $\frac{1}{4}$ —————		3
Sextances ——————— $\frac{1}{6}$ —————		2
Unciae ——————— $\frac{1}{12}$ —————		1

° *de jur. b. & p.* 2. 12. 22.   ᴾ 1 Equ. Caſ. abr. 289.   1 P. Wᵐˢ. 395.

Turkiſh,

Turkifh, and Indian intereft, have been allowed in our courts, to the amount of even twelve *per cent.* For the moderation or exorbitance of intereft depends upon local circumftances; and the refufal to inforce fuch contracts would put a ftop to all foreign trade.

4. The laft general fpecies of contracts, which I have to mention, is that of *debt;* whereby a *chofe* in action, or right to a certain fum of money, is mutually acquired and loft 9. This may be the counterpart of, and arife from, any of the other fpecies of contracts. As, in cafe of a fale, where the price is not paid in ready money, the vendee becomes indebted to the vendor for the fum agreed on; and the vendor has a property in this price, as a *chofe* in action, by means of this contract of debt. In bailment, if the bailee lofes or detains a fum of money bailed to him for any fpecial purpofe, he becomes indebted to the bailor in the fame numerical fum, upon his implied contract, that he fhall execute the truft repofed in him, or repay the money to the bailor. Upon hiring or borrowing, the hirer or borrower, at the fame time that he acquires a property in the thing lent, may alfo become indebted to the lender, upon his contract to reftore the money borrowed, to pay the price or premium of the loan, the hire of the horfe, or the like. Any contract in fhort whereby a determinate fum of money becomes due to any perfon, and is not paid but remains in action merely, is a contract of debt. And, taken in this light, it comprehends a great variety of acquifition; being ufually divided into debts of *record*, debts by *fpecial*, and debts by *fimple* contract.

A Debt of *record* is a fum of money, which appears to be due by the evidence of a court of record. Thus, when any fpecific fum is adjudged to be due from the defendant to the plaintiff, on an action or fuit at law; this is a contract of the higheft nature, being eftablifhed by the fentence of a court of judicature. Recognizances alfo are a fum of money, recognized or acknowleged to be due to the

9 F. N. B. 119.

crown

crown or a fubject, in the prefence of fome court or magiftrate, with a condition that fuch acknowlegement fhall be void upon the appearance of the party, his good behaviour, or the like: and thefe, together with ftatutes merchant and ftatutes ftaple, *&c*, if forfeited by non-performance of the condition, are alfo ranked among this firft and principal clafs of debts, *viz.* debts of record; fince the contract, on which they are founded, is witneffed by the higheft kind of evidence, *viz.* by matter of record.

D E B T S by *fpecialty*, or fpecial contract, are fuch whereby a fum of money becomes, or is acknowleged to be, due by deed or inftrument under feal. Such as by deed of covenant, by deed of fale, by leafe referving rent, or by bond or obligation: which laft we took occafion to explain in the twentieth lecture of the prefent book; and then fhewed that it is an acknowlegement or creation of a debt from the obligor to the obligee, unlefs the obligor performs a condition thereunto ufually annexed, as the payment of rent or money borrowed, the obfervance of a covenant, and the like; on failure of which the bond becomes forfeited and the debt becomes due in law. Thefe are looked upon as the next clafs of debts after thofe of record, being confirmed by fpecial evidence, under feal.

D E B T S by *fimple contract* are fuch, where the contract upon which the obligation arifes is neither afcertained by matter of record, nor yet by deed or fpecial inftrument, but by mere oral evidence, the moft fimple of any; or by notes unfealed, which are capable of a more eafy proof, and (therefore only) better, than a verbal promife. It is eafy to fee into what a vaft variety of obligations this laft clafs may be branched out, through the numerous contracts for money, which are not only expreffed by the parties, but virtually implied in law. Some of thefe we have already occafionally hinted at; and the reft, to avoid repetition, muft be referred to thofe particular heads in the third book of thefe commentaries, where the breach of fuch contracts will be confidered. I fhall only obferve at prefent, that by the ftatute 29 Car. II. c. 3. no executor or adminiftrator fhall be charged upon any fpecial promife to anfwer damages out of his own eftate, and no perfon fhall be charged upon any promife to anfwer for the debt or default of another, or upon any agreement in confideration of marriage, or upon any contract or fale of any real eftate, or upon any agreement that is not to be performed within one year from the making, unlefs the agreement or fome memorandum thereof be in writing, and figned by the party himfelf or by his authority.

But there is one fpecies of debts upon fimple contract, which, being a tranfaction now introduced into all forts of civil life, under the name of *paper credit,* deferves a more particular regard. Thefe are debts by *bills of exchange,* and *promiffory notes.*

A bill *of exchange* is a fecurity, originally invented among merchants in different countries, for the more eafy remittance of money from the one to the other, which has fince fpread itfelf into almoft all pecuniary tranfactions. It is an open letter of requeft from one man to another, defiring him to pay a fum named therein to a third perfon on his account; by which means a man at the moft diftant part of the world may have money remitted to him from any trading country. If A lives in Jamaica, and owes B who lives in England 1000 *l,* now if C be going from England to Jamaica, he may pay B this 1000 *l,* and take a bill of exchange drawn by B in England upon A in Jamaica, and receive it when he comes thither. Thus does B receive his debt, at any diftance of place, by transferring it to C; who carries over his money in paper credit, without danger of robbery or lofs. This method is faid to have been brought into general ufe by the Jews and Lombards, when banifhed for their ufury and other vices; in order the more eafily to draw their effects out of France and England, into thofe countries in which they had chofen to refide. The invention of them was a little earlier: for the Jews were banifhed out of Guienne in 1287, and out

of

of England in 1290 [r]; and in 1236 the ufe of paper credit was introduced into the Mogul empire in China [s]. In common fpeech fuch a bill is frequently called a *draught*, but a *bill of exchange* is the more legal as well as mercantile expreffion. The perfon however, who writes this letter, is called in law the *drawer*, and he to whom it is written the *drawee*; and the third perfon, or negotiator, to whom it is payable (whether fpecially named, or the *bearer* generally) is called the *payee*.

THESE bills are either *foreign*, or *inland*: *foreign*, when drawn by a merchant refiding abroad upon his correfpondent in England, or *vice verfa*; and *inland*, when both the drawer and the drawee refide within the kingdom. Formerly foreign bills of exchange were much more regarded in the eye of the law than inland ones, as being thought of more public concern in the advancement of trade and commerce. But now by two ftatutes, the one 9 & 10 W. III. c. 17. the other 3 & 4 Ann. c. 9. inland bills of exchange are put upon the fame footing as foreign ones; what was the law and cuftom of merchants with regard to the one, and taken notice of merely as fuch [t], being by thofe ftatutes expreffly enacted with regard to the other. So that there is now in law no manner of difference between them.

PROMISSORY notes, or notes of hand, are a plain and direct engagement in writing, to pay a fum fpecified at the time therein limited to a perfon therein named, or fometimes to his order, or often to the bearer at large. Thefe alfo by the fame ftatute 3 & 4 Ann. c. 9. are made affignable and indorfable in like manner as bills of exchange.

THE payee, we may obferve, either of a bill of exchange or promiffory note, has clearly a property vefted in him (not indeed in poffeffion but in action) by the *exprefs* contract of the drawer in the cafe of a promiffory note, and, in the cafe of a bill of exchange, by his *implied* contract; viz. that, provided the drawee

[r] 2 Carte. 203. 206.　　　　　　[t] 1 Roll. Abr. 6.
[s] Mod. Un. Hift. iv. 499.　　L l l 2　　　　does

does not pay the bill, the drawer will : for which reason it is usual, in bills of exchange, to express that the *value* thereof hath been *received* by the drawer[u]; in order to shew the consideration, upon which the implied contract of repayment arises. And this property, so vested, may be transferred and assigned from the payee to any other man; contrary to the general rule of the common law, that no *chose* in action is assignable : which assignment is the life of paper credit. It may therefore be of some use, to mention a few of the principal incidents attending this transfer or assignment, in order to make it regular, and thereby to charge the drawer with the payment of the debt to other persons, than those with whom he originally contracted.

In the first place then the payee, or person to whom or whose *order* such bill of exchange or promissory note is payable, may by indorsement, or writing his name *in dorso* or on the back of it, assign over his whole property to the bearer, or else to another person by name, either of whom is then called the indorsee; and he may assign the same to another, and so on *in infinitum*. And a promissory note, payable to A or *bearer*, is negotiable without any indorsement, and payment thereof may be demanded by any bearer of it[v]. But, in case of a bill of exchange, the payee, or the indorsee, (whether it be a general or particular indorsement) is to go to the drawee, and offer his bill for acceptance; which acceptance (so as to charge the drawer with costs) must be in writing, under or on the back of the bill. If the drawee accepts the bill, either verbally or in writing[w], he then makes himself liable to pay it; this being now a contract on his side, grounded on an acknowlegement that the drawer has effects in his hands, or at least credit sufficient to warrant the payment. If the drawee refuses to accept the bill, and it be of the value of 20 *l.* or upwards, and expressed to be for value received, the payee or indorsee may protest it for *non-acceptance* : which protest must be made in writing, under a copy of such bill

---

[u] Stra. 1212.
[v] 2 Show. 235.—Grant v. Vaughan. T. 4 Geo. III. B. R.
[w] Stra. 1000.

of

of exchange, by fome notary public; or, if no fuch notary be refident in the place, then by any other fubftantial inhabitant in the prefence of two credible witnefles; and notice of fuch proteft muft, within fourteen days after, be given to the drawer.

B U T, in cafe fuch bill be accepted by the drawee, and after acceptance he fails or refufes to pay it within three days after it becomes due (which three days are called days of grace) the payee or indorfee is then to get it protefted for *non-payment*, in the fame manner and by the fame perfons who are to proteft it in cafe of non-acceptance: and fuch proteft muft alfo be notified, within fourteen days after, to the drawer. And he, on producing fuch proteft, either of non-acceptance or non-payment, is bound to make good to the payee, or indorfee, not only the amount of the faid bills, (which he is bound to do within a reafonable time after non-payment, without any proteft, by the rules of the common law ') but alfo intereft and all charges, to be computed from the time of making fuch proteft. But if no proteft be made or notified to the drawer, and any damage accrues by fuch neglect, it fhall fall on the holder of the bill. The bill, when refufed, muft be demanded of the drawer as foon as conveniently may be: for though, when one draws a bill of exchange, he fubjects himfelf to the payment, if the perfon on whom it is drawn refufes either to accept or pay, yet that is with this limitation, that if the bill be not paid, when due, the perfon to whom it is payable fhall in convenient time give the drawer notice thereof; for otherwife the law will imply it paid: fince it would be prejudicial to commerce, if a bill might rife up to charge the drawer at any diftance of time; when in the mean time all reckonings and accounts may be adjufted between the drawer and the drawee ʸ.

I F the bill be an indorfed bill, and the indorfee cannot get the drawee to difchàrge it, he may call upon either the drawer or the indorfor, or if the bill has been negotiated through many

---

ˣ Lord Raym. 993.   ʸ Salk. 127.

hands,

hands, upon any of the indorſors; for each indorſor is a warrantor for the payment of the bill, which is frequently taken in
payment as much (or more) upon the credit of the indorſor, as of
the drawer. And if ſuch indorſor, ſo called upon, has the names
of one or more indorſors prior to his own, to each of whom he
is properly an indorſee, he is alſo at liberty to call upon any of
them to make him ſatisfaction; and ſo upwards. But the firſt
indorſor has nobody to reſort to, but the drawer only.

WHAT has been ſaid of bills of exchange is applicable alſo
to promiſſory notes, that are indorſed over, and negotiated from
one hand to another: only that, in this caſe, as there is no
drawee, there can be no proteſt for non-acceptance; or rather,
the law conſiders a promiſſory note in the light of a bill drawn
by a man upon himſelf, and accepted at the time of drawing.
And, in caſe of non-payment by the drawer, the ſeveral indor-
ſees of a promiſſory note have the ſame remedy, as upon bills of
exchange, againſt the prior indorſors.

CHAPTER THE THIRTY FIRST.

OF TITLE BY BANKRUPTCY.

THE preceding chapter having treated pretty largely of the acquifition of perfonal property by feveral commercial methods, we from thence fhall be eafily led to take into our prefent confideration a tenth method of transferring property, which is that of

X. BANKRUPTCY; a title which we before lightly touched upon[a], fo far as it related to the transfer of the real eftate of the bankrupt. At prefent we are to treat of it more minutely, as it principally relates to the difpofition of chattels, in which the property of perfons concerned in trade more ufually confifts, than in lands or tenements. Let us therefore firft of all confider, 1. *Who* may become a bankrupt: 2. What *acts* make a bankrupt: 3. The *proceedings* on a commiffion of bankrupt: and, 4. In what manner an eftate in goods and chattels may be *transferred* by bankruptcy.

1. WHO may become a bankrupt. A bankrupt was before[b] defined to be "a trader, who fecretes himfelf, or does certain " other acts, tending to defraud his creditors." He was formerly confidered merely in the light of a criminal or offender[c]; and in this fpirit we are told by fir Edward Coke[d], that we have fetched as well the name, as the wickednefs, of bankrupts from foreign

---

[a] See pag. 285.
[b] *Ibid.*
[c] Stat. 1 Jac. I. c. 15. §. 17.
[d] 4 Inft. 277.

nations[e]

nations[e]. But at prefent the laws of bankruptcy are confidered as laws calculated for the benefit of trade, and founded on the principles of humanity as well as juftice; and to that end they confer fome privileges, not only on the creditors, but alfo on the bankrupt or debtor himfelf. On the creditors; by compelling the bankrupt to give up all his effects to their ufe, without any fraudulent concealment : on the debtor; by exempting him from the rigor of the general law, whereby his perfon might be confined at the difcretion of his creditor, though in reality he has nothing to fatisfy the debt; whereas the law of bankrupts, taking into confideration the fudden and unavoidable accidents to which men in trade are liable, has given them the liberty of their perfons, and fome pecuniary emoluments, upon condition they furrender up their whole eftate to be divided among their creditors.

IN this refpect our legiflature feems to have attended to the example of the Roman law. I mean not the terrible law of the twelve tables; whereby the creditors might cut the debtor's body into pieces, and each of them take his proportionable fhare : if indeed that law, *de debitore in partes fecando,* is to be underftood in fo very butcherly a light; which many learned men have with reafon doubted[f]. Nor do I mean thofe lefs inhuman laws (if they may be called fo, as *their* meaning is indifputably certain) of imprifoning the debtor's perfon in chains; fubjecting him to ftripes and hard labour, at the mercy of his rigid creditor; and fometimes felling him, his wife, and children, to perpetual foreign flavery *trans Tiberim*[g] : an oppreffion, which produced fo

---

[e] The word itfelf is derived from the word *bancus* or *banque,* which fignifies the table or counter of a tradefman (Dufrefne. I. 969.) and *ruptus,* broken ; denoting thereby one whofe fhop or place of trade is broken and gone ; though others rather chufe to adopt the word *route,* which in French fignifies a trace or track, and tell us that a bankrupt is one who hath removed his banque, leaving but a trace behind. (4 Inft. 277.) And it is obfervable that the

title of the firft Englifh ftatute concerning this offence, 34 Hen.VIII. c. 4. "againft "fuch perfons as do make bankrupt," is a literal tranflation of the French idiom, *qui font banque route.*

[f] Taylor. *Comment. in L. decemviral.* Bynkerfh. *Obferv. Jur. I.* 1. Heinecc. *Antiqu. III.* 30. 4.

[g] In Pegu, and the adjacent countries in Eaft India, the creditor is entitled to difpofe of the debtor himfelf, and likewife of his

many popular infurrections, and feceffions to the *mons facer*. But I mean the law of *ceffion*, introduced by the chriftian empe-rors; whereby if a debtor ceded, or yielded up, all his fortune to his creditors, he was fecured from being dragged to a goal, " *omni* " *quoque corporali cruciatu femoto*[h]." For, as the emperor juftly obferves [i], " *inhumanum erat fpoliatum fortunis fuis in folidum* " *damnari.*" Thus far was juft and reafonable : but, as the de-parting from one extreme is apt to produce it's oppofite, we find it afterwards enacted [k], that if the debtor by any unforefeen ac-cident was reduced to low circumftances, and would *fwear* that he had not fufficient left to pay his debts, he fhould not be com-pelled to cede or give up even that which he had in his poffeffion : a law, which under a falfe notion of humanity, feems to be fer-tile of perjury, injuftice, and abfurdity.

TH E laws of England, more wifely, have fteered in the middle between both extremes : providing at once againft the inhumanity of the creditor, who is not fuffered to confine an honeft bankrupt after his effects are delivered up; and at the fame time taking care that all his juft debts fhall be paid, fo far as the effects will extend. But ftill they are cautious of encouraging prodigality and extravagance by this indulgence to debtors; and therefore they allow the benefit of the laws of bankruptcy to none but ac-tual *traders*; fince that fet of men are, generally fpeaking, the only perfons liable to accidental loffes, and to an inability of paying their debts, without any fault of their own. If perfons in other fituations of life run in debt without the power of pay-ment, they muft take the confequences of their own indifcretion, even though they meet with fudden accidents that may reduce their fortunes : for the law holds it to be an unjuftifiable prac-tice, for any perfon but a tradefman to encumber himfelf with debts of any confiderable value. If a gentleman, or one in a

his wife and children ; infomuch that he may even violate with impunity the chafti-ty of the debtor's wife : but then, by fo doing, the debt is underftood to be dif-

charged. (Mod. Un. Hift. vii. 128)
[h] *Cod.* 7. 71. *per tot.*
[i] *Inft.* 4. 6. 40.
[k] *Nov.* 135. *c.* 1.

liberal profeſſion, at the time of contracting his debts, has a ſufficient fund to pay them, the delay of payment is a ſpecies of
diſhoneſty, and a temporary injuſtice to his creditor : and if, at
ſuch time, he has no ſufficient fund, the diſhoneſty and injuſtice
is the greater. He cannot therefore murmur, if he ſuffers the
puniſhment which he has voluntarily drawn upon himſelf. But
in mercantile tranſactions the caſe is far otherwiſe. Trade cannot
be carried on without mutual credit on both ſides : the contracting of debts is therefore here not only juſtifiable, but neceſſary.
And if by accidental calamities, as by the loſs of a ſhip in a
tempeſt, the failure of brother traders, or by the non-payment
of perſons out of trade, a merchant or tradeſman becomes incapable of diſcharging his own debts, it is his misfortune and not
his fault. To the misfortunes therefore of debtors the law has
given a compaſſionate remedy, but denied it to their faults : ſince,
at the ſame time that it provides for the ſecurity of commerce,
by enacting that every conſiderable trader may be declared a bankrupt, for the benefit of his creditors as well as himſelf, it has
alſo to diſcourage extravagance declared, that no one ſhall be capable of being made a bankrupt, but only a *trader ;* nor capable
of receiving the full benefit of the ſtatutes, but only an *induſtrious* trader.

T h e firſt ſtatute made concerning any Engliſh bankrupts, was
34 Hen. VIII. c. 4. when trade began firſt to be properly cultivated in England : which has been almoſt totally altered by ſtatute
13 Eliz. c. 7. whereby bankruptcy is confined to ſuch perſons
only as have *uſed the trade of merchandize,* in groſs or by retail,
by way of bargaining, exchange, rechange, bartering, chevi-
ſance[1], or otherwiſe ; or have *ſought their living by buying and
ſelling.* And by ſtatute 21 Jac. I. c. 19. perſons uſing the trade
or profeſſion of a *ſcrivener,* receiving other mens monies and e-
ſtates into their truſt and cuſtody, are alſo made liable to the ſtatutes of bankruptcy : and the benefits, as well as the penal parts
of the law, are extended as well to *aliens* and *denizens* as to na-

---

[1] that is, making contracts. (Dufreſne. II. 569.)

tural

tural born fubjects ; being intended entirely for the protection of trade, in which aliens are often as deeply concerned as natives. By many fubfequent ftatutes, but laftly by ftatute 5 Geo. II. c. 30.[m] *bankers, brokers,* and *factors,* are declared liable to the ftatutes of bankruptcy; and this upon the fame reafon that fcriveners are included by the ftatute of James I. *viz.* for the relief of their creditors; whom they have otherwife more opportunities of defrauding than any other fet of dealers : and they are properly to be looked upon as traders, fince they make merchandize of money, in the fame manner as other merchants do of goods and other moveable chattels. But by the fame act[n], no *farmer, grazier,* or *drover,* fhall (as fuch) be liable to be deemed a bankrupt : for, though they buy and fell corn, and hay, and beafts, in the courfe of hufbandry, yet trade is not their principal, but only a collateral, object; their chief concern being to manure and till the ground, and make the beft advantage of it's produce. And, befides, the fubjecting them to the laws of bankruptcy might be a means of defeating their landlords of the fecurity which the law has given them above all others, for the payment of their referved rents : wherefore alfo, upon a fimilar reafon, a *receiver of the king's taxes* is not capable[o], as fuch, of being a bankrupt; left the king fhould be defeated of thofe extenfive remedies againft his debtors, which are put into his hands by the prerogative. By the fame ftatute[p], no perfon fhall have a commiffion of bankrupt awarded againft him, unlefs at the petition of fome *one* creditor, to whom he owes 100 *l*; or of *two*, to whom he is indebted 150 *l*; or of *more*, to whom all together he is indebted 200 *l*. For the law does not look upon perfons, whofe debts amount to lefs, to be traders confiderable enough, either to enjoy the benefit of the ftatutes, themfelves, or to entitle the creditors, for the benefit of public commerce, to demand the diftribution of their effects.

---

[m] §. 39.   [o] §. ead.
[n] §. 40.   [p] §. 23.

IN the interpretation of thefe feveral ftatutes, it hath been held, that buying only, or felling only, will not qualify a man to be a bankrupt ; but it muft be both buying and felling, and alfo getting a livelyhood by it. As, by exercifing the calling of a merchant, a grocer, a mercer, or, in one general word, a *chapman*, who is one that buys and fells .any thing. But no handicraft occupation (where nothing is bought and fold, and therefore an extenfive credit, for the ftock in trade, is not neceffary to be had) will make a man a regular bankrupt ; as that of a hufbandman, a gardener, and the like, who are paid for their work and labour[q]. Alfo an inn-keeper cannot, as fuch, be a bankrupt[r]: for his gain or livelyhood does not arife from buying and felling in the way of merchandize, but greatly from the ufe of his rooms and furniture, his attendance, and the like : and though he may buy corn and victuals, to fell again at a profit, yet that no more makes him a trader, than a fchoolmafter or other perfon is, that keeps a boarding houfe, and makes confiderable gains by buying and felling what he fpends in the houfe, and fuch a one is clearly not within the ftatutes[s]. But where perfons buy goods, and make them up into faleable commodities, as fhoe-makers, fmiths, and the like ; here, though part of the gain is by bodily labour, and not by buying and felling, yet they are within the ftatutes of bankrupts[t]; for the labour is only in melioration of the commodity, and rendering it more fit for fale.

ONE fingle act of buying and felling will not make a man a trader ; but a repeated practice, and profit by it. Buying and felling bank-ftock, or other government fecurities, will not make a man a bankrupt ; they not being goods, wares, or merchandize, within the intent of the ftatute, by which a profit may be fairly made[u]. Neither will buying and felling under particular reftraints, or for particular purpofes ; as if a commiffioner of the

[q] Cro. Car. 31.   [t] Cro. Car. 31. Skinn. 292.
[r] Cro. Car. 549. Skinn. 291.   [u] 2 P. Wms. 308.
[s] Skinn. 292. 3 Mod. 330.

navy ufes to buy victuals for the fleet, and difpofe of the furplus and refufe, he is not thereby made a trader within the ftatutes ᵂ. An infant, though a trader, cannot be made a bankrupt : for an infant can owe nothing but for neceffaries; and the ftatutes of bankruptcy create no new debts, but only give a fpeedier and more effectual remedy for recovering fuch as were before due : and no perfon can be made a bankrupt for debts, which he is not liable at law to pay ˣ. But a feme-covert in London, being a fole trader according to the cuftom, is liable to a commiffion of bankrupt ʸ.

2. HAVING thus confidered, who may, and who may not, be made a bankrupt, we are to inquire, fecondly, by what *acts* a man may become a bankrupt. A bankrupt is "a trader, who " fecretes himfelf, or does certain other acts, tending to defraud " his creditors." We have hitherto been employed in explaining the former part of this defcription, " a trader :" let us now attend to the latter, " who fecretes himfelf, or does certain other " acts, tending to defraud his creditors." And, in general, whenever fuch a trader, as is before defcribed, hath endeavoured to avoid his creditors or evade their juft demands, this hath been declared by the legiflature to be an act of bankruptcy, upon which a commiffion may be fued out. For in this extrajudicial method of proceeding, which is allowed merely for the benefit of commerce, the law is extremely watchful to detect a man, whofe circumftances are declining, in the firft inftance, or at leaft as early as poffible : that the creditors may receive as large a proportion of their debts as may be; and that a man may not go on wantonly wafting his fubftance, and then claim the benefit of the ftatutes, when he has nothing left to diftribute.

To learn what the particular acts of bankruptcy are, which render a man a bankrupt, we muft confult the feveral ftatutes, and the refolutions formed by the courts thereon. Among thefe

ᵂ 1 Salk. 110. Skin. 292.   ʸ *La Vie* v. *Philips.* M. 6 Geo. III. B. R.
ˣ Lord Raym. 443.

may

may therefore be reckoned, 1. Departing from the realm, whereby a man withdraws himfelf from the jurifdiction and coërcion of the law, with intent to defraud his creditors ². 2. Departing from his own houfe, with intent to fecrete himfelf, and avoid his creditors ³. 3. Keeping in his own houfe, privately, fo as not to be feen or fpoken with by his creditors, except for juft and neceffary caufe; which is likewife conftrued to be an intention to defraud his creditors, by avoiding the procefs of the law ᵇ. 4. Procuring or fuffering himfelf willingly to be arrefted, or outlawed, or imprifoned, without juft and lawful caufe; which is likewife deemed an attempt to defraud his creditors ᶜ. 5. Procuring his money, goods, chattels, and effects to be attached or fequeftered by any legal procefs; which is another plain and direct endeavour to difappoint his creditors of their fecurity ᵈ. 6. Making any fraudulent conveyance to a friend, or fecret truftee, of his lands, tenements, goods, or chattels; which is an act of the fame fufpicious nature with the laft ᵉ. 7. Procuring any protection, not being himfelf privileged by parliament, in order to fcreen his perfon from arrefts; which alfo is an endeavour to elude the juftice of the law ᶠ. 8. Endeavouring or defiring, by any petition to the king, or bill exhibited in any of the king's courts againft any creditors, to compel them to take lefs than their juft debts; or to procraftinate the time of payment, originally contracted for; which are an acknowlegement of either his poverty or his knavery ᵍ. 9. Lying in prifon for two months, or more, upon arreft or other detention for debt, without finding bail, in order to obtain his liberty ʰ. For the inability to procure bail argues a ftrong deficiency in his credit, owing either to his fufpected poverty, or ill character; and his neglect to do it, if able, can arife only from a fraudulent intention: in either of which cafes it is high time for his creditors to look to

---

ᶻ Stat. 13 Eliz. c. 7.
ᵃ *Ibid.* 1 Jac. I. c. 15.
ᵇ Stat. 13 Eliz. c. 7.
ᶜ *Ibid.* 1 Jac. I. c. 15.
ᵈ Stat. 1 Jac. I. c. 15.

ᵉ *Ibid.*
ᶠ Stat. 21 Jac. I. c. 19.
ᵍ *Ibid.*
ʰ *Ibid.*

themfelves,

themselves, and compel a diftribution of his effects. 10. Efca-ping from prifon after an arreft for a juft debt of 100 *l.* or up-wards[i]. For no man would break prifon, that was able and de-firous to procure bail; which brings it within the reafon of the laft cafe. 11. Neglecting to make fatisfaction for any juft debt to the amount of 100 *l.* within two months after fervice of legal procefs, for fuch debt, upon any trader having privilege of par-liament[k].

THESE are the feveral acts of bankruptcy, expreffly defined by the ftatutes relating to this title: which being fo numerous, and the whole law of bankrupts being an innovation on the com-mon law, our courts of juftice have been tender of extending or multiplying acts of bankruptcy by any conftruction, or implica-tion. And therefore fir John Holt held[l], that a man's removing his goods privately, to prevent their being feifed in execution, was no act of bankruptcy. For the ftatutes mention only frau-dulent gifts to third perfons, and procuring them to be feifed by fham procefs, in order to defraud creditors: but this, though a palpable fraud, yet falling within neither of thofe cafes, cannot be adjudged an act of bankruptcy. So alfo it has been determi-ned expreffly, that a banker's ftopping or refufing payment is no act of bankruptcy; for it is not within the defcription of any of the ftatutes, and there may be good reafons for his fo doing, as, fufpicion of forgery, and the like: and if, in confequence of fuch refufal, he is arrefted, and puts in bail, ftill it is no act of bank-ruptcy[m]: but if he goes to prifon, and lies there two months, then, and not before, is he become a bankrupt.

WE have feen *who* may be a bankrupt, and what *acts* will make him fo: let us next confider,

3. THE *proceedings* on a commiffion of bankrupt; fo far as they affect the bankrupt himfelf. And thefe depend entirely on

[i] Stat. 21 Jac. I. c. 19.
[k] Stat. 4 Geo. III. c. 33.
[l] Lord Raym. 725.
[m] 7 Mod. 139.

the

the feveral ftatutes of bankruptcy ⁿ; all which I fhall endeavour
to blend together, and digeft into a concife methodical order.

A n d, firft, there muft be a *petition* to the lord chancellor by
one creditor to the amount of 100 *l*, or by two to the amount of
150 *l*, or by three or more to the amount of 200 *l*; upon which
he grants a *commiffion* to fuch difcreet perfons as to him fhall
feem good, who are then ftiled commiffioners of bankrupt. The
petitioners, to prevent malicious applications, muft be bound in
a fecurity of 200 *l*, to make the party amends in cafe they do
not prove him a bankrupt. And, if on the other hand they receive any money or effects from the bankrupt, as a recompenfe
for fuing out the commiffion, fo as to receive more than their ratable dividends of the bankrupt's eftate, they forfeit not only
what they fhall have fo received, but their whole debt. Thefe
provifions are made, as well to fecure perfons in good credit from
being damnified by malicious petitions, as to prevent knavifh
combinations between the creditors and bankrupt, in order to
obtain the benefit of a commiffion. When the commiffion is a-
warded and iffued, the commiffioners are to meet, at their own
expenfe, and to take an oath for the due execution of their commiffion, and to be allowed a fum not exceeding 20 *s. per diem*
each, at every fitting. And no commiffion of bankrupt fhall
abate, or be void, upon any demife of the crown.

W h e n the commiffioners have received their commiffion,
they are firft to receive proof of the perfon's being a trader, and
having committed fome act of bankruptcy; and then to declare
him a bankrupt, if proved fo; and to give notice thereof in the
gazette, and at the fame time to appoint three meetings. At the
firft of thefe meetings an election muft be made of affignees, or
perfons to whom the bankrupt's eftate fhall be affigned, and in
whom it fhall be vefted for the benefit of the creditors; which
affignees are to be firft named by the commiffioners, and after-

ⁿ 13 Eliz. c 7. 1 Jac. I. c.15. 21 Jac. I. c.19. 7 Geo. I. c.31. 5 Geo. II. c.30. 19 Geo. II.
c. 32. & 24 Geo. II. c. 57.

wards

wards to be approved or rejected at the said meeting by the major part, in value, of the creditors who shall then prove their debts : but no creditor shall be admitted to vote in the choice of assignees, whose debt on the ballance of accounts does not amount to 10*l*. At the second meeting any farther business relating to the commission may be proceeded on. And at the third meeting, at fartheft, which must be on the forty second day after the advertisement in the gazette, the bankrupt, upon notice also personally ferved upon him or left at his usual place of abode, must surrender himself personally to the commissioners, and must thenceforth in all respects conform to the directions of the statutes of bankruptcy; or, in default thereof, shall be guilty of felony without benefit of clergy, and shall suffer death, and his goods and estate shall be distributed among his creditors.

IN case the bankrupt absconds, or is likely to run away, between the time of the commission issued, and the last day of surrender, he may by warrant from any judge or justice of the peace be committed to the county goal, in order to be forthcoming to the commissioners; who are also empowered immediately to grant a warrant for seising his goods and papers.

WHEN the bankrupt appears, the commissioners are to examine him touching all matters relating to his trade and effects. They may also summon before them, and examine, the bankrupt's wife and any other person whatsoever, as to all matters relating to the bankrupt's affairs. And in case any of them shall refuse to answer, or shall not answer fully, to any lawful question, or shall refuse to subscribe such their examination, the commissioners may commit them to prison without bail, till they make and sign a full answer; the commissioners specifying in their warrant of commitment the question so refused to be answered. And any goaler, permitting such persons to escape, or go out of prison, shall forfeit 500 *l*. to the creditors.

TH E brankrupt, upon this examination, is bound upon pain of death to make a full difcovery of all his eftate and effects, as well in expectancy as poffeffion, and how he has difpofed of the fame; together with all books and writings relating thereto : and is to deliver up all in his own power to the commiffioners; (except the neceffary apparel of himfelf, his wife, and his children) or, in cafe he conceals or imbezzles any effects to the amount of 20 *l*, or withholds any books or writings, with intent to defraud his creditors, he fhall be guilty of felony without benefit of clergy °.

AFTER the time allowed to the bankrupt for fuch difcovery is expired, any other perfon voluntarily difcovering any part of his eftate, before unknown to the affignees, fhall be entitled to *five per cent.* out of the effects fo difcovered, and fuch farther reward as the affignees and commiffioners fhall think proper. And any truftee wilfully concealing the eftate of any bankrupt, after the expiration of the two and forty days, fhall forfeit 100*l*, and double the value of the eftate concealed, to the creditors.

HITHERTO every thing is in favour of the creditors; and the law feems to be pretty rigid and fevere againft the bankrupt: but, in cafe he proves honeft, it makes him full amends for all this rigor and feverity. For if the bankrupt hath made an ingenuous difcovery, hath conformed to the directions of the law, and hath acted in all points to the fatisfaction of his creditors; and if they, or four parts in five of them in number and value, (but none of them creditors for lefs than 20 *l*.) will fign a certificate to that purport; the commiffioners are then to authenticate fuch certificate under their hands and feals, and to tranfmit it to the lord chancellor : and he, or two judges whom he fhall ap-

---

° By the laws of Naples all fraudulent bankrupts, particularly fuch as do not furrender themfelves within four days, are punifhed with death : alfo all who conceal the effects of a bankrupt, or fet up a pretended debt to defraud his creditors. (Mod. Un. Hift. xxviii. 320.)

point, on oath made by the bankrupt that fuch certificate was obtained without fraud, may allow the fame; or difallow it, upon caufe fhewn by any of the creditors of the bankrupt.

I F no caufe be fhewn to the contrary, the certificate is allowed of courfe; and then the bankrupt is entitled to a decent and reafonable allowance out of his effects, for his future fupport and maintenance, and to put him in a way of honeft induftry. This allowance is alfo in proportion to his former good behaviour, in the early difcovery of the decline of his affairs, and thereby giving his creditors a larger dividend. For, if his effects will not pay one half of his debts, or ten fhillings in the pound, he is left to the difcretion of the commiffioners and affignees, to have a competent fum allowed him, not exceeding *three per cent:* but if they pay ten fhillings in the pound, he is to be allowed *five per cent*; if twelve fhillings and fixpence, then *feven and a half per cent*; and if fifteen fhillings in the pound, then the bankrupt fhall be allowed *ten per cent:* provided, that fuch allowance do not in the firft cafe exceed 200*l*, in the fecond 250*l*, and in the third 300*l*. ᴾ

BESIDES this allowance, he has alfo an indemnity granted him, of being free and difcharged for ever from all debts owing by him at the time he became a bankrupt; even though judgment fhall have been obtained againft him, and he lies in prifon upon execution for fuch debts; and, for that among other purpofes, all proceedings on commiffions of bankrupt are, on petition, to be entered of record, as a perpetual bar againft actions to be commenced on this account: though, in general, the production of the certificate properly allowed fhall be fufficient evidence of all previ-

---

ᴾ By the Roman law of ceffion, if the debtor acquired any confiderable property fubfequent to the giving up of his all, it was liable to the demands of his creditors. (*Ff*. 42. 3. 4.) But this did not extend to fuch allowance as was left to him on the fcore of compaffion, for the maintenance of himfelf and family. *Si quid mifericordiae caufa ei fuerit relictum, puta menftruum vel annuum, alimentorum nomine, non oportet propter hoc bona ejus iterato venundari: nec enim fraudandus eft alimentis quotidianis.* (*Ibid* l.6.)

ous proceedings. Thus the bankrupt becomes a clear man again; and, by the affiftance of his allowance and his own induftry, may become a ufeful member of the commonwealth : which is the rather to be expected, as he cannot be entitled to thefe benefits, but by the teftimony of his creditors themfelves of his honeft and ingenuous difpofition ; and unlefs his failures have been owing to misfortunes, rather than to mifconduct and extravagance.

F o r no allowance or indemnity fhall be given to a bankrupt, unlefs his certificate be figned and allowed, as before-mentioned; and alfo, if any creditor produces a fictitious debt, and the bankrupt does not make difcovery of it, but fuffers the fair creditors to be impofed upon, he lofes all title to thefe advantages. Neither can he claim them, if he has given with any of his children above 100 *l.* for a marriage portion, unlefs he had at that time fufficient left to pay all his debts ; or if he has loft at any one time 5 *l*, or in the whole 100 *l*, within a twelvemonth before he became bankrupt, by any manner of gaming or wagering whatfoever ; or, within the fame time, has loft to the value of 100 *l.* by ftockjobbing. Alfo, to prevent the too common practice of frequent and fraudulent or carelefs breaking, a mark is fet upon fuch as have been once cleared by a commiffion of bankrupt, or have compounded with their creditors, or have been delivered by an act of infolvency : which is an occafional act, frequently paffed [q] by the legiflature ; whereby all perfons whatfoever, who are either in too low a way of dealing to become bankrupts, or not being in a mercantile ftate of life are not included within the laws of bankruptcy, are difcharged from all fuits and imprifonment, upon delivering up all their eftate and effects to their creditors upon oath, at the feffions or affifes ; in which cafe their perjury or fraud is ufually, as in cafe of bankrupts, punifhed with death. Perfons who have been once cleared by this, or either of the other methods, (of compofition with their creditors, or bankruptcy) and afterwards become bankrupts

[q] Stat. 28 Geo. II. c 13. 32 Geo. II. c. 28. 1 Geo. III. c. 17. 5 Geo. III. c. 41.

again,

again, unlefs they pay full fifteen fhillings in the pound, are only thereby indemnified as to the confinement of their bodies; but any future eftate they fhall acquire remains liable to their creditors, excepting their neceffary apparel, houfehold goods, and the tools and implements of their trades.

T H U S much for the proceedings on a commiffion of bankrupt, fo far as they affect the bankrupt himfelf perfonally. Let us next confider,

4. H o w fuch proceedings affect or transfer the *eftate* and *property* of the bankrupt. The method whereby a *real* eftate, in lands, tenements, and hereditaments, may be transferred by bankruptcy, was fhewn under it's proper head, in a former chapter[r]. At prefent therefore we are only to confider the transfer of things *perfonal* by this operation of law.

B Y virtue of the ftatutes before-mentioned all the perfonal eftate and effects of the bankrupt are confidered as vefted, by the act of bankruptcy, in the future affignees of his commiffioners, whether they be goods in actual *poffeffion,* or debts, contracts, and other chofes in *action;* and the commiffioners by their warrant may caufe any houfe or tenement of the bankrupt to be broken open, in order to enter upon and feize the fame. And, when the affignees are chofen or approved by the creditors, the commiffioners are to affign every thing over to them; and the property of every part of the eftate is thereby as fully vefted in them, as it was in the bankrupt himfelf, and they have the fame remedies to recover it[s].

T H E property vefted in the affignees is the whole that the bankrupt had in himfelf, at the time he committed the firft act of bankruptcy, or that has been vefted in him fince, before his debts are fatisfied or agreed for. Therefore it is ufually faid, that once a bankrupt, and always a bankrupt : by which is meant,

[r] pag. 285.   [s] 12 Mod. 324.

that

that a plain direct act of bankruptcy once committed cannot be purged, or explained away, by any subsequent conduct, as a dubious equivocal act may be [u]; but that, if a commission is afterwards awarded, the commission and the property of the assignees shall have a relation, or reference, back to the first and original act of bankruptcy [u]. Infomuch that all transactions of the bankrupt are from that time abfolutely null and void, either with regard to the alienation of his property, or the receipt of his debts from fuch as are privy to his bankruptcy; for they are no longer his property, or his debts, but thofe of the future assignees. And, if an execution be fued out, but not ferved and executed on the bankrupt's effects till after the act of bankruptcy, it is void as againft the assignees. But the king is not bound by this fictitious relation, nor is within the ftatutes of bankrupts [w]; for if, after the act of bankruptcy committed and before the assignment of his effects, an extent issues for the debt of the crown, the goods are bound thereby [x]. In France this doctrine of relation is carried to a very great length; for there every act of a merchant, for ten days *precedent* to the act of bankruptcy, is prefumed to be fraudulent, and is therefore void [y]. But with us the law ftands upon a more reafonable footing : for, as thefe acts of bankruptcy may fometimes be fecret to all but a few, and it would be prejudicial to trade to carry this notion to it's utmoft length, it is provided by ftatute 19 Geo. II. c. 32. that no money paid by a bankrupt to a *bona fide* or real creditor, in a courfe of trade, even after an act of bankruptcy done, fhall be liable to be refunded. Nor, by ftatute 1 Jac. I. c. 15. fhall any debtor of a bankrupt, that pays him his debt, without knowing of his bankruptcy, be liable to account for it again. The intention of this relative power being only to reach fraudulent transactions, and not to diftrefs the fair trader.

THE assignees may purfue any *legal* method of recovering this property fo vefted in them, by their own authority; but cannot

[t] Salk. 110.
[u] 4 Burr. 32.
[w] Atk. 262.

[x] Viner. Abr. t. creditor and bankr. 104.
[y] Sp. L. b. 29. c. 16.

commence

commence a fuit in *equity*, nor compound any debts owing to the bankrupt, nor refer any matters to arbitration, without the confent of the creditors, or the major part of them in value, at a meeting to be held in purfuance of notice in the gazette.

WHEN they have got in all the effects they can reafonably hope for, and reduced them to ready money, the affignees muft, within twelve months after the commiffion iffued, give one and twenty days notice to the creditors of a meeting for a dividend or diftribution; at which time they muft produce their accounts, and verify them upon oath, if required. And then the commiffioners fhall direct a dividend to be made, at fo much in the pound, to all creditors who have before proved, or fhall then prove, their debts. This dividend muft be made equally, and in a ratable proportion, to all the creditors, according to the *quantity* of their debts; no regard being had to the *quality* of them. Mortgages indeed, for which the creditor has a real fecurity in his own hands, are entirely fafe; for the commiffion of bankrupt reaches only the equity of redemption[z]. So are alfo perfonal debts, where the creditor has a chattel in his hands, as a pledge or pawn for the payment, or has taken the debtor's lands or goods in execution. And, upon the equity of the ftatute 8 Ann. c. 14. (which directs, that, upon all executions of goods being on any premifes demifed to a tenant, one year's rent and no more fhall, if due, be paid to the landlord) it hath alfo been held, that under a commiffion of bankrupt, which is in the nature of a ftatute-execution, the landlord fhall be allowed his arrears of rent to the fame amount, in preference to other creditors, even though he hath neglected to diftrein, while the goods remained on the premifes; which he is otherwife intitled to do for his intire rent, be the *quantum* what it may[a]. But, otherwife, judgments and recognizances, (both which are debts of record, and therefore at other times have a priority) and alfo bonds and obligations by deed or fpecial inftrument (which are called debts by fpecialty, and are ufually the next in order) thefe are all put

[z] Finch. Rep. 466.   [a] Atk. 103, 104.

on a level with debts by mere fimple contract, and all paid *pari paſſu*. Nay, fo far is this matter carried, that, by the expreſs proviſion of the ſtatutes, debts not due at the time of the dividend made, as bonds or notes of hand payable at a future day, ſhall be paid equally with the reſt[b], allowing a diſcount or drawback in proportion. And inſurances, and obligations upon bottomry or *reſpondentia*, *bona fide* made by the bankrupt, though forfeited after the commiſſion is awarded, ſhall be looked upon in the ſame light as debts contracted before any act of bankruptcy.

W I T H I N eighteen months after the commiſſion iſſued, a fecond and final dividend ſhall be made, unleſs all the effects were exhauſted by the firſt. And if any ſurplus remains, after paying every creditor his full debt, it ſhall be reſtored to the bankrupt. This is a caſe which ſometimes happens to men in trade, who involuntarily, or at leaſt unwarily, commit acts of bankruptcy, by abſconding and the like, while their effects are more than ſufficient to pay their creditors. And, if any ſuſpicious or malevolent creditor will take the advantage of ſuch acts, and ſue out a commiſſion, the bankrupt has no remedy, but muſt quietly ſubmit to the effects of his own imprudence; except that, upon ſatisfaction made to all the creditors, the commiſſion may be *ſuperſeded*[c]. This caſe may alſo happen, when a knave is deſirous of defrauding his creditors, and is compelled by a commiſſion to do them that juſtice, which otherwiſe he wanted to evade. And therefore, though the uſual rule is, that all intereſt on debts carrying intereſt ſhall ceaſe from the time of iſſuing the commiſſion, yet, in caſe of a ſurplus left after payment of every debt, ſuch intereſt ſhall again revive, and be chargeable on the bankrupt[d], or his repreſentatives.

[b] Lord Raym. 1549.
[c] 2 Ch. Caſ. 144.
[d] Atk. 244.

CHAPTER THE THIRTY SECOND.

OF TITLE BY TESTAMENT, AND
ADMINISTRATION.

THERE yet remain to be examined, in the prefent chapter, two other methods of acquiring perfonal eftates, *viz.*
by *teftament* and *adminiftration.* And thefe I propofe to confider
in one and the fame view; they being in their nature fo connected and blended together, as makes it impoffible to treat of
them diftinctly, without manifeft tautology and repetition.

XI. XII. IN the purfuit then of this joint fubject, I fhall,
firft, enquire into the original and antiquity of teftaments and
adminiftrations; fhall, fecondly, fhew who is capable of making
a laft will and teftament; fhall, thirdly, confider the nature of
a teftament and it's incidents; fhall, fourthly, fhew what an executor and adminiftrator are, and how they are to be appointed;
and, laftly, fhall felect fome few of the general heads of the office and duty of executors and adminiftrators.

FIRST, as to the *original* of teftaments and adminiftrations.
We have more than once obferved, that, when property came to
be vefted in individuals by the right of occupancy, it became neceffary for the peace of fociety, that this occupancy fhould be
continued, not only in the prefent poffeffor, but in thofe perfons
to whom he fhould think proper to transfer it; which introduced

the doctrine and practice of alienations, gifts, and contracts. But thefe precautions would be very fhort and imperfect, if they were confined to the life only of the occupier ; for then upon his death all his goods would again become common, and create an infinite variety of ftrife and confufion. The law of very many focieties has therefóre given to the proprietor a right of continuing his property after his death, in fuch perfons as he fhall name ; and, in defect of fuch appointment or nomination, the law of every fociety has directed the goods to be vefted in certain particular individuals, exclufive of all other perfons[a]. The former method of acquiring perfonal property, according to the exprefs directions of the deceafed, we call a *teftament :* the latter, which is alfo according to the will of the deceafed, not expreffed indeed but prefumed by the law[b], we call in England an *adminiftration* ; being the fame which the civil lawyers term a fucceffion *ab inteftato,* and which anfwers to the defcent or inheritance of real eftates.

TESTAMENTS are of very high antiquity. We find them in ufe among the antient Hebrews ; though I hardly think the example ufually given[c], of Abraham's complaining[d] that, unlefs he had fome children of his body, his fteward Eliezer of Damafcus would be his heir, is quite conclufive to fhew that he had made him fo by *will.* And indeed a learned writer[e] has adduced this very paffage to prove, that in the patriarchal age, on failure of children or kindred, the fervants born under their mafter's roof fucceeded to the inheritance as heirs at law[f]. But, (to omit what Eufebius and others have related of Noah's teftament, made in *writing* and witneffed under his *feal,* whereby he difpofed of the whole world[g]) I apprehend that a much more authentic inftance of the early ufe of teftaments may be found in the facred writings[h], wherein Jacob bequeaths to his fon Jo-

---

[a] Puff. L. of N. b. 4. c. 10.
[b] *Ibid.* b 4. c. 11.
[c] Barbeyr. Puff. 4. 10. 4. Godolph. Orph. Leg. 1. 1.
[d] Gen. c. 15.

[e] Taylor's elem. civ. law. 517.
[f] See pag. 12.
[g] Selden. *de fucc. Ebr. c.* 24.
[h] Gen. c. 48.

feph

feph a portion of his inheritance double to that of his brethren: which will we find carried into execution many hundred years afterwards, when the pofterity of Jofeph were divided into two diftinct tribes, thofe of Ephraim and Manaffeh, and had two feveral inheritances affigned them ; whereas the defcendents of each of the other patriarchs formed only one fingle tribe, and had only one lot of inheritance. Solon was the firft legiflator that introduced wills into Athens[i]; but in many other parts of Greece they were totally difcountenanced[k]. In Rome they were unknown, till the laws of the twelve tables were compiled, which firft gave the right of bequeathing[l]: and, among the northern nations, particularly among the Germans[m], teftaments were not received into ufe. And this variety may ferve to evince, that the right of making wills, and difpofing of property after death, is merely a creature of the civil ftate[n]; which has permitted it in fome countries, and denied it in others : and, even where it is permitted by law, it is fubjected to different formalities and reftrictions in almoft every nation under heaven[o].

WITH us in England this power of bequeathing is co-eval with the firft rudiments of the law : for we have no traces or memorials of any time when it did not exift. Mention is made of inteftacy, in the old law before the conqueft, as being merely accidental ; and the diftribution of the inteftate's eftate, after payment of the lord's heriot, is then directed to go according to the eftablifhed law. " *Sive quis incuria, five morte repentina, fuerit* " *inteftatus mortuus, dominus tamen nullam rerum fuarum partem* " *(praeter eam quae jure debetur hereoti nomine) fibi affumito. Verum* " *poffeffiones uxori, liberis, et cognatione proximis, pro fuo cuique* " *jure, diftribuantur*[p]." But we are not to imagine, that the power of bequeathing extended originally to *all* a man's perfonal eftate. On the contrary, Glanvil will inform us[q], that by the

[i] Plutarch. *in vita Solon.*
[k] Pott. Antiq. l. 4. c. 15.
[l] *Inft.* 2. 22. 1.
[m] Tacit. *de mor. Germ.* 21.
[n] See pag. 13.

[o] Sp. L. b. 27. c. 1. Vinnius *in Inft. l.2. tit.* 10.
[p] *LL. Canut.* c. 68.
[q] *l.* 2. c. 5.

common

common law, as it ſtood in the reign of Henry the ſecond, a
man's goods were to be divided into three equal parts; of which
one went to his heirs or lineal deſcendants, another to his wife,
and the third was at his own diſpoſal : or if he died without a
wife, he might then diſpoſe of one moiety, and the other went
to his children ; and ſo *e converſo*, if he had no children, the
wife was entitled to one moiety, and he might bequeath the o-
ther : but, if he died without either wife or iſſue, the whole was
at his own diſpoſal ᶠ. The ſhares of the wife and children was
called their *reaſonable* part; and the writ *de rationabili parte bonorum* was given to recover it ˢ.

T H I S continued to be the law of the land at the time of *magna
carta*, which provides, that the king's debts ſhall firſt of all be
levied, and then the reſidue of the goods ſhall go to the executor to perform the will of the deceaſed : and, if nothing be owing
to the crown, " *omnia catalla cedant defuncto ; ſalvis uxori ipſius
" et pueris ſuis rationabilibus partibus ſuis* ᵗ." In the reign of king
Edward the third this right of the wife and children was ſtill
held to be the univerſal or common law ᵘ; though frequently
pleaded as the local cuſtom of Berks, Devon, and other counties ʷ : and ſir Henry Finch lays it down expreſſly ˣ, in the reign
of Charles the firſt, to be the general law of the land. But this
law is at preſent altered by imperceptible degrees, and the deceaſed may now by will bequeath the whole of his goods and
chattels; though we cannot trace out when firſt this alteration

---

ᶠ Bracton. *l.* 2. *c.* 26.   Flet. *l.* 2. *c.* 57.
ˢ F. N. B. 122.
ᵗ 9 Hen. III. c. 18.
ᵘ A widow brought an action of detinue
againſt her huſband's executors, *quod cum
per conſuetudinem totius regni Angliae hactenus
uſitatam et approbatam, uxores debent et ſolent
a tempore &c, habere ſuam rationabilem partem bonorum maritorum ſuorum : ita videlicet,
quod ſi nullos habuerint liberos, tunc medieta-
tem ; et, ſi habuerint, tunc tertiam partem, &c;*
and that her huſband died worth 200,000

marks, without iſſue had between them ;
and thereupon ſhe claimed the moiety.
Some exceptions were taken to the pleadings, and the fact of the huſband's dying
without iſſue was denied ; but the rule of
law, as ſtated in the writ, ſeems to have
been univerſally allowed. *(M.* 30 *Edw.*
III. 25.*)* And a ſimilar caſe occurs in
H. 17 *Edw. III.* 9.
ʷ *Reg. Brev.* 142.   Co. Litt. 176.
ˣ Law. 175.

began.

began. Indeed fir Edward Coke[y] is of opinion, that this never was the general law, but only obtained in particular places by fpecial cuftom : and to eftablifh that doctrine he relies on a paffage in Bracton, which in truth, when compared with the context, makes directly againft his opinion. For Bracton[z] lays down the doctrine of the *reafonable part* to be the common law ; but mentions that as a particular exception, which fir Edward Coke has haftily cited for the general rule. And Glanvil, *magna carta,* Fleta, the year-books, Fitzherbert, and Finch, do all agree with Bracton, that this right to the *pars rationabilis* was by the common law : which alfo continues to this day to be the general law of our fifter kingdom of Scotland[a]. To which we may add, that, whatever may have been the cuftom of later years in many parts of the kingdom, or however it was introduced in derogation of the old common law, the antient method continued in ufe in the province of York, the principality of Wales, and the city of London, till very modern times : when, in order to favour the power of bequeathing, and to reduce the whole kingdom to the fame ftandard, three ftatutes have been provided ; the one 4 & 5 W. & M. c. 2. explained by 2 & 3 Ann. c. 5. for the province of York ; another 7 & 8 W. III. c. 38. for Wales ; and a third, 11 Geo. I. c.18. for London : whereby it is enacted, that perfons within thofe diftricts, and liable to thofe cuftoms, may (if they think proper) difpofe of *all* their perfonal eftates by will ; and the claims of the widow, children, and other relations, to the contrary, are totally barred. Thus is the old common law now utterly abolifhed throughout all the kingdom of England, and a man may devife the whole of his chattels as freely, as he formerly could his third part or moiety. In difpofing of which, he was bound by the cuftom of many places (as was ftated in a former chapter[b]) to remember his lord and the church, by leaving them his two beft chattels, which was the original of heriots and mortuaries ; and afterwards he was left at his own liberty, to bequeath the remainder as he pleafed.

[y] 2 Inft. 33.   [a] Dalrymp. of feud. property. 145.
[z] *l. 2. c. 26. § 2.*   [b] pag 426.

I N

I n cafe a perfon made no difpofition of fuch of his goods as were teftable, whether that were only part or the whole of them, he was, and is, faid to die inteftate ; and in fuch cafes it is faid, that by the old law the king was entitled to feife upon his goods, as the *parens patriae,* and general truftee of the kingdom [c]. This prerogative the king continued to exercife for fome time by his own minifters of juftice ; and probably in the county court, where matters of all kinds were determined : and it was granted as a franchife to many lords of manors, and others, who have to this day a prefcriptive right to grant adminiftration to their inteftate tenants and fuitors, in their own courts baron and other courts, or to have their wills there proved, in cafe they made any difpo-fition [d]. Afterwards the crown, in favour of the church, invefted the prelates with this branch of the prerogative ; which was done, faith Perkins [e], becaufe it was intended by the law, that fpiritual men are of better confcience than laymen, and that they had more knowlege what things would conduce to the benefit of the foul of the deceafed. The goods therefore of inteftates were given to the ordinary by the crown ; and he might feife them, and keep them without wafting, and alfo might give, alien, or fell them at his will, and difpofe of the money *in pios ufus:* and, if he did otherwife, he broke the confidence which the law repofed in him [f]. So that properly the whole intereft and power, which were granted to the ordinary, were only thofe of being the king's almo-ner within his diocefe; in truft to diftribute the inteftate's goods in charity to the poor, or in fuch fuperftitious ufes as the miftaken zeal of the times had denominated pious [g]. And, as he had thus the difpofition of inteftates effects, the probate of wills of courfe followed : for it was thought juft and natural, that the will of the deceafed fhould be proved to the fatisfaction of the prelate, whofe right of diftributing his chattels for the good of his foul was effectually fuperfeded thereby.

[c] 9 Rep. 38.
[d] *Ibid.* 37.
[e] §. 486.

[f] Finch, Law. 173, 174.
[g] Plowd. 277.

T H E

THE goods of the inteſtate being thus veſted in the ordinary upon the moſt ſolemn and conſcientious truſt, the reverend prelates were therefore not accountable to any, but to God and themſelves, for their conduct [h]. But even in Fleta's time it was complained [i], *"quod ordinarii, hujuſmodi bona nomine ecclefiae occu-* *" pantes, nullam vel ſaltem indebitam faciunt diſtributionem."* And to what a length of iniquity this abuſe was carried, moſt evidently appears from a gloſs of pope Innocent IV [k], written about the year 1250; wherein he lays it down for eſtabliſhed canon law, that *" in Britannia tertia pars bonorum decedentium ab inteſtato in* *" opus ecclefiae et pauperum diſpenfanda eſt."* Thus the popiſh clergy took to themſelves [l] (under the name of the church and poor) the whole reſidue of the deceaſed's eſtate, after the *partes ratio-* *nabiles,* or two thirds, of the wife and children were deducted; without paying even his lawful debts, or other charges thereon. For which reaſon it was enacted by the ſtatute of Weſtm. 2. [m] that the ordinary ſhall be bound to pay the debts of the inteſtate ſo far as his goods will extend, in the ſame manner that executors were bound in caſe the deceaſed had left a will : a uſe more truly pious, than any *requiem,* or maſs for his ſoul. This was the firſt check given to that exorbitant power, which the law had entruſted with ordinaries. But, though they were now made liable to the creditors of the inteſtate for their juſt and lawful demands, yet the *reſiduum,* after payment of debts, remained ſtill in their hands, to be applied to whatever purpoſes the conſcience of the ordinary ſhould approve. The flagrant abuſes of which power occaſioned the legiſlature again to interpoſe, in order to prevent the ordinaries from keeping any longer the adminiſtration in their own hands, or thoſe of their immediate de-

---

[h] Plowd. 277.
[i] *l.* 2. *c.* 57. §. 10.
[k] *in Decretal. l.* 5. *t.* 3. c. 42.
[l] The proportion given to the prieſt, and to other pious uſes, was different in different countries. In the archdeaconry of Rich-

mond in Yorkſhire, this proportion was ſettled by a papal bulle *A.D.* 1254. *(Regiſt. honoris de Richm.* 101.*)* and was obſerved till aboliſhed by the ſtatute 26 Hen. VIII. c. 15.
[m] 13 Edw. I. c. 19.

pendents :

pendents : and therefore the ftatute 31 Edw. III. c. 11. provides, that, in cafe of inteftacy, the ordinary fhall depute the neareft and moft lawful friends of the deceafed to adminifter his goods ; which adminiftrators are put upon the fame footing, with regard to fuits and to accounting, as executors appointed by will. This is the original of adminiftrators, as they at prefent ftand ; who are only the officers of the ordinary, appointed by him in purfuance of this ftatute, which fingles out the *next and moft lawful friend* of the inteftate ; who is interpreted[n] to be the *next of blood* that is under no legal difabilities. The ftatute 21 Hen.VIII. c. 5. enlarges a little more the power of the ecclefiaftical judge ; and permits him to grant adminiftration *either* to the widow, *or* the next of kin, *or* to both of them, at his own difcretion ; and, where two or more perfons are in the fame degree of kindred, gives the ordinary his election to accept whichever he pleafes.

Upon this footing ftands the general law of adminiftrations at this day. I fhall, in the farther progrefs of this chapter, mention a few more particulars, with regard to who may, and who may not, be adminiftrator ; and what he is bound to do when he has taken this charge upon him : what has been hitherto remarked only ferving to fhew the original and gradual progrefs of teftaments and adminiftrations ; in what manner the latter was firft of all vefted in the bifhops by the royal indulgence ; and how it was afterwards, by authority of parliament, taken from them in effect, by obliging them to commit all their power to particular perfons nominated expreffly by the law.

I proceed now, *fecondly*, to enquire who may, or may not make a teftament ; or what perfons are abfolutely obliged by law to die inteftate. And this law[o] is entirely prohibitory ; for, regularly, every perfon hath full power and liberty to make a will, that is not under fome fpecial prohibition by law or cuftom : which prohibitions are principally upon three accounts ; for want

---

[n] 9 Rep. 39.   [o] Godolph. Orph. Leg. *p.* 1. *c.* 7.

of fufficient difcretion; for want of fufficient liberty and free will; and on account of their criminal conduct.

1. In the firft fpecies are to be reckoned infants under the age of fourteen if males, and twelve if females; which is the rule of the civil law [p]. For, though fome of our common lawyers have held that an infant of any age (even four years old) might make a teftament [q], and others have denied that under eighteen he is capable [r], yet as the ecclefiaftical court is the judge of every teftator's capacity, this cafe muft be governed by the rules of the ecclefiaftical law. So that no objection can be admitted to the will of an infant of fourteen, merely for want of age: but, if the teftator was not of fufficient difcretion, whether at the age of fourteen or four and twenty, that will overthrow his teftament. Madmen, or otherwife *non compotes,* idiots or natural fools, perfons grown childifh by reafon of old age or diftemper, fuch as have their fenfes befotted with drunkennefs, --- all thefe are incapable, by reafon of mental difability, to make any will fo long as fuch difability lafts. To this clafs alfo may be referred fuch perfons as are *born* deaf, blind, and dumb; who, as they want the common inlets of underftanding, are incapable of having *animum teftandi,* and their teftaments are therefore void.

2. Such perfons, as are inteftable for want of liberty or freedom of will, are by the civil law of various kinds; as prifoners, captives, and the like [s]. But the law of England does not make fuch perfons abfolutely inteftable; but only leaves it to the difcretion of the court to judge, upon the confideration of the particular circumftances of durefs, whether or no fuch perfons could be fuppofed to have *liberum animum teftandi.* And, with regard to feme-coverts, our laws differ ftill more materially from the civil. Among the Romans there was no diftinction; a married woman was as capable of bequeathing as a feme-fole [t]. But with us

---

[p] Godolph. p. 1. c. 8. Wentw. 212.   [r] Co. Litt. 89.
2 Vern. 104. 469. Gilb. Rep. 74.   [s] Godolph. p. 1. c. 9.
[q] Perkins. §. 503.   [t] Ff. 31. 1. 77.

a married woman is not only utterly incapable of devising *lands*, being excepted out of the statute of wills, 34 & 35 Hen. VIII. c. 5. but also she is incapable of making a testament of *chattels*, without the licence of her husband. For all her personal chattels are absolutely his own; and he may dispose of her chattels real, or shall have them to himself if he survives her: it would be therefore extremely inconsistent, to give her a power of defeating that provision of the law, by bequeathing those chattels to another[v]. Yet by her husband's licence she may make a testament[u]; and the husband, upon marriage, frequently covenants with her friends to allow her that licence: but such licence is more properly his assent; for, unless it be given to the particular will in question, it will not be a complete testament, even though the husband beforehand hath given her permission to make a will[w]. Yet it shall be sufficient to repel the husband from his general right of administring his wife's effects; and administration shall be granted to her appointee, with such testamentary paper annexed[x]. So that in reality the woman makes no will at all, but only something like a will[y]; operating in the nature of an appointment, the execution of which the husband by his bond, agreement, or covenant, is bound to allow. A distinction similar to which, we meet with in the civil law. For, though a son who was *in potestate parentis* could not by any means make a formal and legal testament, even though his father permitted it[z], yet he might, with the like permission of his father, make what was called a *donatio mortis causa*[a]. The queen consort is an exception to this general rule, for she may dispose of her chattels by will, without the consent of her lord[b]: and any feme-covert may make her will of goods, which are in her possession *in auter droit*, as executrix or administratix; for these can never be the property of the husband[c]: and, if she has any pinmoney or separate maintenance, it is said she may dispose of her savings thereout by testament, without the control of

[v] 4 Rep. 51.
[u] Dr & St. d. 1. c. 7.
[w] Bro. *Abr. tit devise*. 34. Stra. 891.
[x] *The king v. di Petresworth*. T. 13 Geo. II. B. R.

[y] Cro. Car. 376. 1 Mod. 211.
[z] *Ff*. 28. 1. 6.
[a] *Ff*. 39. 6. 25.
[b] Co. Litt. 133.
[c] Godolph. 1. 10.

her

her hufband[d]. But, if a feme-fole makes her will, and afterwards marries, fuch fubfequent marriage is efteemed a revocation in law, and intirely vacates the will[e].

3. PERSONS incapable of making teftaments, on account of their criminal conduct, are in the firft place all traitors and felons, from the time of conviction; for then their goods and chattels are no longer at their own difpofal, but forfeited to the king. Neither can a *felo de fe* make a will of goods and chattels, for they are forfeited by the act and manner of his death; but he may make a devife of his lands, for they are not fubjected to any forfeiture[f]. Outlaws alfo, though it be but for debt, are incapable of making a will, fo long as the outlawry fubfifts, for their goods and chattels are forfeited during that time[g]. As for perfons guilty of other crimes, fhort of felony, who are by the civil law precluded from making teftaments, (as ufurers, libellers, and others of a worfe ftamp) at the common law their teftaments may be good[h]. And in general the rule is, and has been fo at leaft ever fince Glanvil's time[i], *quod libera fit cujufcunque ultima voluntas.*

LET us next, *thirdly*, confider what this laft will and teftament is, which almoft every one is thus at liberty to make; or the nature and incidents of a teftament. Teftaments both Juftinian[i] and fir Edward Coke[k] agree to be fo called, becaufe they are *teftatio mentis*; an etymon, which feems to favour too much of the conceit; it being plainly a fubftantive derived from the verb *teftari*, in like manner as *juramentum*, *incrementum*, and others, from other verbs. The definition of the old Roman lawyers is much better than their etymology; " *voluntatis nof-* " *trae jufta fententia de eo, quod quis poft mortem fuam fieri velit*[l]:" which may be thus rendered into Englifh, " the legal declara- " tion of a man's intentions, which he wills to be performed af-

[d] Prec. Chan. 44.
[e] 4 Rep. 60. 2 P. Wm. 624.
[f] Plowd. 261.
[g] Fitzh. *Abr. t. defcent.* 16.
[h] Godolph. p. 1. c. 12.

[i] *l.* 7. *c.* 5.
[i] *Inft.* 2. 10.
[k] 1 Inft. 111. 322.
[l] *Ff.* 28. 1. 1.

" te

" ter his death." It is called *fententia* to denote the circumfpec-
tion and prudence with which it is fuppofed to be made : it is
voluntatis noftrae fententia, becaufe it's efficacy depends on it's
declaring the teftator's intention, whence in England it is emphatically ftiled his *will:* it is *jufta fententia* ; that is, drawn,
attefted, and publifhed with all due folemnities and forms of law :
It is *de eo, quod quis poft mortem fuam fieri v 'lit*, becaufe a teftament is of no force till after the death of 'he teftator.

THESE teftaments are divided into two forts ; *written*, and
verbal or *nuncupative* ; of which the former is committed to writing, the latter depends merely upon oral evidence, being declared by the teftator *in extremis* before a fufficient number of witneffes, and afterwards reduced to writing. A *codicil, codicillus*, a
little book or writing, is a fupplement to a will ; or an addition
made by the teftator, and annexed to, and to be taken as part of,
a teftament : being for it's explanation, or alteration, or to make
fome addition to, or elfe fome fubtraction from, the former difpofitions of the teftator [m]. This may alfo be either written or
nuncupative.

BUT, as *nuncupative* wills and codicils, (which were formerly
more in ufe than at prefent, when the art of writing is become
more univerfal) are liable to great impofitions, and may occafion
many perjuries, the ftatute of frauds, 29 Car. II. c. 3. enacts;
1. That no written will fhall be revoked or altered by a fubfequent nuncupative one, except the fame be in the lifetime of the
teftator reduced to writing, and read over to him, and approved ;
and unlefs the fame be proved to have been fo done by the oaths
of three witneffes at the leaft ; who, by ftatute 4 & 5 Ann. c.16.
muft be fuch as are admiffible upon trials at common law. 2. That
no nuncupative will fhall in any wife be good, where the eftate
bequeathed exceeds 30 *l*, unlefs proved by three fuch witneffes,
prefent at the making thereof (the Roman law requiring feven [n])
and unlefs they or fome of them were fpecially required to bear

[m] Godolph. p. 1. c. 1. §. 3.   [n] *Inft*. 2. 10. 14.

witnefs

witnefs thereto by the teftator himfelf, and unlefs it was made in his laft ficknefs, in his own habitation or dwelling-houfe, or where he had been previoufly refident ten days at the leaft, except he be furprized with ficknefs on a journey, or from home, and dies without returning to his dwelling. 3. That no nuncupative will fhall be proved by the witneffes after fix months from the making, unlefs it were put in writing within fix days. Nor fhall it be proved till fourteen days after the death of the teftator, nor till procefs hath firft iffued to call in the widow, or next of kin, to conteft it if they think proper. Thus has the legiflature provided againft any frauds in fetting up nuncupative wills, by fo numerous a train of requifites, that the thing itfelf is fallen into difufe; and hardly ever heard of, but in the only inftance where favour ought to be fhewn to it, when the teftator is furprized by fudden and violent ficknefs. The teftamentary words muft be fpoken with an intent to bequeath, not any loofe idle difcourfe in his illnefs; for he muft require the by-ftanders to bear witnefs of fuch his intention : the will muft be made at home, or among his family or friends, unlefs by unavoidable accident; to prevent impofitions from ftrangers : it muft be in his *laft* ficknefs; for, if he recovers, he may alter his difpofitions, and has time to make a written will : it muft not be proved at too long a diftance from the teftator's death, left the words fhould efcape the memory of the witneffes; nor yet too haftily and without notice, left the family of the teftator fhould be put to inconvenience, or furprized.

As to *written* wills, they need not any witnefs of their publication. I fpeak not here of devifes of lands, which are entirely another thing, a conveyance by ftatute, unknown to the feodal or common law, and not under the fame jurifdiction as perfonal teftaments. But a teftament of chattels, written in the teftator's own hand, though it has neither his name nor feal to it, nor witneffes prefent at it's publication, is good; provided fufficient proof can be had that it is his hand-writing[o]. And though written in another man's hand, and never figned by the teftator, yet

[o] Godolph. p. 1. c. 21. Gilb. Rep. 260.

if

if proved to be according to his inftructions and approved by
him, it hath been held a good teftament of the perfonal eftate [p].
Yet it is the fafer, and more prudent way, and leaves lefs in the
breaft of the ecclefiaftical judge, if it be figned or fealed by the
teftator, and publifhed in the prefence of witneffes; which laft
was always required in the time of Bracton [q]; or, rather, he in
this refpect has implicitly copied the rule of the civil law.

N o teftament is of any effect till after the death of the teftator. "*Nam omne teſtamentum morte confummatum eſt; et voluntas*
"*teſtatoris eſt ambulatoria uſque ad mortem* [r]." And therefore, if
there be many teftaments, the laft overthrows all the former [s]: but
the republication of a former will revokes one of a later date,
and eftablifhes the firft again [t].

H e n c e it follows, that teftaments may be avoided three
ways : 1. If made by a perfon labouring under any of the incapacities before-mentioned : 2. By making another teftament
of a later date: and, 3. By cancelling or revoking it. For, though
I make a laft will and teftament irrevocable in the ftrongeft words,
yet I am at liberty to revoke it : becaufe my own act or words
cannot alter the difpofition of law, fo as to make that irrevocable,
which is in it's own nature revocable [u]. For this, faith lord Bacon [w], would be for a man to deprive himfelf of that, which of
all other things is moft incident to human condition ; and that
is, alteration or repentance. It hath alfo been held, that, without an exprefs revocation, if a man, who hath made his will,
afterwards marries and hath a child, this is a prefumptive or
implied revocation of his former will, which he made in his
ftate of celibacy [x]. The Romans were alfo wont to fet afide teftaments as being *inofficiofa*, deficient in natural duty, if they
difinherited or totally paffed by (without affigning a true and

p Comyns. 452, 3, 4.
q *l.* 2. *c.* 26.
r Co. Litt. 112.
s Litt. §. 168. Perk. 478.

t Perk. 479.
u 8 Rep. 82.
w Elem. c. 19.
x Lord Raym. 441. 1 P. W^ms. 304.

fufficient

fufficient reafon ʸ) any of the children of the teftator ᶻ. But
if the child had any legacy, though ever fo fmall, it was a
proof that the teftator had not loft his memory or his reafon,
which otherwife the law prefumed ; but was then fuppofed to
have acted thus for fome fubftantial caufe : and in fuch cafe no
querela inofficiofi teftamenti was allowed. Hence probably has arifen
that groundlefs vulgar error, of the neceffity of leaving the heir
a fhilling or fome other exprefs legacy, in order to difinherit him
effectually : whereas the law of England makes no fuch wild
fuppofitions of forgetfulnefs or infanity ; and therefore, though
the heir or next of kin be totally omitted, it admits no *querela
inofficiofi,* to fet afide fuch a teftament.

We are next to confider, *fourthly,* what is an executor, and
what is an adminiftrator; and how they are both to be appointed.

An executor is he to whom another man commits by will the
execution of that his laft will and teftament. And all perfons
are capable of being executors, that are capable of making wills,
and many others befides; as feme-coverts, and infants : nay,
even infants unborn, or *in ventre fa mere,* may be made executors ᵃ. But no infant can act as fuch till the age of feventeen
years ; till which time adminiftration muft be granted to fome
other, *durante minore aetate* ᵇ. In like manner as it may be granted *durante abfentia,* or *pendente lite ;* when the executor is out of
the realm ᶜ, or when a fuit is commenced in the ecclefiaftical
court touching the validity of the will ᵈ. This appointment of
an executor is effential to the making of a will ᵉ : and it may be
performed either by exprefs words, or fuch as ftrongly imply the
fame. But if the teftator makes his will, without naming any
executors, or if he names incapable perfons, or if the executors
named refufe to act ; in any of thefe cafes, the ordinary muft

---

ʸ See Book I. ch. 16.
ᶻ *Inft.* 2. 18. 1.
ᵃ Weft. Symb. p. 1. §. 635.
ᵇ Went. Off. Ex. c. 18.

ᶜ 1 Lutw. 342.
ᵈ 2 P. Wᵐˢ. 589, 590.
ᵉ Wentw. c. 1. Plowd. 281.

grant

grant adminiſtration *cum teſtamento annexo* [f] to ſome other perſon; and then the duty of the adminiſtrator, as alſo when he is con-ſtituted only *durante minore aetate, &c*, of another, is very little different from that of an executor. And this was law ſo early as the reign of Henry II, when Glanvil [g] informs us, that " *teſta-*" *menti executores eſſe debent ii, quos teſtator ad hoc elegerit, et cu-*" *ram ipſe commiſerit: ſi vero teſtator nullos ad hoc nominaverit,*" *poſſunt propinqui et conſanguinei ipſius defuncti ad id faciendum ſe*" *ingerere.*"

B u t if the deceaſed died totally inteſtate, without making either will or executors, then general letters of adminiſtration muſt be granted by the ordinary to ſuch adminiſtrator as the ſta-tutes of Edward the third, and Henry the eighth, before-men-tioned, direct. In conſequence of which we may obſerve; 1. That the ordinary is compellable to grant adminiſtration of the goods and chattels of the wife, to the huſband, or his repreſentatives [h]: and, of the huſband's effects, to the widow, or next of kin; but he may grant it to either, or both, at his diſcretion [i]. 2. That, among the kindred, thoſe are to be preferred that are the neareſt in degree to the inteſtate; but, of perſons in equal degree, the ordinary may take which he pleaſes [k] 3. That this *nearneſs* or propinquity of degree ſhall be reckoned according to the com-putation of the civilians [l]; and not of the canoniſts, which the law of England adopts in the deſcent of real eſtates [m]: becauſe in the civil computation the inteſtate himſelf is the *terminus, a quo* the ſeveral degrees are numbered; and not the common an-ceſtor, according to the rule of the canoniſts. And therefore in the firſt place the children, or (on failure of children) the pa-rents of the deceaſed, are intitled to the adminiſtration: both which are indeed in the firſt degree; but with us [n] the children

[f] 1 Roll. Abr. 907. Comb. 20.
[g] *l.* 7. *c.* 6.
[h] Cro. Car. 106. Stat. 29 Car. II. c. 3.
[i] P. Wms. 381.
[j] Salk. 36. Stra. 532.

[k] Stat. 28 Hen. VIII. c. 5. See pag. 496.
[l] Prec. Chanc. 593.
[m] See pag. 203. 207. 224.
[n] Godolph. p. 2. c. 34. §. 1. 2 Vern. 125.

are

are allowed the preference °. Then follow brothers ᴾ, grand-fathers �q, uncles or nephews ʳ, (and the females of each claſs re-ſpectively) and laſtly couſins. 4. The half blood is admitted to the adminiſtration as well as the whole : for they are of the kindred of the inteſtate, and only excluded from inheritances of land upon feodal reaſons. Therefore the brother of the half blood ſhall exclude the uncle of the whole blood ˢ : and the or-dinary may grant adminiſtration to the ſiſter of the half, or the brother of the whole blood, at his own diſcretion ᵗ. 5. If none of the kindred will take out adminiſtration, a creditor may, by cuſtom, do it ᵘ. 6. If the executor refuſes, or dies inteſtate, the adminiſtration may be granted to the reſiduary legatee, in exclu-ſion of the next of kin ʷ. And, laſtly, the ordinary may, in de-fect of all theſe, commit adminiſtration (as he might have done ˣ before the ſtatute Edw. III.) to ſuch diſcreet perſon as he ap-proves of : or may grant him letters *ad colligendum bona defuncti,* which neither make him executor nor adminiſtrator; his only buſineſs being to keep the goods in his ſafe cuſtody ʸ, and to do other acts for the benefit of ſuch as are entitled to the property of the deceaſed ᶻ. If a baſtard, who has no kindred, being *nullius filius,* or any one elſe that has no kindred, dies inteſtate and with-out wife or child, it hath formerly been held ᵃ that the ordinary might ſeiſe his goods, and diſpoſe of them *in pios uſus.* But the

---

° In Germany there was long a diſpute, whether a man's children ſhould inherit his effects during the life of their grandfather; which depends (as we ſhall ſee hereafter) on the ſame principles as the granting of ad-miniſtrations. At laſt it was agreed at the diet of Arenſberg, about the middle of the tenth century, that the point ſhould be de-cided by combat. Accordingly, an equal number of champions being choſen on both ſides, thoſe of the children obtained the victory; and ſo the law was eſtabliſhed in their favour, that the iſſue of a perſon de-ceaſed ſhall be intitled to his goods and chattels in preference to his parents. (Mod. Un. Hiſt. xxix. 28.)

ᴾ Harris *in Nov.* 118. *c.* 2.
q Prec. Chanc. 527. 1 P. Wᵐˢ. 41.
ʳ Atk. 455.
ˢ 1 Ventr. 425.
ᵗ Aleyn. 36. Styl. 74.
ᵘ Salk. 38.
ʷ 1 Sid. 281. 1 Ventr. 219.
ˣ Plowd. 278.
ʸ Went. ch. 14.
ᶻ 2 Inſt. 398.
ᵃ Salk. 37.

ufual courfe now is for fome one to procure letters patent, or other authority, from the king; and then the ordinary of courfe grants adminiftration to fuch appointee of the crown [b].

THE intereft, vefted in an executor by the will of the deceafed, may be continued and kept alive by the will of the fame executor : fo that the executor of A's executor is to all intents and purpofes the executor and reprefentative of A himfelf [c] : but the executor of A's adminiftrator, or the adminiftrator of A's executor, is not the reprefentative of A [d]. For the power of an executor is founded upon the fpecial confidence and actual appointment of the deceafed; and fuch executor is therefore allowed to tranfmit that power to another, in whom he has equal confidence : but the adminiftrator of A is merely the officer of the ordinary, prefcribed to him by act of parliament, in whom the deceafed has repofed no truft at all ; and therefore, on the death of that officer, it refults back to the ordinary to appoint another. And, with regard to the adminiftrator of A's executor, he has clearly no privity or relation to A ; being only commiffioned to adminifter the effects of the inteftate executor, and not of the original teftator. Wherefore, in both thefe cafes, and whenever the courfe of reprefentation from executor to executor is interrupted by any one adminiftration, it is neceffary for the ordinary to commit adminiftration afrefh, *of the goods* of the deceafed *not* adminiftred by the former executor or adminiftrator. And this adminiftrator, *de bonis non*, is the only legal reprefentative of the deceafed in matters of perfonal property [e]. But he may, as well as an original adminiftrator, have only a *limited* or *fpecial* adminiftration committed to his care, viz. of certain fpecific effects, fuch as a term of years and the like ; the reft being committed to others [f].

[b] 3 P. W^ms. 33.
[c] Stat. 25 Edw. III. ft. 5. c. 5. 1 Leon. 275.
[d] Bro. *Abr. tit. adminiftrator.* 7.

[e] Styl. 225.
[f] 1 Roll. Abr. 908. Godolph. p. 2. c. 30. Salk. 36.

HAVING

HAVING thus fhewn what is, and who may be, an executor or adminiftrator, I proceed now, *fifthly* and laftly, to enquire into fome few of the principal points of their office and duty. Thefe in general are very much the fame in both executors and adminiftrators; excepting, firft, that the executor is bound to perform a will, which an adminiftrator is not, unlefs where a teftament is annexed to his adminiftration, and then he differs ftill lefs from an executor : and, fecondly, that an executor may do many acts before he proves the will[g], but an adminiftrator may do nothing till letters of adminiftration are iffued; for the former derives his power from the will and not from the probate[h], the latter owes his entirely to the appointment of the ordinary. If a ftranger takes upon him to act as executor, without any juft authority (as by intermeddling with the goods of the deceafed[i], and many other tranfactions[k]) he is called in law an executor of his own wrong, *de fon tort*, and is liable to all the trouble of an executorfhip, without any of the profits or advantages : but merely doing acts of neceffity or humanity, as locking up the goods, or burying the corpfe of the deceafed, will not amount to fuch an intermeddling, as will charge a man as executor of his own wrong[l]. Such a one cannot bring an action himfelf in right of the deceafed[m], but actions may be brought againft him. And, in all actions by creditors againft fuch an officious intruder, he fhall be named an executor, generally[n]; for the moft obvious conclufion, which ftrangers can form from his conduct, is that he hath a will of the deceafed, wherein he is named executor, but hath not yet taken probate thereof[o]. He is chargeable with the debts of the deceafed, fo far as affets come to his hands[p] : and, as againft creditors in general, fhall be allowed all payments made to any other creditor in the fame or a fuperior degree[q], himfelf

[g] Wentw. ch. 3.
[h] Comyns. 151.
[i] 5 Rep. 33, 34.
[k] Wentw. ch. 14. Stat. 43 Eliz. c. 8.
[l] Dyer. 166.
[m] Bro. *Abr. t. adminiftrator.* 8.
[n] 5 Rep. 31.
[o] 12 Mod. 471.
[p] Dyer. 166.
[q] 1 Chan Caf. 33.

only

only excepted ʳ. And though, as againſt the rightful executor or adminiſtrator, he cannot plead ſuch payment, yet it ſhall be allowed him in mitigation of damages ˢ; unleſs perhaps upon a deficiency of aſſets, whereby the rightful executor may be prevented from ſatisfying his own debt ᵗ. But let us now ſee what are the power and duty of a rightful executor or adminiſtrator.

1. HE muſt *bury* the deceaſed in a manner ſuitable to the eſtate which he leaves behind him. Neceſſary funeral expences are allowed, previous to all other debts and charges; but if the executor or adminiſtrator be extravagant, it is a ſpecies of *devaſtation* or waſte of the ſubſtance of the deceaſed, and ſhall only be prejudicial to himſelf, and not to the creditors or legatees of the deceaſed ᵘ.

2. THE executor, or the adminiſtrator *durante minore aetate,* or *durante abſentia,* or *cum teſtamento annexo,* muſt *prove the will* of the deceaſed : which is done either in *common form,* which is only upon his own oath before the ordinary, or his ſurrogate; or *per teſtes,* in more ſolemn form of law, in caſe the validity of the will be diſputed ʷ. When the will is ſo proved, the original muſt be depoſited in the regiſtry of the ordinary; and a copy thereof in parchment is made out under the ſeal of the ordinary, and delivered to the executor or adminiſtrator, together with a certificate of it's having been proved before him : all which together is uſually ſtiled the *probate.* In defect of any will, the perſon entitled to be adminiſtrator muſt alſo at this period take out letters of adminiſtration under the ſeal of the ordinary; whereby an executorial power to collect and adminiſter, that is, diſpoſe of the goods of the deceaſed, is veſted in him : and he muſt, by ſtatute 22 & 23 Car. II. c. 10. enter into a bond with ſureties, faithfully to execute his truſt. If all the goods of the deceaſed lie within the ſame juriſdiction, a probate before the

ʳ 5 Rep. 30. Moor. 527.
ˢ 12 Mod. 441. 471.
ᵗ Wentw. ch. 14.

ᵘ Salk. 196. Godolph. p. 2. c. 26. §. 2.
ʷ Godolph. p. 1. c. 20. §. 4.

ordinary

ordinary, or an adminiftration granted by him, are the only proper ones : but if the deceafed had *bona notabilia*, or chattels to
the value of a *hundred fhillings*, in two diftinct diocefes or jurifdictions, then the will muft be proved, or adminiftration taken
out, before the metropolitan of the province, by way of fpecial
prerogative[x] ; whence the court where the validity of fuch wills
is tried, and the office where they are regiftered, are called the
prerogative court, and the prerogative office, of the provinces of
Canterbury and York. Lyndewode, who flourifhed in the beginning of the fifteenth century, and was official to arch-bifhop
Chichele, interprets thefe hundred fhillings to fignify *folidos le-
gales* ; of which he tells us feventy two amounted to a pound of
gold, which in his time was valued at fifty nobles or 16 *l.* 13 *s.* 4 *d.*
He therefore computes[y] that the hundred fhillings, which conftituted *bona notabilia*, were then equal in current money to 23 *l.*
3 *s.* 0¼ *d.* This will account for what is faid in our antient
books, that *bona notabilia* in the diocefe of London[z], and indeed
every where elfe[a], were of the value of ten pounds by *compofition :*
for, if we purfue the calculations of Lyndewode to their full extent, and confider that a pound of gold is now almoft equal in value
to an hundred and fifty nobles, we fhall extend the prefent amount
of *bona notabilia* to nearly 70 *l.* But the makers of the canons of
1603 underftood this antient rule to be meant of the fhillings
current in the reign of James I, and have therefore directed[b] that
five pounds fhall for the future be the ftandard of *bona notabilia*,
fo as to make the probate fall within the archiepifcopal prerogative. Which prerogative (properly underftood) is grounded
upon this reafonable foundation : that, as the bifhops were
themfelves originally the adminiftrators to all inteftates in their
own diocefe, and as the prefent adminiftrators are in effect no
other than their officers or fubftitutes, it was impoffible for
the bifhops, or thofe who acted under them, to collect any
goods of the deceafed, other than fuch as lay within their own

[x] 4 Inft. 335.

[y] *Provinc. l.* 3. *t.* 13. *c. item. v. centum. &
c. ftatutum. v. laicis.*

[z] 4 Inft. 335. Godolph. p. 2. c. 22.

[a] Plowd. 281.

[b] can. 92.

diocefes, beyond which their epifcopal authority extends not. But it would be extremely troublefome, if as many adminiftrations were to be granted, as there are diocefes within which the deceafed had *bona notabilia*; befides the uncertainty which creditors and legatees would be at, in cafe different adminiftrators were appointed, to afcertain the fund out of which their demands are to be paid. A prerogative is therefore very prudently vefted in the metropolitan of each province, to make in fuch cafes one adminiftration ferve for all. This accounts very fatisfactorily for the reafon of taking out adminiftration to inteftates, that have large and diffufive property, in the prerogative court: and the probate of wills naturally follows, as was before obferved, the power of granting adminiftrations; in order to fatisfy the ordinary that the deceafed has, in a legal manner, by appointing his own executor, excluded him and his officers from the privilege of adminiftring the effects.

3. THE executor or adminiftrator is to make an *inventory* [c] of all the goods and chattels, whether in poffeffion or action, of the deceafed; which he is to deliver in to the ordinary upon oath, if thereunto lawfully required.

4. HE is to *collect* all the goods and chattels fo inventoried; and to that end he has very large powers and interefts conferred on him by law; being the reprefentative of the deceafed [d], and having the fame property in his goods as the principal had when living, and the fame remedies to recover them. And, if there be two or more executors, a fale or releafe by one of them fhall be good againft all the reft [e]; but in cafe of adminiftrators it is otherwife [f]. Whatever is fo recovered, that is of a faleable nature and may be converted into ready money, is called *affets* in the hands of the executor or adminiftrator [g]; that is, fufficient or enough (from the French *affez*) to make him chargeable to a creditor or legatee, fo far as fuch goods and chattels extend.

---

[c] Stat. 21 Hen. VIII. c. 5.
[d] Co. Litt. 209.
[e] Dyer. 23.
[f] Atk. 460.
[g] See pag. 244.

What-

Whatever affets fo come to his hands he may convert into ready money, to anfwer the demands that may be made upon him: which are the next thing to be confidered; for,

5. THE executor or adminiftrator muft *pay* the *debts* of the deceafed. In payment of debts he muft obferve the rules of priority; otherwife, on deficiency of affets, if he pays thofe of a lower degree firft, he muft anfwer thofe of a higher out of his own eftate. And, firft, he may pay all funeral charges, and the expenfe of proving the will, and the like. Secondly, debts due to the king on record or fpecialty[h]. Thirdly, fuch debts as are by particular ftatutes to be preferred to all others; as the forfeitures for not burying in woollen[i], money due on poors rates[k], for letters to the poft-office[l], and fome others. Fourthly, debts of record; as judgments (docketted according to the ftatute 4 & 5 W. & M. c. 20.) ftatutes, and recognizances[m]. Fifthly, debts due on fpecial contracts; as for rent, (for which the leffor has often a better remedy in his own hands, by diftraining) or upon bonds, covenants, and the like, under feal[n]. Laftly, debts on fimple contracts, viz. upon notes unfealed, and verbal promifes. Among thefe fimple contracts, fervants wages are by fome[o] with reafon preferred to any other: and fo ftood the antient law, according to Bracton[p] and Fleta[q], who reckon, among the firft debts to be paid, *fervitia fervientium et ftipendia famulorum.* Among debts of equal degree, the executor or adminiftrator is allowed to pay himfelf firft; by retaining in his hands fo much as his debt amounts to[r]. But an executor of his own wrong is not allowed to retain: for that would tend to encourage creditors to ftrive who fhould firft take poffeffion of the goods of the deceafed; and would befides be taking advantage of their own wrong, which is contrary to the rule of law[s]. If a

[h] 1 And. 129.
[i] Stat. 30 Car. II. c. 3.
[k] Stat. 17 Geo. II. c. 38.
[l] Stat. 9 Ann. c. 10.
[m] 4 Rep. 60. Cro. Car. 363.
[n] Wentw. ch. 12.

[o] 1 Roll. Abr 927.
[p] *l*. 2. *c*. 26.
[q] *l*. 2. *c*. 57. §. 10.
[r] 10 Mod. 496.
[s] 5 Rep. 30.

creditor

creditor conftitutes his debtor his executor, this is a releafe or difcharge of the debt, whether the executor acts or no [t]; provided there be affets fufficient to pay the teftator's debts: for, though this difcharge of the debt fhall take place of all legacies, yet it were unfair to defraud the teftator's creditors of their juft debts by a releafe which is abfolutely voluntary [u]. Alfo, if no fuit is commenced againft him, the executor may pay any one creditor in equal degree his whole debt, though he has nothing left for the reft: for, without a fuit commenced, the executor has no legal notice of the debt [w].

6. WHEN the debts are all difcharged, the *legacies* claim the next regard; which are to be paid by the executor fo far as his affets will extend: but he may not give himfelf the preference herein, as in the cafe of debts [x].

A LEGACY is a bequeft, or gift, of goods and chattels by teftament; and the perfon to whom it is given is ftiled the legatee: which every perfon is capable of being, unlefs particularly difabled by the common law or ftatutes, as traitors, papifts, and fome others. This bequeft transfers an inchoate property to the legatee; but the legacy is not perfect without the affent of the executor: for if I have a *general* or *pecuniary* legacy of 100 *l*, or a *fpecific* one of a piece of plate, I cannot in either cafe take it without the confent of the executor [y]. For in him all the chattels are vefted; and it is his bufinefs firft of all to fee whether there is a fufficient fund left to pay the debts of the teftator: the rule of equity being, that a man muft be juft, before he is permitted to be generous; or, as Bracton exprefles the fenfe of our antient law [z], "*de bonis defuncti primo deducenda funt ea quae funt* "*neceffitatis, et poftea quae funt utilitatis, et ultimo quae funt vo-* "*luntatis.*" And in cafe of a deficiency of affets, all the *general* legacies muft abate proportionably, in order to pay the debts;

[t] Plowd. 184. Salk. 299.
[u] Salk. 303. 1 Roll. Abr. 921.
[w] Dyer. 32. 2 Leon. 60.

[x] 2 Vern 434. 2 P. W[ms]. 25.
[y] Co. Litt. 111. Aleyn. 39.
[z] *l. 2, c. 26.*

but

but a *specific* legacy (of a piece of plate, a horse, or the like) is not to abate at all, or allow any thing by way of abatement, un-less there be not sufficient without it[a]. Upon the same principle, if the legatees have been paid their legacies, they are afterwards bound to refund a ratable part, in case debts come in, more than sufficient to exhaust the *residuum* after the legacies paid[b]. And this law is as old as Bracton and Fleta, who tell us[c], "*si plura* "*sint debita, vel plus legatum fuerit, ad quae catalla defuncti non* "*sufficiant, fiat ubique defalcatio, excepto regis privilegio.*"

IF the legatee dies before the testator, the legacy is a lost or *lapsed* legacy, and shall sink into the *residuum*. And if a *contin-gent* legacy be left to any one; as, *when* he attains, or *if* he at-tains, the age of twenty one; and he dies before that time; it is a lapsed legacy[d]. But a legacy to one, *to be paid* when he attains the age of twenty one years, is a *vested* legacy; an interest which commences *in praesenti*, although it be *solvendum in futuro :* and, if the legatee dies before that age, his representatives shall receive it out of the testator's personal estate, at the same time that it would have become payable, in case the legatee had lived. This distinction is borrowed from the civil law[e]; and it's adoption in our courts is not so much owing to it's intrinsic equity, as to it's having been before adopted by the ecclesiastical courts. For, since the chancery has a concurrent jurisdiction with them, in regard to the recovery of legacies, it was reasonable that there should be a conformity in their determinations; and that the subject should have the same measure of justice in whatever court he sued[f]. But if such legacies be charged upon a real estate, in both cases they shall lapse for the benefit of the heir[g]; for, with regard to devises affecting lands, the ecclesiastical court hath no concurrent jurisdiction. And, in case of a vested legacy, due immediately, and charged on land or money in the funds, which yield an im-

---

[a] 2 Vern. 111.
[b] *Ibid.* 205.
[c] Bract. *l.* 2. *c.* 26. Flet. *l.* 2. *c.* 57. §.: 1.
[d] Dyer. 59. 1 Equ. Caf. abr. 295.

[e] *Ff.* 35. 1. 1 & 2.
[f] 1 Equ. Caf. abr. 295.
[g] 2 P. W^{ms}. 601.

mediate profit, intereſt ſhall be payable thereon from the teſtator's death ; but if charged only on the perſonal eſtate, which
cannot be immediately got in, it ſhall carry intereſt only from
the end of the year after the death of the teſtator [h].

BESIDES theſe formal legacies, contained in a man's will
and teſtament, there is alſo permitted another death-bed diſpoſition of property ; which is called a donation *cauſa mortis*. And
that is, when a perſon in his laſt ſickneſs, apprehending his diſ-
ſolution near, delivers or cauſes to be delivered to another the
poſſeſſion of any perſonal goods, (under which have been included bonds, and bills drawn by the deceaſed upon his banker) to
keep in caſe of his deceaſe. This gift, if the donor dies, needs
not the aſſent of his executor : yet it ſhall not prevail againſt
creditors ; and is accompanied with this implied truſt, that, if
the donor lives, the property thereof ſhall revert to himſelf, being
only given in contemplation of death, or *mortis cauſa* [i]. This
method of donation might have ſubſiſted in a ſtate of nature, being
always accompanied with delivery of actual poſſeſſion [k] ; and ſo
far differs from a teſtamentary diſpoſition : but ſeems to have been
handed to us from the civil lawyers [l], who themſelves borrowed it
from the Greeks [m].

7. WHEN all the debts and particular legacies are diſcharged,
the ſurplus or *reſiduum* muſt be paid to the reſiduary legatee, if
any be appointed by the will ; and, if there be none, it was long a
ſettled notion that it devolved to the executor's own uſe, by virtue
of his executorſhip [n]. But, whatever ground there might have
been formerly for this opinion, it ſeems now to be underſtood [o]
with this reſtriction ; that, although where the executor has no
legacy at all the *reſiduum* ſhall in general be his own, yet where-

[h] 2 P. Wmſ. 26, 27.
[i] Prec. Chan. 269. 1 P. Wmſ. 406. 441.
3 P. Wmſ. 357.
[k] Law of forfeit. 16.
[l] *Inſt.* 2. 7. 1. *Ff. l.* 39. *t.* 6.
[m] There is a very complete *donatio mortis
cauſa*, in the Odyſſey b. 17. v. 78, made by

Telemachus to his friend Piraeus ; and another by Hercules, in the Alceſtes of Euri-
pides, v. 1020.
[n] Perkins. 525.
[o] Prec. Chanc. 323. 1 P. Wmſ. 7. 544.
2 P. Wmſ. 338. 3 P. Wmſ. 43. 194. Stra. 559.

ever there is fufficient on the face of a will, (by means of a competent legacy or otherwife) to imply that the teftator intended his
executor fhould *not* have the refidue, the undevifed furplus of the
eftate fhall go to the next of kin, the executor then ftanding upon
exactly the fame footing as an adminiftrator: concerning whom indeed there formerly was much debate[p], whether or no he could be
compelled to make any diftribution of the inteftate's eftate. For,
though (after the adminiftration was taken in effect from the ordinary, and transferred to the relations of the deceafed) the fpiritual
court endeavoured to compel a diftribution, and took bonds of the
adminiftrator for that purpofe, they were prohibited by the temporal courts, and the bonds declared void at law[q]. And the right
of the hufband not only to adminifter, but alfo to enjoy exclufively, the effects of his deceafed wife, depends ftill on this doctrine of the common law : the ftatute 29 Car. II. declaring only
that the ftatute of diftributions does not extend to this cafe. But
now thefe controverfies are quite at an end ; for by the ftatute
22 & 23 Car. II. c. 10. it is enacted, that the furplufage of intef-
ftates' eftates, except of femes covert[r], fhall (after the expiration of one full year from the death of the inteftate) be diftributed in the following manner. One third fhall go to the widow of the inteftate, and the refidue in equal proportions to his
children, or, if dead, to their reprefentatives ; that is, their lineal defcendants : if there are no children or legal reprefentatives
fubfifting, then a moiety fhall go to the widow, and a moiety to
the next of kindred in equal degree and their reprefentatives : if
no widow, the whole fhall go to the children : if neither widow
nor children, the whole fhall be diftributed among the next of
kin in equal degree, and their reprefentatives : but no reprefentatives are admitted, among collaterals, farther than the children
of the inteftate's brothers and fifters[s]. The next of kindred, here
referred to, are to be inveftigated by the fame rules of confanguinity, as thofe who are intitled to letters of adminiftration ; of
whom we have fufficiently fpoken[t]. And therefore by this ftatute

---

[p] Godolph. p. 2. c. 32.
[q] 1 Lev. 233. Cart. 125. 2 P. W^ms. 447.
[r] Stat. 29 Car. II. c. 3. §. 25.

[s] Raym. 496. Lord Raym. 571.
[t] pag. 504.

R r r 2   the

the mother, as well as the father, fucceeded to all the perfonal effects of their children, who died inteftate and without wife or iffue : in exclufion of the other fons and daughters, the brothers and fifters of the deceafed. And fo the law ftill remains with refpect to the father; but by ftatute 1 Jac. II. c. 17. if the father be dead, and any of the children die inteftate without wife or iffue, in the lifetime of the mother, fhe and each of the remaining children, or their reprefentatives, fhall divide his effects in equal portions.

It is obvious to obferve, how near a refemblance this ftatute of diftributions bears to our antient Englifh law, *de rationabili parte bonorum*, fpoken of at the beginning of this chapter [u]; and which fir Edward Coke [w] himfelf, though he doubted the generality of it's reftraint on the power of devifing by will, held to be univerfally binding upon the adminiftrator or executor, in the cafe of either a total or partial inteftacy. It alfo bears fome refemblance to the Roman law of fucceffions *ab inteftato* [x] : which, and becaufe the act was alfo penned by an eminent civilian [y], has occafioned a notion that the parliament of England copied it from the Roman praetor : though indeed it is little more than a reftoration, with fome refinements and regulations, of our old conftitutional law ; which prevailed as an eftablifhed right and cuftom from the time of king Canute downwards, many centuries before Juftinian's laws were known or heard of in the weftern parts of Europe. So likewife there is another part of the ftatute of diftributions, where directions are given, that no child of the inteftate, (except his heir at law) on whom he fettled in his lifetime any eftate in lands, or pecuniary portion, equal to the diftributive fhares of the other children, fhall have any part of the furplufage with their brothers and fifters ; but if the eftates fo

[u] pag. 492.
[w] 2 Inft. 33.
[x] The general rule of fuch fucceffions was this : 1. The children or lineal defcendants in equal portions. 2. On failure of thefe, the parents or lineal afcendants, and with them the brethren or fifters of the whole blood ; or, if the parents were dead,

all the brethren and fifters, together with the reprefentatives of a brother or fifter deceafed. 3. The next collateral relations in equal degree. 4. The hufband or wife of the deceafed. (*Ff.* 38. 15. 1. *Nov.* 118. c. 1, 2, 3. 127. c. 1.)
[y] Sir Walter Walker. Lord Raym. 574.

given

given them, by way of advancement, are not quite equivalent to the other fhares, the children fo advanced fhall now have fo much as will make them equal. This juft and equitable provifion hath been alfo faid to be derived from the *collatio bonorum* of the imperial law [z] : which it certainly refembles in fome points, though it differs widely in others. But it may not be amifs to obferve, that, with regard to goods and chattels, this is part of the antient cuftom of London, of the province of York, and of our fifter kingdom of Scotland : and, with regard to lands de-fcending in coparcenary, that it hath always been, and ftill is, the common law of England, under the name of *hotchpot* [a].

BEFORE I quit this fubject, I muft however acknowlege, that the doctrine and limits of reprefentation, laid down in the ftatute of diftributions, feem to have been principally borrowed from the civil law : whereby it will fometimes happen, that perfonal eftates are divided *per capita*, and fometimes *per ftirpes* ; whereas the common law knows no other rule of fucceffion but that *per ftirpes* only [b]. They are divided *per capita*, to every man an equal fhare, when all the claimants claim in their own rights, as in equal degree of kindred, and not *jure repraefentationis*, in the right of another perfon. As if the next of kin be the inteftate's three brothers, A, B, and C; here his eftate is divided into three equal portions, and diftributed *per capita*, one to each : but if one of thefe brothers, A, had been dead leaving three children, and another, B, leaving two ; then the diftribution muft have been *per ftirpes* ; viz. one third to A's three children, another third to B's two children, and the remaining third to C the furviving bro-ther : yet if C had alfo been dead, without iffue, then A's and B's five children, being all in equal degree to the inteftate, would take in their own rights *per capita*, viz. each of them one fifth part [c].

THE ftatute of diftributions expreffly excepts and referves the cuftoms of the city of London, of the province of York, and

<hr>

[z] *Ff.* 37. 6. 1.   [b] See ch. 14. pag. 217.
[a] See ch. 12. pag. 191.   [c] Prec. Chanc. 54.

of

of all other places having peculiar cuſtoms of diſtributing inteſtates' effects. So that, though in thoſe places the reſtraint of deviſing is removed by the ſtatutes formerly mentioned [d], their antient cuſtoms remain in full force, with reſpect to the eſtates of
inteſtates. I ſhall therefore conclude this chapter, and with it
the preſent book, with a few remarks on thoſe cuſtoms.

In the firſt place we may obſerve, that in the city of London [e], and province of York [f], as well as in the kingdom of Scotland [g], and therefore probably alſo in Wales, (concerning which
there is little to be gathered, but from the ſtatute 7 & 8 W. III.
c. 38.) the effects of the inteſtate, after payment of his debts,
are in general divided according to the antient univerſal doctrine
of the *pars rationabilis*. If the deceaſed leaves a widow and children, his ſubſtance (deducting the widow's apparel and furniture
of her bed-chamber, which in London is called the *widow's
chamber*) is divided into three parts; one of which belongs to the
widow, another to the children, and the third to the adminiſtrator : if only a widow, or only children, they ſhall reſpectively,
in either caſe, take one moiety, and the adminiſtrator the other [h]:
if neither widow nor child, the adminiſtrator ſhall have the
whole [i]. And this portion, or *dead man's* part, the adminiſtrator
was wont to apply to his own uſe [k], till the ſtatute 1 Jac. II. c.17.
declared that the ſame ſhould be ſubject to the ſtatutes of diſtribution. So that if a man dies worth 1800*l.* leaving a widow and
two children, the eſtate ſhall be divided into eighteen parts;
whereof the widow ſhall have eight, ſix by the cuſtom and two
by the ſtatute ; and each of the children five, three by the cuſtom
and two by the ſtatute : if he leaves a widow and one child, they
ſhall each have a moiety of the whole, or nine ſuch eighteenth
parts, ſix by the cuſtom and three by the ſtatute : if he leaves
a widow and no child, the widow ſhall have three fourths of
the whole, two by the cuſtom and one by the ſtatute; and the

[d] pag. 493.
[e] Lord Raym. 1329.
[f] 2 Burn. eccl. law. 746.
[g] *Ibid.* 782.

[h] 1 P. W^{ms}. 341. Salk. 246.
[i] 2 Show. 175.
[k] 2 Freem. 85. 1 Vern. 133.

remaining

remaining fourth fhall go by the ftatute to the next of kin. It is alfo to be obferved, that if the wife be provided for by a jointure before marriage, in bar of her cuftomary part, it puts her in a ftate of non-entity, with regard to the cuftom only[l]; but fhe fhall be intitled to her fhare of the dead man's part under the ftatute of diftributions, unlefs barred by fpecial agreement[m]. And if any of the children are advanced by the father in his lifetime with any fum of money (not amounting to their full proportionable part) they fhall bring that portion into hotchpot with the reft of the brothers and fifters, but not with the widow, before they are intitled to any benefit under the cuftom[n]: but, if they are fully advanced, the cuftom intitles them to no farther dividend[o].

THUS far in the main the cuftoms of London and of York agree : but, befides certain other lefs material variations, there are two principal points in which they confiderably differ. One is, that in London the fhare of the children (or orphanage part) is not fully vefted in them till the age of twenty one, before which they cannot difpofe of it by teftament[p] : and, if they die under that age, whether fole or married, their fhare fhall furvive to the other children; but, after the age of twenty one, it is free from any orphanage cuftom, and, in cafe of inteftacy, fhall fall under the ftatute of diftributions[q]. The other, that in the province of York, the heir at common law, who inherits any lands either in fee or in tail, is excluded from any filial portion or reafonable part[r]. But, notwithftanding thefe provincial variations, the cuftoms appear to be fubftantially one and the fame. And, as a fimilar policy formerly prevailed in every part of the ifland, we may fairly conclude the whole to be of Britifh original; or, if derived from the Roman law of fucceffions, to have been drawn from that fountain much earlier than the time of

---

[l] 2 Vern. 665. 3 P. W^ms. 16.
[m] 1 Vern. 15. 2 Chan. Rep. 252.
[n] 2 Freem. 279. 1 Equ. caf. abr. 155.
2 P. W^ms. 526.

[o] 2 P. W^ms. 527.
[p] 2 Vern. 558.
[q] Prec. Chan. 537.
[r] 2 Burn. 754.

Juftinian,

Juſtinian, from whoſe conſtitutions in many points (particularly in the advantages given to the widow) it very conſiderably differs: though it is not improbable that the reſemblances which yet remain may be owing to the Roman uſages; introduced in the time of Claudius Caeſar, (who eſtabliſhed a colony in Britain to inſtruct the natives in legal knowlege[s]) inculcated and diffuſed by Papinian (who preſided at York as *praefectus praetorio* under the emperors Severus and Caracalla[t]) and continued by his ſucceſſors till the final departure of the Romans in the beginning of the fifth century after Chriſt.

[s] Tacit. *Annal. l.* 12. *c.* 32.   •[t] Selden *in Fletam. cap.* 4. §. 3.

THE END OF THE SECOND BOOK.

APPENDIX.

N°. I.

Vetus Carta FEOFFAMENTI.

SCIANT prefentes et futuri, quod ego Willielmus, filius Wil- Premifes.
lielmi de Segenho, dedi, conceffi, et hac prefenti carta mea con-
firmavi, Johanni quondam filio Johannis de Saleford, pro qua-
dam fumma pecunie quam michi dedit pre manibus, unam acram terre
mee arabilis, jacentem in campo de Saleford, juxta terram quondam Ri-
chardi de la Mare : **Habendam et Tenendam** totam predictam acram Habendum, and
terre, cum omnibus ejus pertinentiis, prefato Johanni, et heredibus fuis, Tenendum.
et fuis affignatis, de capitalibus dominis feodi : **Reddendo** et faciendo Reddendum.
annuatim eifdem dominis capitalibus fervitia inde debita et confueta : **Et** Warranty.
ego predictus Willielmus, et heredes mei, et mei affignati, totam predictam acram terre, cum omnibus fuis pertinentiis, predicto Johanni de
Saleford, et heredibus fuis, et fuis affignatis, contra omnes gentes war-
rantizabimus in perpetuum. **In cujus** rei teftimonium huic prefenti car- Conclufion.
te figillum meum appofui : **His** teftibus, Nigello de Saleford, Johanne
de Seybroke, Radulpho clerico de Saleford, Johanne molendario de eadem villa, et aliis. **Data** apud Saleford die Veneris proximo ante fef-
tum fancte Margarete virginis, anno regni regis EDWARDI filii regis
EDWARDI fexto.

(L. S.)

Memorandum, quod die et anno infrafcriptis Livery of feifin
plena et pacifica feifina acre infrafpecificate, cum endorfed.
pertinentiis, data et deliberata fuit per infranomi-
natum Willielmum de Segenho infranominato Johanni de Saleford, in propriis perfonis fuis, fecundum tenorem et effectum carte infrafcripte, in
prefentia Nigelli de Saleford, Johannis de Seybroke, et aliorum.

VOL. II.   *   N°. II.

N°. II.

N°. II.

A modern Conveyance by L E A S E *and* R E L E A S E.

§. I. L E A S E, *or* B A R G A I N *and* S A L E, *for a year.*

Premises. 𝕿𝕳𝕴𝕾 **Indenture**, made the third day of September, in the twenty firſt year of the reign of our ſovereign lord G E O R G E the ſecond by the grace of God king of Great Britain, France, and Ireland, defender of the faith, and ſo forth, and in the year of our Lord one thou-*Parties.* ſand, ſeven hundred, and forty ſeven, between Abraham Barker of Dale Hall in the county of Norfolk, eſquire, and Cecilia his wife, of the one part, and David Edwards of Lincoln's Inn in the county of Middleſex, eſquire, and Francis Golding of the city of Norwich, clerk, of the other part, witneſſeth ; that the ſaid Abraham Barker and Cecilia his *Conſideration.* wife, in conſideration of five ſhillings of lawful money of Great Britain to them in hand paid by the ſaid David Edwards and Francis Golding at or before the enſealing and delivery of theſe preſents, (the receipt whereof is hereby acknowleged,) and for other good cauſes and conſiderations them the ſaid Abraham Barker and Cecilia his wife hereunto *Bargain and* ſpecially moving, **have** bargained and ſold, and by theſe preſents do, *ſale.* and each of them doth, bargain and ſell, unto the ſaid David Edwards *Parcels.* and Francis Golding, their executors, adminiſtrators, and aſſigns, **all** that the capital meſſuage, called Dale Hall in the pariſh of Dale in the ſaid county of Norfolk, wherein the ſaid Abraham Barker and Cecilia his wife now dwell, and all thoſe their lands in the ſaid pariſh of Dale called or known by the name of Wilſon's farm, containing by eſtimation five hundred and forty acres, be the ſame more or leſs, together with all and ſingular houſes, dovehouſes, barns, buildings, ſtables, yards, gardens, orchards, lands, tenements, meadows, paſtures, feedings, commons, woods, underwoods, ways, waters, watercourſes, fiſhings, privileges, profits, eaſements, commodities, advantages, emoluments, hereditaments, and appurtenances whatſoever to the ſaid capital meſſuage and farm belonging or appertaining, or with the ſame uſed or enjoyed, or accepted, reputed, taken, or known, as part, parcel, or member thereof, or as belonging to the ſame or any part thereof ; and the reverſion and reverſions, remainder and remainders, yearly and other rents, *Habendum.* iſſues, and profits thereof, and of every part and parcel thereof : **To have and to hold** the ſaid capital meſſuage, lands, tenements, hereditaments, and all and ſingular other the premiſes herein before mentioned

or

or intended to be bargained and fold, and every part and parcel thereof,   N°. II.
with their and every of their rights, members, and appurtenances, unto
the faid David Edwards and Francis Golding, their executors, adminiftrators, and affigns, from the day next before the day of the date of
thefe prefents, for and during, and unto the full end and term of, one
whole year from thence next enfuing and fully to be complete and ended:
𝔜𝔦𝔢𝔩𝔡𝔦𝔫𝔤 and paying therefore unto the faid Abraham Barker, and Ce-   *Reddendum.*
cilia his wife, and their heirs or affigns, the yearly rent of one peppercorn at the expiration of the faid term, if the fame fhall be lawfully demanded : 𝕿𝔬 𝔱𝔥𝔢 𝔦𝔫𝔱𝔢𝔫𝔱 and purpofe, that by virtue of thefe prefents,   *Intent.*
and of the ftatute for transferring ufes into poffeffion, the faid David Edwards and Francis Golding may be in the actual poffeffion of the premifes,
and be thereby enabled to take and accept a grant and releafe of the freehold, reverfion, and inheritance of the fame premifes, and of every part
and parcel thereof, to them, their heirs, and affigns ; to the ufes, and
upon the trufts, thereof to be declared by another indenture, intended
to bear date the day next after the day of the date hereof. 𝕴𝔫 𝔴𝔦𝔱𝔫𝔢𝔣𝔰 *Conclufion.*
whereof the parties to thefe prefents their hands and feals have fubfcribed
and fet, the day and year firft abovewritten.

Sealed, and delivered, being	
firft duly ftamped, in the	Abraham Barker. (L. S.)
prefence of	Cecilia Barker. (L. S.)
George Carter.	David Edwards. (L. S.)
William Browne.	Francis Golding. (L. S.)

§. 2. *Deed of* RELEASE.

𝕿𝔥𝔦𝔰 𝕴𝔫𝔡𝔢𝔫𝔱𝔲𝔯𝔢 of five parts, made the fourth day of September, *Premifes.*
in the twenty-firft year of the reign of our fovereign lord GEORGE the
fecond by the grace of God king of Great Britain, France, and Ireland, defender of the faith, and fo forth, and in the year of our Lord
one thoufand, feven hundred, and forty-feven, between Abraham *Parties.*
Barker, of Dale Hall in the county of Norfolk, efquire, and Cecilia
his wife, of the firft part ; David Edwards of Lincoln's Inn in the
county of Middlefex, efquire, executor of the laft will and teftament
of Lewis Edwards, of Cowbridge in the county of Glamorgan, gentleman, his late father, deceafed, and Francis Golding of the city of
Norwich, clerk, of the fecond part ; Charles Browne of Enftone in
the county of Oxford, gentleman, and Richard More of the city of
Briftol, merchant, of the third part ; John Barker, efquire, fon and
heir apparent of the faid Abraham Barker, of the fourth part ; and
Katherine Edwards, fpinfter, one of the fifters of the faid David Ed-

N⁰. II.

Recital.
Confideration.

Releafe.

Parcels.

wards, of the fifth part. 𝔚𝔥𝔢𝔯𝔢𝔞𝔰 a marriage is intended, by the per-miffion of God, to be fhortly had and folemnized between the faid John Barker and Katherine Edwards : 𝔑𝔬𝔴 𝔱𝔥𝔦𝔰 𝔍𝔫𝔡𝔢𝔫𝔱𝔲𝔯𝔢 𝔴𝔦𝔱𝔫𝔢𝔰𝔰𝔢𝔱𝔥, that in confideration of the faid intended marriage, and of the fum of five thoufand pounds, of good and lawful money of Great Britain, to the faid Abraham Barker, (by and with the confent and agreement of the faid John Barker, and Katherine Edwards, teftified by their being parties to, and their fealing and delivery of, thefe prefents,) by the faid David Edwards in hand paid at or before the enfealing and delivery here-of, being the marriage portion of the faid Katherine Edwards, bequeath-ed to her by the laft will and teftament of the faid Lewis Edwards, her late father, deceafed ; the receipt and payment whereof the faid Abra-ham Barker doth hereby acknowlege, and thereof, and of every part and parcel thereof, they the faid Abraham Barker, John Barker, and Kathe-rine Edwards, do, and each of them doth, releafe, acquit, and difcharge the faid David Edwards, his executors, and adminiftrators, for ever by thefe prefents : and for providing a competent jointure and provi-fion of maintenance for the faid Katherine Edwards, in cafe fhe fhall, after the faid intended marriage had, furvive and overlive the faid John Barker her intended hufband : and for fettling and affuring the capital meffuage, lands, tenements, and hereditaments, hereinafter mentioned, unto fuch ufes, and upon fuch trufts, as are hereinafter expreffed and declared : and for and in confideration of the fum of five fhillings of lawful money of Great Britain to the faid Abraham Barker and Cecilia his wife in hand paid by the faid David Edwards and Francis Golding, and of ten fhillings of like lawful money to them alfo in hand paid by the faid Charles Browne and Richard More, at or before the enfealing and delivery hereof, (the feveral receipts whereof are hereby refpectively acknowleged,) they the faid Abraham Barker and Cecilia his Wife, 𝔥𝔞𝔳𝔢, and each of them hath, granted, bargained, fold, releafed, and confirmed, and by thefe prefents do, and each of them doth, grant, bargain, fell, releafe, and confirm unto the faid David Edwards and Francis Golding, their heirs and affigns, 𝔞𝔩𝔩 that the ca-pital meffuage called Dale Hall, in the parifh of Dale in the faid county of Norfolk, wherein the faid Abraham Barker and Cecilia his wife now dwell, and all thofe their lands in the faid parifh of Dale called or known by the name of Wilfon's farm, containing by eftimation five hundred and forty acres, be the fame more or lefs, together with all and fingular houfes, dovehoufes, barns, buildings, ftables, yards, gardens, orchards, lands, tenements, meadows, paftures, feedings, commons, woods, underwoods, ways, waters, water-courfes, fifhings, privileges, profits, eafements, commodities, advantages, emoluments, hereditaments, and appurtenances whatfoever to the faid capital mef-fuage and farm belonging or appertaining, or with the fame ufed or enjoyed,

enjoyed, or accepted, reputed, taken, or known, as part, parcel, or member thereof, or as belonging to the fame or any part thereof ; (all which faid premifes are now in the actual poffeffion of the faid David Edwards and Francis Golding, by virtue of a bargain and fale to them thereof made by the faid Abraham Barker and Cecilia his wife for one whole year, in confideration of five fhillings to them paid by the faid David Edwards and Francis Golding, in and by one indenture bearing date the day next before the day of the date hereof, and by force of the ftatute for transferring ufes into poffeffion ;) and the reverfion and reverfions, remainder and remainders, yearly and other rents, iffues, and profits thereof, and every part and parcel thereof, and alfo all the eftate, right, title, intereft, truft, property, claim, and demand whatfoever, both at law and in equity, of them the faid Abraham Barker and Cecilia his wife, in, to, or out of, the faid capital meffuage, lands, tenements, hereditaments, and premifes : **To have and to hold** the faid capital meffuage, lands, tenements, hereditaments, and all and fingular other the premifes herein before mentioned to be hereby granted and releafed, with their and every of their appurtenances, unto the faid David Edwards and Francis Golding, their heirs and affigns, to fuch ufes, upon fuch trufts, and to and for fuch intents and purpofes as are hereinafter mentioned, expreffed, and declared, of and concerning the fame : that is to fay, to the ufe and behoof of the faid Abraham Barker, and Cecilia his wife, according to their feveral and refpective eftates and interefts therein, at the time of, or immediately before, the execution of thefe prefents, until the folemnization of the faid intended marriage : and from and after the folemnization thereof, to the ufe and behoof of the faid John Barker, for and during the term of his natural life; without impeachment of or for any manner of wafte : and from and after the determination of that eftate, then to the ufe of the faid David Edwards and Francis Golding, and their heirs, during the life of the faid John Barker, upon truft to fupport and preferve the contingent ufes and eftates hereinafter limited from being defeated and deftroyed, and for that purpofe to make entries, or bring actions, as the cafe fhall require ; but neverthelefs to permit and fuffer the faid John Barker, and his affigns, during his life, to receive and take the rents and profits thereof, and of every part thereof, to and for his and their own ufe and benefit : and from and after the deceafe of the faid John Barker, then to the ufe and behoof of the faid Katherine Edwards, his intended wife, for and during the term of her natural life, for her jointure, and in lieu, bar, and fatisfaction of her dower and thirds at common law, which fhe can or may have or claim, of, in, to, or out of, all, and every, or any, of the lands, tenements, and hereditaments, whereof or wherein the faid John Barker now is, or at any time or times hereafter during the coverture between them fhall be, feifed of any eftate of freehold

Mention of bargain and fale.

Habendum,

To the ufe of the grantors till marriage :

Then of the hufband for life, fans wafte :

Remainder to truftees to preferve contingent remainders :

Remainder to the wife for life, for her jointure, in bar of dower :

N°. II.

Remainder to o-
ther truftees for
a term, upon
trufts after men-
tioned :

Remainder to the
firft and other
fons of the mar-
riage in tail :

Remainder to the
daughters,

as tenants in
common, in tail :

Remainder to the
hufband in tail :

Remainder to the
hufband's mother
in fee.
The truft of the
term declared;

freehold or inheritance : and from and after the deceafe of the faid
Katherine Edwards, or other fooner determination of the faid eftate,
then to the ufe and behoof of the faid Charles Browne and Richard
More, their executors, adminiftrators, and affigns, for and during,
and unto the full end and term of, five hundred years from thence
next enfuing and fully to be complete and ended, without impeachment
of wafte : upon fuch trufts neverthelefs, and to and for fuch intents
and purpofes, and under and fubject to fuch provifoes and agreements,
as are hereinafter mentioned, and expreffed, and declared of and concerning the fame : and from and after the end, expiration, or other fooner
determination of the faid term of five hundred years, and fubject
thereunto, to the ufe and behoof of the firft fon of the faid John Barker on the body of the faid Katherine Edwards his intended wife to
be begotten, and of the heirs of the body of fuch firft fon lawfully
iffuing ; and for default of fuch iffue, then to the ufe and behoof
of the fecond, third, fourth, fifth, fixth, feventh, eighth, ninth,
tenth, and of all and every other the fon and fons of the faid John
Barker on the body of the faid Katherine Edwards his intended wife
to be begotten, feverally, fucceffively, and in remainder, one after
another, as they and every of them fhall be in feniority of age and
priority of birth, and of the feveral and refpective heirs of the body
and bodies of all and every fuch fon and fons lawfully iffuing ; the
elder of fuch fons, and the heirs of his body iffuing, being always
to be preferred and to take before the younger of fuch fons, and the
heirs of his or their body or bodies iffuing : and for default of fuch
iffue, then to the ufe and behoof of all and every the daughter and
daughters of the faid John Barker on the body of the faid Katherine
Edwards his intended wife to be begotten, to be equally divided between them, (if more than one,) fhare and fhare alike, as tenants in
common and not as jointenants, and of the feveral and refpective
heirs of the body and bodies of all and every fuch daughter and daughters lawfully iffuing : and for default of fuch iffue, then to the ufe
and behoof of the heirs of the body of him the faid John Barker lawfully iffuing : and for default of fuch heirs, then to the ufe and behoof of
the faid Cecilia, the wife of the faid Abraham Barker, and of her heirs
and affigns for ever. And as to, for, and concerning the term of five hundred years herein before limited to the faid Charles Browne and Richard
More, their executors, adminiftrators and affigns, as aforefaid, it is
hereby declared and agreed by and between all the faid parties to thefe
prefents, that the fame is fo limited to them upon the trufts, and to and
for the intents and purpofes, and under and fubject to the provifoes and
agreements, hereinafter mentioned, expreffed, and declared, of and
concerning the fame : that is to fay, in cafe there fhall be an eldeft or
only fon and one more or other child or children of the faid John Barker,

ker, on the body of the faid Katherine, his intended wife to be begotten, then upon truft that they the faid Charles Browne and Richard
More, their executors, adminiftrators, and affigns, by fale or mortgage of the faid term of five hundred years, or by fuch other ways and
means as they or the furvivor of them, or the executors or adminiftrators of fuch furvivor fhall think fit, fhall and do raife and levy, or borrow and take up at intereft, the fum of four thoufand pounds of lawful money of Great Britain, for the portion or portions of fuch other
child and children (befides the eldeft or only fon) as aforefaid, to be
equally divided between them (if more than one) fhare and fhare alike ;
the portion or portions of fuch of them as fhall be a fon or fons to be
paid at his or their refpective age or ages of twenty-one years; and
the portion or portions of fuch of them as fhall be a daughter or daughters to be paid at her or their refpective age or ages of twenty one
years, or day or days of marriage, which fhall firft happen. And upon this further truft, that in the mean time and until the fame portions
fhall become payable as aforefaid, the faid Charles Browne and Richard
More, their executors, adminiftrators, and affigns, fhall and do, by and
out of the rents, iffues, and profits of the premifes aforefaid, raife and
levy fuch competent yearly fum and fums of money for the maintenance
and education of fuch child or children, as fhall not exceed in the whole
the intereft of their refpective portions after the rate of four pounds in
the hundred yearly. **Provided** always, that in cafe any of the fame
children fhall happen to die before his, her, or their portions fhall become payable as aforefaid, then the portion or portions of fuch of them
fo dying fhall go and be paid unto and be equally divided among the furvivor or furvivors of them, when and at fuch time as the original portion
or portions of fuch furviving child or children fhall become payable as
aforefaid. **Provided** alfo, that in cafe there fhall be no fuch child or children of the faid John Barker on the body of the faid Katherine his intended
wife begotten, befides an eldeft or only fon ; or in cafe all and every
fuch child or children fhall happen to die before all or any of their faid
portions fhall become due and payable as aforefaid ; or in cafe the faid
portions, and alfo fuch maintenance as aforefaid, fhall by the faid Charles
Browne and Richard More, their executors, adminiftrators, or affigns,
be raifed and levied by any of the ways and means in that behalf afore-
mentioned ; or in cafe the fame by fuch perfon or perfons as fhall for
the time being be next in reverfion or remainder of the fame premifes
expectant upon the faid term of five hundred years, fhall be paid, or
well and duly fecured to be paid, according to the true intent and
meaning of thefe prefents ; then and in any of the faid cafes, and at
all times thenceforth, the faid term of five hundred years, or fo much
thereof as fhall remain unfold or undifpofed of for the purpofes aforefaid, fhall ceafe, determine, and be utterly void to all intents and
purpofes,

N°. II.

Condition, that
the ules and
eftates hereby
granted fhall be
void, on fettling
other lands of
equal value in
recompenfe.

purpofes, any thing herein contained to the contrary thereof in any wife notwithftanding. Provided alfo, and it is hereby further declared and agreed by and between all the faid parties to thefe prefents, that that in cafe the faid Abraham Barker or Cecilia his wife, at any time during their lives, or the life of the furvivor of them, with the approbation of the faid David Edwards and Francis Golding, or the furvivor of them, or the executors and adminiftrators of fuch furvivor, fhall fettle, convey, and affure other lands and tenements of an eftate of inheritance in fee fimple, in poffeffion, in fome convenient place or places within the realm of England, of equal or better value than the faid capital meffuage, lands, tenements, hereditaments and premifes, hereby granted and releafed, and in lieu, and recompenfe thereof, unto and for fuch and the like ufes, intents, and purpofes, and upon fuch and the like trufts, as the faid capital meffuage, lands, tenements, hereditaments, and premifes are hereby fettled and affured unto and upon, then and in fuch cafe, and at all times from thenceforth, all and every the ufe and ufes, truft and trufts, eftate and eftates herein before limited, expreffed, and declared of or concerning the fame, fhall ceafe, determine, and be utterly void to all intents and purpofes; and the fame capital meffuage, lands, tenements, hereditaments, and premifes, fhall from thenceforth remain and be to and for the only proper ufe and behoof of the faid Abraham Barker or Cecilia his wife, or the furvivor of them, fo fettling, conveying, and affuring fuch other lands and tenements as aforefaid, and of his or her heirs and affigns for ever: and to and for no other ufe, intent, or purpofe whatfoever; any thing herein contained to the contrary thereof in any wife notwithftanding. And, for the confiderations aforefaid, and for barring all eftates tail, and all remainders or reverfions thereupon expectant and depending, if any be now fubfifting and unbarred or otherwife undetermined, of and in the faid capital meffuage, lands, tenements, hereditaments, and premifes, hereby granted and releafed, or mentioned to be hereby granted and releafed, or any of them, or any part thereof, the faid Abraham Barker for himfelf and the faid Cecilia his wife, his and her heirs, executors, and adminiftrators, and the faid John Barker for himfelf, his heirs, executors, and adminiftrators, do, and each of them doth, refpectively covenant, promife, and grant, to and with the faid David Edwards and Francis Golding, their heirs, executors, and adminiftrators, by thefe prefents, that they the faid Abraham Barker and Cecilia his wife, and John Barker, fhall and will, at the cofts and charges of of the faid Abraham Barker, before the end of Michaelmas term next enfuing the date hereof, acknowlege and levy, before his Majefty's juftices of the court of common pleas at Weftminfter, one or more fine or fines, *fur cognizance de droit, come ceo, &c.* with proclamations

according

according to the form of the statutes in that case made and provided, and the usual course of fines in such cases accustomed, unto the said David Edwards, and his heirs, of the said capital messuage, lands, tenements, hereditaments, and premises, by such apt and convenient names, quantities, qualities, number of acres, and other descriptions to ascertain the same, as shall be thought meet: which said fine or fines, so as aforesaid or in any other manner levied and acknowleged, or to be levied and acknowleged, shall be and enure, and shall be adjudged, deemed, construed, and taken, and so are and were meant and intended, to be and enure, and are hereby declared by all the said parties to these presents to be and enure, to the use and behoof of the said David Edwards, and his heirs and assigns; to the intent and purpose that the said David Edwards may, by virtue of the said fine or fines so covenanted and agreed to be levied as aforesaid, be and become perfect tenant of the freehold of the said capital messuage, lands, tenements, hereditaments, and all other the premises, to the end that one or more good and perfect common recovery or recoveries may be thereof had and suffered, in such manner as is hereinafter for that purpose mentioned. And it is hereby declared and agreed by and between all the said parties to these presents, that it shall and may be lawful to and for the said Francis Golding, at the costs and charges of the said Abraham Barker, before the end of Michaelmas term next ensuing the date hereof, to sue forth and prosecute out of his majesty's high court of chancery one more writ or writs of entry *sur disseisin en le post*, returnable before his majesty's justices of the court of common pleas at Westminster, thereby demanding by apt and convenient names, quantities, qualities, number of acres, and other descriptions, the said capital messuage, lands, tenements, hereditaments, and premises, against the said David Edwards; to which said writ, or writs, of entry he the said David Edwards shall appear *gratis*, either in his own proper person, or by his attorney thereto lawfully authorized, and vouch over to warranty the said Abraham Barker, and Cecilia his wife, and John Barker; who shall also *gratis* appear in their proper persons, or by their attorney, or attorneys, thereto lawfully authorized, and enter into the warranty, and vouch over to warranty the common vouchee of the same court; who shall also appear, and after imparlance shall make default; so as judgment shall and may be thereupon had and given for the said Francis Golding, to recover the said capital messuage, lands, tenements, hereditaments, and premises, against the said David Edwards, and for him to recover in value against the said Abraham Barker, and Cecilia his wife, and John Barker, and for them to recover in value against the said common vouchee, and that execution shall and may be thereupon awarded and had accordingly, and all and every other act and thing be done and executed, needful and requisite for the suffering and

N°. II.

in order to make a tenant to the praecipe, that a recovery may be suffered;

to enure

perfecting of such common recovery or recoveries, with vouchers as aforesaid. And it is hereby further declared and agreed by and between all the said parties to these presents, that immediately from and after the suffering and perfecting of the said recovery or recoveries, so as aforesaid, or in any other manner, or at any other time or times, suffered or to be suffered, as well these presents and the assurance hereby made, and the said fine or fines so covenanted to be levied as aforesaid, as also the said recovery or recoveries, and also all and every other fine and fines, recovery and recoveries, conveyances, and assurances in the law whatsoever heretofore had, made, levied, suffered, or executed, or hereafter to be had, made, levied, suffered, or executed, of the said capital messuage, lands, tenements, hereditaments, and premises, or any of them, or any part thereof, by and between the said parties to these presents or any of them, or whereunto they or any of them are or shall be parties or privies, shall be and enure, and shall be adjudged, deemed, construed, and taken, and so are and were meant and intended, to be and enure, and the recoveror or recoverors in the said recovery or recoveries named or to be named, and his or their heirs, shall stand and be seised of the said capital messuage, lands, tenements, hereditaments, and premises, and of every part and parcel *to the preceding* thereof, to the uses, upon the trusts, and to and for the intents and *uses in this deed.* purposes, and under and subject to the provisoes, limitations, and agreements, herein before mentioned, expressed, and declared, of and *Other covenants;* concerning the same. And the said Abraham Barker, party hereunto, doth hereby for himself, his heirs, executors, and administrators, further covenant, promise, grant, and agree, to and with the said David Edwards and Francis Golding, their heirs, executors, and administra- *for quiet enjoy-* tors, in manner and form following; that is to say, that the said capi- *ment,* tal messuage, lands, tenements, hereditaments, and premises, shall and may at all times hereafter remain, continue, and be, to and for the uses and purposes, upon the trusts, and under and subject to the provisoes, limitations, and agreements, hereinbefore mentioned, expressed, and declared, of and concerning the same; and shall and may be peaceably and quietly had, held, and enjoyed accordingly, without any lawful let or interruption of or by the said Abraham Barker or Cecilia his wife, parties hereunto, his or her heirs or assigns, or of or by any other person or persons lawfully claiming or to claim from, by, or under, or in trust for him, her, them, or any of them, or from, by, or under *free from incum-* his or her ancestors, or any of them; and shall so remain, continue, *brances;* and be, free and clear, and freely and clearly acquitted, exonerated, and discharged, or otherwise by the said Abraham Barker, or Cecilia his wife, parties hereunto, his or her heirs, executors, or administrators, well and sufficiently saved, defended, kept harmless, and indemnified of, from, and against all former and other gifts, grants, bargains, sales,

leases,

leafes, mortgages, eftates, titles, troubles, charges, and incumbrances
whatfoever, had, made, done, committed, occafioned, or fuffered, or
to be had, made, done, committed, occafioned, or fuffered, by the faid
Abraham Barker, or Cecilia his wife, or by his or her anceftors, or any
of them, or by his, her, their, or any of their act, means, affent, confent, or procurement: **And moreover** that he the faid Abraham Barker, and Cecilia his wife, parties hereunto, and his and her heirs, and
all other perfons having or lawfully claiming, or which fhall or may
have or lawfully claim, any eftate, right, title, truft, or intereft, at
law or in equity, of, in, to, or out of, the faid capital meffuage, lands,
tenements, hereditaments, and premifes, or any of them, or any part
thereof, by or under or in truft for him, her, them, or any of them,
or by or under his or her anceftors or any of them, fhall and will from
time to time, and at all times hereafter, upon every reafonable requeft,
and at the cofts and charges, of the faid David Edwards and Francis
Golding, or either of them, their or either of their heirs, executors,
or adminiftrators, make, do, and execute, or caufe to be made, done,
and executed, all fuch further and other lawful and reafonable acts,
deeds, conveyances, and affurances in the law whatfoever, for the further, better, more perfect, and abfolute granting, conveying, fettling,
and affuring of the fame capital meffuage, lands, tenements, hereditaments, and premifes, to and for the ufes and purpofes, upon the
trufts, and under and fubject to the provifoes, limitations, and agreements, herein before mentioned, expreffed, and declared, of and concerning the fame, as by the faid David Edwards and Francis Golding
or either of them, their or either of their heirs, executors, or adminiftrators, or their or any of their counfel learned in the law fhall be reafonably advifed, devifed, or required: fo as fuch further affurances
contain in them no further or other warranty or covenants than againft
the perfon or perfons, his, her, or their heirs, who fhall make or do
the fame; and fo as the party or parties, who fhall be requefted to
make fuch further affurances, be not compelled or compellable, for
making or doing thereof, to go and travel above five miles from his,
her, or their then refpective dwellings, or places of abode. **Provided**
laftly, and it is hereby further declared and agreed by and between
all the parties to thefe prefents, that it fhall and may be lawful to and
for the faid Abraham Barker and Cecilia his wife, John Barker and
Katherine his intended wife, and David Edwards, at any time or times
hereafter, during their joint lives, by any writing or writings under
their refpective hands and feals and attefted by two or more credible
witneffes, to revoke, make void, alter, or change all and every or any
the ufe and ufes, eftate and eftates, herein and hereby before limited
and declared, or mentioned or intended to be limited and declared, of
and in the capital meffuage, lands, tenements, hereditaments, and

N°. II.

and for further
affurance.

Power of revo-
cation.

N°. II.

Conclusion.

premises aforesaid, or of and in any part or parcel thereof, and to declare new and other uses of the same, or of any part or parcel thereof, any thing herein contained to the contrary thereof in any wise notwithstanding. In witness whereof the parties to these presents their hands and seals have subscribed and set, the day and year first above written.

Sealed, and delivered, being first duly stamped, in the presence of
George Carter.
William Browne.

Abraham Barker. (L. S.)
Cecilia Barker. (L. S.)
David Edwards. (L. S.)
Francis Golding. (L. S.)
Charles Browne. (L. S.)
Richard More. (L. S.)
John Barker. (L. S.)
Katherine Edwards. (L. S.)

N°. III.

N°. III.

An OBLIGATION, *or* BOND, *with* CONDITION *for the Payment of Money.*

Know all men by thefe prefents, that I David Edwards, of Lincoln's Inn in the county of Middlefex, efquire, am held and firmly bound to Abraham Barker of Dale-Hall in the county of Norfolk, efquire, in ten thoufand pounds of lawful money of Great Britain, to be paid to the faid Abraham Barker, or his certain attorney, executors, adminiftrators, or affigns; for which payment well and truly to be made, I bind myfelf, my heirs, executors, and adminiftrators, firmly by thefe prefents, fealed with my feal. Dated the fourth day of September in the twenty firft year of the reign of our fovereign lord GEORGE the fecond by the grace of God king of Great Britain, France, and Ireland, defender of the faith, and fo forth, and in the year of our Lord one thoufand, feven hundred, and forty feven.

The condition of this obligation is fuch, that if the above bounden David Edwards, his heirs, executors, or adminiftrators, do and fhall well and truly pay, or caufe to be paid, unto the above named Abraham Barker, his executors, adminiftrators, or affigns, the full fum of five thoufand pounds of lawful Britifh money, with lawful intereft for the fame, on the fourth day of March next enfuing the date of the above written obligation, then this obligation fhall be void and of none effect, or elfe fhall be and remain in full force and virtue.

Sealed, and delivered, being   David Edwards. (L. S.)
firft duly ftamped, in the
prefence of
   George Carter.
   William Browne.

N°. IV.

Nº. IV.

A F I N E *of Lands,* fur Cognizance de Droit, come ceo, *&c.*

§. 1. *Writ of Covenant*; *or* P R A E C I P E.

𝕲 𝕮 𝕺 𝕽 𝕲 𝕮 the fecond by the grace of God of Great Britain, France, and Ireland king, defender of the faith, and fo forth ; to the fheriff of Norfolk, greeting. **Command** Abraham Barker, efquire, and Cecilia his wife, and John Barker, efquire, that juftly and without delay they perform to David Edwards, efquire, the covenant made between them of two meffuages, two gardens, three hundred acres of land, one hundred acres of meadow, two hundred acres of pafture, and fifty acres of wood, with the appurtenances, in Dale ; and unlefs they fhall fo do, and if the faid David fhall give you fecurity of profecuting his claim, then fummon by good fummoners the faid Abraham, Cecilia, and John, that they appear before our juftices, at Weftminfter, from the day of faint Michael in one month, to fhew wherefore they have not done it : and have you there the fummoners, and this writ. **Witnefs** ourfelf at Weftminfter, the ninth day of October, in the twenty firft year of our reign.

Sheriff's return. Pledges of { John Doe. profecution, { Richard Roe.   Summoners of the within named Abraham, Cecilia, and John. { John Den. { Richard Fen.

§. 2. *The Licence to agree.*

Norfolk, ⎱ **David Edwards**, efquire, gives to the lord the king ten to wit. ⎰ marks, for licence to agree with Abraham Barker, efquire, of a plea of covenant of two meffuages, two gardens, three hundred acres of land, one hundred acres of meadow, two hundred acres of pafture, and fifty acres of wood, with the appurtenances, in Dale.

§. 3. *The Concord.*

And the agreement is fuch, to wit, that the aforefaid Abraham, Cecilia, and John, have acknowleged the aforefaid tenements, with the

the appurtenances, to be the right of him the faid David, as thofe
which the faid David hath of the gift of the aforefaid Abraham, Cecilia, and John; and thofe they have remifed and quitted claim, from
them and their heirs, to the aforefaid David and his heirs for ever.
And further, the fame Abraham, Cecilia, and John, have granted,
for themfelves and their heirs, that they will warrant to the aforefaid
David, and his heirs, the aforefaid tenements, with the appurtenances,
againft all men for ever. And for this recognition, remife, quit-claim,
warranty, fine, and agreement, the faid David hath given to the faid
Abraham, Cecilia, and John, two hundred pounds fterling.

§. 4. *The Note, or Abftract.*

Norfolk, ⁊ **Between** David Edwards, efquire, complainant, and A-
to wit. ſ braham Barker, efquire, and Cecilia his wife, and John
Barker, efquire, deforciants, of two meſſuages, two gardens, three
hundred acres of land, one hundred acres of meadow, two hundred
acres of pafture, and fifty acres of wood, with the appurtenances, in
Dale, whereupon a plea of covenant was fummoned between them;
to wit, that the faid Abraham, Cecilia, and John, have acknowleged
the aforefaid tenements, with the appurtenances, to be the right of
him the faid David, as thofe which the faid David hath of the gift of the
aforefaid Abraham, Cecilia, and John; and thofe they have remifed
and quitted claim, from them and their heirs, to the aforefaid David
and his heirs for ever. And further, the fame Abraham, Cecilia, and
John, have granted for themfelves, and their heirs, that they will warrant to the aforefaid David, and his heirs, the aforefaid tenements,
with the appurtenances, againft all men for ever. And for this recognition, remife, quit-claim, warranty, fine, and agreement, the faid
David hath given to the faid Abraham, Cecilia, and John, two hundred pounds fterling.

§. 5. *The Foot, Chirograph, or Indentures, of the* FINE.

Norfolk, ⁊ **This is the final agreement,** made in the court of the lord
to wit. ſ the king at Weftminfter, from the day of faint Michael
in one month, in the twenty firft year of the reign of the lord GEORGE
the fecond by the grace of God of Great Britain, France, and Ireland
king, defender of the faith, and fo forth, before John Willes, Thomas
Abney, Thomas Burnet, and Thomas Birch, juftices, and other faith-
ful fubjects of the lord the king then there prefent, between David Edwards, efquire, complainant, and Abraham Barker, efquire, and Cecilia

N°. IV.

cilia his wife, and John Barker, efquire, deforciants, of two meffuages, two gardens, three hundred acres of land, one hundred acres of meadow, two hundred acres of pafture, and fifty acres of wood, with the appurtenances, in Dale, whereupon a plea of covenant was fummoned between them in the fame court; to wit, that the aforefaid Abraham, Cecilia, and John, have acknowleged the aforefaid tenements, to be the right of him the faid David, as thofe which the faid David hath of the gift of the aforefaid Abraham, Cecilia, and John; and thofe they have remifed and quitted claim, from them and their heirs, to the aforefaid David and his heirs for ever. And further, the fame Abraham, Cecilia, and John, have granted for themfelves and their heirs, that they will warrant to the aforefaid David and his heirs, the aforefaid tenements, with the appurtenances, againft all men for ever. And for this recognition, remife, quit-claim, warranty, fine, and agreement, the faid David hath given to the faid Abraham, Cecilia, and John, two hundred pounds fterling.

§. 6. *Proclamations, endorfed upon the* FINE, *according to the Statutes.*

The firft proclamation was made the fixteenth day of November, in the term of faint Michael, in the twenty firft year of the king withinwritten.

The fecond proclamation was made the fourth day of February, in the term of faint Hilary, in the twenty firft year of the king withinwritten.

The third proclamation was made the thirteenth day of May, in the term of Eafter, in the twenty firft year of the king withinwritten.

The fourth proclamation was made the twenty eighth day of June, in the term of the holy Trinity, in the twenty fecond year of the king withinwritten.

N°. V.

N°. V.

A common RECOVERY *of Lands, with* * *double Voucher.*

§. 1. *Writ of Entry* fur Diffeifin *in the* Poft; *or,* PRAECIPE.

𝕲𝕰𝕺𝕽𝕲𝕰 the fecond by the grace of God of Great Britain, France, and Ireland king, defender of the faith, and fo forth; to the fheriff of Norfolk, greeting. **Command** David Edwards, efquire, that juftly and without delay he render to Francis Golding, clerk, two meffuages, two gardens, three hundred acres of land, one hundred acres of meadow, two hundred acres of pafture, and fifty acres of wood, with the appurtenances, in Dale, which he claims to be his right and inheritance, and into which the faid David hath not entry, unlefs after the diffeifin, which Hugh Hunt thereof unjuftly, and without judgment, hath made to the aforefaid Francis, within thirty years now laft paft, as he faith, and whereupon he complains that the aforefaid David deforceth him. And unlefs he fhall fo do, and if the faid Francis fhall give you fecurity of profecuting his claim, then fummon by good fummoners the faid David, that he appear before our juftices at Weftminfter, on the octave of faint Martin, to fhew wherefore he hath not done it: and have you there the fummoners, and this writ. **Witnefs** ourfelf at Weftminfter, the twenty ninth day of October, in the twenty firft year of our reign.

Pledges of { John Doe.	Summoners of the { John Den.	Sheriff's return.
profecution, { Richard Roe.	withinnamed David, { Richard Fen.	

§. 2. *Exemplification of the* RECOVERY *Roll.*

𝕲𝕰𝕺𝕽𝕲𝕰 the fecond by the grace of God of Great Britain, France, and Ireland king, defender of the faith, and fo forth; to all to whom thefe our prefent letters fhall come, greeting. **Know ye,** that among the pleas of land, enrolled at Weftminfter, before Sir John Willes, knight, and his fellows, our juftices of the bench, of the term of faint Michael, in the twenty firft year of our reign, upon the fifty fecond roll it is thus contained. **Entry** returnable on the oc- Return.

* Note, that if the recovery be had with fingle voucher, the parts marked "thus" in §. 2. are omitted.

Nᵒ. V.

Demand againſt
the tenant.

tave of ſaint Martin. Ɲorfolƙ, to wit : Francis Golding, clerk, in his proper perſon demandeth againſt David Edwards, eſquire, two meſſuages, two gardens, three hundred acres of land, one hundred acres of meadow, two hundred acres of paſture, and fifty acres of wood, with the appurtenances, in Dale, as his right and inheritance, and into which the ſaid David hath not entry, unleſs after the diſſeiſin, which Hugh Hunt thereof unjuſtly, and without judgment, hath made to the aforeſaid Francis, within thirty years now laſt paſt. And

Count.

whereupon he ſaith, that he himſelf was ſeiſed of the tenements aforeſaid, with the appurtenances, in his demeſne as of fee and right, in time of peace, in the time of the lord the king that now is, by taking

Eſ, lees.

the profits thereof to the value [* of ſix ſhillings and eight pence, and more, in rents, corn, and graſs :] and into which [the ſaid David hath not entry, unleſs as aforeſaid :] and thereupon he bringeth

Defence of the
tenant.

ſuit, [and good proof.] Aɲɒ the ſaid David in his proper perſon comes and defendeth his right, when [and where the court ſhall

Voucher.

award,] and thereupon voucheth to warranty " John Barker, eſquire ;

"Warranty.

" who is preſent here in court in his proper perſon, and the tenements " aforeſaid with the appurtenances to him freely warranteth, [and

"Demand againſt
"the vouchee.

" prays that the ſaid Francis may count againſt him.] Aɲɒ hereupon " the ſaid Francis demandeth againſt the ſaid John, tenant by his own " warranty, the tenements aforeſaid with the appurtenances, in form

"Count.

" aforeſaid, &c. And whereupon he ſaith, that he himſelf was ſeiſed " of the tenements aforeſaid, with the appurtenances, in his demeſne " as of fee and right, in time of peace, in the time of the lord the king " that now is, by taking the profits thereof to the value, &c. And into

"Defence of the
"vouchee.

" which, &c. And thereupon he bringeth ſuit, &c. Aɲɒ the aforeſaid " John, tenant by his own warranty, defends his right, when, &c. and

"Second voucher.
Warranty.

" thereupon he further voucheth to warranty" Jacob Morland ; who is preſent here in court in his proper perſon, and the tenements aforeſaid,

Demand againſt
the common
vouchee.

with the appurtenances, to him freely warranteth, &c. Aɲɒ hereupon the ſaid Francis demandeth againſt the ſaid Jacob, tenant by his own warranty, the tenements aforeſaid, with the appurtenances, in form

Count.

aforeſaid, &c. And whereupon he ſaith, that he himſelf was ſeiſed of the tenements aforeſaid, with the appurtenances, in his demeſne as of fee and right, in time of peace, in the time of the lord the king that now is, by taking the profits thereof to the value, &c. And into which,

Defence of the
common vouchee.

&c. And thereupon he bringeth ſuit, &c. Aɲɒ the aforeſaid Jacob, tenant by his own warranty, defends his right, when, &c. And ſaith

Plea, nul diſſeiſin.

that the aforeſaid Hugh did not diſſeiſe the aforeſaid Francis of the tenements aforeſaid, as the aforeſaid Francis by his writ and count afore-

---

* The clauſes, between hooks, are no otherwiſe expreſſed in the record than by an &c.

ſaid

faid above doth fuppofe : and of this he puts himfelf upon the coun- N°. V.
try. **And** the aforefaid Francis thereupon craveth leave to imparl ; and
he hath it. And afterwards the aforefaid Francis cometh again here Imparlance.
into court in this fame term in his proper perfon, and the aforefaid Default of the
Jacob, though folemnly called, cometh not again, but hath departed commonvouchee.
in contempt of the court, and maketh default. **Therefore it is confi-** Judgment for the
dered, that the aforefaid Francis do recover his feifin againft the afore- demandant.
faid David of the tenements aforefaid, with the appurtenances ; and Recovery in
that the faid David have of the land of the aforefaid " John, to the value value.
" [of the tenements aforefaid ;] and further, that the faid John, have of
" the land of the faid" Jacob to the value [of the tenements aforefaid.]
And the faid Jacob in mercy. **And** hereupon the faid Francis prays a writ Amercement.
of the lord the king, to be directed to the fheriff of the county aforefaid,
to caufe him to have full feifin of the tenements aforefaid with the appurtenances : and it is granted unto him, returnable here without de- Award of the
lay. Afterwards, that is to fay, the twenty eighth day of November writ of feifin,
in this fame term, here cometh the faid Francis in his proper perfon ; and return.
and the fheriff, namely fir Charles Thompfon, knight, now fendeth,
that he by virtue of the writ aforefaid to him directed, on the twenty
fourth day of the fame month, did caufe the faid Francis to have full
feifin of the tenements aforefaid with the appurtenances, as he was
commanded. **All and fingular** which premifes, at the requeft of the faid Exemplification
Francis, by the tenor of thefe prefents we have held good to be exem- continued.
plified. In teftimony whereof we have caufed our feal, appointed for
fealing writs in the bench aforefaid, to be affixed to thefe prefents.
Witnefs fir John Willes, knight, at Weftminfter, the twenty eighth Tefte.
day of November, in the twenty firft year of our reign.

Cooke.

THE END

Made in the USA
Lexington, KY
16 December 2014